Deep Reinforcemen with Python

Second Edition

Master classic RL, deep RL, distributional RL, inverse RL, and more with OpenAI Gym and TensorFlow

Sudharsan Ravichandiran

BIRMINGHAM - MUMBAI

Deep Reinforcement Learning with Python
Second Edition

Producers: Ben Renow-Clarke and Aarthi Kumaraswamy
Acquisition Editor – Peer Reviews: Divya Mudaliar
Content Development Editor: Bhavesh Amin
Technical Editor: Aniket Shetty
Project Editor: Janice Gonsalves
Copy Editor: Safis Editing
Proofreader: Safis Editing
Indexer: Pratik Shirodkar
Presentation Designer: Pranit Padwal

First published: June 2018

Second edition: September 2020

Production reference: 1300920

Published by Packt Publishing Ltd.

Livery Place

35 Livery Street

Birmingham B3 2PB, UK.

ISBN 978-1-83921-068-6

www.packt.com

To my adorable mom, Kasthuri, and to my beloved dad, Ravichandiran.

- Sudharsan Ravichandiran

packt.com

Subscribe to our online digital library for full access to over 7,000 books and videos, as well as industry leading tools to help you plan your personal development and advance your career. For more information, please visit our website.

Why subscribe?

- Spend less time learning and more time coding with practical eBooks and Videos from over 4,000 industry professionals
- Learn better with Skill Plans built especially for you
- Get a free eBook or video every month
- Fully searchable for easy access to vital information
- Copy and paste, print, and bookmark content

Did you know that Packt offers eBook versions of every book published, with PDF and ePub files available? You can upgrade to the eBook version at www.Packt.com and as a print book customer, you are entitled to a discount on the eBook copy. Get in touch with us at customercare@packtpub.com for more details.

At www.Packt.com, you can also read a collection of free technical articles, sign up for a range of free newsletters, and receive exclusive discounts and offers on Packt books and eBooks.

Contributors

About the author

Sudharsan Ravichandiran is a data scientist, researcher, best-selling author, and YouTuber (search for *Sudharsan reinforcement learning*). He completed his bachelor's in information technology at Anna University. His area of research focuses on practical implementations of deep learning and reinforcement learning, which includes natural language processing and computer vision. He is an open source contributor and loves answering questions on Stack Overflow. He also authored a best-seller, *Hands-On Reinforcement Learning with Python, 1st edition*, published by Packt Publishing.

I would like to thank my most amazing parents and my brother, Karthikeyan, for inspiring and motivating me. My huge thanks to the producer of the book, Aarthi, and the editors, Bhavesh, Aniket, and Janice. Special thanks to the reviewers, Sujit Pal and Valerii Babushkin, for providing their valuable insights and feedback. Without all their support, it would have been impossible to complete this book.

About the reviewers

Sujit Pal is a Technology Research Director at Elsevier Labs, an advanced technology group within the Reed-Elsevier Group of companies. His areas of interests include semantic search, natural language processing, machine learning, and deep learning. At Elsevier, he has worked on several initiatives involving search quality measurement and improvement, image classification and duplicate detection, and annotation and ontology development for medical and scientific corpora. He has co-authored a book on deep learning and writes about technology on his blog *Salmon Run*.

Valerii Babushkin is the senior director of data science at X5 Retail Group, where he leads a team of 100+ people in the area of natural language processing, machine learning, computer vision, data analysis, and A/B testing. Valerii is a Kaggle competitions Grand Master, ranking globally in the top 30. He studied cybernetics at Moscow Polytechnical University and mechatronics at Karlsruhe University of Applied Sciences and has worked with Packt as an author of the *Python Machine Learning Tips, Tricks, and Techniques* course and a technical reviewer for some books on reinforcement learning.

Table of Contents

Preface

With significant enhancement in the quality and quantity of algorithms in recent years, this second edition of *Hands-On Reinforcement Learning with Python* has been revamped into an example-rich guide to learning state-of-the-art **reinforcement learning** (**RL**) and deep RL algorithms with TensorFlow 2 and the OpenAI Gym toolkit.

In addition to exploring RL basics and foundational concepts such as the Bellman equation, Markov decision processes, and dynamic programming, this second edition dives deep into the full spectrum of value-based, policy-based, and actor-critic RL methods. It explores state-of-the-art algorithms such as DQN, TRPO, PPO and ACKTR, DDPG, TD3, and SAC in depth, demystifying the underlying math and demonstrating implementations through simple code examples.

The book has several new chapters dedicated to new RL techniques including distributional RL, imitation learning, inverse RL, and meta RL. You will learn to leverage Stable Baselines, an improvement of OpenAI's baseline library, to implement popular RL algorithms effortlessly. The book concludes with an overview of promising approaches such as meta-learning and imagination augmented agents in research.

Who this book is for

If you're a machine learning developer with little or no experience with neural networks interested in artificial intelligence and want to learn about reinforcement learning from scratch, this book is for you. Basic familiarity with linear algebra, calculus, and Python is required. Some experience with TensorFlow would be a plus.

What this book covers

Chapter 1, Fundamentals of Reinforcement Learning, helps you build a strong foundation on RL concepts. We will learn about the key elements of RL, the Markov decision process, and several important fundamental concepts such as action spaces, policies, episodes, the value function, and the Q function. At the end of the chapter, we will learn about some of the interesting applications of RL and we will also look into the key terms and terminologies frequently used in RL.

Chapter 2, A Guide to the Gym Toolkit, provides a complete guide to OpenAI's Gym toolkit. We will understand several interesting environments provided by Gym in detail by implementing them. We will begin our hands-on RL journey from this chapter by implementing several fundamental RL concepts using Gym.

Chapter 3, The Bellman Equation and Dynamic Programming, will help us understand the Bellman equation in detail with extensive math. Next, we will learn two interesting classic RL algorithms called the value and policy iteration methods, which we can use to find the optimal policy. We will also see how to implement value and policy iteration methods for solving the Frozen Lake problem.

Chapter 4, Monte Carlo Methods, explains the model-free method, Monte Carlo. We will learn what prediction and control tasks are, and then we will look into Monte Carlo prediction and Monte Carlo control methods in detail. Next, we will implement the Monte Carlo method to solve the blackjack game using the Gym toolkit.

Chapter 5, Understanding Temporal Difference Learning, deals with one of the most popular and widely used model-free methods called **Temporal Difference (TD)** learning. First, we will learn how the TD prediction method works in detail, and then we will explore the on-policy TD control method called SARSA and the off-policy TD control method called Q learning in detail. We will also implement TD control methods to solve the Frozen Lake problem using Gym.

Chapter 6, Case Study – The MAB Problem, explains one of the classic problems in RL called the **multi-armed bandit (MAB)** problem. We will start the chapter by understanding what the MAB problem is and then we will learn about several exploration strategies such as epsilon-greedy, softmax exploration, upper confidence bound, and Thompson sampling methods for solving the MAB problem in detail.

Chapter 7, Deep Learning Foundations, helps us to build a strong foundation on deep learning. We will start the chapter by understanding how artificial neural networks work. Then we will learn several interesting deep learning algorithms, such as recurrent neural networks, LSTM networks, convolutional neural networks, and generative adversarial networks.

Chapter 8, A Primer on TensorFlow, deals with one of the most popular deep learning libraries called TensorFlow. We will understand how to use TensorFlow by implementing a neural network to recognize handwritten digits. Next, we will learn to perform several math operations using TensorFlow. Later, we will learn about TensorFlow 2.0 and see how it differs from the previous TensorFlow versions.

Chapter 9, Deep Q Network and Its Variants, enables us to kick-start our deep RL journey. We will learn about one of the most popular deep RL algorithms called the **Deep Q Network (DQN)**. We will understand how DQN works step by step along with the extensive math. We will also implement a DQN to play Atari games. Next, we will explore several interesting variants of DQN, called Double DQN, Dueling DQN, DQN with prioritized experience replay, and DRQN.

Chapter 10, Policy Gradient Method, covers policy gradient methods. We will understand how the policy gradient method works along with the detailed derivation. Next, we will learn several variance reduction methods such as policy gradient with reward-to-go and policy gradient with baseline. We will also understand how to train an agent for the Cart Pole balancing task using policy gradient.

Chapter 11, Actor-Critic Methods – A2C and A3C, deals with several interesting actor-critic methods such as advantage actor-critic and asynchronous advantage actor-critic. We will learn how these actor-critic methods work in detail, and then we will implement them for a mountain car climbing task using OpenAI Gym.

Chapter 12, Learning DDPG, TD3, and SAC, covers state-of-the-art deep RL algorithms such as deep deterministic policy gradient, twin delayed DDPG, and soft actor, along with step by step derivation. We will also learn how to implement the DDPG algorithm for performing the inverted pendulum swing-up task using Gym.

Chapter 13, TRPO, PPO, and ACKTR Methods, deals with several popular policy gradient methods such as TRPO and PPO. We will dive into the math behind TRPO and PPO step by step and understand how TRPO and PPO helps an agent find the optimal policy. Next, we will learn to implement PPO for performing the inverted pendulum swing-up task. At the end, we will learn about the actor-critic method called actor-critic using Kronecker-Factored trust region in detail.

Chapter 14, Distributional Reinforcement Learning, covers distributional RL algorithms. We will begin the chapter by understanding what distributional RL is. Then we will explore several interesting distributional RL algorithms such as categorical DQN, quantile regression DQN, and distributed distributional DDPG.

Chapter 15, Imitation Learning and Inverse RL, explains imitation and inverse RL algorithms. First, we will understand how supervised imitation learning, DAgger, and deep Q learning from demonstrations work in detail. Next, we will learn about maximum entropy inverse RL. At the end of the chapter, we will learn about generative adversarial imitation learning.

Chapter 16, Deep Reinforcement Learning with Stable Baselines, helps us to understand how to implement deep RL algorithms using a library called Stable Baselines. We will learn what Stable Baselines is and how to use it in detail by implementing several interesting Deep RL algorithms such as DQN, A2C, DDPG TRPO, and PPO.

Chapter 17, Reinforcement Learning Frontiers, covers several interesting avenues in RL, such as meta RL, hierarchical RL, and imagination augmented agents in detail.

To get the most out of this book

You need the following software for this book:

- Anaconda
- Python
- Any web browser

Download the example code files

You can download the example code files for this book from your account at http://www.packtpub.com. If you purchased this book elsewhere, you can visit http://www.packtpub.com/support and register to have the files emailed directly to you.

You can download the code files by following these steps:

1. Log in or register at http://www.packtpub.com.
2. Select the **SUPPORT** tab.
3. Click on **Code Downloads & Errata**.
4. Enter the name of the book in the **Search** box and follow the on-screen instructions.

Once the file is downloaded, please make sure that you unzip or extract the folder using the latest version of:

- WinRAR / 7-Zip for Windows

- Zipeg / iZip / UnRarX for Mac
- 7-Zip / PeaZip for Linux

The code bundle for the book is also hosted on GitHub at `https://github.com/PacktPublishing/Deep-Reinforcement-Learning-with-Python`. We also have other code bundles from our rich catalog of books and videos available at `https://github.com/PacktPublishing/`. Check them out!

Download the color images

We also provide a PDF file that has color images of the screenshots/diagrams used in this book. You can download it here: `https://static.packt-cdn.com/downloads/9781839210686_ColorImages.pdf`.

Conventions used

There are a number of text conventions used throughout this book.

`CodeInText`: Indicates code words in text, database table names, folder names, filenames, file extensions, pathnames, dummy URLs, user input, and Twitter handles. For example: "`epsilon_greedy` computes the optimal policy."

A block of code is set as follows:

```
def epsilon_greedy(epsilon):
    if np.random.uniform(0,1) < epsilon:
        return env.action_space.sample()
    else:
        return np.argmax(Q)
```

When we wish to draw your attention to a particular part of a code block, the relevant lines or items are highlighted:

```
def epsilon_greedy(epsilon):
    if np.random.uniform(0,1) < epsilon:
        return env.action_space.sample()
    else:
        return np.argmax(Q)
```

Any command-line input or output is written as follows:

```
source activate universe
```

Bold: Indicates a new term, an important word, or words that you see on the screen, for example, in menus or dialog boxes, also appear in the text like this. For example: "The **Markov Reward Process (MRP)** is an extension of the Markov chain with the reward function."

 Warnings or important notes appear like this.

 Tips and tricks appear like this.

Get in touch

Feedback from our readers is always welcome.

General feedback: Email feedback@packtpub.com, and mention the book's title in the subject of your message. If you have questions about any aspect of this book, please email us at questions@packtpub.com.

Errata: Although we have taken every care to ensure the accuracy of our content, mistakes do happen. If you have found a mistake in this book we would be grateful if you would report this to us. Please visit, http://www.packtpub.com/submit-errata, selecting your book, clicking on the Errata Submission Form link, and entering the details.

Piracy: If you come across any illegal copies of our works in any form on the Internet, we would be grateful if you would provide us with the location address or website name. Please contact us at copyright@packtpub.com with a link to the material.

If you are interested in becoming an author: If there is a topic that you have expertise in and you are interested in either writing or contributing to a book, please visit http://authors.packtpub.com.

Reviews

Please leave a review. Once you have read and used this book, why not leave a review on the site that you purchased it from? Potential readers can then see and use your unbiased opinion to make purchase decisions, we at Packt can understand what you think about our products, and our authors can see your feedback on their book. Thank you!

For more information about Packt, please visit `packtpub.com`.

1

Fundamentals of Reinforcement Learning

Reinforcement Learning (RL) is one of the areas of **Machine Learning (ML)**. Unlike other ML paradigms, such as supervised and unsupervised learning, RL works in a trial and error fashion by interacting with its environment.

RL is one of the most active areas of research in artificial intelligence, and it is believed that RL will take us a step closer towards achieving artificial general intelligence. RL has evolved rapidly in the past few years with a wide variety of applications ranging from building a recommendation system to self-driving cars. The major reason for this evolution is the advent of deep reinforcement learning, which is a combination of deep learning and RL. With the emergence of new RL algorithms and libraries, RL is clearly one of the most promising areas of ML.

In this chapter, we will build a strong foundation in RL by exploring several important and fundamental concepts involved in RL.

In this chapter, we will cover the following topics:

- Key elements of RL
- The basic idea of RL
- The RL algorithm
- How RL differs from other ML paradigms
- The Markov Decision Processes
- Fundamental concepts of RL

- Applications of RL
- RL glossary

We will begin the chapter by defining *Key elements of RL*. This will help explain *The basic idea of RL*.

Key elements of RL

Let's begin by understanding some key elements of RL.

Agent

An agent is a software program that learns to make intelligent decisions. We can say that an agent is a learner in the RL setting. For instance, a chess player can be considered an agent since the player learns to make the best moves (decisions) to win the game. Similarly, Mario in a Super Mario Bros video game can be considered an agent since Mario explores the game and learns to make the best moves in the game.

Environment

The environment is the world of the agent. The agent stays within the environment. For instance, coming back to our chess game, a chessboard is called the environment since the chess player (agent) learns to play the game of chess within the chessboard (environment). Similarly, in Super Mario Bros, the world of Mario is called the environment.

State and action

A state is a position or a moment in the environment that the agent can be in. We learned that the agent stays within the environment, and there can be many positions in the environment that the agent can stay in, and those positions are called states. For instance, in our chess game example, each position on the chessboard is called the state. The state is usually denoted by s.

The agent interacts with the environment and moves from one state to another by performing an action. In the chess game environment, the action is the move performed by the player (agent). The action is usually denoted by a.

Reward

We learned that the agent interacts with an environment by performing an action and moves from one state to another. Based on the action, the agent receives a reward. A reward is nothing but a numerical value, say, +1 for a good action and -1 for a bad action. How do we decide if an action is good or bad?

In our chess game example, if the agent makes a move in which it takes one of the opponent's chess pieces, then it is considered a good action and the agent receives a positive reward. Similarly, if the agent makes a move that leads to the opponent taking the agent's chess piece, then it is considered a bad action and the agent receives a negative reward. The reward is denoted by r.

The basic idea of RL

Let's begin with an analogy. Let's suppose we are teaching a dog (agent) to catch a ball. Instead of teaching the dog explicitly to catch a ball, we just throw a ball and every time the dog catches the ball, we give the dog a cookie (reward). If the dog fails to catch the ball, then we do not give it a cookie. So, the dog will figure out what action caused it to receive a cookie and repeat that action. Thus, the dog will understand that catching the ball caused it to receive a cookie and will attempt to repeat catching the ball. Thus, in this way, the dog will learn to catch a ball while aiming to maximize the cookies it can receive.

Similarly, in an RL setting, we will not teach the agent what to do or how to do it; instead, we will give a reward to the agent for every action it does. We will give a positive reward to the agent when it performs a good action and we will give a negative reward to the agent when it performs a bad action. The agent begins by performing a random action and if the action is good, we then give the agent a positive reward so that the agent understands it has performed a good action and it will repeat that action. If the action performed by the agent is bad, then we will give the agent a negative reward so that the agent will understand it has performed a bad action and it will not repeat that action.

Thus, RL can be viewed as a trial and error learning process where the agent tries out different actions and learns the good action, which gives a positive reward.

In the dog analogy, the dog represents the agent, and giving a cookie to the dog upon it catching the ball is a positive reward and not giving a cookie is a negative reward. So, the dog (agent) explores different actions, which are catching the ball and not catching the ball, and understands that catching the ball is a good action as it brings the dog a positive reward (getting a cookie).

Let's further explore the idea of RL with one more simple example. Let's suppose we want to teach a robot (agent) to walk without hitting a mountain, as *Figure 1.1* shows:

Figure 1.1: Robot walking

We will not teach the robot explicitly to not go in the direction of the mountain. Instead, if the robot hits the mountain and gets stuck, we give the robot a negative reward, say -1. So, the robot will understand that hitting the mountain is the wrong action, and it will not repeat that action:

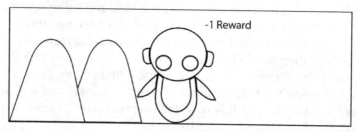

Figure 1.2: Robot hits mountain

Similarly, when the robot walks in the right direction without hitting the mountain, we give the robot a positive reward, say +1. So, the robot will understand that not hitting the mountain is a good action, and it will repeat that action:

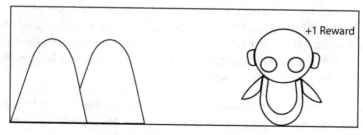

Figure 1.3: Robot avoids mountain

Thus, in the RL setting, the agent explores different actions and learns the best action based on the reward it gets.

Now that we have a basic idea of how RL works, in the upcoming sections, we will go into more detail and also learn the important concepts involved in RL.

The RL algorithm

The steps involved in a typical RL algorithm are as follows:

1. First, the agent interacts with the environment by performing an action.
2. By performing an action, the agent moves from one state to another.
3. Then the agent will receive a reward based on the action it performed.
4. Based on the reward, the agent will understand whether the action is good or bad.
5. If the action was good, that is, if the agent received a positive reward, then the agent will prefer performing that action, else the agent will try performing other actions in search of a positive reward.

RL is basically a trial and error learning process. Now, let's revisit our chess game example. The agent (software program) is the chess player. So, the agent interacts with the environment (chessboard) by performing an action (moves). If the agent gets a positive reward for an action, then it will prefer performing that action; else it will find a different action that gives a positive reward.

Ultimately, the goal of the agent is to maximize the reward it gets. If the agent receives a good reward, then it means it has performed a good action. If the agent performs a good action, then it implies that it can win the game. Thus, the agent learns to win the game by maximizing the reward.

RL agent in the grid world

Let's strengthen our understanding of RL by looking at another simple example. Consider the following grid world environment:

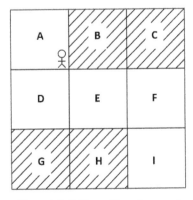

Figure 1.4: Grid world environment

Poth finding
with
STATCS.

The positions **A** to **I** in the environment are called the states of the environment. The goal of the agent is to reach state **I** by starting from state **A** without visiting the shaded states (**B, C, G,** and **H**). Thus, in order to achieve the goal, whenever our agent visits a shaded state, we will give a negative reward (say -1) and when it visits an unshaded state, we will give a positive reward (say +1). The actions in the environment are moving *up, down, right* and *left*. The agent can perform any of these four actions to reach state **I** from state **A**.

The first time the agent interacts with the environment (the first iteration), the agent is unlikely to perform the correct action in each state, and thus it receives a negative reward. That is, in the first iteration, the agent performs a random action in each state, and this may lead the agent to receive a negative reward. But over a series of iterations, the agent learns to perform the correct action in each state through the reward it obtains, helping it achieve the goal. Let us explore this in detail.

Iteration 1

As we learned, in the first iteration, the agent performs a random action in each state. For instance, look at the following figure. In the first iteration, the agent moves *right* from state **A** and reaches the new state **B**. But since **B** is the shaded state, the agent will receive a negative reward and so the agent will understand that moving *right* is not a good action in state **A**. When it visits state **A** next time, it will try out a different action instead of moving *right*:

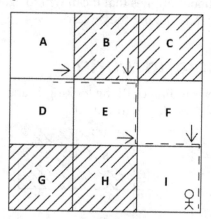

Figure 1.5: Actions taken by the agent in iteration 1

As *Figure 1.5* shows, from state **B**, the agent moves *down* and reaches the new state **E**. Since **E** is an unshaded state, the agent will receive a positive reward, so the agent will understand that moving *down* from state **B** is a good action.

From state **E**, the agent moves *right* and reaches state **F**. Since **F** is an unshaded state, the agent receives a positive reward, and it will understand that moving *right* from state **E** is a good action. From state **F**, the agent moves *down* and reaches the goal state **I** and receives a positive reward, so the agent will understand that moving down from state **F** is a good action.

Iteration 2

In the second iteration, from state **A**, instead of moving *right*, the agent tries out a different action as the agent learned in the previous iteration that moving *right* is not a good action in state **A**.

Thus, as *Figure 1.6* shows, in this iteration the agent moves *down* from state **A** and reaches state **D**. Since **D** is an unshaded state, the agent receives a positive reward and now the agent will understand that moving *down* is a good action in state **A**:

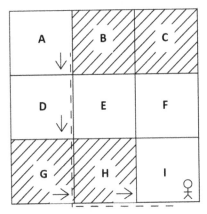

Figure 1.6: Actions taken by the agent in iteration 2

As shown in the preceding figure, from state **D**, the agent moves *down* and reaches state **G**. But since **G** is a shaded state, the agent will receive a negative reward and so the agent will understand that moving *down* is not a good action in state **D**, and when it visits state **D** next time, it will try out a different action instead of moving *down*.

From **G**, the agent moves *right* and reaches state **H**. Since **H** is a shaded state, it will receive a negative reward and understand that moving *right* is not a good action in state **G**.

From **H** it moves *right* and reaches the goal state **I** and receives a positive reward, so the agent will understand that moving *right* from state **H** is a good action.

Iteration 3

In the third iteration, the agent moves *down* from state **A** since, in the second iteration, our agent learned that moving *down* is a good action in state **A**. So, the agent moves *down* from state **A** and reaches the next state, **D**, as *Figure 1.7* shows:

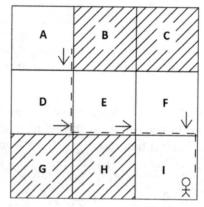

Figure 1.7: Actions taken by the agent in iteration 3

Now, from state **D**, the agent tries a different action instead of moving *down* since in the second iteration our agent learned that moving *down* is not a good action in state **D**. So, in this iteration, the agent moves *right* from state **D** and reaches state **E**.

From state **E**, the agent moves *right* as the agent already learned in the first iteration that moving *right* from state **E** is a good action and reaches state **F**.

Now, from state **F**, the agent moves *down* since the agent learned in the first iteration that moving *down* is a good action in state **F**, and reaches the goal state **I**.

Figure 1.8 shows the result of the third iteration:

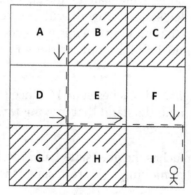

Figure 1.8: The agent reaches the goal state without visiting the shaded states

As we can see, our agent has successfully learned to reach the goal state **I** from state **A** without visiting the shaded states based on the rewards.

In this way, the agent will try out different actions in each state and understand whether an action is good or bad based on the reward it obtains. The goal of the agent is to maximize rewards. So, the agent will always try to perform good actions that give a positive reward, and when the agent performs good actions in each state, then it ultimately leads the agent to achieve the goal.

Note that these iterations are called episodes in RL terminology. We will learn more about episodes later in the chapter.

How RL differs from other ML paradigms

We can categorize ML into three types:

- Supervised learning
- Unsupervised learning
- RL

In supervised learning, the machine learns from training data. The training data consists of a labeled pair of inputs and outputs. So, we train the model (agent) using the training data in such a way that the model can generalize its learning to new unseen data. It is called supervised learning because the training data acts as a supervisor, since it has a labeled pair of inputs and outputs, and it guides the model in learning the given task.

Now, let's understand the difference between supervised and reinforcement learning with an example. Consider the dog analogy we discussed earlier in the chapter. In supervised learning, to teach the dog to catch a ball, we will teach it explicitly by specifying turn left, go right, move forward seven steps, catch the ball, and so on in the form of training data. But in RL, we just throw a ball, and every time the dog catches the ball, we give it a cookie (reward). So, the dog will learn to catch the ball while trying to maximize the cookies (reward) it can get.

Let's consider one more example. Say we want to train the model to play chess using supervised learning. In this case, we will have training data that includes all the moves a player can make in each state, along with labels indicating whether it is a good move or not. Then, we train the model to learn from this training data, whereas in the case of RL, our agent will not be given any sort of training data; instead, we just give a reward to the agent for each action it performs. Then, the agent will learn by interacting with the environment and, based on the reward it gets, it will choose its actions.

Similar to supervised learning, in unsupervised learning, we train the model (agent) based on the training data. But in the case of unsupervised learning, the training data does not contain any labels; that is, it consists of only inputs and not outputs. The goal of unsupervised learning is to determine hidden patterns in the input. There is a common misconception that RL is a kind of unsupervised learning, but it is not. In unsupervised learning, the model learns the hidden structure, whereas, in RL, the model learns by maximizing the reward.

For instance, consider a movie recommendation system. Say we want to recommend a new movie to the user. With unsupervised learning, the model (agent) will find movies similar to the movies the user (or users with a profile similar to the user) has viewed before and recommend new movies to the user.

With RL, the agent constantly receives feedback from the user. This feedback represents rewards (a reward could be ratings the user has given for a movie they have watched, time spent watching a movie, time spent watching trailers, and so on). Based on the rewards, an RL agent will understand the movie preference of the user and then suggest new movies accordingly.

Since the RL agent is learning with the aid of rewards, it can understand if the user's movie preference changes and suggest new movies according to the user's changed movie preference dynamically.

Thus, we can say that in both supervised and unsupervised learning the model (agent) learns based on the given training dataset, whereas in RL the agent learns by directly interacting with the environment. Thus, RL is essentially an interaction between the agent and its environment.

Before moving on to the fundamental concepts of RL, we will introduce a popular process to aid decision-making in an RL environment.

Markov Decision Processes

The **Markov Decision Process (MDP)** provides a mathematical framework for solving the RL problem. Almost all RL problems can be modeled as an MDP. MDPs are widely used for solving various optimization problems. In this section, we will understand what an MDP is and how it is used in RL.

To understand an MDP, first, we need to learn about the Markov property and Markov chain.

The Markov property and Markov chain

The Markov property states that the future depends only on the present and not on the past. The Markov chain, also known as the Markov process, consists of a sequence of states that strictly obey the Markov property; that is, the Markov chain is the probabilistic model that solely depends on the current state to predict the next state and not the previous states, that is, the future is conditionally independent of the past.

For example, if we want to predict the weather and we know that the current state is cloudy, we can predict that the next state could be rainy. We concluded that the next state is likely to be rainy only by considering the current state (cloudy) and not the previous states, which might have been sunny, windy, and so on.

However, the Markov property does not hold for all processes. For instance, throwing a dice (the next state) has no dependency on the previous number that showed up on the dice (the current state).

Moving from one state to another is called a transition, and its probability is called a transition probability. We denote the transition probability by $P(s'|s)$. It indicates the probability of moving from the state s to the next state s'. Say we have three states (cloudy, rainy, and windy) in our Markov chain. Then we can represent the probability of transitioning from one state to another using a table called a Markov table, as shown in *Table 1.1*:

Current State	Next State	Transition Probability
Cloudy	Rainy	0.7
Cloudy	Windy	0.3
Rainy	Rainy	0.8
Rainy	Cloudy	0.2
Windy	Rainy	1.0

Table 1.1: An example of a Markov table

From *Table 1.1*, we can observe that:

- From the state cloudy, we transition to the state rainy with 70% probability and to the state windy with 30% probability.
- From the state rainy, we transition to the same state rainy with 80% probability and to the state cloudy with 20% probability.
- From the state windy, we transition to the state rainy with 100% probability.

We can also represent this transition information of the Markov chain in the form of a state diagram, as shown in *Figure 1.9*:

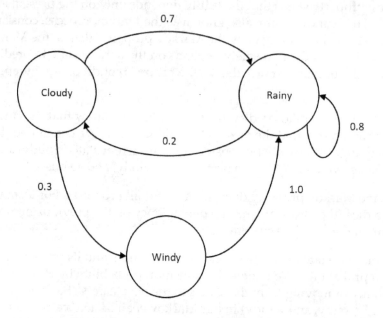

Figure 1.9: A state diagram of a Markov chain

We can also formulate the transition probabilities into a matrix called the transition matrix, as shown in *Figure 1.10*:

$$
\begin{array}{c}
\quad\quad \text{Cloudy} \;\; \text{Rainy} \;\; \text{Windy} \\
\begin{array}{c}
\text{Cloudy} \\
\text{Rainy} \\
\text{Windy}
\end{array}
\begin{bmatrix}
0.0 & 0.7 & 0.3 \\
0.2 & 0.8 & 0.0 \\
0.0 & 1.0 & 0.0
\end{bmatrix}
\end{array}
$$

Figure 1.10: A transition matrix

Thus, to conclude, we can say that the Markov chain or Markov process consists of a set of states along with their transition probabilities.

The Markov Reward Process

The **Markov Reward Process** (**MRP**) is an extension of the Markov chain with the reward function. That is, we learned that the Markov chain consists of states and a transition probability. The MRP consists of states, a transition probability, and also a reward function.

A reward function tells us the reward we obtain in each state. For instance, based on our previous weather example, the reward function tells us the reward we obtain in the state cloudy, the reward we obtain in the state windy, and so on. The reward function is usually denoted by $R(s)$.

Thus, the MRP consists of states s, a transition probability $P(s'|s)$, and a reward function $R(s)$.

The Markov Decision Process

The **Markov Decision Process** (**MDP**) is an extension of the MRP with actions. That is, we learned that the MRP consists of states, a transition probability, and a reward function. The MDP consists of states, a transition probability, a reward function, and also actions. We learned that the Markov property states that the next state is dependent only on the current state and is not based on the previous state. Is the Markov property applicable to the RL setting? Yes! In the RL environment, the agent makes decisions only based on the current state and not based on the past states. So, we can model an RL environment as an MDP.

Let's understand this with an example. Given any environment, we can formulate the environment using an MDP. For instance, let's consider the same grid world environment we learned earlier. *Figure 1.11* shows the grid world environment, and the goal of the agent is to reach state **I** from state **A** without visiting the shaded states:

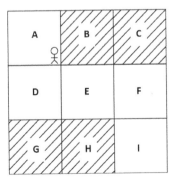

Figure 1.11: Grid world environment

An agent makes a decision (action) in the environment only based on the current state the agent is in and not based on the past state. So, we can formulate our environment as an MDP. We learned that the MDP consists of states, actions, transition probabilities, and a reward function. Now, let's learn how this relates to our RL environment:

States – A set of states present in the environment. Thus, in the grid world environment, we have states **A** to **I**.

Actions – A set of actions that our agent can perform in each state. An agent performs an action and moves from one state to another. Thus, in the grid world environment, the set of actions is *up*, *down*, *left*, and *right*.

Transition probability – The transition probability is denoted by $P(s'|s, a)$. It implies the probability of moving from a state s to the next state s' while performing an action a. If you observe, in the MRP, the transition probability is just $P(s'|s)$, that is, the probability of going from state s to state s', and it doesn't include actions. But in the MDP, we include the actions, and thus the transition probability is denoted by $P(s'|s, a)$.

For example, in our grid world environment, say the transition probability of moving from state **A** to state **B** while performing an action *right* is 100%. This can be expressed as $P(B \,|\, A, \text{right}) = 1.0$. We can also view this in the state diagram, as shown in *Figure 1.12*:

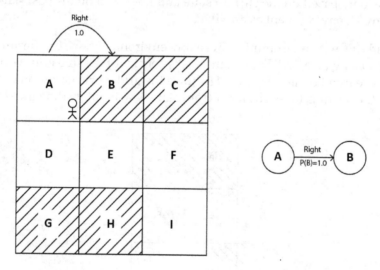

Figure 1.12: Transition probability of moving right from A to B

Suppose our agent is in state **C** and the transition probability of moving from state **C** to state **F** while performing the action *down* is 90%, then it can be expressed as $P(F \mid C, down) = 0.9$. We can also view this in the state diagram, as shown in *Figure 1.13*:

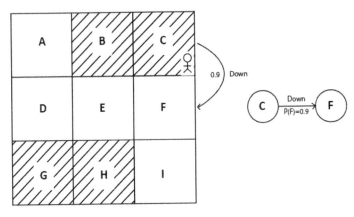

Figure 1.13: Transition probability of moving down from C to F

Reward function - The reward function is denoted by $R(s, a, s')$. It represents the reward our agent obtains while transitioning from state s to state s' while performing an action a.

Say the reward we obtain while transitioning from state **A** to state **B** while performing the action *right* is -1, then it can be expressed as $R(A, right, B) = -1$. We can also view this in the state diagram, as shown in *Figure 1.14*:

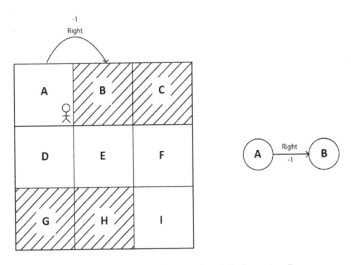

Figure 1.14: Reward of moving right from A to B

Suppose our agent is in state **C** and say the reward we obtain while transitioning from state **C** to state **F** while performing the action *down* is +1, then it can be expressed as $R(C, down, F) = +1$. We can also view this in the state diagram, as shown in *Figure 1.15*:

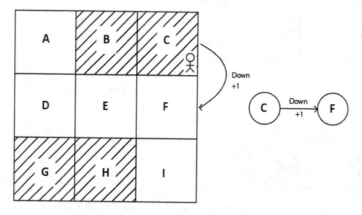

Figure 1.15: Reward of moving down from C to F

Thus, an RL environment can be represented as an MDP with states, actions, transition probability, and the reward function. But wait! What is the use of representing the RL environment using the MDP? We can solve the RL problem easily once we model our environment as the MDP. For instance, once we model our grid world environment using the MDP, then we can easily find how to reach the goal state **I** from state **A** without visiting the shaded states. We will learn more about this in the upcoming chapters. Next, we will go through more essential concepts of RL.

Fundamental concepts of RL

In this section, we will learn about several important fundamental RL concepts.

Math essentials

Before going ahead, let's quickly recap expectation from our high school days, as we will be dealing with expectation throughout the book.

Expectation

Let's say we have a variable X and it has the values 1, 2, 3, 4, 5, 6. To compute the average value of X, we can just sum all the values of X divided by the number of values of X. Thus, the average of X is $(1+2+3+4+5+6)/6 = 3.5$.

Now, let's suppose X is a random variable. The random variable takes values based on a random experiment, such as throwing dice, tossing a coin, and so on. The random variable takes different values with some probabilities. Let's suppose we are throwing a fair dice, then the possible outcomes (X) are 1, 2, 3, 4, 5, and 6 and the probability of occurrence of each of these outcomes is 1/6, as shown in *Table 1.2*:

X	1	2	3	4	5	6
P(x)	1/6	1/6	1/6	1/6	1/6	1/6

Table 1.2: Probabilities of throwing a dice

How can we compute the average value of the random variable X? Since each value has a probability of an occurrence, we can't just take the average. So, instead, we compute the weighted average, that is, the sum of values of X multiplied by their respective probabilities, and this is called expectation. The expectation of a random variable X can be defined as:

$$E(X) = \sum_{i=1}^{N} x_i p(x_i)$$

Thus, the expectation of the random variable X is $E(X) = 1(1/6) + 2(1/6) + 3(1/6) + 4(1/6) + 5(1/6) + 6(1/6) = 3.5$.

The expectation is also known as the expected value. Thus, the expected value of the random variable X is 3.5. Thus, when we say expectation or the expected value of a random variable, it basically means the weighted average.

Now, we will look into the expectation of a function of a random variable. Let $f(x) = x^2$, then we can write:

X	1	2	3	4	5	6
f(x)	1	4	9	16	25	36
P(x)	1/6	1/6	1/6	1/6	1/6	1/6

Table 1.3: Probabilities of throwing a dice

The expectation of a function of a random variable can be computed as:

$$\mathbb{E}_{x \sim p(x)}[f(X)] = \sum_{i=1}^{N} f(x_i)p(x_i)$$

Thus, the expected value of $f(X)$ is given as $E(f(X)) = 1(1/6) + 4(1/6) + 9(1/6) + 16(1/6) + 25(1/6) + 36(1/6) = 15.1$.

Action space

Consider the grid world environment shown in *Figure 1.16*:

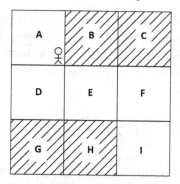

Figure 1.16: Grid world environment

In the preceding grid world environment, the goal of the agent is to reach state **I** starting from state **A** without visiting the shaded states. In each of the states, the agent can perform any of the four actions—*up, down, left,* and *right*—to achieve the goal. The set of all possible actions in the environment is called the action space. Thus, for this grid world environment, the action space will be [*up, down, left, right*].

We can categorize action spaces into two types:

- Discrete action space
- Continuous action space

Discrete action space: When our action space consists of actions that are discrete, then it is called a discrete action space. For instance, in the grid world environment, our action space consists of four discrete actions, which are up, down, left, right, and so it is called a discrete action space.

Continuous action space: When our action space consists of actions that are continuous, then it is called a continuous action space. For instance, let's suppose we are training an agent to drive a car, then our action space will consist of several actions that have continuous values, such as the speed at which we need to drive the car, the number of degrees we need to rotate the wheel, and so on. In cases where our action space consists of actions that are continuous, it is called a continuous action space.

Policy

A policy defines the agent's behavior in an environment. The policy tells the agent what action to perform in each state. For instance, in the grid world environment, we have states **A** to **I** and four possible actions. The policy may tell the agent to move *down* in state **A**, move *right* in state **D**, and so on.

To interact with the environment for the first time, we initialize a random policy, that is, the random policy tells the agent to perform a random action in each state. Thus, in an initial iteration, the agent performs a random action in each state and tries to learn whether the action is good or bad based on the reward it obtains. Over a series of iterations, an agent will learn to perform good actions in each state, which gives a positive reward. Thus, we can say that over a series of iterations, the agent will learn a good policy that gives a positive reward.

This good policy is called the optimal policy. The optimal policy is the policy that gets the agent a good reward and helps the agent to achieve the goal. For instance, in our grid world environment, the optimal policy tells the agent to perform an action in each state such that the agent can reach state **I** from state **A** without visiting the shaded states.

The optimal policy is shown in *Figure 1.17*. As we can observe, the agent selects the action in each state based on the optimal policy and reaches the terminal state **I** from the starting state **A** without visiting the shaded states:

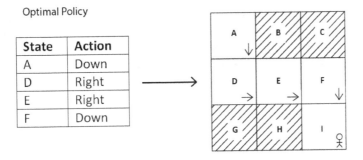

Figure 1.17: The optimal policy in the grid world environment

Thus, the optimal policy tells the agent to perform the correct action in each state so that the agent can receive a good reward.

A policy can be classified as the following:

- A deterministic policy
- A stochastic policy

Deterministic policy

The policy that we just covered is called a deterministic policy. A deterministic policy tells the agent to perform one particular action in a state. Thus, the deterministic policy maps the state to one particular action and is often denoted by μ. Given a state s at a time t, a deterministic policy tells the agent to perform one particular action a. It can be expressed as:

$$a_t = \mu(s_t)$$

For instance, consider our grid world example. Given state **A**, the deterministic policy μ tells the agent to perform the action *down*. This can be expressed as:

$$\mu(A) = \text{Down}$$

Thus, according to the deterministic policy, whenever the agent visits state **A**, it performs the action *down*.

Stochastic policy

Unlike a deterministic policy, a stochastic policy does not map a state directly to one particular action; instead, it maps the state to a probability distribution over an action space.

That is, we learned that given a state, the deterministic policy will tell the agent to perform one particular action in the given state, so whenever the agent visits the state it always performs the same particular action. But with a stochastic policy, given a state, the stochastic policy will return a probability distribution over an action space. So instead of performing the same action every time the agent visits the state, the agent performs different actions each time based on a probability distribution returned by the stochastic policy.

Let's understand this with an example; we know that our grid world environment's action space consists of four actions, which are [*up, down, left, right*]. Given a state **A**, the stochastic policy returns the probability distribution over the action space as [0.10,0.70,0.10,0.10]. Now, whenever the agent visits state **A**, instead of selecting the same particular action every time, the agent selects *up* 10% of the time, *down* 70% of the time, *left* 10% of the time, and *right* 10% of the time.

The difference between the deterministic policy and stochastic policy is shown in *Figure 1.18*. As we can observe, the deterministic policy maps the state to one particular action, whereas the stochastic policy maps the state to the probability distribution over an action space:

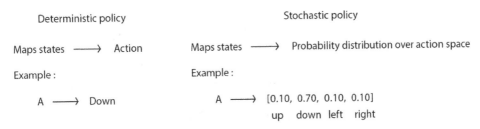

Figure 1.18: The difference between deterministic and stochastic policies

Thus, the stochastic policy maps the state to a probability distribution over the action space and is often denoted by π. Say we have a state s and action a at a time t, then we can express the stochastic policy as:

$$a_t \sim \pi(s_t)$$

Or it can also be expressed as $\pi(a_t|s_t)$.

We can categorize the stochastic policy into two types:

- Categorical policy
- Gaussian policy

Categorical policy

A stochastic policy is called a categorical policy when the action space is discrete. That is, the stochastic policy uses a categorical probability distribution over the action space to select actions when the action space is discrete. For instance, in the grid world environment from the previous example, we select actions based on a categorical probability distribution (discrete distribution) as the action space of the environment is discrete. As *Figure 1.19* shows, given state **A**, we select an action based on the categorical probability distribution over the action space:

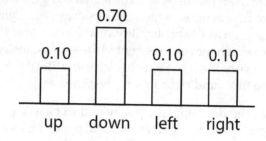

Figure 1.19: Probability of next move from state A for a discrete action space

Gaussian policy

A stochastic policy is called a Gaussian policy when our action space is continuous. That is, the stochastic policy uses a Gaussian probability distribution over the action space to select actions when the action space is continuous. Let's understand this with a simple example. Suppose we are training an agent to drive a car and say we have one continuous action in our action space. Let the action be the speed of the car, and the value of the speed of the car ranges from 0 to 150 kmph. Then, the stochastic policy uses the Gaussian distribution over the action space to select an action, as *Figure 1.20* shows:

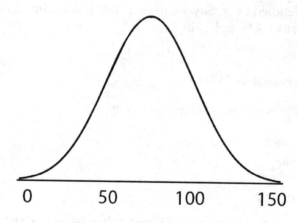

Figure 1.20: Gaussian distribution

We will learn more about the Gaussian policy in the upcoming chapters.

Episode

The agent interacts with the environment by performing some actions, starting from the initial state and reaches the final state. This agent-environment interaction starting from the initial state until the final state is called an episode. For instance, in a car racing video game, the agent plays the game by starting from the initial state (the starting point of the race) and reaches the final state (the endpoint of the race). This is considered an episode. An episode is also often called a trajectory (the path taken by the agent) and it is denoted by τ.

An agent can play the game for any number of episodes, and each episode is independent of the others. What is the use of playing the game for multiple episodes? In order to learn the optimal policy, that is, the policy that tells the agent to perform the correct action in each state, the agent plays the game for many episodes.

For example, let's say we are playing a car racing game; the first time, we may not win the game, so we play the game several times to understand more about the game and discover some good strategies for winning the game. Similarly, in the first episode, the agent may not win the game and it plays the game for several episodes to understand more about the game environment and good strategies to win the game.

Say we begin the game from an initial state at a time step $t = 0$ and reach the final state at a time step T, then the episode information consists of the agent-environment interaction, such as state, action, and reward, starting from the initial state until the final state, that is, $(s_0, a_0, r_0, s_1, a_1, r_1, \ldots, s_T)$.

Figure 1.21 shows an example of an episode/trajectory:

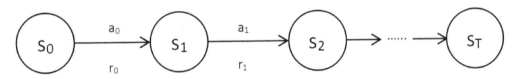

Figure 1.21: An example of an episode

Let's strengthen our understanding of the episode and the optimal policy with the grid world environment. We learned that in the grid world environment, the goal of our agent is to reach the final state **I** starting from the initial state **A** without visiting the shaded states. An agent receives a +1 reward when it visits the unshaded states and a -1 reward when it visits the shaded states.

When we say generate an episode, it means going from the initial state to the final state. The agent generates the first episode using a random policy and explores the environment and over several episodes, it will learn the optimal policy.

Episode 1

As the *Figure 1.22* shows, in the first episode, the agent uses a random policy and selects a random action in each state from the initial state until the final state and observes the reward:

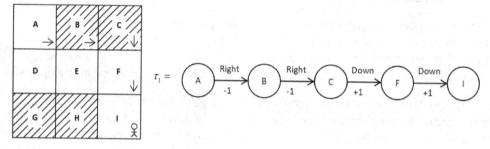

Figure 1.22: Episode 1

Episode 2

In the second episode, the agent tries a different policy to avoid the negative rewards it received in the previous episode. For instance, as we can observe in the previous episode, the agent selected the action *right* in state **A** and received a negative reward, so in this episode, instead of selecting the action *right* in state **A**, it tries a different action, say *down*, as shown in *Figure 1.23*:

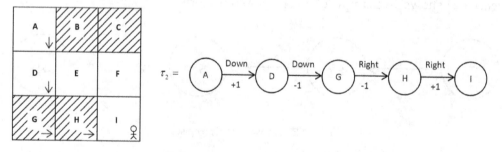

Figure 1.23: Episode 2

Episode n

Thus, over a series of episodes, the agent learns the optimal policy, that is, the policy that takes the agent to the final state **I** from state **A** without visiting the shaded states, as *Figure 1.24* shows:

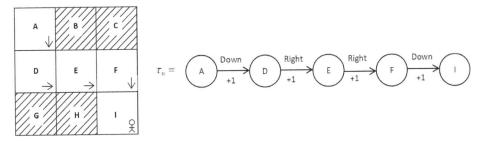

Figure 1.24: Episode n

Episodic and continuous tasks

An RL task can be categorized as:

- An episodic task
- A continuous task

Episodic task: As the name suggests, an episodic task is one that has a terminal/ final state. That is, episodic tasks are tasks made up of episodes and thus they have a terminal state. For example, in a car racing game, we start from the starting point (initial state) and reach the destination (terminal state).

Continuous task: Unlike episodic tasks, continuous tasks do not contain any episodes and so they don't have any terminal state. For example, a personal assistance robot does not have a terminal state.

Horizon

Horizon is the time step until which the agent interacts with the environment. We can classify the horizon into two categories:

- Finite horizon
- Infinite horizon

Finite horizon: If the agent-environment interaction stops at a particular time step, then the horizon is called a finite horizon. For instance, in episodic tasks, an agent interacts with the environment by starting from the initial state at time step $t = 0$ and reaches the final state at time step T. Since the agent-environment interaction stops at time step T, it is considered a finite horizon.

Infinite horizon: If the agent-environment interaction never stops, then it is called an infinite horizon. For instance, we learned that a continuous task has no terminal states. This means the agent-environment interaction will never stop in a continuous task and so it is considered an infinite horizon.

Return and discount factor

A return can be defined as the sum of the rewards obtained by the agent in an episode. The return is often denoted by R or G. Say the agent starts from the initial state at time step $t = 0$ and reaches the final state at time step T, then the return obtained by the agent is given as:

$$R(\tau) = r_0 + r_1 + r_2 + \ldots + r_T$$

$$R(\tau) = \sum_{t=0}^{T} r_t$$

Let's understand this with an example; consider the trajectory (episode) τ:

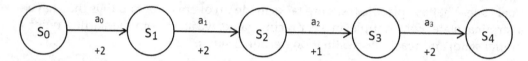

Figure 1.25: Trajectory/episode τ

The return of the trajectory is the sum of the rewards, that is, $R(\tau) = 2 + 2 + 1 + 2 = 7$.

Thus, we can say that the goal of our agent is to maximize the return, that is, maximize the sum of rewards (cumulative rewards) obtained over the episode. How can we maximize the return? We can maximize the return if we perform the correct action in each state. Okay, how can we perform the correct action in each state? We can perform the correct action in each state by using the optimal policy. Thus, we can maximize the return using the optimal policy. Thus, the optimal policy is the policy that gets our agent the maximum return (sum of rewards) by performing the correct action in each state.

Okay, how can we define the return for continuous tasks? We learned that in continuous tasks there are no terminal states, so we can define the return as a sum of rewards up to infinity:

$$R(\tau) = r_0 + r_1 + r_2 + \ldots + r_\infty$$

But how can we maximize the return that just sums to infinity? We introduce a new term called discount factor γ and rewrite our return as:

$$R(\tau) = \gamma^0 r_0 + \gamma^1 r_1 + \gamma^2 r_2 + \ldots + \gamma^n r_\infty$$

$$R(\tau) = \sum_{t=0}^{\infty} \gamma^t r_t$$

Okay, but how is this discount factor γ helping us? It helps us in preventing the return from reaching infinity by deciding how much importance we give to future rewards and immediate rewards. The value of the discount factor ranges from 0 to 1. When we set the discount factor to a small value (close to 0), it implies that we give more importance to immediate rewards than to future rewards. When we set the discount factor to a high value (close to 1), it implies that we give more importance to future rewards than to immediate rewards. Let's understand this with an example with different discount factor values.

Small discount factor

Let's set the discount factor to a small value, say 0.2, that is, let's set $\gamma = 0.2$, then we can write:

$$
\begin{aligned}
R &= (\gamma)^0 r_0 + (\gamma)^1 r_1 + (\gamma)^2 r_2 + \ldots \\
&= (0.2)^0 r_0 + (0.2)^1 r_1 + (0.2)^2 r_2 + \ldots \\
&= (1) r_0 + (0.2) r_1 + (0.04) r_2 + \ldots
\end{aligned}
$$

From this equation, we can observe that the reward at each time step is weighted by a discount factor. As the time steps increase, the discount factor (weight) decreases and thus the importance of rewards at future time steps also decreases. That is, from the equation, we can observe that:

- At time step 0, the reward r_0 is weighted by a discount factor of 1.
- At time step 1, the reward r_1 is weighted by a heavily decreased discount factor of 0.2.
- At time step 2, the reward r_2 is weighted by a heavily decreased discount factor of 0.04.

As we can observe, the discount factor is heavily decreased for the subsequent time steps and more importance is given to the immediate reward r_0 than the rewards obtained at the future time steps. Thus, when we set the discount factor to a small value, we give more importance to the immediate reward than future rewards.

Large discount factor

Let's set the discount factor to a high value, say 0.9, that is, let's set, $\gamma = 0.9$, then we can write:

$$
\begin{aligned}
R &= (\gamma)^0 r_0 + (\gamma)^1 r_1 + (\gamma)^2 r_2 + \ldots \\
&= (0.9)^0 r_0 + (0.9)^1 r_1 + (0.9)^2 r_2 + \ldots \\
&= (1) r_0 + (0.9) r_1 + (0.81) r_2 + \ldots
\end{aligned}
$$

From this equation, we can infer that as the time step increases the discount factor (weight) decreases; however, it is not decreasing heavily (unlike the previous case) since here we started off with $\gamma = 0.9$. So, in this case, we can say that we give more importance to future rewards. That is, from the equation, we can observe that:

- At time step 0, the reward r_0 is weighted by a discount factor of 1.
- At time step 1, the reward r_1 is weighted by a slightly decreased discount factor of 0.9.
- At time step 2, the reward r_2 is weighted by a slightly decreased discount factor of 0.81.

As we can observe, the discount factor is decreased for subsequent time steps but unlike the previous case, the discount factor is not decreased heavily. Thus, when we set the discount factor to a high value, we give more importance to future rewards than the immediate reward.

What happens when we set the discount factor to 0?

When we set the discount factor to 0, that is $\gamma = 0$, it implies that we consider only the immediate reward r_0 and not the reward obtained from the future time steps. Thus, when we set the discount factor to 0, then the agent will never learn as it will consider only the immediate reward r_0, as shown here:

$$
\begin{aligned}
R &= (\gamma)^0 r_0 + (\gamma)^1 r_1 + (\gamma)^2 r_2 + \ldots \\
&= (0)^0 r_0 + (0)^1 r_1 + (0)^2 r_2 + \ldots \\
&= (1) r_0 + (0) r_1 + (0) r_2 + \ldots \\
&= r_0
\end{aligned}
$$

As we can observe, when we set $\gamma = 0$, our return will be just the immediate reward r_0.

What happens when we set the discount factor to 1?

When we set the discount factor to 1, that is $\gamma = 1$, it implies that we consider all the future rewards. Thus, when we set the discount factor to 1, then the agent will learn forever, looking for all the future rewards, which may lead to infinity, as shown here:

$$
\begin{aligned}
R &= (\gamma)^0 r_0 + (\gamma)^1 r_1 + (\gamma)^2 r_2 + \cdots \\
&= (1)^0 r_0 + (1)^1 r_1 + (1)^2 r_2 + \cdots \\
&= r_0 + r_1 + r_2 + \cdots
\end{aligned}
$$

As we can observe, when we set $\gamma = 1$, then our return will be the sum of rewards up to infinity.

Thus, we have learned that when we set the discount factor to 0, the agent will never learn, considering only the immediate reward, and when we set the discount factor to 1 the agent will learn forever, looking for the future rewards that lead to infinity. So, the optimal value of the discount factor lies between 0.2 and 0.8.

But the question is, why should we care about immediate and future rewards? We give importance to immediate and future rewards depending on the tasks. In some tasks, future rewards are more desirable than immediate rewards, and vice versa. In a chess game, the goal is to defeat the opponent's king. If we give more importance to the immediate reward, which is acquired by actions such as our pawn defeating any opposing chessman, then the agent will learn to perform this sub-goal instead of learning the actual goal. So, in this case, we give greater importance to future rewards than the immediate reward, whereas in some cases, we prefer immediate rewards over future rewards. Would you prefer chocolates if I gave them to you today or 13 days later?

In the following two sections, we'll analyze the two fundamental functions of RL.

The value function

The value function, also called the state value function, denotes the value of the state. The value of a state is the return an agent would obtain starting from that state following policy π. The value of a state or value function is usually denoted by $V(s)$ and it can be expressed as:

$$
V^\pi(s) = [R(\tau)|s_0 = s]
$$

where $s_0 = s$ implies that the starting state is s. The value of a state is called the state value.

Let's understand the value function with an example. Let's suppose we generate the trajectory τ following some policy π in our grid world environment, as shown in *Figure 1.26*:

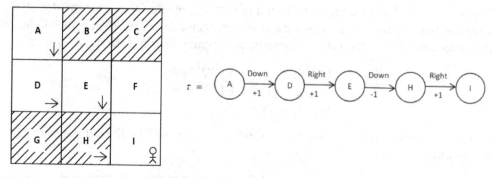

Figure 1.26: A value function example

Now, how do we compute the value of all the states in our trajectory? We learned that the value of a state is the return (sum of rewards) an agent would obtain starting from that state following policy π. The preceding trajectory is generated using policy π, thus we can say that the value of a state is the return (sum of rewards) of the trajectory starting from that state:

- The value of state **A** is the return of the trajectory starting from state **A**. Thus, $V(A) = 1+1+ -1+1 = 2$.

- The value of state **D** is the return of the trajectory starting from state **D**. Thus, $V(D) = 1-1+1= 1$.

- The value of state **E** is the return of the trajectory starting from state **E**. Thus, $V(E) = -1+1 = 0$.

- The value of state **H** is the return of the trajectory starting from state **H**. Thus, $V(H) = 1$.

What about the value of the final state **I**? We learned the value of a state is the return (sum of rewards) starting from that state. We know that we obtain a reward when we transition from one state to another. Since **I** is the final state, we don't make any transition from the final state, so there is no reward and thus no value for the final state **I**.

In a nutshell, the value of a state is the return of the trajectory starting from that state.

Wait! There is a small change here: instead of taking the return directly as a value of a state, we will use the expected return. Thus, the value function or the value of state s can be defined as the expected return that the agent would obtain starting from state s following policy π. It can be expressed as:

$$V^\pi(s) = \underset{\tau \sim \pi}{\mathbb{E}} \left[R(\tau) | s_0 = s \right]$$

Now, the question is why expected return? Why we can't we just compute the value of a state as a return directly? Because our return is the random variable and it takes different values with some probability.

Let's understand this with a simple example. Suppose we have a stochastic policy π. We learned that unlike the deterministic policy, which maps the state to the action directly, the stochastic policy maps the state to the probability distribution over the action space. Thus, the stochastic policy selects actions based on a probability distribution.

Let's suppose we are in state **A** and the stochastic policy returns the probability distribution over the action space as $[0.0, 0.80, 0.00, 0.20]$. It implies that with the stochastic policy, in state **A**, we perform the action *down* 80% of the time, that is, $\pi(down|A) = 0.8$, and the action *right* 20% of the time, that is $\pi(right|A) = 0.20$.

Thus, in state **A**, our stochastic policy π selects the action *down* 80% of the time and the action *right* 20% of the time, and say our stochastic policy selects the action *right* in states **D** and **E** and the action *down* in states **B** and **F** 100% of the time.

First, we generate an episode τ_1 using our stochastic policy π, as shown in *Figure 1.27*:

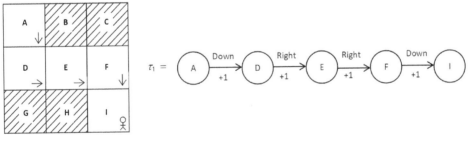

Figure 1.27: Episode τ_1

For better understanding, let's focus only on the value of state **A**. The value of state **A** is the return (sum of rewards) of the trajectory starting from state **A**. Thus, $V(A) = R(\tau_1) = 1 + 1 + 1 + 1 = 4$.

Say we generate another episode τ_2 using the same given stochastic policy π, as shown in *Figure 1.28*:

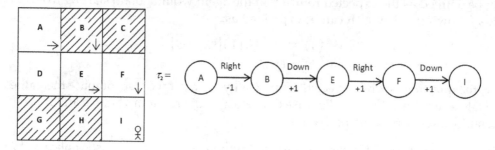

Figure 1.28: Episode τ_2

The value of state **A** is the return (sum of rewards) of the trajectory from state **A**. Thus, $V(A) = R(\tau_2) = -1 + 1 + 1 + 1 = 2$.

As you may observe, although we use the same policy, the values of state **A** in trajectories τ_1 and τ_2 are different. This is because our policy is a stochastic policy and it performs the action *down* in state **A** 80% of the time and the action *right* in state **A** 20% of the time. So, when we generate a trajectory using policy π, the trajectory τ_1 will occur 80% of the time and the trajectory τ_2 will occur 20% of the time. Thus, the return will be 4 for 80% of the time and 2 for 20% of the time.

Thus, instead of taking the value of the state as a return directly, we will take the expected return, since the return takes different values with some probability. The expected return is basically the weighted average, that is, the sum of the return multiplied by their probability. Thus, we can write:

$$V^\pi(s) = \mathop{\mathbb{E}}_{\tau \sim \pi} [R(\tau)|s_0 = s]$$

The value of a state **A** can be obtained as:

$$V^\pi(A) = \mathop{\mathbb{E}}_{\tau \sim \pi} [R(\tau)|s_0 = A]$$

$$= \sum_i R(\tau_i)\pi(a_i|A)$$

$$= R(\tau_1)\pi(\text{down}|A) + R(\tau_2)\pi(\text{right}|A)$$
$$= 4(0.8) + 2(0.2)$$
$$= 3.6$$

Thus, the value of a state is the expected return of the trajectory starting from that state.

Note that the value function depends on the policy, that is, the value of the state varies based on the policy we choose. There can be many different value functions according to different policies. The optimal value function $V^*(s)$ yields the maximum value compared to all the other value functions. It can be expressed as:

$$V^*(s) = \max_{\pi} V^{\pi}(s)$$

For example, let's say we have two policies π_1 and π_2. Let the value of state s using policy π_1 be $V^{\pi_1}(s) = 13$ and the value of state s using policy π_2 be $V^{\pi_2}(s) = 11$. Then the optimal value of state s will be $V^*(s) = 13$ as it is the maximum. The policy that gives the maximum state value is called the optimal policy π^*. Thus, in this case, π_1 is the optimal policy as it gives the maximum state value.

We can view the value function in a table called a value table. Let's say we have two states s_0 and s_1, then the value function can be represented as:

State	Value
s_0	7
s_1	11

Table 1.4: Value table

From the value table, we can tell that it is better to be in state s_1 than state s_0 as s_1 has a higher value. Thus, we can say that state s_1 is the optimal state.

Q function

A Q function, also called the state-action value function, denotes the value of a state-action pair. The value of a state-action pair is the return the agent would obtain starting from state s and performing action a following policy π. The value of a state-action pair or Q function is usually denoted by $Q(s,a)$ and is known as the Q value or state-action value. It is expressed as:

$$Q^{\pi}(s, a) = [R(\tau)|s_0 = s, a_0 = a]$$

Note that the only difference between the value function and Q function is that in the value function we compute the value of a state, whereas in the Q function we compute the value of a state-action pair. Let's understand the Q function with an example. Consider the trajectory in *Figure 1.29* generated using policy π:

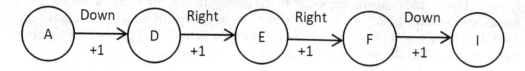

Figure 1.29: A trajectory/episode example

We learned that the Q function computes the value of a state-action pair. Say we need to compute the Q value of state-action pair **A**-*down*. That is the Q value of moving *down* in state **A**. Then the Q value will be the return of our trajectory starting from state **A** and performing the action *down*:

$$Q^\pi(A, \text{down}) = [R(\tau)|s_0 = A, a_0 = \text{down}]$$

$$Q(A, \text{down}) = 1 + 1 + 1 + 1 = 4$$

Let's suppose we need to compute the Q value of the state-action pair **D**-*right*. That is the Q value of moving *right* in state **D**. The Q value will be the return of our trajectory starting from state **D** and performing the action *right*:

$$Q^\pi(A, \text{right}) = [R(\tau)|s_0 = D, a_0 = \text{right}]$$

$$Q(A, \text{right}) = 1 + 1 + 1 = 3$$

Similarly, we can compute the Q value for all the state-action pairs. Similar to what we learned about the value function, instead of taking the return directly as the Q value of a state-action pair, we use the expected return because the return is the random variable and it takes different values with some probability. So, we can redefine our Q function as:

$$Q^\pi(s, a) = \underset{\tau \sim \pi}{\mathbb{E}} [R(\tau)|s_0 = s, a_0 = a]$$

It implies that the Q value is the expected return the agent would obtain starting from state s and performing action a following policy π.

Similar to the value function, the Q function depends on the policy, that is, the Q value varies based on the policy we choose. There can be many different Q functions according to different policies. The optimal Q function is the one that has the maximum Q value over other Q functions, and it can be expressed as:

$$Q^*(s, a) = \max_\pi Q^\pi(s, a)$$

The optimal policy π^* is the policy that gives the maximum Q value.

Like the value function, the Q function can be viewed in a table. It is called a Q table. Let's say we have two states s_0 and s_1, and two actions 0 and 1; then the Q function can be represented as follows:

State	Action	Value
s_0	0	9
s_0	1	11
s_1	0	17
s_1	1	13

Table 1.5: Q table

As we can observe, the Q table represents the Q values of all possible state-action pairs. We learned that the optimal policy is the policy that gets our agent the maximum return (sum of rewards). We can extract the optimal policy from the Q table by just selecting the action that has the maximum Q value in each state. Thus, our optimal policy will select action 1 in state s_0 and action 0 in state s_1 since they have a high Q value, as shown in *Table 1.6*:

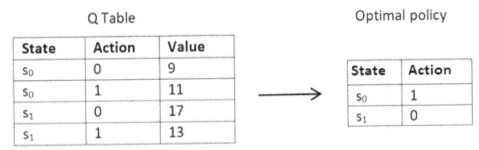

Table 1.6: Optimal policy extracted from the Q table

Thus, we can extract the optimal policy by computing the Q function.

Model-based and model-free learning

Now, let's look into two different types of learning called model-based and model-free learning.

Model-based learning: In model-based learning, an agent will have a complete description of the environment. We know that the transition probability tells us the probability of moving from state s to the next state s' by performing action a. The reward function tells us the reward we would obtain while moving from state s to the next state s' by performing action a. When the agent knows the model dynamics of its environment, that is, when the agent knows the transition probability of its environment, then the learning is called model-based learning. Thus, in model-based learning, the agent uses the model dynamics to find the optimal policy.

Model-free learning: Model-free learning is when the agent does not know the model dynamics of its environment. That is, in model-free learning, an agent tries to find the optimal policy without the model dynamics.

Next, we'll discover the different types of environment an agent works within.

Different types of environments

At the beginning of the chapter, we learned that the environment is the world of the agent and the agent lives/stays within the environment. We can categorize the environment into different types.

Deterministic and stochastic environments

Deterministic environment: In a deterministic environment, we are certain that when an agent performs action a in state s, then it always reaches state s'. For example, let's consider our grid world environment. Say the agent is in state **A**, and when it moves *down* from state **A**, it always reaches state **D**. Hence the environment is called a deterministic environment:

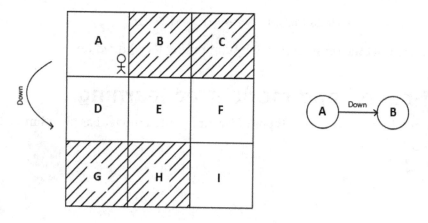

Figure 1.30: Deterministic environment

Stochastic environment: In a stochastic environment, we cannot say that by performing action *a* in state *s* the agent always reaches state s' because there will be some randomness associated with the stochastic environment. For example, let's suppose our grid world environment is a stochastic environment. Say our agent is in state **A**; now if it moves *down* from state **A**, then the agent doesn't always reach state **D**. Instead, it reaches state **D** 70% of the time and state **B** 30% of the time. That is, if the agent moves *down* in state **A**, then the agent reaches state **D** with 70% probability and state **B** with 30% probability, as *Figure 1.31* shows:

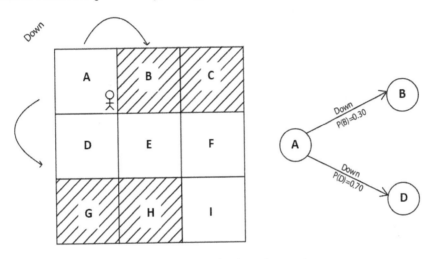

Figure 1.31: Stochastic environment

Discrete and continuous environments

Discrete environment: A discrete environment is one where the environment's action space is discrete. For instance, in the grid world environment, we have a discrete action space, which consists of the actions [*up, down, left, right*] and thus our grid world environment is discrete.

Continuous environment: A continuous environment is one where the environment's action space is continuous. For instance, suppose we are training an agent to drive a car, then our action space will be continuous, with several continuous actions such as changing the car's speed, the number of degrees the agent needs to rotate the wheel, and so on. In such a case, our environment's action space is continuous.

Episodic and non-episodic environments

Episodic environment: In an episodic environment, an agent's current action will not affect future actions, and thus an episodic environment is also called a non-sequential environment.

Non-episodic environment: In a non-episodic environment, an agent's current action will affect future actions, and thus a non-episodic environment is also called a sequential environment. For example, a chessboard is a sequential environment since the agent's current action will affect future actions in a chess match.

Single and multi-agent environments

- **Single-agent environment**: When our environment consists of only a single agent, then it is called a single-agent environment.

- **Multi-agent environment**: When our environment consists of multiple agents, then it is called a multi-agent environment.

We have covered a lot of concepts of RL. Now, we'll finish the chapter by looking at some exciting applications of RL.

Applications of RL

RL has evolved rapidly over the past couple of years with a wide range of applications ranging from playing games to self-driving cars. One of the major reasons for this evolution is due to **Deep Reinforcement Learning (DRL)**, which is a combination of RL and deep learning. We will learn about the various state-of-the-art deep RL algorithms in the upcoming chapters, so be excited! In this section, we will look at some real-life applications of RL:

- **Manufacturing**: In manufacturing, intelligent robots are trained using RL to place objects in the right position. The use of intelligent robots reduces labor costs and increases productivity.

- **Dynamic pricing**: One of the popular applications of RL is dynamic pricing. Dynamic pricing implies that we change the price of products based on demand and supply. We can train the RL agent for the dynamic pricing of products with the goal of maximizing revenue.

- **Inventory management**: RL is used extensively in inventory management, which is a crucial business activity. Some of these activities include supply chain management, demand forecasting, and handling several warehouse operations (such as placing products in warehouses to manage space efficiently).

- **Recommendation system**: RL is widely used in building a recommendation system where the behavior of the user constantly changes. For instance, in music recommendation systems, the behavior or the music preferences of the user changes from time to time. So, in those cases using an RL agent can be very useful as the agent constantly learns by interacting with the environment.

- **Neural architecture search**: In order for a neural network to perform a given task with good accuracy, the architecture of the network is very important, and it has to be properly designed. With RL, we can automate the process of complex neural architecture search by training the agent to find the best neural architecture for a given task with the goal of maximizing the accuracy.

- **Natural Language Processing (NLP)**: With the increase in popularity of deep reinforcement algorithms, RL has been widely used in several NLP tasks, such as abstractive text summarization, chatbots, and more.

- **Finance**: RL is widely used in financial portfolio management, which is the process of constant redistribution of a fund into different financial products. RL is also used in predicting and trading in commercial transaction markets. JP Morgan has successfully used RL to provide better trade execution results for large orders.

RL glossary

We have learned several important and fundamental concepts of RL. In this section, we revisit several important terms that are very useful for understanding the upcoming chapters.

Agent: The agent is the software program that learns to make intelligent decisions, such as a software program that plays chess intelligently.

Environment: The environment is the world of the agent. If we continue with the chess example, a chessboard is the environment where the agent plays chess.

State: A state is a position or a moment in the environment that the agent can be in. For example, all the positions on the chessboard are called states.

Action: The agent interacts with the environment by performing an action and moves from one state to another, for example, moves made by chessmen are actions.

Reward: A reward is a numerical value that the agent receives based on its action. Consider a reward as a point. For instance, an agent receives +1 point (reward) for a good action and -1 point (reward) for a bad action.

Action space: The set of all possible actions in the environment is called the action space. The action space is called a discrete action space when our action space consists of discrete actions, and the action space is called a continuous action space when our actions space consists of continuous actions.

Policy: The agent makes a decision based on the policy. A policy tells the agent what action to perform in each state. It can be considered the brain of an agent. A policy is called a deterministic policy if it exactly maps a state to a particular action. Unlike a deterministic policy, a stochastic policy maps the state to a probability distribution over the action space. The optimal policy is the one that gives the maximum reward.

Episode: The agent-environment interaction from the initial state to the terminal state is called an episode. An episode is often called a trajectory or rollout.

Episodic and continuous task: An RL task is called an episodic task if it has a terminal state, and it is called a continuous task if it does not have a terminal state.

Horizon: The horizon can be considered an agent's lifespan, that is, the time step until which the agent interacts with the environment. The horizon is called a finite horizon if the agent-environment interaction stops at a particular time step, and it is called an infinite horizon when the agent environment interaction continues forever.

Return: Return is the sum of rewards received by the agent in an episode.

Discount factor: The discount factor helps to control whether we want to give importance to the immediate reward or future rewards. The value of the discount factor ranges from 0 to 1. A discount factor close to 0 implies that we give more importance to immediate rewards, while a discount factor close to 1 implies that we give more importance to future rewards than immediate rewards.

Value function: The value function or the value of the state is the expected return that an agent would get starting from state s following policy π.

Q function: The Q function or the value of a state-action pair implies the expected return an agent would obtain starting from state s and performing action a following policy π.

Model-based and model-free learning: When the agent tries to learn the optimal policy with the model dynamics, then it is called model-based learning; and when the agent tries to learn the optimal policy without the model dynamics, then it is called model-free learning.

Deterministic and stochastic environment: When an agent performs action *a* in state *s* and it reaches state *s'* every time, then the environment is called a deterministic environment. When an agent performs action *a* in state *s* and it reaches different states every time based on some probability distribution, then the environment is called a stochastic environment.

Summary

We started the chapter by understanding the basic idea of RL. We learned that RL is a trial and error learning process and the learning in RL happens based on a reward. We then explored the difference between RL and the other ML paradigms, such as supervised and unsupervised learning. Going ahead, we learned about the MDP and how the RL environment can be modeled as an MDP. Next, we understood several important fundamental concepts involved in RL, and at the end of the chapter we looked into some real-life applications of RL.

Thus, in this chapter, we have learned several fundamental concepts of RL. In the next chapter, we will begin our *Hands-on reinforcement learning* journey by implementing all the fundamental concepts we have learned in this chapter using the popular toolkit called Gym.

Questions

Let's evaluate our newly acquired knowledge by answering these questions:

1. How does RL differ from other ML paradigms?
2. What is called the environment in the RL setting?
3. What is the difference between a deterministic and a stochastic policy?
4. What is an episode?
5. Why do we need a discount factor?
6. How does the value function differ from the Q function?
7. What is the difference between deterministic and stochastic environments?

Further reading

For further information, refer to the following link:

Reinforcement Learning: A Survey by *L. P. Kaelbling, M. L. Littman, A. W. Moore*, available at https://arxiv.org/abs/cs/9605103

2
A Guide to the Gym Toolkit

OpenAI is an **artificial intelligence (AI)** research organization that aims to build **artificial general intelligence (AGI)**. OpenAI provides a famous toolkit called Gym for training a reinforcement learning agent.

Let's suppose we need to train our agent to drive a car. We need an environment to train the agent. Can we train our agent in the real-world environment to drive a car? No, because we have learned that reinforcement learning (RL) is a trial-and-error learning process, so while we train our agent, it will make a lot of mistakes during learning. For example, let's suppose our agent hits another vehicle, and it receives a negative reward. It will then learn that hitting other vehicles is not a good action and will try not to perform this action again. But we cannot train the RL agent in the real-world environment by hitting other vehicles, right? That is why we use simulators and train the RL agent in the simulated environments.

There are many toolkits that provide a simulated environment for training an RL agent. One such popular toolkit is Gym. Gym provides a variety of environments for training an RL agent ranging from classic control tasks to Atari game environments. We can train our RL agent to learn in these simulated environments using various RL algorithms. In this chapter, first, we will install Gym and then we will explore various Gym environments. We will also get hands-on with the concepts we have learned in the previous chapter by experimenting with the Gym environment.

Throughout the book, we will use the Gym toolkit for building and evaluating reinforcement learning algorithms, so in this chapter, we will make ourselves familiar with the Gym toolkit.

In this chapter, we will learn about the following topics:

- Setting up our machine
- Installing Anaconda and Gym
- Understanding the Gym environment
- Generating an episode in the Gym environment
- Exploring more Gym environments
- Cart-Pole balancing with the random agent
- An agent playing the Tennis game

Setting up our machine

In this section, we will learn how to install several dependencies that are required for running the code used throughout the book. First, we will learn how to install Anaconda and then we will explore how to install Gym.

Installing Anaconda

Anaconda is an open-source distribution of Python. It is widely used for scientific computing and processing large volumes of data. It provides an excellent package management environment, and it supports Windows, Mac, and Linux operating systems. Anaconda comes with Python installed, along with popular packages used for scientific computing such as NumPy, SciPy, and so on.

To download Anaconda, visit `https://www.anaconda.com/download/`, where you will see an option for downloading Anaconda for different platforms. If you are using Windows or macOS, you can directly download the graphical installer according to your machine architecture and install Anaconda using the graphical installer.

If you are using Linux, follow these steps:

1. Open the Terminal and type the following command to download Anaconda:

```
wget https://repo.continuum.io/archive/Anaconda3-5.0.1-
Linux-x86_64.sh
```

2. After downloading, we can install Anaconda using the following command:

```
bash Anaconda3-5.0.1-Linux-x86_64.sh
```

After the successful installation of Anaconda, we need to create a virtual environment. What is the need for a virtual environment? Say we are working on project A, which uses NumPy version 1.14, and project B, which uses NumPy version 1.13. So, to work on project B we either downgrade NumPy or reinstall NumPy. In each project, we use different libraries with different versions that are not applicable to the other projects. Instead of downgrading or upgrading versions or reinstalling libraries every time for a new project, we use a virtual environment.

The virtual environment is just an isolated environment for a particular project so that each project can have its own dependencies and will not affect other projects. We will create a virtual environment using the following command and name our environment universe:

```
conda create --name universe python=3.6 anaconda
```

Note that we use Python version 3.6. Once the virtual environment is created, we can activate it using the following command:

```
source activate universe
```

That's it! Now that we have learned how to install Anaconda and create a virtual environment, in the next section, we will learn how to install Gym.

Installing the Gym toolkit

In this section, we will learn how to install the Gym toolkit. Before going ahead, first, let's activate our virtual environment, universe:

```
source activate universe
```

Now, install the following dependencies:

```
sudo apt-get update
sudo apt-get install golang libcupti-dev libjpeg-turbo8-dev make tmux
htop chromium-browser git cmake zlib1g-dev libjpeg-dev xvfb libav-tools
xorg-dev python-opengl libboost-all-dev libsdl2-dev swig
conda install pip six libgcc swig
conda install opencv
```

We can install Gym directly using pip. Note that throughout the book, we will use Gym version 0.15.4. We can install Gym using the following command:

```
pip install gym==0.15.4
```

We can also install Gym by cloning the Gym repository as follows:

```
cd ~
git clone https://github.com/openai/gym.git
cd gym
pip install -e '.[all]'
```

Common error fixes

Just in case, if you get any of the following errors while installing Gym, the following commands will help:

- **Failed building wheel for pachi-py** or **failed building wheel for pachi-py atari-py**:

  ```
  sudo apt-get update
  sudo apt-get install xvfb libav-tools xorg-dev libsdl2-dev swig
  cmake
  ```

- **Failed building wheel for mujoco-py**:

  ```
  git clone https://github.com/openai/mujoco-py.git
  cd mujoco-py

  sudo apt-get update
  sudo apt-get install libgl1-mesa-dev libgl1-mesa-glx libosmesa6-
  dev python3-pip python3-numpy python3-scipy

  pip3 install -r requirements.txt
  sudo python3 setup.py install
  ```

- **error: command 'gcc' failed with exit status 1**:

  ```
  sudo apt-get update

  sudo apt-get install python-dev
  sudo apt-get install libevent-dev
  ```

Now that we have successfully installed Gym, in the next section, let's kickstart our hands-on reinforcement learning journey.

Creating our first Gym environment

We have learned that Gym provides a variety of environments for training a reinforcement learning agent. To clearly understand how the Gym environment is designed, we will start with the basic Gym environment. After that, we will understand other complex Gym environments.

Let's introduce one of the simplest environments called the Frozen Lake environment. *Figure 2.1* shows the Frozen Lake environment. As we can observe, in the Frozen Lake environment, the goal of the agent is to start from the initial state **S** and reach the goal state **G**:

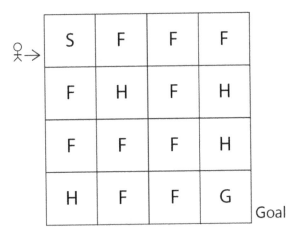

Figure 2.1: The Frozen Lake environment

In the preceding environment, the following apply:

- **S** denotes the starting state
- **F** denotes the frozen state
- **H** denotes the hole state
- **G** denotes the goal state

So, the agent has to start from state **S** and reach the goal state **G**. But one issue is that if the agent visits state **H**, which is the hole state, then the agent will fall into the hole and die as shown in *Figure 2.2*:

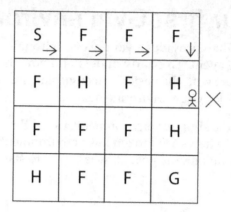

Figure 2.2: The agent falls down a hole

So, we need to make sure that the agent starts from **S** and reaches **G** without falling into the hole state **H** as shown in *Figure 2.3*:

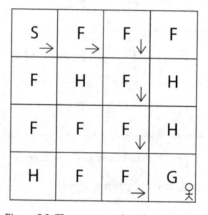

Figure 2.3: The agent reaches the goal state

Each grid box in the preceding environment is called a state, thus we have 16 states (**S** to **G**) and we have 4 possible actions, which are *up, down, left*, and *right*. We learned that our goal is to reach the state **G** from **S** without visiting **H**. So, we assign +1 reward for the goal state **G** and 0 for all other states.

Thus, we have learned how the Frozen Lake environment works. Now, to train our agent in the Frozen Lake environment, first, we need to create the environment by coding it from scratch in Python. But luckily we don't have to do that! Since Gym provides various environments, we can directly import the Gym toolkit and create a Frozen Lake environment.

Now, we will learn how to create our Frozen Lake environment using Gym. Before running any code, make sure that you have activated our virtual environment universe. First, let's import the Gym library:

```
import gym
```

Next, we can create a Gym environment using the make function. The make function requires the environment id as a parameter. In Gym, the id of the Frozen Lake environment is FrozenLake-v0. So, we can create our Frozen Lake environment as follows:

```
env = gym.make("FrozenLake-v0")
```

After creating the environment, we can see how our environment looks like using the render function:

```
env.render()
```

The preceding code renders the following environment:

Figure 2.4: Gym's Frozen Lake environment

As we can observe, the Frozen Lake environment consists of 16 states (**S** to **G**) as we learned. The state **S** is highlighted indicating that it is our current state, that is, the agent is in the state **S**. So whenever we create an environment, an agent will always begin from the initial state, which in our case is state **S**.

That's it! Creating the environment using Gym is that simple. In the next section, we will understand more about the Gym environment by relating all the concepts we have learned in the previous chapter.

Exploring the environment

In the previous chapter, we learned that the reinforcement learning environment can be modeled as a **Markov decision process (MDP)** and an MDP consists of the following:

- **States**: A set of states present in the environment.
- **Actions**: A set of actions that the agent can perform in each state.
- **Transition probability**: The transition probability is denoted by $P(s'|s, a)$. It implies the probability of moving from a state s to the state s' while performing an action a.
- **Reward function**: The reward function is denoted by $R(s, a, s')$. It implies the reward the agent obtains moving from a state s to the state s' while performing an action a.

Let's now understand how to obtain all the above information from the Frozen Lake environment we just created using Gym.

States

A state space consists of all of our states. We can obtain the number of states in our environment by just typing env.observation_space as follows:

```
print(env.observation_space)
```

The preceding code will print:

```
Discrete(16)
```

It implies that we have 16 discrete states in our state space starting from state **S** to **G**. Note that, in Gym, the states will be encoded as a number, so the state **S** will be encoded as 0, state **F** will be encoded as 1, and so on as *Figure 2.5* shows:

Figure 2.5: Sixteen discrete states

Actions

We learned that the action space consists of all the possible actions in the environment. We can obtain the action space by using `env.action_space`:

```
print(env.action_space)
```

The preceding code will print:

```
Discrete(4)
```

It shows that we have 4 discrete actions in our action space, which are *left*, *down*, *right*, and *up*. Note that, similar to states, actions also will be encoded into numbers as shown in *Table 2.1*:

Number	Action
0	Left
1	Down
2	Right
3	Up

Table 2.1: Four discrete actions

Transition probability and reward function

Now, let's look at how to obtain the transition probability and the reward function. We learned that in the stochastic environment, we cannot say that by performing some action *a*, the agent will always reach the next state *s'* exactly because there will be some randomness associated with the stochastic environment, and by performing an action *a* in the state *s*, the agent reaches the next state *s'* with some probability.

Let's suppose we are in state 2 (**F**). Now, if we perform action 1 (*down*) in state 2, we can reach state 6 as shown in *Figure 2.6*:

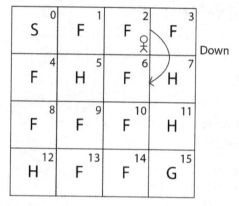

Figure 2.6: The agent performing a down action from state 2

Our Frozen Lake environment is a stochastic environment. When our environment is stochastic, we won't always reach state 6 by performing action 1 (*down*) in state 2; we also reach other states with some probability. So when we perform an action 1 (*down*) in state 2, we reach state 1 with probability 0.33333, we reach state 6 with probability 0.33333, and we reach state 3 with probability 0.33333 as shown in *Figure 2.7*:

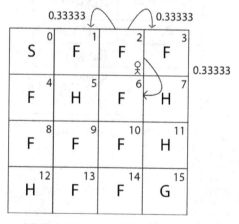

Figure 2.7: Transition probability of the agent in state 2

As we can see, in a stochastic environment we reach the next states with some probability. Now, let's learn how to obtain this transition probability using the Gym environment.

We can obtain the transition probability and the reward function by just typing `env.P[state][action]`. So, to obtain the transition probability of moving from state **S** to the other states by performing the action *right*, we can type `env.P[S][right]`. But we cannot just type state **S** and action *right* directly since they are encoded as numbers. We learned that state **S** is encoded as 0 and the action *right* is encoded as 2, so, to obtain the transition probability of state **S** by performing the action *right*, we type `env.P[0][2]` as the following shows:

```
print(env.P[0][2])
```

The above code will print:

```
[(0.33333, 4, 0.0, False),
 (0.33333, 1, 0.0, False),
 (0.33333, 0, 0.0, False)]
```

What does this imply? Our output is in the form of `[(transition probability, next state, reward, Is terminal state?)]`. It implies that if we perform an action 2 (*right*) in state 0 (**S**) then:

- We reach state 4 (**F**) with probability 0.33333 and receive 0 reward.
- We reach state 1 (**F**) with probability 0.33333 and receive 0 reward.
- We reach the same state 0 (**S**) with probability 0.33333 and receive 0 reward.

Figure 2.8 shows the transition probability:

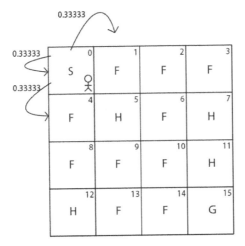

Figure 2.8: Transition probability of the agent in state 0

Thus, when we type env.P[state][action], we get the result in the form of [(transition probability, next state, reward, Is terminal state?)]. The last value is Boolean and tells us whether the next state is a terminal state. Since 4, 1, and 0 are not terminal states, it is given as false.

The output of env.P[0][2] is shown in *Table 2.2* for more clarity:

Transition Probability	Next State	Reward	Is terminal state
0.33333	4(F)	0.0	False
0.33333	1(F)	0.0	False
0.33333	0(S)	0.0	False

Table 2.2: Output of env.P[0][2]

Let's understand this with one more example. Let's suppose we are in state 3 (F) as *Figure 2.9* shows:

Figure 2.9: The agent in state 3

Say we perform action 1 (*down*) in state 3 (F). Then the transition probability of state 3 (F) by performing action 1 (*down*) can be obtained as the following shows:

```
print(env.P[3][1])
```

The preceding code will print:

```
[(0.33333, 2, 0.0, False),
 (0.33333, 7, 0.0, True),
 (0.33333, 3, 0.0, False)]
```

As we learned, our output is in the form of [(transition probability, next state, reward, Is terminal state?)]. It implies that if we perform action 1 (*down*) in state 3 (**F**) then:

- We reach state 2 (**F**) with probability 0.33333 and receive 0 reward.
- We reach state 7 (**H**) with probability 0.33333 and receive 0 reward.
- We reach the same state 3 (**F**) with probability 0.33333 and receive 0 reward.

Figure 2.10 shows the transition probability:

Figure 2.10: Transition probabilities of the agent in state 3

The output of env.P[3][1] is shown in *Table 2.3* for more clarity:

Transition Probability	Next State	Reward	Is terminal State
0.33333	2(F)	0.0	False
0.33333	7(H)	0.0	True
0.33333	3(F)	0.0	False

Table 2.3: Output of env.P[3][1]

As we can observe, in the second row of our output, we have (0.33333, 7, 0.0, True), and the last value here is marked as True. It implies that state 7 is a terminal state. That is, if we perform action 1 (*down*) in state 3 (**F**) then we reach state 7 (**H**) with 0.33333 probability, and since 7 (**H**) is a hole, the agent dies if it reaches state 7 (**H**). Thus 7(**H**) is a terminal state and so it is marked as True.

Thus, we have learned how to obtain the state space, action space, transition probability, and the reward function using the Gym environment. In the next section, we will learn how to generate an episode.

Generating an episode in the Gym environment

We learned that the agent-environment interaction starting from an initial state until the terminal state is called an episode. In this section, we will learn how to generate an episode in the Gym environment.

Before we begin, we initialize the state by resetting our environment; resetting puts our agent back to the initial state. We can reset our environment using the `reset()` function as shown as follows:

```
state = env.reset()
```

Action selection

In order for the agent to interact with the environment, it has to perform some action in the environment. So, first, let's learn how to perform an action in the Gym environment. Let's suppose we are in state 3 (**F**) as *Figure 2.11* shows:

Figure 2.11: The agent is in state 3 in the Frozen Lake environment

Say we need to perform action 1 (*down*) and move to the new state 7 (**H**). How can we do that? We can perform an action using the `step` function. We just need to input our action as a parameter to the `step` function. So, we can perform action 1 (*down*) in state 3 (**F**) using the `step` function as follows:

```
env.step(1)
```

Now, let's render our environment using the `render` function:

```
env.render()
```

As shown in *Figure 2.12*, the agent performs action 1 (*down*) in state 3 (**F**) and reaches the next state 7 (**H**):

Figure 2.12: The agent in state 7 in the Frozen Lake environment

Note that whenever we make an action using env.step(), it outputs a tuple containing 4 values. So, when we take action 1 (*down*) in state 3 (**F**) using env. step(1), it gives the output as:

```
(7, 0.0, True, {'prob': 0.33333})
```

As you might have guessed, it implies that when we perform action 1 (*down*) in state 3 (**F**):

- We reach the next state 7 (**H**).
- The agent receives the reward 0.0.
- Since the next state 7 (**H**) is a terminal state, it is marked as True.
- We reach the next state 7 (**H**) with a probability of 0.33333.

So, we can just store this information as:

```
(next_state, reward, done, info) = env.step(1)
```

Thus:

- next_state represents the next state.
- reward represents the obtained reward.
- done implies whether our episode has ended. That is, if the next state is a terminal state, then our episode will end, so done will be marked as True else it will be marked as False.
- info — Apart from the transition probability, in some cases, we also obtain other information saved as info, which is used for debugging purposes.

We can also sample action from our action space and perform a random action to explore our environment. We can sample an action using the `sample` function:

```
random_action = env.action_space.sample()
```

After we have sampled an action from our action space, then we perform our sampled action using our step function:

```
next_state, reward, done, info = env.step(random_action)
```

Now that we have learned how to select actions in the environment, let's see how to generate an episode.

Generating an episode

Now let's learn how to generate an episode. The episode is the agent environment interaction starting from the initial state to the terminal state. The agent interacts with the environment by performing some action in each state. An episode ends if the agent reaches the terminal state. So, in the Frozen Lake environment, the episode will end if the agent reaches the terminal state, which is either the hole state (**H**) or goal state (**G**).

Let's understand how to generate an episode with the random policy. We learned that the random policy selects a random action in each state. So, we will generate an episode by taking random actions in each state. So for each time step in the episode, we take a random action in each state and our episode will end if the agent reaches the terminal state.

First, let's set the number of time steps:

```
num_timesteps = 20
```

For each time step:

```
for t in range(num_timesteps):
```

Randomly select an action by sampling from the action space:

```
    random_action = env.action_space.sample()
```

Perform the selected action:

```
    next_state, reward, done, info = env.step(random_action)
```

If the next state is the terminal state, then break. This implies that our episode ends:

```
if done:
    break
```

The preceding complete snippet is provided for clarity. The following code denotes that on every time step, we select an action by randomly sampling from the action space, and our episode will end if the agent reaches the terminal state:

```
import gym
env = gym.make("FrozenLake-v0")

state = env.reset()

print('Time Step 0 :')
env.render()

num_timesteps = 20

for t in range(num_timesteps):
    random_action = env.action_space.sample()

    new_state, reward, done, info = env.step(random_action)
    print ('Time Step {} :'.format(t+1))


    env.render()

    if done:
        break
```

The preceding code will print something similar to *Figure 2.13*. Note that you might get a different result each time you run the preceding code since the agent is taking a random action in each time step.

As we can observe from the following output, on each time step, the agent takes a random action in each state and our episode ends once the agent reaches the terminal state. As *Figure 2.13* shows, in time step 4, the agent reaches the terminal state **H**, and so the episode ends:

Time Step 0 :

```
S F F F
F HF H
F F F H
HF F G
```

Time Step 1 :
(right)

```
S F F F
F HF H
F F F H
HF F G
```

Time Step 2 :
(right)

```
S F F F
F HF H
F F F H
HF F G
```

Time Step 3 :
(right)

```
S F F F
F HF H
F F F H
HF F G
```

Time Step 4 :
(down)

```
S F F F
F HF H
F F F H
HF F G
```

Figure 2.13: Actions taken by the agent in each time step

Instead of generating one episode, we can also generate a series of episodes by taking some random action in each state:

```
import gym
env = gym.make("FrozenLake-v0")
```

```
num_episodes = 10
num_timesteps = 20

for i in range(num_episodes):

    state = env.reset()
    print('Time Step 0 :')
    env.render()

    for t in range(num_timesteps):
        random_action = env.action_space.sample()

        new_state, reward, done, info = env.step(random_action)
        print ('Time Step {} :'.format(t+1))


        env.render()
        if done:
            break
```

Thus, we can generate an episode by selecting a random action in each state by sampling from the action space. But wait! What is the use of this? Why do we even need to generate an episode?

In the previous chapter, we learned that an agent can find the optimal policy (that is, the correct action in each state) by generating several episodes. But in the preceding example, we just took random actions in each state over all the episodes. How can the agent find the optimal policy? So, in the case of the Frozen Lake environment, how can the agent find the optimal policy that tells the agent to reach state **G** from state **S** without visiting the hole states **H**?

This is where we need a reinforcement learning algorithm. Reinforcement learning is all about finding the optimal policy, that is, the policy that tells us what action to perform in each state. We will learn how to find the optimal policy by generating a series of episodes using various reinforcement learning algorithms in the upcoming chapters. In this chapter, we will focus on getting acquainted with the Gym environment and various Gym functionalities as we will be using the Gym environment throughout the course of the book.

So far we have understood how the Gym environment works using the basic Frozen Lake environment, but Gym has so many other functionalities and also several interesting environments. In the next section, we will learn about the other Gym environments along with exploring the functionalities of Gym.

More Gym environments

In this section, we will explore several interesting Gym environments, along with exploring different functionalities of Gym.

Classic control environments

Gym provides environments for several classic control tasks such as Cart-Pole balancing, swinging up an inverted pendulum, mountain car climbing, and so on. Let's understand how to create a Gym environment for a Cart-Pole balancing task. The Cart-Pole environment is shown below:

Figure 2.14: Cart-Pole example

Cart-Pole balancing is one of the classical control problems. As shown in *Figure 2.14*, the pole is attached to the cart and the goal of our agent is to balance the pole on the cart, that is, the goal of our agent is to keep the pole standing straight up on the cart as shown in *Figure 2.15*:

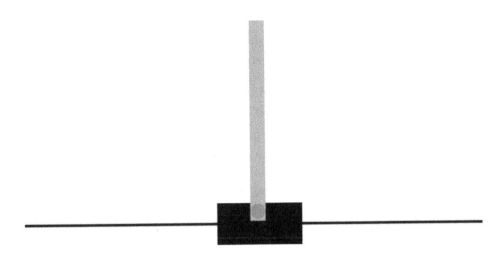

Figure 2.15: The goal is to keep the pole straight up

So the agent tries to push the cart left and right to keep the pole standing straight on the cart. Thus our agent performs two actions, which are pushing the cart to the left and pushing the cart to the right, to keep the pole standing straight on the cart. You can also check out this very interesting video, `https://youtu.be/qMlcsc43-1g`, which shows how the RL agent balances the pole on the cart by moving the cart left and right.

Now, let's learn how to create the Cart-Pole environment using Gym. The environment id of the Cart-Pole environment in Gym is `CartPole-v0`, so we can just use our `make` function to create the Cart-Pole environment as shown below:

```
env = gym.make("CartPole-v0")
```

After creating the environment, we can view our environment using the `render` function:

```
env.render()
```

We can also close the rendered environment using the `close` function:

```
env.close()
```

State space

Now, let's look at the state space of our Cart-Pole environment. Wait! What are the states here? In the Frozen Lake environment, we had 16 discrete states from **S** to **G**. But how can we describe the states here? Can we describe the state by cart position? Yes! Note that the cart position is a continuous value. So, in this case, our state space will be continuous values, unlike the Frozen Lake environment where our state space had discrete values (**S** to **G**).

But with just the cart position alone we cannot describe the state of the environment completely. So we include cart velocity, pole angle, and pole velocity at the tip. So we can describe our state space by an array of values as shown as follows:

```
array([cart position, cart velocity, pole angle, pole velocity at the
tip])
```

Note that all of these values are continuous, that is:

1. The value of the cart position ranges from `-4.8` to `4.8`.
2. The value of the cart velocity ranges from `-Inf` to `Inf` ($-\infty$ to ∞).
3. The value of the pole angle ranges from `-0.418` radians to `0.418` radians.
4. The value of the pole velocity at the tip ranges from `-Inf` to `Inf`.

Thus, our state space contains an array of continuous values. Let's learn how we can obtain this from Gym. In order to get the state space, we can just type `env.observation_space` as shown as follows:

```
print(env.observation_space)
```

The preceding code will print:

```
Box(4,)
```

`Box` implies that our state space consists of continuous values and not discrete values. That is, in the Frozen Lake environment, we obtained the state space as `Discrete(16)`, which shows that we have 16 discrete states (**S** to **G**). But now we have our state space denoted as `Box(4,)`, which implies that our state space is continuous and consists of an array of 4 values.

For example, let's reset our environment and see how our initial state space will look like. We can reset the environment using the `reset` function:

```
print(env.reset())
```

The preceding code will print:

```
array([ 0.02002635, -0.0228838 ,  0.01248453,  0.04931007])
```

Note that here the state space is randomly initialized and so we will get different values every time we run the preceding code.

The result of the preceding code implies that our initial state space consists of an array of 4 values that denote the cart position, cart velocity, pole angle, and pole velocity at the tip, respectively. That is:

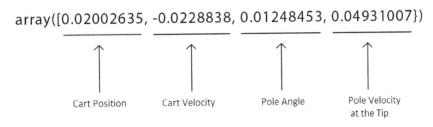

Figure 2.16: Initial state space

Okay, how can we obtain the maximum and minimum values of our state space? We can obtain the maximum values of our state space using env.observation_space.high and the minimum values of our state space using env.observation_space.low.

For example, let's look at the maximum value of our state space:

```
print(env.observation_space.high)
```

The preceding code will print:

```
[4.8000002e+00 3.4028235e+38 4.1887903e-01 3.4028235e+38]
```

It implies that:

1. The maximum value of the cart position is 4.8.
2. We learned that the maximum value of the cart velocity is +Inf, and we know that infinity is not really a number, so it is represented using the largest positive real value 3.4028235e+38.
3. The maximum value of the pole angle is 0.418 radians.
4. The maximum value of the pole velocity at the tip is +Inf, so it is represented using the largest positive real value 3.4028235e+38.

Similarly, we can obtain the minimum value of our state space as:

```
print(env.observation_space.low)
```

The preceding code will print:

```
[-4.8000002e+00 -3.4028235e+38 -4.1887903e-01 -3.4028235e+38]
```

It states that:

1. The minimum value of the cart position is -4.8.
2. We learned that the minimum value of the cart velocity is -Inf, and we know that infinity is not really a number, so it is represented using the largest negative real value -3.4028235e+38.
3. The minimum value of the pole angle is -0.418 radians.
4. The minimum value of the pole velocity at the tip is -Inf, so it is represented using the largest negative real value -3.4028235e+38.

Action space

Now, let's look at the action space. We already learned that in the Cart-Pole environment we perform two actions, which are pushing the cart to the left and pushing the cart to the right, and thus the action space is discrete since we have only two discrete actions.

In order to get the action space, we can just type env.action_space as the following shows:

```
print(env.action_space)
```

The preceding code will print:

```
Discrete(2)
```

As we can observe, Discrete(2) implies that our action space is discrete, and we have two actions in our action space. Note that the actions will be encoded into numbers as shown in *Table 2.4*:

Number	Action
0	Push cart to the left
1	Push cart to the right

Table 2.4: Two possible actions

Cart-Pole balancing with random policy

Let's create an agent with the random policy, that is, we create the agent that selects a random action in the environment and tries to balance the pole. The agent receives a +1 reward every time the pole stands straight up on the cart. We will generate over 100 episodes, and we will see the return (sum of rewards) obtained over each episode. Let's learn this step by step.

First, let's create our Cart-Pole environment:

```
import gym
env = gym.make('CartPole-v0')
```

Set the number of episodes and number of time steps in the episode:

```
num_episodes = 100
num_timesteps = 50
```

For each episode:

```
for i in range(num_episodes):
```

Set the return to 0:

```
Return = 0
```

Initialize the state by resetting the environment:

```
state = env.reset()
```

For each step in the episode:

```
for t in range(num_timesteps):
```

Render the environment:

```
env.render()
```

Randomly select an action by sampling from the environment:

```
random_action = env.action_space.sample()
```

Perform the randomly selected action:

```
next_state, reward, done, info = env.step(random_action)
```

Update the return:

```
Return = Return + reward
```

If the next state is a terminal state then end the episode:

```
if done:
    break
```

For every 10 episodes, print the return (sum of rewards):

```
if i%10==0:
    print('Episode: {}, Return: {}'.format(i, Return))
```

Close the environment:

```
env.close()
```

The preceding code will output the sum of rewards obtained over every 10 episodes:

```
Episode: 0, Return: 14.0
Episode: 10, Return: 31.0
Episode: 20, Return: 16.0
Episode: 30, Return: 9.0
Episode: 40, Return: 18.0
Episode: 50, Return: 13.0
Episode: 60, Return: 25.0
Episode: 70, Return: 21.0
Episode: 80, Return: 17.0
Episode: 90, Return: 14.0
```

Thus, we have learned about one of the interesting and classic control problems called Cart-Pole balancing and how to create the Cart-Pole balancing environment using Gym. Gym provides several other classic control environments as shown in *Figure 2.17*:

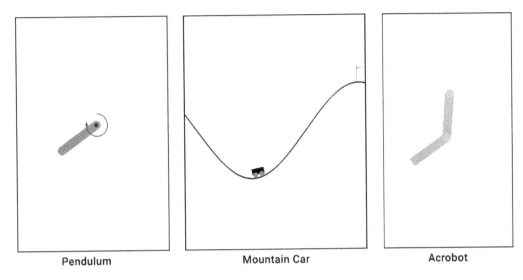

Figure 2.17: Classic control environments

You can also do some experimentation by creating any of the above environments using Gym. We can check all the classic control environments offered by Gym here: `https://gym.openai.com/envs/#classic_control`.

Atari game environments

Are you a fan of Atari games? If yes, then this section will interest you. Atari 2600 is a video game console from a game company called Atari. The Atari game console provides several popular games, which include Pong, Space Invaders, Ms. Pac-Man, Break Out, Centipede, and many more. Training our reinforcement learning agent to play Atari games is an interesting as well as challenging task. Often, most of the RL algorithms will be tested out on Atari game environments to evaluate the accuracy of the algorithm.

In this section, we will learn how to create the Atari game environment using Gym. Gym provides about 59 Atari game environments including Pong, Space Invaders, Air Raid, Asteroids, Centipede, Ms. Pac-Man, and so on. Some of the Atari game environments provided by Gym are shown in *Figure 2.18* to keep you excited:

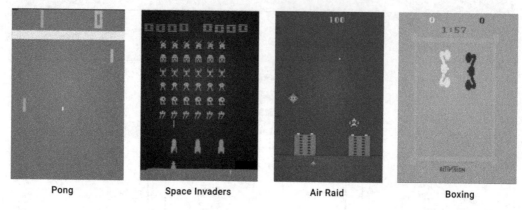

Pong   Space Invaders   Air Raid   Boxing

Figure 2.18: Atari game environments

In Gym, every Atari game environment has 12 different variants. Let's understand this with the Pong game environment. The Pong game environment will have 12 different variants as explained in the following sections.

General environment

- **Pong-v0 and Pong-v4**: We can create a Pong environment with the environment id as Pong-v0 or Pong-v4. Okay, what about the state of our environment? Since we are dealing with the game environment, we can just take the image of our game screen as our state. But we can't deal with the raw image directly so we will take the pixel values of our game screen as the state. We will learn more about this in the upcoming section.

- **Pong-ram-v0 and Pong-ram-v4**: This is similar to Pong-v0 and Pong-v4, respectively. However, here, the state of the environment is the RAM of the Atari machine, which is just the 128 bytes instead of the game screen's pixel values.

Deterministic environment

- **PongDeterministic-v0 and PongDeterministic-v4**: In this type, as the name suggests, the initial position of the game will be the same every time we initialize the environment, and the state of the environment is the pixel values of the game screen.

- **Pong-ramDeterministic-v0 and Pong-ramDeterministic-v4**: This is similar to PongDeterministic-v0 and PongDeterministic-v4, respectively, but here the state is the RAM of the Atari machine.

No frame skipping

- **PongNoFrameskip-v0 and PongNoFrameskip-v4**: In this type, no game frame is skipped; all game screens are visible to the agent and the state is the pixel value of the game screen.

- **Pong-ramNoFrameskip-v0 and Pong-ramNoFrameskip-v4**: This is similar to PongNoFrameskip-v0 and PongNoFrameskip-v4, but here the state is the RAM of the Atari machine.

Thus in the Atari environment, the state of our environment will be either the game screen or the RAM of the Atari machine. Note that similar to the Pong game, all other Atari games have the id in the same fashion in the Gym environment. For example, suppose we want to create a deterministic Space Invaders environment; then we can just create it with the id `SpaceInvadersDeterministic-v0`. Say we want to create a Space Invaders environment with no frame skipping; then we can create it with the id `SpaceInvadersNoFrameskip-v0`.

We can check out all the Atari game environments offered by Gym here: `https://gym.openai.com/envs/#atari`.

State and action space

Now, let's explore the state space and action space of the Atari game environments in detail.

State space

In this section, let's understand the state space of the Atari games in the Gym environment. Let's learn this with the Pong game. We learned that in the Atari environment, the state of the environment will be either the game screen's pixel values or the RAM of the Atari machine. First, let's understand the state space where the state of the environment is the game screen's pixel values.

Let's create a Pong environment with the `make` function:

```
env = gym.make("Pong-v0")
```

Here, the game screen is the state of our environment. So, we will just take the image of the game screen as the state. However, we can't deal with the raw images directly, so we will take the pixel values of the image (game screen) as our state. The dimension of the image pixel will be 3 containing the image height, image width, and the number of the channel.

Thus, the state of our environment will be an array containing the pixel values of the game screen:

```
[Image height, image width, number of the channel]
```

Note that the pixel values range from 0 to 255. In order to get the state space, we can just type env.observation_space as the following shows:

```
print(env.observation_space)
```

The preceding code will print:

```
Box(210, 160, 3)
```

This indicates that our state space is a 3D array with a shape of [210,160,3]. As we've learned, 210 denotes the height of the image, 160 denotes the width of the image, and 3 represents the number of channels.

For example, we can reset our environment and see how the initial state space looks like. We can reset the environment using the reset function:

```
print(env.reset())
```

The preceding code will print an array representing the initial game screen's pixel value.

Now, let's create a Pong environment where the state of our environment is the RAM of the Atari machine instead of the game screen's pixel value:

```
env = gym.make("Pong-ram-v0")
```

Let's look at the state space:

```
print(env.observation_space)
```

The preceding code will print:

```
Box(128,)
```

This implies that our state space is a 1D array containing 128 values. We can reset our environment and see how the initial state space looks like:

```
print(env.reset())
```

Note that this applies to all Atari games in the Gym environment, for example, if we create a space invaders environment with the state of our environment as the game screen's pixel value, then our state space will be a 3D array with a shape of `Box(210, 160, 3)`. However, if we create the Space Invaders environment with the state of our environment as the RAM of Atari machine, then our state space will be an array with a shape of `Box(128,)`.

Action space

Let's now explore the action space. In general, the Atari game environment has 18 actions in the action space, and the actions are encoded from 0 to 17 as shown in *Table 2.5*:

Name	Action
0	Noop
1	Fire
2	Up
3	Right
4	Left
5	Down
6	Up Right
7	Up Left
8	Down Right
9	Down Left
10	Up Fire
11	Right Fire
12	Left Fire
13	Down Fire
14	Up Right Fire
15	Up Left Fire
16	Down Right Fire
17	Down Left Fire

Table 2.5: Atari game environment actions

Note that all the preceding 18 actions are not applicable to all the Atari game environments and the action space varies from game to game. For instance, some games use only the first six of the preceding actions as their action space, and some games use only the first nine of the preceding actions as their action space, while others use all of the preceding 18 actions. Let's understand this with an example using the Pong game:

```
env = gym.make("Pong-v0")
print(env.action_space)
```

The preceding code will print:

```
Discrete(6)
```

The code shows that we have 6 actions in the Pong action space, and the actions are encoded from 0 to 5. So the possible actions in the Pong game are noop (no action), fire, up, right, left, and down.

Let's now look at the action space of the Road Runner game. Just in case you have not come across this game before, the game screen looks like this:

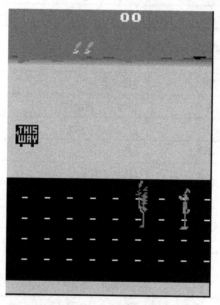

Figure 2.19: The Road Runner environment

Let's see the action space of the Road Runner game:

```
env = gym.make("RoadRunner-v0")
print(env.action_space)
```

The preceding code will print:

```
Discrete(18)
```

This shows us that the action space in the Road Runner game includes all 18 actions.

An agent playing the Tennis game

In this section, let's explore how to create an agent to play the Tennis game. Let's create an agent with a random policy, meaning that the agent will select an action randomly from the action space and perform the randomly selected action.

First, let's create our Tennis environment:

```
import gym
env = gym.make('Tennis-v0')
```

Let's view the Tennis environment:

```
env.render()
```

The preceding code will display the following:

Figure 2.20: The Tennis game environment

Set the number of episodes and the number of time steps in the episode:

```
num_episodes = 100
num_timesteps = 50
```

For each episode:

```
for i in range(num_episodes):
```

Set the return to 0:

```
Return = 0
```

Initialize the state by resetting the environment:

```
state = env.reset()
```

For each step in the episode:

```
for t in range(num_timesteps):
```

Render the environment:

```
env.render()
```

Randomly select an action by sampling from the environment:

```
random_action = env.action_space.sample()
```

Perform the randomly selected action:

```
next_state, reward, done, info = env.step(random_action)
```

Update the return:

```
Return = Return + reward
```

If the next state is a terminal state, then end the episode:

```
if done:
    break
```

For every 10 episodes, print the return (sum of rewards):

```
if i%10==0:
    print('Episode: {}, Return: {}'.format(i, Return))
```

Close the environment:

```
env.close()
```

The preceding code will output the return (sum of rewards) obtained over every 10 episodes:

```
Episode: 0, Return: -1.0
Episode: 10, Return: -1.0
Episode: 20, Return: 0.0
Episode: 30, Return: -1.0
Episode: 40, Return: -1.0
Episode: 50, Return: -1.0
Episode: 60, Return: 0.0
Episode: 70, Return: 0.0
Episode: 80, Return: -1.0
Episode: 90, Return: 0.0
```

Recording the game

We have just learned how to create an agent that randomly selects an action from the action space and plays the Tennis game. Can we also record the game played by the agent and save it as a video? Yes! Gym provides a wrapper class, which we can use to save the agent's gameplay as video.

To record the game, our system should support FFmpeg. FFmpeg is a framework used for processing media files. So before moving ahead, make sure that your system provides FFmpeg support.

We can record our game using the `Monitor` wrapper as the following code shows. It takes three parameters: the environment; the directory where we want to save our recordings; and the force option. If we set `force = False`, it implies that we need to create a new directory every time we want to save new recordings, and when we set `force = True`, old recordings in the directory will be cleared out and replaced by new recordings:

```
env = gym.wrappers.Monitor(env, 'recording', force=True)
```

We just need to add the preceding line of code after creating our environment. Let's take a simple example and see how the recordings work. Let's make our agent randomly play the Tennis game for a single episode and record the agent's gameplay as a video:

```
import gym
env = gym.make('Tennis-v0')

#Record the game
env = gym.wrappers.Monitor(env, 'recording', force=True)

env.reset()

for _ in range(5000):

    env.render()
    action = env.action_space.sample()
    next_state, reward, done, info = env.step(action)


    if done:
        break
env.close()
```

Once the episode ends, we will see a new directory called **recording** and we can find the video file in MP4 format in this directory, which has our agent's gameplay as shown in *Figure 2.21*:

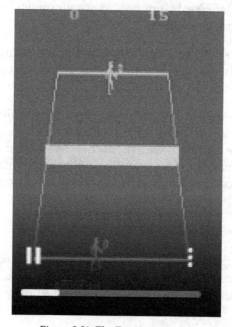

Figure 2.21: The Tennis gameplay

Other environments

Apart from the classic control and the Atari game environments we've discussed, Gym also provides several different categories of the environment. Let's find out more about them.

Box2D

Box2D is the 2D simulator that is majorly used for training our agent to perform continuous control tasks, such as walking. For example, Gym provides a Box2D environment called `BipedalWalker-v2`, which we can use to train our agent to walk. The `BipedalWalker-v2` environment is shown in *Figure 2.22*:

Figure 2.22: The Bipedal Walker environment

We can check out several other Box2D environments offered by Gym here: `https://gym.openai.com/envs/#box2d`.

MuJoCo

Mujoco stands for **Multi-Joint dynamics with Contact** and is one of the most popular simulators used for training our agent to perform continuous control tasks. For example, MuJoCo provides an interesting environment called HumanoidStandup-v2, which we can use to train our agent to stand up. The HumanoidStandup-v2 environment is shown in *Figure 2.23*:

Figure 2.23: The Humanoid Stand Up environment

We can check out several other Mujoco environments offered by Gym here: https:// gym.openai.com/envs/#mujoco.

Robotics

Gym provides several environments for performing goal-based tasks for the fetch and shadow hand robots. For example, Gym provides an environment called HandManipulateBlock-v0, which we can use to train our agent to orient a box using a robotic hand. The HandManipulateBlock-v0 environment is shown in *Figure 2.24*:

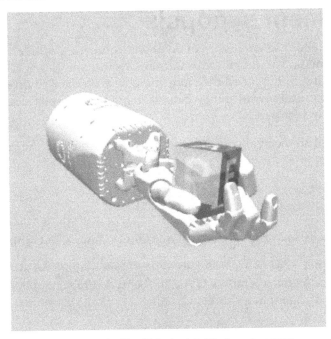

Figure 2.24: The Hand Manipulate Block environment

We can check out the several robotics environments offered by Gym here: `https://gym.openai.com/envs/#robotics`.

Toy text

Toy text is the simplest text-based environment. We already learned about one such environment at the beginning of this chapter, which is the Frozen Lake environment. We can check out other interesting toy text environments offered by Gym here: `https://gym.openai.com/envs/#toy_text`.

Algorithms

Instead of using our RL agent to play games, can we make use of our agent to solve some interesting problems? Yes! The algorithmic environment provides several interesting problems like copying a given sequence, performing addition, and so on. We can make use of the RL agent to solve these problems by learning how to perform computation. For instance, Gym provides an environment called `ReversedAddition-v0`, which we can use to train our agent to add multiple digit numbers.

We can check the algorithmic environments offered by Gym here: `https://gym.openai.com/envs/#algorithmic`.

Environment synopsis

We have learned about several types of Gym environment. Wouldn't it be nice if we could have information about all the environments in a single place? Yes! The Gym wiki provides a description of all the environments with their environment id, state space, action space, and reward range in a table: `https://github.com/openai/gym/wiki/Table-of-environments`.

We can also check all the available environments in Gym using the `registry.all()` method:

```
from gym import envs
print(envs.registry.all())
```

The preceding code will print all the available environments in Gym.

Thus, in this chapter, we have learned about the Gym toolkit and also several interesting environments offered by Gym. In the upcoming chapters, we will learn how to train our RL agent in a Gym environment to find the optimal policy.

Summary

We started the chapter by understanding how to set up our machine by installing Anaconda and the Gym toolkit. We learned how to create a Gym environment using the `gym.make()` function. Later, we also explored how to obtain the state space of the environment using `env.observation_space` and the action space of the environment using `env.action_space`. We then learned how to obtain the transition probability and reward function of the environment using `env.P`. Following this, we also learned how to generate an episode using the Gym environment. We understood that in each step of the episode we select an action using the `env.step()` function.

We understood the classic control methods in the Gym environment. We learned about the continuous state space of the classic control environments and how they are stored in an array. We also learned how to balance a pole using a random agent. Later, we learned about interesting Atari game environments, and how Atari game environments are named in Gym, and then we explored their state space and action space. We also learned how to record the agent's gameplay using the wrapper class, and at the end of the chapter, we discovered other environments offered by Gym.

In the next chapter, we will learn how to find the optimal policy using two interesting algorithms called value iteration and policy iteration.

Questions

Let's evaluate our newly gained knowledge by answering the following questions:

1. What is the use of a Gym toolkit?
2. How do we create an environment in Gym?
3. How do we obtain the action space of the Gym environment?
4. How do we visualize the Gym environment?
5. Name some classic control environments offered by Gym.
6. How do we generate an episode using the Gym environment?
7. What is the state space of Atari Gym environments?
8. How do we record the agent's gameplay?

Further reading

Check out the following resources for more information:

- To learn more about Gym, go to `http://gym.openai.com/docs/`.
- We can also check out the Gym repository to understand how Gym environments are coded: `https://github.com/openai/gym`.

3

The Bellman Equation and Dynamic Programming

In the previous chapter, we learned that in reinforcement learning our goal is to find the optimal policy. The optimal policy is the policy that selects the correct action in each state so that the agent can get the maximum return and achieve its goal. In this chapter, we'll learn about two interesting classic reinforcement learning algorithms called the value and policy iteration methods, which we can use to find the optimal policy.

Before diving into the value and policy iteration methods directly, first, we will learn about the Bellman equation. The Bellman equation is ubiquitous in reinforcement learning and it is used for finding the optimal value and Q functions. We will understand what the Bellman equation is and how it finds the optimal value and Q functions.

After understanding the Bellman equation, we will learn about two interesting dynamic programming methods called value and policy iterations, which use the Bellman equation to find the optimal policy. At the end of the chapter, we will learn how to solve the Frozen Lake problem by finding an optimal policy using the value and policy iteration methods.

In this chapter, we will learn about the following topics:

- The Bellman equation
- The Bellman optimality equation
- The relationship between the value and Q functions

- Dynamic programming – value and policy iteration methods
- Solving the Frozen Lake problem using value and policy iteration

The Bellman equation

The Bellman equation, named after Richard Bellman, helps us solve the **Markov decision process (MDP)**. When we say solve the MDP, we mean finding the optimal policy.

As stated in the introduction of the chapter, the Bellman equation is ubiquitous in reinforcement learning and is widely used for finding the optimal value and Q functions recursively. Computing the optimal value and Q functions is very important because once we have the optimal value or optimal Q function, then we can use them to derive the optimal policy.

In this section, we'll learn what exactly the Bellman equation is and how we can use it to find the optimal value and Q functions.

The Bellman equation of the value function

The Bellman equation states that the value of a state can be obtained as a sum of the immediate reward and the discounted value of the next state. Say we perform an action a in state s and move to the next state s' and obtain a reward r, then the Bellman equation of the value function can be expressed as:

$$V(s) = R(s, a, s') + \gamma V(s')$$

In the above equation, the following applies:

- $R(s, a, s')$ implies the immediate reward obtained while performing an action a in state s and moving to the next state s'
- γ is the discount factor
- $V(s')$ implies the value of the next state

Let's understand the Bellman equation with an example. Say we generate a trajectory τ using some policy π:

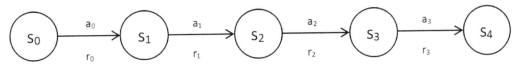

Figure 3.1: Trajectory

Let's suppose we need to compute the value of state s_2. According to the Bellman equation, the value of state s_2 is given as:

$$V(s_2) = R(s_2, a_2, s_3) + \gamma V(s_3)$$

In the preceding equation, $R(s_2, a_2, s_3)$ implies the immediate reward we obtain while performing an action a_2 in state s_2 and moving to state s_3. From the trajectory, we can tell that the immediate reward $R(s_2, a_2, s_3)$ is r_2. And the term $\gamma V(s_3)$ is the discounted value of the next state.

Thus, according to the Bellman equation, the value of state s_2 is given as:

$$V(s_2) = r_2 + \gamma V(s_3)$$

Thus, the Bellman equation of the value function can be expressed as:

$$V^\pi(s) = R(s, a, s') + \gamma V^\pi(s')$$

Where the superscript π implies that we are using policy π. The right-hand side term $R(s, a, s') + \gamma V^\pi(s')$ is often called the **Bellman backup**.

The preceding Bellman equation works only when we have a deterministic environment. Let's suppose our environment is stochastic, then in that case, when we perform an action a in state s, it is not guaranteed that our next state will always be s'; it could be some other states too. For instance, look at the trajectory in *Figure 3.2*.

As we can see, when we perform an action a_1 in state s_1, with a probability 0.7, we reach state s_2, and with a probability 0.3, we reach state s_3:

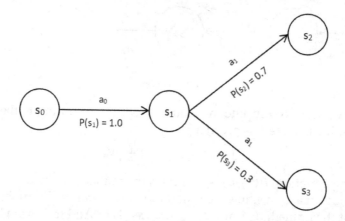

Figure 3.2: Transition probability of performing action a_1 in state s_1

Thus, when we perform action a_1 in state s_1, there is a 70% chance the next state will be s_2 and a 30% chance the next state will be s_3. We learned that the Bellman equation is a sum of immediate reward and the discounted value of the next state. But when our next state is not guaranteed due to the stochasticity present in the environment, how can we define our Bellman equation?

In this case, we can slightly modify our Bellman equation with the expectations (the weighted average), that is, a sum of the Bellman backup multiplied by the corresponding transition probability of the next state:

$$V^\pi(s) = \sum_{s'} P(s'|s, a)[R(s, a, s') + \gamma V^\pi(s')]$$

In the preceding equation, the following applies:

- $P(s'|s, a)$ denotes the transition probability of reaching s' by performing an action a in state s
- $[R(s, a, s') + \gamma V^\pi(s')]$ denotes the Bellman backup

Let's understand this equation better by considering the same trajectory we just used. As we notice, when we perform an action a_1 in state s_1, we go to s_2 with a probability of 0.70 and s_3 with a probability of 0.30. Thus, we can write:

$$V(s_1) = P(s_2|s_1, a_1)[R(s_1, a_1, s_2) + V(s_2)] + P(s_3|s_1, a_1)[R(s_1, a_1, s_3) + V(s_3)]$$

$$V(s_1) = 0.70[R(s_1, a_1, s_2) + V(s_2)] + 0.30[R(s_1, a_1, s_3) + V(s_3)]$$

Thus, the Bellman equation of the value function including the stochasticity present in the environment using the expectation (weighted average) is expressed as:

$$V^\pi(s) = \sum_{s'} P(s'|s, a)[R(s, a, s') + \gamma V^\pi(s')]$$

Okay, but what if our policy is a stochastic policy? We learned that with a stochastic policy, we select actions based on a probability distribution; that is, instead of performing the same action in a state, we select an action based on the probability distribution over the action space. Let's understand this with a different trajectory, shown in *Figure 3.3*. As we see, in state s_1, with a probability of 0.8, we select action a_1 and reach state s_2, and with a probability of 0.2, we select action a_2 and reach state s_3:

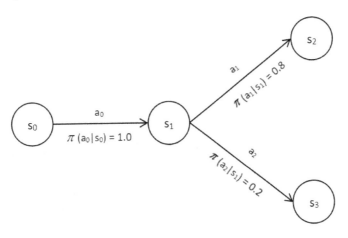

Figure 3.3: Trajectory using a stochastic policy

Thus, when we use a stochastic policy, our next state will not always be the same; it will be different states with some probability. Now, how can we define the Bellman equation including the stochastic policy?

- We learned that to include the stochasticity present in the environment in the Bellman equation, we took the expectation (the weighted average), that is, a sum of the Bellman backup multiplied by the corresponding transition probability of the next state.

- Similarly, to include the stochastic nature of the policy in the Bellman equation, we can use the expectation (the weighted average), that is, a sum of the Bellman backup multiplied by the corresponding probability of action.

Thus, our final Bellman equation of the value function can be written as:

$$V^{\pi}(s) = \sum_a \pi(a|s) \sum_{s'} P(s'|s,a)[R(s,a,s') + \gamma V^{\pi}(s')] \tag{1}$$

The preceding equation is also known as the **Bellman expectation equation** of the value function. We can also express the above equation in expectation form. Let's recollect the definition of expectation:

$$\mathbb{E}_{x \sim p(x)}[f(X)] = \sum_x p(x)f(x)$$

In equation (1), $f(x) = R(s,a,s') + \gamma V^{\pi}(s')$ and $P(x) = P(s'|s,a)$ and $\pi(a|s)$ which denote the probability of the stochastic environment and stochastic policy, respectively.

Thus, we can write the Bellman equation of the value function as:

$$V^{\pi}(s) = \underset{\substack{a \sim \pi \\ s' \sim P}}{\mathbb{E}}[R(s,a,s') + \gamma V^{\pi}(s')] \tag{2}$$

The Bellman equation of the Q function

Now, let's learn how to compute the Bellman equation of the state-action value function, that is, the Q function. The Bellman equation of the Q function is very similar to the Bellman equation of the value function except for a small difference. Similar to the Bellman equation of the value function, the Bellman equation of the Q function states that the Q value of a state-action pair can be obtained as a sum of the immediate reward and the discounted Q value of the next state-action pair:

$$Q(s,a) = R(s,a,s') + \gamma Q(s',a')$$

In the preceding equation, the following applies:

- $R(s,a,s')$ implies the immediate reward obtained while performing an action a in state s and moving to the next state s'
- γ is the discount factor
- $Q(s',a')$ is the Q value of the next state-action pair

Let's understand this with an example. Say we generate a trajectory τ using some policy π as shown in *Figure 3.4*:

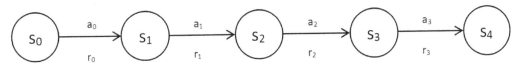

Figure 3.4: Trajectory

Let's suppose we need to compute the Q value of a state-action pair (s_2, a_2). Then, according to the Bellman equation, we can write:

$$Q(s_2, a_2) = R(s_2, a_2, s_3) + \gamma Q(s_3, a_3)$$

In the above equation, $R(s_2, a_2, a_3)$ represents the immediate reward we obtain while performing an action a_2 in state s_2 and moving to state s_3. From the preceding trajectory, we can tell that the immediate reward $R(s_2, a_2, s_3)$ is r_2. And the term $\gamma Q(s_3, a_3)$ represents the discounted Q value of the next state-action pair. Thus:

$$Q(s_2, a_2) = r_2 + \gamma Q(s_3, a_3)$$

Thus, the Bellman equation for the Q function can be expressed as:

$$Q^\pi(s, a) = R(s, a, s') + \gamma Q^\pi(s', a')$$

Where the superscript π implies that we are using the policy π and the right-hand side term $R(s, a, s') + \gamma Q^\pi(s', a')$ is the **Bellman backup**.

Similar to what we learned in the Bellman equation of the value function, the preceding Bellman equation works only when we have a deterministic environment because in the stochastic environment our next state will not always be the same and it will be based on a probability distribution. Suppose we have a stochastic environment, then when we perform an action a in state s. It is not guaranteed that our next state will always be s'; it could be some other states too with some probability.

So, just like we did in the previous section, we can use the expectation (the weighted average), that is, a sum of the Bellman backup multiplied by their corresponding transition probability of the next state, and rewrite our Bellman equation of the Q function as:

$$Q^\pi(s, a) = \sum_{s'} P(s'|s, a) [R(s, a, s') + \gamma Q^\pi(s', a')]$$

Similarly, when we use a stochastic policy, our next state will not always be the same; it will be different states with some probability. So, to include the stochastic nature of the policy, we can rewrite our Bellman equation with the expectation (the weighted average), that is, a sum of Bellman backup multiplied by the corresponding probability of action, just like we did in the Bellman equation of the value function. Thus, the Bellman equation of the Q function is given as:

$$Q^{\pi}(s,a) = \sum_a \pi(a|s) \sum_{s'} P(s'|s,a)\left[R(s,a,s') + \gamma Q^{\pi}(s',a')\right]$$

But wait! There is a small change in the above equation. Why do we need to add the term $\sum_a \pi(a|s)$ in the case of a Q function? Because in the value function $V(s)$, we are given only a state s and we choose an action a based on the policy π. So, we added the term $\sum_a \pi(a|s)$ to include the stochastic nature of the policy. But in the case of the Q function $Q(s, a)$, we will be given both state s and action a, so we don't need to add the term $\sum_a \pi(a|s)$ in our equation since we are not selecting any action a based on the policy π.

However, if you look at the above equation, we need to select action a' based on the policy π while computing the Q value of the next state-action pair $Q(s', a')$ since a' will not be given. So, we can just place the term $\sum_{a'} \pi(a'|s')$ before the Q value of the next state-action pair. Thus, our final Bellman equation of the Q function can be written as:

$$Q^{\pi}(s,a) = \sum_{s'} P(s'|s,a)\left[R(s,a,s') + \gamma \sum_{a'} \pi(a'|s')Q^{\pi}(s',a')\right] \qquad (3)$$

Equation (3) is also known as the Bellman expectation equation of the Q function. We can also express the equation (3) in expectation form as:

$$Q^{\pi}(s,a) = \mathbb{E}_{s'\sim P}[R(s,a,s') + \gamma \mathbb{E}_{a'\sim\pi}Q^{\pi}(s',a')] \qquad (4)$$

Now that we have understood what the Bellman expectation equation is, in the next section, we will learn about the Bellman optimality equation and explore how it is useful for finding the optimal Bellman value and Q functions.

The Bellman optimality equation

The Bellman optimality equation gives the optimal Bellman value and Q functions. First, let's look at the optimal Bellman value function. We learned that the Bellman equation of the value function is expressed as:

$$V^\pi(s) = \mathop{\mathbb{E}}_{\substack{a \sim \pi \\ s' \sim P}} [R(s, a, s') + \gamma V^\pi(s')]$$

In the first chapter, we learned that the value function depends on the policy, that is, the value of the state varies based on the policy we choose. There can be many different value functions according to different policies. The optimal value function, $V^*(s)$ is the one that yields the maximum value compared to all the other value functions. Similarly, there can be many different Bellman value functions according to different policies. The optimal Bellman value function is the one that has the maximum value.

Okay, how can we compute the optimal Bellman value function that has the maximum value?

We can compute the optimal Bellman value function by selecting the action that gives the maximum value. But we don't know which action gives the maximum value, so, we compute the value of state using all possible actions, and then we select the maximum value as the value of the state.

That is, instead of using some policy π to select the action, we compute the value of the state using all possible actions, and then we select the maximum value as the value of the state. Since we are not using any policy, we can remove the expectation over the policy π and add the max over the action and express our optimal Bellman value function as:

$$V^*(s) = \max_a \mathbb{E}_{s' \sim P}[R(s, a, s') + \gamma V^*(s')] \qquad (5)$$

It's just the same as the Bellman equation, except here we are taking a maximum over all the possible actions instead of the expectation (weighted average) over the policy since we are only interested in the maximum value. Let's understand this with an example. Say we are in a state s and we have two possible actions in the state. Let the actions be 0 and 1. Then $V^*(s)$ is given as:

$$V^*(s) = \max \begin{pmatrix} \mathbb{E}_{s' \sim P}[R(s, 0, s') + \gamma V^*(s')] \\ \mathbb{E}_{s' \sim P}[R(s, 1, s') + \gamma V^*(s')] \end{pmatrix}$$

As we can observe from the above equation, we compute the state value using all possible actions (0 and 1) and then select the maximum value as the value of the state.

Now, let's look at the optimal Bellman Q function. We learned that the Bellman equation of the Q function is expressed as:

$$Q^{\pi}(s, a) = \mathbb{E}_{s' \sim P}[R(s, a, s') + \gamma \mathbb{E}_{a' \sim \pi} Q^{\pi}(s', a')]$$

Just like we learned with the optimal Bellman value function, instead of using the policy to select action a' in the next state s', we choose all possible actions in that state s' and compute the maximum Q value. It can be expressed as:

$$Q^{*}(s, a) = \mathbb{E}_{s' \sim P}\left[R(s, a, s') + \gamma \max_{a'} Q^{*}(s', a')\right] \tag{6}$$

Let's understand this with an example. Say we are in a state s with an action a. We perform action a in state s and reach the next state s'. We need to compute the Q value for the next state s'. There can be many actions in state s'. Let's say we have two actions 0 and 1 in state s'. Then we can write the optimal Bellman Q function as:

$$Q^{*}(s, a) = \mathbb{E}_{s' \sim P}[R(s, a, s') + \gamma \max \begin{pmatrix} Q^{*}(s', 0) \\ Q^{*}(s', 1) \end{pmatrix}]$$

Thus, to summarize, the Bellman optimality equations of the value function and Q function are:

$$V^{*}(s) = \max_{a} \mathbb{E}_{s' \sim P}[R(s, a, s') + \gamma V^{*}(s')]$$

$$Q^{*}(s, a) = \mathbb{E}_{s' \sim P}\left[R(s, a, s') + \gamma \max_{a'} Q^{*}(s', a')\right]$$

We can also expand the expectation and rewrite the preceding Bellman optimality equations as:

$$V^{*}(s) = \max_{a} \sum_{s'} P(s'|s, a)[R(s, a, s') + \gamma V^{*}(s')]$$

$$Q^{*}(s, a) = \sum_{s'} P(s'|s, a)[R(s, a, s') + \gamma \max_{a'} Q^{*}(s', a')]$$

The relationship between the value and Q functions

Let's take a little detour and recap the value and Q functions we covered in *Chapter 1, Fundamentals of Reinforcement Learning*. We learned that the value of a state (value function) denotes the expected return starting from that state following a policy π:

$$V^\pi(s) = \underset{\tau \sim \pi}{\mathbb{E}} [R(\tau)|s_0 = s]$$

Similarly, the Q value of a state-action pair (Q function) represents the expected return starting from that state-action pair following a policy π:

$$Q^\pi(s, a) = \underset{\tau \sim \pi}{\mathbb{E}} [R(\tau)|s_0 = s, a_0 = a]$$

We learned that the optimal value function gives the maximum state-value:

$$V^*(s) = \max_\pi V^\pi(s)$$

And the optimal Q function gives the maximum state-action value (Q value):

$$Q^\pi(s, a) = \max_\pi Q^\pi(s, a)$$

Can we derive some relation between the optimal value function and optimal Q function? We know that the optimal value function has the maximum expected return when we start from a state s and the optimal Q function has the maximum expected return when we start from state s performing some action a. So, we can say that the optimal value function is the maximum of optimal Q value over all possible actions, and it can be expressed as follows (that is, we can derive V from Q):

$$V^*(s) = \max_a Q^*(s, a)$$

Alright, now let's get back to our Bellman equations. Before going ahead, let's just recap the Bellman equations:

- **Bellman expectation equation of the value function and Q function:**

  - $$V^\pi(s) = \sum_a \pi(a|s) \sum_{s'} P(s'|s, a)[R(s, a, s') + \gamma V^\pi(s')]$$

  - $$Q^\pi(s, a) = \sum_{s'} P(s'|s, a) [R(s, a, s') + \gamma \sum_{a'} \pi(a'|s')Q^\pi(s', a')]$$

- **Bellman optimality equation of the value function and Q function:**

  - $$V^*(s) = \max_a \sum_{s'} P(s'|s, a)[R(s, a, s') + \gamma V^*(s')]$$

  - $$Q^*(s, a) = \sum_{s'} P(s'|s, a)[R(s, a, s') + \gamma \max_{a'} Q^*(s', a')]$$

We learned that the optimal Bellman Q function is expressed as:

$$Q^*(s, a) = \sum_{s'} P(s'|s, a)[R(s, a, s') + \gamma \max_{a'} Q^*(s', a')]$$

If we have an optimal value function $V^*(s)$, then we can use it to derive the preceding optimal Bellman Q function, (that is, we can derive Q from V):

$$Q^*(s, a) = \sum_{s'} P(s'|s, a)[R(s, a, s') + \gamma V^*(s')]$$

The preceding equation is one of the most useful identities in reinforcement learning, and we will see how it will help us in finding the optimal policy in the upcoming section.

Thus, to summarize, we learned that we can derive V from Q:

$$V^*(s) = \max_a Q^*(s, a) \tag{7}$$

And derive Q from V:

$$Q^*(s, a) = \sum_{s'} P(s'|s, a)[R(s, a, s') + \gamma V^*(s')] \tag{8}$$

Substituting equation (8) in equation (7), we can write:

$$V^*(s) = \max_a \sum_{s'} P(s'|s, a)[R(s, a, s') + \gamma V^*(s')]$$

As we can observe, we just obtained the optimal Bellman value function. Now that we understand the Bellman equation and the relationship between the value and the Q function, we can move on to the next section on how to make use of these equations to find the optimal policy.

Dynamic programming

Dynamic programming (DP) is a technique for solving complex problems. In DP, instead of solving a complex problem as a whole, we break the problem into simple sub-problems, then for each sub-problem, we compute and store the solution. If the same subproblem occurs, we don't recompute; instead, we use the already computed solution. Thus, DP helps in drastically minimizing the computation time. It has its applications in a wide variety of fields including computer science, mathematics, bioinformatics, and so on.

Now, we will learn about two important methods that use DP to find the optimal policy. The two methods are:

- Value iteration
- Policy iteration

Note that dynamic programming is a model-based method meaning that it will help us to find the optimal policy only when the model dynamics (transition probability) of the environment are known. If we don't have the model dynamics, we cannot apply DP methods.

 The upcoming sections are explained with manual calculations, for a better understanding, follow along with a pen and paper.

Value iteration

In the value iteration method, we try to find the optimal policy. We learned that the optimal policy is the one that tells the agent to perform the correct action in each state. In order to find the optimal policy, first, we compute the optimal value function and once we have the optimal value function, we can use it to derive the optimal policy. Okay, how can we compute the optimal value function? We can use our optimal Bellman equation of the value function. We learned that, according to the Bellman optimality equation, the optimal value function can be computed as:

$$V^*(s) = \max_a \sum_{s'} P(s'|s, a)[R(s, a, s') + \gamma V^*(s')] \qquad (9)$$

In the *The relationship between the value and Q functions* section, we learned that given the value function, we can derive the Q function:

$$Q^*(s, a) = \sum_{s'} P(s'|s, a)[R(s, a, s') + \gamma V^*(s')] \qquad (10)$$

Substituting (10) in (9), we can write:

$$V^*(s) = \max_a Q^*(s, a)$$

Thus, we can compute the optimal value function by just taking the maximum over the optimal Q function. So, in order to compute the value of a state, we compute the Q value for all state-action pairs. Then, we select the maximum Q value as the value of the state.

Let's understand this with an example. Say we have two states, s_0 and s_1, and we have two possible actions in these states; let the actions be 0 and 1. First, we compute the Q value for all possible state-action pairs. *Table 3.1* shows the Q values for all possible state-action pairs:

State	Action	Value
s_0	0	2.7
s_0	1	3
s_1	0	4
s_1	1	2

Table 3.1: Q values of all possible state-action pairs

Then, in each state, we select the maximum Q value as the optimal value of a state. Thus, the value of state s_0 is 3 and the value of state s_1 is 4. The optimal value of the state (value function) is shown *Table 3.2*:

State	Value
s_0	3
s_1	4

Table 3.2: Optimal state values

Once we obtain the optimal value function, we can use it to extract the optimal policy.

Now that we have a basic understanding of how the value iteration method finds the optimal value function, in the next section, we will go into detail and learn how exactly the value iteration method works and how it finds the optimal policy from the optimal value function.

The value iteration algorithm

The algorithm of value iteration is given as follows:

1. Compute the optimal value function by taking the maximum over the Q function, that is, $V^*(s) = \max_a Q^*(s, a)$

2. Extract the optimal policy from the computed optimal value function

Let's go into detail and learn exactly how the above two steps work. For better understanding, let's perform the value iteration manually. Consider the small grid world environment shown in *Figure 3.5*. Let's say we are in state **A** and our goal is to reach state **C** without visiting the shaded state **B**, and say we have two actions, $0-$left/right, and $1-$up/down:

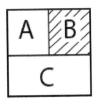

Figure 3.5: Grid world environment

Can you think of what the optimal policy is here? The optimal policy here is the one that tells us to perform action 1 in state **A** so that we can reach **C** without visiting **B**. Now we will see how to find this optimal policy using value iteration.

Table 3.3 shows the model dynamics of state **A**:

State	Action	Next State	Transition Probability	Reward Function
(s)	(a)	(s')	$P(s'\|s,a)$ or $P_{ss'}^a$	$R(s,a,s')$ or $R_{ss'}^a$
A	0	A	0.1	0
A	0	B	0.8	-1
A	0	C	0.1	1
A	1	A	0.1	0
A	1	B	0.0	-1
A	1	C	0.9	0

Table 3.3: Model dynamics of state A

Step 1 – Compute the optimal value function

We can compute the optimal value function by computing the maximum over the Q function.

$$V^*(s) = \max_a Q^*(s, a)$$

That is, we compute the Q value for all state-action pairs and then we select the maximum Q value as the value of a state.

The Q value for a state s and action a can be computed as:

$$Q(s, a) = \sum_{s'} P(s'|s, a)[R(s, a, s') + \gamma V(s')]$$

For notation simplicity, we can denote $P(s'|s, a)$ by $P_{ss'}^a$ and $R(s, a, s')$ by $R_{ss'}^a$ and rewrite the preceding equation as:

$$Q(s, a) = \sum_{s'} P_{ss'}^a [R_{ss'}^a + \gamma V(s')] \qquad (11)$$

Thus, using the preceding equation, we can compute the Q function. If you look at the equation, to compute the Q function, we need the transition probability $P_{ss'}^a$, the reward function $R_{ss'}^a$, and the value of the next state $V(s')$. The model dynamics provide us with the transition probability $P_{ss'}^a$ and the reward function $R_{ss'}^a$. But what about the value of the next state $V(s')$? We don't know the value of any states yet. So, we will initialize the value function (state values) with random values or zeros as shown in *Table 3.4* and compute the Q function.

State	Value
A	0
B	0
C	0

Table 3.4: Initial value table

Iteration 1:

Let's compute the Q value of state **A**. We have two actions in state **A**, which are 0 and 1. So, first let's compute the Q value for state **A** and action 0 (note that we use the discount factor $\gamma = 1$ throughout this section):

$$
\begin{aligned}
Q(A, 0) &= P_{AA}^0 [R_{AA}^0 + \gamma V(A)] + P_{AB}^0 [R_{AB}^0 + \gamma V(B)] + P_{AC}^0 [R_{AC}^0 + \gamma V(C)] \\
&= 0.1(0 + 0) + 0.8(-1 + 0) + 0.1(1 + 0) \\
&= -0.7
\end{aligned}
$$

Now, let's compute the Q value for state **A** and action 1:

$$
\begin{aligned}
Q(A, 1) &= P_{AA}^1 [R_{AA}^1 + \gamma V(A)] + P_{AB}^1 [R_{AB}^1 + \gamma V(B)] + P_{AC}^1 [R_{AC}^1 + \gamma V(C)] \\
&= 0.1(0 + 0) + 0.0(-1 + 0) + 0.9(1 + 0) \\
&= 0.9
\end{aligned}
$$

After computing the Q values for both the actions in state **A**, we can update the Q table as shown in *Table 3.5*:

State	Action	Value
A	0	- 0.7
A	1	0.9
B	0	
B	1	
C	0	
C	1	

Table 3.5: Q table

We learned that the optimal value of a state is just the max of the Q function. That is, $V^*(s) = \max_a Q^*(s, a)$. By looking at *Table 3.5*, we can say that the value of state **A**, $V(A)$, is $Q(A, 1)$ since $Q(A, 1)$ has a higher value than $Q(A, 0)$. Thus, $V(A) = 0.9$.

We can update the value of state **A** in our value table as shown in *Table 3.6*:

State	Value
A	0.9
B	0
C	0

Table 3.6: Updated value table

Similarly, in order to compute the value of state **B**, $V(B)$, we compute the Q value of $Q(B, 0)$ and $Q(B, 1)$ and select the highest Q value as the value of state **B**. In the same way, to compute the values of other states, we compute the Q value for all state-action pairs and select the maximum Q value as the value of a state.

After computing the value of all the states, our updated value table may resemble *Table 3.7*. This is the result of the first iteration:

State	Value
A	0.9
B	- 0.2
C	0.5

Table 3.7: Value table from iteration 1

However, the value function (value table) shown in *Table 3.7* obtained as a result of the first iteration is not an optimal one. But why? We learned that the optimal value function is the maximum of the optimal Q function. That is, $V^*(s) = \max_a Q^*(s, a)$. Thus to find the optimal value function, we need the optimal Q function. But the Q function may not be an optimal one in the first iteration as we computed the Q function based on the randomly initialized state values.

As the following shows, when we started off computing the Q function, we used the randomly initialized state values.

$$V^*(s) = \max_a Q^*(s, a)$$

$$\sum_{s'} P_{ss'}^a [R_{ss'}^a + \gamma V(s')]$$

Random Values

So, what we can do is, in the next iteration, while computing the Q function, we can use the updated state values obtained as a result of the first iteration.

That is, in the second iteration, to compute the value function, we compute the Q value of all state-action pairs and select the maximum Q value as the value of a state. In order to compute the Q value, we need to know the state values, in the first iteration, we used the randomly initialized state values. But in the second iteration, we use the updated state values (value table) obtained from the first iteration as the following shows:

$$V^*(s) = \max_a Q^*(s,a)$$

$$\downarrow \quad \sum_{s'} P_{ss'}^a [R_{ss'}^a + \gamma V(s')]$$

↳ Use state values from 1st iteration

Iteration 2:

Let's compute the Q value of state **A**. Remember that while computing the Q value, we use the updated state values from the previous iteration.

First, let's compute the Q value of state **A** and action 0:

$$
\begin{aligned}
Q(A, 0) &= P_{AA}^0 [R_{AA}^0 + \gamma V(A)] + P_{AB}^0 [R_{AB}^0 + \gamma V(B)] + P_{AC}^0 [R_{AC}^0 + \gamma V(C)] \\
&= 0.1(0 + 0.9) + 0.8(-1 - 0.2) + 0.1(1 + 0.5) \\
&= -0.72
\end{aligned}
$$

Now, let's compute the Q value for state **A** and action 1:

$$
\begin{aligned}
Q(A, 1) &= P_{AA}^1 [R_{AA}^1 + \gamma V(A)] + P_{AB}^1 [R_{AB}^1 + \gamma V(B)] + P_{AC}^1 [R_{AC}^1 + \gamma V(C)] \\
&= 0.1(0 + 0.9) + 0.0(-1 - 0.2) + 0.9(1 + 0.5) \\
&= 1.44
\end{aligned}
$$

As we may observe, since the Q value of action 1 in state A is higher than action 0, the value of state A becomes 1.44. Similarly, we compute the value for all the states and update the value table. *Table 3.8* shows the updated value table:

State	Value
A	1.44
B	- 0.50
C	1.0

Table 3.8: Value table from iteration 2

Iteration 3:

We repeat the same steps we saw in the previous iteration and compute the value of all the states by selecting the maximum Q value. Remember that while computing the Q value, we use the updated state values (value table) obtained from the previous iteration. So, we use the updated state values from iteration 2 to compute the Q value.

Table 3.9 shows the updated state values obtained as a result of the third iteration:

State	Value
A	1.94
B	- 0.70
C	1.3

Table 3.9: Value table from iteration 3

So, we repeat these steps for many iterations until we find the optimal value function. But how can we understand whether we have found the optimal value function or not? When the value function (value table) does not change over iterations or when it changes by a very small fraction, then we can say that we have attained convergence, that is, we have found an optimal value function.

Okay, how can we find out whether the value table is changing or not changing from the previous iteration? We can calculate the difference between the value table obtained from the previous iteration and the value table obtained from the current iteration. If the difference is very small—say, the difference is less than a very small threshold number—then we can say that we have attained convergence as there is not much change in the value function.

For example, let's suppose *Table 3.10* shows the value table obtained as a result of **iteration 4**:

State	Value
A	1.94
B	- 0.70
C	1.3

Table 3.10: Value table from iteration 4

As we can notice, the difference between the value table obtained as a result of iteration 4 and iteration 3 is very small. So, we can say that we have attained convergence and we take the value table obtained as a result of iteration 4 as our optimal value function. Please note that the above example is just for better understanding; in practice, we cannot attain convergence in just four iterations — it usually takes many iterations.

Now that we have found the optimal value function, in the next step, we will use this optimal value function to extract an optimal policy.

Step 2 – Extract the optimal policy from the optimal value function obtained from step 1

As a result of *Step 1*, we obtained the optimal value function:

State	Value
A	1.95
B	- 0.72
C	1.3

Table 3.11: Optimal value table (value function)

Now, how can we extract the optimal policy from the obtained optimal value function?

We generally use the Q function to compute the policy. We know that the Q function gives the Q value for every state-action pair. Once we have the Q values for all state-action pairs, we extract the policy by selecting the action that has the maximum Q value in each state. For example, consider the Q table in *Table 3.12*. It shows the Q values for all state-action pairs. Now we can extract the policy from the Q function (Q table) by selecting action 1 in the state s_0 and action 0 in the state s_1 as they have the maximum Q value.

State	Action	Value
s_0	0	1
s_0	1	4
s_1	0	7
s_1	1	2

Table 3.12: Q table

Okay, now we compute the Q function using the optimal value function obtained from *Step 1*. Once we have the Q function, then we extract the policy by selecting the action that has the maximum Q value in each state. Since we are computing the Q function using the optimal value function, the policy extracted from the Q function will be the optimal policy.

We learned that the Q function can be computed as:

$$Q(s, a) = \sum_{s'} P_{ss'}^a [R_{ss'}^a + \gamma V(s')]$$

Now, while computing Q values, we use the optimal value function we obtained from *step 1*. After computing the Q function, we can extract the optimal policy by selecting the action that has the maximum Q value:

$$\pi^* = \arg\max_a Q(s, a)$$

For instance, let's compute the Q value for all actions in state **A** using the optimal value function. The Q value for action 0 in state **A** is computed as:

$$
\begin{aligned}
Q(A, 0) &= P_{AA}^0[R_{AA}^0 + \gamma V(A)] + P_{AB}^0[R_{AB}^0 + \gamma V(B)] + P_{AC}^0[R_{AC}^0 + \gamma V(C)] \\
&= 0.1(0 + 1.95) + 0.8(-1 - 0.72) + 0.1(1 + 1.3) \\
&= -0.951
\end{aligned}
$$

The Q value for action 1 in state **A** is computed as:

$$
\begin{aligned}
Q(A, 1) &= P_{AA}^1[R_{AA}^1 + \gamma V(A)] + P_{AB}^1[R_{AB}^1 + \gamma V(B)] + P_{AC}^1[R_{AC}^1 + \gamma V(C)] \\
&= 0.1(0 + 1.95) + 0.0(-1 - 0.72) + 0.9(1 + 1.3) \\
&= 2.26
\end{aligned}
$$

Since $Q(A, 1)$ is higher than $Q(A, 0)$, our optimal policy will select action 1 as the optimal action in state **A**. *Table 3.13* shows the Q table after computing the Q values for all state-action pairs using the optimal value function:

State	Action	Value
A	0	-0.95
A	1	2.26
B	0	-0.5
B	1	0.5
C	0	-1.1
C	1	1.4

Table 3.13: Q table

From this Q table, we pick the action in each state that has the maximum value as an optimal policy. Thus, our optimal policy would select action 1 in state **A**, action 1 in state **B**, and action 1 in state **C**.

Thus, according to our optimal policy, if we perform action 1 in state **A**, we can reach state **C** without visiting state **B**.

In this section, we learned how to compute the optimal policy using the value iteration method. In the next section, we will learn how to implement the value iteration method to compute the optimal policy in the Frozen Lake environment using the Gym toolkit.

Solving the Frozen Lake problem with value iteration

In the previous chapter, we learned about the Frozen Lake environment. The Frozen Lake environment is shown in *Figure 3.6*:

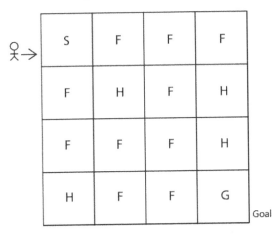

Figure 3.6: Frozen Lake environment

Let's recap the Frozen Lake environment a bit. In the Frozen Lake environment shown in *Figure 3.6*, the following applies:

- **S** implies the starting state
- **F** implies the frozen states
- **H** implies the hole states
- **G** implies the goal state

We learned that in the Frozen Lake environment, our goal is to reach the goal state **G** from the starting state **S** without visiting the hole states **H**. That is, while trying to reach the goal state **G** from the starting state **S**, if the agent visits the hole states **H**, then it will fall into the hole and die as *Figure 3.7* shows:

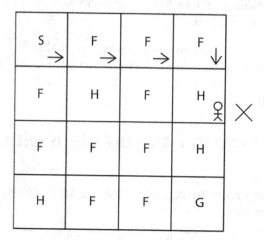

Figure 3.7: Agent falling into the hole

So, we want the agent to avoid the hole states **H** to reach the goal state **G** as shown in the following:

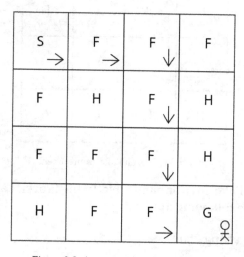

Figure 3.8: Agent reaches the goal state

How can we achieve this goal? That is, how can we reach state **G** from **S** without visiting **H**? We learned that the optimal policy tells the agent to perform the correct action in each state. So, if we find the optimal policy, then we can reach state **G** from **S** without visiting state **H**. Okay, how can we find the optimal policy? We can use the value iteration method we just learned to find the optimal policy.

Remember that all our states (**S** to **G**) will be encoded from 0 to 16 and all four actions—*left, down, up, right*—will be encoded from 0 to 3 in the Gym toolkit.

In this section, we will learn how to find the optimal policy using the value iteration method so that the agent can reach state **G** from **S** without visiting **H**.

First, let's import the necessary libraries:

```
import gym
import numpy as np
```

Now, let's create the Frozen Lake environment using Gym:

```
env = gym.make('FrozenLake-v0')
```

Let's look at the Frozen Lake environment using the render function:

```
env.render()
```

The preceding code will display:

Figure 3.9: Gym Frozen Lake environment

As we can notice, our agent is in state **S** and it has to reach state **G** without visiting the **H** states. So, let's learn how to compute the optimal policy using the value iteration method.

In the value iteration method, we perform two steps:

1. Compute the optimal value function by taking the maximum over the Q function, that is, $V^*(s) = \max_a Q^*(s, a)$
2. Extract the optimal policy from the computed optimal value function

First, let's learn how to compute the optimal value function, and then we will see how to extract the optimal policy from the computed optimal value function.

Computing the optimal value function

We will define a function called `value_iteration` where we compute the optimal value function iteratively by taking the maximum over the Q function, that is, $V^*(s) = \max_a Q^*(s, a)$. For better understanding, let's closely look at every line of the function, and then we'll look at the complete function at the end, which will provide more clarity.

Define the `value_iteration` function, which takes the environment as a parameter:

```
def value_iteration(env):
```

Set the number of iterations:

```
    num_iterations = 1000
```

Set the threshold number for checking the convergence of the value function:

```
    threshold = 1e-20
```

We also set the discount factor γ to 1:

```
    gamma = 1.0
```

Now, we will initialize the value table by setting the value of all states to zero:

```
    value_table = np.zeros(env.observation_space.n)
```

For every iteration:

```
    for i in range(num_iterations):
```

Update the value table, that is, we learned that on every iteration, we use the updated value table (state values) from the previous iteration:

```
        updated_value_table = np.copy(value_table)
```

Now, we compute the value function (state value) by taking the maximum of the Q value:

$$V^*(s) = \max_a Q^*(s, a)$$

$$\text{Where } Q(s, a) = \sum_{s'} P_{ss'}^a [R_{ss'}^a + \gamma V(s')].$$

Thus, for each state, we compute the Q values of all the actions in the state and then we update the value of the state as the one that has the maximum Q value:

```
for s in range(env.observation_space.n):
```

Compute the Q value of all the actions, $Q(s, a) = \sum_{s'} P_{ss'}^a [R_{ss'}^a + \gamma V(s')]$:

```
Q_values = [sum([prob*(r + gamma * updated_value_table[s_])
                for prob, s_, r, _ in env.P[s][a]])
                for a in range(env.action_space.n)]
```

Update the value of the state as a maximum Q value, $V^*(s) = \max_a Q^*(s, a)$:

```
value_table[s] = max(Q_values)
```

After computing the value table, that is, the value of all the states, we check whether the difference between the value table obtained in the current iteration and the previous iteration is less than or equal to a threshold value. If the difference is less than the threshold, then we break the loop and return the value table as our optimal value function as the following code shows:

```
    if (np.sum(np.fabs(updated_value_table - value_table)) <=
threshold):
            break

    return value_table
```

The following complete snippet of the `value_iteration` function is shown to provide more clarity:

```
def value_iteration(env):

    num_iterations = 1000
    threshold = 1e-20
    gamma = 1.0
```

```
    value_table = np.zeros(env.observation_space.n)

    for i in range(num_iterations):

        updated_value_table = np.copy(value_table)

        for s in range(env.observation_space.n):

            Q_values = [sum([prob*(r + gamma * updated_value_table[s_])
                            for prob, s_, r, _ in env.P[s][a]])
                                for a in range(env.action_space.n)]

            value_table[s] = max(Q_values)


        if (np.sum(np.fabs(updated_value_table - value_table)) <=
threshold):
                break

    return value_table
```

Now that we have computed the optimal value function by taking the maximum of the Q values, let's see how to extract the optimal policy from the optimal value function.

Extracting the optimal policy from the optimal value function

In the previous step, we computed the optimal value function. Now, let's see how to extract the optimal policy from the computed optimal value function.

First, we define a function called `extract_policy`, which takes `value_table` as a parameter:

```
def extract_policy(value_table):
```

Set the discount factor γ to 1:

```
gamma = 1.0
```

First, we initialize the policy with zeros, that is, we set the actions for all the states to be zero:

```
policy = np.zeros(env.observation_space.n)
```

Now, we compute the Q function using the optimal value function obtained from the previous step. We learned that the Q function can be computed as:

$$Q(s, a) = \sum_{s'} P^a_{ss'} [R^a_{ss'} + \gamma V(s')]$$

After computing the Q function, we can extract the policy by selecting the action that has the maximum Q value. Since we are computing the Q function using the optimal value function, the policy extracted from the Q function will be the optimal policy.

$$\pi^* = \arg\max_a Q(s, a)$$

As the following code shows, for each state, we compute the Q values for all the actions in the state and then we extract the policy by selecting the action that has the maximum Q value.

For each state:

```
for s in range(env.observation_space.n):
```

Compute the Q value of all the actions in the state, $Q(s, a) = \sum_{s'} P^a_{ss'} [R^a_{ss'} + \gamma V(s')]$:

```
Q_values = [sum([prob*(r + gamma * value_table[s_])
                for prob, s_, r, _ in env.P[s][a]])
                for a in range(env.action_space.n)]
```

Extract the policy by selecting the action that has the maximum Q value, $\pi^* = \arg\max_a Q(s, a)$:

```
policy[s] = np.argmax(np.array(Q_values))
```

```
return policy
```

The complete snippet of the `extract_policy` function is shown here to give us more clarity:

```
def extract_policy(value_table):

    gamma = 1.0

    policy = np.zeros(env.observation_space.n)

    for s in range(env.observation_space.n):

        Q_values = [sum([prob*(r + gamma * value_table[s_])
                        for prob, s_, r, _ in env.P[s][a]])
                            for a in range(env.action_space.n)]

        policy[s] = np.argmax(np.array(Q_values))

    return policy
```

That's it! Now, we will see how to extract the optimal policy in our Frozen Lake environment.

Putting it all together

We learned that in the Frozen Lake environment, our goal is to find the optimal policy that selects the correct action in each state so that we can reach state **G** from state **A** without visiting the hole states.

First, we compute the optimal value function using our `value_iteration` function by passing our Frozen Lake environment as the parameter:

```
optimal_value_function = value_iteration(env)
```

Next, we extract the optimal policy from the optimal value function using our `extract_policy` function:

```
optimal_policy = extract_policy(optimal_value_function)
```

We can print the obtained optimal policy:

```
print(optimal_policy)
```

The preceding code will print the following. As we can observe, our optimal policy tells us to perform the correct action in each state:

```
[0. 3. 3. 3. 0. 0. 0. 0. 3. 1. 0. 0. 0. 2. 1. 0.]
```

Now that we have learned what value iteration is and how to perform the value iteration method to compute the optimal policy in our Frozen Lake environment, in the next section, we will learn about another interesting method, called policy iteration.

Policy iteration

In the value iteration method, first, we computed the optimal value function by taking the maximum over the Q function (Q values) iteratively. Once we found the optimal value function, we used it to extract the optimal policy. Whereas in policy iteration we try to compute the optimal value function using the policy iteratively, once we found the optimal value function, we can use it to extract the optimal policy.

First, let's learn how to compute the value function using a policy. Say we have a policy π, how can we compute the value function using the policy π? Here, we can use our Bellman equation. We learned that according to the Bellman equation, we can compute the value function using the policy π as the following shows:

$$V^{\pi}(s) = \sum_a \pi(a|s) \sum_{s'} P(s'|s,a)[R(s,a,s') + \gamma V^{\pi}(s')]$$

Let's suppose our policy is a deterministic policy, so we can remove the term $\sum_a \pi(a|s)$ from the preceding equation since there is no stochasticity in the policy and rewrite our Bellman equation as:

$$V^{\pi}(s) = \sum_{s'} P(s'|s,a)[R(s,a,s') + \gamma V^{\pi}(s')]$$

For notation simplicity, we can denote $P(s'|s,a)$ by $P_{ss'}^a$ and $R(s,a,s')$ with $R_{ss'}^a$ and rewrite the preceding equation as:

$$V^{\pi}(s) = \sum_{s'} P_{ss'}^a [R_{ss'}^a + \gamma V(s')]$$

Thus using the above equation we can compute the value function using a policy. Our goal is to find the optimal value function because once we have found the optimal value function, we can use it to extract the optimal policy.

We will not be given any policy as an input. So, we will initialize the random policy and compute the value function using the random policy. Then we check if the computed value function is optimal or not. It will not be optimal since it is computed based on the random policy.

So, we will extract a new policy from the computed value function, then we will use the extracted new policy to compute the new value function, and then we will check if the new value function is optimal. If it's optimal we will stop, else we repeat these steps for a series of iterations. For a better understanding, look at the following steps:

Iteration 1: Let π_0 be the random policy. We use this random policy to compute the value function V^{π_0}. Our value function will not be optimal as it is computed based on the random policy. So, from V^{π_0}, we extract a new policy π_1.

Iteration 2: Now, we use the new policy π_1 derived from the previous iteration to compute the new value function V^{π_1}, then we check if V^{π_1} is optimal. If it is optimal, we stop, else from this value function V^{π_1}, we extract a new policy π_2.

Iteration 3: Now, we use the new policy π_2 derived from the previous iteration to compute the new value function V^{π_2}, then we check if V^{π_2} is optimal. If it is optimal, we stop, else from this value function V^{π_2}, we extract a new policy π_3.

We repeat this process for many iterations until we find the optimal value function V^{π^*} as the following shows:

$$\pi_0 \to V^{\pi_0} \to \pi_1 \to V^{\pi_1} \to \pi_2 \to V^{\pi_2} \to \pi_3 \to V^{\pi_3} \to \cdots \to \pi^* \to V^{\pi^*}$$

The preceding step is called policy evaluation and improvement. Policy evaluation implies that at each step we evaluate the policy by checking if the value function computed using that policy is optimal. Policy improvement means that at each step we find the new improved policy to compute the optimal value function.

Once we have found the optimal value function V^{π^*}, then it implies that we have also found the optimal policy. That is, if V^{π^*} is optimal, then the policy that is used to compute V^{π^*} will be an optimal policy.

To get a better understanding of how policy iteration works, let's look into the below steps with pseudocode. In the first iteration, we will initialize a random policy and use it to compute the value function:

```
policy = random_policy
value_function = compute_value_function(policy)
```

Since we computed the value function using the random policy, the computed value function will not be optimal. So, we need to find a new policy with which we can compute the optimal value function.

So, we extract a new policy from the value function computed using a random policy:

```
new_policy = extract_policy(value_function)
```

Now, we will use this new policy to compute the new value function:

```
policy = new_policy
value_function = compute_value_function(policy)
```

If the new value function is optimal, we stop, else we repeat the preceding steps for a number of iterations until we find the optimal value function. The following pseudocode gives us a better understanding:

```
policy = random_policy
for i in range(num_iterations):
    value_function = compute_value_function(policy)
    new_policy = extract_policy(value_function)

    if value_function = optimal:
        break
    else:
        policy = new_policy
```

Wait! How do we say our value function is optimal? If the value function is not changing over iterations, then we can say that our value function is optimal. Okay, how can we check if the value function is not changing over iterations?

We learned that we compute the value function using a policy. If the policy is not changing over iterations, then our value function also doesn't change over the iterations. Thus, when the policy doesn't change over iterations, then we can say that we have found the optimal value function.

Thus, over a series of iterations when the policy and new policy become the same, then we can say that we obtained the optimal value function. The following final pseudocode is given for clarity:

```
policy = random_policy
for i in range(num_iterations):
    value_function = compute_value_function(policy)
    new_policy = extract_policy(value_function)
```

```
    if policy == new_policy:
        break
else:
    policy = new_policy
```

Thus, when the policy is not changing, that is, when the policy and new policy become the same, then we can say that we obtained the optimal value function and the policy that is used to compute the optimal value function will be the optimal policy.

Remember that in the value iteration method, we compute the optimal value function using the maximum over Q function (Q value) iteratively and once we have found the optimal value function, we extract the optimal policy from it. But in the policy iteration method, we compute the optimal value function using the policy iteratively and once we have found the optimal value function, then the policy that is used to compute the optimal value function will be the optimal policy.

Now that we have a basic understanding of how the policy iteration method works, in the next section, we will get into the details and learn how to compute policy iteration manually.

Algorithm – policy iteration

The steps of the policy iteration algorithm is given as follows:

1. Initialize a random policy
2. Compute the value function using the given policy
3. Extract a new policy using the value function obtained from *step 2*
4. If the extracted policy is the same as the policy used in *step 2*, then stop, else send the extracted new policy to *step 2* and repeat *steps 2* to *4*

Now, let's get into the details and learn how exactly the preceding steps work. For a clear understanding, let's perform policy iteration manually. Let's take the same grid world environment we used in the value iteration method. Let's say we are in state **A** and our goal is to reach state **C** without visiting the shaded state **B**, and say we have two actions, 0 – *left/right* and 1 – *up/down*:

Figure 3.10: Grid world environment

We know that in the above environment, the optimal policy is the one that tells us to perform action 1 in state **A** so that we can reach **C** without visiting **B**. Now, we will see how to find this optimal policy using policy iteration.

Table 3.14 shows the model dynamics of state **A**:

State	Action	Next State	Transition Probability	Reward Function
(s)	(a)	(s')	$P(s' \mid s, a)$ or $P^a_{ss'}$	$R(s, a, s')$ or $R^a_{ss'}$
A	0	A	0.1	0
A	0	B	0.8	-1
A	0	C	0.1	1
A	1	A	0.1	0
A	1	B	0.0	-1
A	1	C	0.9	0

Table 3.14: Model dynamics of state A

Step 1 – Initialize a random policy

First, we will initialize a random policy. As the following shows, our random policy tells us to perform action 1 in state **A**, 0 in state **B**, and action 1 in state **C**:

$$A \rightarrow 1$$
$$B \rightarrow 0$$
$$C \rightarrow 1$$

Step 2 – Compute the value function using the given policy

This step is exactly the same as how we computed the value function in value iteration but with a small difference. In value iteration, we computed the value function by taking the maximum over the Q function. But here in policy iteration, we will compute the value function using the policy.

To understand this step better, let's quickly recollect how we compute the value function in value iteration. In value iteration, we compute the optimal value function as the maximum over the optimal Q function as the following shows:

$$V^*(s) = \max_a Q^*(s, a)$$

$$\text{where } Q^*(s, a) = P^a_{ss'}[R^a_{ss'} + \gamma V(s')]$$

In policy iteration, we compute the value function using a policy π, unlike value iteration, where we computed the value function using the maximum over the Q function. The value function using a policy π can be computed as:

$$V^\pi(s) = \sum_{s'} P_{ss'}^a [R_{ss'}^a + \gamma V^\pi(s')]$$

If you look at the preceding equation, to compute the value function, we need the transition probability $P_{ss'}^a$, the reward function $R_{ss'}^a$ and the value of the next state $V(s')$. The values of the transition probability $P_{ss'}^a$ and the reward function $R_{ss'}^a$ can be obtained from the model dynamics. But what about the value of the next state $V(s')$? We don't know the value of any states yet. So, we will initialize the value function (state values) with random values or zeros as *Figure 3.15* shows and compute the value function:

State	Value
A	0
B	0
C	0

Table 3.15: Initial value table

Iteration 1:

Let's compute the value of state **A** (note that here, we only compute the value for the action given by the policy, unlike in value iteration, where we computed the Q value for all the actions in the state and selected the maximum value).

So, the action given by the policy for state **A** is 1 and we can compute the value of state **A** as the following shows (note that we have used a discount factor $\gamma = 1$ throughout this section):

$$
\begin{aligned}
V(A) &= P_{AA}^1[R_{AA}^1 + \gamma V(A)] + P_{AB}^1[R_{AB}^1 + \gamma V(B)] + P_{AC}^1[R_{AC}^1 + \gamma V(C)] \\
&= 0.1(0+0) + 0.0(-1+0) + 0.9(1+0) \\
&= 0.9
\end{aligned}
$$

Similarly, we compute the value for all the states using the action given by the policy. *Table 3.16* shows the updated state values obtained as a result of the first iteration:

State	Value
A	0.9
B	- 0.2
C	0.1

Table 3.16: Value table from iteration 1

However, the value function (value table) shown in *Table 3.16* obtained as a result of the first iteration will not be accurate. That is, the state values (value function) will not be accurate according to the given policy.

Note that unlike the value iteration method, here we are not checking whether our value function is optimal or not; we just check whether our value function is accurately computed according to the given policy.

The value function will not be accurate because when we started off computing the value function using the given policy, we used the randomly initialized state values:

$$V^{\pi}(s) = \sum_{s'} P_{ss'}^{a}[R_{ss'}^{a} + \gamma V^{\pi}(s')]$$

$\llcorner\rightarrow$ Random Values

So, in the next iteration, while computing the value function, we will use the updated state values obtained as a result of the first iteration:

$$V^{\pi}(s) = \sum_{s'} P_{ss'}^{a}[R_{ss'}^{a} + \gamma V^{\pi}(s')]$$

$\llcorner\rightarrow$ Use state values from 1st iteration

Iteration 2:

Now, in iteration 2, we compute the value function using the policy π. Remember that while computing the value function, we will use the updated state values (value table) obtained from iteration 1.

For instance, let's compute the value of state A:

$$
\begin{aligned}
V(A) &= P^1_{AA}[R^1_{AA} + \gamma V(A)] + P^1_{AB}[R^1_{AB} + \gamma V(B)] + P^1_{AC}[R^1_{AC} + \gamma V(C)] \\
&= 0.1(0 + 0.9) + 0.0(-1 - 0.2) + 0.9(1 + 0.1) \\
&= 1.08
\end{aligned}
$$

Similarly, we compute the value for all the states using the action given by the policy. *Table 3.17* shows the updated state values obtained as a result of the second iteration:

State	Value
A	1.08
B	- 0.5
C	0.5

Table 3.17: Value table from iteration 2

Iteration 3:

Similarly, in iteration 3, we compute the value function using the policy π and while computing the value function, we will use the updated state values (value table) obtained from iteration 2.

Table 3.18 shows the updated state values obtained from the third iteration:

State	Value
A	1.45
B	- 0.9
C	0.6

Table 3.18: Value table from iteration 3

We repeat this for many iterations until the value table does not change or changes very little over iterations. For example, let's suppose *Table 3.19* shows the value table obtained as a result of **iteration 4**:

State	Value
A	1.46
B	- 0.9
C	0.61

Table 3.19: Value table from iteration 4

As we can see, the difference between the value tables obtained from iteration 4 and iteration 3 is very small. So, we can say that the value table is not changing much over iterations and we stop at this iteration and take this as our final value function.

Step 3 – Extract a new policy using the value function obtained from the previous step

As a result of *step 2*, we obtained the value function, which is computed using the given random policy. However, this value function will not be optimal as it is computed using the random policy. So will extract a new policy from the value function obtained in the previous step. The value function (value table) obtained from the previous step is shown in *Table 3.20*:

State	Value
A	1.46
B	- 0.9
C	0.61

Table 3.20: Value table from the previous step

Okay, how can we extract a new policy from the value function? (Hint: This step is exactly the same as how we extracted a policy given the value function in *step 2* of the value iteration method.)

In order to extract a new policy, we compute the Q function using the value function (value table) obtained from the previous step. Once we compute the Q function, we pick up actions in each state that have the maximum value as a new policy. We know that the Q function can be computed as:

$$Q(s, a) = \sum_{s'} P_{ss'}^a [R_{ss'}^a + \gamma V(s')]$$

Now, while computing Q values, we use the value function we obtained from the previous step.

For instance, let's compute the Q value for all actions in state **A** using the value function obtained from the previous step. The Q value for action 0 in state **A** is computed as:

$$
\begin{aligned}
Q(A, 0) &= P_{AA}^0[R_{AA}^0 + \gamma V(A)] + P_{AB}^0[R_{AB}^0 + \gamma V(B)] + P_{AC}^0[R_{AC}^0 + \gamma V(C)] \\
&= 0.1(0 + 1.46) + 0.8(-1 - 0.9) + 0.1(1 + 0.61) \\
&= -1.21
\end{aligned}
$$

The Q value for action 1 in state **A** is computed as:

$$
\begin{aligned}
Q(A, 1) &= P_{AA}^1[R_{AA}^1 + \gamma V(A)] + P_{AB}^1[R_{AB}^1 + \gamma V(B)] + P_{AC}^1[R_{AC}^1 + \gamma V(C)] \\
&= 0.1(0 + 1.46) + 0.0(-1 - 0.9) + 0.9(1 + 0.61) \\
&= 1.59
\end{aligned}
$$

Table 3.21 shows the Q table after computing the Q values for all state-action pairs:

State	Action	Value
A	0	- 1.21
A	1	1.59
B	0	0.1
B	1	0.0
C	0	0.5
C	1	0.0

Table 3.21: Q table

From this Q table, we pick up actions in each state that have the maximum value as a new policy.

$$
\begin{aligned}
A &\rightarrow 1 \\
B &\rightarrow 0 \\
C &\rightarrow 0
\end{aligned}
$$

Step 4 – Check the new policy

Now we will check if the extracted new policy from *step 3* is the same as the policy we used in *step 2*. If it is the same, then we stop, else we send the extracted new policy to *step 2* and repeat *steps 2* to *4*.

Thus, in this section, we learned how to compute the optimal policy using the policy iteration method. In the next section, we will learn how to implement the policy iteration method to compute the optimal policy in the Frozen Lake environment using the Gym toolkit.

Solving the Frozen Lake problem with policy iteration

We learned that in the Frozen Lake environment, our goal is to reach the goal state **G** from the starting state **S** without visiting the hole states **H**. Now, let's learn how to compute the optimal policy using the policy iteration method in the Frozen Lake environment.

First, let's import the necessary libraries:

```
import gym
import numpy as np
```

Now, let's create the Frozen Lake environment using Gym:

```
env = gym.make('FrozenLake-v0')
```

We learned that in the policy iteration, we compute the value function using the policy iteratively. Once we have found the optimal value function, then the policy that is used to compute the optimal value function will be the optimal policy.

So, first, let's learn how to compute the value function using the policy.

Computing the value function using the policy

This step is exactly the same as how we computed the value function in the value iteration method but with a small difference. Here, we compute the value function using the policy but in the value iteration method, we compute the value function by taking the maximum over Q values. Now, let's learn how to define a function that computes the value function using the given policy.

Let's define a function called `compute_value_function`, which takes the policy as a parameter:

```
def compute_value_function(policy):
```

Now, let's define the number of iterations:

```
num_iterations = 1000
```

Define the threshold value:

```
threshold = 1e-20
```

Set the discount factor γ value to 1.0:

```
gamma = 1.0
```

Now, we will initialize the value table by setting all the state values to zero:

```
value_table = np.zeros(env.observation_space.n)
```

For every iteration:

```
for i in range(num_iterations):
```

Update the value table; that is, we learned that on every iteration, we use the updated value table (state values) from the previous iteration:

```
updated_value_table = np.copy(value_table)
```

Now, we compute the value function using the given policy. We learned that a value function can be computed according to some policy π as follows:

$$V^{\pi}(s) = \sum_{s'} P_{ss'}^{a} [R_{ss'}^{a} + \gamma V^{\pi}(s')]$$

Thus, for each state, we select the action according to the policy and then we update the value of the state using the selected action as follows.

For each state:

```
for s in range(env.observation_space.n):
```

Select the action in the state according to the policy:

```
a = policy[s]
```

Compute the value of the state using the selected action,

$$V^\pi(s) = \sum_{s'} P^a_{ss'}[R^a_{ss'} + \gamma V^\pi(s')]:$$

```
            value_table[s] = sum(
                [prob * (r + gamma * updated_value_table[s_])
                    for prob, s_, r, _ in env.P[s][a]])
```

After computing the value table, that is, the value of all the states, we check whether the difference between the value table obtained in the current iteration and the previous iteration is less than or equal to a threshold value. If it is less, then we break the loop and return the value table as an accurate value function of the given policy:

```
        if (np.sum(np.fabs(updated_value_table - value_table)) <=
    threshold):
                break

    return value_table
```

Now that we have computed the value function of the policy, let's see how to extract the policy from the value function.

Extracting the policy from the value function

This step is exactly the same as how we extracted the policy from the value function in the value iteration method. Thus, similar to what we learned in the value iteration method, we define a function called extract_policy to extract a policy given the value function:

```
def extract_policy(value_table):

    gamma = 1.0
    policy = np.zeros(env.observation_space.n)
    for s in range(env.observation_space.n):

        Q_values = [sum([prob*(r + gamma * value_table[s_])
                            for prob, s_, r, _ in env.P[s][a]])
                                for a in range(env.action_space.n)]

        policy[s] = np.argmax(np.array(Q_values))

    return policy
```

Putting it all together

First, let's define a function called `policy_iteration`, which takes the environment as a parameter:

```
def policy_iteration(env):
```

Set the number of iterations:

```
    num_iterations = 1000
```

We learned that in the policy iteration method, we begin by initializing a random policy. So, we will initialize the random policy, which selects the action 0 in all the states:

```
    policy = np.zeros(env.observation_space.n)
```

For every iteration:

```
    for i in range(num_iterations):
```

Compute the value function using the policy:

```
        value_function = compute_value_function(policy)
```

Extract the new policy from the computed value function:

```
        new_policy = extract_policy(value_function)
```

If `policy` and `new_policy` are the same, then break the loop:

```
        if (np.all(policy == new_policy)):
            break
```

Else update the current `policy` to `new_policy`

```
        policy = new_policy
```

```
    return policy
```

Now, let's learn how to perform policy iteration and find the optimal policy in the Frozen Lake environment. So, we just feed the Frozen Lake environment to our `policy_iteration` function as shown here and get the optimal policy:

```
optimal_policy = policy_iteration(env)
```

We can print the optimal policy:

```
print(optimal_policy)
```

The preceding code will print the following:

```
array([0., 3., 3., 3., 0., 0., 0., 0., 3., 1., 0., 0., 0., 2., 1., 0.])
```

As we can observe, our optimal policy tells us to perform the correct action in each state. Thus, we learned how to perform the policy iteration method to compute the optimal policy.

Is DP applicable to all environments?

In dynamic programming, that is, in the value and policy iteration methods, we try to find the optimal policy.

Value iteration: In the value iteration method, we compute the optimal value function by taking the maximum over the Q function (Q values) iteratively:

$$V^*(s) = \max_a Q^*(s, a)$$

Where $Q(s, a) = \sum_{s'} P_{SS'}^a [R_{SS'}^a + \gamma V(s')]$. After finding the optimal value function, we extract the optimal policy from it.

Policy iteration: In the policy iteration method, we compute the optimal value function using the policy iteratively:

$$V^\pi(s) = \sum_{s'} P_{SS'}^a [R_{SS'}^a + \gamma V^\pi(s')]$$

We will start off with the random policy and compute the value function. Once we have found the optimal value function, then the policy that is used to create the optimal value function will be the optimal policy.

If you look at the preceding two equations, in order to find the optimal policy, we compute the value function and Q function. But to compute the value and the Q function, we need to know the transition probability $P_{SS'}^a$ of the environment, and when we don't know the transition probability of the environment, we cannot compute the value and the Q function in order to find the optimal policy.

That is, dynamic programming is a model-based method and to apply this method, we need to know the model dynamics (transition probability) of the environment, and when we don't know the model dynamics, we cannot apply the dynamic programming method.

Okay, how can we find the optimal policy when we don't know the model dynamics of the environment? In such a case, we can use model-free methods. In the next chapter, we will learn about one of the interesting model-free methods, called Monte Carlo, and how it is used to find the optimal policy without requiring the model dynamics.

Summary

We started off the chapter by understanding the Bellman equation of the value and Q functions. We learned that, according to the Bellman equation, the value of a state is the sum of the immediate reward, and the discounted value of the next state and the value of a state-action pair is the sum of the immediate reward and the discounted value of the next state-action pair. Then we learned about the optimal Bellman value function and the Q function, which gives the maximum value.

Moving forward, we learned about the relation between the value and Q functions. We learned that the value function can be extracted from the Q function as $V^*(s) = \max_a Q^*(s, a)$ and then we learned that the Q function can be extracted from the value function as $Q^*(s, a) = \sum_{s'} P(s'|s, a)[R(s, a, s') + \gamma V^*(s')]$.

Later we learned about two interesting methods called value iteration and policy iteration, which use dynamic programming to find the optimal policy.

In the value iteration method, first, we compute the optimal value function by taking the maximum over the Q function iteratively. Once we have found the optimal value function, then we use it to extract the optimal policy. In the policy iteration method, we try to compute the optimal value function using the policy iteratively. Once we have found the optimal value function, then the policy that is used to create the optimal value function will be extracted as the optimal policy.

Questions

Let's try answering the following questions to assess our knowledge of what we learned in this chapter:

1. Define the Bellman equation.
2. What is the difference between the Bellman expectation and Bellman optimality equations?
3. How do we derive the value function from the Q function?
4. How do we derive the Q function from the value function?
5. What are the steps involved in value iteration?
6. What are the steps involved in policy iteration?
7. How does policy iteration differ from value iteration?

4

Monte Carlo Methods

In the previous chapter, we learned how to compute the optimal policy using two interesting dynamic programming methods called value and policy iteration. Dynamic programming is a model-based method and it requires the model dynamics of the environment to compute the value and Q functions in order to find the optimal policy.

But let's suppose we don't have the model dynamics of the environment. In that case, how do we compute the value and Q functions? Here is where we use model-free methods. Model-free methods do not require the model dynamics of the environment to compute the value and Q functions in order to find the optimal policy. One such popular model-free method is the **Monte Carlo (MC)** method.

We will begin the chapter by understanding what the MC method is, then we will look into two important types of tasks in reinforcement learning called prediction and control tasks. Later, we will learn how the Monte Carlo method is used in reinforcement learning and how it is beneficial compared to the dynamic programming method we learned about in the previous chapter. Moving forward, we will understand what the MC prediction method is and the different types of MC prediction methods. We will also learn how to train an agent to play blackjack with the MC prediction method.

Going ahead, we will learn about the Monte Carlo control method and different types of Monte Carlo control methods. Following this, we will learn how to train an agent to play blackjack with the MC control method.

To summarize, in this chapter, we will learn about the following topics:

- Understanding the Monte Carlo method
- Prediction and control tasks
- The Monte Carlo prediction method
- Playing blackjack with the MC prediction method
- The Monte Carlo control method
- Playing blackjack with the MC control method

Understanding the Monte Carlo method

Before understanding how the Monte Carlo method is useful in reinforcement learning, first, let's understand what the Monte Carlo method is and how it works. The Monte Carlo method is a statistical technique used to find an approximate solution through sampling.

For instance, the Monte Carlo method approximates the expectation of a random variable by sampling, and when the sample size is greater, the approximation will be better. Let's suppose we have a random variable X and say we need to compute the expected value of X; that is $E(X)$, then we can compute it by taking the sum of the values of X multiplied by their respective probabilities as follows:

$$E(X) = \sum_{i=1}^{N} x_i p(x_i)$$

But instead of computing the expectation like this, can we approximate it with the Monte Carlo method? Yes! We can estimate the expected value of X by just sampling the values of X for some N times and compute the average value of X as the expected value of X as follows:

$$\mathbb{E}_{x \sim p(x)}[X] \approx \frac{1}{N} \sum_{i} x_i$$

When N is larger our approximation will be better. Thus, with the Monte Carlo method, we can approximate the solution through sampling and our approximation will be better when the sample size is large.

In the upcoming sections, we will learn how exactly the Monte Carlo method is used in reinforcement learning.

Prediction and control tasks

In reinforcement learning, we perform two important tasks, and they are:

- The prediction task
- The control task

Prediction task

In the prediction task, a policy π is given as an input and we try to predict the value function or Q function using the given policy. But what is the use of doing this? Our goal is to evaluate the given policy. That is, we need to determine whether the given policy is good or bad. How can we determine that? If the agent obtains a good return using the given policy then we can say that our policy is good. Thus, to evaluate the given policy, we need to understand what the return the agent would obtain if it uses the given policy. To obtain the return, we predict the value function or Q function using the given policy.

That is, we learned that the value function or value of a state denotes the expected return an agent would obtain starting from that state following some policy π. Thus, by predicting the value function using the given policy π, we can understand what the expected return the agent would obtain in each state if it uses the given policy π. If the return is good then we can say that the given policy is good.

Similarly, we learned that the Q function or Q value denotes the expected return the agent would obtain starting from the state s and an action a following the policy π. Thus, predicting the Q function using the given policy π, we can understand what the expected return the agent would obtain in each state-action pair if it uses the given policy. If the return is good then we can say that the given policy is good.

Thus, we can evaluate the given policy π by computing the value and Q functions.

Note that, in the prediction task, we don't make any change to the given input policy. We keep the given policy as fixed and predict the value function or Q function using the given policy and obtain the expected return. Based on the expected return, we evaluate the given policy.

Control task

Unlike the prediction task, in the control task, we will not be given any policy as an input. In the control task, our goal is to find the optimal policy. So, we will start off by initializing a random policy and we try to find the optimal policy iteratively. That is, we try to find an optimal policy that gives the maximum return.

Thus, in a nutshell, in the prediction task, we evaluate the given input policy by predicting the value function or Q function, which helps us to understand the expected return an agent would get if it uses the given policy, while in the control task our goal is to find the optimal policy and we will not be given any policy as input; so we will start off by initializing a random policy and we try to find the optimal policy iteratively.

Now that we have understood what prediction and control tasks are, in the next section, we will learn how to use the Monte Carlo method for performing the prediction and control tasks.

Monte Carlo prediction

In this section, we will learn how to use the Monte Carlo method to perform the prediction task. We have learned that in the prediction task, we will be given a policy and we predict the value function or Q function using the given policy to evaluate it. First, we will learn how to predict the value function using the given policy with the Monte Carlo method. Later, we will look into predicting the Q function using the given policy. Alright, let's get started with the section.

Why do we need the Monte Carlo method for predicting the value function of the given policy? Why can't we predict the value function using the dynamic programming methods we learned about in the previous chapter? We learned that in order to compute the value function using the dynamic programming method, we need to know the model dynamics (transition probability), and when we don't know the model dynamics, we use the model-free methods.

The Monte Carlo method is a model-free method, meaning that it doesn't require the model dynamics to compute the value function.

First, let's recap the definition of the value function. The value function or the value of the state s can be defined as the expected return the agent would obtain starting from the state s and following the policy π. It can be expressed as:

$$V^{\pi}(s) = \mathop{\mathbb{E}}_{\tau \sim \pi} [R(\tau)|s_0 = s]$$

Okay, how can we estimate the value of the state (value function) using the Monte Carlo method? At the beginning of the chapter, we learned that the Monte Carlo method approximates the expected value of a random variable by sampling, and when the sample size is greater, the approximation will be better. Can we leverage this concept of the Monte Carlo method to predict the value of a state? Yes!

In order to approximate the value of the state using the Monte Carlo method, we sample episodes (trajectories) following the given policy π for some N times and then we compute the value of the state as the average return of a state across the sampled episodes, and it can be expressed as:

$$V(s) \approx \frac{1}{N} \sum_{i=1}^{N} R_i(s)$$

From the preceding equation, we can understand that the value of a state s can be approximated by computing the average return of the state s across some N episodes. Our approximation will be better when N is higher.

In a nutshell, in the Monte Carlo prediction method, we approximate the value of a state by taking the average return of a state across N episodes instead of taking the expected return.

Okay, let's get a better understanding of how the Monte Carlo method estimates the value of a state (value function) with an example. Let's take our favorite grid world environment we covered in *Chapter 1, Fundamentals of Reinforcement Learning*, as shown in *Figure 4.1*. Our goal is to reach the state **I** from the state **A** without visiting the shaded states, and the agent receives +1 reward when it visits the unshaded states and -1 reward when it visits the shaded states:

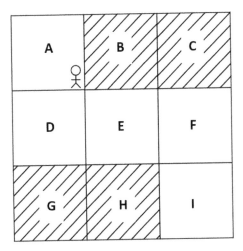

Figure 4.1: Grid world environment

Let's say we have a stochastic policy π. Let's suppose, in state **A**, our stochastic policy π selects action *down* 80% of time and action *right* 20% of the time, and it selects action *right* in states **D** and **E** and action *down* in states **B** and **F** 100% of the time.

First, we generate an episode τ_1 using our given stochastic policy π as *Figure 4.2* shows:

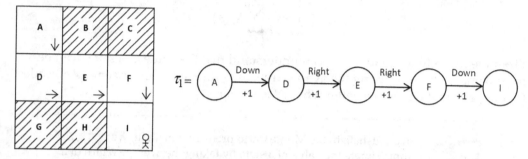

Figure 4.2: Episode τ_1

For a better understanding, let's focus only on state **A**. Let's now compute the return of state **A**. The return of a state is the sum of the rewards of the trajectory starting from that state. Thus, the return of state **A** is computed as $R_1(A) = 1+1+1+1 = 4$ where the subscript 1 in R_1 indicates the return from episode 1.

Say we generate another episode τ_2 using the same given stochastic policy π as *Figure 4.3* shows:

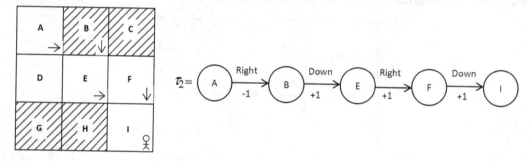

Figure 4.3: Episode τ_2

Let's now compute the return of state **A**. The return of state **A** is $R_2(A) = -1+1+1+1 = 2$.

Say we generate another episode τ_3 using the same given stochastic policy π as *Figure 4.4* shows:

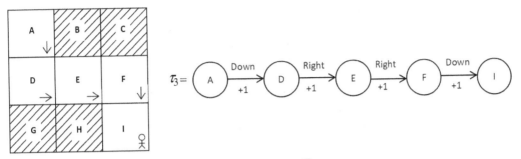

Figure 4.4: Episode τ_3

Let's now compute the return of state **A**. The return of state **A** is $R_3(A) = 1+1+1+1 = 4$.

Thus, we generated three episodes and computed the return of state **A** in all three episodes. Now, how can we compute the value of the state **A**? We learned that in the Monte Carlo method, the value of a state can be approximated by computing the average return of the state across some N episodes (trajectories):

$$V(s) \approx \frac{1}{N}\sum_{i=1}^{N} R_i(s)$$

We need to compute the value of state **A**, so we can compute it by just taking the average return of the state **A** across the N episodes as:

$$V(A) \approx \frac{1}{N}\sum_{i=1}^{N} R_i(A)$$

We generated three episodes, thus:

$$V(A) \approx \frac{1}{3}\sum_{i=1}^{3} R_i(A)$$

$$V(A) = \frac{1}{3}(R_1(A) + R_2(A) + R_3(A))$$

$$V(A) = \frac{4 + 2 + 4}{3} = 3.3$$

Thus, the value of state **A** is 3.3. Similarly, we can compute the value of all other states by just taking the average return of the state across the three episodes.

For easier understanding, in the preceding example, we only generated three episodes. In order to find a better and more accurate estimate of the value of the state, we should generate many episodes (not just three) and compute the average return of the state as the value of the state.

Thus, in the Monte Carlo prediction method, to predict the value of a state (value function) using the given input policy π, we generate some N episodes using the given policy and then we compute the value of a state as the average return of the state across these N episodes.

 Note that while computing the return of the state, we can also include the discount factor and compute the discounted return, but for simplicity let's not include the discount factor.

Now, that we have a basic understanding of how the Monte Carlo prediction method predicts the value function of the given policy, let's look into more detail by understanding the algorithm of the Monte Carlo prediction method in the next section.

MC prediction algorithm

The Monte Carlo prediction algorithm is given as follows:

1. Let total_return(s) be the sum of return of a state across several episodes and $N(s)$ be the counter, that is, the number of times a state is visited across several episodes. Initialize total_return(s) and $N(s)$ as zero for all the states. The policy π is given as input.

2. For M number of iterations:

    1. Generate an episode using the policy π
    2. Store all the rewards obtained in the episode in the list called rewards
    3. For each step t in the episode:

        1. Compute the return of state s_t as $R(s_t) = $ sum(rewards[t:])
        2. Update the total return of state s_t as total_returns(s_t) = total_return(s_t) + $R(s_t)$
        3. Update the counter as $N(s_t) = N(s_t) + 1$

3. Compute the value of a state by just taking the average, that is:

$$V(s) = \frac{\text{total\_return}(s)}{N(s)}$$

The preceding algorithm implies that the value of the state is just the average return of the state across several episodes.

To get a better understanding of how exactly the preceding algorithm works, let's take a simple example and compute the value of each state manually. Say we need to compute the value of three states s_0, s_1, and s_2. We know that we obtain a reward when we transition from one state to another. Thus, the reward for the final state will be 0 as we don't make any transitions from the final state. Hence, the value of the final state s_2 will be zero. Now, we need to find the value of two states s_0 and s_1.

> The upcoming sections are explained with manual calculations, for a better understanding, follow along with a pen and paper.

Step 1:

Initialize the total_returns(s) and N(s) for all the states to zero as *Table 4.1* shows:

State	total_return(s)	N(s)
s_0	0	0
s_1	0	0

Table 4.1: Initial values

Say we are given a stochastic policy π; in state s_0 our stochastic policy selects the action 0 for 50% of the time and action 1 for 50% of the time, and it selects action 1 in state s_1 for 100% of the time.

Step 2: Iteration 1:

Generate an episode using the given input policy π, as *Figure 4.5* shows:

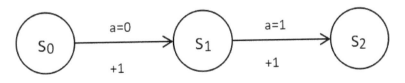

Figure 4.5: Generating an episode using the given policy π

Store all rewards obtained in the episode in the list called rewards. Thus, rewards = $[1, 1]$.

First, we compute the return of the state s_0 (sum of rewards from s_0):

$$\begin{aligned} R(s_0) &= \text{sum(rewards}[0:]) \\ &= \text{sum}([1, 1]) \\ &= 2 \end{aligned}$$

Update the total return of the state s_0 in our table as:

$$\begin{aligned} \text{total\_returns}(s_0) &= \text{total\_returns}(s_0) + R(s_0) \\ &= 0 + 2 = 2 \end{aligned}$$

Update the number of times the state s_0 is visited in our table as:

$$\begin{aligned} N(s_0) &= N(s_0) + 1 \\ &= 0 + 1 = 1 \end{aligned}$$

Now, let's compute the return of the state s_1 (sum of rewards from s_1):

$$\begin{aligned} R(s_1) &= \text{sum(rewards}[1:]) \\ &= \text{sum}([1]) \\ &= 1 \end{aligned}$$

Update the total return of the state s_1 in our table as:

$$\begin{aligned} \text{total\_returns}(s_1) &= \text{total\_returns}(s_1) + R(s_1) \\ &= 0 + 1 = 1 \end{aligned}$$

Update the number of times the state s_1 is visited in our table as:

$$\begin{aligned} N(s_1) &= N(s_1) + 1 \\ &= 0 + 1 = 1 \end{aligned}$$

Our updated table, after iteration 1, is as follows:

State	total_return(s)	N(s)
s_0	2	1
s_1	1	1

Table 4.2: Updated table after the first iteration

Iteration 2:

Say we generate another episode using the same given policy π as *Figure 4.6* shows:

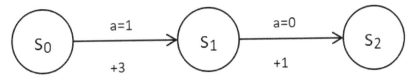

Figure 4.6: Generating an episode using the given policy π

Store all rewards obtained in the episode in the list called rewards. Thus, rewards = [3, 1].

First, we compute the return of the state s_0 (sum of rewards from s_0):

$$
\begin{aligned}
R(s_0) &= \text{sum(rewards}[0:]) \\
&= \text{sum}([3, 1]) \\
&= 4
\end{aligned}
$$

Update the total return of the state s_0 in our table as:

$$
\begin{aligned}
\text{total\_returns}(s_0) &= \text{total\_returns}(s_0) + R(s_0) \\
&= 2 + 4 = 6
\end{aligned}
$$

Update the number of times the state s_0 is visited in our table as:

$$
\begin{aligned}
N(s_0) &= N(s_0) + 1 \\
&= 1 + 1 = 2
\end{aligned}
$$

Now, let's compute the return of the state s_1 (sum of rewards from s_1):

$$
\begin{aligned}
R(s_1) &= \text{sum(rewards}[1:]) \\
&= \text{sum}([1]) \\
&= 1
\end{aligned}
$$

Update the return of the state s_1 in our table as:

$$
\begin{aligned}
\text{total\_returns}(s_1) &= \text{total\_returns}(s_1) + R(s_1) \\
&= 1 + 1 = 2
\end{aligned}
$$

Update the number of times the state is visited:

$$N(s_1) = N(s_1) + 1$$
$$= 1 + 1 = 2$$

Our updated table after the second iteration is as follows:

State	total_return(s)	N(s)
s_0	6	2
s_1	2	2

Table 4.3: Updated table after the second iteration

Since we are computing manually, for simplicity, let's stop at two iterations; that is, we just generate only two episodes.

Step 3:

Now, we can compute the value of the state as:

$$V(s) = \frac{\text{total\_returns}(s)}{N(s)}$$

Thus:

$$V(s_0) = \frac{\text{total\_return}(s_0)}{N(s_0)} = \frac{6}{2} = 3$$

$$V(s_1) = \frac{\text{total\_return}(s_1)}{N(s_1)} = \frac{2}{2} = 1$$

Thus, we computed the value of the state by just taking the average return across multiple episodes. Note that in the preceding example, for our manual calculation, we just generated two episodes, but for a better estimation of the value of the state, we generate several episodes and then we compute the average return across those episodes (not just 2).

Types of MC prediction

We just learned how the Monte Carlo prediction algorithm works. We can categorize the Monte Carlo prediction algorithm into two types:

- First-visit Monte Carlo
- Every-visit Monte Carlo

First-visit Monte Carlo

We learned that in the MC prediction method, we estimate the value of the state by just taking the average return of the state across multiple episodes. We know that in each episode a state can be visited multiple times. In the first-visit Monte Carlo method, if the same state is visited again in the same episode, we don't compute the return for that state again. For example, consider a case where an agent is playing snakes and ladders. If the agent lands on a snake, then there is a good chance that the agent will return to a state that it had visited earlier. So, when the agent revisits the same state, we don't compute the return for that state for the second time.

The following shows the algorithm of first-visit MC; as the point in bold says, we compute the return for the state s_t only if it is occurring for the first time in the episode:

1. Let total_return(s) be the sum of return of a state across several episodes and $N(s)$ be the counter, that is, the number of times a state is visited across several episodes. Initialize total_return(s) and $N(s)$ as zero for all the states. The policy π is given as input

2. For M number of iterations:

    1. Generate an episode using the policy π

    2. Store all the rewards obtained in the episode in the list called rewards

    3. For each step t in the episode:

       If the state s_t is occurring for the first time in the episode:

       1. Compute the return of the state s_t as $R(s_t) = \text{sum(rewards[t:])}$

       2. Update the total return of the state s_t as total_return(s_t) = total_return(s_t) + $R(s_t)$

       3. Update the counter as $N(s_t) = N(s_t) + 1$

3. Compute the value of a state by just taking the average, that is:

$$V(s) = \frac{\text{total\_return}(s)}{N(s)}$$

Every-visit Monte Carlo

As you might have guessed, every-visit Monte Carlo is just the opposite of first-visit Monte Carlo. Here, we compute the return every time a state is visited in the episode. The algorithm of every-visit Monte Carlo is the same as the one we saw earlier at the beginning of this section and it is as follows:

1. Let total_return(s) be the sum of the return of a state across several episodes and $N(s)$ be the counter, that is, the number of times a state is visited across several episodes. Initialize total_return(s) and $N(s)$ as zero for all the states. The policy π is given as input

2. For M number of iterations:

    1. Generate an episode using the policy π
    2. Store all the rewards obtained in the episode in the list called rewards
    3. For each step t in the episode:

        1. Compute the return of the state s_t as $R(s_t) = \text{sum(rewards[t:])}$
        2. Update the total return of the state s_t as total_return(s_t) = total_return(s_t) + $R(s_t)$
        3. Update the counter as $N(s_t) = N(s_t) + 1$

3. Compute the value of a state by just taking the average, that is:

$$V(s) = \frac{\text{total\_return}(s)}{N(s)}$$

Remember that the only difference between the first-visit MC and every-visit MC methods is that in the first-visit MC method, we compute the return for a state only for its first time of occurrence in the episode but in the every-visit MC method, the return of the state is computed every time the state is visited in an episode. We can choose between first-visit MC and every-visit MC based on the problem that we are trying to solve.

Now that we have understood how the Monte Carlo prediction method predicts the value function of the given policy, in the next section, we will learn how to implement the Monte Carlo prediction method.

Implementing the Monte Carlo prediction method

If you love playing card games then this section is definitely going to be interesting for you. In this section, we will learn how to play blackjack with the Monte Carlo prediction method. Before diving in, let's understand how the blackjack game works and its rules.

Understanding the blackjack game

Blackjack, also known as **21**, is one of the most popular card games. The game consists of a player and a dealer. The goal of the player is to have the value of the sum of all their cards be 21 or a larger value than the sum of the dealer's cards while not exceeding 21. If one of these criteria is met then the player wins the game; else the dealer wins the game. Let's understand this in more detail.

The values of the cards **Jack (J)**, **King (K)**, and **Queen (Q)** will be considered as 10. The value of the **Ace (A)** can be 1 or 11, depending on the player's choice. That is, the player can decide whether the value of an **Ace** should be 1 or 11 during the game. The value of the rest of the cards (**2 to 10**) is just their face value. For instance, the value of the card **2** will be 2, the value of the card **3** will be 3, and so on.

We learned that the game consists of a player and a dealer. There can be many players at a time but only one dealer. All the players compete with the dealer and not with other players. Let's consider a case where there is only one player and a dealer. Let's understand blackjack by playing the game along with different cases. Let's suppose we are the player and we are competing with the dealer.

Case 1: When the player wins the game

Initially, a player is given two cards. Both of these cards are face up, that is, both of the player's cards are visible to the dealer. Similarly, the dealer is also given two cards. But one of the dealer's cards is face up, and the other is face down. That is, the dealer shows only one of their cards.

As we can see in *Figure 4.7*, the player has two cards (both face up) and the dealer also has two cards (only one face up):

Dealer $\longrightarrow$

Player $\longrightarrow$

Figure 4.7: The player has 20, and the dealer has 2 with one card face down

Now, the player performs either of the two actions, which are **Hit** and **Stand**. If we (the player) perform the action **hit,** then we get one more card. If we perform **stand,** then it implies that we don't need any more cards and tells the dealer to show all their cards. Whoever has a sum of cards value equal to 21 or a larger value than the other player but not exceeding 21 wins the game.

We learned that the value of **J**, **K**, and **Q** is 10. As shown in *Figure 4.7*, we have cards **J** and **K**, which sums to 20 (10+10). Thus, the total value our cards is already a large number and it didn't exceed 21. So we **stand**, and this action tells the dealer to show their cards. As we can observe in *Figure 4.8*, the dealer has now shown all their cards and the total value of the dealer's cards is 12 and the total value of our (the player's) cards is 20, which is larger and also didn't exceed 21, so we win the game.

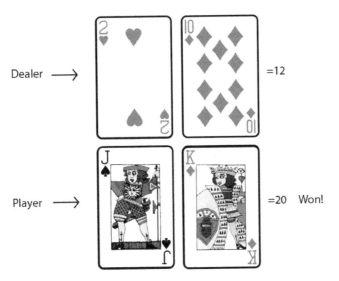

Dealer ⟶ ... =12

Player ⟶ ... =20 Won!

Figure 4.8: The player wins!

Case 2: When the player loses the game

Figure 4.9 shows we have two cards and the dealer also has two cards and only one of the dealer's card is visible to us:

Dealer ⟶

Player ⟶

Figure 4.9: The player has 13, and the dealer has 7 with one card face down

Now, we have to decide whether we should (perform the action) hit or stand. *Figure 4.9* shows we have two cards, **K** and **3**, which sums to 13 (10+3). Let's be a little optimistic and hope that the total value of the dealer's cards will not be greater than ours. So we **stand,** and this action tells the dealer to show their cards. As we can observe in *Figure 4.10*, the sum of the dealer's card is 17, but ours is only 13, so we lose the game. That is, the dealer has got a larger value than us, and it did not exceed 21, so the dealer wins the game, and we lose:

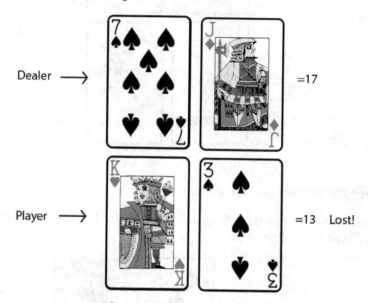

Figure 4.10: The dealer wins!

Case 3: When the player goes bust

Figure 4.11 shows we have two cards and the dealer also has two cards but only one of the dealer's cards is visible to us:

Figure 4.11: The player has 8, and the dealer has 10 with one card face down

Now, we have to decide whether we should (perform the action) hit or stand. We learned that the goal of the game is to have a sum of cards value of 21, or a larger value than the dealer while not exceeding 21. Right now, the total value of our cards is just 3+5 = 8. Thus, we (perform the action) **hit** so that we can make our sum value larger. After we **hit**, we receive a new card as shown in *Figure 4.12*:

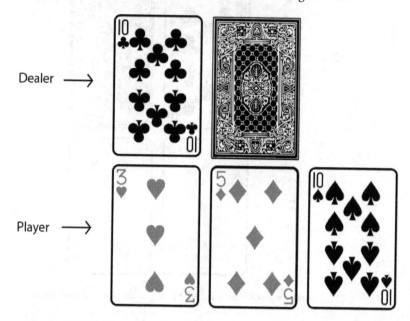

Figure 4.12: The player has 18, and the dealer has 10 with one card face down

As we can observe, we got a new card. Now, the total value of our cards is 3+5+10 = 18. Again, we need to decide whether we should (perform the action) hit or stand. Let's be a little greedy and (perform the action) **hit** so that we can make our sum value a little larger. As shown in *Figure 4.13*, we **hit** and received one more card but now the total value of our cards becomes 3+5+10+10 = 28, which exceeds 21, and this is called a **bust** and we lose the game:

Figure 4.13: The player goes bust!

Case 4: Useable Ace

We learned that the value of the **Ace** can be either 1 or 11, and the player can decide the value of the **ace** during the game. Let's learn how this works. As *Figure 4.14* shows, we have been given two cards and the dealer also has two cards and only one of the dealer's cards is face up:

Figure 4.14: The player has 10, and the dealer has 5 with one card face down

As we can see, the total value of our cards is 5+5 = 10. Thus, we **hit** so that we can make our sum value larger. As *Figure 4.15* shows, after performing the hit action we received a new card, which is an **Ace**. Now, we can decide the value of the **Ace** to be either 1 or 11. If we consider the value of **Ace** to be 1, then the total value of our cards will be 5+5+1 = 11. But if we consider the value of the **Ace** to be 11, then the total value of our cards will be 5+5+11 = 21. In this case, we consider the value of our **Ace** to be 11 so that our sum value becomes 21.

Thus, we set the value of the **Ace** to be 11 and win the game, and in this case, the **Ace** is called the usable **Ace** since it helped us to win the game:

Figure 4.15: The player uses the **Ace** as 11 and wins the game

Case 5: Non-usable Ace

Figure 4.16 shows we have two cards and the dealer has two cards with one face up:

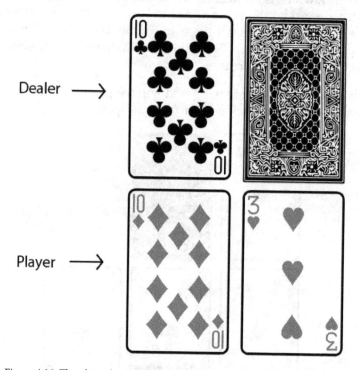

Figure 4.16: The player has 13, and the dealer has 10 with one card face down

As we can observe, the total value of our cards is 13 (10+3). We (perform the action) **hit** so that we can make our sum value a little larger:

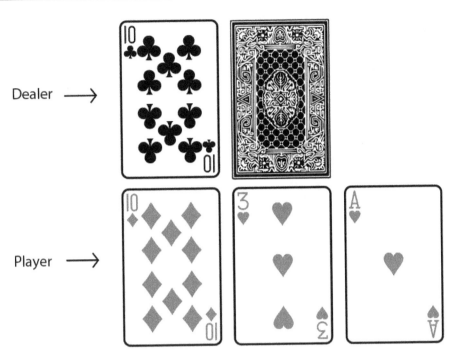

Figure 4.17: The player has to use the **Ace** as a 1 else they go bust

As *Figure 4.17* shows, we **hit** and received a new card, which is an **Ace**. Now we can decide the value of **Ace** to be 1 or 11. If we choose 11, then our sum value becomes 10+3+11 = 23. As we can observe, when we set our ace to 11, then our sum value exceeds 21, and we lose the game. Thus, instead of choosing **Ace** = 11, we set the **Ace** value to be 1; so our sum value becomes 10+3+1 = 14.

Again, we need to decide whether we should (perform the action) hit or stand. Let's say we stand hoping that the dealer sum value will be lower than ours. As *Figure 4.18* shows, after performing the stand action, both of the dealer's cards are shown, and the sum of the dealer's card is 20, but ours is just 14, and so we lose the game, and in this case, the **Ace** is called a **non-usable Ace** since it did not help us to win the game.

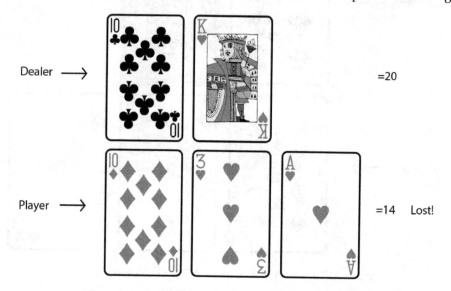

Figure 4.18: The player has 14, and the dealer has 20 and wins

Case 6: When the game is a draw

If both the player and the dealer's sum of cards value is the same, say 20, then the game is called a draw.

Now that we have understood how to play blackjack, let's implement the Monte Carlo prediction method in the blackjack game. But before going ahead, first, let's learn how the blackjack environment is designed in Gym.

The blackjack environment in the Gym library

Import the Gym library:

```
import gym
```

The environment id of blackjack is `Blackjack-v0`. So, we can create the blackjack game using the `make` function as shown as follows:

```
env = gym.make('Blackjack-v0')
```

Now, let's look at the state of the blackjack environment; we can just reset our environment and look at the initial state:

```
print(env.reset())
```

Note that every time we run the preceding code, we might get a different result, as the initial state is randomly initialized. The preceding code will print something like this:

```
(15, 9, True)
```

As we can observe, our state is represented as a tuple, but what does this mean? We learned that in the blackjack game, we will be given two cards and we also get to see one of the dealer's cards. Thus, 15 implies that the value of the sum of our cards, 9 implies the face value of one of the dealer's cards, True implies that we have a usable ace, and it will be False if we don't have a usable ace.

Thus, in the blackjack environment the state is represented as a tuple consisting of three values:

1. The value of the sum of our cards
2. The face value of one of the dealer's card
3. Boolean value—True if we have a useable ace and False if we don't have a useable ace

Let's look at the action space of our blackjack environment:

```
print(env.action_space)
```

The preceding code will print:

```
Discrete(2)
```

As we can observe, it implies that we have two actions in our action space, which are 0 and 1:

- The action **stand** is represented by 0
- The action **hit** is represented by 1

Okay, what about the reward? The reward will be assigned as follows:

- **+1.0** reward if we win the game
- **-1.0** reward if we lose the game
- **0** reward if the game is a draw

Now that we have understood how the blackjack environment is designed in Gym, let's start implementing the MC prediction method in the blackjack game. First, we will look at every-visit MC and then we will learn how to implement first-visit MC prediction.

Every-visit MC prediction with the blackjack game

To understand this section clearly, you should recap the every-visit Monte Carlo method we learned earlier. Let's now understand how to implement every-visit MC prediction with the blackjack game step by step:

Import the necessary libraries:

```
import gym
import pandas as pd
from collections import defaultdict
```

Create a blackjack environment:

```
env = gym.make('Blackjack-v0')
```

Defining a policy

We learned that in the prediction method, we will be given an input policy and we predict the value function of the given input policy. So, now, we first define a policy function that acts as an input policy. That is, we define the input policy whose value function will be predicted in the upcoming steps.

As shown in the following code, our policy function takes the state as an input and if the **state[0]**, the sum of our cards, value, is greater than 19, then it will return action **0** (stand), else it will return action **1** (hit):

```
def policy(state):
    return 0 if state[0] > 19 else 1
```

We defined an optimal policy: it makes more sense to perform an action 0 (stand) when our sum value is already greater than 19. That is, when the sum value is greater than 19 we don't have to perform a 1 (hit) action and receive a new card, which may cause us to lose the game or bust.

For example, let's generate an initial state by resetting the environment as shown as follows:

```
state = env.reset()
print(state)
```

Suppose the preceding code prints the following:

```
(20, 5, False)
```

As we can notice, `state[0]` = `20`; that is, the value of the sum of our cards is 20, so in this case, our policy will return the action 0 (stand) as the following shows:

```
print(policy(state))
```

The preceding code will print:

```
0
```

Now that we have defined the policy, in the next sections, we will predict the value function (state values) of this policy.

Generating an episode

Next, we generate an episode using the given policy, so we define a function called `generate_episode`, which takes the policy as an input and generates the episode using the given policy.

First, let's set the number of time steps:

```
num_timesteps = 100
```

For a clear understanding, let's look into the function line by line:

```
def generate_episode(policy):
```

Let's define a list called `episode` for storing the episode:

```
    episode = []
```

Initialize the state by resetting the environment:

```
    state = env.reset()
```

Then for each time step:

```
    for t in range(num_timesteps):
```

Select the action according to the given policy:

```
        action = policy(state)
```

Perform the action and store the next state information:

```
next_state, reward, done, info = env.step(action)
```

Store the state, action, and reward into our episode list:

```
episode.append((state, action, reward))
```

If the next state is a final state then break the loop, else update the next state to the current state:

```
if done:
    break

state = next_state


return episode
```

Let's take a look at what the output of our generate_episode function looks like. Note that we generate an episode using the policy we defined earlier:

```
print(generate_episode(policy))
```

The preceding code will print something like the following:

```
[((10, 2, False), 1, 0), ((20, 2, False), 0, 1.0)]
```

As we can observe our output is in the form of **[(state, action, reward)]**. As shown previously, we have two states in our episode. We performed action 1 (hit) in the state (10, 2, False) and received a 0 reward, and we performed action 0 (stand) in the state (20, 2, False) and received a reward of 1.0.

Now that we have learned how to generate an episode using the given policy, next, we will look at how to compute the value of the state (value function) using the every-visit MC method.

Computing the value function

We learned that in order to predict the value function, we generate several episodes using the given policy and compute the value of the state as an average return across several episodes. Let's see how to implement that.

First, we define the `total_return` and `N` as a dictionary for storing the total return and the number of times the state is visited across episodes respectively:

```
total_return = defaultdict(float)
N = defaultdict(int)
```

Set the number of iterations, that is, the number of episodes, we want to generate:

```
num_iterations = 500000
```

Then, for every iteration:

```
for i in range(num_iterations):
```

Generate the episode using the given policy; that is, generate an episode using the policy function we defined earlier:

```
episode = generate_episode(policy)
```

Store all the states, actions, and rewards obtained from the episode:

```
states, actions, rewards = zip(*episode)
```

Then, for each step in the episode:

```
for t, state in enumerate(states):
```

Compute the return R of the state as the sum of rewards, $R(s_t) = \text{sum(rewards[t:])}$:

```
R = (sum(rewards[t:]))
```

Update the `total_return` of the state as total_return(s_t) = total_return(s_t) + $R(s_t)$:

```
total_return[state] =  total_return[state] + R
```

Update the number of times the state is visited in the episode as $N(s_t) = N(s_t) + 1$:

```
N[state] =  N[state] + 1
```

After computing the `total_return` and `N` we can just convert them into a pandas data frame for a better understanding. Note that this is just to give a clear understanding of the algorithm; we don't necessarily have to convert to the pandas data frame, we can also implement this efficiently just by using the dictionary.

Convert the `total_returns` dictionary into a data frame:

```
total_return = pd.DataFrame(total_return.items(),columns=['state',
'total_return'])
```

Convert the counter `N` dictionary into a data frame:

```
N = pd.DataFrame(N.items(),columns=['state', 'N'])
```

Merge the two data frames on states:

```
df = pd.merge(total_return, N, on="state")
```

Look at the first few rows of the data frame:

```
df.head(10)
```

The preceding code will display the following. As we can observe, we have the total return and the number of times the state is visited:

	state	total_return	N
0	(7, 10, False)	-52.0	98
1	(11, 10, False)	6.0	190
2	(15, 10, False)	-219.0	394
3	(12, 10, False)	-160.0	331
4	(18, 10, False)	-269.0	406
5	(14, 10, True)	-21.0	49
6	(21, 10, True)	176.0	193
7	(16, 4, False)	-55.0	83
8	(10, 10, False)	-23.0	150
9	(20, 10, False)	275.0	585

Figure 4.19: The total return and the number of times a state has been visited

Next, we can compute the value of the state as the average return:

$$V(s) = \frac{\text{total\_return}(s)}{N(s)}$$

Thus, we can write:

```
df['value'] = df['total_return']/df['N']
```

Let's look at the first few rows of the data frame:

```
df.head(10)
```

The preceding code will display something like this:

	state	total_return	N	value
0	(7, 10, False)	-52.0	98	-0.530612
1	(11, 10, False)	6.0	190	0.031579
2	(15, 10, False)	-219.0	394	-0.555838
3	(12, 10, False)	-160.0	331	-0.483384
4	(18, 10, False)	-269.0	406	-0.662562
5	(14, 10, True)	-21.0	49	-0.428571
6	(21, 10, True)	176.0	193	0.911917
7	(16, 4, False)	-55.0	83	-0.662651
8	(10, 10, False)	-23.0	150	-0.153333
9	(20, 10, False)	275.0	585	0.470085

Figure 4.20: The value is calculated as the average of the return of each state

As we can observe, we now have the value of the state, which is just the average of a return of the state across several episodes. Thus, we have successfully predicted the value function of the given policy using the every-visit MC method.

Okay, let's check the value of some states and understand how accurately our value function is estimated according to the given policy. Recall that when we started off, to generate episodes, we used the optimal policy, which selects the action 0 (stand) when the sum value is greater than 19 and the action 1 (hit) when the sum value is lower than 19.

Let's evaluate the value of the state (21,9,False), as we can observe, the value of the sum of our cards is already 21 and so this is a good state and should have a high value. Let's see what our estimated value of the state is:

```
df[df['state']==(21,9,False)]['value'].values
```

The preceding will print something like this:

```
array([1.0])
```

As we can observe, the value of the state is high.

Now, let's check the value of the state (5,8,False). As we can notice, the value of the sum of our cards is just 5 and even the one dealer's single card has a high value, 8; in this case, the value of the state should be lower. Let's see what our estimated value of the state is:

```
df[df['state']==(5,8,False)]['value'].values
```

The preceding code will print something like this:

```
array([-1.0])
```

As we can notice, the value of the state is lower.

Thus, we learned how to predict the value function of the given policy using the every-visit MC prediction method. In the next section, we will look at how to compute the value of the state using the first-visit MC method.

First-visit MC prediction with the blackjack game

Predicting the value function using the first-visit MC method is exactly the same as how we predicted the value function using the every-visit MC method, except that here we compute the return of a state only for its first time of occurrence in the episode. The code for first-visit MC is the same as what we have seen in every-visit MC except here, we compute the return only for its first time of occurrence as shown in the following highlighted code:

```
for i in range(num_iterations):

    episode = generate_episode(env,policy)
    states, actions, rewards = zip(*episode)

    for t, state in enumerate(states):
        if state not in states[0:t]:
```

```
R = (sum(rewards[t:]))
total_return[state] = total_return[state] + R
N[state] = N[state] + 1
```

You can obtain the complete code from the GitHub repo of the book and you will get results similar to what we saw in the every-visit MC section.

Thus, we learned how to predict the value function of the given policy using the first-visit and every-visit MC methods.

Incremental mean updates

In both first-visit MC and every-visit MC, we estimate the value of a state as an average (arithmetic mean) return of the state across several episodes as shown as follows:

$$V(s) = \frac{\text{total\_return}(s)}{N(s)}$$

Instead of using the arithmetic mean to approximate the value of the state, we can also use the incremental mean, and it is expressed as:

$$N(s_t) = N(s_t) + 1$$

$$V(s_t) = V(s_t) + \frac{1}{N(s_t)}(R_t - V(s_t))$$

But why do we need incremental mean? Consider our environment as non-stationary. In that case, we don't have to take the return of the state from all the episodes and compute the average. As the environment is non-stationary we can ignore returns from earlier episodes and use only the returns from the latest episodes for computing the average. Thus, we can compute the value of the state using the incremental mean as shown as follows:

$$V(s_t) = V(s_t) + \alpha(R_t - V(s_t))$$

Where $\alpha = 1/N(s_t)$ and R_t is the return of the state s_t.

MC prediction (Q function)

So far, we have learned how to predict the value function of the given policy using the Monte Carlo method. In this section, we will see how to predict the Q function of the given policy using the Monte Carlo method.

Predicting the Q function of the given policy using the MC method is exactly the same as how we predicted the value function in the previous section except that here we use the return of the state-action pair, whereas in the case of the value function we used the return of the state. That is, just like we approximated the value of a state (value function) by computing the average return of the state across several episodes, we can also approximate the value of a state-action pair (Q function) by computing the average return of the state-action pair across several episodes.

Thus, we generate several episodes using the given policy π, then, we calculate the total_return(s, a), the sum of the return of the state-action pair across several episodes, and also we calculate $N(s, a)$, the number of times the state-action pair is visited across several episodes. Then we compute the Q function or Q value as the average return of the state-action pair as shown as follows:

$$Q(s, a) = \frac{\text{total\_return}(s, a)}{N(s, a)}$$

For instance, let consider a small example. Say we have two states s_0 and s_1 and we have two possible actions 0 and 1. Now, we compute total_return(s, a) and $N(s, a)$. Let's say our table after computation looks like *Table 4.4*:

State	Action	total_return(s,a)	N(s,a)
s_0	0	4	2
s_0	1	2	2
s_1	0	2	2
s_1	1	2	1

Table 4.4: The result of two actions in two states

Once we have this, we can compute the Q value by just taking the average, that is:

$$Q(s, a) = \frac{\text{total\_return}(s, a)}{N(s, a)}$$

Thus, we can compute the Q value for all state-action pairs as:

$$Q(s_0, 0) = \text{total\_return}(s_0, 0)/N(s_0, 0) = 4/2 = 2$$

$$Q(s_0, 1) = \text{total\_return}(s_0, 1)/N(s_0, 1) = 2/2 = 1$$

$$Q(s_1, 0) = \text{total\_return}(s_1, 0)/N(s_1, 0) = 2/2 = 1$$

$$Q(s_1, 1) = \text{total\_return}(s_1, 1)/N(s_1, 1) = 2/1 = 2$$

The algorithm for predicting the Q function using the Monte Carlo method is as follows. As we can see, it is exactly the same as how we predicted the value function using the return of the state except that here we predict the Q function using the return of a state-action pair:

1. Let total_return(*s, a*) be the sum of the return of a state-action pair across several episodes and $N(s, a)$ be the number of times a state-action pair is visited across several episodes. Initialize total_return(*s, a*) and $N(s, a)$ for all state-action pairs to zero. The policy π is given as input

2. For M number of iterations:

   1. Generate an episode using policy π

   2. Store all rewards obtained in the episode in the list called rewards

   3. For each step t in the episode:

      1. Compute return for the state-action pair, $R(s_t, a_t) = \text{sum}(\text{rewards}[t:])$

      2. Update the total return of the state-action pair, total_return(*s_t, a_t*) = total_return(*s_t, a_t*) + R(*s_t, a_t*)

      3. Update the counter as $N(s_t, a_t) = N(s_t, a_t) + 1$

3. Compute the Q function (Q value) by just taking the average, that is:

$$Q(s, a) = \frac{\text{total\_return}(s, a)}{N(s, a)}$$

Recall that in the MC prediction of the value function, we learned two types of MC— first-visit MC and every-visit MC. In first-visit MC, we compute the return of the state only for the first time the state is visited in the episode and in every-visit MC we compute the return of the state every time the state is visited in the episode.

Similarly, in the MC prediction of the Q function, we have two types of MC—first-visit MC and every-visit MC. In first-visit MC, we compute the return of the state-action pair only for the first time the state-action pair is visited in the episode and in every-visit MC we compute the return of the state-action pair every time the state-action pair is visited in the episode.

As mentioned in the previous section, instead of using the arithmetic mean, we can also use the incremental mean. We learned that the value of a state can be computed using the incremental mean as:

$$V(s_t) = V(s_t) + \alpha\big(R_t - V(s_t)\big)$$

Similarly, we can also compute the Q value using the incremental mean as shown as follows:

$$Q(s_t, a_t) = Q(s_t, a_t) + \alpha\big(R_t - Q(s_t, a_t)\big)$$

Now that we have learned how to perform the prediction task using the Monte Carlo method, in the next section, we will learn how to perform the control task using the Monte Carlo method.

Monte Carlo control

In the control task, our goal is to find the optimal policy. Unlike the prediction task, here, we will not be given any policy as an input. So, we will begin by initializing a random policy, and then we try to find the optimal policy iteratively. That is, we try to find an optimal policy that gives the maximum return. In this section, we will learn how to perform the control task to find the optimal policy using the Monte Carlo method.

Okay, we learned that in the control task our goal is to find the optimal policy. First, how can we compute a policy? We learned that the policy can be extracted from the Q function. That is, if we have a Q function, then we can extract policy by selecting an action in each state that has the maximum Q value as the following shows:

$$\pi = \arg\max_a Q(s, a)$$

So, to compute a policy, we need to compute the Q function. But how can we compute the Q function? We can compute the Q function similarly to what we learned in the MC prediction method. That is, in the MC prediction method, we learned that when given a policy, we can generate several episodes using that policy and compute the Q function (Q value) as the average return of the state-action pair across several episodes.

We can perform the same step here to compute the Q function. But in the control method, we are not given any policy as input. So, we will initialize a random policy, and then we compute the Q function using the random policy. That is, just like we learned in the prediction method, we generate several episodes using our random policy. Then we compute the Q function (Q value) as the average return of a state-action pair across several episodes as the following shows:

$$Q(s, a) = \frac{total\_return(s, a)}{N(s, a)}$$

Let's suppose after computing the Q function as the average return of the state-action pair, our Q function looks like *Table 4.5*:

State	Action	Value
s_0	0	2
s_0	1	1
s_1	0	1
s_1	1	2

Table 4.5: The Q table

From the preceding Q function, we can extract a new policy by selecting an action in each state that has the maximum Q value. That is, $\pi = \arg\max_a Q(s, a)$. Thus, our new policy selects action 0 in state s_0 and action 1 in state s_1 as it has the maximum Q value.

However, this new policy will not be an optimal policy because this new policy is extracted from the Q function, which is computed using the random policy. That is, we initialized a random policy and generated several episodes using the random policy, then we computed the Q function by taking the average return of the state-action pair across several episodes. Thus, we are using the random policy to compute the Q function and so the new policy extracted from the Q function will not be an optimal policy.

But now that we have extracted a new policy from the Q function, we can use this new policy to generate episodes in the next iteration and compute the new Q function. Then, from this new Q function, we extract a new policy. We repeat these steps iteratively until we find the optimal policy. This is explained clearly in the following steps:

Iteration 1 – Let π_0 be the random policy. We use this random policy to generate an episode, and then we compute the Q function Q^{π_0} by taking the average return of the state-action pair. Then, from this Q function Q^{π_0}, we extract a new policy π_1. This new policy π_1 will not be an optimal policy since it is extracted from the Q function, which is computed using the random policy.

Iteration 2 – So, we use the new policy π_1 derived from the previous iteration to generate an episode and compute the new Q function Q^{π_1} as average return of a state-action pair. Then, from this Q function Q^{π_1}, we extract a new policy π_2. If the policy π_2 is optimal we stop, else we go to iteration 3.

Iteration 3 – Now, we use the new policy π_2 derived from the previous iteration to generate an episode and compute the new Q function Q^{π_2}. Then, from this Q function Q^{π_2}, we extract a new policy π_3. If π_3 is optimal we stop, else we go to the next iteration.

We repeat this process for several iterations until we find the optimal policy π^* as shown in *Figure 4.21*:

$$\pi_0 \rightarrow Q^{\pi_0} \rightarrow \pi_1 \rightarrow Q^{\pi_1} \rightarrow \pi_2 \rightarrow Q^{\pi_2} \rightarrow \pi_3 \rightarrow Q^{\pi_3} \rightarrow \cdots \rightarrow \pi^* \rightarrow Q^{\pi^*}$$

Figure 4.21: The path to finding the optimal policy

This step is called policy evaluation and improvement and is similar to the policy iteration method we covered in *Chapter 3, The Bellman Equation and Dynamic Programming*. Policy evaluation implies that at each step we evaluate the policy. Policy improvement implies that at each step we are improving the policy by taking the maximum Q value. Note that here, we select the policy in a greedy manner meaning that we are selecting policy π by just taking the maximum Q value, and so we can call our policy a greedy policy.

Now that we have a basic understanding of how the MC control method works, in the next section, we will look into the algorithm of the MC control method and learn about it in more detail.

MC control algorithm

The following steps show the Monte Carlo control algorithm. As we can observe, unlike the MC prediction method, here, we will not be given any policy. So, we start off by initializing the random policy and use the random policy to generate an episode in the first iteration. Then, we will compute the Q function (Q value) as the average return of the state-action pair.

Once we have the Q function, we extract a new policy by selecting an action in each state that has the maximum Q value. In the next iteration, we use the extracted new policy to generate an episode and compute the new Q function (Q value) as the average return of the state-action pair. We repeat these steps for many iterations to find the optimal policy.

One more thing, we need to observe that just as we learned in the first-visit MC prediction method, here, we compute the return of the state-action pair only for the first time a state-action pair is visited in the episode.

For a better understanding, we can compare the MC control algorithm with the MC prediction of the Q function. One difference we can observe is that, here, we compute the Q function in each iteration. But if you notice, in the MC prediction of the Q function, we compute the Q function after all the iterations. The reason for computing the Q function in every iteration here is that we need the Q function to extract the new policy so that we can use the extracted new policy in the next iteration to generate an episode:

1. Let total_return(s, a) be the sum of the return of a state-action pair across several episodes and $N(s, a)$ be the number of times a state-action pair is visited across several episodes. Initialize total_return(s, a) and $N(s, a)$ for all state-action pairs to zero and initialize a random policy π

2. For M number of iterations:

   1. Generate an episode using policy π

   2. Store all rewards obtained in the episode in the list called rewards

   3. For each step t in the episode:

      If (s_t, a_t) is occurring for the first time in the episode:

      1. Compute the return of a state-action pair, $R(s_t, a_t) =$ sum(rewards[t:])

      2. Update the total return of the state-action pair as, total_return(s_t, a_t) = total_return(s_t, a_t) + $R(s_t, a_t)$

      3. Update the counter as $N(s_t, a_t) = N(s_t, a_t) + 1$

      4. Compute the Q value by just taking the average, that is,

      $$Q(s_t, a_t) = \frac{\text{total\_return}(s_t, a_t)}{N(s_t, a_t)}$$

   4. Compute the new updated policy π using the Q function:

   $$\pi = \arg \max_a Q(s, a)$$

From the preceding algorithm, we can observe that we generate an episode using the policy π. Then for each step in the episode, we compute the return of state-action pair and compute the Q function $Q(s_t, a_t)$ as an average return, then from this Q function, we extract a new policy π. We repeat this step iteratively to find the optimal policy π. Thus, we learned how to perform the control task using the Monte Carlo method.

We can classify the control methods into two types:

- On-policy control
- Off-policy control

On-policy control – In the on-policy control method, the agent behaves using one policy and also tries to improve the same policy. That is, in the on-policy method, we generate episodes using one policy and also improve the same policy iteratively to find the optimal policy. For instance, the MC control method, which we just learned above, can be called on-policy MC control as we are generating episodes using a policy π, and we also try to improve the same policy π on every iteration to compute the optimal policy.

Off-policy control – In the off-policy control method, the agent behaves using one policy b and tries to improve a different policy π. That is, in the off-policy method, we generate episodes using one policy and we try to improve the different policy iteratively to find the optimal policy.

We will learn how exactly the preceding two control methods work in detail in the upcoming sections.

On-policy Monte Carlo control

There are two types of on-policy Monte Carlo control methods:

- Monte Carlo exploring starts
- Monte Carlo with the epsilon-greedy policy

Monte Carlo exploring starts

We have already learned how the Monte Carlo control method works. One thing we may want to take into account is exploration. There can be several actions in a state: some actions will be optimal, while others won't. To understand whether an action is optimal or not, the agent has to explore by performing that action. If the agent never explores a particular action in a state, then it will never know whether it is a good action or not. So, how can we solve this? That is, how can we ensure enough exploration? Here is where Monte Carlo exploring starts helps us.

In the MC exploring starts method, we set all state-action pairs to a non-zero probability for being the initial state-action pair. So before generating an episode, first, we choose the initial state-action pair randomly and then we generate the episode starting from this initial state-action pair following the policy π. Then, in every iteration, our policy will be updated as a greedy policy (selecting the max Q value; see the next section on *Monte Carlo with the epsilon-greedy policy* for more details).

The following steps show the algorithm of MC control exploring starts. It is essentially the same as what we learned earlier for the MC control algorithm section, except that here, we select an initial state-action pair and generate episodes starting from this initial state-action pair as shown in the bold point:

1. Let total_return(s, a) be the sum of the return of a state-action pair across several episodes and $N(s, a)$ be the number of times a state-action pair is visited across several episodes. Initialize total_return(s, a) and $N(s, a)$ for all state-action pairs to zero and initialize a random policy π

2. For M number of iterations:

    1. **Select the initial state s_0 and initial action a_0 randomly such that all state-action pairs have a probability greater than 0**

    2. Generate an episode from the selected initial state s_0 and action a_0 using policy π

    3. Store all the rewards obtained in the episode in the list called rewards

    4. For each step t in the episode:

        If (s_t, a_t) is occurring for the first time in the episode:

        1. Compute the return of a state-action pair, $R(s_t, a_t) =$ sum(rewards[t:])

        2. Update the total return of the state-action pair as total_return$(s_t, a_t) =$ total_return$(s_t, a_t) + R(s_t, a_t)$

        3. Update the counter as $N(s_t, a_t) = N(s_t, a_t) + 1$

        4. Compute the Q value by just taking the average, that is,

$$Q(s_t, a_t) = \frac{\text{total\_return}(s_t, a_t)}{N(s_t, a_t)}$$

    5. Compute the updated policy π using the Q function:

$$\pi = \arg \max_a Q(s, a)$$

One of the major drawbacks of the exploring starts method is that it is not applicable to every environment. That is, we can't just randomly choose any state-action pair as an initial state-action pair because in some environments there can be only one state-action pair that can act as an initial state-action pair. So we can't randomly select the state-action pair as the initial state-action pair.

For example, suppose we are training an agent to play a car racing game; we can't start the episode in a random position as the initial state and a random action as the initial action because we have a fixed single starting state and action as the initial state and action.

Thus, to overcome the problem in exploring starts, in the next section, we will learn about the Monte Carlo control method with a new type of policy called the epsilon-greedy policy.

Monte Carlo with the epsilon-greedy policy

Before going ahead, first, let us understand what the epsilon-greedy policy is as it is ubiquitous in reinforcement learning.

First, let's learn what a greedy policy is. A greedy policy is one that selects the best action available at the moment. For instance, let's say we are in some state **A** and we have four possible actions in the state. Let the actions be *up, down, left,* and *right*. But let's suppose our agent has explored only two actions, *up* and *right*, in the state **A**; the Q value of actions *up* and *right* in the state **A** are shown in *Table 4.6*:

State	Action	Value
A	up	3
A	right	1

Table 4.6: The agent has only explored two actions in state A

We learned that the greedy policy selects the best action available at the moment. So the greedy policy checks the Q table and selects the action that has the maximum Q value in state **A**. As we can see, the action *up* has the maximum Q value. So our greedy policy selects the action *up* in state **A**.

But one problem with the greedy policy is that it never explores the other possible actions; instead, it always picks the best action available at the moment. In the preceding example, the greedy policy always selects the action *up*. But there could be other actions in state **A** that might be more optimal than the action *up* that the agent has not explored yet. That is, we still have two more actions—*down* and *left*—in state **A** that the agent has not explored yet, and they might be more optimal than the action *up*.

So, now the question is whether the agent should explore all the other actions in the state and select the best action as the one that has the maximum Q value or exploit the best action out of already-explored actions. This is called an **exploration-exploitation dilemma.**

Say there are many routes from our work to home and we have explored only two routes so far. Thus, to reach home, we can select the route that takes us home most quickly out of the two routes we have explored. However, there are still many other routes that we have not explored yet that might be even better than our current optimal route. The question is whether we should explore new routes (exploration) or whether we should always use our current optimal route (exploitation).

To avoid this dilemma, we introduce a new policy called the epsilon-greedy policy. Here, all actions are tried with a non-zero probability (epsilon). With a probability epsilon, we explore different actions randomly and with a probability 1-epsilon, we choose an action that has the maximum Q value. That is, with a probability epsilon, we select a random action (exploration) and with a probability 1-epsilon we select the best action (exploitation).

In the epsilon-greedy policy, if we set the value of epsilon to 0, then it becomes a greedy policy (only exploitation), and when we set the value of epsilon to 1, then we will always end up doing only the exploration. So, the value of epsilon has to be chosen optimally between 0 and 1.

Say we set epsilon = 0.5; then we will generate a random number from the uniform distribution and if the random number is less than epsilon (0.5), then we select a random action (exploration), but if the random number is greater than or equal to epsilon then we select the best action, that is, the action that has the maximum Q value (exploitation).

So, in this way, we explore actions that we haven't seen before with the probability epsilon and select the best actions out of the explored actions with the probability 1-epsilon. As *Figure 4.22* shows, if the random number we generated from the uniform distribution is less than epsilon, then we choose a random action. If the random number is greater than or equal to epsilon, then we choose the best action:

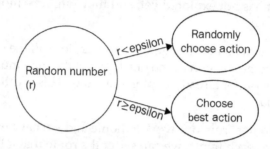

Figure 4.22: Epsilon-greedy policy

The following snippet shows the Python code for the epsilon-greedy policy:

```python
def epsilon_greedy_policy(state, epsilon):
    if random.uniform(0,1) < epsilon:
        return env.action_space.sample()
    else:
        return max(list(range(env.action_space.n)), key = lambda x:
q[(state,x)])
```

Now that we have understood what an epsilon-greedy policy is, and how it is used to solve the exploration-exploitation dilemma, in the next section, we will look at how to use the epsilon-greedy policy in the Monte Carlo control method.

The MC control algorithm with the epsilon-greedy policy

The algorithm of Monte Carlo control with the epsilon-greedy policy is essentially the same as the MC control algorithm we learned earlier except that here we select actions based on the epsilon-greedy policy to avoid the exploration-exploitation dilemma. The following steps show the algorithm of Monte Carlo with the epsilon-greedy policy:

1. Let total_return(s, a) be the sum of the return of a state-action pair across several episodes and $N(s, a)$ be the number of times a state-action pair is visited across several episodes. Initialize total_return(s, a) and $N(s, a)$ for all state-action pairs to zero and initialize a random policy π

2. For M number of iterations:

   1. Generate an episode using policy π

   2. Store all rewards obtained in the episode in the list called rewards

   3. For each step t in the episode:

      If (s_t, a_t) is occurring for the first time in the episode:

      1. Compute the return of a state-action pair, $R(s_t, a_t) = $ sum(rewards[t:])

      2. Update the total return of the state-action pair as total_return(s_t, a_t) = total_return(s_t, a_t) + $R(s_t, a_t)$

      3. Update the counter as $N(s_t, a_t) = N(s_t, a_t) + 1$

      4. Compute the Q value by just taking the average, that is,

$$Q(s_t, a_t) = \frac{\text{total\_return}(s_t, a_t)}{N(s_t, a_t)}$$

   4. Compute the updated policy π using the Q function. Let $a^* = \arg \max_a Q(s, a)$. The policy π selects the best action a^* with probability $1 - \epsilon$ and random action with probability ϵ

As we can observe, in every iteration, we generate the episode using the policy π and also we try to improve the same policy π in every iteration to compute the optimal policy.

Implementing on-policy MC control

Now, let's learn how to implement the MC control method with the epsilon-greedy policy to play the blackjack game; that is, we will see how can we use the MC control method to find the optimal policy in the blackjack game.

First, let's import the necessary libraries:

```
import gym
import pandas as pd
import random
from collections import defaultdict
```

Create a blackjack environment:

```
env = gym.make('Blackjack-v0')
```

Initialize the dictionary for storing the Q values:

```
Q = defaultdict(float)
```

Initialize the dictionary for storing the total return of the state-action pair:

```
total_return = defaultdict(float)
```

Initialize the dictionary for storing the count of the number of times a state-action pair is visited:

```
N = defaultdict(int)
```

Define the epsilon-greedy policy

We learned that we select actions based on the epsilon-greedy policy, so we define a function called `epsilon_greedy_policy`, which takes the state and Q value as an input and returns the action to be performed in the given state:

```
def epsilon_greedy_policy(state,Q):
```

Set the epsilon value to 0.5:

```
epsilon = 0.5
```

Sample a random value from the uniform distribution; if the sampled value is less than epsilon then we select a random action, else we select the best action that has the maximum Q value as shown:

```
if random.uniform(0,1) < epsilon:
    return env.action_space.sample()
else:
    return max(list(range(env.action_space.n)), key = lambda x:
Q[(state,x)])
```

Generating an episode

Now, let's generate an episode using the epsilon-greedy policy. We define a function called `generate_episode`, which takes the Q value as an input and returns the episode.

First, let's set the number of time steps:

```
num_timesteps = 100
```

Now, let's define the function:

```
def generate_episode(Q):
```

Initialize a list for storing the episode:

```
episode = []
```

Initialize the state using the reset function:

```
state = env.reset()
```

Then for each time step:

```
for t in range(num_timesteps):
```

Select the action according to the epsilon-greedy policy:

```
action = epsilon_greedy_policy(state,Q)
```

Perform the selected action and store the next state information:

```
next_state, reward, done, info = env.step(action)
```

Store the state, action, and reward in the episode list:

```
episode.append((state, action, reward))
```

If the next state is the final state then break the loop, else update the next state to the current state:

```
if done:
    break

state = next_state

return episode
```

Computing the optimal policy

Now, let's learn how to compute the optimal policy. First, let's set the number of iterations, that is, the number of episodes, we want to generate:

```
num_iterations = 500000
```

For each iteration:

```
for i in range(num_iterations):
```

We learned that in the on-policy control method, we will not be given any policy as an input. So, we initialize a random policy in the first iteration and improve the policy iteratively by computing the Q value. Since we extract the policy from the Q function, we don't have to explicitly define the policy. As the Q value improves, the policy also improves implicitly. That is, in the first iteration, we generate the episode by extracting the policy (epsilon-greedy) from the initialized Q function. Over a series of iterations, we will find the optimal Q function, and hence we also find the optimal policy.

So, here we pass our initialized Q function to generate an episode:

```
episode = generate_episode(Q)
```

Get all the state-action pairs in the episode:

```
all_state_action_pairs = [(s, a) for (s,a,r) in episode]
```

Store all the rewards obtained in the episode in the rewards list:

```
rewards = [r for (s,a,r) in episode]
```

For each step in the episode:

```
for t, (state, action,_) in enumerate(episode):
```

If the state-action pair is occurring for the first time in the episode:

```
if not (state, action) in all_state_action_pairs[0:t]:
```

Compute the return R of the state-action pair as the sum of rewards, $R(s_t, a_t) =$ sum(rewards[t:]):

```
R = sum(rewards[t:])
```

Update the total return of the state-action pair as total_return(s_t, a_t) = total_return(s_t, a_t) + $R(s_t, a_t)$:

```
total_return[(state,action)] = total_return[(state,action)]
+ R
```

Update the number of times the state-action pair is visited as $N(s_t, a_t) = N(s_t, a_t) + 1$:

```
N[(state, action)] += 1
```

Compute the Q value by just taking the average, that is,

$$Q(s_t, a_t) = \frac{\text{total\_return}(s_t, a_t):}{N(s_t, a_t)}$$

```
Q[(state,action)] = total_return[(state, action)] /
N[(state, action)]
```

Thus on every iteration, the Q value improves and so does the policy.

After all the iterations, we can have a look at the Q value of each state-action pair in the pandas data frame for more clarity. First, let's convert the Q value dictionary into a pandas data frame:

```
df = pd.DataFrame(Q.items(),columns=['state_action pair','value'])
```

Let's look at the first few rows of the data frame:

```
df.head(11)
```

	state_action pair	value
0	((12, 10, False), 0)	-0.562372
1	((12, 10, False), 1)	-0.496164
2	((14, 3, True), 0)	-0.222222
3	((14, 3, True), 1)	0.086957
4	((19, 2, False), 0)	0.354545
5	((19, 2, False), 1)	-0.695122
6	((16, 10, False), 0)	-0.530662
7	((14, 5, False), 0)	-0.112782
8	((17, 9, True), 0)	-0.333333
9	((20, 9, False), 1)	-0.861789
10	((19, 10, False), 0)	-0.014479

Figure 4.23: The Q values of the state-action pairs

As we can observe, we have the Q values for all the state-action pairs. Now we can extract the policy by selecting the action that has the maximum Q value in each state. For instance, say we are in the state (21,8, True). Now, should we perform action 0 (stand) or action 1 (hit)? It makes more sense to perform action 0 (stand) here, since the value of the sum of our cards is already 21, and if we perform action 1 (hit) our game will lead to a bust.

Note that due to stochasticity, you might get different results than those shown here.

Let's look at the Q values of all the actions in this state, (21,8, True):

```
df[124:126]
```

The preceding code will print the following:

	state_action pair	value
124	((21, 8, True), 0)	0.936782
125	((21, 8, True), 1)	-0.123077

Figure 4.24: The Q values of the state (21,8, True)

As we can observe, we have a maximum Q value for action 0 (stand) compared to action 1 (hit). So, we perform action 0 in the state (21,8, True). Similarly, in this way, we can extract the policy by selecting the action in each state that has the maximum Q value.

In the next section, we will learn about an off-policy control method that uses two different policies.

Off-policy Monte Carlo control

Off-policy Monte Carlo is another interesting Monte Carlo control method. In the off-policy method, we use two policies called the behavior policy and the target policy. As the name suggests, we behave (generate episodes) using the behavior policy and we try to improve the other policy called the target policy.

In the on-policy method, we generate an episode using the policy π and we improve the same policy π iteratively to find the optimal policy. But in the off-policy method, we generate an episode using a policy called the behavior policy b and we try to iteratively improve a different policy called the target policy π.

That is, in the on-policy method, we learned that the agent generates an episode using the policy π. Then for each step in the episode, we compute the return of the state-action pair and compute the Q function $Q(s_t, a_t)$ as an average return, then from this Q function, we extract a new policy π. We repeat this step iteratively to find the optimal policy π.

But in the off-policy method, the agent generates an episode using a policy called the behavior policy b. Then for each step in the episode, we compute the return of the state-action pair and compute the Q function $Q(s_t, a_t)$ as an average return, then from this Q function, we extract a new policy called the target policy π. We repeat this step iteratively to find the optimal target policy π.

The behavior policy will usually be set to the epsilon-greedy policy and thus the agent explores the environment with the epsilon-greedy policy and generates an episode. Unlike the behavior policy, the target policy is set to be the greedy policy and so the target policy will always select the best action in each state.

Let's now understand how the off-policy Monte Carlo method works exactly. First, we will initialize the Q function with random values. Then we generate an episode using the behavior policy, which is the epsilon-greedy policy. That is, from the Q function we select the best action (the action that has the max Q value) with probability 1-epsilon and we select the random action with probability epsilon. Then for each step in the episode, we compute the return of the state-action pair and compute the Q function $Q(s_t, a_t)$ as an average return. Instead of using the arithmetic mean to compute the Q function, we can use the incremental mean. We can compute the Q function using the incremental mean as shown as follows:

$$Q(s_t, a_t) = Q(s_t, a_t) + \alpha\big(R_t - Q(s_t, a_t)\big)$$

After computing the Q function, we extract the target policy π by selecting an action in each state that has the maximum Q value as shown as follows:

$$\pi(s_t) = \arg\max_a Q(s_t, a)$$

The algorithm is given as follows:

1. Initialize the Q function $Q(s, a)$ with random values, set the behavior policy b to be epsilon-greedy, and also set the target policy π to be greedy policy.

2. For M number of episodes:
    1. Generate an episode using the behavior policy b
    2. Initialize return R to 0

3. For each step t in the episode, $t = T-1, T-2, ..., 0$:

    1. Compute the return as $R = R + r_{t+1}$

    2. Compute the Q value as $Q(s_t, a_t) = Q(s_t, a_t) + \alpha(R_t - Q(s_t, a_t))$

    3. Compute the target policy $\pi(s_t) = \arg\max_a Q(s_t, a)$

3. Return the target policy π

As we can observe from the preceding algorithm, first we set the Q values of all the state-action pairs to random values and then we generate an episode using the behavior policy. Then on each step of the episode, we compute the updated Q function (Q values) using the incremental mean and then we extract the target policy from the updated Q function. As we can notice, on every iteration, the Q function is constantly improving and since we are extracting the target policy from the Q function, our target policy will also be improving on every iteration.

Also, note that since it is an off-policy method, the episode is generated using the behavior policy and we try to improve the target policy.

But wait! There is a small issue here. Since we are finding the target policy π from the Q function, which is computed based on the episodes generated by a different policy called the behavior policy, our target policy will be inaccurate. This is because the distribution of the behavior policy and the target policy will be different. So, to correct this, we introduce a new technique called **importance sampling**. This is a technique for estimating the values of one distribution when given samples from another.

Let us say we want to compute the expectation of a function $f(x)$ where the value of x is sampled from the distribution $p(x)$ that is, $x \sim p(x)$; then we can write:

$$\mathbb{E}_{x \sim p(x)}[f(x)] = \int_x p(x)f(x)dx$$

With the importance sampling method, we estimate the expectation using a different distribution $q(x)$; that is, instead of sampling x from $p(x)$ we use a different distribution $q(x)$ as shown as follows:

$$\mathbb{E}[f(x)] \approx \int_x f(x)\frac{p(x)}{q(x)}q(x)dx$$

$$\mathbb{E}[f(x)] \approx \frac{1}{N}\sum_i f(x_i)\frac{p(x_i)}{q(x_i)}$$

The ratio $\frac{p(x)}{q(x)}$ is called the importance sampling ratio or importance correction.

Okay, how does importance sampling help us? We learned that with importance sampling, we can estimate the value of one distribution by sampling from another using the importance sampling ratio. In off-policy control, we can estimate the target policy with the samples (episodes) from the behavior policy using the importance sampling ratio.

Importance sampling has two types:

- Ordinary importance sampling
- Weighted importance sampling

In ordinary importance sampling, the importance sampling ratio will be the ratio of the target policy to the behavior policy $\frac{\pi(a|s)}{b(a|s)}$ and in weighted importance sampling, the importance sampling ratio will be the weighted ratio of the target policy to the behavior policy $W\frac{\pi(a|s)}{b(a|s)}$.

Let's now understand how we use weighted importance sampling in the off-policy Monte Carlo method. Let W be the weight and $C(s_t, a_t)$ denote the cumulative sum of weights across all the episodes. We learned that we compute the Q function (Q values) using the incremental mean as:

$$Q(s_t, a_t) = Q(s_t, a_t) + \alpha(R_t - Q(s_t, a_t))$$

Now, we slightly modify our Q function computation with the weighted importance sampling as shown as follows:

$$Q(s_t, a_t) = Q(s_t, a_t) + \frac{W}{C(s_t, a_t)}(R_t - Q(s_t, a_t))$$

The algorithm of the off-policy Monte Carlo method is shown next. First, we generate an episode using the behavior policy and then we initialize return R to 0 and the weight W to 1. Then on every step of the episode, we compute the return and update the cumulative weight as $C(s_t, a_t) = C(s_t, a_t) + W$. After updating the cumulative weights, we update the Q value as $Q(s_t, a_t) = Q(s_t, a_t) + \frac{W}{C(s_t, a_t)}(R_t - Q(s_t, a_t))$.

From the Q value, we extract the target policy as $\pi(s_t) = \arg\max\limits_{a} Q(s_t, a)$. When the action a_t given by the behavior policy and the target policy is not the same then we break the loop and generate the next episode; else we update the weight as

$$W = W\frac{1}{b(a_t|s_t)}.$$

The complete algorithm of the off-policy Monte Carlo method is explained in the following steps:

1. Initialize the Q function $Q(s, a)$ with random values, set the behavior policy b to be epsilon-greedy, and target policy π to be greedy policy and initialize the cumulative weights as $C(s, a) = 0$

2. For M number of episodes:

   1. Generate an episode using the behavior policy b
   2. Initialize return R to 0 and weight W to 1
   3. For each step t in the episode, $t = T\text{-}1, T\text{-}2,..., 0$:

      1. Compute the return as $R = R + r_{t+1}$
      2. Update the cumulative weights $C(s_t, a_t) = C(s_t, a_t) + W$
      3. Update the Q value as

         $$Q(s_t, a_t) = Q(s_t, a_t) + \frac{W}{C(s_t, a_t)}(R_t - Q(s_t, a_t))$$

      4. Compute the target policy $\pi(s_t) = \arg\max\limits_{a} Q(s_t, a)$
      5. If $a_t \neq \pi(s_t)$ then break
      6. Update the weight as $W = W\frac{1}{b(a_t|s_t)}$

3. Return the target policy π

Is the MC method applicable to all tasks?

We learned that Monte Carlo is a model-free method, and so it doesn't require the model dynamics of the environment to compute the value and Q function in order to find the optimal policy. The Monte Carlo method computes the value function and Q function by just taking the average return of the state and the average return of the state-action pair, respectively.

But one issue with the Monte Carlo method is that it is applicable only to episodic tasks. We learned that in the Monte Carlo method, we compute the value of the state by taking the average return of the state and the return is the sum of rewards of the episode. But when there is no episode, that is, if our task is a continuous task (non-episodic task), then we cannot apply the Monte Carlo method.

Okay, how do we compute the value of the state where we have a continuous task and also where we don't know the model dynamics of the environment? Here is where we use another interesting model-free method called temporal difference learning. In the next chapter, we will learn exactly how temporal difference learning works.

Summary

We started the chapter by understanding what the Monte Carlo method is. We learned that in the Monte Carlo method, we approximate the expectation of a random variable by sampling, and when the sample size is greater, the approximation will be better. Then we learned about the prediction and control tasks. In the prediction task, we evaluate the given policy by predicting the value function or Q function, which helps us to understand the expected return an agent would get if it uses the given policy. In the control task, our goal is to find the optimal policy, and we will not be given any policy as input, so we start by initializing a random policy and we try to find the optimal policy iteratively.

Moving forward, we learned how to use the Monte Carlo method to perform the prediction task. We learned that the value of a state and the value of a state-action pair can be computed by just taking the average return of the state and an average return of state-action pair across several episodes, respectively.

We also learned about the first-visit MC and every-visit MC methods. In first-visit MC, we compute the return only for the first time the state is visited in the episode, and in every-visit MC, we compute the return every time the state is visited in the episode.

Following this, we explored how to perform a control task using the Monte Carlo method. We learned about two different types of control methods—on-policy and off-policy control.

In the on-policy method, we generate episodes using one policy and also improve the same policy iteratively to find the optimal policy. We first learned about the Monte Carlo control exploring starts method where we set all the state-action pairs to a non-zero probability to ensure exploration. Later, we learned about Monte Carlo control with an epsilon-greedy policy where we select a random action (exploration) with probability epsilon, and with probability 1-epsilon we select the best action (exploitation).

At the end of the chapter, we discussed the off-policy Monte Carlo control method where we use two different policies called the behavior policy, for generating the episode, and the target policy, for finding the optimal policy.

Questions

Let's assess our knowledge of the Monte Carlo methods by answering the following questions:

1. What is the Monte Carlo method?
2. Why is the Monte Carlo method preferred over dynamic programming?
3. How do prediction tasks differ from control tasks?
4. How does the MC prediction method predict the value function?
5. What is the difference between first-visit MC and every-visit MC?
6. Why do we use incremental mean updates?
7. How does on-policy control differ from off-policy control?
8. What is the epsilon-greedy policy?

5
Understanding Temporal Difference Learning

Temporal difference (TD) learning is one of the most popular and widely used model-free methods. The reason for this is that TD learning combines the advantages of both the **dynamic programming** (DP) method and the **Monte Carlo** (MC) method we covered in the previous chapters.

We will begin the chapter by understanding how exactly TD learning is beneficial compared to DP and MC methods. Later, we will learn how to perform the prediction task using TD learning. Going forward, we will learn how to perform TD control tasks with an on-policy TD control method called SARSA and an off-policy TD control method called Q learning.

We will also learn how to find the optimal policy in the Frozen Lake environment using SARSA and the Q learning method. At the end of the chapter, we will compare the DP, MC, and TD methods.

Thus, in this chapter, we will learn about the following topics:

- TD learning
- TD prediction method
- TD control method
- On-policy TD control – SARSA
- Off-policy TD control – Q learning
- Implementing SARSA and Q learning to find the optimal policy

- The difference between Q learning and SARSA
- Comparing the DP, MC, and TD methods

TD learning

The TD learning algorithm was introduced by Richard S. Sutton in 1988. In the introduction of the chapter, we learned that the reason the TD method became popular is that it combines the advantages of DP and the MC method. But what are those advantages?

First, let's recap quickly the advantages and disadvantages of DP and the MC method.

Dynamic programming — The advantage of the DP method is that it uses the Bellman equation to compute the value of a state. That is, we have learned that according to the Bellman equation, the value of a state can be obtained as the sum of the immediate reward and the discounted value of the next state. This is called bootstrapping. That is, to compute the value of a state, we don't have to wait till the end of the episode, instead, using the Bellman equation, we can estimate the value of a state just based on the value of the next state, and this is called bootstrapping.

Remember how we estimated the value function in DP methods (value and policy iteration)? We estimated the value function (the value of a state) as:

$$V(s) = \sum_{s'} P_{ss'}^{a} \left[R_{ss'}^{a} + \gamma V(s') \right]$$

As you may recollect, we learned that in order to find the value of a state, we didn't have to wait till the end of the episode. Instead, we bootstrap, that is, we estimate the value of the current state $V(s)$ by estimating the value of the next state $V(s')$.

However, the disadvantage of DP is that we can apply the DP method only when we know the model dynamics of the environment. That is, DP is a model-based method and we should know the transition probability in order to use it. When we don't know the model dynamics of the environment, we cannot apply the DP method.

Monte Carlo method — The advantage of the MC method is that it is a model-free method, which means that it does not require the model dynamics of the environment to be known in order to estimate the value and Q functions.

However, the disadvantage of the MC method is that in order to estimate the state value or Q value we need to wait until the end of the episode, and if the episode is long then it will cost us a lot of time. Also, we cannot apply MC methods to continuous tasks (non-episodic tasks).

Now, let's get back to TD learning. The TD learning algorithm takes the benefits of the DP and the MC methods into account. So, just like in DP, we perform bootstrapping so that we don't have to wait until the end of an episode to compute the state value or Q value, and just like the MC method, it is a model-free method and so it does not require the model dynamics of the environment to compute the state value or Q value. Now that we have the basic idea behind the TD learning algorithm, let's get into the details and learn exactly how it works.

Similar to what we learned in *Chapter 4*, *Monte Carlo Methods*, we can use the TD learning algorithm for both the prediction and control tasks, and so we can categorize TD learning into:

- TD prediction
- TD control

We learned what the prediction and control methods mean in the previous chapter. Let's recap that a bit before going forward.

In the prediction method, a policy is given as an input and we try to predict the value function or Q function using the given policy. If we predict the value function using the given policy, then we can say how good it is for the agent to be in each state if it uses the given policy. That is, we can say what the expected return an agent can get in each state if it acts according to the given policy.

In the control method, we are not given a policy as input, and the goal in the control method is to find the optimal policy. So, we initialize a random policy and then we try to find the optimal policy iteratively. That is, we try to find an optimal policy that gives us the maximum return.

First, let's see how to use TD learning to perform prediction task, and then we will learn how to use TD learning for the control task.

TD prediction

In the TD prediction method, the policy is given as input and we try to estimate the value function using the given policy. TD learning bootstraps like DP, so it does not have to wait till the end of the episode, and like the MC method, it does not require the model dynamics of the environment to compute the value function or the Q function. Now, let's see how the update rule of TD learning is designed, taking the preceding advantages into account.

In the MC method, we estimate the value of a state by taking its return:

$$V(s) \approx R(s)$$

However, a single return value cannot approximate the value of a state perfectly. So, we generate N episodes and compute the value of a state as the average return of a state across N episodes:

$$V(s) \approx \frac{1}{N} \sum_{i=1}^{N} R_i(s)$$

But with the MC method, we need to wait until the end of the episode to compute the value of a state and when the episode is long, it takes a lot of time. One more problem with the MC method is that we cannot apply it to non-episodic tasks (continuous tasks).

So, in TD learning, we make use of bootstrapping and estimate the value of a state as:

$$V(s) \approx r + \gamma V(s')$$

The preceding equation tells us that we can estimate the value of the state by only taking the immediate reward r and the discounted value of the next state $\gamma V(s')$. As you may observe from the preceding equation, similar to what we learned in DP methods (value and policy iteration), we perform bootstrapping but here we don't need to know the model dynamics.

Thus, using TD learning, the value of a state is approximated as:

$$V(s) \approx r + \gamma V(s')$$

However, a single value of $r + \gamma V(s')$ cannot approximate the value of a state perfectly. So, we can take a mean value and instead of taking an arithmetic mean, we can use the incremental mean.

In the MC method, we learned how to use the incremental mean to estimate the value of the state and it given as follows:

$$V(s) = V(s) + \alpha\big(R - V(s)\big)$$

Similarly, here in TD learning, we can use the incremental mean and estimate the value of the state, as shown here:

$$V(s) = V(s) + \alpha(r + \gamma V(s') - V(s))$$

This equation is called the TD learning update rule. As we can observe, the only difference between the TD learning and the MC method is that to compute the value of the state, in the MC method, we use the full return R, which is computed using the complete episode, whereas in the TD learning method, we use the bootstrap estimate $r + \gamma V(s')$ so that we don't have to wait until the end of the episode to compute the value of the state. Thus, we can apply TD learning to non-episodic tasks as well. The following shows the difference between the MC method and TD learning:

Monte Carlo Method   TD Learning

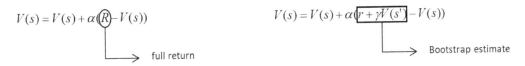

$$V(s) = V(s) + \alpha(R - V(s))$$ $$V(s) = V(s) + \alpha(r + \gamma V(s') - V(s))$$

→ full return   → Bootstrap estimate

Figure 5.1: A comparison between MC and TD learning

Thus, our TD learning update rule is:

$$V(s) = V(s) + \alpha(r + \gamma V(s') - V(s))$$

We learned that $r + \gamma V(s')$ is an estimate of the value of state $V(s)$. So, we can call $r + \gamma V(s')$ the TD target. Thus, subtracting $V(s)$ from $r + \gamma V(s')$ implies that we are subtracting the predicted value from the target value, and this is usually called the TD error. Okay, what about that α? It is basically the learning rate, also called the step size. That is:

$$V(s) = V(s) + \alpha(r + \gamma V(s') - V(s))$$

Learning rate   TD error

Our TD learning update rule basically implies:

Value of a state = value of a state + learning rate (reward + discount factor(value of next state) - value of a state)

Now that we have seen the TD learning update rule and how TD learning is used to estimate the value of a state, in the next section, we will look into the TD prediction algorithm and get a clearer understanding of the TD learning method.

TD prediction algorithm

We learned that, in the prediction task, given a policy, we estimate the value function using the given policy. So, we can say what the expected return an agent can obtain in each state if it acts according to the given policy.

We learned that the TD learning update rule is given as:

$$V(s) = V(s) + \alpha(r + \gamma V(s') - V(s))$$

Thus, using this equation, we can estimate the value function of the given policy.

Before looking into the algorithm directly, for better understanding, first, let's manually calculate and see how exactly the value of a state is estimated using the TD learning update rule.

 The upcoming sections are explained with manual calculations, for a better understanding, follow along with a pen and paper.

Let's explore TD prediction with the Frozen Lake environment. We have learned that in the Frozen Lake environment, the goal of the agent is to reach the goal state **G** from the starting state **S** without visiting the hole states **H**. If the agent visits state **G**, we assign a reward of 1 and if it visits any other states, we assign a reward of 0. *Figure 5.2* shows the Frozen Lake environment:

	1	2	3	4
1	S	F	F	F
2	F	H	F	H
3	F	F	F	H
4	H	F	F	G

Figure 5.2: The Frozen Lake environment

We have four actions in our action space, which are *up, down, left*, and *right*, and we have 16 states from **S** to **G**. Instead of encoding the states and actions into numbers, for easier understanding, let's just keep them as they are. That is, let's just denote each action by the strings *up, down, left*, and *right*, and let's denote each state by their position in the grid. That is, the first state **S** is denoted by **(1,1)** and the second state **F** is denoted by **(1,2)** and so on to the last state **G**, which is denoted by **(4,4)**.

Now, let's learn how to perform TD prediction in the Frozen Lake environment. We know that in the TD prediction method, we will be given a policy and we predict the value function (state value) using a given policy. Let's suppose we are given the following policy. It basically tells us what action to perform in each state:

State	Action
(1,1)	Right
(1,2)	Right
(1,3)	Left
⋮	⋮
(4,4)	Down

Table 5.1: A policy

Now, we will see how to estimate the value function of the preceding policy using the TD learning method. Before going ahead, first, we initialize the values of all the states with random values, as shown here:

	1	2	3	4
1	S	F	F	F
2	F	H	F	H
3	F	F	F	F
4	H	F	F	G

State	Value
(1,1)	0.9
(1,2)	0.6
(1,3)	0.8
⋮	⋮
(4,4)	0.7

Figure 5.3: Initialize the states with random values

Say we are in state **(1,1)** and as per the given policy we take the *right* action and move to the next state **(1,2)**, and we receive a reward r of 0. Let's keep the learning rate α as 0.1 and the discount factor γ as 1 throughout this section. Now, how can we update the value of the state?

Recall the TD update equation:

$$V(s) = V(s) + \alpha(r + \gamma V(s') - V(s))$$

Substituting the value of state $V(s)$ with $V(1,1)$ and the next state $V(s')$ with $V(1,2)$ in the preceding equation, we can write:

$$V(1, 1) = V(1, 1) + \alpha(r + \gamma V(1, 2) - V(1, 1))$$

Substituting the reward $r = 0$, the learning rate $\alpha = 0.1$, and the discount factor $\gamma = 1$, we can write:

$$V(1, 1) = V(1, 1) + 0.1(0 + 1 \times V(1, 2) - V(1, 1))$$

We can get the state values from the value table shown earlier. That is, from the preceding value table, we can observe that the value of state **(1,1)** is 0.9 and the value of the next state **(1,2)** is 0.6. Substituting these values in the preceding equation, we can write:

$$V(1, 1) = 0.9 + 0.1(0 + 1 \times 0.6 - 0.9)$$

Thus, the value of state **(1,1)** becomes:

$$V(1, 1) = 0.87$$

So, we update the value of state **(1,1)** as **0.87** in the value table, as *Figure 5.4* shows:

Figure 5.4: The value of state (1,1) is updated

Now we are in state **(1,2)**. We select the *right* action according to the given policy in state **(1,2)** and move to the next state **(1,3)** and receive a reward *r* of 0. We can compute the value of the state as:

$$V(s) = V(s) + \alpha(r + \gamma V(s') - V(s))$$

Substituting the value of state $V(s)$ with $V(1,2)$ and the next state $V(s')$ with $V(1,3)$, we can write:

$$V(1, 2) = V(1, 2) + \alpha(r + \gamma V(1, 3) - V(1, 2))$$

Substituting the reward $r = 0$, the learning rate $\alpha = 0.1$, and the discount factor $\gamma = 1$, we can write:

$$V(1,2) = V(1,2) + 0.1(0 + 1 \times V(1,3) - V(1,2))$$

From the preceding value table, we can observe that the value of state **(1,2)** is 0.6 and the value of the next state **(1,3)** is 0.8, so we can write:

$$V(1,2) = 0.6 + 0.1(0 + 1 \times 0.8 - 0.6)$$

Thus, the value of state **(1,2)** becomes:

$$V(1,2) = 0.62$$

So, we update the value of state **(1,2)** to **0.62** in the value table, as *Figure 5.5* shows:

State	Value
(1,1)	0.87
(1,2)	0.62
(1,3)	0.8
⋮	⋮
(4,4)	0.7

Figure 5.5: The value of state (1,2) is updated

Now we are in state **(1,3)**. We select the *left* action according to our policy and move to the next state **(1,2)** and receive a reward r of 0. We can compute the value of the state as:

$$V(s) = V(s) + \alpha(r + \gamma V(s') - V(s))$$

Substituting the value of state $V(s)$ with $V(1,3)$ and the next state $V(s')$ with $V(1,2)$, we have:

$$V(1,3) = V(1,3) + \alpha(r + \gamma V(1,2) - V(1,3))$$

Substituting the reward $r = 0$, the learning rate $\alpha = 0.1$, and the discount factor $\gamma = 1$, we can write:

$$V(1,3) = V(1,3) + 0.1(0 + 1 \times V(1,2) - V(1,3))$$

Note that we use the updated values in every step, that is, the value of state **(1,2)** is updated with 0.62 in the previous step, as shown in the preceding value table. So, we substitute $V(1,2)$ with 0.62 and $V(1,3)$ with 0.8:

$$V(1,3) = 0.8 + 0.1(0 + 1 \times 0.62 - 0.8)$$

Thus, the value of state **(1,3)** becomes:

$$V(1,3) = 0.782$$

So, we update the value of state **(1,3)** to **0.782** in the value table, as *Figure 5.6* shows:

Figure 5.6: The value of state (1,3) is updated

Thus, in this way, we compute the value of every state using the given policy. However, computing the value of the state just for one episode will not be accurate. So, we repeat these steps for several episodes and compute the accurate estimates of the state value (the value function).

The TD prediction algorithm is given as follows:

1. Initialize a value function $V(s)$ with random values. A policy π is given.
2. For each episode:

    1. Initialize state s
    2. For each step in the episode:

        1. Perform an action a in state s according to given policy π, get the reward r, and move to the next state s'
        2. Update the value of the state to
           $$V(s) = V(s) + \alpha(r + \gamma V(s') - V(s))$$
        3. Update $s = s'$ (this step implies we are changing the next state s' to the current state s)
        4. If s is not the terminal state, repeat *steps 1 to 4*

Now that we have learned how the TD prediction method predicts the value function of the given policy, in the next section, let's learn how to implement the TD prediction method to predict the value of states in the Frozen Lake environment.

Predicting the value of states in the Frozen Lake environment

We have learned that in the prediction method, the policy is given as an input and we predict the value function using the given policy. So, let's initialize a random policy and predict the value function (state values) of the Frozen Lake environment using the random policy.

First, let's import the necessary libraries:

```
import gym
import pandas as pd
```

Now, we create the Frozen Lake environment using Gym:

```
env = gym.make('FrozenLake-v0')
```

Define the random policy, which returns the random action by sampling from the action space:

```
def random_policy():
    return env.action_space.sample()
```

Let's define the dictionary for storing the value of states, and we initialize the value of all the states to 0.0:

```
V = {}
for s in range(env.observation_space.n):
    V[s]=0.0
```

Initialize the discount factor γ and the learning rate α:

```
alpha = 0.85
gamma = 0.90
```

Set the number of episodes and the number of time steps in each episode:

```
num_episodes = 50000
num_timesteps = 1000
```

Compute the values of the states

Now, let's compute the value function (state values) using the given random policy.

For each episode:

```
for i in range(num_episodes):
```

Initialize the state by resetting the environment:

```
s = env.reset()
```

For every step in the episode:

```
for t in range(num_timesteps):
```

Select an action according to random policy:

```
a = random_policy()
```

Perform the selected action and store the next state information:

```
s_, r, done, _ = env.step(a)
```

Compute the value of the state as $V(s) = V(s) + \alpha(r + \gamma V(s') - V(s))$:

```
V[s] += alpha * (r + gamma * V[s_]-V[s])
```

Update the next state to the current state $s = s'$:

```
s = s_
```

If the current state is the terminal state, then break:

```
if done:
    break
```

After all the iterations, we will have values of all the states according to the given random policy.

Evaluating the values of the states

Now, let's evaluate our value function (state values). First, let's convert our value dictionary to a pandas data frame for more clarity:

```
df = pd.DataFrame(list(V.items()), columns=['state', 'value'])
```

Before checking the values of the states, let's recollect that in Gym, all the states in the Frozen Lake environment will be encoded into numbers. Since we have 16 states, all the states will be encoded into numbers from 0 to 15 as *Figure 5.7* shows:

0 S	1 F	2 F	3 F
4 F	5 H	6 F	7 H
8 F	9 F	10 F	11 H
12 H	13 F	14 F	15 G

Figure 5.7: States encoded as numbers

Now, Let's check the value of the states:

```
df
```

The preceding code will print:

	state	value
0	0	0.1241807
1	1	0.0024911
2	2	0.0001897
3	3	0.0000000
4	4	0.0242708
5	5	0.0000000
6	6	0.0008208
7	7	0.0000000
8	8	0.1605379
9	9	0.0230677
10	10	0.0035581
11	11	0.0000000
12	12	0.0000000
13	13	0.4063436
14	14	0.8770302
15	15	0.0000000

Figure 5.8: Value table

As we can observe, we now have the values of all the states. The value of state 14 is high since we can reach goal state 15 from state 14 easily, and also, as we can see, the values of all the terminal states (hole states and the goal state) are zero.

Note that since we have initialized a random policy, you might get varying results every time you run the previous code.

Now that we have understood how TD learning can be used for prediction tasks, in the next section, we will learn how to use TD learning for control tasks.

TD control

In the control method, our goal is to find the optimal policy, so we will start off with an initial random policy and then we will try to find the optimal policy iteratively. In the previous chapter, we learned that the control method can be classified into two categories:

- On-policy control
- Off-policy control

We learned what on-policy and off-policy control means in the previous chapter. Let's recap that a bit before going ahead. In the **on-policy control**, the agent behaves using one policy and tries to improve the same policy. That is, in the on-policy method, we generate episodes using one policy and improve the same policy iteratively to find the optimal policy. In the **off-policy control** method, the agent behaves using one policy and tries to improve a different policy. That is, in the off-policy method, we generate episodes using one policy and we try to improve a different policy iteratively to find the optimal policy.

Now, we will learn how to perform control tasks using TD learning. First, we will learn how to perform on-policy TD control and then we will learn about off-policy TD control.

On-policy TD control – SARSA

In this section, we will look into the popular on-policy TD control algorithm called **SARSA**, which stands for **State-Action-Reward-State-Action**. We know that in TD control our goal is to find the optimal policy. First, how can we extract a policy? We can extract the policy from the Q function. That is, once we have the Q function then we can extract policy by selecting the action in each state that has the maximum Q value.

Okay, how can we compute the Q function in TD learning? First, let's recall how we compute the value function. In TD learning, the value function is computed as:

$$V(s) = V(s) + \alpha(r + \gamma V(s') - V(s))$$

We can just rewrite this update rule in terms of the Q function as:

$$Q(s, a) = Q(s, a) + \alpha\big(r + \gamma Q(s', a') - Q(s, a)\big)$$

Now, we compute the Q function using the preceding TD learning update rule, and then we extract a policy from them. We can also call the preceding update rule as the SARSA update rule.

But wait! In the prediction method, we were given a policy as input, so we acted in the environment using that policy and computed the value function. But here, we don't have a policy as input. So how can we act in the environment?

So, first we initialize the Q function with random values or with zeros. Then we extract a policy from this randomly initialized Q function and act in the environment. Our initial policy will definitely not be optimal as it is extracted from the randomly initialized Q function, but on every episode, we will update the Q function (Q values). So, on every episode, we can use the updated Q function to extract a new policy. Thus, we will obtain the optimal policy after a series of episodes.

One important point we need to note is that in the SARSA method, instead of making our policy act greedily, we use the epsilon-greedy policy. That is, in a greedy policy, we always select the action that has the maximum Q value. But, with the epsilon-greedy policy we select a random action with probability epsilon, and we select the best action (the action with the maximum Q value) with probability 1-epsilon.

Before looking into the algorithm directly, for a better understanding, first, let's manually calculate and see how exactly the Q function (Q value) is estimated using the SARSA update rule and how we can find the optimal policy.

Let us consider the same Frozen Lake environment. Before going ahead, we initialize our Q table (Q function) with random values. *Figure 5.9* shows the Frozen Lake environment along with the Q table containing random values:

	1	2	3	4
1	S	F	F	F
2	F	H	F	H
3	F	F	F	H
4	H	F	F	G

State	Action	Value
(1,1)	Up	0.5
⋮	⋮	⋮
(4,2)	Up	0.3
(4,2)	Down	0.5
(4,2)	Left	0.1
(4,2)	Right	0.8
⋮	⋮	⋮
(4,4)	Right	0.5

Figure 5.9: The Frozen Lake environment and Q table with random values

Suppose we are in state **(4,2)**. Now we need to select an action in this state. How can we select an action? We learned that in the SARSA method, we select an action based on the epsilon-greedy policy. With probability epsilon, we select a random action and with probability 1-epsilon we select the best action (the action that has the maximum Q value). Suppose we use a probability 1-epsilon and select the best action. So, in state **(4,2)**, we move *right* as it has the highest Q value compared to the other actions, as shown here:

	1	2	3	4
1	S	F	F	F
2	F	H	F	H
3	F	F	F	H
4	H	F	F	G

State	Action	Value
(1,1)	Up	0.5
⋮	⋮	⋮
(4,2)	Up	0.3
(4,2)	Down	0.5
(4,2)	Left	0.1
(4,2)	Right	0.8
⋮	⋮	⋮
(4,4)	Right	0.5

Figure 5.10: Our agent is in state (4,2)

Okay, so, we perform the *right* action in state **(4,2)** and move to the next state **(4,3)** as *Figure 5.11* shows:

	1	2	3	4
1	S	F	F	F
2	F	H	F	H
3	F	F	F	H
4	H	F	F	G

Right

State	Action	Value
(1,1)	Up	0.5
⋮	⋮	⋮
(4,2)	Up	0.3
(4,2)	Down	0.5
(4,2)	Left	0.1
(4,2)	Right	0.8
⋮	⋮	⋮
(4,4)	Right	0.5

Figure 5.11: We perform the action with the maximum Q value in state (4,2)

Thus, we moved *right* in state **(4,2)** to the next state **(4,3)** and received a reward r of 0. Let's keep the learning rate α at 0.1, and the discount factor γ at 1. Now, how can we update the Q value?

Let recall our SARSA update rule:

$$Q(s,a) = Q(s,a) + \alpha(r + \gamma Q(s',a') - Q(s,a))$$

Substituting the state-action pair $Q(s,a)$ with $Q((4,2),\text{right})$ and the next state s' with **(4,3)** in the preceding equation, we can write:

$$Q((4,2),\text{right}) = Q((4,2),\text{right}) + \alpha(r + \gamma Q((4,3),a') - Q(4,2),\text{right})$$

Substituting the reward $r = 0$, the learning rate $\alpha = 0.1$, and the discount factor $\gamma = 1$, we can write:

$$Q((4,2),\text{right}) = Q((4,2),\text{right}) + 0.1(0 + 1 \times Q((4,3),a') - Q(4,2),\text{right})$$

From the previous Q table, we can observe that the Q value of $Q((4,2),\text{right})$ is **0.8**. Thus, substituting $Q((4,2),\text{right})$ with **0.8**, we can rewrite the preceding equation as:

$$Q((4,2),\text{right}) = 0.8 + 0.1(0 + 1 \times Q((4,3),a') - 0.8)$$

Okay, what about the term $Q((4,3),a')$? As you can see in the preceding equation, we have the term $Q((4,3),a')$, which represents the Q value of the next state-action pair.

Because we have moved to the next state **(4,3)**, we need to select an action in this state in order to compute the Q value of the next state-action pair. So, we use our same epsilon-greedy policy to select the action. That is, we select a random action with a probability of epsilon, or we select the best action that has the maximum Q value with a probability of 1-epsilon.

Suppose we use probability epsilon and select the random action. In state **(4,3)**, we select the *right* action randomly, as *Figure 5.12* shows. As you can see, although the *right* action does not have the maximum Q value, we selected it randomly with probability epsilon:

	1	2	3	4
1	S	F	F	F
2	F	H	F	H
3	F	F	F	H
4	H	F	F	G

State	Action	Value
(1,1)	Up	0.5
⋮	⋮	⋮
(4,2)	Left	0.1
(4,2)	Right	0.8
(4,3)	Up	0.1
(4,3)	Down	0.3
(4,3)	Left	1.0
(4,3)	Right	0.9
⋮	⋮	⋮
(4,4)	Right	0.5

Figure 5.12: We perform a random action in state (4,3)

Thus, now our update rule becomes:

$$Q((4,2), \text{right}) = 0.8 + 0.1\big(0 + 1 \times Q((4,3), \text{right}) - 0.8\big)$$

From the preceding Q table, we can see that the Q value of **Q((4,3), right)** is **0.9**. Thus, substituting the value of **Q((4,3), right)** with **0.9**, we can rewrite the above equation as:

$$Q((4,2), \text{right}) = 0.8 + 0.1(0 + 1(0.9) - 0.8)$$

Thus, our Q value becomes:

$$Q((4,2), \text{right}) = 0.81$$

Thus, in this way, we update the Q function by updating the Q value of the state-action pair in each step of the episode. After completing an episode, we extract a new policy from the updated Q function and uses this new policy to act in the environment. (Remember that our policy is always an epsilon-greedy policy). We repeat this steps for several episodes to find the optimal policy. The SARSA algorithm given in the following will help us understand this better.

The SARSA algorithm is given as follows:

1. Initialize a Q function $Q(s, a)$ with random values
2. For each episode:

    1. Initialize state s
    2. Extract a policy from $Q(s, a)$ and select an action a to perform in state s
    3. For each step in the episode:

        1. Perform the action a and move to the next state s' and observe the reward r
        2. In state s', select the action a' using the epsilon-greedy policy
        3. Update the Q value to
        $$Q(s, a) = Q(s, a) + \alpha(r + \gamma Q(s', a') - Q(s, a))$$
        4. Update $s = s'$ and $a = a'$ (update the next state s'-action a' pair to the current state s-action a pair)
        5. If s is not a terminal state, repeat *steps 1 to 5*

Now that we have learned how the SARSA algorithm works, in the next section, let's implement the SARSA algorithm to find the optimal policy.

Computing the optimal policy using SARSA

Now, let's implement SARSA to find the optimal policy in the Frozen Lake environment.

First, let's import the necessary libraries:

```
import gym
import random
```

Now, we create the Frozen Lake environment using Gym:

```
env = gym.make('FrozenLake-v0')
```

Let's define the dictionary for storing the Q value of the state-action pair and initialize the Q value of all the state-action pairs to `0.0`:

```
Q = {}
for s in range(env.observation_space.n):
    for a in range(env.action_space.n):
        Q[(s,a)] = 0.0
```

Now, let's define the epsilon-greedy policy. We generate a random number from the uniform distribution and if the random number is less than epsilon, we select the random action, else we select the best action that has the maximum Q value:

```
def epsilon_greedy(state, epsilon):
    if random.uniform(0,1) < epsilon:
        return env.action_space.sample()
    else:
        return max(list(range(env.action_space.n)), key = lambda x:
Q[(state,x)])
```

Initialize the discount factor γ, the learning rate α, and the epsilon value:

```
alpha = 0.85
gamma = 0.90
epsilon = 0.8
```

Set the number of episodes and number of time steps in the episode:

```
num_episodes = 50000
num_timesteps = 1000
```

Compute the policy

For each episode:

```
for i in range(num_episodes):
```

Initialize the state by resetting the environment:

```
s = env.reset()
```

Select the action using the epsilon-greedy policy:

```
a = epsilon_greedy(s,epsilon)
```

For each step in the episode:

```
for t in range(num_timesteps):
```

Perform the selected action and store the next state information:

```
s_, r, done, _ = env.step(a)
```

Select the action a' in the next state s' using the epsilon-greedy policy:

```
a_ = epsilon_greedy(s_,epsilon)
```

Compute the Q value of the state-action pair as
$Q(s, a) = Q(s, a) + \alpha(r + \gamma Q(s', a') - Q(s, a))$:

```
Q[(s,a)] += alpha * (r + gamma * Q[(s_,a_)]-Q[(s,a)])
```

Update $s = s'$ and $a = a'$ (update the next state s'-action a' pair to the current state s-action a pair):

```
s = s_
a = a_
```

If the current state is the terminal state, then break:

```
if done:
    break
```

Note that on every iteration we update the Q function. After all the iterations, we will have the optimal Q function. Once we have the optimal Q function then we can extract the optimal policy by selecting the action that has the maximum Q value in each state.

Off-policy TD control – Q learning

In this section, we will learn the off-policy TD control algorithm called Q learning. It is one of the very popular algorithms in reinforcement learning, and we will see that this algorithm keeps coming up in other chapters too. Q learning is an off-policy algorithm, meaning that we use two different policies, one policy for behaving in the environment (selecting an action in the environment) and the other for finding the optimal policy.

We learned that in the SARSA method, we select action a in state s using the epsilon-greedy policy, move to the next state s', and update the Q value using the update rule shown here:

$$Q(s, a) = Q(s, a) + \alpha(r + \gamma Q(s', a') - Q(s, a))$$

In the preceding equation, in order to compute the Q value of next state-action pair, $Q(s', a')$, we need to select an action. So, we select the action using the same epsilon-greedy policy and update the Q value of the next state-action pair.

But unlike SARSA, in Q learning, we use two different policies. One is the epsilon-greedy policy and the other is a greedy policy. To select an action in the environment we use an epsilon-greedy policy, but while updating the Q value of the next state-action pair we use a greedy policy.

That is, we select action a in state s using the epsilon-greedy policy and move to the next state s' and update the Q value using the update rule shown below:

$$Q(s, a) = Q(s, a) + \alpha\big(r + \gamma Q(s', a') - Q(s, a)\big)$$

In the preceding equation, in order to compute the Q value of the next state-action pair, $Q(s', a')$, we need to select an action. Here, we select the action using the greedy policy and update the Q value of the next state-action pair. We know that the greedy policy always selects the action that has the maximum value. So, we can modify the equation to:

$$Q(s, a) = Q(s, a) + \alpha\left(r + \gamma \max_{a'} Q(s', a') - Q(s, a)\right)$$

As we can observe from the preceding equation, the **max** operator implies that in state s', we select the action a' that has the maximum Q value.

Thus, to sum up, in the Q learning method we select an action in the environment using the epsilon-greedy policy, but while computing the Q value of the next state-action pair we use the greedy policy. Thus, update rule of Q learning is given as:

$$Q(s, a) = Q(s, a) + \alpha\left(r + \gamma \max_{a'} Q(s', a') - Q(s, a)\right)$$

Let's understand this better by manually calculating the Q value using our Q learning update rule. Let's use the same Frozen Lake example. We initialize our Q table with random values. *Figure 5.13* shows the Frozen Lake environment, along with the Q table containing random values:

	1	2	3	4
1	S	F	F	F
2	F	H	F	H
3	F	F	F	H
4	H	F	F	G

State	Action	Value
(1,1)	Up	0.5
⋮	⋮	⋮
(3,2)	Up	0.1
(3,2)	Down	0.8
(3,2)	Left	0.5
(3,2)	Right	0.6
⋮	⋮	⋮
(4,4)	Right	0.5

Figure 5.13: The Frozen Lake environment with a randomly initialized Q table

Suppose we are in state **(3,2)**. Now, we need to select some action in this state. How can we select an action? We select an action using the epsilon-greedy policy. So, with probability epsilon, we select a random action and with probability 1-epsilon we select the best action that has the maximum Q value.

Say we use probability 1-epsilon and select the best action. So, in state **(3,2)**, we select the *down* action as it has the highest Q value compared to other actions in that state, as *Figure 5.14* shows:

	1	2	3	4
1	S	F	F	F
2	F	H	F	H
3	F	F	F	H
4	H	F	F	G

State	Action	Value
(1,1)	Up	0.5
⋮	⋮	⋮
(3,2)	Up	0.1
(3,2)	Down	0.8
(3,2)	Left	0.5
(3,2)	Right	0.6
⋮	⋮	⋮
(4,4)	Right	0.5

Figure 5.14: We perform the action with the maximum Q value in state (3,2)

Okay, so, we perform the *down* action in state **(3,2)** and move to the next state **(4,2)**, as *Figure 5.15* shows:

State	Action	Value
(1,1)	Up	0.5
⋮	⋮	⋮
(3,2)	Up	0.1
(3,2)	Down	0.8
(3,2)	Left	0.5
(3,2)	Right	0.6
⋮	⋮	⋮
(4,4)	Right	0.5

Figure 5.15: We move down to state (4,2)

Thus, we move *down* in state **(3,2)** to the next state **(4,2)** and receive a reward *r* of 0. Let's keep the learning rate α as 0.1, and the discount factor γ as 1. Now, how can we update the Q value?

Let's recall our Q learning update rule:

$$Q(s, a) = Q(s, a) + \alpha \left(r + \gamma \max_{a'} Q(s', a') - Q(s, a) \right)$$

Substituting the state-action pair $Q(s,a)$ with $Q((3,2),\text{down})$ and the next state s' with **(4,2)** in the preceding equation, we can write:

$$Q((3, 2), \text{down}) = Q((3, 2), \text{down}) + \alpha \left(r + \gamma \max_{a'} Q((4, 2), a') - Q(3, 2), \text{down} \right)$$

Substituting the reward, $r = 0$, the learning rate $\alpha = 0.1$, and the discount factor $\gamma = 1$, we can write:

$$Q((3,2), \text{down}) = Q((3,2), \text{down}) + 0.1 \left(0 + 1 \times \max_{a'} Q((4, 2), a') - Q(3, 2), \text{down} \right)$$

From the previous Q table, we can observe that the Q value of $Q((3,2), \text{down})$ is **0.8**. Thus, substituting $Q((3,2), \text{down})$ with **0.8**, we can rewrite the preceding equation as:

$$Q((3,2), \text{down}) = 0.8 + 0.1\left(0 + 1 \times \max_{a'} Q\big((4,2), a'\big) - 0.8\right)$$

As we can observe, in the preceding equation we have the term $\max_{a} Q\big((4,2), a'\big)$, which represents the Q value of the next state-action pair as we moved to the new state **(4,2)**. In order to compute the Q value for the next state, first we need to select an action. Here, we select an action using the greedy policy, that is, the action that has maximum Q value.

As *Figure 5.16* shows, the *right* action has the maximum Q value in state **(4,2)**. So, we select the *right* action and update the Q value of the next state-action pair:

State	Action	Value
(1,1)	Up	0.5
⋮	⋮	⋮
(4,2)	Up	0.3
(4,2)	Down	0.5
(4,2)	Left	0.1
(4,2)	Right	0.8
⋮	⋮	⋮
(4,4)	Right	0.5

Figure 5.16: We perform the action with the maximum Q value in state (4,2)

Thus, now our update rule becomes:

$$Q((3,2), \text{down}) = 0.8 + 0.1\big(0 + 1 \times Q((4,2), \text{right}) - 0.8\big)$$

From the previous Q table, we can observe that the Q value of $Q((4,2), \text{right})$ is **0.8**. Thus, substituting the value of $Q((4,2), \text{right})$ with **0.8**, we can rewrite the above equation as:

$$Q((3,2), \text{down}) = 0.8 + 0.1(0 + 1 \times 0.8 - 0.8)$$

Thus, our Q value becomes:

$$Q((3, 2), \text{down} = 0.8$$

Similarly, we update the Q value for all state-action pairs. That is, we select an action in the environment using an epsilon-greedy policy, and while updating the Q value of the next state-action pair we use the greedy policy. Thus, we update the Q value for every state-action pair.

Thus, in this way, we update the Q function by updating the Q value of the state-action pair in each step of the episode. We will extract a new policy from the updated Q function on every step of the episode and uses this new policy. (Remember that we select an action in the environment using epsilon-greedy policy but while updating Q value of the next state-action pair we use the greedy policy). After several episodes, we will have the optimal Q function. The Q learning algorithm given in the following will help us to understand this better.

The Q learning algorithm is given as follows:

1. Initialize a Q function $Q(s, a)$ with random values
2. For each episode:

    1. Initialize state s
    2. For each step in the episode:

        1. Extract a policy from $Q(s, a)$ and select an action a to perform in state s
        2. Perform the action a, move to the next state s', and observe the reward r
        3. Update the Q value as
            $$Q(s, a) = Q(s, a) + \alpha \left(r + \gamma \max_{a'} Q(s'a') - Q(s, a) \right)$$
        4. Update $s = s'$ (update the next state s' to the current state s)
        5. If s is not a terminal state, repeat *steps 1 to 5*

Now that we have learned how the Q learning algorithm works, in the next section, let's implement Q learning to find the optimal policy.

Computing the optimal policy using Q learning

Now, let's implement Q learning to find the optimal policy in the Frozen Lake environment.

First, let's import the necessary libraries:

```
import gym
import numpy as np
import random
```

Now, we create the Frozen Lake environment using Gym:

```
env = gym.make('FrozenLake-v0')
```

Let's define the dictionary for storing the Q values of the state-action pairs, and initialize the Q values of all the state-action pairs to `0.0`:

```
Q = {}
for s in range(env.observation_space.n):
    for a in range(env.action_space.n):
        Q[(s,a)] = 0.0
```

Now, let's define the epsilon-greedy policy. We generate a random number from the uniform distribution, and if the random number is less than epsilon we select the random action, else we select the best action that has the maximum Q value:

```
def epsilon_greedy(state, epsilon):
    if random.uniform(0,1) < epsilon:
        return env.action_space.sample()
    else:
        return max(list(range(env.action_space.n)), key = lambda x:
Q[(state,x)])
```

Initialize the discount factor γ, the learning rate α, and the epsilon value:

```
alpha = 0.85
gamma = 0.90
epsilon = 0.8
```

Set the number of episodes and the number of time steps in the episode:

```
num_episodes = 50000
num_timesteps = 1000
```

Compute the policy.

For each episode:

```
for i in range(num_episodes):
```

Initialize the state by resetting the environment:

```
s = env.reset()
```

For each step in the episode:

```
for t in range(num_timesteps):
```

Select the action using the epsilon-greedy policy:

```
a = epsilon_greedy(s,epsilon)
```

Perform the selected action and store the next state information:

```
s_, r, done, _ = env.step(a)
```

Now, let's compute the Q value of the state-action pair as $Q(s,a) = Q(s,a) + \alpha\left(r + \gamma \max_{a'} Q(s',a') - Q(s,a)\right)$.

First, select the action a' that has the maximum Q value in the next state s':

```
a_ = np.argmax([Q[(s_, a)] for a in range(env.action_space.n)])
```

Now, we can compute the Q value of the state-action pair as:

```
Q[(s,a)] += alpha * (r + gamma * Q[(s_,a_)]-Q[(s,a)])
```

Update $s = s'$ (update the next state s' to the current state s):

```
s = s_
```

If the current state is the terminal state, then break:

```
if done:
    break
```

After all the iterations, we will have the optimal Q function. Then we can extract the optimal policy by selecting the action that has the maximum Q value in each state.

The difference between Q learning and SARSA

Understanding the difference between Q learning and SARSA is very important. So, let's do a little recap on how Q learning and SARSA differ.

SARSA is an on-policy algorithm, meaning that we use a single epsilon-greedy policy for selecting an action in the environment and also to compute the Q value of the next state-action pair. The update rule of SARSA is given as follows:

$$Q(s,a) = Q(s,a) + \alpha\big(r + \gamma Q(s',a') - Q(s,a)\big)$$

Q learning is an off-policy algorithm, meaning that we use an epsilon-greedy policy for selecting an action in the environment, but to compute the Q value of next state-action pair we use a greedy policy. The update rule of Q learning is given as follows:

$$Q(s,a) = Q(s,a) + \alpha\left(r + \gamma \max_{a'} Q(s',a') - Q(s,a)\right)$$

Comparing the DP, MC, and TD methods

So far, we have learned several interesting and important reinforcement learning algorithms, such as DP (value iteration and policy iteration), MC methods, and TD learning methods, to find the optimal policy. These are called the key algorithms in classic reinforcement learning, and understanding the differences between these three algorithms is very important. So, in this section, we will recap the differences between the DP, MC, and TD learning methods.

Dynamic programming (**DP**), that is, the value and policy iteration methods, is a model-based method, meaning that we compute the optimal policy using the model dynamics of the environment. We cannot apply the DP method when we don't have the model dynamics of the environment.

We also learned about the **Monte Carlo** (**MC**) method. MC is a model-free method, meaning that we compute the optimal policy without using the model dynamics of the environment. But one problem we face with the MC method is that it is applicable only to episodic tasks and not to continuous tasks.

We learned about another interesting model-free method called **temporal difference** (**TD**) learning. TD learning takes advantage of both DP by bootstrapping and the MC method by being model free.

Many congratulations on learning about all the important reinforcement learning algorithms. In the next chapter, we will look into a case study called the multi-armed bandit problem.

Summary

We started off the chapter by understanding what TD learning is and how it takes advantage of both DP and the MC method. We learned that, just like DP, TD learning bootstraps, and just like the MC method, TD learning is a model-free method.

Later, we learned how to perform a prediction task using TD learning, and then we looked into the algorithm of the TD prediction method.

Going forward, we learned how to use TD learning for a control task. First, we learned about the on-policy TD control method called SARSA, and then we learned about the off-policy TD control method called Q learning. We also learned how to find the optimal policy in the Frozen Lake environment using the SARSA and Q learning methods.

We also learned the difference between SARSA and Q learning methods. We understood that SARSA is an on-policy algorithm, meaning that we use a single epsilon-greedy policy to select an action in the environment and also to compute the Q value of the next state-action pair, whereas Q learning is an off-policy algorithm, meaning that we use an epsilon-greedy policy to select an action in the environment but to compute the Q value of the next state-action pair we use a greedy policy. At the end of the chapter, we compared the DP, MC, and TD methods.

In the next chapter, we will look into an interesting problem called the multi-armed bandit problem.

Questions

Let's evaluate our newly acquired knowledge by answering the following questions:

1. How does TD learning differ from the MC method?
2. What is the advantage of using the TD learning method?
3. What is TD error?
4. What is the update rule of TD learning?
5. How does the TD prediction method work?
6. What is SARSA?
7. How does Q learning differ from SARSA?

Further reading

For further information, refer to the following link:

- **Learning to Predict by the Methods of Temporal Differences** by *Richard S. Sutton*, available at https://link.springer.com/content/pdf/10.1007/BF00115009.pdf

6
Case Study – The MAB Problem

So far in the previous chapters, we have learned the fundamental concepts of reinforcement learning and also several interesting reinforcement learning algorithms. We learned about a model-based method called dynamic programming and a model-free method called the Monte Carlo method, and then we learned about the temporal difference method, which combines the advantages of dynamic programming and the Monte Carlo method.

In this chapter, we will learn about one of the classic problems in reinforcement learning called the **multi-armed bandit** (**MAB**) problem. We start the chapter by understanding the MAB problem, and then we will learn about several exploration strategies, called epsilon-greedy, softmax exploration, upper confidence bound, and Thompson sampling, for solving the MAB problem. Following this, we will learn how a MAB is useful in real-world use cases.

Moving forward, we will understand how to find the best advertisement banner that is clicked on most frequently by users by framing it as a MAB problem. At the end of the chapter, we will learn about contextual bandits and how they are used in different use cases.

In this chapter, we will learn about the following:

- The MAB problem
- The epsilon-greedy method
- Softmax exploration

- The upper confidence bound algorithm
- The Thompson sampling algorithm
- Applications of MAB
- Finding the best advertisement banner using MAB
- Contextual bandits

The MAB problem

The MAB problem is one of the classic problems in reinforcement learning. A MAB is a slot machine where we pull the arm (lever) and get a payout (reward) based on some probability distribution. A single slot machine is called a one-armed bandit and when there are multiple slot machines it is called a MAB or k-armed bandit, where k denotes the number of slot machines.

Figure 6.1 shows a 3-armed bandit:

Figure 6.1: 3-armed bandit slot machines

Slot machines are one of the most popular games in the casino, where we pull the arm and get a reward. If we get 0 reward then we lose the game, and if we get +1 reward then we win the game. There can be several slot machines, and each slot machine is referred to as an arm. For instance, slot machine 1 is referred to as arm 1, slot machine 2 is referred to as arm 2, and so on. Thus, whenever we say arm n, it actually means that we are referring to slot machine n.

Each arm has its own probability distribution indicating the probability of winning and losing the game. For example, let's suppose we have two arms. Let the probability of winning if we pull arm 1 (slot machine 1) be 0.7 and the probability of winning if we pull arm 2 (slot machine 2) be 0.5.

Then, if we pull arm 1, 70% of the time we win the game and get the +1 reward, and if we pull arm 2, then 50% of the time we win the game and get the +1 reward.

Thus, we can say that pulling arm 1 is desirable as it makes us win the game 70% of the time. However, this probability distribution of the arm (slot machine) will not be given to us. We need to find out which arm helps us to win the game most of the time and gives us a good reward.

Okay, how can we find this?

Say we pulled arm 1 once and received a +1 reward, and we pulled arm 2 once and received a 0 reward. Since arm 1 gives a +1 reward, we cannot come to the conclusion that arm 1 is the best arm immediately after pulling it only once. We need to pull both of the arms many times and compute the average reward we obtain from each of the arms, and then we can select the arm that gives the maximum average reward as the best arm.

Let's denote the arm by a and define the average reward by pulling the arm a as:

$$Q(a) = \frac{\text{Sum of rewards obtained from the arm}}{\text{Number of times the arm was pulled}}$$

Where $Q(a)$ denotes the average reward of arm a.

The optimal arm a^* is the one that gives us the maximum average reward, that is:

$$a^* = \arg\max_a Q(a)$$

Okay, we have learned that the arm that gives the maximum average reward is the optimal arm. But how can we find this?

We play the game for several rounds and we can pull only one arm in each round. Say in the first round we pull arm 1 and observe the reward, and in the second round we pull arm 2 and observe the reward. Similarly, in every round, we keep pulling arm 1 or arm 2 and observe the reward. After completing several rounds of the game, we compute the average reward of each of the arms, and then we select the arm that has the maximum average reward as the best arm.

But this is not a good approach to find the best arm. Say we have 20 arms; if we keep pulling a different arm in each round, then in most of the rounds we will lose the game and get a 0 reward. Along with finding the best arm, our goal should be to minimize the cost of identifying the best arm, and this is usually referred to as regret.

Thus, we need to find the best arm while minimizing regret. That is, we need to find the best arm, but we don't want to end up selecting the arms that make us lose the game in most of the rounds.

So, should we explore a different arm in each round, or should we select only the arm that got us a good reward in the previous rounds? This leads to a situation called the exploration-exploitation dilemma, which we learned about in *Chapter 4, Monte Carlo Methods.* So, to resolve this, we use the epsilon-greedy method and select the arm that got us a good reward in the previous rounds with probability 1-epsilon and select the random arm with probability epsilon. After completing several rounds, we select the best arm as the one that has the maximum average reward.

Similar to the epsilon-greedy method, there are several different exploration strategies that help us to overcome the exploration-exploitation dilemma. In the upcoming section, we will learn more about several different exploration strategies in detail and how they help us to find the optimal arm, but first let's look at creating a bandit.

Creating a bandit in the Gym

Before going ahead, let's learn how to create a bandit environment with the Gym toolkit. The Gym does not come with a prepackaged bandit environment. So, we need to create a bandit environment and integrate it with the Gym. Instead of creating the bandit environment from scratch, we will use the open-source version of the bandit environment provided by Jesse Cooper.

First, let's clone the Gym bandits repository:

```
git clone https://github.com/JKCooper2/gym-bandits
```

Next, we can install it using pip:

```
cd gym-bandits
pip install -e .
```

After installation, we import gym_bandits and also the gym library:

```
import gym_bandits
import gym
```

gym_bandits provides several versions of the bandit environment. We can examine the different bandit versions at https://github.com/JKCooper2/gym-bandits.

Let's just create a simple 2-armed bandit whose environment ID is
`BanditTwoArmedHighLowFixed-v0`:

```
env = gym.make("BanditTwoArmedHighLowFixed-v0")
```

Since we created a 2-armed bandit, our action space will be 2 (as there are two arms),
as shown here:

```
print(env.action_space.n)
```

The preceding code will print:

```
2
```

We can also check the probability distribution of the arm with:

```
print(env.p_dist)
```

The preceding code will print:

```
[0.8, 0.2]
```

It indicates that, with arm 1, we win the game 80% of the time and with arm 2, we
win the game 20% of the time. Our goal is to find out whether pulling arm 1 or arm 2
makes us win the game most of the time.

Now that we have learned how to create bandit environments in the Gym, in the
next section, we will explore different exploration strategies to solve the MAB
problem and we will implement them with the Gym.

Exploration strategies

At the beginning of the chapter, we learned about the exploration-exploitation
dilemma in the MAB problem. To overcome this, we use different exploration
strategies and find the best arm. The different exploration strategies are listed here:

- Epsilon-greedy
- Softmax exploration
- Upper confidence bound
- Thomson sampling

Now, we will explore all of these exploration strategies in detail and implement them
to find the best arm.

Epsilon-greedy

We learned about the epsilon-greedy algorithm in the previous chapters. With epsilon-greedy, we select the best arm with a probability 1-epsilon and we select a random arm with a probability epsilon. Let's take a simple example and learn how to find the best arm with the epsilon-greedy method in more detail.

Say we have two arms—arm 1 and arm 2. Suppose with arm 1 we win the game 80% of the time and with arm 2 we win the game 20% of the time. So, we can say that arm 1 is the best arm as it makes us win the game 80% of the time. Now, let's learn how to find this with the epsilon-greedy method.

First, we initialize the count (the number of times the arm is pulled), sum_rewards (the sum of rewards obtained from pulling the arm), and Q (the average reward obtained by pulling the arm), as *Table 6.1* shows:

arm	count	sum_rewards	Q
arm 1	0	0	0
arm 2	0	0	0

Table 6.1: Initialize the variables with zero

Round 1:

Say, in round 1 of the game, we select a random arm with a probability epsilon, and suppose we randomly pull arm 1 and observe the reward. Let the reward obtained by pulling arm 1 be 1. So, we update our table with count of arm 1 set to 1, and sum_rewards of arm 1 set to 1, and thus the average reward Q of arm 1 after round 1 is 1 as *Table 6.2* shows:

arm	count	sum_rewards	Q
arm 1	1	1	1
arm 2	0	0	0

Table 6.2: Results after round 1

Round 2:

Say, in round 2, we select the best arm with a probability 1-epsilon. The best arm is the one that has the maximum average reward. So, we check our table to see which arm has the maximum average reward. Since arm 1 has the maximum average reward, we pull arm 1 and observe the reward and let the reward obtained from pulling arm 1 be 1.

So, we update our table with count of arm 1 to 2 and sum_rewards of arm 1 to 2, and thus the average reward Q of arm 1 after round 2 is 1 as *Table 6.3* shows:

arm	count	sum_rewards	Q
arm 1	2	2	1
arm 2	0	0	0

Table 6.3: Results after round 2

Round 3:

Say, in round 3, we select a random arm with a probability epsilon. Suppose we randomly pull arm 2 and observe the reward. Let the reward obtained by pulling arm 2 be 0. So, we update our table with count of arm 2 set to 1 and sum_rewards of arm 2 set to 0, and thus the average reward Q of arm 2 after round 3 is 0 as *Table 6.4* shows:

arm	count	sum_rewards	Q
arm 1	2	2	1
arm 2	1	0	0

Table 6.4: Results after round 3

Round 4:

Say, in round 4, we select the best arm with a probability 1-epsilon. So, we pull arm 1 since it has the maximum average reward. Let the reward obtained by pulling arm 1 be 0 this time. Now, we update our table with count of arm 1 to 3 and sum_rewards of arm 2 to 2, and thus the average reward Q of arm 1 after round 4 will be 0.66 as *Table 6.5* shows:

arm	count	sum_rewards	Q
arm 1	3	2	0.66
arm 2	1	0	0

Table 6.5: Results after round 4

We repeat this process for several rounds; that is, for several rounds of the game, we pull the best arm with a probability 1-epsilon and we pull a random arm with probability epsilon.

Table 6.6 shows the updated table after 100 rounds of the game:

arm	count	sum_rewards	Q
arm 1	75	61	0.81
arm 2	25	2	0.08

Table 6.6: Results after 100 rounds

From *Table 6.6*, we can conclude that arm 1 is the best arm since it has the maximum average reward.

Implementing epsilon-greedy

Now, let's learn to implement the epsilon-greedy method to find the best arm. First, let's import the necessary libraries:

```
import gym
import gym_bandits
import numpy as np
```

For better understanding, let's create the bandit with only two arms:

```
env = gym.make("BanditTwoArmedHighLowFixed-v0")
```

Let's check the probability distribution of the arm:

```
print(env.p_dist)
```

The preceding code will print:

```
[0.8, 0.2]
```

We can observe that with arm 1 we win the game with 80% probability and with arm 2 we win the game with 20% probability. Here, the best arm is arm 1, as with arm 1 we win the game with 80% probability. Now, let's see how to find this best arm using the epsilon-greedy method.

First, let's initialize the variables.

Initialize the count for storing the number of times an arm is pulled:

```
count = np.zeros(2)
```

Initialize `sum_rewards` for storing the sum of rewards of each arm:

```
sum_rewards = np.zeros(2)
```

Initialize Q for storing the average reward of each arm:

```
Q = np.zeros(2)
```

Set the number of rounds (iterations):

```
num_rounds = 100
```

Now, let's define the `epsilon_greedy` function.

First, we generate a random number from a uniform distribution. If the random number is less than epsilon, then we pull the random arm; else, we pull the best arm that has the maximum average reward, as shown here:

```
def epsilon_greedy(epsilon):

    if np.random.uniform(0,1) < epsilon:
        return env.action_space.sample()
    else:
        return np.argmax(Q)
```

Now, let's play the game and try to find the best arm using the epsilon-greedy method.

For each round:

```
for i in range(num_rounds):
```

Select the arm based on the epsilon-greedy method:

```
arm = epsilon_greedy(epsilon=0.5)
```

Pull the arm and store the reward and next state information:

```
next_state, reward, done, info = env.step(arm)
```

Increment the count of the arm by 1:

```
count[arm] += 1
```

Update the sum of rewards of the arm:

```
sum_rewards[arm]+=reward
```

Update the average reward of the arm:

```
Q[arm] = sum_rewards[arm]/count[arm]
```

After all the rounds, we look at the average reward obtained from each of the arms:

```
print(Q)
```

The preceding code will print something like this:

```
[0.83783784 0.34615385]
```

Now, we can select the optimal arm as the one that has the maximum average reward:

$$a^* = \arg\max_a Q(a)$$

Since arm 1 has a higher average reward than arm 2, our optimal arm will be arm 1:

```
print('The optimal arm is arm {}'.format(np.argmax(Q)+1))
```

The preceding code will print:

```
The optimal arm is arm 1
```

Thus, we have found the optimal arm using the epsilon-greedy method.

Softmax exploration

Softmax exploration, also known as Boltzmann exploration, is another useful exploration strategy for finding the optimal arm.

In the epsilon-greedy policy, we learned that we select the best arm with probability 1-epsilon and a random arm with probability epsilon. As you may have noticed, in the epsilon-greedy policy, all the non-best arms are explored equally. That is, all the non-best arms have a uniform probability of being selected. For example, say we have 4 arms and arm 1 is the best arm. Then we explore the non-best arms – [arm 2, arm 3, arm 4] – uniformly.

Say arm 3 is never a good arm and it always gives a reward of 0. In this case, instead of exploring arm 3 again, we can spend more time exploring arm 2 and arm 4. But the problem with the epsilon-greedy method is that we explore all the non-best arms equally. So, all the non-best arms – [arm 2, arm 3, arm 4] – will be explored equally.

To avoid this, if we can give priority to arm 2 and arm 4 over arm 3, then we can explore arm 2 and arm 4 more than arm 3.

Okay, but how can we give priority to the arms? We can give priority to the arms by assigning a probability to all the arms based on the average reward Q. The arm that has the maximum average reward will have high probability, and all the non-best arms have a probability proportional to their average reward.

For instance, as *Table 6.7* shows, arm 1 is the best arm as it has a high average reward Q. So, we assign a high probability to arm 1. Arms 2, 3, and 4 are the non-best arms, and we need to explore them. As we can observe, arm 3 has an average reward of 0. So, instead of selecting all the non-best arms uniformly, we give more priority to arms 2 and 4 than arm 3. So, the probability of arm 2 and 4 will be high compared to arm 3:

arm	Q
arm 1	0.84
arm 2	0.24
arm 3	0.0
arm 4	0.13

Table 6.7: Average reward for a 4-armed bandit

Thus, in softmax exploration, we select the arms based on a probability. The probability of each arm is directly proportional to its average reward:

$$p_t(a) \propto Q_t(a)$$

But wait, the probabilities should sum to 1, right? The average reward (Q value) will not sum to 1. So, we convert them into probabilities with the softmax function, as shown here:

$$P_t(a) \propto \frac{\exp(Q_t(a))}{\sum_{i=1}^{n} \exp(Q_t(i))} \qquad (1)$$

So, now the arm will be selected based on the probability. However, in the initial rounds we will not know the correct average reward of each arm, so selecting the arm based on the probability of average reward will be inaccurate in the initial rounds. To avoid this, we introduce a new parameter called T. T is called the temperature parameter.

We can rewrite the preceding equation with the temperature T, as shown here:

$$P_t(a) \propto \frac{\exp(Q_t(a)/T)}{\sum_{i=1}^{n} \exp(Q_t(i)/T)} \qquad (2)$$

Okay, how will this T help us? When T is high, all the arms have an equal probability of being selected and when T is low, the arm that has the maximum average reward will have a high probability. So, we set T to a high number in the initial rounds, and after a series of rounds we reduce the value of T. This means that in the initial round we explore all the arms equally and after a series of rounds, we select the best arm that has a high probability.

Let's understand this with a simple example. Say we have four arms, arm 1 to arm 4. Suppose we pull arm 1 and receive a reward of 1. Then the average reward of arm 1 will be 1 and the average reward of all other arms will be 0, as *Table 6.8* shows:

arm	Q
arm 1	1
arm 2	0
arm 3	0
arm 4	0

Table 6.8: Average reward for each arm

Now, if we convert the average reward to probabilities using the softmax function given in equation (1), then our probabilities look like the following:

arm	Q	probability
arm 1	1	0.475
arm 2	0	0.174
arm 3	0	0.174
arm 4	0	0.174

Table 6.9: Probability of each arm

As we can observe, we have a 47% probability for arm 1 and a 17% probability for all other arms. But we cannot assign a high probability to arm 1 by just pulling arm 1 once. So, we set T to a high number, say $T = 30$, and calculate the probabilities based on equation (2). Now our probabilities become:

arm	Q	probability
arm 1	1	0.253
arm 2	0	0.248
arm 3	0	0.248
arm 4	0	0.248

Table 6.10: Probability of each arm with T=30

As we can see, now all the arms have equal probabilities of being selected. Now we explore the arms based on this probability and over a series of rounds, the T value will be reduced, and we will have a high probability to the best arm. Let's suppose after some 30 rounds, the average reward of all the arms is:

arm	Q
arm 1	0.84
arm 2	0.24
arm 3	0.0
arm 4	0.13

Table 6.11: Average reward for each arm after 30+ rounds

We learned that the value of T is reduced over several rounds. Suppose the value of T is reduced and it is now 0.3 ($T=0.3$); then the probabilities will become:

arm	Q	probability
arm 1	0.84	0.775
arm 2	0.24	0.104
arm 3	0.0	0.047
arm 4	0.13	0.072

Table 6.12: Probabilities for each arm with T now set to 0.3

As we can see, arm 1 has a high probability compared to other arms. So, we select arm 1 as the best arm and explore the non-best arms – [arm 2, arm 3, arm 4] – based on their probabilities in the next rounds.

Thus, in the initial round, we don't know which arm is the best arm. So instead of assigning a high probability to the arm based on the average reward, we assign an equal probability to all the arms in the initial round with a high value of T and over a series of rounds, we reduce the value of T and assign a high probability to the arm that has a high average reward.

Implementing softmax exploration

Now, let's learn how to implement softmax exploration to find the best arm. First, let's import the necessary libraries:

```
import gym
import gym_bandits
import numpy as np
```

Let's take the same two-armed bandit we saw in the epsilon-greedy section:

```
env = gym.make("BanditTwoArmedHighLowFixed-v0")
```

Now, let's initialize the variables.

Initialize count for storing the number of times an arm is pulled:

```
count = np.zeros(2)
```

Initialize sum_rewards for storing the sum of rewards of each arm:

```
sum_rewards = np.zeros(2)
```

Initialize Q for storing the average reward of each arm:

```
Q = np.zeros(2)
```

Set the number of rounds (iterations):

```
num_rounds = 100
```

Now, we define the softmax function with the temperature T:

$$P_t(a) = \frac{\exp(Q_t(a)/T)}{\sum_{i=1}^{n} \exp(Q_t(i)/T)}$$

```
def softmax(T):
```

Compute the probability of each arm based on the preceding equation:

```
denom = sum([np.exp(i/T) for i in Q])
probs = [np.exp(i/T)/denom for i in Q]
```

Select the arm based on the computed probability distribution of arms:

```
arm = np.random.choice(env.action_space.n, p=probs)


return arm
```

Now, let's play the game and try to find the best arm using the softmax exploration method.

Let's begin by setting the temperature T to a high number, say, 50:

```
T = 50
```

For each round:

```
for i in range(num_rounds):
```

Select the arm based on the softmax exploration method:

```
arm = softmax(T)
```

Pull the arm and store the reward and next state information:

```
next_state, reward, done, info = env.step(arm)
```

Increment the count of the arm by 1:

```
count[arm] += 1
```

Update the sum of rewards of the arm:

```
sum_rewards[arm]+=reward
```

Update the average reward of the arm:

```
Q[arm] = sum_rewards[arm]/count[arm]
```

Reduce the temperature T:

```
T = T*0.99
```

After all the rounds, we check the Q value, that is, the average reward of all the arms:

```
print(Q)
```

The preceding code will print something like this:

```
[0.77700348 0.1971831 ]
```

As we can see, arm 1 has a higher average reward than arm 2, so we select arm 1 as the optimal arm:

```
print('The optimal arm is arm {}'.format(np.argmax(Q)+1))
```

The preceding code prints:

```
The optimal arm is arm 1
```

Thus, we have found the optimal arm using the softmax exploration method.

Upper confidence bound

In this section, we will explore another interesting algorithm called **upper confidence bound (UCB)** for handling the exploration-exploitation dilemma. The UCB algorithm is based on a principle called optimism in the face of uncertainty. Let's take a simple example and understand how exactly the UCB algorithm works.

Suppose we have two arms – arm 1 and arm 2. Let's say we played the game for 20 rounds by pulling arm 1 and arm 2 randomly and found that the mean reward of arm 1 is 0.6 and the mean reward of arm 2 is 0.5. But how can we be sure that this mean reward is actually accurate? That is, how can we be sure that this mean reward represents the true mean (population mean)? This is where we use the confidence interval.

The confidence interval denotes the interval within which the true value lies. So, in our setting, the confidence interval denotes the interval within which the true mean reward of the arm lies.

For instance, from *Figure 6.2*, we can see that the confidence interval of arm 1 is 0.2 to 0.9, which indicates that the mean reward of arm 1 lies in the range of 0.2 to 0.9. 0.2 is the lower confidence bound and 0.9 is the upper confidence bound. Similarly, we can observe that the confidence interval of arm 2 is 0.5 to 0.7, which indicates that the mean reward of arm 2 lies in the range of 0.5 to 0.7. where 0.5 is the lower confidence bound and 0.7 is the upper confidence bound:

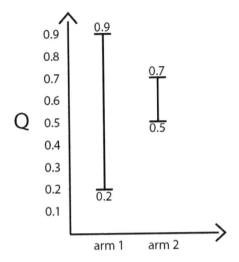

Figure 6.2: Confidence intervals for arms 1 and 2

Okay, from *Figure 6.2*, we can see the confidence intervals of arm 1 and arm 2. Now, how can we make a decision? That is, how can we decide whether to pull arm 1 or arm 2? If we look closely, we can see that the confidence interval of arm 1 is large and the confidence interval of arm 2 is small.

When the confidence interval is large, we are uncertain about the mean value. Since the confidence interval of arm 1 is large (0.2 to 0.9), we are not sure what reward we would obtain by pulling arm 1 because the average reward varies from as low as 0.2 to as high as 0.9. So, there is a lot of uncertainty in arm 1 and we are not sure whether arm 1 gives a high reward or a low reward.

When the confidence interval is small, then we are certain about the mean value. Since the confidence interval of arm 2 is small (0.5 to 0.7), we can be sure that we will get a good reward by pulling arm 2 as our average reward is in the range of 0.5 to 0.7.

But what is the reason for the confidence interval of arm 2 being small and the confidence interval of arm 1 being large? At the beginning of the section, we learned that we played the game for 20 rounds by pulling arm 1 and arm 2 randomly and computed the mean reward of arm 1 and arm 2. Say arm 2 has been pulled 15 times and arm 1 has been pulled only 5 times. Since arm 2 has been pulled many times, the confidence interval of arm 2 is small and it denotes a certain mean reward. Since arm 1 has been pulled fewer times, the confidence interval of the arm is large and it denotes an uncertain mean reward. Thus, it indicates that arm 2 has been explored a lot more than arm 1.

Okay, coming back to our question, should we pull arm 1 or arm 2? In UCB, we always select the arm that has a high upper confidence bound, so in our example, we select arm 1 since it has a high upper confidence bound of 0.9. But why do we have to select the arm that has the highest upper confidence bound? Selecting the arm with the highest upper bound helps us to select the arm that gives the maximum reward.

But there is a small catch here. When the confidence interval is large, we will not be sure about the mean reward. For instance, in our example, we select arm 1 since it has a high upper confidence bound of 0.9; however, since the confidence interval of arm 1 is large, our mean reward could be anywhere from 0.2 to 0.9, and so we can even get a low reward. But that's okay, we still select arm 1 as it promotes exploration. When the arm is explored well, then the confidence interval gets smaller.

As we play the game for several rounds by selecting the arm that has a high UCB, our confidence interval of both arms will get narrower and denote a more accurate mean value. For instance, as we can see in *Figure 6.3*, after playing the game for several rounds, the confidence interval of both the arms becomes small and denotes a more accurate mean value:

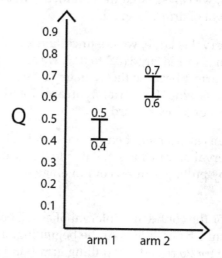

Figure 6.3: Confidence intervals for arms 1 and 2 after several rounds

From *Figure 6.3*, we can see that the confidence interval of both arms is small and we have a more accurate mean, and since in UCB we select arm that has the highest UCB, we select arm 2 as the best arm.

Thus, in UCB, we always select the arm that has the highest upper confidence bound. In the initial rounds, we may not select the best arm as the confidence interval of the arms will be large in the initial round. But over a series of rounds, the confidence interval gets smaller and we select the best arm.

Let $N(a)$ be the number of times arm a was pulled and t be the total number of rounds, then the upper confidence bound of arm a can be computed as:

$$\text{UCB}(a) = Q(a) + \sqrt{\frac{2\log(t)}{N(a)}} \qquad (3)$$

We select the arm that has the highest upper confidence bound as the best arm:

$$a^* = \arg\max_a \text{UCB}(a)$$

The algorithm of UCB is given as follows:

1. Select the arm whose upper confidence bound is high
2. Pull the arm and receive a reward
3. Update the arm's mean reward and confidence interval
4. Repeat *steps 1* to *3* for several rounds

Implementing UCB

Now, let's learn how to implement the UCB algorithm to find the best arm.

First, let's import the necessary libraries:

```
import gym
import gym_bandits
import numpy as np
```

Let's create the same two-armed bandit we saw in the previous section:

```
env = gym.make("BanditTwoArmedHighLowFixed-v0")
```

Now, let's initialize the variables.

Initialize count for storing the number of times an arm is pulled:

```
count = np.zeros(2)
```

Initialize `sum_rewards` for storing the sum of rewards of each arm:

```
sum_rewards = np.zeros(2)
```

Initialize `Q` for storing the average reward of each arm:

```
Q = np.zeros(2)
```

Set the number of rounds (iterations):

```
num_rounds = 100
```

Now, we define the **UCB function**, which returns the best arm as the one that has the highest UCB:

```
def UCB(i):
```

Initialize the numpy array for storing the UCB of all the arms:

```
ucb = np.zeros(2)
```

Before computing the UCB, we explore all the arms at least once, so for the first 2 rounds, we directly select the arm corresponding to the round number:

```
if i < 2:
    return i
```

If the round is greater than 2, then we compute the UCB of all the arms as specified in equation (3) and return the arm that has the highest UCB:

```
else:
    for arm in range(2):
        ucb[arm] = Q[arm] + np.sqrt((2*np.log(sum(count))) /
count[arm])

    return (np.argmax(ucb))
```

Now, let's play the game and try to find the best arm using the UCB method.

For each round:

```
for i in range(num_rounds):
```

Select the arm based on the UCB method:

```
arm = UCB(i)
```

Pull the arm and store the reward and next state information:

```
next_state, reward, done, info = env.step(arm)
```

Increment the count of the arm by 1:

```
count[arm] += 1
```

Update the sum of rewards of the arm:

```
sum_rewards[arm]+=reward
```

Update the average reward of the arm:

```
Q[arm] = sum_rewards[arm]/count[arm]
```

After all the rounds, we can select the optimal arm as the one that has the maximum average reward:

```
print('The optimal arm is arm {}'.format(np.argmax(Q)+1))
```

The preceding code will print:

```
The optimal arm is arm 1
```

Thus, we found the optimal arm using the UCB method.

Thompson sampling

Thompson sampling (TS) is another interesting exploration strategy to overcome the exploration-exploitation dilemma and it is based on a beta distribution. So, before diving into Thompson sampling, let's first understand the beta distribution. The beta distribution is a probability distribution function and it is expressed as:

$$f(x) = \frac{1}{B(\alpha, \beta)} x^{\alpha-1}(1-x)^{\beta-1}$$

Where $B(\alpha, \beta) = \frac{\Gamma(\alpha)\Gamma(\beta)}{\Gamma(\alpha+\beta)}$ and $\Gamma(.)$ is the gamma function.

The shape of the distribution is controlled by the two parameters α and β. When the values of α and β are the same, then we will have a symmetric distribution.

For instance, as *Figure 6.4* shows, since the value of α and β is equal to two we have a symmetric distribution:

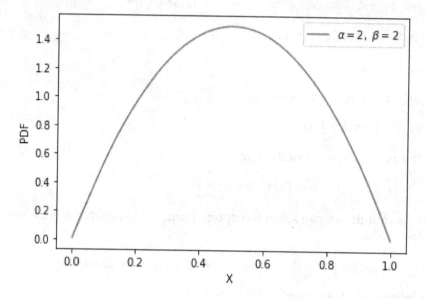

Figure 6.4: Symmetric beta distribution

When the value of α is higher than β then we will have a probability closer to 1 than 0. For instance, as *Figure 6.5* shows, since the value of $\alpha = 9$ and $\beta = 2$, we have a high probability closer to 1 than 0:

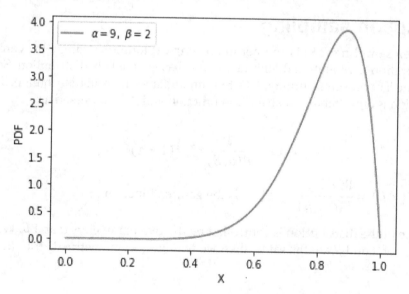

Figure 6.5: Beta distribution where $\alpha > \beta$

When the value of β is higher than α then we will have a high probability closer to 0 than 1. For instance, as shown in the following plot, since the value of $\alpha = 2$ and $\beta = 9$, we have a high probability closer to 0 than 1:

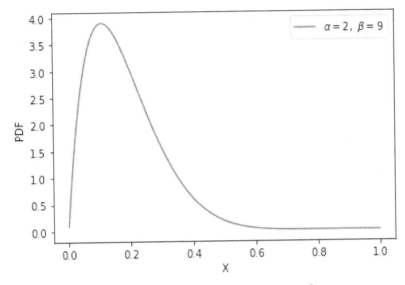

Figure 6.6: Gamma distribution where $\alpha < \beta$

Now that we have a basic idea of the beta distribution, let's explore how Thompson sampling works and how it uses the beta distribution. Understanding the true distribution of each arm is very important because once we know the true distribution of the arm, then we can easily understand whether the arm will give us a good reward; that is, we can understand whether pulling the arm will help us to win the game. For example, let's say we have two arms – arm 1 and arm 2. *Figure 6.7* shows the true distribution of the two arms:

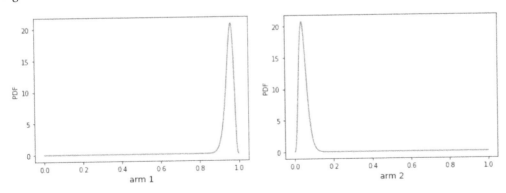

Figure 6.7: True distributions for arms 1 and 2

From *Figure 6.7*, we can see that it is better to pull arm 1 than arm 2 because arm 1 has a high probability close to 1, but arm 2 has a high probability close to 0. So, if we pull arm 1, we get a reward of 1 and win the game, but if we pull arm 2 we get a reward of 0 and lose the game. Thus, once we know the true distribution of the arms then we can understand which arm is the best arm.

But how can we learn the true distribution of arm 1 and arm 2? This is where we use the Thompson sampling method. Thompson sampling is a probabilistic method and it is based on a prior distribution.

First, we take *n* samples from arm 1 and arm 2 and compute their distribution. However, in the initial iterations, the computed distributions of arm 1 and arm 2 will not be the same as the true distribution, and so we will call this the prior distribution. As *Figure 6.8* shows, we have the prior distribution of arm 1 and arm 2, and it varies from the true distribution:

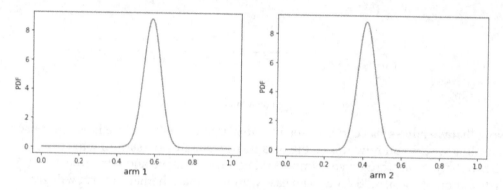

Figure 6.8: Prior distributions for arms 1 and 2

But over a series of iterations, we learn the true distribution of arm 1 and arm 2 and, as *Figure 6.9* shows, the prior distributions of the arms look the same as the true distribution after a series of iterations:

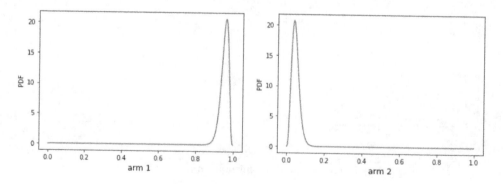

Figure 6.9: The prior distributions move closer to the true distributions

Once we have learned the true distributions of all the arms, then we can easily select the best arm. Okay, but how exactly do we learn the true distribution? Let's explore this in more detail.

Here, we use the beta distribution as a prior distribution. Say we have two arms, so we will have two beta distributions (prior distributions), and we initialize both α and β to the same value, say 3, as *Figure 6.10* shows:

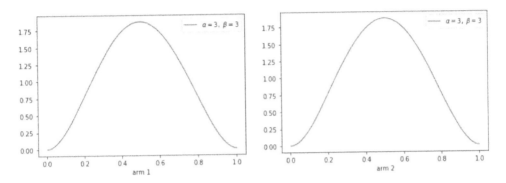

Figure 6.10: Initialized prior distributions for arms 1 and 2 look the same

As we can see, since we initialized alpha and beta to the same value, the beta distributions of arm 1 and arm 2 look the same.

In the first round, we just randomly sample a value from these two distributions and select the arm that has the maximum sampled value. Let's say the sampled value of arm 1 is high, so in this case, we pull arm 1. Say we win the game by pulling arm 1, then we update the distribution of arm 1 by incrementing the alpha value of the distribution by 1; that is, we update the alpha value as $\alpha = \alpha + 1$. As *Figure 6.11* shows, the alpha value of the distribution of arm 1 is incremented, and as we can see, arm 1's beta distribution has slightly high probability closer to 1 compared to arm 2:

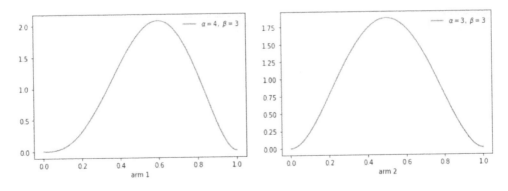

Figure 6.11: Prior distributions for arms 1 and 2 after round 1

In the next round, we again sample a value randomly from these two distributions and select the arm that has the maximum sampled value. Suppose, in this round as well, we got the maximum sampled value from arm 1. Then we pull the arm 1 again. Say we win the game by pulling arm 1, then we update the distribution of arm 1 by updating the alpha value to $\alpha = \alpha + 1$. As *Figure 6.12* shows, the alpha value of arm 1's distribution is incremented, and arm 1's beta distribution has a slightly high probability close to 1:

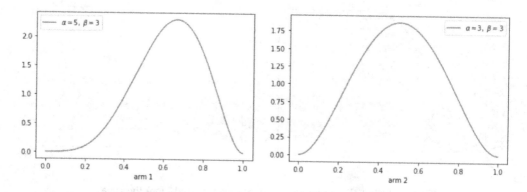

Figure 6.12: Prior distributions for arms 1 and 2 after round 2

Similarly, in the next round, we again randomly sample a value from these distributions and pull the arm that has the maximum value. Say this time we got the maximum value from arm 2, so we pull arm 2 and play the game. Suppose we lose the game by pulling arm 2. Then we update the distribution of arm 2 by updating the beta value as $\beta = \beta + 1$. As *Figure 6.13* shows, the beta value of arm 2's distribution is incremented and the beta distribution of arm 2 has a slightly high probability close to 0:

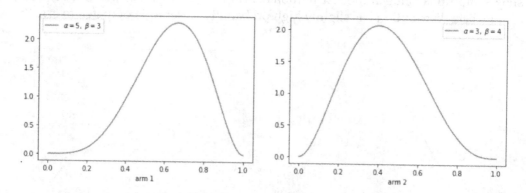

Figure 6.13: Prior distributions for arms 1 and 2 after round 3

Again, in the next round, we randomly sample a value from the beta distribution of arm 1 and arm 2. Say the sampled value of arm 2 is high, so we pull arm 2. Say we lose the game again by pulling arm 2. Then we update the distribution of arm 2 by updating the beta value as $\beta = \beta + 1$. As *Figure 6.14* shows, the beta value of arm 2's distribution is incremented by 1 and also arm 2's beta distribution has a slightly high probability close to 0:

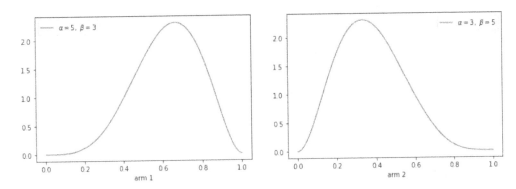

Figure 6.14: Prior distributions for arms 1 and 2 after round 4

Okay, so, did you notice what we are doing here? We are essentially increasing the alpha value of the distribution of the arm if we win the game by pulling that arm, else we increase the beta value. If we do this repeatedly for several rounds, then we can learn the true distribution of the arm. Say after several rounds, our distribution will look like *Figure 6.15*. As we can see, the distributions of both arms resemble the true distributions:

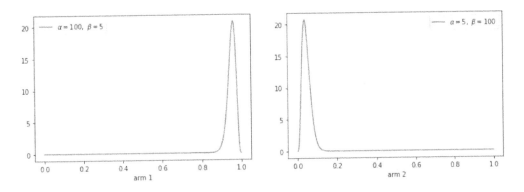

Figure 6.15: Prior distributions for arms 1 and 2 after several rounds

Now if we sample a value from each of these distributions, then the sampled value will always be high from arm 1 and we always pull arm 1 and win the game.

The steps involved in the Thomson sampling method are given here:

1. Initialize the beta distribution with alpha and beta set to equal values for all k arms

2. Sample a value from the beta distribution of all k arms

3. Pull the arm whose sampled value is high

4. If we win the game, then update the alpha value of the distribution to $\alpha = \alpha + 1$

5. If we lose the game, then update the beta value of the distribution to $\beta = \beta + 1$

6. Repeat *steps* 2 to 5 for many rounds

Implementing Thompson sampling

Now, let's learn how to implement the Thompson sampling method to find the best arm.

First, let's import the necessary libraries:

```
import gym
import gym_bandits
import numpy as np
```

For better understanding, let's create the same two-armed bandit we saw in the previous section:

```
env = gym.make("BanditTwoArmedHighLowFixed-v0")
```

Now, let's initialize the variables.

Initialize count for storing the number of times an arm is pulled:

```
count = np.zeros(2)
```

Initialize sum_rewards for storing the sum of rewards of each arm:

```
sum_rewards = np.zeros(2)
```

Initialize Q for storing the average reward of each arm:

```
Q = np.zeros(2)
```

Initialize the alpha value as 1 for both arms:

```
alpha = np.ones(2)
```

Initialize the beta value as 1 for both arms:

```
beta = np.ones(2)
```

Set the number of rounds (iterations):

```
num_rounds = 100
```

Now, let's define the `thompson_sampling` function.

As the following code shows, we randomly sample values from the beta distributions of both arms and return the arm that has the maximum sampled value:

```
def thompson_sampling(alpha,beta):

    samples = [np.random.beta(alpha[i]+1,beta[i]+1) for i in range(2)]

    return np.argmax(samples)
```

Now, let's play the game and try to find the best arm using the Thompson sampling method.

For each round:

```
for i in range(num_rounds):
```

Select the arm based on the Thompson sampling method:

```
arm = thompson_sampling(alpha,beta)
```

Pull the arm and store the reward and next state information:

```
next_state, reward, done, info = env.step(arm)
```

Increment the count of the arm by 1:

```
count[arm] += 1
```

Update the sum of rewards of the arm:

```
sum_rewards[arm]+=reward
```

Update the average reward of the arm:

```
Q[arm] = sum_rewards[arm]/count[arm]
```

If we win the game, that is, if the reward is equal to 1, then we update the value of alpha to $\alpha = \alpha + 1$, else we update the value of beta to $\beta = \beta + 1$:

```
if reward==1:
    alpha[arm] = alpha[arm] + 1
else:
    beta[arm] = beta[arm] + 1
```

After all the rounds, we can select the optimal arm as the one that has the highest average reward:

```
print('The optimal arm is arm {}'.format(np.argmax(Q)+1))
```

The preceding code will print:

```
The optimal arm is arm 1
```

Thus, we found the optimal arm using the Thompson sampling method.

Applications of MAB

So far, we have learned about the MAB problem and how can we solve it using various exploration strategies. But our goal is not to just use these algorithms for playing slot machines. We can apply the various exploration strategies to several different use cases.

For instance, bandits can be used as an alternative to AB testing. AB testing is one of the most commonly used classic methods of testing. Say we have two versions of the landing page of our website. Suppose we want to know which version of the landing page is most liked by the users. In this case, we conduct AB testing to understand which version of the landing page is most liked by the users. So, we show version 1 of the landing page to a particular set of users and version 2 of the landing page to other set of users. Then we measure several metrics, such as click-through rate, average time spent on the website, and so on, to understand which version of the landing page is most liked by the users. Once we understand which version of the landing page is most liked by the users, then we will start showing that version to all the users.

Thus, in AB testing, we schedule a separate time for exploration and exploitation. That is, AB testing has two different dedicated periods for exploration and exploitation. But the problem with AB testing is that it will incur high regret. We can minimize the regret using the various exploration strategies that we have used to solve the MAB problem. So, instead of performing complete exploration and exploitation separately, we can perform exploration and exploitation simultaneously in an adaptive fashion with the various exploration strategies we learned in the previous sections.

Bandits are widely used for website optimization, maximizing conversion rates, online advertisements, campaigning, and so on.

Finding the best advertisement banner using bandits

In this section, let's see how to find the best advertisement banner using bandits. Suppose we are running a website and we have five different banners for a single advertisement on our website, and say we want to figure out which advertisement banner is most liked by the users.

We can frame this problem as a MAB problem. The five advertisement banners represent the five arms of the bandit, and we assign +1 reward if the user clicks the advertisement and 0 reward if the user does not click the advertisement. So, to find out which advertisement banner is most clicked by the users, that is, which advertisement banner can give us the maximum reward, we can use various exploration strategies. In this section, let's just use an epsilon-greedy method to find the best advertisement banner.

First, let's import the necessary libraries:

```
import pandas as pd
import numpy as np
import matplotlib.pyplot as plt
import seaborn as sns
%matplotlib inline
plt.style.use('ggplot')
```

Creating a dataset

Now, let's create a dataset. We generate a dataset with five columns denoting the five advertisement banners, and we generate 100,000 rows, where the values in the rows will be either 0 or 1, indicating whether the advertisement banner has been clicked (1) or not clicked (0) by the user:

```
df = pd.DataFrame()
for i in range(5):
    df['Banner_type_'+str(i)] = np.random.randint(0,2,100000)
```

Let's look at the first few rows of our dataset:

```
df.head()
```

The preceding code will print the following. As we can see, we have the five advertisement banners (0 to 4) and the rows consisting of values of 0 or 1, indicating whether the banner has been clicked (1) or not clicked (0).

	Banner_type_0	Banner_type_1	Banner_type_2	Banner_type_3	Banner_type_4
0	0	1	1	0	1
1	1	0	1	0	1
2	0	1	1	0	1
3	1	1	1	0	1
4	0	0	1	1	0

Figure 6.14: Clicks per banner

Initialize the variables

Now, let's initialize some of the important variables.

Set the number of iterations:

```
num_iterations = 100000
```

Define the number of banners:

```
num_banner = 5
```

Initialize count for storing the number of times the banner was clicked:

```
count = np.zeros(num_banner)
```

Initialize sum_rewards for storing the sum of rewards obtained from each banner:

```
sum_rewards = np.zeros(num_banner)
```

Initialize Q for storing the mean reward of each banner:

```
Q = np.zeros(num_banner)
```

Define a list for storing the selected banners:

```
banner_selected = []
```

Define the epsilon-greedy method

Now, let's define the epsilon-greedy method. We generate a random value from a uniform distribution. If the random value is less than epsilon, then we select the random banner; else, we select the best banner that has the maximum average reward:

```
def epsilon_greedy_policy(epsilon):

    if np.random.uniform(0,1) < epsilon:
        return np.random.choice(num_banner)
    else:
        return np.argmax(Q)
```

Run the bandit test

Now, we run the epsilon-greedy policy to find out which advertisement banner is the best.

For each iteration:

```
for i in range(num_iterations):
```

Select the banner using the epsilon-greedy policy:

```
banner = epsilon_greedy_policy(0.5)
```

Get the reward of the banner:

```
reward = df.values[i, banner]
```

Increment the counter:

```
count[banner] += 1
```

Store the sum of rewards:

```
sum_rewards[banner]+=reward
```

Compute the average reward:

```
Q[banner] = sum_rewards[banner]/count[banner]
```

Store the banner to the banner selected list:

```
banner_selected.append(banner)
```

After all the rounds, we can select the best banner as the one that has the maximum average reward:

```
print( 'The best banner is banner {}'.format(np.argmax(Q)))
```

The preceding code will print:

```
The best banner is banner 2
```

We can also plot and see which banner is selected the most often:

```
ax = sns.countplot(banner_selected)
ax.set(xlabel='Banner', ylabel='Count')
plt.show()
```

The preceding code will plot the following. As we can see, banner 2 is selected most often:

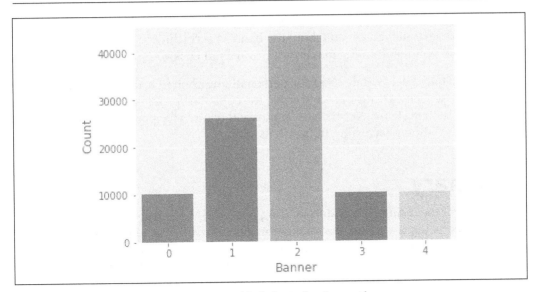

Figure 6.15: Banner 2 is the best advertisement banner

Thus, we have learned how to find the best advertisement banner by framing our problem as a MAB problem.

Contextual bandits

We just learned how to use bandits to find the best advertisement banner for the users. But the banner preference varies from user to user. That is, user A likes banner 1, but user B might like banner 3, and so on. Each user has their own preferences. So, we have to personalize advertisement banners according to each user. How can we do that? This is where we use contextual bandits.

In the MAB problem, we just perform the action and receive a reward. But with contextual bandits, we take actions based on the state of the environment and the state holds the context.

For instance, in the advertisement banner example, the state specifies the user behavior and we will take action (show the banner) according to the state (user behavior) that will result in the maximum reward (ad clicks).

Contextual bandits are widely used for personalizing content according to the user's behavior. They are also used to solve the cold-start problems faced by recommendation systems. Netflix uses contextual bandits for personalizing the artwork for TV shows according to user behavior.

Summary

We started off the chapter by understanding what the MAB problem is and how it can be solved using several exploration strategies. We first learned about the epsilon-greedy method, where we select a random arm with a probability epsilon and select the best arm with a probability 1-epsilon. Next, we learned about the softmax exploration method, where we select the arm based on the probability distribution, and the probability of each arm is proportional to the average reward.

Following this, we learned about the UCB algorithm, where we select the arm that has the highest upper confidence bound. Then, we explored the Thomspon sampling method, where we learned the distributions of the arms based on the beta distribution.

Moving forward, we learned how MAB can be used as an alternative to AB testing and how can we find the best advertisement banner by framing the problem as a MAB problem. At the end of the chapter, we also had an overview of contextual bandits.

In the next chapter, we will learn about several interesting deep learning algorithms that are essential for deep reinforcement learning.

Questions

Let's evaluate the knowledge we gained in this chapter by answering the following questions:

1. What is a MAB problem?
2. How does the epsilon-greedy policy select an arm?
3. What is the significance of T in softmax exploration?
4. How do we compute the upper confidence bound?

5. What happens when the value of alpha is higher than the value of beta in the beta distribution?

6. What are the steps involved in Thompson sampling?

7. What are contextual bandits?

Further reading

For more information, check out these interesting resources:

- **Introduction to Multi-Armed Bandits** by *Aleksandrs Slivkins*, `https://arxiv.org/pdf/1904.07272.pdf`

- **A Survey on Practical Applications of Multi-Armed and Contextual Bandits** by *Djallel Bouneffouf, Irina Rish*, `https://arxiv.org/pdf/1904.10040.pdf`

- **Collaborative Filtering Bandits** by *Shuai Li, Alexandros Karatzoglou, Claudio Gentile*, `https://arxiv.org/pdf/1502.03473.pdf`

7
Deep Learning Foundations

So far in the previous chapters, we have learned how several reinforcement learning algorithms work and how they find the optimal policy. In the upcoming chapters, we will learn about **Deep Reinforcement Learning** (DRL), which is a combination of deep learning and reinforcement learning. To understand DRL, we need to have a strong foundation in deep learning. So, in this chapter, we will learn several important deep learning algorithms.

Deep learning is a subset of machine learning and it is all about neural networks. Deep learning has been around for a decade, but the reason it is so popular right now is because of the computational advancements and availability of huge volumes of data. With this huge volume of data, deep learning algorithms can outperform classic machine learning algorithms.

We will start off the chapter by understanding what biological and artificial neurons are, and then we will learn about **Artificial Neural Networks** (ANNs) and how to implement them. Moving forward, we will learn about several interesting deep learning algorithms such as the **Recurrent Neural Network** (RNN), **Long Short-Term Memory** (LSTM), **Convolutional Neural Network** (CNN), and **Generative Adversarial Network** (GAN).

In this chapter, we will learn about the following:

- Biological and artificial neurons
- ANNs
- RNNs
- LSTM RNNs

- CNNs
- GANs

Let's begin the chapter by understanding how biological and artificial neurons work.

Biological and artificial neurons

Before going ahead, first, we will explore what neurons are and how neurons in our brain actually work, and then we will learn about artificial neurons.

A **neuron** can be defined as the basic computational unit of the human brain. Neurons are the fundamental units of our brain and nervous system. Our brain encompasses approximately 100 billion neurons. Each and every neuron is connected to one another through a structure called a **synapse**, which is accountable for receiving input from the external environment via sensory organs, for sending motor instructions to our muscles, and for performing other activities.

A neuron can also receive inputs from other neurons through a branchlike structure called a **dendrite**. These inputs are strengthened or weakened; that is, they are weighted according to their importance and then they are summed together in the cell body called the **soma**. From the cell body, these summed inputs are processed and move through the **axons** and are sent to the other neurons.

Figure 7.1 shows a basic single biological neuron:

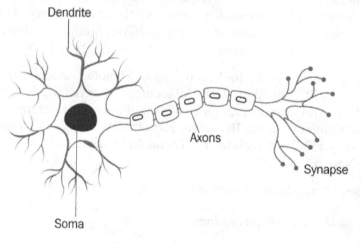

Figure 7.1: Biological neuron

Now, let's see how artificial neurons work. Let's suppose we have three inputs x_1, x_2, and x_3, to predict the output y. These inputs are multiplied by weights w_1, w_2, and w_3 and are summed together as follows:

$$x_1.w_1 + x_2.w_2 + x_3.w_3$$

But why are we multiplying these inputs by weights? Because all of the inputs are not equally important in calculating the output y. Let's say that x_2 is more important in calculating the output compared to the other two inputs. Then, we assign a higher value to w_2 than the other two weights. So, upon multiplying weights with inputs, x_2 will have a higher value than the other two inputs. In simple terms, weights are used for strengthening the inputs. After multiplying inputs with the weights, we sum them together and we add a value called bias, b:

$$z = (x_1.w_1 + x_2.w_2 + x_3.w_3) + b$$

If you look at the preceding equation closely, it may look familiar. Doesn't z look like the equation of linear regression? Isn't it just the equation of a straight line? We know that the equation of a straight line is given as:

$$z = mx + b$$

Here, m is the weights (coefficients), x is the input, and b is the bias (intercept).

Well, yes. Then, what is the difference between neurons and linear regression? In neurons, we introduce non-linearity to the result, z, by applying a function $f(.)$ called the **activation** or **transfer function**. Thus, our output becomes:

$$y = f(z)$$

Figure 7.2 shows a single artificial neuron:

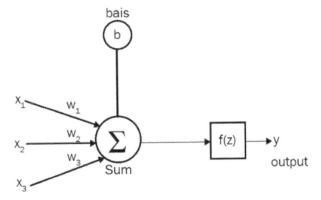

Figure 7.2: Artificial neuron

So, a neuron takes the input, x, multiples it by weights, w, and adds bias, b, forms z, and then we apply the activation function on z and get the output, y.

ANN and its layers

While neurons are really cool, we cannot just use a single neuron to perform complex tasks. This is the reason our brain has billions of neurons, stacked in layers, forming a network. Similarly, artificial neurons are arranged in layers. Each and every layer will be connected in such a way that information is passed from one layer to another.

A typical ANN consists of the following layers:

- Input layer
- Hidden layer
- Output layer

Each layer has a collection of neurons, and the neurons in one layer interact with all the neurons in the other layers. However, neurons in the same layer will not interact with one another. This is simply because neurons from the adjacent layers have connections or edges between them; however, neurons in the same layer do not have any connections. We use the term **nodes** or **units** to represent the neurons in the ANN.

Figure 7.3 shows a typical ANN:

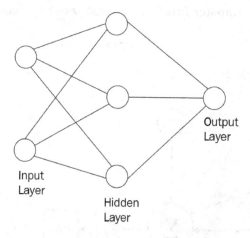

Figure 7.3: ANN

Input layer

The **input layer** is where we feed input to the network. The number of neurons in the input layer is the number of inputs we feed to the network. Each input will have some influence on predicting the output. However, no computation is performed in the input layer; it is just used for passing information from the outside world to the network.

Hidden layer

Any layer between the input layer and the output layer is called a **hidden layer**. It processes the input received from the input layer. The hidden layer is responsible for deriving complex relationships between input and output. That is, the hidden layer identifies the pattern in the dataset. It is majorly responsible for learning the data representation and for extracting the features.

There can be any number of hidden layers; however, we have to choose a number of hidden layers according to our use case. For a very simple problem, we can just use one hidden layer, but while performing complex tasks such as image recognition, we use many hidden layers, where each layer is responsible for extracting important features. The network is called a **deep neural network** when we have many hidden layers.

Output layer

After processing the input, the hidden layer sends its result to the output layer. As the name suggests, the output layer emits the output. The number of neurons in the output layer is based on the type of problem we want our network to solve.

If it is a binary classification, then the number of neurons in the output layer is one, and it tells us which class the input belongs to. If it is a multi-class classification say, with five classes, and if we want to get the probability of each class as an output, then the number of neurons in the output layer is five, each emitting the probability. If it is a regression problem, then we have one neuron in the output layer.

Exploring activation functions

An **activation function**, also known as a **transfer function**, plays a vital role in neural networks. It is used to introduce non-linearity in neural networks. As we learned before, we apply the activation function to the input, which is multiplied by weights and added to the bias, that is, $f(z)$, where $z = (input * weights) + bias$ and $f(.)$ is the activation function.

If we do not apply the activation function, then a neuron simply resembles the linear regression. The aim of the activation function is to introduce a non-linear transformation to learn the complex underlying patterns in the data.

Now let's look at some of the interesting commonly used activation functions.

The sigmoid function

The **sigmoid function** is one of the most commonly used activation functions. It scales the value between 0 and 1. The sigmoid function can be defined as follows:

$$f(x) = \frac{1}{1 + e^{-x}}$$

It is an S-shaped curve shown in *Figure 7.4*:

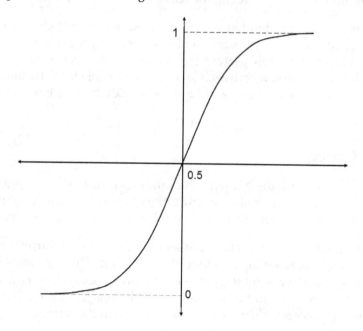

Figure 7.4: Sigmoid function

It is differentiable, meaning that we can find the slope of the curve at any two points. It is **monotonic**, which implies it is either entirely non-increasing or non-decreasing. The sigmoid function is also known as a **logistic** function. As we know that probability lies between 0 and 1, and since the sigmoid function squashes the value between 0 and 1, it is used for predicting the probability of output.

The tanh function

A **hyperbolic tangent (tanh)** function outputs the value between -1 to +1 and is expressed as follows:

$$f(x) = \frac{1 - e^{-2x}}{1 + e^{-2x}}$$

It also resembles the S-shaped curve. Unlike the sigmoid function, which is centered on 0.5, the tanh function is 0-centered, as shown in the following diagram:

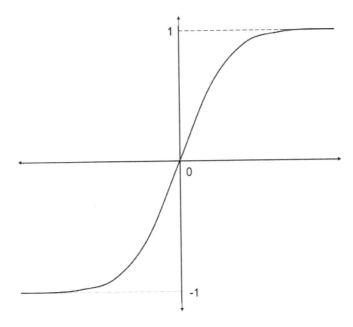

Figure 7.5: tanh function

The Rectified Linear Unit function

The **Rectified Linear Unit (ReLU)** function is another one of the most commonly used activation functions. It outputs a value from zero to infinity. It is basically a **piecewise** function and can be expressed as follows:

$$f(x) = \begin{cases} 0 & for\ x < 0 \\ x & for\ x \geq 0 \end{cases}$$

That is, $f(x)$ returns zero when the value of x is less than zero and $f(x)$ returns x when the value of x is greater than or equal to zero. It can also be expressed as follows:

$$f(x) = \max(0, x)$$

Figure 7.6 shows the ReLU function:

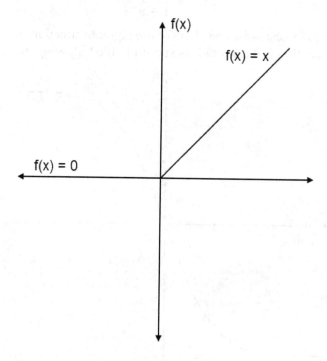

Figure 7.6: ReLU function

As we can see in the preceding diagram, when we feed any negative input to the ReLU function, it converts the negative input to zero.

The softmax function

The **softmax function** is basically the generalization of the sigmoid function. It is usually applied to the final layer of the network and while performing multi-class classification tasks. It gives the probabilities of each class for being output and thus, the sum of softmax values will always equal 1.

It can be represented as follows:

$$f(x_i) = \frac{e^{x_i}}{\sum_j e^{x_j}}$$

As shown in the *Figure 7.7*, the softmax function converts its inputs to probabilities:

$$\begin{bmatrix} 0.5 \\ 1.3 \\ 1.1 \end{bmatrix} \rightarrow \boxed{\text{Softmax}} \rightarrow \begin{bmatrix} 0.198 \\ 0.440 \\ 0.360 \end{bmatrix}$$

Figure 7.7: Softmax function

Now that we have learned about different activation functions, in the next section, we will learn about forward propagation in ANNs.

Forward propagation in ANNs

In this section, we will see how an ANN learns where neurons are stacked up in layers. The number of layers in a network is equal to the number of hidden layers plus the number of output layers. We don't take the input layer into account when calculating the number of layers in a network. Consider a two-layer neural network with one input layer, x, one hidden layer, h, and one output layer, y, as shown in the following diagram:

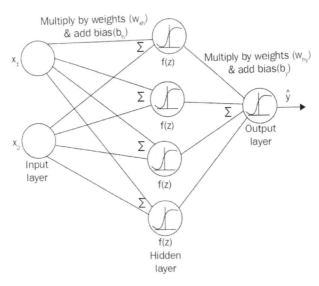

Figure 7.8: Forward propagation in ANN

Let's consider we have two inputs, x_1 and x_2, and we have to predict the output, $\hat{y}$. Since we have two inputs, the number of neurons in the input layer is two. We set the number of neurons in the hidden layer to four, and the number of neurons in the output layer to one. Now, the inputs are multiplied by weights, and then we add bias and propagate the resultant value to the hidden layer where the activation function is applied.

Before that, we need to initialize the weight matrix. In the real world, we don't know which input is more important than the other so that we can weight them and compute the output. Therefore, we randomly initialize the weights and bias value. The weight and the bias value between the input to the hidden layer are represented by W_{xh} and b_h, respectively. What about the dimensions of the weight matrix? The dimensions of the weight matrix must be *the number of neurons in the current layer* x *the number of neurons in the next layer*. Why is that?

Because it is a basic matrix multiplication rule. To multiply any two matrices, AB, the number of columns in matrix A must be equal to the number of rows in matrix B. So, the dimension of the weight matrix, W_{xh}, should be *the number of neurons in the input layer* x *the number of neurons in the hidden layer*, that is, 2 x 4:

$$z_1 = X W_{xh} + b_h$$

The preceding equation represents, z_1 = input × weights + bias. Now, this is passed to the hidden layer. In the hidden layer, we apply an activation function to z_1. Let's use the sigmoid σ activation function. Then, we can write:

$$a_1 = \sigma(z_1)$$

After applying the activation function, we again multiply result a_1 by a new weight matrix and add a new bias value that is flowing between the hidden layer and the output layer. We can denote this weight matrix and bias as W_{hy} and b_y, respectively. The dimension of the weight matrix, W_{hy}, will be *the number of neurons in the hidden layer* x *the number of neurons in the output layer*. Since we have four neurons in the hidden layer and one neuron in the output layer, the W_{hy} matrix dimension will be 4 x 1. So, we multiply a_1 by the weight matrix, W_{hy}, and add bias, b_y, and pass the result z_2 to the next layer, which is the output layer:

$$z_2 = a_1 W_{hy} + b_y$$

Now, in the output layer, we apply the sigmoid function to z_2, which will result in an output value:

$$\hat{y} = \sigma(z_2)$$

This whole process from the input layer to the output layer is known as **forward propagation**. Thus, in order to predict the output value, inputs are propagated from the input layer to the output layer. During this propagation, they are multiplied by their respective weights on each layer and an activation function is applied on top of them. The complete forward propagation steps are given as follows:

$$z_1 = XW_{xh} + b_h$$

$$a_1 = \sigma(z_1)$$

$$z_2 = a_1 W_{hy} + b_y$$

$$\hat{y} = \sigma(z_2)$$

The preceding forward propagation steps can be implemented in Python as follows:

```
def forward_prop(X):
    z1 = np.dot(X,Wxh) + bh
    a1 = sigmoid(z1)
    z2 = np.dot(a1,Why) + by
    y_hat = sigmoid(z2)

    return y_hat
```

Forward propagation is cool, isn't it? But how do we know whether the output generated by the neural network is correct? We define a new function called the **cost function** (J), also known as the **loss function** (L), which tells us how well our neural network is performing. There are many different cost functions. We will use the mean squared error as a cost function, which can be defined as the mean of the squared difference between the actual output and the predicted output:

$$J = \frac{1}{n} \sum_{i=1}^{n} (y_i - \hat{y}_i)^2$$

Here, n is the number of training samples, y is the actual output, and $\hat{y}$ is the predicted output.

Okay, so we learned that a cost function is used for assessing our neural network; that is, it tells us how good our neural network is at predicting the output. But the question is where is our network actually learning? In forward propagation, the network is just trying to predict the output. But how does it learn to predict the correct output? In the next section, we will examine this.

How does an ANN learn?

If the cost or loss is very high, then it means that our network is not predicting the correct output. So, our objective is to minimize the cost function so that our neural network predictions will be better. How can we minimize the cost function? That is, how can we minimize the loss/cost? We learned that the neural network makes predictions using forward propagation. So, if we can change some values in the forward propagation, we can predict the correct output and minimize the loss. But what values can we change in the forward propagation? Obviously, we can't change input and output. We are now left with weights and bias values. Remember that we just initialized weight matrices randomly. Since the weights are random, they are not going to be perfect. Now, we will update these weight matrices (W_{xh} and W_{hy}) in such a way that our neural network gives a correct output. How do we update these weight matrices? Here comes a new technique called **gradient descent**.

With gradient descent, the neural network learns the optimal values of the randomly initialized weight matrices. With the optimal values of weights, our network can predict the correct output and minimize the loss.

Now, we will explore how the optimal values of weights are learned using gradient descent. Gradient descent is one of the most commonly used optimization algorithms. It is used for minimizing the cost function, which allows us to minimize the error and obtain the lowest possible error value. But how does gradient descent find the optimal weights? Let's begin with an analogy.

Imagine we are on top of a hill, as shown in the following diagram, and we want to reach the lowest point on the hill. There could be many regions that look like the lowest points on the hill, but we have to reach the point that is actually the lowest of all.

That is, we should not be stuck at a point believing it is the lowest point when the global lowest point exists:

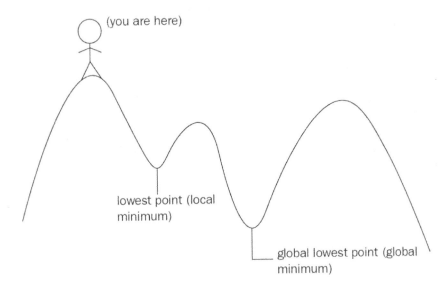

Figure 7.9: Analogy of gradient descent

Similarly, we can represent our cost function as follows. It is a plot of cost against weights. Our objective is to minimize the cost function. That is, we have to reach the lowest point where the cost is the minimum. The solid dark point in the following diagram shows the randomly initialized weights. If we move this point downward, then we can reach the point where the cost is the minimum:

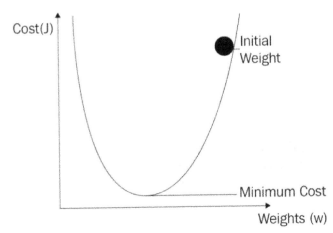

Figure 7.10: Gradient descent

But how can we move this point (initial weight) downward? How can we descend and reach the lowest point? Gradients are used for moving from one point to another. So, we can move this point (initial weight) by calculating a gradient of the cost function with respect to that point (initial weights), which is $\frac{\partial J}{\partial W}$.

Gradients are the derivatives that are actually the slope of a tangent line, as illustrated in the following diagram. So, by calculating the gradient, we descend (move downward) and reach the lowest point where the cost is the minimum. Gradient descent is a first-order optimization algorithm, which means we only take into account the first derivative when performing the updates:

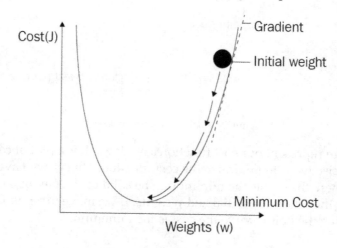

Figure 7.11: Gradient descent

Thus, with gradient descent, we move our weights to a position where the cost is minimum. But still, how do we update the weights?

As a result of forward propagation, we are in the output layer. We will now **backpropagate** the network from the output layer to the input layer and calculate the gradient of the cost function with respect to all the weights between the output and the input layer so that we can minimize the error. After calculating gradients, we update our old weights using the weight update rule:

$$W = W - \alpha \frac{\partial J}{\partial W}$$

This implies *weights = weights -a* x *gradients*.

What is α? It is called the **learning rate**. As shown in the following diagram, if the learning rate is small, then we take a small step downward and our gradient descent can be slow.

If the learning rate is large, then we take a large step and our gradient descent will be fast, but we might fail to reach the global minimum and become stuck at a local minimum. So, the learning rate should be chosen optimally:

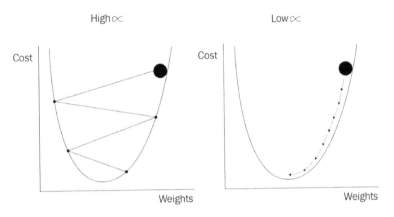

Figure 7.12: Effect of learning rate

This whole process of backpropagating the network from the output layer to the input layer and updating the weights of the network using gradient descent to minimize the loss is called **backpropagation**. Now that we have a basic understanding of backpropagation, we will strengthen our understanding by learning about this in detail, step by step. We are going to look at some interesting math, so put on your calculus hats and follow the steps.

So, we have two weights, one W_{xh}, which is the input to hidden layer weights, and the other W_{hy}, which is the hidden to output layer weights. We need to find the optimal values for these two weights that will give us the fewest errors. So, we need to calculate the derivative of the cost function J with respect to these weights. Since we are backpropagating, that is, going from the output layer to the input layer, our first weight will be W_{hy}. So, now we need to calculate the derivative of J with respect to W_{hy}. How do we calculate the derivative? First, let's recall our cost function, J:

$$J = \frac{1}{n}\sum_{i=1}^{n}(y_i - \hat{y}_i)^2$$

We cannot calculate the derivative directly from the preceding equation since there is no W_{hy} term. So, instead of calculating the derivative directly, we calculate the partial derivative. Let's recall our forward propagation equation:

$$\hat{y} = \sigma(z_2)$$

$$z_2 = a_1 W_{hy} + b_y$$

First, we will calculate a partial derivative with respect to $\hat{y}$, and then from $\hat{y}$ we will calculate the partial derivative with respect to z_2. From z_2, we can directly calculate our derivative W_{hy}. It is basically the chain rule. So, the derivative of J with respect to W_{hy} becomes as follows:

$$\frac{\partial J}{\partial W_{hy}} = \frac{\partial J}{\partial \hat{y}} \cdot \frac{\partial \hat{y}}{\partial z_2} \cdot \frac{dz_2}{dW_{hy}} \tag{1}$$

Now, we will compute each of the terms in the preceding equation:

$$\frac{\partial J}{\partial \hat{y}} = (y - \hat{y})$$

$$\frac{\partial \hat{y}}{\partial z_2} = \sigma'(z_2)$$

Here, σ' is the derivative of our sigmoid activation function. We know that the sigmoid function is $\sigma(z) = \frac{1}{1 + e^{-z}}$, so the derivative of the sigmoid function would be $\sigma'(z) = \frac{e^z}{(1 + e^{-z})^2}$.

Next we have:

$$\frac{dz_2}{dW_{hy}} = a_1$$

Thus, substituting all the preceding terms in equation *(1)* we can write:

$$\frac{\partial J}{dW_{hy}} = (y - \hat{y}).\sigma'(z_2).a_1 \tag{2}$$

Now we need to compute a derivative of J with respect to our next weight, W_{xh}.

Similarly, we cannot calculate the derivative of W_{xh} directly from J as we don't have any W_{xh} terms in J. So, we need to use the chain rule. Let's recall the forward propagation steps again:

$$\hat{y} = \sigma(z_2)$$

$$z_2 = a_1 W_{hy} + b_y$$

$$a_1 = \sigma(z_1)$$

$$z_1 = X W_{xh} + b_h$$

Now, according to the chain rule, the derivative of J with respect to W_{xh} is given as:

$$\frac{\partial J}{\partial W_{xh}} = \frac{\partial J}{\partial \hat{y}} \cdot \frac{\partial \hat{y}}{\partial z_2} \cdot \frac{dz_2}{\partial a_1} \cdot \frac{\partial a_1}{\partial z_1} \cdot \frac{dz_1}{dW_{xh}} \qquad (3)$$

We have already seen how to compute the first two terms in the preceding equation; now, we will see how to compute the rest of the terms:

$$\frac{dz_2}{\partial a_1} = W_{hy}$$

$$\frac{\partial a_1}{\partial z_1} = \sigma'(z_1)$$

$$\frac{dz_1}{dW_{xh}} = X$$

Thus, substituting all the preceding terms in equation (3), we can write:

$$\frac{\partial J}{\partial W_{xh}} = (y - \hat{y}) . \sigma'(z_2) . W_{hy} . \sigma'(z_1) . x \qquad (4)$$

After we have computed gradients for both weights, W_{hy} and W_{xh}, we will update our initial weights according to the weight update rule:

$$W_{hy} = W_{hy} - \alpha \frac{\partial J}{\partial W_{hy}} \qquad (5)$$

$$W_{xy} = W_{xy} - \alpha \frac{\partial J}{\partial W_{xh}} \qquad (6)$$

That's it! This is how we update the weights of a network and minimize the loss. Now, let's see how to implement the backpropagation algorithm in Python.

In both the equations (2) and (4), we have the term $(y - \hat{y}) . \sigma'(z_2)$, so instead of computing them again and again, we just call them `delta2`:

```
delta2 = np.multiply(-(y-yHat),sigmoidPrime(z2))
```

Now, we compute the gradient with respect to W_{hy}. Refer to equation (2):

```
dJ_dWhy = np.dot(a1.T,delta2)
```

We compute the gradient with respect to W_{xh}. Refer to equation *(4)*:

```
delta1 = np.dot(delta2,Why.T)*sigmoidPrime(z1)


dJ_dWxh = np.dot(X.T,delta1)
```

We will update the weights according to our weight update rule equation *(5)* and *(6)* as follows:

```
Wxh = Wxh - alpha * dJ_dWhy
Why = Why - alpha * dJ_dWxh
```

The complete code for the backpropagation is given as follows:

```
def backword_prop(y_hat, z1, a1, z2):
    delta2 = np.multiply(-(y-y_hat),sigmoid_derivative(z2))
    dJ_dWhy = np.dot(a1.T, delta2)

    delta1 = np.dot(delta2,Why.T)*sigmoid_derivative(z1)
    dJ_dWxh = np.dot(X.T, delta1)

    Wxh = Wxh - alpha * dJ_dWhy
    Why = Why - alpha * dJ_dWxh

    return Wxh,Why
```

That's it. Apart from this, there are different variants of gradient descent methods such as stochastic gradient descent, mini-batch gradient descent, Adam, RMSprop, and more.

Before moving on, let's familiarize ourselves with some of the frequently used terminology in neural networks:

- **Forward pass**: Forward pass implies forward propagating from the input layer to the output layer.
- **Backward pass**: Backward pass implies backpropagating from the output layer to the input layer.

- **Epoch**: The epoch specifies the number of times the neural network sees our whole training data. So, we can say one epoch is equal to one forward pass and one backward pass for all training samples.
- **Batch size**: The batch size specifies the number of training samples we use in one forward pass and one backward pass.
- **Number of iterations**: The number of iterations implies the number of passes where *one pass = one forward pass + one backward pass*.

Say that we have 12,000 training samples and our batch size is 6,000. Then it will take us two iterations to complete one epoch. That is, in the first iteration, we pass the first 6,000 samples and perform a forward pass and a backward pass; in the second iteration, we pass the next 6,000 samples and perform a forward pass and a backward pass. After two iterations, our neural network will see the whole 12,000 training samples, which makes it one epoch.

Putting it all together

Putting all the concepts we have learned so far together, we will see how to build a neural network from scratch. We will understand how the neural network learns to perform the XOR gate operation. The XOR gate returns 1 only when exactly only one of its inputs is 1, else it returns 0, as shown in *Table 7.1*:

Input(x)		Output(y)
x_1	x_2	y
0	0	0
0	1	1
1	0	1
1	1	0

Table 7.1: XOR operation

Building a neural network from scratch

To perform the XOR gate operation, we build a simple two-layer neural network, as shown in the following diagram. As you can see, we have an input layer with two nodes, a hidden layer with five nodes and an output layer comprising one node:

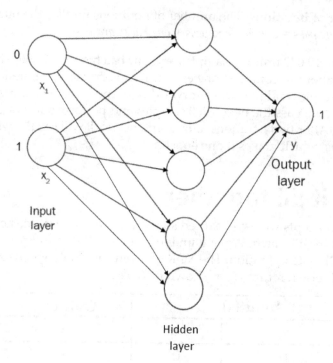

Figure 7.13: ANN

We will understand step-by-step how a neural network learns the XOR logic:

1. First, import the libraries:

    ```
    import numpy as np
    import matplotlib.pyplot as plt
    %matplotlib inline
    ```

2. Prepare the data as shown in the preceding XOR table:

    ```
    X = np.array([ [0, 1], [1, 0], [1, 1],[0, 0] ])
    y = np.array([ [1], [1], [0], [0]])
    ```

3. Define the number of nodes in each layer:

```
num_input = 2
num_hidden = 5
num_output = 1
```

4. Initialize the weights and bias randomly. First, we initialize the input to hidden layer weights:

```
Wxh = np.random.randn(num_input,num_hidden)
bh = np.zeros((1,num_hidden))
```

5. Now, we initialize the hidden to output layer weights:

```
Why = np.random.randn (num_hidden,num_output)
by = np.zeros((1,num_output))
```

6. Define the sigmoid activation function:

```
def sigmoid(z):
    return 1 / (1+np.exp(-z))
```

7. Define the derivative of the sigmoid function:

```
def sigmoid_derivative(z):
    return np.exp(-z)/((1+np.exp(-z))**2)
```

8. Define the forward propagation:

```
def forward_prop(x,Wxh,Why):
    z1 = np.dot(x,Wxh) + bh
    a1 = sigmoid(z1)
    z2 = np.dot(a1,Why) + by
    y_hat = sigmoid(z2)

    return z1,a1,z2,y_hat
```

9. Define the backward propagation:

```
def backword_prop(y_hat, z1, a1, z2):
    delta2 = np.multiply(-(y-y_hat),sigmoid_derivative(z2))
    dJ_dWhy = np.dot(a1.T, delta2)
    delta1 = np.dot(delta2,Why.T)*sigmoid_derivative(z1)
    dJ_dWxh = np.dot(x.T, delta1)

    return dJ_dWxh, dJ_dWhy
```

10. Define the cost function:

```
def cost_function(y, y_hat):
    J = 0.5*sum((y-y_hat)**2)

    return J
```

11. Set the learning rate and the number of training iterations:

```
alpha = 0.01
num_iterations = 5000
```

12. Now, let's start training the network with the following code:

```
cost =[]

for i in range(num_iterations):
    z1,a1,z2,y_hat = forward_prop(X,Wxh,Why)
    dJ_dWxh, dJ_dWhy = backword_prop(y_hat, z1, a1, z2)

    #update weights
    Wxh = Wxh -alpha * dJ_dWxh
    Why = Why -alpha * dJ_dWhy

    #compute cost
    c = cost_function(y, y_hat)

    cost.append(c)
```

13. Plot the cost function:

```
plt.grid()
plt.plot(range(num_iterations),cost)

plt.title('Cost Function')
plt.xlabel('Training Iterations')
plt.ylabel('Cost')
```

As you can observe in the following plot, the loss decreases over the training iterations:

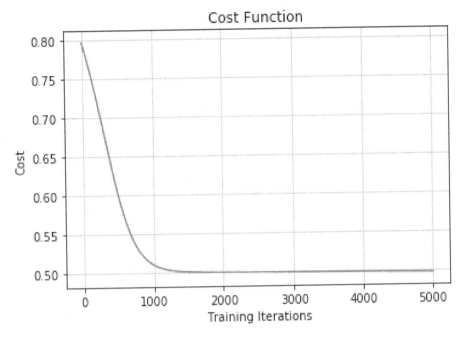

Figure 7.14: Cost function

Thus, we have an overall understanding of ANNs and how they learn.

Recurrent Neural Networks

The sun rises in the _____.

If we were asked to predict the blank term in the preceding sentence, we would probably say east. Why would we predict that the word east would be the right word here? Because we read the whole sentence, understood the context, and predicted that the word east would be an appropriate word to complete the sentence.

If we use a feedforward neural network (the one we learned in the previous section) to predict the blank, it would not predict the right word. This is due to the fact that in feedforward networks, each input is independent of other input and they make predictions based only on the current input, and they don't remember previous input.

Thus, the input to the network will just be the word preceding the blank, which is the word *the*. With this word alone as an input, our network cannot predict the correct word, because it doesn't know the context of the sentence, which means that it doesn't know the previous set of words to understand the context of the sentence and to predict an appropriate next word.

Here is where we use **Recurrent Neural Networks** (**RNNs**). They predict output not only based on the current input, but also on the previous hidden state. Why do they have to predict the output based on the current input and the previous hidden state? Why can't they just use the current input and the previous input?

This is because the previous input will only store information about the previous word, while the previous hidden state will capture the contextual information about all the words in the sentence that the network has seen so far. Basically, the previous hidden state acts like memory, and it captures the context of the sentence. With this context and the current input, we can predict the relevant word.

For instance, let's take the same sentence, *The sun rises in the _____.* As shown in the following figure, we first pass the word *the* as an input, and then we pass the next word, *sun*, as input; but along with this, we also pass the previous hidden state, h_0. So, every time we pass the input word, we also pass a previous hidden state as an input.

In the final step, we pass the word *the*, and also the previous hidden state h_3, which captures the contextual information about the sequence of words that the network has seen so far. Thus, h_3 acts as the memory and stores information about all the previous words that the network has seen. With h_3 and the current input word (*the*), we can predict the relevant next word:

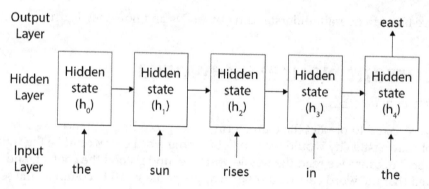

Figure 7.15: RNN

In a nutshell, an RNN uses the previous hidden state as memory, which captures and stores the contextual information (input) that the network has seen so far.

RNNs are widely applied for use cases that involve sequential data, such as time series, text, audio, speech, video, weather, and much more. They have been greatly used in various **natural language processing** (**NLP**) tasks, such as language translation, sentiment analysis, text generation, and so on.

The difference between feedforward networks and RNNs

A comparison between an RNN and a feedforward network is shown in the *Figure 7.16*:

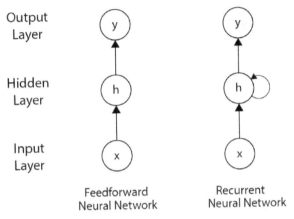

Figure 7.16: Difference between feedforward network and RNN

As you can observe in the preceding diagram, the RNN contains a looped connection in the hidden layer, which implies that we use the previous hidden state along with the input to predict the output.

Still confused? Let's look at the following unrolled version of an RNN. But wait; what is the unrolled version of an RNN?

It means that we roll out the network for a complete sequence. Let's suppose that we have an input sentence with T words; then, we will have 0 to $T-1$ layers, one for each word, as shown in *Figure 7.17*:

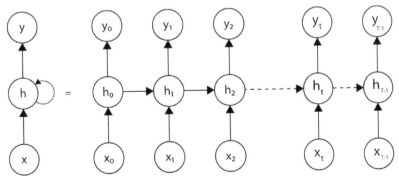

Figure 7.17: Unrolled RNN

As you can see in *Figure 7.17*, at the time step $t = 1$, the output y_1 is predicted based on the current input x_1 and the previous hidden state h_0. Similarly, at time step $t = 2$, y_2 is predicted using the current input x_2 and the previous hidden state h_1. This is how an RNN works; it takes the current input and the previous hidden state to predict the output.

Forward propagation in RNNs

Let's look at how an RNN uses forward propagation to predict the output; but before we jump right in, let's get familiar with the notations:

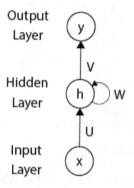

Figure 7.18: Forward propagation in RNN

The preceding figure illustrates the following:

- U represents the input to hidden layer weight matrix
- W represents the hidden to hidden layer weight matrix
- V represents the hidden to output layer weight matrix

The hidden state h at a time step t can be computed as follows:

$$h_t = \tanh (Ux_t + Wh_{t-1})$$

That is, *the hidden state at a time step, t = tanh([input to hidden layer weight x input] + [hidden to hidden layer weight x previous hidden state]).*

The output at a time step t can be computed as follows:

$$\hat{y}_t = \text{softmax}(Vh_t)$$

That is, *the output at a time step, t = softmax (hidden to output layer weight x hidden state at a time t).*

We can also represent RNNs as shown in the following figure. As you can see, the hidden layer is represented by an RNN block, which implies that our network is an RNN, and previous hidden states are used in predicting the output:

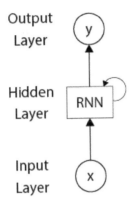

Figure 7.19: Forward propagation in an RNN

Figure 7.20 shows how forward propagation works in an unrolled version of an RNN:

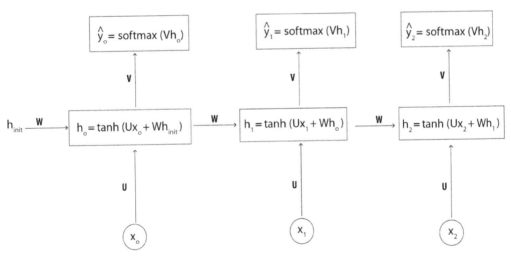

Figure 7.20: Unrolled version – forward propagation in an RNN

We initialize the initial hidden state h_{init} with random values. As you can see in the preceding figure, the output, $\hat{y}_0$, is predicted based on the current input, x_0 and the previous hidden state, which is an initial hidden state, h_{init}, using the following formula:

$$h_0 = \tanh(Ux_0 + Wh_{init})$$

$$\hat{y}_0 = softmax(Vh_0)$$

Similarly, look at how the output, $\hat{y}_1$, is computed. It takes the current input, x_1, and the previous hidden state, h_0:

$$h_1 = \tanh(Ux_1 + Wh_0)$$

$$\hat{y}_1 = softmax(Vh_1)$$

Thus, in forward propagation to predict the output, RNN uses the current input and the previous hidden state.

Backpropagating through time

We just learned how forward propagation works in RNNs and how it predicts the output. Now, we compute the loss, L, at each time step, t, to determine how well the RNN has predicted the output. We use the cross-entropy loss as our loss function. The loss L at a time step t can be given as follows:

$$L_t = -y_t \log(\hat{y}_t)$$

Here, y_t is the actual output, and $\hat{y}_t$ is the predicted output at a time step t.

The final loss is a sum of the loss at all the time steps. Suppose that we have $T - 1$ layers; then, the final loss can be given as follows:

$$L = \sum_{j=0}^{T-1} L_j$$

Figure 7.21 shows that the final loss is obtained by the sum of loss at all the time steps:

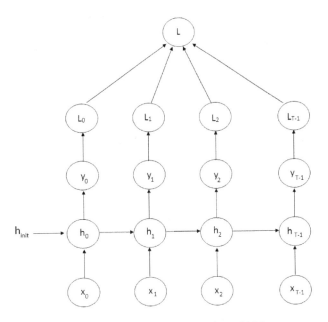

Figure 7.21: Backpropagation in an RNN

We computed the loss, now our goal is to minimize the loss. How can we minimize the loss? We can minimize the loss by finding the optimal weights of the RNN. As we learned, we have three weights in RNNs: input to hidden, U, hidden to hidden, W, and hidden to output, V.

We need to find optimal values for all of these three weights to minimize the loss. We can use our favorite gradient descent algorithm to find the optimal weights. We begin by calculating the gradients of the loss function with respect to all the weights; then, we update the weights according to the weight update rule as follows:

$$V = V - \alpha \frac{\partial L}{\partial V}$$

$$W = W - \alpha \frac{\partial L}{\partial W}$$

$$U = U - \alpha \frac{\partial L}{\partial U}$$

However, we have a problem with the RNN. The gradient calculation involves calculating the gradient with respect to the activation function. When we calculate the gradient with respect to the sigmoid or tanh function, the gradient will become very small. When we further backpropagate the network over many time steps and multiply the gradients, the gradients will tend to get smaller and smaller. This is called a vanishing gradient problem.

Since the gradient vanishes over time, we cannot learn information about long-term dependencies, that is, RNNs cannot retain information for a long time in the memory. The vanishing gradient problem occurs not only in RNNs but also in other deep networks where we have many hidden layers and when we use sigmoid/tanh functions.

One solution to avoid vanishing gradient problem is to use ReLU as an activation function. However, we have a variant of the RNN called **Long Short-Term Memory (LSTM)**, which can solve the vanishing gradient problem effectively. We will see how it works in the upcoming section.

LSTM to the rescue

While backpropagating an RNN, we learned about a problem called **vanishing gradients**. Due to the vanishing gradient problem, we cannot train the network properly, and this causes the RNN to not retain long sequences in the memory. To understand what we mean by this, let's consider a small sentence:

The sky is __.

An RNN can easily predict the blank as *blue* based on the information it has seen, but it cannot cover the long-term dependencies. What does that mean? Let's consider the following sentence to understand the problem better:

Archie lived in China for 13 years. He loves listening to good music. He is a fan of comics. He is fluent in ____.

Now, if we were asked to predict the missing word in the preceding sentence, we would predict it as *Chinese*, but how did we predict that? We simply remembered the previous sentences and understood that Archie lived for 13 years in China. This led us to the conclusion that Archie might be fluent in Chinese. An RNN, on the other hand, cannot retain all of this information in its memory to say that Archie is fluent in Chinese.

Due to the vanishing gradient problem, it cannot recollect/remember information for a long time in its memory. That is, when the input sequence is long, the RNN memory (hidden state) cannot hold all the information. To alleviate this, we use an LSTM cell.

LSTM is a variant of an RNN that resolves the vanishing gradient problem and retains information in the memory as long as it is required. Basically, RNN cells are replaced with LSTM cells in the hidden units, as shown in *Figure 7.22*:

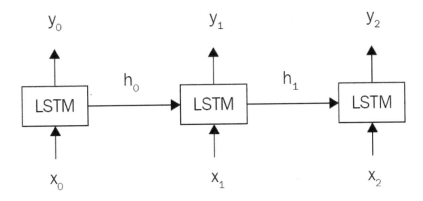

Figure 7.22: LSTM network

In the next section, we will understand how the LSTM cells works.

Understanding the LSTM cell

What makes LSTM cells so special? How do LSTM cells achieve long-term dependency? How does it know what information to keep and what information to discard from the memory?

This is all achieved by special structures called **gates**. As shown in the following diagram, a typical LSTM cell consists of three special gates called the input gate, output gate, and forget gate:

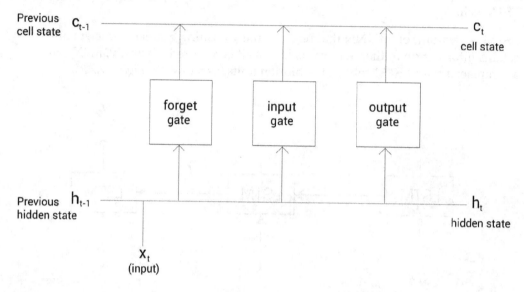

Figure 7.23: LSTM gates

These three gates are responsible for deciding what information to add, output, and forget from the memory. With these gates, an LSTM cell effectively keeps information in the memory only as long as required. *Figure 7.24* shows a typical LSTM cell:

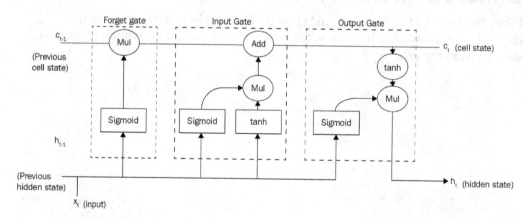

Figure 7.24: LSTM cell

If you look at the LSTM cell, the top horizontal line is called the cell state. It is where the information flows. Information on the cell state will be constantly updated by LSTM gates. Now, we will see the function of these gates:

Forget gate: The forget gate is responsible for deciding what information should not be in the cell state. Look at the following statement:

Harry is a good singer. He lives in New York. Zayn is also a good singer.

As soon as we start talking about Zayn, the network will understand that the subject has been changed from Harry to Zayn and the information about Harry is no longer required. Now, the forget gate will remove/forget information about Harry from the cell state.

Input gate: The input gate is responsible for deciding what information should be stored in the memory. Let's consider the same example:

Harry is a good singer. He lives in New York. Zayn is also a good singer.

So, after the forget gate removes information from the cell state, the input gate decides what information has to be in the memory. Here, since the information about Harry is removed from the cell state by the forget gate, the input gate decides to update the cell state with the information about Zayn.

Output gate: The output gate is responsible for deciding what information should be shown from the cell state at a time, *t*. Now, consider the following sentence:

Zayn's debut album was a huge success. Congrats _____.

Here, congrats is an adjective which is used to describe a noun. The output layer will predict Zayn (noun), to fill in the blank.

Thus, using LSTM, we can overcome the vanishing gradient problem faced in RNN. In the next section, we will learn another interesting algorithm called the **Convolutional Neural Network (CNN)**.

What are CNNs?

A CNN, also known as a **ConvNet**, is one of the most widely used deep learning algorithms for computer vision tasks. Let's say we are performing an image-recognition task. Consider the following image.

We want our CNN to recognize that it contains a horse:

Figure 7.25: Image containing a horse

How can we do that? When we feed the image to a computer, it basically converts it into a matrix of pixel values. The pixel values range from 0 to 255, and the dimensions of this matrix will be of [*image width* x *image height* x *number of channels*]. A grayscale image has one channel, and colored images have three channels, **red, green, and blue (RGB)**.

Let's say we have a colored input image with a width of 11 and a height of 11, that is 11 x 11, then our matrix dimension would be *[11 x 11 x 3]*. As you can see in *[11 x 11 x 3]*, 11 x 11 represents the image width and height and 3 represents the channel number, as we have a colored image. So, we will have a 3D matrix.

But it is hard to visualize a 3D matrix, so, for the sake of understanding, let's consider a grayscale image as our input. Since the grayscale image has only one channel, we will get a 2D matrix.

As shown in the following diagram, the input grayscale image will be converted into a matrix of pixel values ranging from 0 to 255, with the pixel values representing the intensity of pixels at that point:

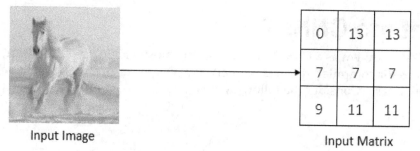

Input Image   Input Matrix

Figure 7.26: Input image is converted to matrix of pixel values

The values given in the input matrix are just arbitrary values for our understanding.

Okay, now we have an input matrix of pixel values. What happens next? How does the CNN come to understand that the image contains a horse? CNNs consists of the following three important layers:

- The convolutional layer
- The pooling layer
- The fully connected layer

With the help of these three layers, the CNN recognizes that the image contains a horse. Now we will explore each of these layers in detail.

Convolutional layers

The convolutional layer is the first and core layer of the CNN. It is one of the building blocks of a CNN and is used for extracting important features from the image.

We have an image of a horse. What do you think are the features that will help us to understand that this is an image of a horse? We can say body structure, face, legs, tail, and so on. But how does the CNN understand these features? This is where we use a convolution operation that will extract all the important features from the image that characterize the horse. So, the convolution operation helps us to understand what the image is all about.

Okay, what exactly is this convolution operation? How it is performed? How does it extract the important features? Let's look at this in detail.

As we know, every input image is represented by a matrix of pixel values. Apart from the input matrix, we also have another matrix called the **filter matrix**.

The filter matrix is also known as a **kernel**, or simply a **filter**, as shown in the *Figure 7.27*:

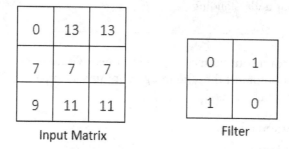

Input Matrix   Filter

Figure 7.27: Input and filter matrix

We take the filter matrix, slide it over the input matrix by one pixel, perform element-wise multiplication, sum the results, and produce a single number. That's pretty confusing, isn't it? Let's understand this better with the aid of the following diagram:

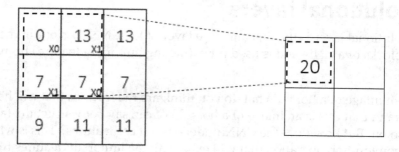

Figure 7.28: Convolution operation

As you can see in the previous diagram, we took the filter matrix and placed it on top of the input matrix, performed element-wise multiplication, summed their results, and produced the single number. This is demonstrated as follows:

$$(0 * 0) + (13 * 1) + (7 * 1) + (7 * 0) = 20$$

Now, we slide the filter over the input matrix by one pixel and perform the same steps, as shown in *Figure 7.29*:

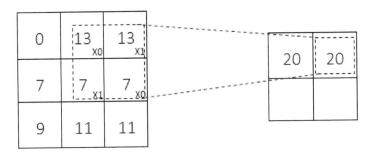

Figure 7.29: Convolution operation

This is demonstrated as follows:

$$(13 * 0) + (13 * 1) + (7 * 1) + (7 * 0) = 20$$

Again, we slide the filter matrix by one pixel and perform the same operation, as shown in *Figure 7.30*:

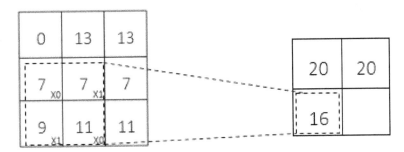

Figure 7.30: Convolution operation

This is demonstrated as follows:

$$(7 * 0) + (7 * 1) + (9 * 1) + (11 * 0) = 16$$

Now, again, we slide the filter matrix over the input matrix by one pixel and perform the same operation, as shown in *Figure 7.31*:

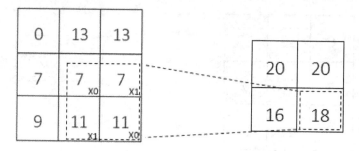

Figure 7.31: Convolution operation

That is:

$$(7 * 0) + (7 * 1) + (11 * 1) + (11 * 0) = 18$$

Okay. What are we doing here? We are basically sliding the filter matrix over the entire input matrix by one pixel, performing element-wise multiplication and summing their results, which creates a new matrix called a **feature map** or **activation map**. This is called the **convolution operation**.

As we've learned, the convolution operation is used to extract features, and the new matrix, that is, the feature maps, represents the extracted features. If we plot the feature maps, then we can see the features extracted by the convolution operation.

Figure 7.32 shows the actual image (the input image) and the convolved image (the feature map). We can see that our filter has detected the edges from the actual image as a feature:

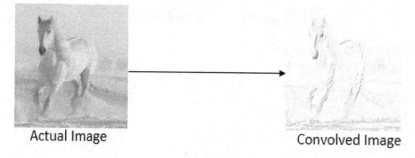

Actual Image   Convolved Image

Figure 7.32: Conversion of actual image to convolved image

Various filters are used for extracting different features from the image. For instance, if we use a sharpen filter, $\begin{bmatrix} 0 & -1 & 0 \\ -1 & 5 & -1 \\ 0 & 1 & 0 \end{bmatrix}$, then it will sharpen our image, as shown in the following figure:

Figure 7.33: Sharpened image

Thus, we have learned that with filters, we can extract important features from the image using the convolution operation. So, instead of using one filter, we can use multiple filters to extract different features from the image and produce multiple feature maps. So, the depth of the feature map will be the number of filters. If we use seven filters to extract different features from the image, then the depth of our feature map will be seven:

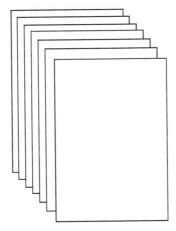

Feature map of depth 7

Figure 7.34: Feature maps

Okay, we have learned that different filters extract different features from the image. But the question is, how can we set the correct values for the filter matrix so that we can extract the important features from the image? Worry not! We just initialize the filter matrix randomly, and the optimal values of the filter matrix, with which we can extract the important features from the images, will be learned through backpropagation. However, we just need to specify the size of the filter and the number of filters we want to use.

Strides

We have just learned how a convolution operation works. We slide over the input matrix with the filter matrix by one pixel and perform the convolution operation. But we don't have to only slide over the input matrix by one pixel, we can also slide over the input matrix by any number of pixels.

The number of pixels we slide over the input matrix by the filter matrix is called a **stride**.

If we set the stride to 2, then we slide over the input matrix with the filter matrix by two pixels. *Figure 7.35* shows a convolution operation with a stride of 2:

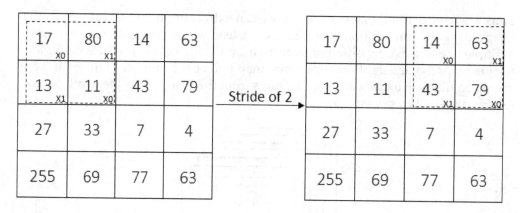

Figure 7.35: Stride operation

But how do we choose the stride number? We just learned that a stride is the number of pixels along that we move our filter matrix. So, when the stride is set to a small number, we can encode a more detailed representation of the image than when the stride is set to a large number. However, a stride with a high value takes less time to compute than one with a low value.

Padding

With the convolution operation, we are sliding over the input matrix with a filter matrix. But in some cases, the filter does not perfectly fit the input matrix. What do we mean by that? For example, let's say we are performing a convolution operation with a stride of 2. There exists a situation where, when we move our filter matrix by two pixels, it reaches the border and the filter matrix does not fit the input matrix. That is, some part of our filter matrix is outside the input matrix, as shown in the following diagram:

17	80	14	63
13	11	43	79
27	33	7	4
255	89	77	63

Figure 7.36: Padding operation

In this case, we perform padding. We can simply pad the input matrix with zeros so that the filter can fit the input matrix, as shown in *Figure 7.37*. Padding with zeros on the input matrix is called **same padding** or **zero padding**:

17	80	14	63	0
13	11	43	79	0
27	33	7	4	
255	89	77	63	

Figure 7.37: Same padding

Instead of padding them with zeros, we can also simply discard the region of the input matrix where the filter doesn't fit in. This is called **valid padding**:

Figure 7.38: Valid padding

Pooling layers

Okay. Now, we are done with the convolution operation. As a result of the convolution operation, we have some feature maps. But the feature maps are too large in dimension. In order to reduce the dimensions of feature maps, we perform a pooling operation. This reduces the dimensions of the feature maps and keeps only the necessary details so that the amount of computation can be reduced.

For example, to recognize a horse from the image, we need to extract and keep only the features of the horse; we can simply discard unwanted features, such as the background of the image and more. A pooling operation is also called a **downsampling** or **subsampling** operation, and it makes the CNN translation invariant. Thus, the pooling layer reduces spatial dimensions by keeping only the important features.

There are different types of pooling operations, including max pooling, average pooling, and sum pooling.

In max pooling, we slide over the filter on the input matrix and simply take the maximum value from the filter window, as *Figure 7.39* shows:

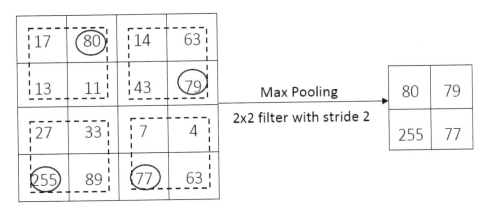

Figure 7.39: Max pooling

In average pooling, we take the average value of the input matrix within the filter window, and in sum pooling, we sum all the values of the input matrix within the filter window.

Fully connected layers

So far, we've learned how convolutional and pooling layers work. A CNN can have multiple convolutional layers and pooling layers. However, these layers will only extract features from the input image and produce the feature map; that is, they are just the feature extractors.

Given any image, convolutional layers extract features from the image and produce a feature map. Now, we need to classify these extracted features. So, we need an algorithm that can classify these extracted features and tell us whether the extracted features are the features of a horse, or something else. In order to make this classification, we use a feedforward neural network. We flatten the feature map and convert it into a vector, and feed it as an input to the feedforward network.

The feedforward network takes this flattened feature map as an input, applies an activation function, such as sigmoid, and returns the output, stating whether the image contains a horse or not; this is called a fully connected layer and is shown in the following diagram:

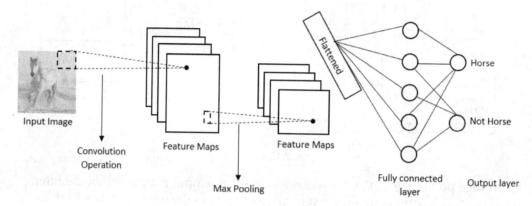

Figure 7.40: Fully connected layer

Let's see how all this fits together.

The architecture of CNNs

Figure 7.41 shows the architecture of a CNN:

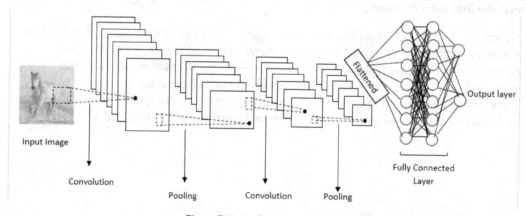

Figure 7.41: Architecture of CNN

As you will notice, first we feed the input image to the convolutional layer, where we apply the convolution operation to extract important features from the image and create the feature maps. We then pass the feature maps to the pooling layer, where the dimensions of the feature maps will be reduced.

As shown in the previous diagram, we can have multiple convolutional and pooling layers, and we should also note that the pooling layer does not necessarily have to be there after every convolutional layer; there can be many convolutional layers followed by a pooling layer.

So, after the convolutional and pooling layers, we flatten the resultant feature maps and feed it to a fully connected layer, which is basically a feedforward neural network that classifies the given input image based on the feature maps.

Now that we have learned how CNNs work, in the next section, we will learn about another interesting algorithm called the generative adversarial network.

Generative adversarial networks

Generative Adversarial Networks (GANs) was first introduced by Ian J Goodfellow, Jean Pouget-Abadie, Mehdi Mirza, Bing Xu, David Warde-Farley, Sherjil Ozair, Aaron Courville, and Yoshua Bengio in their paper, *Generative Adversarial Networks*, in 2014.

GANs are used extensively for generating new data points. They can be applied to any type of dataset, but they are popularly used for generating images. Some of the applications of GANs include generating realistic human faces, converting grayscale images to colored images, translating text descriptions into realistic images, and many more.

GANs have evolved so much in recent years that they can generate a very realistic image. The following figure shows the evolution of GANs in generating images over the course of five years:

Figure 7.42: Evolution of GANs over the years

Excited about GANs already? Now, we will see how exactly they work. Before going ahead, let's consider a simple analogy. Let's say you are the police and your task is to find counterfeit money, and the role of the counterfeiter is to create fake money and cheat the police.

The counterfeiter constantly tries to create fake money in a way that is so realistic that it cannot be differentiated from the real money. But the police have to identify whether the money is real or fake. So, the counterfeiter and the police essentially play a two-player game where one tries to defeat the other. GANs work something like this. They consist of two important components:

- Generator
- Discriminator

You can perceive the generator as analogous to the counterfeiter, while the discriminator is analogous to the police. That is, the role of the generator is to create fake money, and the role of the discriminator is to identify whether the money is fake or real.

Without going into detail, first, we will get a basic understanding of GANs. Let's say we want our GAN to generate handwritten digits. How can we do that? First, we will take a dataset containing a collection of handwritten digits; say, the MNIST dataset. The generator learns the distribution of images in our dataset. Thus, it learns the distribution of handwritten digits in our training set. Once, it learns the distribution of the images in our dataset, and we feed a random noise to the generator, it will convert the random noise into a new handwritten digit similar to the one in our training set based on the learned distribution:

Figure 7.43: Generator

The goal of the discriminator is to perform a classification task. Given an image, it classifies it as real or fake; that is, whether the image is from the training set or the image is generated by the generator:

Figure 7.44: Discriminator

The generator component of GAN is basically a generative model, and the discriminator component is basically a discriminative model. Thus, the generator learns the distribution of the class and the discriminator learns the decision boundary of a class.

As *Figure 7.45* shows, we feed random noise to the generator, and it then converts this random noise into a new image similar to the one we have in our training set, but not exactly the same as the images in the training set. The image generated by the generator is called a fake image, and the images in our training set are called real images. We feed both the real and fake images to the discriminator, which tells us the probability of them being real. It returns 0 if the image is fake and 1 if the image is real:

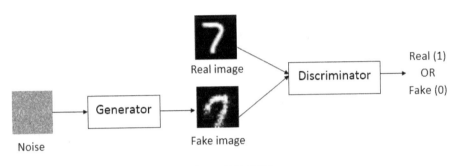

Figure 7.45: GAN

Now that we have a basic understanding of generators and discriminators, we will study each of the components in detail.

Breaking down the generator

The generator component of a GAN is a generative model. When we say the generative model, there are two types of generative models—an **implicit** and an **explicit** density model. The implicit density model does not use any explicit density function to learn the probability distribution, whereas the explicit density model, as the name suggests, uses an explicit density function. GANs falls into the first category. That is, they are an implicit density model. Let's study in detail and understand how GANs are an implicit density model.

Let's say we have a generator, G. It is basically a neural network parametrized by θ_g. The role of the generator network is to generate new images. How do they do that? What should be the input to the generator?

We sample a random noise, z, from a normal or uniform distribution, P_z. We feed this random noise, z, as an input to the generator and then it converts this noise to an image:

$$G(z; \theta_g)$$

Surprising, isn't it? How does the generator convert random noise to a realistic image?

Let's say we have a dataset containing a collection of human faces and we want our generator to generate a new human face. First, the generator learns all the features of the face by learning the probability distribution of the images in our training set. Once the generator learns the correct probability distribution, it can generate totally new human faces.

But how does the generator learn the distribution of the training set? That is, how does the generator learn the distribution of images of human faces in the training set?

A generator is nothing but a neural network. So, what happens is that the neural network learns the distribution of the images in our training set implicitly; let's call this distribution a generator distribution, P_g. At the first iteration, the generator generates a really noisy image. But over a series of iterations, it learns the exact probability distribution of our training set and learns to generate a correct image by tuning its θ_g parameter.

 It is important to note that we are not using the uniform distribution P_z for learning the distribution of our training set. It is only used for sampling random noise, and we feed this random noise as an input to the generator. The generator network implicitly learns the distribution of our training set and we call this distribution a generator distribution, P_g and that is why we call our generator network an implicit density model.

Now that we understand the generator, let's move on to the discriminator.

Breaking down the discriminator

As the name suggests, the discriminator is a discriminative model. Let's say we have a discriminator, D. It is also a neural network and it is parametrized by θ_d.

The goal of the discriminator is to discriminate between two classes. That is, given an image x, it has to identify whether the image is from a real distribution or a fake distribution (generator distribution). That is, the discriminator has to identify whether the given input image is from the training set or the fake image generated by the generator:

$$D(x; \theta_d)$$

Let's call the distribution of our training set the real data distribution, which is represented by P_r. We know that the generator distribution is represented by P_g.

So, the discriminator D essentially tries to discriminate whether the image x is from P_r or P_g.

How do they learn, though?

So far, we just studied the role of the generator and discriminator, but how do they learn exactly? How does the generator learn to generate new realistic images and how does the discriminator learn to discriminate between images correctly?

We know that the goal of the generator is to generate an image in such a way as to fool the discriminator into believing that the generated image is from a real distribution.

In the first iteration, the generator generates a noisy image. When we feed this image to the discriminator, it can easily detect that the image is from a generator distribution. The generator takes this as a loss and tries to improve itself, as its goal is to fool the discriminator. That is, if the generator knows that the discriminator is easily detecting the generated image as a fake image, then it means that it is not generating an image similar to those in the training set. This implies that it has not learned the probability distribution of the training set yet.

So, the generator tunes its parameters in such a way as to learn the correct probability distribution of the training set. As we know that the generator is a neural network, we simply update the parameters of the network through backpropagation. Once it has learned the probability distribution of the real images, then it can generate images similar to the ones in the training set.

Okay, what about the discriminator? How does it learn? As we know, the role of the discriminator is to discriminate between real and fake images.

If the discriminator incorrectly classifies the generated image; that is, if the discriminator classifies the fake image as a real image, then it implies that the discriminator has not learned to differentiate between the real and fake image. So, we update the parameter of the discriminator network through backpropagation to make the discriminator learn to classify between real and fake images.

So, basically, the generator is trying to fool the discriminator by learning the real data distribution, P_r, and the discriminator is trying to find out whether the image is from a real or fake distribution. Now the question is, when do we stop training the network in light of the fact that the generator and discriminator are competing against each other?

Basically, the goal of the GAN is to generate images similar to the one in the training set. Say we want to generate a human face—we learn the distribution of images in the training set and generate new faces. So, for a generator, we need to find the optimal discriminator. What do we mean by that?

We know that a generator distribution is represented by P_g and the real data distribution is represented by P_r. If the generator learns the real data distribution perfectly, then P_g equals P_r, as *Figure 7.46* shows:

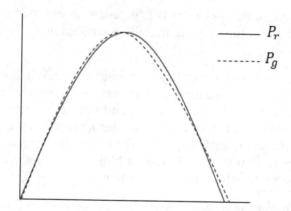

Figure 7.46: Generator and real data distribution

When $P_g = P_r$, then the discriminator cannot differentiate between whether the input image is from a real or a fake distribution, so it will just return 0.5 as a probability, as the discriminator will become confused between the two distributions when they are the same.

So, for a generator, the optimal discriminator can be given as follows:

$$D(x) = \frac{P_r(x)}{P_r(x) + P_g(x)} = \frac{1}{2}$$

So, when the discriminator just returns the probability of 0.5 for all the generator images, then we can say that the generator has learned the distribution of images in our training set and has fooled the discriminator successfully.

Architecture of a GAN

Figure 7.47 shows the architecture of a GAN:

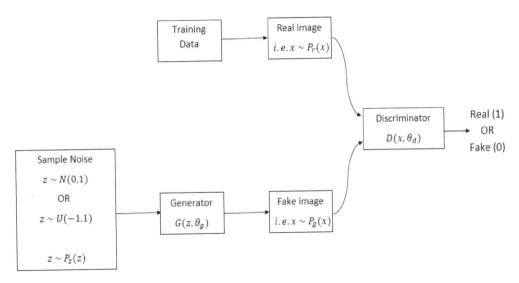

Figure 7.47: Architecture of GAN

As shown in the preceding diagram, generator G takes the random noise, z, as input by sampling from a uniform or normal distribution and generates a fake image by implicitly learning the distribution of the training set.

We sample an image, x, from the real data distribution, $x \sim P_r(x)$, and fake data distribution, $x \sim P_g(x)$, and feed it to the discriminator, D. We feed real and fake images to the discriminator and the discriminator performs a binary classification task. That is, it returns 0 when the image is fake and 1 when the image is real.

Demystifying the loss function

Now we will examine the loss function of the GAN. Before going ahead, let's recap the notation:

- A noise that is fed as an input to the generator is represented by z
- The uniform or normal distribution from which the noise z is sampled is represented by P_z
- An input image is represented by x
- The real data distribution or the distribution of our training set is represented by P_r
- The fake data distribution or the distribution of the generator is represented by P_g

When we write $x \sim P_r(x)$, it implies that image x is sampled from the real distribution, P_r. Similarly, $x \sim P_g(x)$ denotes that image x is sampled from the generator distribution, P_g, and $z \sim P_z(z)$ implies that the generator input, z, is sampled from the uniform distribution, P_z.

We've learned that both the generator and discriminator are neural networks and both of them update their parameters through backpropagation. We now need to find the optimal generator parameter, θ_g, and the discriminator parameter, θ_d.

Discriminator loss

Now we will look at the loss function of the discriminator. We know that the goal of the discriminator is to classify whether the image is a real or a fake image. Let's denote the discriminator by D.

The loss function of the discriminator is given as follows:

$$\max_d L(D, G) = \mathbb{E}_{x \sim P_r(x)}[\log D(x; \theta_d)] + \mathbb{E}_{z \sim P_z(z)}\left[\log\left(1 - D\left(G\left(z; \theta_g\right); \theta_d\right)\right)\right]$$

What does this mean, though? Let's understand each of the terms one by one.

First term

Let's look at the first term:

$$\mathbb{E}_{x \sim P_r(x)}\log(D(x))$$

Here, $x \sim P_r(x)$ implies that we are sampling input x from the real data distribution, P_r, so x is a real image.

$D(x)$ implies that we are feeding the input image x to the discriminator D, and the discriminator will return the probability of input image x to be a real image. As x is sampled from real data distribution P_r, we know that x is a real image. So, we need to maximize the probability of $D(x)$:

$$max\ D(x)$$

But instead of maximizing raw probabilities, we maximize log probabilities, so, we can write the following:

$$max\ log D(x)$$

So, our final equation becomes the following:

$$max\ \mathbb{E}_{x \sim P_r(x)} log\ [D(x)]$$

$\mathbb{E}_{x \sim P_r(x)} log\ [D(x)]$ represents the expectations of the log-likelihood of input images sampled from the real data distribution being real.

Second term

Now, let's look at the second term:

$$\mathbb{E}_{z \sim P_z(z)}[log\ (1 - D(G(z)))]$$

Here, $z \sim P_z(z)$ shows that we are sampling a random noise z from the uniform distribution P_z. $G(z)$ implies that the generator G takes the random noise z as an input and returns a fake image based on its implicitly learned distribution P_g.

$D(G(z))$ implies that we are feeding the fake image generated by the generator to the discriminator D and it will return the probability of the fake input image being a real image.

If we subtract $D(G(z))$ from 1, then it will return the probability of the fake input image being a fake image:

$$1 - D(G(z))$$

Since we know z is not a real image, the discriminator will maximize this probability. That is, the discriminator maximizes the probability of z being classified as a fake image, so we write:

$$max\ 1 - D(G(z))$$

Instead of maximizing raw probabilities, we maximize the log probability:

$$max \log \left(1 - D\big(G(z)\big)\right)$$

$\mathbb{E}_{z \sim P_z(z)} \left[\log \left(1 - D\big(G(z)\big)\right)\right]$ implies the expectations of the log likelihood of the input images generated by the generator being fake.

Final term

So, combining these two terms, the loss function of the discriminator is given as follows:

$$\max_d L(D, G) = \mathbb{E}_{x \sim P_r(x)}[\log D(x; \theta_d)] + \mathbb{E}_{z \sim P_z(z)} \left[\log \left(1 - D\big(G(z; \theta_g); \theta_d\big)\right)\right]$$

Here, θ_g and θ_d are the parameters of the generator and discriminator network respectively. So, the discriminator's goal is to find the right θ_d so that it can classify the image correctly.

Generator loss

The loss function of the generator is given as follows:

$$\min_g L(D, G) = \mathbb{E}_{z \sim P_z(z)} \left[\log \left(1 - D\big(G(z; \theta_g); \theta_d\big)\right)\right]$$

We know that the goal of the generator is to fool the discriminator to classify the fake image as a real image.

In the *Discriminator loss* section, we saw that $\mathbb{E}_{z \sim P_z(z)} \left[\log \left(1 - D\big(G(z)\big)\right)\right]$ implies the probability of classifying the fake input image as a fake image, and the discriminator maximizes the probabilities for correctly classifying the fake image as fake.

But the generator wants to minimize this probability. As the generator wants to fool the discriminator, it minimizes this probability of a fake input image being classified as fake by the discriminator. Thus, the loss function of the generator can be expressed as follows:

$$\min_g L(D, G) = \mathbb{E}_{z \sim P_z(z)} \left[\log \left(1 - D\big(G(z; \theta_g); \theta_d\big)\right)\right]$$

Total loss

We just learned the loss function of the generator and the discriminator combining these two losses, and we write our final loss function as follows:

$$\min_{G} \max_{D} L(D, G) = \mathbb{E}_{x \sim P_r(x)}[\log D(x)] + \mathbb{E}_{z \sim P_z(z)}\left[\log\left(1 - D(G(z))\right)\right]$$

So, our objective function is basically a min-max objective function, that is, a maximization for the discriminator and a minimization for the generator, and we find the optimal generator parameter, θ_g, and discriminator parameter, θ_d, through backpropagating the respective networks.

So, we perform gradient ascent; that is, maximization on the discriminator:

$$\nabla \theta_d \frac{1}{m} \sum_{i=1}^{m}\left[\log D(x^{(i)}) + \log\left(1 - D\left(G(z^{(i)})\right)\right)\right]$$

And, we perform gradient descent; that is, minimization on the generator:

$$\nabla \theta_g \frac{1}{m} \sum_{i=1}^{m} \log\left(1 - D\left(G(z^{(i)})\right)\right)$$

Summary

We started off the chapter by understanding biological and artificial neurons. Then we learned about ANNs and their layers. We learned different types of activation functions and how they are used to introduce nonlinearity in the network.

Later, we learned about the forward and backward propagation in the neural network. Next, we learned how to implement an ANN. Moving on, we learned about RNNs and how they differ from feedforward networks. Next, we learned about the variant of the RNN called LSTM. Going forward, we learned about CNNs, how they use different types of layers, and the architecture of CNNs in detail.

At the end of the chapter, we learned about an interesting algorithm called GAN. We understood the generator and discriminator component of GAN and we also explored the architecture of GAN in detail. Followed by that, we examined the loss function of GAN in detail.

In the next chapter, we will learn about one of the most popularly used deep learning frameworks, called TensorFlow.

Questions

Let's assess our understanding of deep learning algorithms by answering the following questions:

1. What is the activation function?
2. Define the softmax function.
3. What is an epoch?
4. What are some of the applications of RNNs?
5. Explain the vanishing gradient problem.
6. What are the different types of pooling operations?
7. Explain the generator and discriminator components of GANs.

Further reading

- To learn more about deep learning algorithms, you can check out my book **Hands-on Deep Learning Algorithms with Python**, also published by Packt, at https://www.packtpub.com/in/big-data-and-business-intelligence/hands-deep-learning-algorithms-python.

8
A Primer on TensorFlow

TensorFlow is one of the most popular deep learning libraries. In upcoming chapters, we will use TensorFlow to build deep reinforcement models. So, in this chapter, we will get ourselves familiar with TensorFlow and its functionalities.

We will learn about what computational graphs are and how TensorFlow uses them. We will also explore TensorBoard, which is a visualization tool provided by TensorFlow used for visualizing models. Going forward, we will understand how to build a neural network with TensorFlow to perform handwritten digit classification.

Moving on, we will learn about TensorFlow 2.0, which is the latest version of TensorFlow. We will understand how TensorFlow 2.0 differs from its previous versions and how it uses Keras as its high-level API.

In this chapter, we will learn about the following:

- TensorFlow
- Computational graphs and sessions
- Variables, constants, and placeholders
- TensorBoard
- Handwritten digit classification in TensorFlow
- Math operations in TensorFlow
- TensorFlow 2.0 and Keras

What is TensorFlow?

TensorFlow is an open source software library from Google, which is extensively used for numerical computation. It is one of the most used libraries for building deep learning models. It is highly scalable and runs on multiple platforms, such as Windows, Linux, macOS, and Android. It was originally developed by the researchers and engineers of the Google Brain team.

TensorFlow supports execution on everything, including CPUs, GPUs, TPUs, which are tensor processing units, and mobile and embedded platforms. Due to its flexible architecture and ease of deployment, it has become a popular choice of library among many researchers and scientists for building deep learning models.

In TensorFlow, every computation is represented by a data flow graph, also known as a **computational graph**, where nodes represent operations, such as addition or multiplication, and edges represent tensors. Data flow graphs can also be shared and executed on many different platforms. TensorFlow provides a visualization tool, called TensorBoard, for visualizing data flow graphs.

TensorFlow 2.0 is the latest version of TensorFlow. In the upcoming chapters, we will use TensorFlow 2.0 for building deep reinforcement learning models. However, it is important to understand how TensorFlow 1.x works. So, first, we will learn to use TensorFlow 1.x and then we will look into TensorFlow 2.0.

You can install TensorFlow easily through `pip` by just typing the following command in your terminal:

```
pip install tensorflow==1.13.1
```

We can check the successful installation of TensorFlow by running the following simple `Hello TensorFlow!` program:

```
import tensorflow as tf

hello = tf.constant("Hello TensorFlow!")
sess = tf.Session()
print(sess.run(hello))
```

The preceding program should print `Hello TensorFlow!`. If you get any errors, then you probably have not installed TensorFlow correctly.

Understanding computational graphs and sessions

As we have learned, every computation in TensorFlow is represented by a computational graph. They consist of several nodes and edges, where nodes are mathematical operations, such as addition and multiplication, and edges are tensors. Computational graphs are very efficient at optimizing resources and promote distributed computing.

A computational graph consists of several TensorFlow operations, arranged in a graph of nodes.

A computational graph helps us to understand the network architecture when we work on building a really complex neural network. For instance, let's consider a simple layer, $h = \text{Relu}(WX + b)$. Its computational graph would be represented as follows:

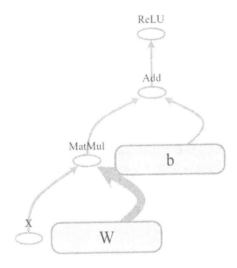

Figure 8.1: Computational graph

There are two types of dependency in the computational graph, called direct and indirect dependency. Say we have node b, the input of which is dependent on the output of node a; this type of dependency is called **direct dependency**, as shown in the following code:

```
a = tf.multiply(8,5)
b = tf.multiply(a,1)
```

When node b doesn't depend on node a for its input, it is called **indirect dependency,** as shown in the following code:

```
a = tf.multiply(8,5)
b = tf.multiply(4,3)
```

So, if we can understand these dependencies, we can distribute the independent computations in the available resources and reduce the computation time. Whenever we import TensorFlow, a default graph is created automatically and all of the nodes we create are associated with the default graph. We can also create our own graphs instead of using the default graph, and this is useful when building multiple models that do not depend on one another. A TensorFlow graph can be created using tf.Graph(), as follows:

```
graph = tf.Graph()

with graph.as_default():
        z = tf.add(x, y, name='Add')
```

If we want to clear the default graph (that is, if we want to clear the previously defined variables and operations in the graph), then we can do this using tf.reset_default_graph().

Sessions

As mentioned in the previous section, a computational graph with operations on its nodes and tensors to its edges is created, and in order to execute the graph, we use a TensorFlow session.

A TensorFlow session can be created using tf.Session(), as shown in the following code:

```
sess = tf.Session()
```

After creating the session, we can execute our graph, using the sess.run() method.

Every computation in TensorFlow is represented by a computational graph, so we need to run a computational graph for everything. That is, in order to compute anything on TensorFlow, we need to create a TensorFlow session.

Let's execute the following code to multiply two numbers:

```
a = tf.multiply(3,3)
print(a)
```

Instead of printing 9, the preceding code will print a TensorFlow object, `Tensor("Mul:0", shape=(), dtype=int32)`.

As we discussed earlier, whenever we import TensorFlow, a default computational graph is automatically created and all nodes are attached to the graph. Hence, when we print a, it just returns the TensorFlow object because the value for a is not computed yet, as the computation graph has not been executed.

In order to execute the graph, we need to initialize and run the TensorFlow session, as follows:

```
a = tf.multiply(3,3)
with tf.Session as sess:
    print(sess.run(a))
```

The preceding code prints 9.

Now that we have learned about sessions, in the next section, we will learn about variables, constants, and placeholders.

Variables, constants, and placeholders

Variables, constants, and placeholders are fundamental elements of TensorFlow. However, there is always confusion between these three. Let's look at each element, one by one, and learn the difference between them.

Variables

Variables are containers used to store values. Variables are used as input to several other operations in a computational graph. A variable can be created using the `tf.Variable()` function, as shown in the following code:

```
x = tf.Variable(13)
```

Let's create a variable called W, using `tf.Variable()`, as follows:

```
W = tf.Variable(tf.random_normal([500, 111], stddev=0.35),
name="weights")
```

As you can see in the preceding code, we create a variable, W, by randomly drawing values from a normal distribution with a standard deviation of 0.35.

What is that name parameter in `tf.Variable()`?

It is used to set the name of the variable in the computational graph. So, in the preceding code, Python saves the variable as W but in the TensorFlow graph, it will be saved as weights.

After defining a variable, we need to initialize all of the variables in the computational graph. That can be done using tf.global_variables_initializer().

Once we create a session, we run the initialization operation, which initializes all of the defined variables, and only then can we run the other operations, as shown in the following code:

```
x = tf.Variable(1212)
init = tf.global_variables_initializer()

with tf.Session() as sess:
  sess.run(init)
  print(sess.run(x))
```

Constants

Constants, unlike variables, cannot have their values changed. That is, constants are immutable. Once they are assigned values, they cannot be changed throughout the program. We can create constants using tf.constant(), as the following code shows:

```
x = tf.constant(13)
```

Placeholders and feed dictionaries

We can think of placeholders as variables, where we only define the type and dimension, but do not assign a value. Values for the placeholders will be fed at runtime. We feed data to computational graphs using placeholders. Placeholders are defined with no values.

A placeholder can be defined using tf.placeholder(). It takes an optional argument called shape, which denotes the dimensions of the data. If shape is set to None, then we can feed data of any size at runtime. A placeholder can be defined as follows:

```
x = tf.placeholder("float", shape=None)
```

 To put it in simple terms, we use tf.Variable to store data and tf.placeholder to feed in external data.

Let's consider a simple example to better understand placeholders:

```
x = tf.placeholder("float", None)
y = x+3

with tf.Session() as sess:
    result = sess.run(y)
    print(result)
```

If we run the preceding code, then it will return an error because we are trying to compute y, where y= x+3 and x is a placeholder whose value is not assigned. As we have learned, values for the placeholders will be assigned at runtime. We assign the values of the placeholder using the feed_dict parameter. The feed_dict parameter is basically a dictionary where the key represents the name of the placeholder, and the value represents the value of the placeholder.

As you can see in the following code, we set feed_dict = {x:5}, which implies that the value for the x placeholder is 5:

```
with tf.Session() as sess:
    result = sess.run(y, feed_dict={x: 5})
    print(result)
```

The preceding code returns 8.0.

That's it. In the next section, we will learn about TensorBoard.

Introducing TensorBoard

TensorBoard is TensorFlow's visualization tool, which can be used to visualize a computational graph. It can also be used to plot various quantitative metrics and the results of several intermediate calculations. When we are training a really deep neural network, it becomes confusing when we have to debug the network. So, if we can visualize the computational graph in TensorBoard, we can easily understand such complex models, debug them, and optimize them. TensorBoard also supports sharing.

As shown in *Figure 8.2*, the TensorBoard panel consists of several tabs—**SCALARS, IMAGES, AUDIO, GRAPHS, DISTRIBUTIONS, HISTOGRAMS**, and **EMBEDDINGS**:

Figure 8.2: TensorBoard

The tabs are pretty self-explanatory. The **SCALARS** tab shows useful information about the scalar variables we use in our program. For example, it shows how the value of a scalar variable called loss changes over several iterations.

The **GRAPHS** tab shows the computational graph. The **DISTRIBUTIONS** and **HISTOGRAMS** tabs show the distribution of a variable. For example, our model's weight distribution and histogram can be seen under these tabs. The **EMBEDDINGS** tab is used for visualizing high-dimensional vectors, such as word embeddings.

Let's build a basic computational graph and visualize it in TensorBoard. Let's say we have four constants, shown as follows:

```
x = tf.constant(1,name='x')
y = tf.constant(1,name='y')
a = tf.constant(3,name='a')
b = tf.constant(3,name='b')
```

Let's multiply x and y and a and b and save them as prod1 and prod2, as shown in the following code:

```
prod1 = tf.multiply(x,y,name='prod1')
prod2 = tf.multiply(a,b,name='prod2')
```

Add prod1 and prod2 and store them in sum:

```
sum = tf.add(prod1,prod2,name='sum')
```

Now, we can visualize all of these operations in TensorBoard. To visualize in TensorBoard, we first need to save our event files. That can be done using tf.summary.FileWriter(). It takes two important parameters, logdir and graph.

As the name suggests, logdir specifies the directory where we want to store the graph, and graph specifies which graph we want to store:

```
with tf.Session() as sess:
    writer = tf.summary.FileWriter(logdir='./graphs',graph=sess.graph)
    print(sess.run(sum))
```

In the preceding code, ./graphs is the directory where we are storing our event file, and sess.graph specifies the current graph in our TensorFlow session. So, we are storing the current graph of the TensorFlow session in the graphs directory.

To start TensorBoard, go to your Terminal, locate the working directory, and type the following:

```
tensorboard --logdir=graphs --port=8000
```

The `logdir` parameter indicates the directory where the event file is stored and `port` is the port number. Once you run the preceding command, open your browser and type `http://localhost:8000/`.

In the TensorBoard panel, under the **GRAPHS** tab, you can see the computational graph:

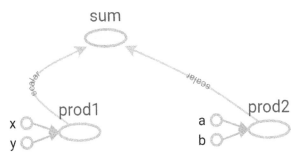

Figure 8.3: Computational graph

As you may notice, all of the operations we have defined are clearly shown in the graph.

Creating a name scope

Scoping is used to reduce complexity and helps us to better understand a model by grouping related nodes together. Having a name scope helps us to group similar operations in a graph. This comes in handy when we are building a complex architecture. Scoping can be created using `tf.name_scope()`. In the previous example, we performed two operations, `Product` and `sum`. We can simply group them into two different name scopes as `Product` and `sum`.

In the previous section, we saw how `prod1` and `prod2` perform multiplication and compute the result. We'll define a name scope called `Product`, and group the `prod1` and `prod2` operations, as shown in the following code:

```
with tf.name_scope("Product"):
    with tf.name_scope("prod1"):
        prod1 = tf.multiply(x,y,name='prod1')

    with tf.name_scope("prod2"):
        prod2 = tf.multiply(a,b,name='prod2')
```

Now, define the name scope for `sum`:

```
with tf.name_scope("sum"):
    sum = tf.add(prod1,prod2,name='sum')
```

Store the file in the graphs directory:

```
with tf.Session() as sess:
    writer = tf.summary.FileWriter('./graphs', sess.graph)
    print(sess.run(sum))
```

Visualize the graph in TensorBoard:

```
tensorboard --logdir=graphs --port=8000
```

As you may notice, now, we have only two nodes, **sum** and **Product**:

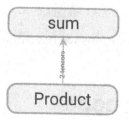

Figure 8.4: A computational graph

Once we double-click on the nodes, we can see how the computation is happening. As you can see, the **prod1** and **prod2** nodes are grouped under the **Product** scope, and their results are sent to the **sum** node, where they will be added. You can see how the **prod1** and **prod2** nodes compute their value:

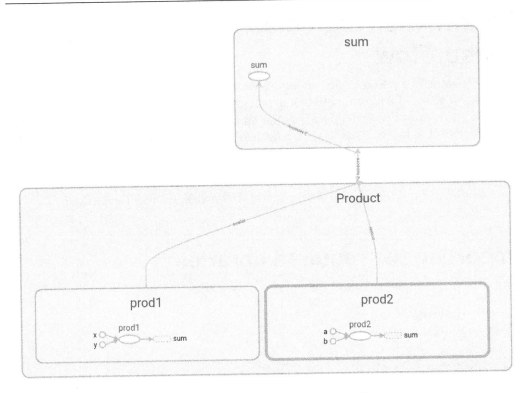

Figure 8.5: A computational graph in detail

The preceding graph is just a simple example. When we are working on a complex project with a lot of operations, name scoping helps us to group similar operations together and enables us to understand the computational graph better.

Now that we have learned about TensorFlow, in the next section, let's see how to build handwritten digit classification using TensorFlow.

Handwritten digit classification using TensorFlow

Putting together all the concepts we have learned so far, we will see how we can use TensorFlow to build a neural network to recognize handwritten digits. If you have been playing around with deep learning of late, then you must have come across the MNIST dataset. It has been called the *hello world* of deep learning. It consists of 55,000 data points of handwritten digits (0 to 9).

In this section, we will see how we can use our neural network to recognize these handwritten digits, and we will get the hang of TensorFlow and TensorBoard.

Importing the required libraries

As a first step, let's import all of the required libraries:

```
import warnings
warnings.filterwarnings('ignore')

import tensorflow as tf
from tensorflow.examples.tutorials.mnist import input_data
tf.logging.set_verbosity(tf.logging.ERROR)

import matplotlib.pyplot as plt
%matplotlib inline
```

Loading the dataset

Load the dataset, using the following code:

```
mnist = input_data.read_data_sets("data/mnist", one_hot=True)
```

In the preceding code, data/mnist implies the location where we store the MNIST dataset, and one_hot=True implies that we are one-hot encoding the labels (0 to 9).

We will see what we have in our data by executing the following code:

```
print("No of images in training set {}".format(mnist.train.images.
shape))
print("No of labels in training set {}".format(mnist.train.labels.
shape))
```

```
print("No of images in test set {}".format(mnist.test.images.shape))
print("No of labels in test set {}".format(mnist.test.labels.shape))

No of images in training set (55000, 784)
No of labels in training set (55000, 10)
No of images in test set (10000, 784)
No of labels in test set (10000, 10)
```

We have 55000 images in the training set, each image is of size 784, and we have 10 labels, which are actually 0 to 9. Similarly, we have 10000 images in the test set.

Now, we'll plot an input image to see what it looks like:

```
img1 = mnist.train.images[0].reshape(28,28)
plt.imshow(img1, cmap='Greys')
```

Thus, our input image looks like the following:

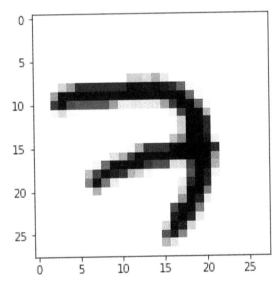

Figure 8.6: Image of the digit 7 from the training set

Defining the number of neurons in each layer

We'll build a four-layer neural network with three hidden layers and one output layer. As the size of the input image is 784, we set num_input to 784, and since we have 10 handwritten digits (0 to 9), we set 10 neurons in the output layer.

We define the number of neurons in each layer as follows:

```
#number of neurons in input layer
num_input = 784


#num of neurons in hidden layer 1
num_hidden1 = 512


#num of neurons in hidden layer 2
num_hidden2 = 256


#num of neurons in hidden layer 3
num_hidden_3 = 128


#num of neurons in output layer
num_output = 10
```

Defining placeholders

As we have learned, we first need to define the placeholders for `input` and `output`. Values for the placeholders will be fed in at runtime through `feed_dict`:

```
with tf.name_scope('input'):
    X = tf.placeholder("float", [None, num_input])

with tf.name_scope('output'):
    Y = tf.placeholder("float", [None, num_output])
```

Since we have a four-layer network, we have four weights and four biases. We initialize our weights by drawing values from the truncated normal distribution with a standard deviation of 0.1. Remember, the dimensions of the weight matrix should be *the number of neurons in the previous layer* x *the number of neurons in the current layer*. For instance, the dimensions of weight matrix w3 should be *the number of neurons in hidden layer 2* x *the number of neurons in hidden layer 3*.

We often define all of the weights in a dictionary, as follows:

```
with tf.name_scope('weights'):

weights = {
 'w1': tf.Variable(tf.truncated_normal([num_input, num_hidden1],
stddev=0.1),name='weight_1'),
 'w2': tf.Variable(tf.truncated_normal([num_hidden1, num_hidden2],
```

```
stddev=0.1),name='weight_2'),
   'w3': tf.Variable(tf.truncated_normal([num_hidden2, num_hidden_3],
stddev=0.1),name='weight_3'),
   'out': tf.Variable(tf.truncated_normal([num_hidden_3, num_output],
stddev=0.1),name='weight_4'),
 }
```

The shape of the bias should be the number of neurons in the current layer. For instance, the dimension of the b2 bias is the number of neurons in hidden layer 2. We set the bias value as a constant; 0.1 in all of the layers:

```
with tf.name_scope('biases'):

    biases = {
        'b1': tf.Variable(tf.constant(0.1, shape=[num_
hidden1]),name='bias_1'),
        'b2': tf.Variable(tf.constant(0.1, shape=[num_
hidden2]),name='bias_2'),
        'b3': tf.Variable(tf.constant(0.1, shape=[num_
hidden_3]),name='bias_3'),
        'out': tf.Variable(tf.constant(0.1, shape=[num_
output]),name='bias_4')
    }
```

Forward propagation

Now we'll define the forward propagation operation. We'll use ReLU activations in all layers. In the last layers, we'll apply sigmoid activation, as shown in the following code:

```
with tf.name_scope('Model'):

    with tf.name_scope('layer1'):
        layer_1 = tf.nn.relu(tf.add(tf.matmul(X, weights['w1']),
biases['b1']) )

    with tf.name_scope('layer2'):
        layer_2 = tf.nn.relu(tf.add(tf.matmul(layer_1, weights['w2']),
biases['b2']))

    with tf.name_scope('layer3'):
        layer_3 = tf.nn.relu(tf.add(tf.matmul(layer_2, weights['w3']),
biases['b3']))
```

```
with tf.name_scope('output_layer'):
        y_hat = tf.nn.sigmoid(tf.matmul(layer_3, weights['out']) +
biases['out'])
```

Computing loss and backpropagation

Next, we'll define our loss function. We'll use softmax cross-entropy as our loss function. TensorFlow provides the `tf.nn.softmax_cross_entropy_with_logits()` function for computing softmax cross-entropy loss. It takes two parameters as inputs, `logits` and `labels`:

- The `logits` parameter specifies the `logits` predicted by our network; for example, `y_hat`
- The `labels` parameter specifies the actual labels; for example, true labels, `Y`

We take the mean of the `loss` function using `tf.reduce_mean()`:

```
with tf.name_scope('Loss'):
        loss = tf.reduce_mean(tf.nn.softmax_cross_entropy_with_
logits(logits=y_hat,labels=Y))
```

Now, we need to minimize the loss using backpropagation. Don't worry! We don't have to calculate the derivatives of all the weights manually. Instead, we can use TensorFlow's `optimizer`:

```
learning_rate = 1e-4
optimizer = tf.train.AdamOptimizer(learning_rate).minimize(loss)
```

Computing accuracy

We calculate the accuracy of our model as follows:

- The `y_hat` parameter denotes the predicted probability for each class of our model. Since we have 10 classes, we will have 10 probabilities. If the probability is high at position 7, then it means that our network predicts the input image as digit 7 with high probability. The `tf.argmax()` function returns the index of the largest value. Thus, `tf.argmax(y_hat,1)` gives the index where the probability is high. Thus, if the probability is high at index 7, then it returns 7.

- The Y parameter denotes the actual labels, and they are the one-hot encoded values. That is, the Y parameter consists of zeros everywhere except at the position of the actual image, where it has a value of 1. For instance, if the input image is 7, then Y has a value of 0 at all indices except at index 7, where it has a value of 1. Thus, `tf.argmax(Y,1)` returns 7 because that is where we have a high value, 1.

Thus, `tf.argmax(y_hat,1)` gives the predicted digit, and `tf.argmax(Y,1)` gives us the actual digit.

The `tf.equal(x, y)` function takes x and y as inputs and returns the truth value of ($x == y$) element-wise. Thus, `correct_pred = tf.equal(predicted_digit,actual_digit)` consists of `True` where the actual and predicted digits are the same, and `False` where the actual and predicted digits are not the same. We convert the Boolean values in `correct_pred` into float values using TensorFlow's cast operation, `tf.cast(correct_pred, tf.float32)`. After converting them into float values, we take the average using `tf.reduce_mean()`.

Thus, `tf.reduce_mean(tf.cast(correct_pred, tf.float32))` gives us the average correct predictions:

```
with tf.name_scope('Accuracy'):

    predicted_digit = tf.argmax(y_hat, 1)
    actual_digit = tf.argmax(Y, 1)

    correct_pred = tf.equal(predicted_digit,actual_digit)
    accuracy = tf.reduce_mean(tf.cast(correct_pred, tf.float32))
```

Creating a summary

We can also visualize how the loss and accuracy of our model changes during several iterations in TensorBoard. So, we use `tf.summary()` to get the summary of the variable. Since the loss and accuracy are scalar variables, we use `tf.summary.scalar()`, as shown in the following code:

```
tf.summary.scalar("Accuracy", accuracy)
tf.summary.scalar("Loss", loss)
```

Next, we merge all of the summaries we use in our graph, using `tf.summary.merge_all()`. We do this because when we have many summaries, running and storing them would become inefficient, so we run them once in our session instead of running them multiple times:

```
merge_summary = tf.summary.merge_all()
```

Training the model

Now, it is time to train our model. As we have learned, first, we need to initialize all of the variables:

```
init = tf.global_variables_initializer()
```

Define the batch size, number of iterations, and learning rate, as follows:

```
learning_rate = 1e-4
num_iterations = 1000
batch_size = 128
```

Start the TensorFlow session:

```
with tf.Session() as sess:
```

Initialize all the variables:

```
    sess.run(init)
```

Save the event files:

```
    summary_writer = tf.summary.FileWriter('./graphs', graph=tf.get_
default_graph()
```

Train the model for a number of iterations:

```
    for i in range(num_iterations):
```

Get a batch of data according to the batch size:

```
batch_x, batch_y = mnist.train.next_batch(batch_size)
```

Train the network:

```
sess.run(optimizer, feed_dict={ X: batch_x, Y: batch_y})
```

Print loss and accuracy for every 100th iteration:

```
if i % 100 == 0:

    batch_loss, batch_accuracy,summary = sess.run(
        [loss, accuracy, merge_summary],
        feed_dict={X: batch_x, Y: batch_y}
        )

    #store all the summaries
    summary_writer.add_summary(summary, i)

    print('Iteration: {}, Loss: {}, Accuracy: {}'.
format(i,batch_loss,batch_accuracy))
```

As you may notice from the following output, the loss decreases and the accuracy increases over various training iterations:

```
Iteration: 0, Loss: 2.30789709091, Accuracy: 0.1171875
Iteration: 100, Loss: 1.76062202454, Accuracy: 0.859375
Iteration: 200, Loss: 1.60075569153, Accuracy: 0.9375
Iteration: 300, Loss: 1.60388696194, Accuracy: 0.890625
Iteration: 400, Loss: 1.59523034096, Accuracy: 0.921875
Iteration: 500, Loss: 1.58489584923, Accuracy: 0.859375
Iteration: 600, Loss: 1.51407408714, Accuracy: 0.953125
Iteration: 700, Loss: 1.53311181068, Accuracy: 0.9296875
Iteration: 800, Loss: 1.57677125931, Accuracy: 0.875
Iteration: 900, Loss: 1.52060437202, Accuracy: 0.9453125
```

Visualizing graphs in TensorBoard

After training, we can visualize our computational graph in TensorBoard, as shown in *Figure 8.7*. As you can see, our **Model** takes **input**, **weights**, and **biases** as input and returns the output. We compute **Loss** and **Accuracy** based on the output of the model. We minimize the loss by calculating **gradients** and updating **weights**:

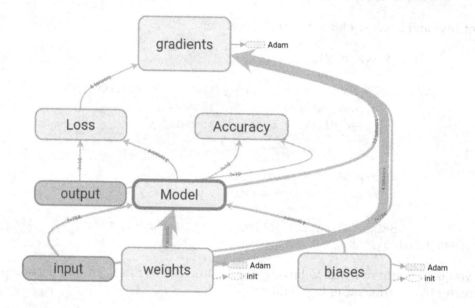

Figure 8.7: Computational graph

If we double-click and expand **Model**, we can see that we have three hidden layers and one output layer:

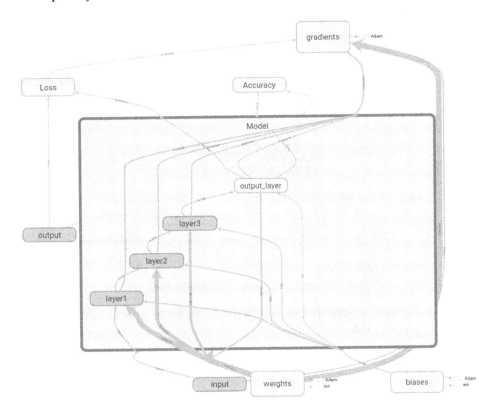

Figure 8.8: Expanding the Model node

Similarly, we can double-click and see every node. For instance, if we open **weights**, we can see how the four weights are initialized using truncated normal distribution, and how it is updated using the Adam optimizer:

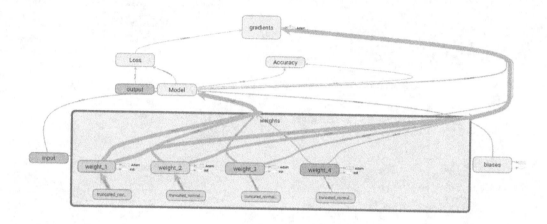

Figure 8.9: Expanding the weights node

As we have learned, the computational graph helps us to understand what is happening on each node.

We can see how the accuracy is being calculated by double-clicking on the **Accuracy** node:

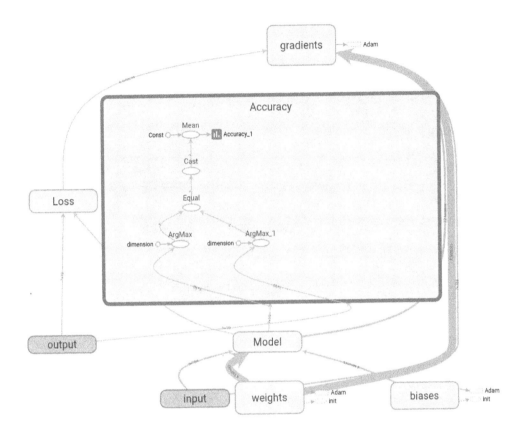

Figure 8.10: Expanding the Accuracy node

Remember that we also stored a summary of our `loss` and `accuracy` variables. We can find them under the **SCALARS** tab in TensorBoard. *Figure 8.11* shows how the loss decreases over iterations:

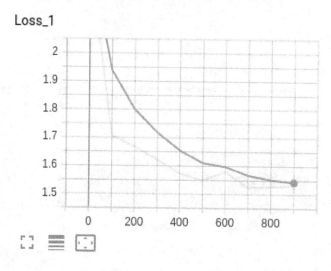

Figure 8.11: Plot of the loss function

Figure 8.12 shows how accuracy increases over iterations:

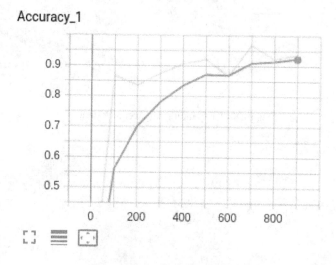

Figure 8.12 Plot of accuracy

That's it. In the next section, we will learn about another interesting feature in TensorFlow called eager execution.

Introducing eager execution

Eager execution in TensorFlow is more Pythonic and allows rapid prototyping. Unlike graph mode, where we need to construct a graph every time we want to perform any operation, eager execution follows the imperative programming paradigm, where any operation can be performed immediately, without having to create a graph, just like we do in Python. Hence, with eager execution, we can say goodbye to sessions and placeholders. It also makes the debugging process easier with an immediate runtime error, unlike graph mode. For instance, in graph mode, to compute anything, we run the session. As shown in the following code, to evaluate the value of z, we have to run the TensorFlow session:

```
x = tf.constant(11)
y = tf.constant(11)
z = x*y

with tf.Session() as sess:
    print(sess.run(z))
```

With eager execution, we don't need to create a session; we can simply compute z, just like we do in Python. In order to enable eager execution, just call the `tf.enable_eager_execution()` function:

```
x = tf.constant(11)
y = tf.constant(11)
z = x*y

print(z)
```

It will return the following:

```
<tf.Tensor: id=789, shape=(), dtype=int32, numpy=121>
```

In order to get the output value, we can print the following:

```
z.numpy()

121
```

Although eager execution enables the imperative programming paradigm, in this book, we will investigate most of the examples in non-eager mode to better understand the algorithms from scratch. In the next section, we will see how to perform math operations using TensorFlow.

Math operations in TensorFlow

Now, we will explore some of the operations in TensorFlow using eager execution mode:

```
x = tf.constant([1., 2., 3.])
y = tf.constant([3., 2., 1.])
```

Let's start with some basic arithmetic operations.

Use `tf.add` to add two numbers:

```
sum = tf.add(x,y)
sum.numpy()
```

```
array([4., 4., 4.], dtype=float32)
```

The `tf.subtract` function is used for finding the difference between two numbers:

```
difference = tf.subtract(x,y)
difference.numpy()
```

```
array([-2., 0., 2.], dtype=float32)
```

The `tf.multiply` function is used for multiplying two numbers:

```
product = tf.multiply(x,y)
product.numpy()
```

```
array([3., 4., 3.], dtype=float32)
```

Divide two numbers using `tf.divide`:

```
division = tf.divide(x,y)
division.numpy()
```

```
array([0.33333334, 1.        , 3.        ], dtype=float32)
```

The dot product can be computed as follows:

```
dot_product = tf.reduce_sum(tf.multiply(x, y))
dot_product.numpy()
```

```
10.0
```

Next, let's find the index of the minimum and maximum elements:

```
x = tf.constant([10, 0, 13, 9])
```

The index of the minimum value is computed using `tf.argmin()`:

```
tf.argmin(x).numpy()
```

```
1
```

The index of the maximum value is computed using `tf.argmax()`:

```
tf.argmax(x).numpy()
```

```
2
```

Run the following code to find the squared difference between x and y:

```
x = tf.Variable([1,3,5,7,11])
y = tf.Variable([1])

tf.math.squared_difference(x,y).numpy()
```

```
[  0,   4,  16,  36, 100]
```

Let's try typecasting; that is, converting from one data type into another.

Print the type of x:

```
print(x.dtype)
```

```
tf.int32
```

We can convert the type of x, which is `tf.int32`, into `tf.float32`, using `tf.cast`, as shown in the following code:

```
x = tf.cast(x, dtype=tf.float32)
```

Now, check the x type. It will be `tf.float32`, as follows:

```
print(x.dtype)
```

```
tf.float32
```

Concatenate the two matrices:

```
x = [[3,6,9], [7,7,7]]
y = [[4,5,6], [5,5,5]]
```

Concatenate the matrices row-wise:

```
tf.concat([x, y], 0).numpy()
```

```
array([[3, 6, 9],
       [7, 7, 7],
       [4, 5, 6],
       [5, 5, 5]], dtype=int32)
```

Use the following code to concatenate the matrices column-wise:

```
tf.concat([x, y], 1).numpy()
```

```
array([[3, 6, 9, 4, 5, 6],
       [7, 7, 7, 5, 5, 5]], dtype=int32)
```

Stack the x matrix using the stack function:

```
tf.stack(x, axis=1).numpy()
```

```
array([[3, 7],
       [6, 7],
       [9, 7]], dtype=int32)
```

Now, let's see how to perform the reduce_mean operation:

```
x = tf.Variable([[1.0, 5.0], [2.0, 3.0]])
```

```
x.numpy()
```

```
array([[1., 5.],
       [2., 3.]]
```

Compute the mean value of x; that is, $(1.0 + 5.0 + 2.0 + 3.0) / 4$:

```
tf.reduce_mean(input_tensor=x).numpy()
```

```
2.75
```

Compute the mean across the row; that is, $(1.0+5.0)/2$, $(2.0+3.0)/2$:

```
tf.reduce_mean(input_tensor=x, axis=0).numpy()
```

```
array([1.5, 4. ], dtype=float32)
```

Compute the mean across the column; that is, $(1.0+5.0)/2.0$, $(2.0+3.0)/2.0$:

```
tf.reduce_mean(input_tensor=x, axis=1, keepdims=True).numpy()
```

```
array([[3. ],
       [2.5]], dtype=float32)
```

Draw random values from the probability distributions:

```
tf.random.normal(shape=(3,2), mean=10.0, stddev=2.0).numpy()
```

```
tf.random.uniform(shape = (3,2), minval=0, maxval=None, dtype=tf.
float32,).numpy()
```

Compute the softmax probabilities:

```
x = tf.constant([7., 2., 5.])
```

```
tf.nn.softmax(x).numpy()
```

```
array([0.8756006 , 0.00589975, 0.11849965], dtype=float32)
```

Now, we'll look at how to compute the gradients.

Define the `square` function:

```
def square(x):
    return tf.multiply(x, x)
```

The gradients can be computed for the preceding `square` function using `tf.GradientTape`, as follows:

```
with tf.GradientTape(persistent=True) as tape:
    print(square(6.).numpy())
```

```
36.0
```

TensorFlow 2.0 and Keras

TensorFlow 2.0 has got some really cool features. It sets the eager execution mode by default. It provides a simplified workflow and uses Keras as the main API for building deep learning models. It is also backward compatible with TensorFlow 1.x versions.

To install TensorFlow 2.0, open your Terminal and type the following command:

```
pip install tensorflow==2.0.0-alpha0
```

Since TensorFlow 2.0 uses Keras as a high-level API, we will look at how Keras works in the next section.

Bonjour Keras

Keras is another popularly used deep learning library. It was developed by François Chollet at Google. It is well known for its fast prototyping, and it makes model building simple. It is a high-level library, meaning that it does not perform any low-level operations on its own, such as convolution. It uses a backend engine for doing that, such as TensorFlow. The Keras API is available in tf.keras, and TensorFlow 2.0 uses it as the primary API.

Building a model in Keras involves four important steps:

1. Defining the model
2. Compiling the model
3. Fitting the model
4. Evaluating the model

Defining the model

The first step is defining the model. Keras provides two different APIs to define the model:

- The sequential API
- The functional API

Defining a sequential model

In a sequential model, we stack each layer, one above another:

```
from keras.models import Sequential
from keras.layers import Dense
```

First, let's define our model as a `Sequential()` model, as follows:

```
model = Sequential()
```

Now, define the first layer, as shown in the following code:

```
model.add(Dense(13, input_dim=7, activation='relu'))
```

In the preceding code, `Dense` implies a fully connected layer, `input_dim` implies the dimension of our input, and `activation` specifies the activation function that we use. We can stack up as many layers as we want, one above another.

Define the next layer with the `relu` activation function, as follows:

```
model.add(Dense(7, activation='relu'))
```

Define the output layer with the `sigmoid` activation function:

```
model.add(Dense(1, activation='sigmoid'))
```

The final code block of the sequential model is shown as follows. As you can see, the Keras code is much simpler than the TensorFlow code:

```
model = Sequential()
model.add(Dense(13, input_dim=7, activation='relu'))
model.add(Dense(7, activation='relu'))
model.add(Dense(1, activation='sigmoid'))
```

Defining a functional model

A functional model provides more flexibility than a sequential model. For instance, in a functional model, we can easily connect any layer to another layer, whereas, in a sequential model, each layer is in a stack, one above another. A functional model comes in handy when creating complex models, such as directed acyclic graphs, models with multiple input values, multiple output values, and shared layers. Now, we will see how to define a functional model in Keras.

The first step is to define the input dimensions:

```
input = Input(shape=(2,))
```

Now, we'll define our first fully connected layer with 10 neurons and relu activation, using the Dense class, as shown:

```
layer1 = Dense(10, activation='relu')
```

We defined layer1, but where is the input to layer1 coming from? We need to specify the input to layer1 in a bracket notation at the end, as shown:

```
layer1 = Dense(10, activation='relu')(input)
```

We define the next layer, layer2, with 13 neurons and relu activation. The input to layer2 comes from layer1, so that is added in the bracket at the end, as shown in the following code:

```
layer2 = Dense(10, activation='relu')(layer1)
```

Now, we can define the output layer with the sigmoid activation function. Input to the output layer comes from layer2, so that is added in bracket at the end:

```
output = Dense(1, activation='sigmoid')(layer2)
```

After defining all of the layers, we define the model using a Model class, where we need to specify inputs and outputs, as follows:

```
model = Model(inputs=input, outputs=output)
```

The complete code for the functional model is shown here:

```
input = Input(shape=(2,))
layer1 = Dense(10, activation='relu')(input)
layer2 = Dense(10, activation='relu')(layer1)
output = Dense(1, activation='sigmoid')(layer2)
model = Model(inputs=input, outputs=output)
```

Compiling the model

Now that we have defined the model, the next step is to compile it. In this phase, we set up how the model should learn. We define three parameters when compiling the model:

- The `optimizer` parameter: This defines the optimization algorithm we want to use; for example, the gradient descent.

- The `loss` parameter: This is the objective function that we are trying to minimize; for example, the mean squared error or cross-entropy loss.

- The `metrics` parameter: This is the metric through which we want to assess the model's performance; for example, `accuracy`. We can also specify more than one metric.

Run the following code to compile the model:

```
model.compile(loss='binary_crossentropy', optimizer='sgd',
metrics=['accuracy'])
```

Training the model

We defined and also compiled the model. Now, we will train the model. Training the model can be done using the `fit` function. We specify our features, x; labels, y; the number of epochs we want to train the model for; and `batch_size`, as follows:

```
model.fit(x=data, y=labels, epochs=100, batch_size=10)
```

Evaluating the model

After training the model, we will evaluate the model on the test set:

```
model.evaluate(x=data_test,y=labels_test)
```

We can also evaluate the model on the same train set, and that will help us to understand the training accuracy:

```
model.evaluate(x=data,y=labels)
```

That's it. Let's see how to use TensorFlow for the MNIST digit classification task in the next section.

MNIST digit classification using TensorFlow 2.0

Now, we will see how we can perform MNIST handwritten digit classification, using TensorFlow 2.0. It requires only a few lines of code compared to TensorFlow 1.x. As we have learned, TensorFlow 2.0 uses Keras as its high-level API; we just need to add `tf.keras` to the Keras code.

Let's start by loading the dataset:

```
mnist = tf.keras.datasets.mnist
```

Create a training set and a test set with the following code:

```
(x_train,y_train), (x_test, y_test) = mnist.load_data()
```

Normalize the train and test sets by dividing the values of x by the maximum value of x; that is, 255.0:

```
x_train, x_test = tf.cast(x_train/255.0, tf.float32), tf.cast(x_
test/255.0, tf.float32)
y_train, y_test = tf.cast(y_train,tf.int64),tf.cast(y_test,tf.int64)
```

Define the sequential model as follows:

```
model = tf.keras.models.Sequential()
```

Now, let's add layers to the model. We use a three-layer network with the ReLU function in the hidden layer and softmax in the final layer:

```
model.add(tf.keras.layers.Flatten())
model.add(tf.keras.layers.Dense(256, activation="relu"))
model.add(tf.keras.layers.Dense(128, activation="relu"))
model.add(tf.keras.layers.Dense(10, activation="softmax"))
```

Compile the model by running the following line of code:

```
model.compile(optimizer='sgd', loss='sparse_categorical_crossentropy',
metrics=['accuracy'])
```

Train the model:

```
model.fit(x_train, y_train, batch_size=32, epochs=10)
```

Evaluate the model:

```
model.evaluate(x_test, y_test)
```

That's it! Writing code with the Keras API is that simple.

Summary

We started off this chapter by understanding TensorFlow and how it uses computational graphs. We learned that computation in TensorFlow is represented by a computational graph, which consists of several nodes and edges, where nodes are mathematical operations, such as addition and multiplication, and edges are tensors.

Next, we learned that variables are containers used to store values, and they are used as input to several other operations in a computational graph. We also learned that placeholders are like variables, where we only define the type and dimension but do not assign the values, and the values for the placeholders are fed at runtime. Moving forward, we learned about TensorBoard, which is TensorFlow's visualization tool and can be used to visualize a computational graph. We also explored eager execution, which is more Pythonic and allows rapid prototyping.

We understood that, unlike graph mode, where we need to construct a graph every time to perform any operation, eager execution follows the imperative programming paradigm, where any operation can be performed immediately, without having to create a graph, just like we do in Python.

In the next chapter, we begin our **deep reinforcement learning (DRL)** journey by understanding one of the popular DRL algorithms, called the **Deep Q Network (DQN)**.

Questions

Let's put our knowledge of TensorFlow to the test by answering the following questions:

1. What is a TensorFlow session?
2. Define a placeholder.
3. What is TensorBoard?
4. Why is eager execution mode useful?
5. What are all the steps involved in building a model using Keras?
6. How does Keras's functional model differ from its sequential model?

Further reading

You can learn more about TensorFlow by checking its official documentation at `https://www.tensorflow.org/tutorials`.

9
Deep Q Network and Its Variants

In this chapter, let's get started with one of the most popular **Deep Reinforcement Learning (DRL)** algorithms called **Deep Q Network (DQN)**. Understanding DQN is very important as many of the state-of-the-art DRL algorithms are based on DQN. The DQN algorithm was first proposed by researchers at Google's DeepMind in 2013 in the paper *Playing Atari with Deep Reinforcement Learning.* They described the DQN architecture and explained why it was so effective at playing Atari games with human-level accuracy. We begin the chapter by learning what exactly a deep Q network is, and how it is used in reinforcement learning. Next, we will deep dive into the algorithm of DQN. Then we will learn how to implement DQN to play Atari games.

After learning about DQN, we will cover several variants of DQN, such as double DQN, DQN with prioritized experience replay, dueling DQN, and the deep recurrent Q network in detail.

In this chapter, we will cover the following topics:

- What is DQN?
- The DQN algorithm
- Playing Atari games with DQN
- Double DQN
- DQN with prioritized experience replay
- The dueling DQN
- The deep recurrent Q network

What is DQN?

The objective of reinforcement learning is to find the optimal policy, that is, the policy that gives us the maximum return (the sum of rewards of the episode). In order to compute the policy, first we compute the Q function. Once we have the Q function, then we extract the policy by selecting an action in each state that has the maximum Q value. For instance, let's suppose we have two states **A** and **B** and our action space consists of two actions; let the actions be *up* and *down*. So, in order to find which action to perform in state **A** and **B**, first we compute the Q value of all state-action pairs, as *Table 9.1* shows:

State	Action	Value
A	up	17
A	down	10
B	up	11
B	down	20

Table 9.1: Q-value of state-action pairs

Once we have the Q value of all state-action pairs, then we select the action in each state that has the maximum Q value. So, we select the action *up* in state **A** and *down* in state **B** as they have the maximum Q value. We improve the Q function on every iteration and once we have the optimal Q function, then we can extract the optimal policy from it.

Now, let's revisit our grid world environment, as shown in *Figure 9.1*:

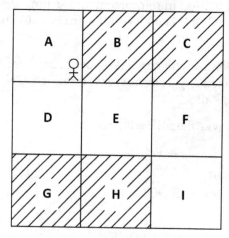

Figure 9.1: Grid world environment

We learned that in the grid world environment, the goal of our agent is to reach state I from state **A** without visiting the shaded states, and in each state, the agent has to perform one of the four actions—*up, down, left, right.*

To compute the policy, first we compute the Q values of all state-action pairs. Here, the number of states is 9 (**A** to **I**) and we have 4 actions in our action space, so our Q table will consist of 9 x 4 = 36 rows containing the Q values of all possible state-action pairs. Once we obtain the Q values, then we extract the policy by selecting the action in each state that has the maximum Q value. But is it a good approach to compute the Q value exhaustively for all state-action pairs? Let's explore this in more detail.

Let's suppose we have an environment where we have 1,000 states and 50 possible actions in each state. In this case, our Q table will consist of 1,000 x 50 = 50,000 rows containing the Q values of all possible state-action pairs. In cases like this, where our environment consists of a large number of states and actions, it will be very expensive to compute the Q values of all possible state-action pairs in an exhaustive fashion.

Instead of computing Q values in this way, can we approximate them using any function approximator, such as a neural network? Yes! We can parameterize our Q function by a parameter θ and compute the Q value where the parameter θ is just the parameter of our neural network. So, we just feed the state of the environment to a neural network and it will return the Q value of all possible actions in that state. Once we obtain the Q values, then we can select the best action as the one that has the maximum Q value.

For example, let's consider our grid world environment. As *Figure 9.2* shows, we just feed state **D** as an input to the network and it returns the Q value of all actions in state **D**, which are *up, down, left,* and *right,* as output. Then, we select the action that has the maximum Q value. Since action *right* has a maximum Q value, we select action *right* in the state **D**:

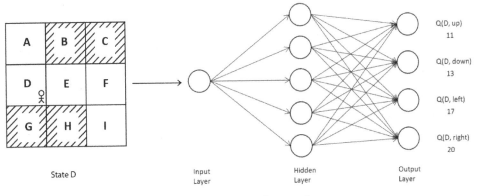

Figure 9.2: Deep Q network

Since we are using a neural network to approximate the Q value, the neural network is called the Q network, and if we use a deep neural network to approximate the Q value, then the deep neural network is called a **deep Q network (DQN)**.

We can denote our Q function by $Q_\theta(s, a)$, where the parameter θ in subscript indicates that our Q function is parameterized by θ, and θ is just the parameter of our neural network.

We initialize the network parameter θ with random values and approximate the Q function (Q values), but since we initialized θ with random values, the approximated Q function will not be optimal. So, we train the network for several iterations by finding the optimal parameter θ. Once we find the optimal θ, we will have the optimal Q function. Then we can extract the optimal policy from the optimal Q function.

Okay, but how can we train our network? What about the training data and the loss function? Is it a classification or regression task? Now that we have a basic understanding of how DQN works, in the next section, we will get into the details and address all these questions.

Understanding DQN

In this section, we will understand how exactly DQN works. We learned that we use DQN to approximate the Q value of all the actions in the given input state. The Q value is just a continuous number, so we are essentially using our DQN to perform a regression task.

Okay, what about the training data? We use a buffer called a replay buffer to collect the agent's experience and, based on this experience, we train our network. Let's explore the replay buffer in detail.

Replay buffer

We know that the agent makes a transition from a state s to the next state s' by performing some action a, and then receives a reward r. We can save this transition information (s, a, r, s') in a buffer called a replay buffer or experience replay. The replay buffer is usually denoted by $\mathcal{D}$. This transition information is basically the agent's experience. We store the agent's experience over several episodes in the replay buffer. The key idea of using the replay buffer to store the agent's experience is that we can train our DQN with experience (transition) sampled from the buffer. A replay buffer is shown here:

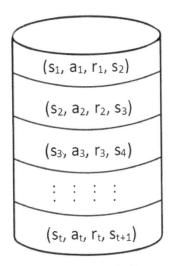

Figure 9.3: Replay buffer

The following steps help us to understand how we store the transition information in the replay buffer $\mathcal{D}$:

1. Initialize the replay buffer $\mathcal{D}$.
2. For each episode perform *step 3*.
3. For each step in the episode:
    1. Make a transition, that is, perform an action a in the state s, move to the next state s', and receive the reward r.
    2. Store the transition information (s, a, r, s') in the replay buffer $\mathcal{D}$.

As explained in the preceding steps, we collect the agent's transition information over many episodes and save it in the replay buffer. To understand this clearly, let's consider our favorite grid world environment. Let's suppose we have the following two episodes/trajectories:

Episode 1:

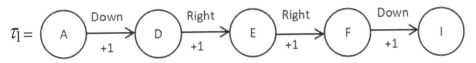

Figure 9.4: Trajectory 1

Episode 2:

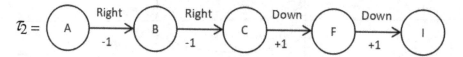

Figure 9.5: Trajectory 2

Now, this information will be stored in the replay buffer, as *Figure 9.6* shows:

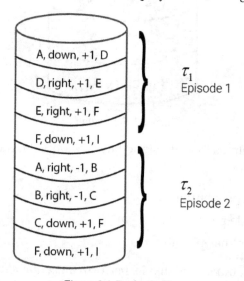

Figure 9.6: Replay buffer

As *Figure 9.6* shows, we store the transition information by stacking it sequentially one after another. We train the network by sampling a minibatch of transitions from the replay buffer. Wait! There is a small issue here. Since we are stacking up the agent's experience (transition) one after another sequentially, the agent's experience will be highly correlated. For example, as shown in the preceding figure, transitions will be correlated with the rows above and below. If we train our network with this correlated experience then our neural network will easily overfit. So, to combat this, we sample a random minibatch of transitions from the replay buffer and train the network.

Note that the replay buffer is of limited size, that is, a replay buffer will store only a fixed amount of the agent's experience. So, when the buffer is full we replace the old experience with new experience. A replay buffer is usually implemented as a queue structure (first in first out) rather than a list. So, if the buffer is full when new experience comes in, we remove the old experience and add the new experience into the buffer.

We have learned that we train our network by randomly sampling a minibatch of experience from the buffer. But how exactly does the training happen? How does our network learn to approximate the optimal Q function using this minibatch of samples? This is exactly what we discuss in the next section.

Loss function

We learned that in DQN, our goal is to predict the Q value, which is just a continuous value. Thus, in DQN we basically perform a regression task. We generally use the **mean squared error (MSE)** as the loss function for the regression task. MSE can be defined as the average squared difference between the target value and the predicted value, as shown here:

$$\text{MSE} = \frac{1}{K} \sum_{i=1}^{K} (y_i - \hat{y}_i)^2$$

Where y is the target value, $\hat{y}$ is the predicted value, and K is the number of training samples.

Now, let's learn how to use MSE in the DQN and train the network. We can train our network by minimizing the MSE between the target Q value and predicted Q value. First, how can we obtain the target Q value? Our target Q value should be the optimal Q value so that we can train our network by minimizing the error between the optimal Q value and predicted Q value. But how can we compute the optimal Q value? This is where the Bellman equation helps us. In *Chapter 3, The Bellman Equation and Dynamic Programming*, we learned that the optimal Q value can be obtained using the Bellman optimality equation:

$$Q^*(s, a) = \mathbb{E}_{s' \sim P}[R(s, a, s') + \gamma \max_{a'} Q^*(s', a')]$$

where $R(s, a, s')$ represents the immediate reward r that we obtain while performing an action a in state s and moving to the next state s', so we can just denote $R(s, a, s')$ by r:

$$Q^*(s, a) = \mathbb{E}_{s' \sim P}\left[r + \gamma \max_{a'} Q^*(s', a')\right]$$

In the preceding equation, we can remove the expectation. We will approximate the expectation by sampling K number of transitions from the replay buffer and taking the average value; we will learn more about this in a while.

Thus, according to the Bellman optimality equation, the optimal Q value is just the sum of the reward and the discounted maximum Q value of the next state-action pair, that is:

$$Q^*(s,a) = r + \gamma \max_{a'} Q^*(s',a') \qquad (1)$$

So, we can define our loss as the difference between the target value (the optimal Q value) and the predicted value (the Q value predicted by the DQN) and express the loss function L as:

$$L(\theta) = Q^*(s,a) - Q_\theta(s,a)$$

Substituting equation (1) in the preceding equation, we can write:

$$L(\theta) = r + \gamma \max_{a'} Q(s',a') - Q_\theta(s,a)$$

We know that we compute the predicted Q value using the network parameterized by θ. How can we compute the target value? That is, we learned that the target value is the sum of the reward and the discounted maximum Q value of the next state-action pair. How do we compute the Q value of the next state-action pair?

$$L(\theta) = r + \gamma \max_{a'} \boxed{Q(s',a')} - Q_\theta(s,a)$$

How do we compute this?

Similar to the predicted Q value, we can compute the Q value of the next state-action pair in the target using the same DQN parameterized by θ. So, we can rewrite our loss function as:

$$L(\theta) = r + \gamma \max_{a'} Q_\theta(s',a') - Q_\theta(s,a)$$

As shown, both the target value and the predicted Q value are parameterized by θ.

Instead of computing the loss as just the difference between the target Q value and the predicted Q value, we use MSE as our loss function. We learned that we store the agent's experience in a buffer called a replay buffer. So, we randomly sample a minibatch of K number of transitions (s, a, r, s') from the replay buffer and train the network by minimizing the MSE, as shown here:

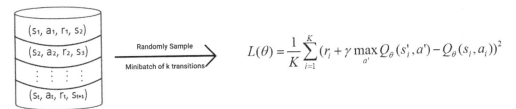

Figure 9.7: Loss function of DQN

Thus, our loss function can be expressed as:

$$L(\theta) = \frac{1}{K} \sum_{i=1}^{K} (r_i + \gamma \max_{a'} Q_\theta(s_i', a') - Q_\theta(s_i, a_i))^2$$

For simplicity of notation, we can denote the target value by y and rewrite the preceding equation as:

$$L(\theta) = \frac{1}{K} \sum_{i=1}^{K} (y_i - Q_\theta(s_i, a_i))^2$$

Where $y_i = r_i + \gamma \max_{a'} Q_\theta(s_i', a')$. We have learned that the target value is just the sum of the reward and the discounted maximum Q value of the next state-action pair. But what if the next state s' is a terminal state? If the next state s' is terminal then we cannot compute the Q value as we don't take any action in the terminal state, so in that case, the target value will be just the reward, as shown here:

$$y_i = \begin{cases} r_i & \text{if } s' \text{ is terminal} \\ r_i + \gamma \max_{a'} Q_\theta(s_i', a') & \text{if } s' \text{ is not terminal} \end{cases}$$

Thus, our loss function is given as:

$$L(\theta) = \frac{1}{K} \sum_{i=1}^{K} (y_i - Q_\theta(s_i, a_i))^2$$

We train our network by minimizing the loss function. We can minimize the loss function by finding the optimal parameter θ. So, we use gradient descent to find the optimal parameter θ. We compute the gradient of our loss function $\nabla_\theta L(\theta)$ and update our network parameter θ as:

$$\theta = \theta - \alpha \nabla_\theta L(\theta)$$

Target network

In the last section, we learned that we train the network by minimizing the loss function, which is the MSE between the target value and the predicted value, as shown here:

$$L(\theta) = \frac{1}{K} \sum_{i=1}^{K} (r_i + \gamma \max_{a'} Q_\theta(s_i', a') - Q_\theta(s_i, a_i))^2$$

However, there is a small issue with our loss function. We have learned that the target value is just the sum of the reward and the discounted maximum Q value of the next state-action pair. We compute this Q value of the next state-action pair in the target and predicted Q values using the same network parameterized by θ, as shown here:

$$L(\theta) = \frac{1}{K} \sum_{i=1}^{K} (r_i + \gamma \max_{a'} \underbrace{Q_\theta(s_i', a')}_{\text{Compute using } \theta} - \underbrace{Q_\theta(s_i, a_i)}_{\text{Compute using } \theta})^2$$

The problem is since the target and predicted value depend on the same parameter θ, this will cause instability in the MSE and the network learns poorly. It also causes a lot of divergence during training.

Let's understand this with a simple example. We will take arbitrary numbers to make it easier to understand. We know that we try to minimize the difference between the target value and the predicted value. So, on every iteration, we compute the gradient of loss and update our network parameter θ so that we can make our predicted value the same as the target value.

Let's suppose in iteration 1, the target value is 13 and the predicted value is 11. So, we update our parameter θ to match the predicted value to the target value, which is 13. But in the next iteration, the target value changes to 15 and the predicted value becomes 13 since we updated our network parameter θ. So, again we update our parameter θ to match the predicted value to the target value, which is now 15. But in the next iteration, the target value changes to 17 and the predicted value becomes 15 since we updated our network parameter θ.

As *Table 9.2* shows, on every iteration, the predicted value tries to be the same as the target value, which keeps on changing:

Target value	Predicted value
13	11
15	13
17	15

Table 9.2: Target and predicted value

This is because the predicted and target values both depend on the same parameter θ. If we update θ, then both the target and predicted values change. Thus, the predicted value keeps on trying to be the same as the target value, but the target value keeps on changing due to the update on the network parameter θ.

How can we avoid this? Can we freeze the target value for a while and compute only the predicted value so that our predicted value matches the target value? Yes! To do this, we introduce another neural network called a target network for computing the Q value of the next state-action pair in the target. The parameter of the target network is represented by θ'. So, our main deep Q network, which is used for predicting Q values, learns the optimal parameter θ using gradient descent. The target network is frozen for a while and then the target network parameter θ' is updated by just copying the main deep Q network parameter θ. Freezing the target network for a while and then updating its parameter θ' with the main network parameter θ stabilizes the training.

So, now our loss function can be rewritten as:

$$L(\theta) = \frac{1}{K} \sum_{i=1}^{K} (r_i + \gamma \max_{a'} Q_{\theta'}(s_i', a') - Q_\theta(s_i, a_i))^2$$

Thus, the Q value of the next state-action pair in the target is computed by the target network parameterized by θ', and the predicted Q value is computed by our main network parameterized by θ:

$$L(\theta) = \frac{1}{K} \sum_{i=1}^{K} (r_i + \gamma \max_{a'} Q_{\theta'}(s_i', a') - Q_\theta(s_i, a_i))^2$$

Compute using θ' Compute using θ

For notation simplicity, we can represent our target value by y and rewrite the preceding equation as:

$$L(\theta) = \frac{1}{K} \sum_{i=1}^{K} (y_i - Q_\theta(s_i, a_i))^2$$

Where $y_i = r_i + \gamma \max_{a'} Q_{\theta'}(s_i', a')$.

We have learned about several concepts concerning DQN, including the experience replay, the loss function, and the target network. In the next section, we will put all these concepts together and see how DQN works.

Putting it all together

First, we initialize the main network parameter θ with random values. We learned that the target network parameter is just a copy of the main network. So, we initialize the target network parameter θ' by just copying the main network parameter θ. We also initialize the replay buffer $\mathcal{D}$.

Now, for each step in the episode, we feed the state of the environment to our network and it outputs the Q values of all possible actions in that state. Then, we select the action that has the maximum Q value:

$$a = \arg\max_a Q_\theta(s, a)$$

If we only select the action that has the highest Q value, then we will not explore any new actions. So, to avoid this, we select actions using the epsilon-greedy policy. With the epsilon-greedy policy, we select a random action with probability epsilon and with probability 1-epsilon, we select the best action that has the maximum Q value.

Note that, since we initialized our network parameter θ with random values, the action we select by taking the maximum Q value will not be the optimal action. But that's okay, we simply perform the selected action, move to the next state, and obtain the reward. If the action is good then we will receive a positive reward, and if it is bad then the reward will be negative. We store all this transition information (s, a, r, s') in the replay buffer $\mathcal{D}$.

Next, we randomly sample a minibatch of K transitions from the replay buffer and compute the loss. We have learned that our loss function is computed as:

$$L(\theta) = \frac{1}{K} \sum_{i=1}^{K} (y_i - Q_\theta(s_i, a_i))^2$$

Where y_i is the target value, that is, $y_i = r_i + \gamma \max_{a'} Q_{\theta'}(s_i', a')$.

In the initial iterations, the loss will be very high since our network parameter θ is just random values. To minimize the loss, we compute the gradients of the loss and update our network parameter θ as:

$$\theta = \theta - \alpha \nabla_\theta L(\theta)$$

We don't update the target network parameter θ' in every time step. We freeze the target network parameter θ' for several time steps and then we copy the main network parameter θ to the target network parameter θ'.

We keep repeating the preceding steps for several episodes to approximate the optimal Q value. Once we have the optimal Q value, we extract the optimal policy from them. To give us a more detailed understanding, the algorithm of DQN is given in the next section.

The DQN algorithm

The DQN algorithm is given in the following steps:

1. Initialize the main network parameter θ with random values
2. Initialize the target network parameter θ' by copying the main network parameter θ
3. Initialize the replay buffer $\mathcal{D}$
4. For N number of episodes, perform *step 5*
5. For each step in the episode, that is, for $t = 0, \ldots, T\text{-}1$:

    1. Observe the state s and select an action using the epsilon-greedy policy, that is, with probability epsilon, select random action a and with probability 1-epsilon, select the action $a = \arg\max_a Q_\theta(s, a)$

    2. Perform the selected action and move to the next state s' and obtain the reward r

3. Store the transition information in the replay buffer $\mathcal{D}$

4. Randomly sample a minibatch of K transitions from the replay buffer $\mathcal{D}$

5. Compute the target value, that is, $y_i = r_i + \gamma \max_{a'} Q_{\theta'}(s_i', a')$

6. Compute the loss, $L(\theta) = \dfrac{1}{K} \sum_{i=1}^{K} (y_i - Q_\theta(s_i, a_i))^2$

7. Compute the gradients of the loss and update the main network parameter θ using gradient descent: $\theta = \theta - \alpha \nabla_\theta L(\theta)$

8. Freeze the target network parameter θ' for several time steps and then update it by just copying the main network parameter θ

Now that we have understood how DQN works, in this next section, we will learn how to implement it.

Playing Atari games using DQN

The Atari 2600 is a popular video game console from a game company called Atari. The Atari game console provides several popular games, such as Pong, Space Invaders, Ms. Pac-Man, Breakout, Centipede, and many more. In this section, we will learn how to build a DQN for playing the Atari games. First, let's explore the architecture of the DQN for playing the Atari games.

Architecture of the DQN

In the Atari environment, the image of the game screen is the state of the environment. So, we just feed the image of the game screen as input to the DQN and it returns the Q values of all the actions in the state. Since we are dealing with images, instead of using a vanilla deep neural network for approximating the Q value, we can use a **convolutional neural network (CNN)** since it is very effective for handling images.

Thus, now our DQN is a CNN. We feed the image of the game screen (the game state) as input to the CNN, and it outputs the Q values of all the actions in the state.

As *Figure 9.8* shows, given the image of the game screen, the convolutional layers extract features from the image and produce a feature map. Next, we flatten the feature map and feed the flattened feature map as input to the feedforward network. The feedforward network takes this flattened feature map as input and returns the Q values of all the actions in the state:

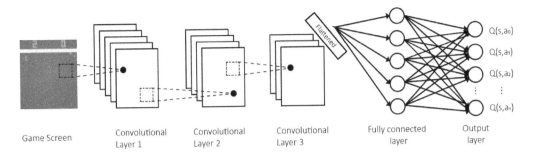

Figure 9.8: Architecture of a DQN

Note that we don't perform a pooling operation. A pooling operation is useful when we perform tasks such as object detection, image classification, and so on where we don't consider the position of the object in the image and we just want to know whether the desired object is present in the image. For example, if we want to identify whether there is a dog in an image, we only look for whether a dog is present in the image and we don't check the position of the dog in the image. Thus, in this case, a pooling operation is used to identify whether there is a dog in the image irrespective of the position of the dog.

But in our setting, a pooling operation should not be performed because to understand the current game state, the position is very important. For example, in the Pong, we just don't want to classify if there is a ball on the game screen. We want to know the position of the ball so that we can make a better action. Thus, we don't include the pooling operation in our DQN architecture.

Now that we have understood the architecture of the DQN to play Atari games, in the next section, we will start implementing it.

Getting hands-on with the DQN

Let's implement the DQN to play the Ms Pacman game. First, let's import the necessary libraries:

```
import random
import gym
import numpy as np
from collections import deque
from tensorflow.keras.models import Sequential
from tensorflow.keras.layers import Dense, Activation, Flatten, Conv2D,
MaxPooling2D
from tensorflow.keras.optimizers import Adam
```

Now, let's create the Ms Pacman game environment using Gym:

```
env = gym.make("MsPacman-v0")
```

Set the state size:

```
state_size = (88, 80, 1)
```

Get the number of actions:

```
action_size = env.action_space.n
```

Preprocess the game screen

We learned that we feed the game state (an image of the game screen) as input to the DQN, which is a CNN, and it outputs the Q values of all the actions in the state. However, directly feeding the raw game screen image is not efficient, since the raw game screen size will be 210 x 160 x 3. This will be computationally expensive.

To avoid this, we preprocess the game screen and then feed the preprocessed game screen to the DQN. First, we crop and resize the game screen image, convert the image to grayscale, normalize it, and then reshape the image to 88 x 80 x 1. Next, we feed this preprocessed game screen image as input to the CNN, which returns the Q values.

Now, let's define a function called `preprocess_state`, which takes the game state (image of the game screen) as an input and returns the preprocessed game state:

```
color = np.array([210, 164, 74]).mean()

def preprocess_state(state):
```

Crop and resize the image:

```
    image = state[1:176:2, ::2]
```

Convert the image to grayscale:

```
    image = image.mean(axis=2)
```

Improve the image contrast:

```
    image[image==color] = 0
```

Normalize the image:

```
image = (image - 128) / 128 - 1
```

Reshape and return the image:

```
image = np.expand_dims(image.reshape(88, 80, 1), axis=0)

return image
```

Defining the DQN class

Let's define the class called DQN where we will implement the DQN algorithm. For a clear understanding, let's look into the code line by line. You can also access the complete code from the GitHub repository of the book:

```
class DQN:
```

Defining the init method

First, let's define the init method

```
def __init__(self, state_size, action_size):
```

Define the state size:

```
self.state_size = state_size
```

Define the action size:

```
self.action_size = action_size
```

Define the replay buffer:

```
self.replay_buffer = deque(maxlen=5000)
```

Define the discount factor:

```
self.gamma = 0.9
```

Define the epsilon value:

```
self.epsilon = 0.8
```

Define the update rate at which we want to update the target network:

```
self.update_rate = 1000
```

Define the main network:

```
self.main_network = self.build_network()
```

Define the target network:

```
self.target_network = self.build_network()
```

Copy the weights of the main network to the target network:

```
self.target_network.set_weights(self.main_network.get_weights())
```

Building the DQN

Now, let's build the DQN. We have learned that to play Atari games, we use a CNN as the DQN, which takes the image of the game screen as an input and returns the Q values. We define the DQN with three convolutional layers. The convolutional layers extract the features from the image and output the feature maps, and then we flatten the feature map obtained by the convolutional layers and feed the flattened feature maps to the feedforward network (the fully connected layer), which returns the Q values:

```
def build_network(self):
```

Define the first convolutional layer:

```
model = Sequential()
model.add(Conv2D(32, (8, 8), strides=4, padding='same', input_shape=self.state_size))
model.add(Activation('relu'))
```

Define the second convolutional layer:

```
model.add(Conv2D(64, (4, 4), strides=2, padding='same'))
model.add(Activation('relu'))
```

Define the third convolutional layer:

```
model.add(Conv2D(64, (3, 3), strides=1, padding='same'))
model.add(Activation('relu'))
```

Flatten the feature maps obtained as a result of the third convolutional layer:

```
model.add(Flatten())
```

Feed the flattened maps to the fully connected layer:

```
model.add(Dense(512, activation='relu'))
model.add(Dense(self.action_size, activation='linear'))
```

Compile the model with loss as MSE:

```
model.compile(loss='mse', optimizer=Adam())
```

Return the model:

```
return model
```

Storing the transition

We have learned that we train the DQN by randomly sampling a minibatch of transitions from the replay buffer. So, we define a function called `store_transition`, which stores the transition information in the replay buffer:

```
def store_transistion(self, state, action,
                      reward, next_state, done):
    self.replay_buffer.append((state, action,
                               reward, next_state, done))
```

Defining the epsilon-greedy policy

We learned that in DQN, to take care of exploration-exploitation trade-off, we select action using the epsilon-greedy policy. So, now we define the function called `epsilon_greedy` for selecting an action using the epsilon-greedy policy:

```
def epsilon_greedy(self, state):
    if random.uniform(0,1) < self.epsilon:
        return np.random.randint(self.action_size)
    Q_values = self.main_network.predict(state)
    return np.argmax(Q_values[0])
```

Define the training

Now let's define a function called `train` for the training network:

```
def train(self, batch_size):
```

Sample a minibatch of transitions from the replay buffer:

```
minibatch = random.sample(self.replay_buffer, batch_size)
```

Compute the target value using the target network:

```
for state, action, reward, next_state, done in minibatch:
    if not done:
        target_Q = (reward + self.gamma * np.amax(
            self.target_network.predict(next_state)))
    else:
        target_Q = reward
```

Compute the predicted value using the main network and store the predicted value in the Q_values:

```
Q_values = self.main_network.predict(state)
```

Update the target value:

```
Q_values[0][action] = target_Q
```

Train the main network:

```
self.main_network.fit(state, Q_values, epochs=1,
                    verbose=0)
```

Updating the target network

Now, let's define the function called `update_target_network` for updating the target network weights by copying from the main network:

```
def update_target_network(self):
    self.target_network.set_weights(self.main_network.get_
weights())
```

Training the DQN

Now, let's train the network. First, let's set the number of episodes we want to train the network for:

```
num_episodes = 500
```

Define the number of time steps:

```
num_timesteps = 20000
```

Define the batch size:

```
batch_size = 8
```

Set the number of past game screens we want to consider:

```
num_screens = 4
```

Instantiate the DQN class:

```
dqn = DQN(state_size, action_size)
```

Set done to `False`:

```
done = False
```

Initialize the `time_step`:

```
time_step = 0
```

For each episode:

```
for i in range(num_episodes):
```

Set `Return` to 0:

```
    Return = 0
```

Preprocess the game screen:

```
    state = preprocess_state(env.reset())
```

For each step in the episode:

```
    for t in range(num_timesteps):
```

Render the environment:

```
env.render()
```

Update the time step:

```
time_step += 1
```

Update the target network:

```
if time_step % dqn.update_rate == 0:
    dqn.update_target_network()
```

Select the action:

```
action = dqn.epsilon_greedy(state)
```

Perform the selected action:

```
next_state, reward, done, _ = env.step(action)
```

Preprocess the next state:

```
next_state = preprocess_state(next_state)
```

Store the transition information:

```
dqn.store_transistion(state, action, reward, next_state, done)
```

Update the current state to the next state:

```
state = next_state
```

Update the return value:

```
Return += reward
```

If the episode is done, then print the return:

```
if done:
    print('Episode: ',i, ',' 'Return', Return)
    break
```

If the number of transitions in the replay buffer is greater than the batch size, then train the network:

```
if len(dqn.replay_buffer) > batch_size:
    dqn.train(batch_size)
```

By rendering the environment, we can also observe how the agent learns to play the game over a series of episodes:

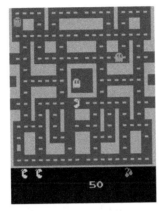

Figure 9.9: DQN agent learning to play

Now that we have learned how DQNs work and how to build a DQN to play Atari games, in the next section, we will learn an interesting variant of DQN called the double DQN.

The double DQN

We have learned that in DQN, the target value is computed as:

$$y = r + \gamma \max_{a'} Q_{\theta'}(s', a')$$

One of the problems with a DQN is that it tends to overestimate the Q value of the next state-action pair in the target:

$$y = r + \gamma \underbrace{\max_{a'} Q_{\theta'}(s', a')}_{\downarrow}$$

Overestimates Q Value

This overestimation is due to the presence of the max operator. Let's see how this overestimation happens with an example. Suppose we are in a state s' and we have three actions a_1, a_2, and a_3. Assume a_3 is the optimal action in the state s'. When we estimate the Q values of all the actions in state s', the estimated Q value will have some noise and differ from the actual value. Say, due to the noise, action a_2 will get a higher Q value than the optimal action a_3.

We know that the target value is computed as:

$$y = r + \gamma \max_{a'=\{a_1,a_2,a_3\}} Q_{\theta'}(s',a')$$

Now, if we select the best action as the one that has the maximum value then we will end up selecting the action a_2 instead of optimal action a_3, as shown here:

$$y = r + \gamma Q_{\theta'}(s',a_2)$$

So, how can we get rid of this overestimation? We can get rid of this overestimation by just modifying our target value computation as:

$$y = r + \gamma Q_{\theta'}(s', \arg\max_{a'} Q_{\theta}(s',a'))$$

As we can observe, now we have two Q functions in our target value computation. One Q function parameterized by the main network parameter θ is used for action selection, and the other Q function parameterized by the target network parameter θ' is used for Q value computation.

Let's understand the preceding equation by breaking it down into two steps:

- **Action selection**: First, we compute the Q values of all the next state-action pairs using the main network parameterized by θ, and then we select action a', which has the maximum Q value:

$$y = r + \gamma Q_{\theta'}(s', \underline{\arg\max_{a'} Q_{\theta}(s',a')})$$
$$\downarrow$$

Select the action a', which has
the maximum Q value computed
by main network θ

- **Q value computation**: Once we have selected action a', then we compute the Q value using the target network parameterized by θ' for the selected action a':

$$y = r + \gamma \underline{Q_{\theta'}(s',a')}$$
$$\downarrow$$

Compute the Q value for the
selected action a' using target
network θ'

Let's understand this with an example. Let's suppose state s' is E, then we can write:

$$y = r + \gamma Q_{\theta'}(E, \arg\max_{a'} Q_\theta(E, a'))$$

First, we compute the Q values of all actions in state E using the main network parameterized by θ, and then we select the action that has the maximum Q value. Let's suppose the action that has the maximum Q value is *right*:

$$y = r + \gamma Q_{\theta'}(E, \underbrace{\arg\max_{a'} Q_\theta(E, a')}_{\downarrow})$$
$$\text{Right}$$

Now, we can compute the Q value using the target network parameterized by θ' with the action selected by the main network, which is *right*. Thus, we can write:

$$y = r + \gamma Q_{\theta'}(E, \text{right})$$

Still not clear? The difference between how we compute the target value in DQN and double DQN is shown here:

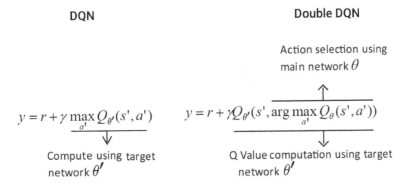

Figure 9.10: Difference between a DQN and double DQN

Thus, we learned that in a double DQN, we compute the target value using two Q functions. One Q function parameterized by the main network parameter θ used for selecting the action that has the maximum Q value, and the other Q function parameterized by target network parameter θ' computes the Q value using the action selected by the main network:

$$y = r + \gamma Q_{\theta'}(s', \arg\max_{a'} Q_\theta(s', a'))$$

Apart from target value computation, double DQN works exactly the same as DQN. To give us more clarity, the algorithm of double DQN is given in the next section.

The double DQN algorithm

The algorithm of double DQN is shown here. As we can see, except the target value computation (the bold step), the rest of the steps are exactly the same as in the DQN:

1. Initialize the main network parameter θ with random values

2. Initialize the target network parameter θ' by copying the main network parameter θ

3. Initialize the replay buffer $\mathcal{D}$

4. For N number of episodes repeat *step 5*

5. For each step in the episode, that is, for $t = 0, \ldots, T\text{-}1$:

    1. Observe the state s and select an action using the epsilon-greedy policy, that is, with probability epsilon, select a random action a with probability 1-epsilon; select the action: $a = \arg\max_a Q_\theta(s, a)$

    2. Perform the selected action, move to the next state s', and obtain the reward r

    3. Store the transition information in the replay buffer $\mathcal{D}$

    4. Randomly sample a minibatch of K transitions from the replay buffer $\mathcal{D}$

    5. **Compute the target value, that is,**
    $$y_i = r_i + \gamma Q_{\theta'}(s_i', \arg\max_{a'} Q_\theta(s_i', a'))$$

    6. Compute the loss, $L(\theta) = \dfrac{1}{K} \sum_{i=1}^{K} (y_i - Q_\theta(s_i, a_i))^2$

    7. Compute the gradients of the loss and update the main network parameter θ using gradient descent: $\theta = \theta - \alpha \nabla_\theta L(\theta)$

    8. Freeze the target network parameter θ' for several time steps and then update it by just copying the main network parameter θ

Now that we have learned how the double DQN works, in the next section, we will learn about an interesting variant of DQN called DQN with prioritized experience replay.

DQN with prioritized experience replay

We learned that in DQN, we randomly sample a minibatch of K transitions from the replay buffer and train the network. Instead of doing this, can we assign some priority to each transition in the replay buffer and sample the transitions that had high priority for learning?

Yes, but first, why do we need to assign priority for the transition, and how can we decide which transition should be given more priority than the others? Let's explore this more in detail.

The TD error δ is the difference between the target value and the predicted value, as shown here:

$$\delta = r + \gamma \max_{a'} Q_{\theta'}(s', a') - Q_{\theta}(s, a)$$

A transition that has a high TD error implies that the transition is not correct, and so we need to learn more about that transition to minimize the error. A transition that has a low TD error implies that the transition is already good. We can always learn more from our mistakes rather than only focusing on what we are already good at, right? Similarly, we can learn more from the transitions that have a high TD error than those that have a low TD error. Thus, we can assign more priority to the transitions that have a high TD error and less priority to transitions that have a low TD error.

We know that the transition information consists of (s, a, r, s'), and along with this information, we also add priority p and store the transition with the priority in our replay buffer as (s, a, r, s', p). The following figure shows the replay buffer containing transitions along with the priority:

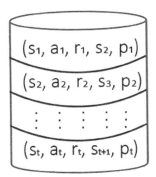

Figure 9.11: Prioritized replay buffer

In the next section, we will learn how to prioritize our transitions using the TD error based on two different types of prioritization methods.

Types of prioritization

We can prioritize our transition using the following two methods:

- Proportional prioritization
- Rank-based prioritization

Proportional prioritization

We learned that the transition can be prioritized using the TD error, so the priority p of the transition i will be just its TD error:

$$p_i = |\delta_i|$$

Note that we take the absolute value of the TD error as a priority to keep the priority positive. Okay, what about a transition that has a TD error of zero? Say we have a transition i and its TD error is 0, then the priority of the transition i will just be 0:

$$p_i = 0$$

But setting the priority of the transition to zero is not desirable, and if we set the priority of a transition to zero then that particular transition will not be used in our training at all. So, to avoid this issue, we will add a small value called epsilon to our TD error. So, even if the TD error is zero, we will still have a small priority due to the epsilon. To be more precise, adding an epsilon to the TD error guarantees that there will be no transition with zero priority. Thus, our priority can be modified as:

$$p_i = |\delta_i| + \epsilon$$

Instead of having the priority as a raw number, we can convert it into a probability so that we will have priorities ranging from 0 to 1. We can convert the priority to a probability as shown here:

$$P(i) = \frac{p_i}{\sum_k p_k}$$

The preceding equation calculates the probability P of the transition i.

Can we also control the amount of prioritization? That is, instead of sampling only the prioritized transition, can we also take a random transition? Yes! To do this, we introduce a new parameter called α and rewrite our equation as follows. When the value of α is high, say 1, then we sample only the transitions that have high priority and when the value of α is low, say 0, then we sample a random transition:

$$P(i) = \frac{p_i{}^\alpha}{\sum_k p_k{}^\alpha}$$

Thus, we have learned how to assign priority to a transition using the proportional prioritization method. In the next section, we will learn another prioritization method called rank-based prioritization.

Rank-based prioritization

Rank-based prioritization is the simplest type of prioritization. Here, we assign priority based on the rank of a transition. What is the rank of a transition? The rank of a transition i can be defined as the location of the transition in the replay buffer where the transitions are sorted from high TD error to low TD error.

Thus, we can define the priority of the transition i using rank as:

$$p_i = \frac{1}{\text{Rank}(i)}$$

Just as we learned in the previous section, we convert the priority into probability:

$$P(i) = \frac{p_i}{\sum_k p_k}$$

Similar to what we learned in the previous section, we can add a parameter α to control the amount of prioritization and express our final equation as:

$$P(i) = \frac{p_i{}^\alpha}{\sum_k p_k{}^\alpha}$$

Correcting the bias

We have learned how to prioritize the transitions using two methods—proportional prioritization and rank-based prioritization. But the problem with these methods is that we will be highly biased towards the samples that have high priority. That is, when we give more importance to samples that have a high TD error, it essentially means that we are learning only from a subset of samples that have a high TD error.

Okay, what's the issue with this? It will lead to the problem of overfitting, and our agent will be highly biased to those transitions that have a high TD error. To combat this, we use importance weights w. The importance weights help us to reduce the weights of transitions that have occurred many times. The importance weight w of the transition i can be expressed as:

$$w_i = \left(\frac{1}{N} \cdot \frac{1}{P(i)} \right)^\beta$$

In the preceding expression, N denotes the length of our replay buffer and $P(i)$ denotes the probability of the transition i. Okay, what's that parameter β? It controls the importance weight. We start off with small values of β, from 0.4 and anneal it toward 1.

Thus, in this section, we have learned how to prioritize transitions in DQN with prioritized experience replay. In the next section, we will learn about another interesting variant of DQN called dueling DQN.

The dueling DQN

Before going ahead, let's learn about one of the most important functions in reinforcement learning, called the advantage function. The advantage function is defined as the difference between the Q function and the value function, and it is expressed as:

$$A(s,a) = Q(s,a) - V(s)$$

Okay, but what's the use of an advantage function? What does it signify? First, let's recall the Q function and the value function:

- **Q function**: The Q function gives the expected return an agent would obtain starting from state s, performing action a, and following the policy π.
- **Value function**: The value function gives the expected return an agent would obtain starting from state s and following the policy π.

Now if we think intuitively, what's the difference between the Q function and the value function? The Q function gives us the value of a state-action pair, while the value function gives the value of a state irrespective of the action. Now, the difference between the Q function and the value function tells us how good the action a is compared to the average actions in state s.

Thus, the advantage function tells us that in state s, how good the action a is compared to the average actions. Now that we have understood what the advantage function is, let's see why and how we can make use of it in the DQN.

Understanding the dueling DQN

We have learned that in a DQN, we feed the state as input and our network computes the Q value for all actions in that state. Instead of computing the Q values in this way, can we compute the Q values using the advantage function? We have learned that the advantage function is given as:

$$A(s,a) = Q(s,a) - V(s)$$

We can rewrite the preceding equation as:

$$Q(s, a) = V(s) + A(s, a)$$

As we can see from the preceding equation, we can compute the Q value just by adding the value function and the advantage function together. Wait! Why do we have to do this? What's wrong with computing the Q value directly?

Let's suppose we are in some state s and we have 20 possible actions to perform in this state. Computing the Q values of all these 20 actions in state s is not going to be useful because most of the actions will not have any effect on the state, and also most of the actions will have a similar Q value. What do we mean by that? Let's understand this with the grid world environment shown in *Figure 9.12*:

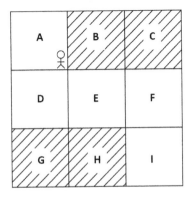

Figure 9.12: Grid world environment

As we can see, the agent is in state **A**. In this case, what is the use of computing the Q value of the action *up* in state **A**? Moving *up* will have no effect in state **A**, and it's not going to take the agent anywhere. Similarly, think of an environment where our action space is huge, say 100. In this case, most of the actions will not have any effect in the given state. Also, when the action space is large, most of the actions will have a similar Q value.

Now, let's talk about the value of a state. Note that not all the states are important for an agent. There could be a state that always gives a bad reward no matter what action we perform. In that case, it is not useful to compute the Q value of all possible actions in the state if we know that the state is always going to give us a bad reward.

Thus, to solve this we can compute the Q function as the sum of the value function and the advantage function. That is, with the value function, we can understand whether a state is valuable or not without computing the values of all actions in the state. And with the advantage function, we can understand whether an action is really good or it just gives us the same value as all the other actions.

Now that we have a basic idea of dueling DQN, let's explore the architecture of dueling DQN in the next section.

The architecture of a dueling DQN

We have learned that in a dueling DQN, the Q values can be computed as:

$$Q(s, a) = V(s) + A(s, a)$$

How can we design our neural network to emit Q values in this way? We can break the final layer of our network into two streams. The first stream computes the value function and the second stream computes the advantage function. Given any state as input, the value stream gives the value of a state, while the advantage stream gives the advantage of all possible actions in the given state. For instance, as *Figure 9.13* shows, we feed the game state (game screen) as an input to the network. The value stream computes the value of a state while the advantage stream computes the advantage values of all actions in the state:

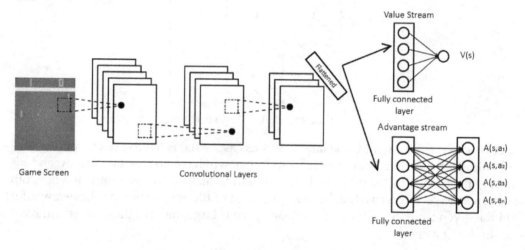

Figure 9.13: Architecture of a dueling DQN

We learned that we compute the Q value by adding the state value and the advantage value together, so we combine the value stream and the advantage stream using another layer called the aggregate layer, and compute the Q value as *Figure 9.14* shows.

Thus, the value stream computes the state value, the advantage stream computes the advantage value, and the aggregate layer sums these streams and computes the Q value:

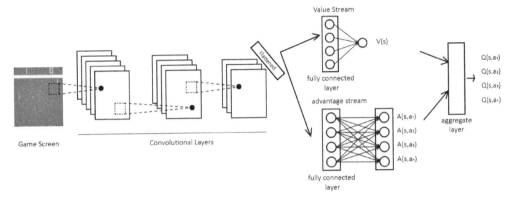

Figure 9.14: Architecture of a dueling DQN including an aggregate layer

But there is a small issue here. Just summing the state value and advantage value in the aggregate layer and computing the Q value leads us to a problem of identifiability.

So, to combat this problem, we make the advantage function to have zero advantage for the selected action. We can achieve this by subtracting the average advantage value, that is, the average advantage of all actions in the action space, as shown here:

$$Q(s,a) = V(s) + \left(A(s,a) - \frac{1}{\mathcal{A}} \sum_{a'} A(s,a') \right)$$

Where $\mathcal{A}$ denotes the length of the action space.

Thus, we can write our final equation for computing the Q value with parameters as:

$$Q(s,a; \theta, \alpha, \beta) = V(s; \theta, \beta) + \left(A(s,a; \theta, \alpha) - \frac{1}{\mathcal{A}} \sum_{a'} A(s,a'; \theta, \alpha) \right)$$

In the preceding equation, θ is the parameter of the convolutional network, β is the parameter of the value stream, and α is the parameter of the advantage stream. After computing the Q value, we can select the action:

$$a = \arg\max_{a} Q(s, a; \theta, \alpha, \beta)$$

Thus, the only difference between a dueling DQN and DQN is that in a dueling DQN, instead of computing the Q values directly, we compute them by combining the state value and the advantage value.

In the next section, we will explore another variant of DQN called deep recurrent Q network.

The deep recurrent Q network

The **deep recurrent Q network** (**DRQN**) is just the same as a DQN but with recurrent layers. But what's the use of recurrent layers in DQN? To answer this question, first, let's understand the problem called **Partially Observable Markov Decision Process (POMDP)**.

An environment is called a POMDP when we have a limited set of information available about the environment. So far, in the previous chapters, we have seen a fully observable MDP where we know all possible actions and states—although we might be unaware of transition and reward probabilities, we had complete knowledge of the environment. For example, in the frozen lake environment, we had complete knowledge of all the states and actions of the environment.

But most real-world environments are only partially observable; we cannot see all the states. For instance, consider an agent learning to walk in a real-world environment. In this case, the agent will not have complete knowledge of the environment (the real world); it will have no information outside its view.

Thus, in a POMDP, states provide only partial information, but keeping the information about past states in the memory will help the agent to understand more about the nature of the environment and find the optimal policy. Thus, in POMDP, we need to retain information about past states in order to take the optimal action.

So, can we take advantage of recurrent neural networks to understand and retain information about the past states as long as it is required? Yes, the **Long Short-Term Memory Recurrent Neural Network (LSTM RNN)** is very useful for retaining, forgetting, and updating the information as required. So, we can use the LSTM layer in the DQN to retain information about the past states as long as it is required. Retaining information about the past states helps when we have the problem of POMDP.

Now that we have a basic understanding of why we need DRQN and how it solves the problem of POMDP, in the next section, we will look into the architecture of DRQN.

The architecture of a DRQN

Figure 9.15 shows the architecture of a DRQN. As we can see, it is similar to the DQN architecture except that it has an LSTM layer:

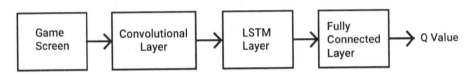

Figure 9.15: Architecture of a DRQN

We pass the game screen as an input to the convolutional layer. The convolutional layer convolves the image and produces a feature map. The resulting feature map is then passed to the LSTM layer. The LSTM layer has memory to hold information. So, it retains information about important previous game states and updates its memory over time steps as required. Then, we feed the hidden state from the LSTM layer to the fully connected layer, which outputs the Q value.

Figure 9.16 helps us to understand how exactly DRQN works. Let's suppose we need to compute the Q value for the state s_t and the action a_t. Unlike DQN, we don't just compute the Q value as $Q(s_t, a_t)$ directly. As we can see, along with the current state s_t, we also use the hidden state h_t to compute the Q value. The reason for using the hidden state is that it holds information about the past game states in memory.

Since we are using the LSTM cells, the hidden state h_t will consist of information about the past game states in the memory as long as it is required:

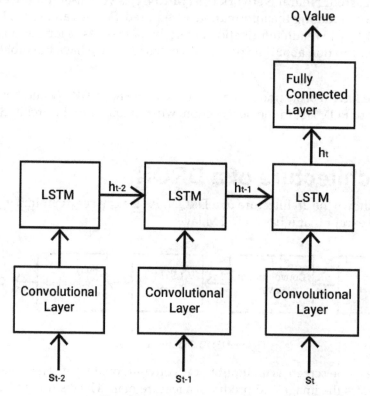

Figure 9.16: Architecture of DRQN

Except for this change, DRQN works just like DQN. Wait. What about the replay buffer? In DQN, we learned that we store the transition information in the replay buffer and train our network by sampling a minibatch of experience. We also learned that the transition information is placed sequentially in the replay buffer one after another, so to avoid the correlated experience, we randomly sample a minibatch of experience from the replay buffer and train the network.

But in the case of a DRQN, we need sequential information so that our network can retain information from past game states. Thus we need sequential information but also we don't want to overfit the network by training with correlated experience. How can we achieve this?

To achieve this, in a DRQN, we randomly sample a minibatch of episodes rather than a random minibatch of transitions. That is, we know that in the episode, we will have transition information that follows sequentially, so we take a random minibatch of episodes and in each episode we will have the transition information that is placed sequentially. So, in this way, we can accommodate both randomization and also the transition information that follows one another. This is called **bootstrapped sequential updates**.

After sampling the minibatch of episodes randomly, then we can train the DRQN just like we trained the DQN network by minimizing the MSE loss. To learn more, you can refer to the DRQN paper given in the *Further reading* section.

Summary

We started the chapter by learning what deep Q networks are and how they are used to approximate the Q value. We learned that in a DQN, we use a buffer called the replay buffer to store the agent's experience. Then, we randomly sample a minibatch of experience from the replay buffer and train the network by minimizing the MSE. Moving on, we looked at the algorithm of DQN in more detail, and then we learned how to implement DQN to play Atari games.

Following this, we learned that the DQN overestimates the target value due to the max operator. So, we used double DQN, where we have two Q functions in our target value computation. One Q function parameterized by the main network parameter θ is used for action selection, and the other Q function parameterized by the target network parameter θ' is used for Q value computation.

Going ahead, we learned about the DQN with prioritized experience replay, where the transition is prioritized based on the TD error. We explored two different types of prioritization methods called proportional prioritization and rank-based prioritization.

Next, we learned about another interesting variant of DQN called dueling DQN. In dueling DQN, instead of computing Q values directly, we compute them using two streams called the value stream and the advantage stream.

At the end of the chapter, we learned about DRQN and how they solve the problem of partially observable Markov decision processes.

In the next chapter, we will learn about another popular algorithm called policy gradient.

Questions

Let's evaluate our understanding of DQN and its variants by answering the following questions:

1. Why do we need a DQN?
2. What is the replay buffer?
3. Why do we need the target network?
4. How does a double DQN differ from a DQN?
5. Why do we have to prioritize the transitions?
6. What is the advantage function?
7. Why do we need LSTM layers in a DRQN?

Further reading

For more information, we can refer to the following papers:

- **Playing Atari with Deep Reinforcement Learning** by *Volodymyr Mnih, et al.,* https://arxiv.org/pdf/1312.5602.pdf

- **Deep Reinforcement Learning with Double Q-learning** by *Hado van Hasselt, Arthur Guez, David Silver,* https://arxiv.org/pdf/1509.06461.pdf

- **Prioritized Experience Replay** by *Tom Schaul, John Quan, Ioannis Antonoglou and David Silver,* https://arxiv.org/pdf/1511.05952.pdf

- **Dueling Network Architectures for Deep Reinforcement Learning** by *Ziyu Wang, Tom Schaul, Matteo Hessel, Hado van Hasselt, Marc Lanctot, Nando de Freitas,* https://arxiv.org/pdf/1511.06581.pdf

- **Deep Recurrent Q-Learning for Partially Observable MDPs** by *Matthew Hausknecht and Peter Stone,* https://arxiv.org/pdf/1507.06527.pdf

10

Policy Gradient Method

In the previous chapters, we learned how to use value-based reinforcement learning algorithms to compute the optimal policy. That is, we learned that with value-based methods, we compute the optimal Q function iteratively and from the optimal Q function, we extract the optimal policy. In this chapter, we will learn about policy-based methods, where we can compute the optimal policy without having to compute the optimal Q function.

We will start the chapter by looking at the disadvantages of computing a policy from the Q function, and then we will learn how policy-based methods learn the optimal policy directly without computing the Q function. Next, we will examine one of the most popular policy-based methods, called the policy gradient. We will first take a broad overview of the policy gradient algorithm, and then we will learn more about it in detail.

Going forward, we will also learn how to derive the policy gradient step by step and examine the algorithm of the policy gradient method in more detail. At the end of the chapter, we will learn about the variance reduction techniques in the policy gradient method.

In this chapter, we will learn the following topics:

- Why policy-based methods?
- Policy gradient intuition
- Deriving the policy gradient
- Algorithm of policy gradient
- Policy gradient with reward-to-go

- Policy gradient with baseline
- Algorithm of policy gradient with baseline

Why policy-based methods?

The objective of reinforcement learning is to find the optimal policy, which is the policy that provides the maximum return. So far, we have learned several different algorithms for computing the optimal policy, and all these algorithms have been value-based methods. Wait, what are value-based methods? Let's recap what value-based methods are, and the problems associated with them, and then we will learn about policy-based methods. Recapping is always good, isn't it?

With value-based methods, we extract the optimal policy from the optimal Q function (Q values), meaning we compute the Q values of all state-action pairs to find the policy. We extract the policy by selecting an action in each state that has the maximum Q value. For instance, let's say we have two states s_0 and s_1 and our action space has two actions; let the actions be 0 and 1. First, we compute the Q value of all the state-action pairs, as shown in the following table. Now, we extract policy from the Q function (Q values) by selecting action 0 in state s_0 and action 1 in state s_1 as they have the maximum Q value:

State	Action	Value
s_0	0	10
s_0	1	5
s_1	0	10
s_1	1	11

Table 10.1: Q table

Later, we learned that it is difficult to compute the Q function when our environment has a large number of states and actions as it would be expensive to compute the Q values of all possible state-action pairs. So, we resorted to the **Deep Q Network (DQN)**. In DQN, we used a neural network to approximate the Q function (Q value). Given a state, the network will return the Q values of all possible actions in that state. For instance, consider the grid world environment. Given a state, our DQN will return the Q values of all possible actions in that state. Then we select the action that has the highest Q value. As we can see in *Figure 10.1*, given state **E**, DQN returns the Q value of all possible actions (*up, down, left, right*). Then we select the *right* action in state **E** since it has the maximum Q value:

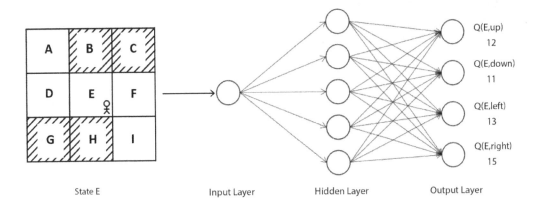

Figure 10.1: DQN

Thus, in value-based methods, we improve the Q function iteratively, and once we have the optimal Q function, then we extract optimal policy by selecting the action in each state that has the maximum Q value.

One of the disadvantages of the value-based method is that it is suitable only for discrete environments (environments with a discrete action space), and we cannot apply value-based methods in continuous environments (environments with a continuous action space).

We have learned that a discrete action space has a discrete set of actions; for example, the grid world environment has discrete actions (up, down, left, and right) and the continuous action space consists of actions that are continuous values, for example, controlling the speed of a car.

So far, we have only dealt with a discrete environment where we had a discrete action space, so we easily computed the Q value of all possible state-action pairs. But how can we compute the Q value of all possible state-action pairs when our action space is continuous? Say we are training an agent to drive a car and say we have one continuous action in our action space. Let the action be the speed of the car and the value of the speed of the car ranges from 0 to 150 kmph. In this case, how can we compute the Q value of all possible state-action pairs with the action being a continuous value?

In this case, we can discretize the continuous actions into speed (0 to 10) as action 1, speed (10 to 20) as action 2, and so on. After discretization, we can compute the Q value of all possible state-action pairs. However, discretization is not always desirable. We might lose several important features and we might end up in an action space with a huge set of actions.

Most real-world problems have continuous action space, say, a self-driving car, or a robot learning to walk and more. Apart from having a continuous action space they also have a high dimension. Thus, the DQN and other value-based methods cannot deal with the continuous action space effectively.

So, we use the policy-based methods. With policy-based methods, we don't need to compute the Q function (Q values) to find the optimal policy; instead, we can compute them directly. That is, we don't need the Q function to extract the policy. Policy-based methods have several advantages over value-based methods, and they can handle both discrete and continuous action spaces.

We learned that DQN takes care of the exploration-exploitation dilemma by using the epsilon-greedy policy. With the epsilon-greedy policy, we either select the best action with the probability 1-epsilon or a random action with the probability epsilon. Most policy-based methods use a stochastic policy. We know that with a stochastic policy, we select actions based on the probability distribution over the action space, which allows the agent to explore different actions instead of performing the same action every time. Thus, policy-based methods take care of the exploration-exploitation trade-off implicitly by using a stochastic policy. However, there are several policy-based methods that use a deterministic policy as well. We will learn more about them in the upcoming chapters.

Okay, how do policy-based methods work, exactly? How do they find an optimal policy without computing the Q function? We will learn about this in the next section. Now that we have a basic understanding of what a policy gradient method is, and also the disadvantages of value-based methods, in the next section we will learn about a fundamental and interesting policy-based method called policy gradient.

Policy gradient intuition

Policy gradient is one of the most popular algorithms in deep reinforcement learning. As we have learned, policy gradient is a policy-based method by which we can find the optimal policy without computing the Q function. It finds the optimal policy by directly parameterizing the policy using some parameter θ.

The policy gradient method uses a stochastic policy. We have learned that with a stochastic policy, we select an action based on the probability distribution over the action space. Say we have a stochastic policy π, then it gives the probability of taking an action a given the state s. It can be denoted by $\pi(a|s)$. In the policy gradient method, we use a parameterized policy, so we can denote our policy as $\pi_\theta(a|s)$, where θ indicates that our policy is parameterized.

Wait! What do we mean when we say a parameterized policy? What is it exactly? Remember with DQN, we learned that we parameterize our Q function to compute the Q value? We can do the same here, except instead of parameterizing the Q function, we will directly parameterize the policy to compute the optimal policy. That is, we can use any function approximator to learn the optimal policy, and θ is the parameter of our function approximator. We generally use a neural network as our function approximator. Thus, we have a policy π parameterized by θ where θ is the parameter of the neural network.

Say we have a neural network with a parameter θ. First, we feed the state of the environment as an input to the network and it will output the probability of all the actions that can be performed in the state. That is, it outputs a probability distribution over an action space. We have learned that with policy gradient, we use a stochastic policy. So, the stochastic policy selects an action based on the probability distribution given by the neural network. In this way, we can directly compute the policy without using the Q function.

Let's understand how the policy gradient method works with an example. Let's take our favorite grid world environment for better understanding. We know that in the grid world environment our action space has four possible actions: *up, down, left,* and *right.*

Given any state as an input, the neural network will output the probability distribution over the action space. That is, as shown in *Figure 10.2,* when we feed the state E as an input to the network, it will return the probability distribution over all actions in our action space. Now, our stochastic policy will select an action based on the probability distribution given by the neural network. So, it will select action *up* 10% of the time, *down* 10% of the time, *left* 10% of the time, and *right* 70% of the time:

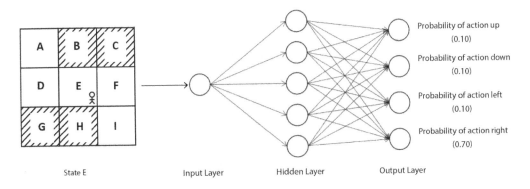

Figure 10.2: A policy network

We should not get confused with the DQN and the policy gradient method. With DQN, we feed the state as an input to the network, and it returns the Q values of all possible actions in that state, then we select an action that has a maximum Q value. But in the policy gradient method, we feed the state as input to the network, and it returns the probability distribution over an action space, and our stochastic policy uses the probability distribution returned by the neural network to select an action.

Okay, in the policy gradient method, the network returns the probability distribution (action probabilities) over the action space, but how accurate are the probabilities? How does the network learn?

Unlike supervised learning, here we will not have any labeled data to train our network. So, our network does not know the correct action to perform in the given state; that is, the network does not know which action gives the maximum reward. So, the action probabilities given by our neural network will not be accurate in the initial iterations, and thus we might get a bad reward.

But that is fine. We simply select the action based on the probability distribution given by the network, store the reward, and move to the next state until the end of the episode. That is, we play an episode and store the states, actions, and rewards. Now, this becomes our training data. If we win the episode, that is, if we get a positive return or high return (the sum of the rewards of the episode), then we increase the probability of all the actions that we took in each state until the end of the episode. If we get a negative return or low return, then we decrease the probability of all the actions that we took in each state until the end of the episode.

Let's understand this with an example. Say we have states s_1 to s_8 and our goal is to reach state s_8. Say our action space consists of only two actions: *left and right*. So, when we feed any state to the network, then it will return the probability distribution over the two actions.

Consider the following trajectory (episode) τ_1, where we select an action in each state based on the probability distribution returned by the network using a stochastic policy:

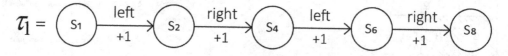

Figure 10.3: Trajectory τ_1

The return of this trajectory is $R(\tau_1) = 1 + 1 + 1 + 1 = 4$. Since we got a positive return, we increase the probabilities of all the actions that we took in each state until the end of the episode. That is, we increase the probabilities of action *left* in s_1, action *right* in s_2, and so on until the end of the episode.

Let's suppose we generate another trajectory τ_2, where we select an action in each state based on the probability distribution returned by the network using a stochastic policy, as shown in *Figure 10.4*:

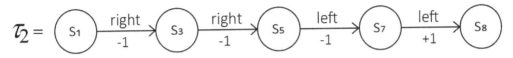

Figure 10.4: Trajectory τ_2

The return of this trajectory is $R(\tau_2) = -1 - 1 - 1 + 1 = -2$. Since we got a negative return, we decrease the probabilities of all the actions that we took in each state until the end of the episode. That is, we will decrease the probabilities of action *right* in s_1, action *right* in s_3, and so on until the end of the episode.

Okay, but how exactly do we increase and decrease these probabilities? We learned that if the return of the trajectory is positive, then we increase the probabilities of all actions in the episode, else we decrease it. How can we do this exactly? This is where backpropagation helps us. We know that we train the neural network by backpropagation.

So, during backpropagation, the network calculates gradients and updates the parameters of the network θ. Gradients updates are in such a way that actions yielding high return will get high probabilities and actions yielding low return will get low probabilities.

In a nutshell, in the policy gradient method, we use a neural network to find the optimal policy. We initialize the network parameter θ with random values. We feed the state as an input to the network and it will return the action probabilities. In the initial iteration, since the network is not trained with any data, it will give random action probabilities. But we select actions based on the action probability distribution given by the network and store the state, action, and reward until the end of the episode. Now, this becomes our training data. If we win the episode, that is, if we get a high return, then we assign high probabilities to all the actions of the episode, else we assign low probabilities to all the actions of the episode.

Since we are using a neural network to find the optimal policy, we can call this neural network a policy network. Now that we have a basic understanding of the policy gradient method, in the next section, we will learn how exactly the neural network finds the optimal policy; that is, we will learn how exactly the gradient computation happens and how we train the network.

Understanding the policy gradient

In the last section, we learned that, in the policy gradient method, we update the gradients in such a way that actions yielding a high return will get a high probability, and actions yielding a low return will get a low probability. In this section, we will learn how exactly we do that.

The goal of the policy gradient method is to find the optimal parameter θ of the neural network so that the network returns the correct probability distribution over the action space. Thus, the objective of our network is to assign high probabilities to actions that maximize the expected return of the trajectory. So, we can write our objective function J as:

$$J(\theta) = E_{\tau \sim \pi_\theta(\tau)}[R(\tau)]$$

In the preceding equation, the following applies:

- τ is the trajectory.
- $\tau \sim \pi_\theta(\tau)$ denotes that we are sampling the trajectory based on the policy π given by network parameterized by θ.
- $R(\tau)$ is the return of the trajectory τ.

Thus, maximizing our objective function maximizes the return of the trajectory. How can we maximize the preceding objective function? We generally deal with minimization problems, where we minimize the loss function (objective function) by calculating the gradients of our loss function and updating the parameter using gradient descent. But here, our goal is to maximize the objective function, so we calculate the gradients of our objective function and perform gradient ascent. That is:

$$\theta = \theta + \alpha \nabla_\theta J(\theta)$$

Where $\nabla_\theta J(\theta)$ implies the gradients of our objective function. Thus, we can find the optimal parameter θ of our network using gradient ascent.

The gradient $\nabla_\theta J(\theta)$ is derived as $\nabla_\theta J(\theta) = \mathbb{E}_{\tau \sim \pi_\theta(\tau)}[\nabla_\theta \log \pi_\theta(a_t|s_t)R(\tau)]$. We will learn how exactly we derived this gradient in the next section. In this section, let's focus only on getting a good fundamental understanding of the policy gradient.

We learned that we update our network parameter with:

$$\theta = \theta + \alpha \nabla_\theta J(\theta)$$

Substituting the value of gradient, our parameter update equation becomes:

$$\theta = \theta + \alpha \nabla_\theta \log \pi_\theta(a_t|s_t)R(\tau)$$

In the preceding equation, the following applies:

- $\log \pi_\theta(a_t|s_t)$ represents the log probability of taking an action a given the state s at a time t.
- $R(\tau)$ represents the return of the trajectory.

We learned that we update the gradients in such a way that actions yielding a high return will get a high probability, and actions yielding a low return will get a low probability. Let's now see how exactly we are doing that.

Case 1:

Suppose we generate an episode (trajectory) using the policy π_θ, where θ is the parameter of the network. After generating the episode, we compute the return of the episode. If the return of the episode is negative, say -1, that is, $R(\tau) = -1$, then we decrease the probability of all the actions that we took in each state until the end of the episode.

We learned that our parameter update equation is given as:

$$\theta = \theta + \alpha \nabla_\theta \log \pi_\theta(a_t|s_t)R(\tau)$$

In the preceding equation, multiplying $\log \pi_\theta(a_t|s_t)$ by the negative return $R(\tau) = -1$ implies that we are decreasing the log probability of action a_t in state s_t. Thus, we perform a negative update. That is:

For each step in the episode, $t = 0, \ldots, T\text{-}1$, we update the parameter θ as:

$$\theta = \theta + \alpha \nabla_\theta \log \pi_\theta(a_t|s_t)(-1)$$

It implies that we are decreasing the probability of all the actions that we took in each state until the end of the episode.

Case 2:

Suppose we generate an episode (trajectory) using the policy π_θ, where θ is the parameter of the network. After generating the episode, we compute the return of the episode. If the return of the episode is positive, say +1, that is, $R(\tau) = +1$, then we increase the probability of all the actions that we took in each state until the end of the episode.

We learned that our parameter update equation is given as:

$$\theta = \theta + \alpha \nabla_\theta \log \pi_\theta(a_t|s_t)R(\tau)$$

In the preceding equation, multiplying $\log \pi_\theta(a_t|s_t)$ by the positive return, $R(\tau) = +1$, means that we are increasing the log probability of action a_t in the state s_t. Thus, we perform a positive update. That is:

For each step in the episode, $t = 0, \ldots, T\text{-}1$, we update the parameter θ as:

$$\theta = \theta + \alpha \nabla_\theta \log \pi_\theta(a_t|s_t)(+1)$$

Thus, if we get a positive return then we increase the probability of all the actions performed in that episode, else we will decrease the probability.

We learned that, for each step in the episode, $t = 0, \ldots, T\text{-}1$, we update the parameter θ as:

$$\theta = \theta + \alpha \nabla_\theta \log \pi_\theta(a_t|s_t)R(\tau)$$

We can simply denote the preceding equation as:

$$\theta = \theta + \alpha \sum_{t=0}^{T-1} \nabla_\theta \log \pi_\theta(a_t|s_t)R(\tau)$$

Thus, if the episode (trajectory) gives a high return, we will increase the probabilities of all the actions of the episode, else we decrease the probabilities. We learned that $\nabla_\theta J(\theta) = \mathbb{E}_{\tau \sim \pi_\theta(\tau)}[\nabla_\theta \log \pi_\theta(a_t|s_t)R(\tau)]$. What about that expectation? We have not included that in our update equation yet. When we looked at the Monte Carlo method, we learned that we can approximate the expectation using the average. Thus, using the Monte Carlo approximation method, we change the expectation term to the sum over N trajectories. So, our update equation becomes:

$$\theta = \theta + \alpha \frac{1}{N} \sum_{i=1}^{N} \sum_{t=0}^{T-1} \nabla_\theta \log \pi_\theta(a_t|s_t) R(\tau)$$

It shows that instead of updating the parameter based on a single trajectory, we collect a set of N trajectories following the policy π_θ and update the parameter based on the average value, that is:

$$\theta = \theta + \alpha \underbrace{\frac{1}{N} \sum_{i=1}^{N}}_{} \underbrace{\sum_{t=0}^{T-1} \nabla_\theta \log \pi_\theta(a_t \mid s_t) R(\tau)}_{}$$

Sum over N For each step in the
trajectories   trajectory

Thus, first, we collect N number of trajectories $\{\tau^i\}_{i=1}^{N}$ following the policy π_θ and compute the gradient as:

$$\nabla_\theta J(\theta) = \frac{1}{N} \sum_{i=1}^{N} \left[\sum_{t=0}^{T-1} \nabla_\theta \log \pi_\theta(a_t|s_t) R(\tau) \right]$$

And then we update our parameter as:

$$\theta = \theta + \alpha \nabla_\theta J(\theta)$$

But we can't find the optimal parameter θ by updating the parameter for just one iteration. So, we repeat the previous step for many iterations to find the optimal parameter.

Now that we have a fundamental understanding of how policy gradient method work, in the next section, we will learn how to derive the policy gradient $\nabla_\theta J(\theta)$. After that, we will learn about the policy gradient algorithm in detail step by step.

Deriving the policy gradient

In this section, we will get into more details and learn how to compute the gradient $\nabla_\theta J(\theta)$ and how it is equal to $\mathbb{E}_{\tau \sim \pi_\theta(\tau)}[\nabla_\theta \log \pi_\theta(a_t|s_t) R(\tau)]$.

Let's deep dive into the interesting math and see how to calculate the derivative of our objective function J with respect to the model parameter θ in simple steps. Don't get intimidated by the upcoming equations, it's actually a pretty simple derivation. Before going ahead, let's revise some math prerequisites in order to understand our derivation better.

Definition of the expectation:

Let X be a discrete random variable whose **probability mass function (pmf)** is given as $p(x)$. Let f be a function of a discrete random variable X. Then the expectation of a function $f(X)$ can be defined as:

$$\mathbb{E}_{x \sim p(x)}[f(X)] = \sum_x p(x)f(x) \qquad (1)$$

Let X be a continuous random variable whose **probability density function (pdf)** is given as $p(x)$. Let f be a function of a continuous random variable X. Then the expectation of a function $f(X)$ can be defined as:

$$\mathbb{E}_{x \sim p(x)}[f(X)] = \int_x p(x)f(x)dx \qquad (2)$$

A log derivative trick is given as:

$$\nabla_\theta \log x = \frac{\nabla_\theta x}{x} \qquad (3)$$

We learned that the objective of our network is to maximize the expected return of the trajectory. Thus, we can write our objective function J as:

$$J(\theta) = E_{\tau \sim \pi_\theta(\tau)}[R(\tau)] \qquad (4)$$

In the preceding equation, the following applies:

- τ is the trajectory.
- $\tau \sim \pi_\theta(\tau)$ shows that we are sampling the trajectory based on the policy π given by network parameterized by θ.
- $R(\tau)$ is the return of the trajectory.

As we can see, our objective function, equation (4), is in the expectation form. From the definition of the expectation given in equation (2), we can expand the expectation and rewrite equation (4) as:

$$J(\theta) = \int \pi_\theta(\tau) R(\tau) d\tau$$

Now, we calculate the derivative of our objective function J with respect to θ:

$$\nabla_\theta J(\theta) = \int \nabla_\theta \pi_\theta(\tau) R(\tau) d\tau$$

Multiplying and dividing by $\pi_\theta(\tau)$, we can write:

$$\nabla_\theta J(\theta) = \int \nabla_\theta \pi_\theta(\tau) \frac{\pi_\theta(\tau)}{\pi_\theta(\tau)} R(\tau) d\tau$$

Rearranging the preceding equation, we can write:

$$\nabla_\theta J(\theta) = \int \pi_\theta(\tau) \frac{\nabla_\theta \pi_\theta(\tau)}{\pi_\theta(\tau)} R(\tau) d\tau$$

From equation (3), substituting $\nabla_\theta \log \pi_\theta(\tau) = \dfrac{\nabla_\theta \pi_\theta(\tau)}{\pi_\theta(\tau)}$ in the preceding equation, we can write:

$$\nabla_\theta J(\theta) = \int \pi_\theta(\tau) \nabla_\theta \log \pi_\theta(\tau) R(\tau) d\tau$$

From the definition of expectation given in equation (2), we can rewrite the preceding equation in expectation form as:

$$\nabla_\theta J(\theta) = \mathbb{E}_{\tau \sim \pi_\theta(\tau)}[\nabla_\theta \log \pi_\theta(\tau) R(\tau)] \tag{5}$$

The preceding equation gives us the gradient of the objective function. But we still haven't solved the equation yet. As we can see, in the preceding equation we have the term $\nabla_\theta \log \pi_\theta(\tau)$. Now we will see how we can compute that.

The probability distribution of trajectory can be given as:

$$\pi_\theta(\tau) = p(s_0) \prod_{t=0}^{T-1} \pi_\theta(a_t|s_t) \, p\,(s_{t+1}|s_t, a_t)$$

Where $p(s_0)$ is the initial state distribution. Taking the log on both sides, we can write:

$$\log \pi_\theta(\tau) = \log \left[p(s_0) \prod_{t=0}^{T-1} [\pi_\theta(a_t|s_t) \, p \, (s_{t+1}|s_t, a_t)] \right]$$

We know that the log of a product is equal to the sum of the logs, that is, $\log(ab) = \log a + \log b$. Applying this log rule to the preceding equation, we can write:

$$\log \pi_\theta(\tau) = \log p(s_0) + \log \prod_{t=0}^{T-1} [\pi_\theta(a_t|s_t) \, p \, (s_{t+1}|s_t, a_t)]$$

Again, we apply the same rule, log of product = sum of logs, and change the log Π to Σ logs, as shown here:

$$\log \pi_\theta(\tau) = \log p(s_0) + \sum_{t=0}^{T-1} \log \pi_\theta(a_t|s_t) + \log p \, (s_{t+1}|s_t, a_t)$$

Now, we compute the derivate with respect to θ:

$$\nabla_\theta \log \pi_\theta(\tau) = \nabla_\theta \left[\log p(s_0) + \sum_{t=0}^{T-1} \log \pi_\theta(a_t|s_t) + \log p \, (s_{t+1}|s_t, a_t) \right]$$

Note that we are calculating derivative with respect to θ and, as we can see in the preceding equation, the first and last term on the **right-hand side (RHS)** does not depend on the θ, and so they will become zero while calculating derivative. Thus our equation becomes:

$$\nabla_\theta \log \pi_\theta(\tau) = \sum_{t=0}^{T-1} \nabla_\theta \log \pi_\theta(a_t|s_t)$$

Now that we have found the value for $\nabla_\theta \log \pi_\theta(\tau)$, substituting this in equation (5) we can write:

$$\nabla_\theta J(\theta) = \mathbb{E}_{\tau \sim \pi_\theta(\tau)} \left[\sum_{t=0}^{T-1} \nabla_\theta \log \pi_\theta(a_t|s_t) R(\tau) \right]$$

That's it. But can we also get rid of that expectation? Yes! We can use a Monte Carlo approximation method and change the expectation to the sum over N trajectories. So, our final gradient becomes:

$$\nabla_\theta J(\theta) \approx \frac{1}{N} \sum_{i=1}^{N} \left[\sum_{t=0}^{T-1} \nabla_\theta \log \pi_\theta(a_t|s_t) R(\tau) \right] \tag{6}$$

Equation (6) shows that instead of updating a parameter based on a single trajectory, we collect N number of trajectories and update the parameter based on its average value over N trajectories.

Thus, after computing the gradient, we can update our parameter as:

$$\theta = \theta + \alpha \nabla_\theta J(\theta)$$

Thus, in this section, we have learned how to derive a policy gradient. In the next section, we will get into more details and learn about the policy gradient algorithm step by step.

Algorithm – policy gradient

The policy gradient algorithm we discussed so far is often called REINFORCE or **Monte Carlo policy gradient**. The algorithm of the REINFORCE method is given in the following steps:

1. Initialize the network parameter θ with random values
2. Generate N trajectories $\{\tau^i\}_{i=1}^N$ following the policy π_θ
3. Compute the return of the trajectory $R(\tau)$
4. Compute the gradients

$$\nabla_\theta J(\theta) = \frac{1}{N} \sum_{i=1}^{N} \left[\sum_{t=0}^{T-1} \nabla_\theta \log \pi_\theta(a_t|s_t) R(\tau) \right]$$

5. Update the network parameter as $\theta = \theta + \alpha \nabla_\theta J(\theta)$

6. Repeat *steps* 2 to 5 for several iterations

As we can see from this algorithm, the parameter θ is getting updated in every iteration. Since we are using the parameterized policy π_θ, our policy is getting updated in every iteration.

The policy gradient algorithm we just learned is an on-policy method, as we are using only a single policy. That is, we are using a policy to generate trajectories and we are also improving the same policy by updating the network parameter θ in every iteration.

We learned that with the policy gradient method (the REINFORCE method), we use a policy network that returns the probability distribution over the action space and then we select an action based on the probability distribution returned by our network using a stochastic policy. But this applies only to a discrete action space, and we use categorical policy as our stochastic policy.

What if our action space is continuous? That is, when the action space is continuous, how can we select actions? Here, our policy network cannot return the probability distribution over the action space as the action space is continuous. So, in this case, our policy network will return the mean and variance of the action as output, and then we generate a Gaussian distribution using this mean and variance and select an action by sampling from this Gaussian distribution using the Gaussian policy. We will learn more about this in the upcoming chapters. Thus, we can apply the policy gradient method to both discrete and continuous action spaces. Next, we will look at two methods to reduce the variance of policy gradient updates.

Variance reduction methods

In the previous section, we learned one of the simplest policy gradient methods, called the REINFORCE method. One major issue we face with the policy gradient method we learned in the previous section is that the gradient, $\nabla_\theta J(\theta)$, will have high variance in each update. The high variance is basically due to the major difference in the episodic returns. That is, we learned that policy gradient is the on-policy method, which means that we improve the same policy with which we are generating episodes in every iteration. Since the policy is getting improved on every iteration, our return varies greatly in each episode and it introduces a high variance in the gradient updates. When the gradients have high variance, then it will take a lot of time to attain convergence.

Thus, now we will learn the following two important methods to reduce the variance:

- Policy gradients with reward-to-go (causality)
- Policy gradients with baseline

Policy gradient with reward-to-go

We learned that the policy gradient is computed as:

$$\nabla_\theta J(\theta) = \frac{1}{N} \sum_{i=1}^{N} \left[\sum_{t=0}^{T-1} \nabla_\theta \log \pi_\theta(a_t|s_t) R(\tau) \right]$$

Now, we make a small change in the preceding equation. We know that the return of the trajectory is the sum of the rewards of that trajectory, that is:

$$R(\tau) = \sum_{t=0}^{T-1} r_t$$

Instead of using the return of trajectory $R(\tau)$, we use something called reward-to-go R_t. Reward-to-go is basically the return of the trajectory starting from state s_t. That is, instead of multiplying the log probabilities by the return of the full trajectory $R(\tau)$ in every step of the episode, we multiply them by the reward-to-go R_t. The reward-to-go implies the return of the trajectory starting from state s_t. But why do we have to do this? Let's understand this in more detail with an example.

We learned that we generate N number of trajectories and compute the gradient as:

$$\nabla_\theta J(\theta) = \frac{1}{N} \sum_{i=1}^{N} \left[\sum_{t=0}^{T-1} \nabla_\theta \log \pi_\theta(a_t|s_t) R(\tau) \right]$$

For better understanding, let's take only one trajectory by setting $N=1$, so we can write:

$$\nabla_\theta J(\theta) = \sum_{t=0}^{T-1} \nabla_\theta \log \pi_\theta(a_t|s_t) R(\tau)$$

Say, we generated the following trajectory with the policy π_θ:

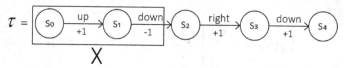

Figure 10.5: Trajectory

The return of the preceding trajectory is $R(\tau) = +1 - 1 + 1 + 1 = 2$.

Now, we can compute gradient as:

$$\nabla_\theta J(\theta) = \nabla_\theta \log \pi_\theta(up|s_0)R(\tau) + \nabla_\theta \log \pi_\theta(down|s_1)R(\tau) + \nabla_\theta \log \pi_\theta(right|s_2)R(\tau)$$
$$+\nabla_\theta \log \pi_\theta(down|s_3)R(\tau)$$

As we can observe from the preceding equation, in every step of the episode, we are multiplying the log probability of the action by the return of the full trajectory $R(\tau)$, which is 2 in the preceding example.

Let's suppose we want to know how good the action *right* is in the state s_2. If we understand that the action *right* is a good action in the state s_2, then we can increase the probability of moving *right* in the state s_2, else we decrease it. Okay, how can we tell whether the action *right* is good in the state s_2? As we learned in the previous section (when discussing the REINFORCE method), if the return of the trajectory $R(\tau)$ is high, then we increase the probability of the action *right* in the state s_2, else we decrease it.

But we don't have to do that now. Instead, we can compute the return (the sum of the rewards of the trajectory) only starting from the state s_2 because there is no use in including all the rewards that we obtain from the trajectory before taking the action *right* in the state s_2. As *Figure 10.6* shows, including all the rewards that we obtain before taking the action *right* in the state s_2 will not help us understand how good the action *right* is in the state s_2:

$\tau = $ So ──up──> S1 ──down──> S2 ──right──> S3 ──down──> S4
        +1   -1   +1   +1

X

Figure 10.6: Trajectory

Thus, instead of taking the complete return of the trajectory in all the steps of the episode, we use reward-to-go R_t, which is the return of the trajectory starting from the state s_t.

Thus, now we can write:

$$\nabla_\theta J(\theta) = \nabla_\theta \log \pi_\theta(up|s_0)R_0 + \nabla_\theta \log \pi_\theta(down|s_1)R_1 + \nabla_\theta \log \pi_\theta(right|s_2)R_2$$
$$+\nabla_\theta \log \pi_\theta(down|s_3)R_3$$

Where R_0 indicates the return of the trajectory starting from the state s_0, R_1 indicates the return of the trajectory starting from the state s_1, and so on. If R_0 is high value, then we increase the probability of the action *up* in the state s_0, else we decrease it. If R_1 is high value, then we increase the probability of the action *down* in the state s_1, else we decrease it.

Thus, now, we can define the reward-to-go as:

$$R_t = \sum_{t'=0}^{T-1} r(s_{t'}, a_{t'})$$

The preceding equation states that the reward-to-go R_t is the sum of rewards of the trajectory starting from the state s_t. Thus, now we can rewrite our gradient with reward-to-go instead of the return of the trajectory as:

$$\nabla_\theta J(\theta) = \frac{1}{N} \sum_{i=1}^{N} \left[\sum_{t=0}^{T-1} \nabla_\theta \log \pi_\theta(a_t | s_t) \sum_{t'=0}^{T-1} r(s_{t'}, a_{t'}) \right]$$

We can simply express the preceding equation as:

$$\nabla_\theta J(\theta) = \frac{1}{N} \sum_{i=1}^{N} \left[\sum_{t=0}^{T-1} \nabla_\theta \log \pi_\theta(a_t | s_t) R_t \right]$$

Where the reward-to-go is $R_t = \sum_{t'=0}^{T-1} r(s_{t'}, a_{t'})$.

After computing the gradient, we update the parameter as:

$$\theta = \theta + \alpha \nabla_\theta J(\theta)$$

Now that we have understood what policy gradient with reward-to-go is, in the next section, we will look into the algorithm for more clarity.

Algorithm – Reward-to-go policy gradient

The algorithm of policy gradient with reward-to-go is similar to the REINFORCE method, except now we compute the reward-to-go (return of the trajectory starting from a state s_t) instead of using the full return of the trajectory, as shown here:

1. Initialize the network parameter θ with random values
2. Generate N number of trajectories $\{\tau^i\}_{i=1}^{N}$ following the policy π_θ
3. Compute the return (reward-to-go) R_t
4. Compute the gradients:

$$\nabla_\theta J(\theta) = \frac{1}{N} \sum_{i=1}^{N} \left[\sum_{t=0}^{T-1} \nabla_\theta \log \pi_\theta(a_t|s_t) R_t \right]$$

5. Update the network parameter as $\theta = \theta + \alpha \nabla_\theta J(\theta)$
6. Repeat *steps* 2 to 5 for several iterations

From the preceding algorithm, we can observe that we are using reward-to-go instead of the return of the trajectory. To get a clear understanding of how the reward-to-go policy gradient works, let's implement it in the next section.

Cart pole balancing with policy gradient

Now, let's learn how to implement the policy gradient algorithm with reward-to-go for the cart pole balancing task.

For a clear understanding of how the policy gradient method works, we use TensorFlow in the non-eager mode by disabling TensorFlow 2 behavior.

First, let's import the necessary libraries:

```
import tensorflow.compat.v1 as tf
tf.disable_v2_behavior()
import numpy as np
import gym
```

Create the cart pole environment using gym:

```
env = gym.make('CartPole-v0')
```

Get the state shape:

```
state_shape = env.observation_space.shape[0]
```

Get the number of actions:

```
num_actions = env.action_space.n
```

Computing discounted and normalized reward

Instead of using the rewards directly, we can use the discounted and normalized rewards.

Set the discount factor, γ:

```
gamma = 0.95
```

Let's define a function called `discount_and_normalize_rewards` for computing the discounted and normalized rewards:

```
def discount_and_normalize_rewards(episode_rewards):
```

Initialize an array for storing the discounted rewards:

```
discounted_rewards = np.zeros_like(episode_rewards)
```

Compute the discounted reward:

```
reward_to_go = 0.0
for i in reversed(range(len(episode_rewards))):
    reward_to_go = reward_to_go * gamma + episode_rewards[i]
    discounted_rewards[i] = reward_to_go
```

Normalize and return the reward:

```
discounted_rewards -= np.mean(discounted_rewards)
discounted_rewards /= np.std(discounted_rewards)

return discounted_rewards
```

Building the policy network

First, let's define the placeholder for the state:

```
state_ph = tf.placeholder(tf.float32, [None, state_shape], name="state_ph")
```

Define the placeholder for the action:

```
action_ph = tf.placeholder(tf.int32, [None, num_actions], name="action_ph")
```

Define the placeholder for the discounted reward:

```
discounted_rewards_ph = tf.placeholder(tf.float32, [None,],
name="discounted_rewards")
```

Define layer 1:

```
layer1 = tf.layers.dense(state_ph, units=32, activation=tf.nn.relu)
```

Define layer 2. Note that the number of units in layer 2 is set to the number of actions:

```
layer2 = tf.layers.dense(layer1, units=num_actions)
```

Obtain the probability distribution over the action space as an output of the network by applying the softmax function to the result of layer 2:

```
prob_dist = tf.nn.softmax(layer2)
```

We learned that we compute gradient as:

$$\nabla_\theta J(\theta) = \frac{1}{N} \sum_{i=1}^{N} \left[\sum_{t=0}^{T-1} \nabla_\theta \log \pi_\theta (a_t | s_t) R_t \right]$$

After computing the gradient, we update the parameter of the network using gradient ascent:

$$\theta = \theta + \alpha \nabla_\theta J(\theta)$$

However, it is a standard convention to perform minimization rather than maximization. So, we can convert the preceding maximization objective into the minimization objective by just adding a negative sign. We can implement this using `tf.nn.softmax_cross_entropy_with_logits_v2`. Thus, we can define the negative log policy as:

```
neg_log_policy = tf.nn.softmax_cross_entropy_with_logits_v2(logits =
layer2, labels = action_ph)
```

Now, let's define the loss:

```
loss = tf.reduce_mean(neg_log_policy * discounted_rewards_ph)
```

Define the train operation for minimizing the loss using the Adam optimizer:

```
train = tf.train.AdamOptimizer(0.01).minimize(loss)
```

Training the network

Now, let's train the network for several iterations. For simplicity, let's just generate one episode in every iteration.

Set the number of iterations:

```
num_iterations = 1000
```

Start the TensorFlow session:

```
with tf.Session() as sess:
```

Initialize all the TensorFlow variables:

```
sess.run(tf.global_variables_initializer())
```

For every iteration:

```
for i in range(num_iterations):
```

Initialize an empty list for storing the states, actions, and rewards obtained in the episode:

```
episode_states, episode_actions, episode_rewards = [],[],[]
```

Set done to `False`:

```
done = False
```

Initialize the Return:

```
Return = 0
```

Initialize the state by resetting the environment:

```
state = env.reset()
```

While the episode is not over:

```
while not done:
```

Reshape the state:

```
state = state.reshape([1,4])
```

Feed the state to the policy network and the network returns the probability distribution over the action space as output, which becomes our stochastic policy π:

```
pi = sess.run(prob_dist, feed_dict={state_ph: state})
```

Now, we select an action using this stochastic policy:

```
a = np.random.choice(range(pi.shape[1]), p=pi.ravel())
```

Perform the selected action:

```
next_state, reward, done, info = env.step(a)
```

Render the environment:

```
env.render()
```

Update the return:

```
Return += reward
```

One-hot encode the action:

```
action = np.zeros(num_actions)
action[a] = 1
```

Store the state, action, and reward in their respective lists:

```
episode_states.append(state)
episode_actions.append(action)
episode_rewards.append(reward)
```

Update the state to the next state:

```
state=next_state
```

Compute the discounted and normalized reward:

```
        discounted_rewards= discount_and_normalize_rewards(episode_
    rewards)
```

Define the feed dictionary:

```
        feed_dict = {state_ph: np.vstack(np.array(episode_states)),
                     action_ph: np.vstack(np.array(episode_actions)),
                     discounted_rewards_ph: discounted_rewards
                    }
```

Train the network:

```
        loss_, _ = sess.run([loss, train], feed_dict=feed_dict)
```

Print the return for every 10 iterations:

```
        if i%10==0:
            print("Iteration:{}, Return: {}".format(i,Return))
```

Now that we have learned how to implement the policy gradient algorithm with reward-to-go, in the next section, we will learn another interesting variance reduction technique called policy gradient with baseline.

Policy gradient with baseline

We have learned that we find the optimal policy by using a neural network and we update the parameter of our network using gradient ascent:

$$\theta = \theta + \alpha \nabla_\theta J(\theta)$$

Where the value of the gradient is:

$$\nabla_\theta J(\theta) \approx \frac{1}{N} \sum_{i=1}^{N} \left[\sum_{t=0}^{T-1} \nabla_\theta \log \pi_\theta(a_t | s_t) R_t \right]$$

Now, to reduce variance, we introduce a new function called a baseline function. Subtracting the baseline b from the return (reward-to-go) R_t reduces the variance, so we can rewrite the gradient as:

$$\nabla_\theta J(\theta) \approx \frac{1}{N} \sum_{i=1}^{N} \left[\sum_{t=0}^{T-1} \nabla_\theta \log \pi_\theta(a_t|s_t) \ (R_t - b) \right]$$

Wait. What is the baseline function? And how does subtracting it from R_t reduce the variance? The purpose of the baseline is to reduce the variance in the return. Thus, if the baseline b is a value that can give us the expected return from the state the agent is in, then subtracting b in every step will reduce the variance in the return.

There are several choices for the baseline functions. We can choose any function as a baseline function but the baseline function should not depend on our network parameter. A simple baseline could be the average return of the sampled trajectories:

$$b = \frac{1}{N} \sum_{i=1}^{N} R(\tau)$$

Thus, subtracting current return R_t and the average return helps us to reduce variance. As we can see, our baseline function doesn't depend on the network parameter θ. So, we can use any function as a baseline function and it should not affect our network parameter θ.

One of the most popular functions of the baseline is the value function. We learned that the value function or the value of a state is the expected return an agent would obtain starting from that state following the policy π. Thus, subtracting the value of a state (the expected return) and the current return R_t can reduce the variance. So, we can rewrite our gradient as:

$$\nabla_\theta J(\theta) \approx \frac{1}{N} \sum_{i=1}^{N} \left[\sum_{t=0}^{T-1} \nabla_\theta \log \pi_\theta(a_t|s_t) \ (R_t - V(s_t)) \right]$$

Other than the value function, we can also use different baseline functions such as the Q function, the advantage function, and more. We will learn more about them in the next chapter.

But now the question is how can we learn the baseline function? Say we are using the value function as the baseline function. How can we learn the optimal value function? Just like we are approximating the policy, we can also approximate the value function using another neural network parameterized by ϕ.

That is, we use another network for approximating the value function (the value of a state) and we can call this network a value network. Okay, how can we train this value network?

Since the value of the state is a continuous value, we can train the network by minimizing the **mean squared error** (**MSE**). The MSE can be defined as the mean squared difference between the actual return R_t and the predicted return $V_\phi(s_t)$. Thus, the objective function of the value network can be defined as:

$$J(\phi) = \frac{1}{N} \sum_{i=1}^{N} \sum_{t=0}^{T-1} \left(R_t - V_\phi(s_t) \right)^2$$

We can minimize the error using the gradient descent and update the network parameter as:

$$\phi = \phi - \alpha \nabla_\phi J(\phi)$$

Thus, in the policy gradient with the baseline method, we minimize the variance in the gradient updates by using the baseline function. A baseline function can be any function and it should not depend on the network parameter θ. We use the value function as a baseline function, then to approximate the value function we use a different neural network parameterized by ϕ, and we find the optimal value function by minimizing the MSE.

In a nutshell, in the policy gradient with the baseline function, we use two neural networks:

Policy network parameterized by θ: This finds the optimal policy by performing gradient ascent:

$$\nabla_\theta J(\theta) \approx \frac{1}{N} \sum_{i=1}^{N} \left[\sum_{t=0}^{T-1} \nabla_\theta \log \pi_\theta(a_t|s_t) \ (R_t - V_\phi(s_t)) \right]$$

$$\theta = \theta + \alpha \nabla_\theta J(\theta)$$

Value network parameterized by ϕ: This is used to correct the variance in the gradient update by acting as a baseline, and it finds the optimal value of a state by performing gradient descent:

$$J(\phi) = \frac{1}{N} \sum_{i=1}^{N} \sum_{t=0}^{T-1} \left(R_t - V_\phi(s_t) \right)^2$$

$$\phi = \phi - \alpha \nabla_\phi J(\phi)$$

Note that the policy gradient with the baseline function is often referred to as the **REINFORCE with baseline** method.

Now that we have seen how the policy gradient method with baseline works by using a policy and a value network, in the next section we will look into the algorithm to get more clarity.

Algorithm – REINFORCE with baseline

The algorithm of the policy gradient method with the baseline function (REINFORCE with baseline) is shown here:

1. Initialize the policy network parameter θ and value network parameter ϕ

2. Generate N number of trajectories $\{\tau^i\}_{i=1}^{N}$ following the policy π_θ

3. Compute the return (reward-to-go) R_t

4. Compute the policy gradient:

$$\nabla_\theta J(\theta) = \frac{1}{N} \sum_{i=1}^{N} \left[\sum_{t=0}^{T-1} \nabla_\theta \log \pi_\theta(a_t|s_t) \; (R_t - V_\phi(s_t)) \right]$$

5. Update the policy network parameter θ using gradient ascent as
$\theta = \theta + \alpha \nabla_\theta J(\theta)$

6. Compute the MSE of the value network:

$$J(\phi) = \frac{1}{N} \sum_{i=1}^{N} \sum_{t=0}^{T-1} \left(R_t - V_\phi(s_t) \right)^2$$

7. Compute gradients $\nabla_\phi J(\phi)$ and update the value network parameter ϕ using gradient descent as $\phi = \phi - \alpha \nabla_\phi J(\phi)$

8. Repeat *steps 2* to *7* for several iterations

Summary

We started off the chapter by learning that with value-based methods, we extract the optimal policy from the optimal Q function (Q values). Then we learned that it is difficult to compute the Q function when our action space is continuous. We can discretize the action space; however, discretization is not always desirable, and it leads to the loss of several important features and an action space with a huge set of actions.

So, we resorted to the policy-based method. In the policy-based method, we compute the optimal policy without the Q function. We learned about one of the most popular policy-based methods called the policy gradient, in which we find the optimal policy directly by parameterizing the policy using some parameter θ.

We also learned that in the policy gradient method, we select actions based on the action probability distribution given by the network, and if we win the episode, that is, if we get a high return, then we assign high probabilities to all the actions in the episode, else we assign low probabilities to all the actions in the episode. Later, we learned how to derive the policy gradient step by step, and then we looked into the algorithm of policy gradient method in more detail.

Moving forward, we learned about the variance reduction methods such as reward-to-go and the policy gradient method with the baseline function. In the policy gradient method with the baseline function, we use two networks called the policy and value network. The role of the policy network is to find the optimal policy, and the role of the value network is to correct the gradient updates in the policy network by estimating the value function.

In the next chapter, we will learn about another interesting set of algorithms called the actor-critic methods.

Questions

Let's evaluate our understanding of the policy gradient method by answering the following questions:

1. What is a value-based method?
2. Why do we need a policy-based method?
3. How does the policy gradient method work?
4. How do we compute the gradient in the policy gradient method?
5. What is a reward-to-go?
6. What is the policy gradient with the baseline function?
7. Define the baseline function.

Further reading

For more information about the policy gradient, we can refer to the following paper:

- **Policy Gradient Methods for Reinforcement Learning with Function Approximation** by *Richard S. Sutton et al.,* https://papers.nips.cc/paper/1713-policy-gradient-methods-for-reinforcement-learning-with-function-approximation.pdf

11

Actor-Critic
Methods – A2C and A3C

So far, we have covered two types of methods for learning the optimal policy. One is the value-based method, and the other is the policy-based method. In the value-based method, we use the Q function to extract the optimal policy. In the policy-based method, we compute the optimal policy without using the Q function.

In this chapter, we will learn about another interesting method called the actor-critic method for finding the optimal policy. The actor-critic method makes use of both the value-based and policy-based methods. We will begin the chapter by understanding what the actor-critic method is and how it makes use of value-based and policy-based methods. We will acquire a basic understanding of actor-critic methods, and then we will learn about them in detail.

Moving on, we will also learn how actor-critic differs from the policy gradient with baseline method, and we will learn the algorithm of the actor-critic method in detail. Next, we will understand what **Advantage Actor-Critic** (**A2C**) is, and how it makes use of the advantage function.

At the end of the chapter, we will learn about one of the most popularly used actor-critic algorithms, called **Asynchronous Advantage Actor-Critic** (**A3C**). We will understand what A3C is and the details of how it works along with its architecture.

In this chapter, we will cover the following topics:

- Overview of the actor-critic method
- Understanding the actor-critic method
- The actor-critic method algorithm
- Advantage actor-critic (A2C)
- Asynchronous advantage actor-critic (A3C)
- The architecture of asynchronous advantage actor-critic (A3C)
- Mountain car climbing using A3C

Let's begin the chapter by getting a basic understanding of the actor-critic method.

Overview of the actor-critic method

The actor-critic method is one of the most popular algorithms in deep reinforcement learning. Several modern deep reinforcement learning algorithms are designed based on actor-critic methods. The actor-critic method lies at the intersection of value-based and policy-based methods. That is, it takes advantage of both value-based and policy-based methods.

In this section, without going into further detail, first, let's acquire a basic understanding of how the actor-critic method works and then, in the next section, we will get into more detail and understand the math behind the actor-critic method.

Actor-critic, as the name suggests, consists of two types of network—the actor network and the critic network. The role of the actor network is to find an optimal policy, while the role of the critic network is to evaluate the policy produced by the actor network. So, we can think of the critic network as a feedback network that evaluates and guides the actor network in finding the optimal policy, as *Figure 11.1* shows:

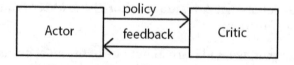

Figure 11.1: The actor-critic network

Okay, so what actually are the actor and critic networks? How do they work together and improve the policy? The actor network is basically the policy network, and it finds the optimal policy using a policy gradient method. The critic network is basically the value network, and it estimates the state value.

Thus, using its state value, the critic network evaluates the action produced by the actor network and sends its feedback to the actor. Based on the critic's feedback, the actor network then updates its parameter.

Thus, in the actor-critic method, we use two networks—the actor network (policy network), which computes the policy, and the critic network (value network), which evaluates the policy produced by the actor network by computing the value function (state values). Isn't this similar to something we just learned in the previous chapter?

Yes! If you recall, it is similar to the policy gradient method with the baseline (REINFORCE with baseline) we learned in the previous chapter. Similar to REINFORCE with baseline, here also, we have an actor (policy network) and a critic (value network) network. However, actor-critic is NOT the same as REINFORCE with baseline. In the REINFORCE with baseline method, we learned that we use a value network as the baseline and it helps to reduce the variance in the gradient updates. In the actor-critic method as well, we use the critic to reduce variance in the gradient updates of the actor, but it also helps to improve the policy iteratively in an online fashion. The distinction between these two will be made clear in the next section.

Now that we have a basic understanding of the actor-critic method, in the next section, we will learn how the actor-critic method works in detail.

Understanding the actor-critic method

In the REINFORCE with baseline method, we learned that we have two networks—policy and value networks. The policy network finds the optimal policy, while the value network acts as a baseline and corrects the variance in the gradient updates. Similar to REINFORCE with baseline, the actor-critic method also consists of a policy network, known as the actor network, and the value network, known as the critic network.

The fundamental difference between the REINFORCE with baseline method and the actor-critic method is that in the REINFORCE with baseline method, we update the parameter of the network at the end of an episode. But in the actor-critic method, we update the parameter of the network at every step of the episode. But why do we have to do this? What is the use of updating the network parameter at every step of the episode? Let's explore this in further detail.

We can think of the REINFORCE with baseline method being similar to the **Monte Carlo (MC)** method, which we covered in *Chapter 4, Monte Carlo Methods*, and the actor-critic method being similar to the TD learning method, which we covered in *Chapter 5, Understanding Temporal Difference Learning*. So, first, let's recap these two methods.

In the MC method, to compute the value of a state, we generate some N trajectories and compute the value of a state as an average return of a state across the N trajectories. We learned that when the trajectory is too long, then the MC method will take us a lot of time to compute the value of the state and is also unsuitable for non-episodic tasks. So, we resorted to the TD learning method.

In the TD learning method, we learned that instead of waiting until the end of the episode to compute the value of the state, we can make use of bootstrapping and estimate the value of the state as the sum of the immediate reward and the discounted value of the next state.

Now, let's see how the MC and TD methods relate to the REINFORCE with baseline and actor-critic methods, respectively.

First, let's recall what we learned in the REINFORCE with baseline method. In the REINFORCE with baseline method, we generate N number of trajectories using the policy π_θ and compute the gradient as:

$$\nabla_\theta J(\theta) = \frac{1}{N} \sum_{i=1}^{N} \left[\sum_{t=0}^{T-1} \nabla_\theta \log \pi_\theta(a_t|s_t) \ (R_t - V_\phi(s_t)) \right]$$

As we can observe, in order to compute the gradients, we need a complete trajectory. That is, as the following equation shows, in order to compute the gradient, we need to compute the return of the trajectory. We know that the return is the sum of rewards of the trajectory, so in order to compute the return (reward-to-go), first, we need a complete trajectory generated using the policy π_θ. So, we generate several trajectories using the policy π_θ and then we compute the gradient:

$$\nabla_\theta J(\theta) = \frac{1}{N} \sum_{i=1}^{N} \left[\sum_{t=0}^{T-1} \nabla_\theta \log \pi_\theta(a_t \mid s_t) (\underbrace{R_t} - V_\phi(s_t)) \right]$$

Return of a trajectory

After computing the gradients, we update the parameter as:

$$\theta = \theta + \alpha \nabla_\theta J(\theta)$$

Instead of generating the complete trajectory and then computing the return, can we make use of bootstrapping, as we learned in TD learning? Yes! In the actor-critic method, we approximate the return by just taking the immediate reward and the discounted value of the next state as:

$$R \approx r + \gamma V(s')$$

Where r is the immediate reward and $\gamma V(s')$ is the discounted value of the next state.

So, we can rewrite the policy gradient by replacing the return R by the bootstrap estimate, $r + \gamma V(s')$, as shown here:

$$\nabla_\theta J(\theta) = \nabla_\theta \log \pi_\theta (a_t | s_t)(r + \gamma V_\phi(s'_t) - V_\phi(s_t))$$

Now, we don't have to wait till the end of the episode to compute the return. Instead, we bootstrap, compute the gradient, and update the network parameter at every step of the episode.

The difference between how we compute the gradient and update the parameter of the policy network in REINFORCE with baseline and the actor-critic method is shown in *Figure 11.2*. As we can observe in REINFORCE with baseline, first we generate complete episodes (trajectories), and then we update the parameter of the network. Whereas, in the actor-critic method, we update the parameter of the network at every step of the episode:

REINFORCE with baseline

Generate some N number of trajectories $\{\tau^i\}_{i=1}^N$ following the policy π_θ

Compute the policy gradient, $\nabla_\theta J(\theta) = \frac{1}{N} \sum_{i=1}^{N} \left[\sum_{t=0}^{T-1} \nabla_\theta \log \pi_\theta (a_t | s_t)(R_t - V_\phi(s_t)) \right]$

Update the policy network parameter θ using gradient ascent as $\theta = \theta + \alpha \nabla_\theta J(\theta)$

Actor Critic

For each step in the episode :

Select an action using the policy π_θ

Take the action a_t in the state s_t, observe the reward r and move to next state s'_t

Compute the policy gradients, $\nabla_\theta J(\theta) = \nabla_\theta \log \pi_\theta (a_t | s_t)(r + \gamma V_\phi(s'_t) - V_\phi(s_t))$

Update the policy network parameter $\theta = \theta + \alpha \nabla_\theta J(\theta)$

Figure 11.2: The difference between the REINFORCE with baseline and actor-critic methods

Okay, what about the critic network (value network)? How can we update the parameter of the critic network? Similar to the actor network, we update the parameter of the critic network at every step of the episode. The loss of the critic network is the TD error, which is the difference between the target value of the state and the value of the state predicted by the network. The target value of the state can be computed as the sum of reward and the discounted value of the next state value. Thus, the loss of the critic network is expressed as:

$$J(\phi) = r + \gamma V_\phi(s'_t) - V_\phi(s_t)$$

Where $r + \gamma V_\phi(s'_t)$ is the target value of the state and $V_\phi(s_t)$ is the predicted value of the state.

After computing the loss of the critic network, we compute gradients $\nabla_\phi J(\phi)$ and update the parameter ϕ of the critic network at every step of the episode using gradient descent:

$$\phi = \phi - \alpha \nabla_\phi J(\phi)$$

Now that we have learned how the actor (policy network) and critic (value network) work in the actor-critic method; let's look at the algorithm of the actor-critic method in the next section for more clarity.

The actor-critic algorithm

The steps for the actor-critic algorithm are:

1. Initialize the actor network parameter θ and the critic network parameter ϕ
2. For N number of episodes, repeat *step 3*
3. For each step in the episode, that is, for $t = 0,. \ldots, T\text{-}1$:
   1. Select an action using the policy, $a_t \sim \pi_\theta(s_t)$
   2. Take the action a_t in the state s_t, observe the reward r, and move to the next state s'_t
   3. Compute the policy gradients:
   $$\nabla_\theta J(\theta) = \nabla_\theta \log \pi_\theta(a_t|s_t)(r + \gamma V_\phi(s'_t) - V_\phi(s_t))$$
   4. Update the actor network parameter θ using gradient ascent:
   $$\theta = \theta + \alpha \nabla_\theta J(\theta)$$
   5. Compute the loss of the critic network:
   $$J(\phi) = r + \gamma V_\phi(s'_t) - V_\phi(s_t)$$
   6. Compute gradients $\nabla_\phi J(\phi)$ and update the critic network parameter ϕ using gradient descent:
   $$\phi = \phi - \alpha \nabla_\phi J(\phi)$$

As we can observe from the preceding algorithm, the actor network (policy network) parameter is being updated at every step of the episode. So, in each step of the episode, we select an action based on the updated policy while the critic network (value network) parameter is also getting updated at every step, and thus the critic also improves at evaluating the actor network at every step of the episode. While with the REINFORCE with baseline method, we only update the parameter of the network after generating the complete episodes.

One more important difference we should note down between the REINFORCE with baseline and the actor-critic method is that, in the REINFORCE with baseline we use the full return of the trajectory whereas in the actor-critic method we use the bootstrapped return.

The actor-critic algorithm we just learned is often referred to as the **Advantage Actor-Critic** (**A2C**). In the next section, we will look into the advantage function and learn why our algorithm is called the advantage actor-critic in more detail.

Advantage actor-critic (A2C)

Before moving on, first, let's recall the advantage function. The advantage function is defined as the difference between the Q function and the value function. We can express the advantage function as:

$$A(s, a) = Q(s, a) - V(s) \qquad\qquad (1)$$

The advantage function tells us, in state s, how good action a is compared to the average actions.

In A2C, we compute the policy gradient with the advantage function. So, first, let's see how to compute the advantage function. We know that the advantage function is the difference between the Q function and the value function, that is, $Q(s, a) - V(s)$, so we can use two function approximators (neural networks), one for estimating the Q function and the other for estimating the value function. Then, we can subtract the values of these two networks to get the advantage value. But this will definitely not be an optimal method and, computationally, it will be expensive.

So, we can approximate the Q value as:

$$Q(s, a) \approx r + \gamma V(s')$$

But how can we approximate the Q value like this? Do you recall in *Chapter 3, The Bellman Equation and Dynamic Programming*, in *The relationship between the value and Q functions* section, we learned we could derive the Q function from the value function? Using that identify, we can approximate the Q function as the sum of the immediate reward and the discounted value of the next state.

Substituting the preceding Q value in the advantage function, equation (1), we can write the following:

$$A(s, a) = r + \gamma V(s') - V(s)$$

Thus, now we have the advantage function. We learned that in A2C, we compute the policy gradient with the advantage function. So, we can write this:

$$\nabla_\theta J(\theta) = \nabla_\theta \log \pi_\theta(a_t|s_t) A(s,a)$$

Expanding the advantage function, we can write the following:

$$\nabla_\theta J(\theta) = \nabla_\theta \log \pi_\theta(a_t|s_t) \left(r + \gamma V_\phi(s_t') - V_\phi(s_t) \right)$$

As we can observe, our policy gradient is now computed using the advantage function:

$$\nabla_\theta J(\theta) = \nabla_\theta \log \pi_\theta(a_t \mid s_t)(r + \gamma V_\phi(s_t') - V_\phi(s_t))$$

$$\downarrow \qquad \downarrow$$

$$Q(s,a) \quad - \quad V(s)$$

Now, check the preceding equation with how we computed the gradient in the previous section. We can observe that both are essentially the same. Thus, the A2C method is the same as what we learned in the previous section.

Asynchronous advantage actor-critic (A3C)

Asynchronous advantage actor-critic, hereinafter referred to as A3C, is one of the popular actor-critic algorithms. The main idea behind the asynchronous advantage actor-critic method is that it uses several agents for learning in parallel and aggregates their overall experience.

In A3C, we will have two types of networks, one is a global network (global agent), and the other is the worker network (worker agent). We will have many worker agents, each worker agent uses a different exploration policy, and they learn in their own copy of the environment and collect experience. Then, the experience obtained from these worker agents is aggregated and sent to the global agent. The global agent aggregates the learning.

Now that we have a very basic idea of how A3C works, let's go into more detail.

The three As

Before diving in, let's first learn what the three A's in A3C signify.

Asynchronous: Asynchronous implies the way A3C works. That is, instead of having a single agent that tries to learn the optimal policy, here, we have multiple agents that interact with the environment. Since we have multiple agents interacting with the environment at the same time, we provide copies of the environment to every agent so that each agent can then interact with their own copy of the environment. So, all these multiple agents are called worker agents and we have a separate agent called the global agent. All the worker agents report to the global agent asynchronously and the global agent aggregates the learning.

Advantage: We have already learned what an advantage function is in the previous section. An advantage function can be defined as the difference between the Q function and the value function.

Actor-critic: Each of the worker networks (worker agents) and the global network (global agent) basically follow an actor-critic architecture. That is, each of the agents consists of an actor network for estimating the policy and the critic network for evaluating the policy produced by the actor network.

Now, let us move on to the architecture of A3C and understand how A3C works in detail.

The architecture of A3C

Now, let's understand the architecture of A3C. The architecture of A3C is shown in the following figure:

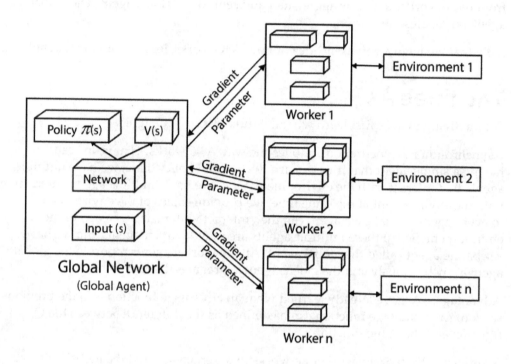

Figure 11.3: The architecture of A3C

As we can observe from the preceding figure, we have multiple worker agents and each worker agent interacts with their own copies of the environment and collects experience. We can also observe that each worker agent follows an actor-critic architecture. So, the worker agents compute the actor network loss (policy loss) and critic network loss (value loss).

In the previous section, we learned that our actor network is updated by computing the policy gradient:

$$\nabla_\theta J(\theta) = \nabla_\theta \log \pi_\theta(a_t | s_t) \left(r + \gamma V_\phi(s_t') - V_\phi(s_t) \right)$$

Thus, the actor loss is basically the following:

$$J(\theta) = \log \pi_\theta(a_t|s_t)\left(r + \gamma V_\phi(s'_t) - V_\phi(s_t)\right)$$

As we can observe, actor loss is the product of log probability of the action and the TD error. Now, we add a new term to our actor loss called the entropy (measure of randomness) of the policy and redefine the actor loss as:

$$J(\theta) = \log \pi_\theta(a_t|s_t)\left(r + \gamma V_\phi(s'_t) - V_\phi(s_t)\right) + \beta H(\pi(s))$$

Where $H(\pi)$ denotes the entropy of the policy. Adding the entropy of the policy promotes sufficient exploration, and the parameter β is used to control the significance of the entropy.

The critic loss is just the mean squared TD error.

After computing the losses of the actor and critic networks, worker agents compute the gradients of the loss and then they send those gradients to the global agent. That is, the worker agents compute the gradients and their gradients are asynchronously accumulated to the global agent. The global agent updates their parameters using the asynchronously received gradients from the worker agents. Then, the global agent sends the updated parameter periodically to the worker agents, so now the worker agents will get updated.

In this way, each worker agent computes loss, calculates gradients, and sends those gradients to the global agent asynchronously. Thus, the global agent parameter is updated by gradients received from the worker agents. Then, the global agent sends the updated parameter to the worker agents periodically.

Since we have many worker agents interacting with their own copies of the environment and aggregating the information to the global network, there will be low to no correlation between the experiences.

The steps involved in A3C are:

1. The worker agent interacts with their own copies of the environment.
2. Each worker follows a different policy and collects the experience.
3. Next, the worker agents compute the losses of the actor and critic networks.

4. After computing the loss, they calculate gradients of the loss, and send those gradients to the global agent asynchronously.

5. The global agent updates their parameters with the gradients received from the worker agents.

6. Now, the updated parameter from the global agent will be sent to the worker agents periodically.

We repeat the preceding steps for several iterations to find the optimal policy. To get a clear understanding of how A3C works, in the next section, we will learn how to implement it.

Mountain car climbing using A3C

Let's implement the A3C algorithm for the mountain car climbing task. In the mountain car climbing environment, a car is placed between two mountains and the goal of the agent is to drive up the mountain on the right. But the problem is, the agent can't drive up the mountain in one pass. So, the agent has to drive back and forth to build momentum to drive up the mountain on the right. A high reward will be assigned if our agent spends less energy while driving up. *Figure 11.4* shows the mountain car environment:

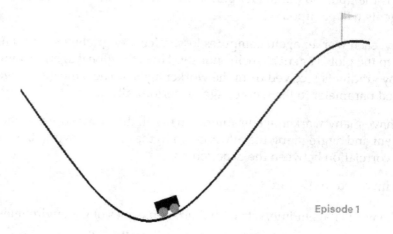

Figure 11.4: The mountain car environment

The code used in this section is adapted from the open source implementation of A3C (https://github.com/stefanbo92/A3C-Continuous) provided by Stefan Boschenriedter.

First, let's import the necessary libraries:

```
import warnings
warnings.filterwarnings('ignore')

import gym
import multiprocessing
import threading
import numpy as np
import os
import shutil
import matplotlib.pyplot as plt
import tensorflow.compat.v1 as tf
tf.disable_v2_behavior()
```

Creating the mountain car environment

Let's create a mountain car environment using Gym. Note that our mountain car environment is a continuous environment, meaning that our action space is continuous:

```
env = gym.make('MountainCarContinuous-v0')
```

Get the state shape of the environment:

```
state_shape = env.observation_space.shape[0]
```

Get the action shape of the environment:

```
action_shape = env.action_space.shape[0]
```

Note that we created the continuous mountain car environment, and thus our action space consists of continuous values. So, we get the bounds of our action space:

```
action_bound = [env.action_space.low, env.action_space.high]
```

Defining the variables

Now, let's define some of the important variables.

Define the number of workers as the number of CPUs:

```
num_workers = multiprocessing.cpu_count()
```

Define the number of episodes:

```
num_episodes = 2000
```

Define the number of time steps:

```
num_timesteps = 200
```

Define the global network (global agent) scope:

```
global_net_scope = 'Global_Net'
```

Define the time step at which we want to update the global network:

```
update_global = 10
```

Define the discount factor, γ:

```
gamma = 0.90
```

Define the beta value:

```
beta = 0.01
```

Define the directory where we want to store the logs:

```
log_dir = 'logs'
```

Defining the actor-critic class

We learned that in A3C, both the global and worker agents follow the actor-critic architecture. So, let's define the class called ActorCritic, where we will implement the actor-critic algorithm. For a clear understanding, let's look into the code line by line. You can also access the complete code from the book's GitHub repository.

```
class ActorCritic(object):
```

Defining the init method:

First, let's define the init method:

```
def __init__(self, scope, sess, globalAC=None):
```

Initialize the TensorFlow session:

```
self.sess=sess
```

Define the actor network optimizer as RMS prop:

```
self.actor_optimizer = tf.train.RMSPropOptimizer(0.0001,
name='RMSPropA')
```

Define the critic network optimizer as RMS prop:

```
self.critic_optimizer = tf.train.RMSPropOptimizer(0.001,
name='RMSPropC')
```

If the scope is the global network (global agent):

```
if scope == global_net_scope:
    with tf.variable_scope(scope):
```

Define the placeholder for the state:

```
self.state = tf.placeholder(tf.float32, [None, state_
shape], 'state')
```

Build the global network (global agent) and get the actor and critic parameters:

```
self.actor_params, self.critic_params = self.build_
network(scope)[-2:]
```

If the network is not the global network, then:

```
else:
    with tf.variable_scope(scope):
```

Define the placeholder for the state:

```
self.state = tf.placeholder(tf.float32, [None, state_
shape], 'state')
```

We learned that our environment is the continuous environment, so our actor network (policy network) returns the mean and variance of the action and then we build the action distribution out of this mean and variance and select the action based on this action distribution.

Define the placeholder to obtain the action distribution:

```
self.action_dist = tf.placeholder(tf.float32, [None,
action_shape], 'action')
```

Define the placeholder for the target value:

```
self.target_value = tf.placeholder(tf.float32, [None,
1], 'Vtarget')
```

Build the worker network (worker agent) and get the mean and variance of the action, the value of the state, and the actor and critic network parameters:

```
mean, variance, self.value, self.actor_params, self.
critic_params = self.build_network(scope)
```

Compute the TD error, which is the difference between the target value of the state and its predicted value:

```
td_error = tf.subtract(self.target_value, self.value,
name='TD_error')
```

Now, let's define the critic network loss:

```
with tf.name_scope('critic_loss'):
    self.critic_loss = tf.reduce_mean(tf.square(td_
error))
```

Create a normal distribution based on the mean and variance of the action:

```
normal_dist = tf.distributions.Normal(mean, variance)
```

Now, let's define the actor network loss. We learned that the loss of the actor network is defined as:

$$\text{Actor Loss} = \log(\pi(a|s)) * \text{TD error} + \beta H(\pi)$$

```
with tf.name_scope('actor_loss'):
```

Compute the log probability of the action:

```
log_prob = normal_dist.log_prob(self.action_dist)
```

Define the entropy of the policy:

```
entropy_pi = normal_dist.entropy()
```

Compute the actor network loss:

```
self.loss = log_prob * td_error + (beta * entropy_
pi)

self.actor_loss = tf.reduce_mean(-self.loss)
```

Select the action based on the normal distribution:

```
with tf.name_scope('select_action'):
    self.action = tf.clip_by_value(tf.squeeze(normal_
dist.sample(1), axis=0), action_bound[0], action_bound[1])
```

Compute the gradients of the actor and critic network losses of the worker agent (local agent):

```
with tf.name_scope('local_grad'):
    self.actor_grads = tf.gradients(self.actor_loss,
self.actor_params)
    self.critic_grads = tf.gradients(self.critic_loss,
self.critic_params)
```

Now, let's perform the sync operation:

```
with tf.name_scope('sync'):
```

After computing the gradients of the losses of the actor and critic networks, the worker agents send (push) those gradients to the global agent:

```
with tf.name_scope('push'):
    self.update_actor_params = self.actor_optimizer.
apply_gradients(zip(self.actor_grads, globalAC.actor_params))
    self.update_critic_params = self.critic_optimizer.
apply_gradients(zip(self.critic_grads, globalAC.critic_params))
```

The global agent updates their parameters with the gradients received from the worker agents (local agents). Then, the worker agents pull the updated parameters from the global agent:

```
with tf.name_scope('pull'):
    self.pull_actor_params = [l_p.assign(g_p) for l_p,
g_p in zip(self.actor_params, globalAC.actor_params)]
    self.pull_critic_params = [l_p.assign(g_p) for l_p,
g_p in zip(self.critic_params, globalAC.critic_params)]
```

Building the network

Now, let's define the function for building the actor-critic network:

```
def build_network(self, scope):
```

Initialize the weight:

```
w_init = tf.random_normal_initializer(0., .1)
```

Define the actor network, which returns the mean and variance of the action:

```
with tf.variable_scope('actor'):
    l_a = tf.layers.dense(self.state, 200, tf.nn.relu, kernel_
initializer=w_init, name='la')
    mean = tf.layers.dense(l_a, action_shape, tf.nn.
tanh,kernel_initializer=w_init, name='mean')
    variance = tf.layers.dense(l_a, action_shape, tf.nn.
softplus, kernel_initializer=w_init, name='variance')
```

Define the critic network, which returns the value of the state:

```
with tf.variable_scope('critic'):
    l_c = tf.layers.dense(self.state, 100, tf.nn.relu, kernel_
initializer=w_init, name='lc')
    value = tf.layers.dense(l_c, 1, kernel_initializer=w_init,
name='value')
```

Get the parameters of the actor and critic networks:

```
actor_params = tf.get_collection(tf.GraphKeys.TRAINABLE_
VARIABLES, scope=scope + '/actor')
critic_params = tf.get_collection(tf.GraphKeys.TRAINABLE_
VARIABLES, scope=scope + '/critic')
```

Return the mean and variance of the action produced by the actor network, the value of the state computed by the critic network, and the parameters of the actor and critic networks:

```
return mean, variance, value, actor_params, critic_params
```

Updating the global network

Let's define a function called update_global to update the parameters of the global network with the gradients of loss computed by the worker networks, that is, the push operation:

```
    def update_global(self, feed_dict):
        self.sess.run([self.update_actor_params, self.update_critic_
params], feed_dict)
```

Updating the worker network

We also define a function called `pull_from_global` to update the parameters of the worker networks by pulling from the global network, that is, the pull operation:

```
    def pull_from_global(self):
        self.sess.run([self.pull_actor_params, self.pull_critic_
params])
```

Selecting the action

Define a function called `select_action` to select the action:

```
    def select_action(self, state):

        state = state[np.newaxis, :]

        return self.sess.run(self.action, {self.state: state})[0]
```

Defining the worker class

Let's define the class called `Worker`, where we will implement the worker agent:

```
  class Worker(object):
```

Defining the init method

First, let's define the `init` method:

```
    def __init__(self, name, globalAC, sess):
```

We learned that each worker agent works with their own copies of the environment. So, let's create a mountain car environment:

```
        self.env = gym.make('MountainCarContinuous-v0').unwrapped
```

Define the name of the worker:

```
self.name = name
```

Create an object for our `ActorCritic` class:

```
self.AC = ActorCritic(name, sess, globalAC)
```

Initialize a TensorFlow session:

```
self.sess=sess
```

Define a function called `work` for the worker to learn:

```
def work(self):
    global global_rewards, global_episodes
```

Initialize the time step:

```
total_step = 1
```

Initialize a list to store the states, actions, and rewards:

```
batch_states, batch_actions, batch_rewards = [], [], []
```

When the global episodes are less than the number of episodes and the coordinator is active:

```
while not coord.should_stop() and global_episodes < num_episodes:
```

Initialize the state by resetting the environment:

```
state = self.env.reset()
```

Initialize the return:

```
Return = 0
```

For each step in the environment:

```
for t in range(num_timesteps):
```

Render the environment of only the worker 0:

```
if self.name == 'W_0':
    self.env.render()
```

Select the action:

```
action = self.AC.select_action(state)
```

Perform the selected action:

```
next_state, reward, done, _ = self.env.step(action)
```

Set done to `True` if we have reached the final step of the episode `else` set to `False`:

```
done = True if t == num_timesteps - 1 else False
```

Update the return:

```
Return += reward
```

Store the state, action, and reward in the lists:

```
batch_states.append(state)
batch_actions.append(action)
batch_rewards.append((reward+8)/8)
```

Now, let's update the global network. If done is `True`, then set the value of the next state to 0 `else` compute the value of the next state:

```
if total_step % update_global == 0 or done:
    if done:
        v_s_ = 0
    else:
        v_s_ = self.sess.run(self.AC.value, {self.
AC.state: next_state[np.newaxis, :]})[0, 0]
```

Compute the target value, which is $r + \gamma V(s')$:

```
batch_target_value = []

for reward in batch_rewards[::-1]:
    v_s_ = reward + gamma * v_s_
    batch_target_value.append(v_s_)
```

Reverse the target value:

```
batch_target_value.reverse()
```

Stack the state, action, and target value:

```
                batch_states, batch_actions, batch_target_value =
np.vstack(batch_states), np.vstack(batch_actions), np.vstack(batch_
target_value)
```

Define the feed dictionary:

```
            feed_dict = {
                    self.AC.state: batch_states,
                    self.AC. action_dist: batch_actions,
                    self.AC.target_value: batch_target_
value,

                    }
```

Update the global network:

```
            self.AC.update_global(feed_dict)
```

Empty the lists:

```
            batch_states, batch_actions, batch_rewards = [],
    [], []
```

Update the worker network by pulling the parameters from the global network:

```
            self.AC.pull_from_global()
```

Update the state to the next state and increment the total step:

```
            state = next_state
            total_step += 1
```

Update the global rewards:

```
            if done:
                if len(global_rewards) < 5:
                    global_rewards.append(Return)
                else:
                    global_rewards.append(Return)
                    global_rewards[-1] =(np.mean(global_
    rewards[-5:]))

                global_episodes += 1
                break
```

Training the network

Now, let's start training the network. Initialize the global rewards list and also initialize the global episodes counter:

```
global_rewards = []
global_episodes = 0
```

Start the TensorFlow session:

```
sess = tf.Session()
```

Create a global agent:

```
with tf.device("/cpu:0"):

    global_agent = ActorCritic(global_net_scope,sess)
```

Create *n* number of worker agents:

```
    worker_agents = []

    for i in range(num_workers):
        i_name = 'W_%i' % i
        worker_agents.append(Worker(i_name, global_agent,sess))
```

Create the TensorFlow coordinator:

```
coord = tf.train.Coordinator()
```

Initialize all the TensorFlow variables:

```
sess.run(tf.global_variables_initializer())
```

Store the TensorFlow computational graph in the log directory:

```
if os.path.exists(log_dir):
    shutil.rmtree(log_dir)

tf.summary.FileWriter(log_dir, sess.graph)
```

Now, run the worker threads:

```
worker_threads = []

for worker in worker_agents:
```

```
    job = lambda: worker.work()
    t = threading.Thread(target=job)
    t.start()
    worker_threads.append(t)

coord.join(worker_threads)
```

For a better understanding of the A3C architecture, let's take a look at the computational graph of A3C in the next section.

Visualizing the computational graph

As we can observe, we have four worker agents (worker networks) and one global agent (global network):

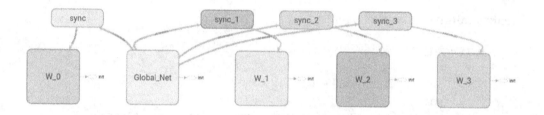

Figure 11.5: A computation graph of A3C

Let's take a look at the architecture of the worker agent. As we can observe, our worker agents follow the actor-critic architecture:

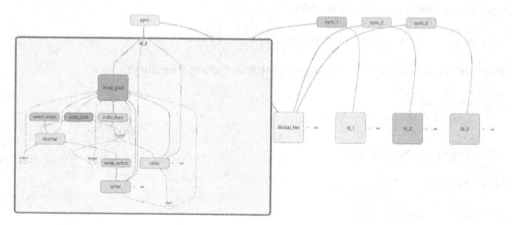

Figure 11.6: A computation graph of A3C with the W_0 node expanded

Now, let's examine the sync node. As *Figure 11.7* shows, we have two operations in the sync node, called *push* and *pull*:

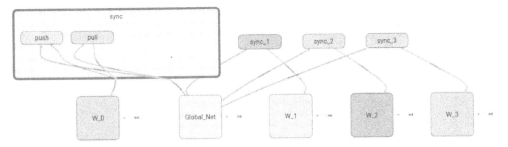

Figure 11.7: A computation graph of A3C showing the push and pull operations of the sync node

After computing the gradients of the losses of the actor and critic networks, the worker agent pushes those gradients to the global agent:

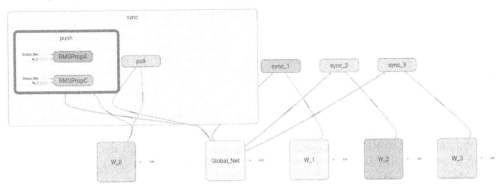

Figure 11.8: A computation graph of A3C—worker agents push their gradients to the global agent

The global agent updates their parameters with the gradients received from the worker agents. Then, the worker agents pull the updated parameters from the global agent:

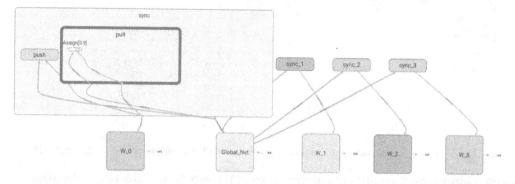

Figure 11.9: A computation graph of A3C – worker agents pull updated parameters from the global agent

Now that we have learned how A3C works, in the next section, let's revisit the A2C method.

A2C revisited

We can design our A2C algorithm with many worker agents, just like the A3C algorithm. However, unlike A3C, A2C is a synchronous algorithm, meaning that in A2C, we can have multiple worker agents, each interacting with their own copies of the environment, and all the worker agents perform synchronous updates, unlike A3C, where the worker agents perform asynchronous updates.

That is, in A2C, each worker agent interacts with the environment, computes losses, and calculates gradients. However, it won't send those gradients to the global network independently. Instead, it waits for all other worker agents to finish their work and then updates the weights to the global network in a synchronous fashion. Performing synchronous weight updates reduces the inconsistency introduced by A3C.

Summary

We started the chapter by understanding what the actor-critic method is. We learned that in the actor-critic method, the actor computes the optimal policy, and the critic evaluates the policy computed by the actor network by estimating the value function. Next, we learned how the actor-critic method differs from the policy gradient method with the baseline.

We learned that in the policy gradient method with the baseline, first, we generate complete episodes (trajectories), and then we update the parameter of the network. Whereas, in the actor-critic method, we update the parameter of the network at every step of the episode. Moving forward, we learned what the advantage actor-critic algorithm is and how it uses the advantage function in the gradient update.

At the end of the chapter, we learned about another interesting actor-critic algorithm, called asynchronous advantage actor-critic method. We learned that A3C consists of several worker agents and one global agent. All the worker agents send their gradients to the global agent asynchronously and then the global agent updates their parameters with gradients received from the worker agents. After updating the parameters, the global agent sends the updated parameters to the worker agents periodically.

Hence, in this chapter, we learned about two interesting actor-critic algorithms – A2C and A3C. In the next chapter, we will understand several state-of-the-art actor-critic algorithms, including DDPG, TD3, and SAC.

Questions

Let's assess our understanding of the actor-critic method by answering the following questions:

1. What is the actor-critic method?
2. What is the role of the actor and critic networks?
3. How does the actor-critic method differ from the policy gradient with the baseline method?
4. What is the gradient update equation of the actor network?
5. How does A2C work?
6. What does *asynchronous* mean in A3C?
7. How does A2C differ from A3C?

Further reading

To learn more, refer to the following paper:

- *Asynchronous Methods for Deep Reinforcement Learning*, by Volodymyr Mnih et al.: https://arxiv.org/pdf/1602.01783.pdf

12

Learning DDPG, TD3, and SAC

In the previous chapter, we learned about interesting actor-critic methods, such as **Advantage Actor-Critic (A2C)** and **Asynchronous Advantage Actor-Critic (A3C)**. In this chapter, we will learn several state-of-the-art actor-critic methods. We will start off the chapter by understanding one of the popular actor-critic methods called **Deep Deterministic Policy Gradient (DDPG)**. DDPG is used only in continuous environments, that is, environments with a continuous action space. We will understand what DDPG is and how it works in detail. We will also learn the DDPG algorithm step by step.

Going forward, we will learn about the **Twin Delayed Deep Deterministic Policy Gradient (TD3)**. TD3 is an improvement over the DDPG algorithm and includes several interesting features that solve the problems faced in DDPG. We will understand the key features of TD3 in detail and also look into the algorithm of TD3 step by step.

Finally, we will learn about another interesting actor-critic algorithm, called **Soft Actor-Critic (SAC)**. We will learn what SAC is and how it works using the entropy term in the objective function. We will look into the actor and critic components of SAC in detail and then learn the algorithm of SAC step by step.

In this chapter, we will learn the following topics:

- Deep deterministic policy gradient (DDPG)
- The components of DDPG
- The DDPG algorithm
- Twin delayed deep deterministic policy gradient (TD3)
- The key features of TD3
- The TD3 algorithm
- Soft actor-critic (SAC)
- The components of SAC
- The SAC algorithm

Deep deterministic policy gradient

DDPG is an off-policy, model-free algorithm, designed for environments where the action space is continuous. In the previous chapter, we learned how the actor-critic method works. DDPG is an actor-critic method where the actor estimates the policy using the policy gradient, and the critic evaluates the policy produced by the actor using the Q function.

DDPG uses the policy network as an actor and deep Q network as a critic. One important difference between the DPPG and actor-critic algorithms we learned in the previous chapter is that DDPG tries to learn a deterministic policy instead of a stochastic policy.

First, we will get an intuitive understanding of how DDPG works and then we will look into the algorithm in detail.

An overview of DDPG

DDPG is an actor-critic method that takes advantage of both the policy-based method and the value-based method. It uses a deterministic policy μ instead of a stochastic policy π.

We learned that a deterministic policy tells the agent to perform one particular action in a given state, meaning a deterministic policy maps the state to one particular action:

$$a = \mu(s)$$

Whereas a stochastic policy maps the state to the probability distribution over the action space:

$$a \sim \pi(s)$$

In a deterministic policy, whenever the agent visits the state, it always performs the same particular action. But with a stochastic policy, instead of performing the same action every time the agent visits the state, the agent performs a different action each time based on a probability distribution over the action space.

Now, we will look into an overview of the actor and critic networks in the DDPG algorithm.

Actor

The actor in DDPG is basically the policy network. The goal of the actor is to learn the mapping between the state and action. That is, the role of the actor is to learn the optimal policy that gives the maximum return. So, the actor uses the policy gradient method to learn the optimal policy.

Critic

The critic is basically the value network. The goal of the critic is to evaluate the action produced by the actor network. How does the critic network evaluate the action produced by the actor network? Let's suppose we have a Q function; can we evaluate an action using the Q function? Yes! First, let's take a little detour and recap the use of the Q function.

We know that the Q function gives the expected return that an agent would obtain starting from state s and performing an action a following a particular policy. The expected return produced by the Q function is often called the Q value. Thus, given a state and action, we obtain a Q value:

- If the Q value is high, then we can say that the action performed in that state is a good action. That is, if the Q value is high, meaning the expected return is high when we perform an action a in state s, we can say that the action a is a good action.

- If the Q value is low, then we can say that the action performed in that state is not a good action. That is, if the Q value is low, meaning the expected return is low when we perform an action a in state s, we can say that the action a is not a good action.

Okay, now how can the critic network evaluate an action produced by the actor network based on the Q function (Q value)? Let's suppose the actor network performs a *down* action in state **A**. So, now, the critic computes the Q value of moving *down* in state **A**. If the Q value is high, then the critic network gives feedback to the actor network that the action *down* is a good action in state **A**. If the Q value is low, then the critic network gives feedback to the actor network that the *down* action is not a good action in state **A**, and so the actor network tries to perform a different action in state **A**.

Thus, with the Q function, the critic network can evaluate the action performed by the actor network. But wait, how can the critic network learn the Q function? Because only if it knows the Q function can it evaluate the action performed by the actor. So, how does the critic network learn the Q function? Here is where we use the **deep Q network (DQN)**. We learned that with the DQN, we can use the neural network to approximate the Q function. So, now, we use the DQN as the critic network to compute the Q function.

Thus, in a nutshell, DDPG is an actor-critic method and so it takes advantage of policy-based and value-based methods. DDPG consists of an actor that is a policy network and uses the policy gradient method to learn the optimal policy and the critic, which is a deep Q network, and it evaluates the action produced by the actor.

DDPG components

Now that we have a basic understanding of how the DDPG algorithm works, let's go into further detail. We will understand how exactly the actor and critic networks work by looking at them separately.

Critic network

We learned that the critic network is basically the DQN and it uses the DQN to estimate the Q value. Now, let's learn how the critic network uses the DQN to estimate the Q value in more detail, along with a recap of the DQN.

The critic evaluates the action produced by the actor. Thus, the input to the critic will be the state and also the action produced by the actor in that state, and the critic returns the Q value of the given state-action pair, as shown *Figure 12.1*:

Figure 12.1: The critic network

To approximate the Q value in the critic, we can use the deep neural network, and if we use the deep neural network to approximate the Q value, then the network is called the DQN. Since we are using the neural network to approximate the Q value in the critic, we can represent the Q function with $Q_\theta(s, a)$, where θ is the parameter of the network.

Thus, in the critic network, we approximate the Q value using the DQN and the parameter of the critic network is represented by θ, as shown in *Figure 12.2*:

Figure 12.2: The critic network

As we can observe from *Figure 12.2*, given state s and the action a produced by the actor, the critic network returns the Q value.

Now, let's look at how to obtain the action a produced by the actor. We learned that the actor is basically the policy network and it uses a policy gradient to learn the optimal policy. In DDPG, we learn a deterministic policy instead of a stochastic policy, so we can denote the policy with μ instead of π. The parameter of the actor network is represented by ϕ. So, we can represent our parameterized policy as μ_ϕ.

Given a state s as the input, the actor network returns the action a to be performed in that state:

$$a = \mu_\phi(s)$$

Thus, the critic network takes state s and action $a = \mu_\phi(s)$ produced by the actor network in that state as input and returns the Q value, as shown in *Figure 12.3*:

Figure 12.3: The critic network

Okay, how can we train the critic network (DQN)? We generally train the network by minimizing the loss as the difference between the target value and predicted value. So, we can train the critic network by minimizing the loss as the difference between the target Q value and the Q value predicted by the network. But how can we obtain the target Q value? The target Q value is the optimal Q value and we can obtain the optimal Q value using the Bellman equation.

We learned that the optimal Q function (Q value) can be obtained by using the Bellman optimality equation. Thus, the optimal Q function can be obtained using the Bellman optimality equation as follows:

$$Q^*(s, a) = \mathbb{E}_{s' \sim P}\left[R(s, a, s') + \gamma \max_{a'} Q^*(s', a')\right]$$

We know that $R(s, a, s')$ represents the immediate reward r we obtain while performing an action a in state s and moving to the next state s', so we can just denote $R(s, a, s')$ with r:

$$Q^*(s, a) = \underset{s' \sim P}{E}\left[r + \gamma \max_{a'} Q^*(s', a')\right]$$

In the preceding equation, we can remove the expectation. We will approximate the expectation by sampling K number of transitions from the replay buffer and taking the average value. We will learn more about this in a while. So, we can express the target Q value as the sum of the immediate reward and discounted maximum Q value of the next state-action pair, as shown here:

$$Q^*(s, a) = r + \gamma \max_{a'} Q(s', a')$$

Thus, we can represent the loss function of the critic network as the difference between the target value (optimal Bellman Q value) and the predicted value (the Q value predicted by the critic network):

$$L(\theta) = r + \gamma \max_{a'} Q_\theta(s', a') - Q_\theta(s, a)$$

Here, the action a is the action produced by the actor network, that is, $a = \mu_\phi(s)$.

Instead of using the loss as simply the difference between the target value and the predicted value, we can use the mean squared error as our loss function. We know that in the DQN, we use the replay buffer and store the transitions as (s, a, r, s'). So, we randomly sample a minibatch of K number of transitions from the replay buffer and train the network by minimizing the mean squared loss between the target value (optimal Bellman Q value) and the predicted value (Q value predicted by the critic network). Thus, our loss function is given as:

$$L(\theta) = \frac{1}{K}\sum_{i=1}^{K}(r_i + \gamma \max_{a'} Q_\theta(s'_i, a') - Q_\theta(s_i, a_i))^2$$

From the preceding equation, we can observe that both the target and predicted Q functions are parameterized by the same parameter θ. This will cause instability in the mean squared error and the network will learn poorly.

So, we introduce another neural network to learn the target value, and it is usually referred to as the target critic network. The parameter of the target critic network is represented by θ'. Our main critic network, which is used to predict Q values, learns the correct parameter θ using gradient descent. The target critic network parameter θ' is updated by just copying the parameter of the main critic network θ.

Thus, the loss function of the critic network can be written as:

$$L(\theta) = \frac{1}{K} \sum_{i=1}^{K} \left(r_i + \gamma \max_{a'} Q_{\theta'}(s_i', a') - Q_{\theta}(s_i, a_i) \right)^2 \qquad (1)$$

Remember that the action a_i in the preceding equation is the action produced by the actor network, that is, $a_i = \mu_\phi(s_i)$.

There is a small problem in the target value computation in our loss function due to the presence of the max term, as shown here:

$$L(\theta) = \frac{1}{K} \sum_{i=1}^{K} (r_i + \gamma \underbrace{\max_{a'}}_{\text{max term}} Q_{\theta'}(s_i', a') - Q_{\theta}(s_i, a_i))^2$$

The max term means that we compute the Q value of all possible actions a' in state s' and select the action a' as the one that has the maximum Q value. But when the action space is continuous, we cannot compute the Q value of all possible actions a' in state s'. So, we need to get rid of the max term in our loss function. How can we do that?

Just as we use the target network in the critic, we can use a target actor network, and the parameter of the target actor network is denoted by ϕ'. Now, instead of selecting the action a' as the one that has the maximum Q value, we can generate an action a' using the target actor network, that is, $a' = \mu_{\phi'}(s')$.

Thus, as shown in *Figure 12.4*, to compute the Q value of the next state-action pair in the target, we feed state s' and the action a' produced by the target actor network parameterized by ϕ' to the target critic network, and it returns the Q value of the next state-action pair:

Figure 12.4: The target critic network

Thus, in our loss function, equation (1), we can remove the max term and instead of a', we can write $\mu_{\phi'}(s')$, as shown here:

$$L(\theta) = \frac{1}{K}\sum_i \left(r_i + \gamma Q_{\theta'}(s_i', \mu_{\phi'}(s_i')) - Q_\theta(s_i, a_i)\right)^2$$

To maintain a uniform notation, let's represent the loss function with J:

$$J(\theta) = \frac{1}{K}\sum_i \left(r_i + \gamma Q_{\theta'}\left(s_i', \mu_{\phi'}(s_i')\right) - Q_\theta(s_i, a_i)\right)^2$$

To reduce the clutter, we can denote the target value with y and write:

$$J(\theta) = \frac{1}{K}\sum_i (y_i - Q_\theta(s_i, a_i))^2$$

Where y_i is the target value of the critic, that is, $y_i = r_i + \gamma Q_{\theta'}\left(s_i', \mu_{\phi'}(s_i')\right)$, and the action a_i is the action produced by the main actor network, that is, $a_i = \mu_\phi(s_i)$.

To minimize the loss, we compute the gradients of the objective function $\nabla_\theta J(\theta)$ and update the main critic network parameter θ by performing gradient descent:

$$\theta = \theta - \alpha\nabla_\theta J(\theta)$$

Okay, what about the target critic network parameter θ'? How can we update it? We can update the parameter of the target critic network by just copying the parameter of the main critic network parameter θ as shown here:

$$\theta' = \tau\theta + (1 - \tau)\theta'$$

This is usually called the soft replacement and the value of τ is often set to 0.001.

Thus, we learned how the critic network uses the DQN to compute the Q value to evaluate the action produced by the actor network. In the next section, we will learn how the actor network learns the optimal policy.

Actor network

We have already learned that the actor network is the policy network and it uses the policy gradient to compute the optimal policy. We also learned that we represent the parameter of the actor network with ϕ, and so the parameterized policy is represented with μ_ϕ.

The actor network takes state s as an input and returns the action a:

$$a = \mu_\phi(s)$$

One important point that we may want to note down here is that we are using a deterministic policy. Since we are using a deterministic policy, we need to take care of the exploration-exploitation dilemma, because we know that a deterministic policy always selects the same action and doesn't explore new actions, unlike a stochastic policy, which selects different actions based on the probability distribution over the action space.

Okay, how can we explore new actions while using a deterministic policy? Note that DDPG is designed for an environment where the action space is continuous. Thus, we are using a deterministic policy in the continuous action space.

Unlike the discrete action space, in the continuous action space, we have continuous values. So, to explore new actions, we can just add some noise $\mathcal{N}$ to the action produced by the actor network since the action is a continuous value. We generate this noise using a process called the Ornstein-Uhlenbeck random process. So, our modified action can be represented as:

$$a = \mu_\phi(s) + \mathcal{N}$$

For example, say the action $\mu_\phi(s)$ produced by the actor network is 13. Suppose the noise $\mathcal{N}$ is 0.1, then our action becomes $a = 13 + 0.1 = 13.1$.

We learned that the critic network is represented by $Q_\theta(s, a)$ and it evaluates the action produced by the actor using the Q value. If the Q value is high, then the critic tells the actor that it has produced a good action but when the Q value is low, then the critic tells the actor that it has produced a bad action.

But wait! We learned that it is difficult to compute the Q value when the action space is continuous. That is, when the action space is continuous, it is difficult to compute the Q value of all possible actions in the state and take the maximum Q value. That is why we resorted to the policy gradient method. But now, we are computing the Q value with a continuous action space. How will this work?

Note that, here in DDPG, we are not computing the Q value of all possible state-action pairs. We simply compute the Q value of state s and action a produced by the actor network.

The goal of the actor is to make the critic tell that the action it has produced is a good action. That is, the actor wants to get good feedback from the critic network. When does the critic give good feedback to the actor? The critic gives good feedback when the action produced by the actor has a maximum Q value. That is, if the action produced by the actor has a maximum Q value, then the critic tells the actor that it has produced a good action. So, the actor tries to generate an action in such a way that it can maximize the Q value produced by the critic.

Thus, the objective function of the actor is to generate an action that maximizes the Q value produced by the critic network. So, we can write the objective function of the actor as:

$$J(\phi) = Q_\theta(s, a)$$

Where the action $a = \mu_\phi(s)$. Maximizing the above objective function $J(\phi)$ implies that we are maximizing the Q value produced by the critic network. Okay, how can we maximize the preceding objective function? We can maximize the objective function by performing gradient ascent and update the actor network parameter as:

$$\phi = \phi + \alpha \nabla_\phi J(\phi)$$

Wait. Instead of updating the actor network parameter ϕ just for a single state s, we sample K number of states from the replay buffer $\mathcal{D}$ and update the parameter. So, now our objective function becomes:

$$J(\phi) = \frac{1}{K} \sum_i Q_\theta(s_i, a)$$

Where the action $a = \mu_\phi(s_i)$. Maximizing the preceding objective function implies that the actor tries to generate actions in such a way that it maximizes the Q value over all the sampled states. We can maximize the objective function by performing gradient ascent and update the actor network parameter as:

$$\phi = \phi + \alpha \nabla_\phi J(\phi)$$

To summarize, the objective of the actor is to generate action in such a way that it maximizes the Q value produced by the critic. So, we perform gradient ascent and update the actor network parameter.

Okay, what about the parameter of the target actor network? How can we update it? We can update the parameter of the target actor network by just copying the parameter of the main actor network parameter ϕ by soft replacement, as shown here:

$$\phi' = \tau\phi + (1 - \tau)\phi'$$

Now that we have understood how actor and critic networks work, let's get a good understanding of what we have learned so far and how DDPG works exactly by putting all the concepts together.

Putting it all together

To avoid getting lost in notations, first, let's recollect the notations to understand DDPG better. We use four networks, two actor networks and two critic networks:

- The main critic network parameter is represented by θ
- The target critic network parameter is represented by θ'
- The main actor network parameter is represented by ϕ
- The target actor network parameter is represented by ϕ'

Note that DDPG is an actor-critic method, and so its parameters will be updated at every step of the episode, unlike the policy gradient method, where we generate complete episodes and then update the parameter. Okay, let's get started and understand how DDPG works.

First, we initialize the main critic network parameter θ and the main actor network parameter ϕ with random values. We learned that the target network parameter is just a copy of the main network parameter. So, we initialize the target critic network parameter θ' by just copying the main critic network parameter θ. Similarly, we initialize the target actor network parameter ϕ' by just copying the main actor network parameter ϕ. We also initialize the replay buffer $\mathcal{D}$.

Now, for each step in the episode, first, we select an action, a, using the actor network:

$$a = \mu_\phi(s)$$

However, instead of using the action a directly, to ensure exploration, we add some noise $\mathcal{N}$, and so the action becomes:

$$a = \mu_\phi(s) + \mathcal{N}$$

Then, we perform the action a, move to the next state s', and get the reward r. We store this transition information in a replay buffer $\mathcal{D}$.

Next, we randomly sample a minibatch of K transitions (s, a, r, s') from the replay buffer. These K transitions will be used for updating both our critic and actor network.

First, let us compute the loss of the critic network. We learned that the loss function of the critic network is:

$$J(\theta) = \frac{1}{K} \sum_i (y_i - Q_\theta(s_i, a_i))^2$$

Where y_i is the target value of the critic, that is, $y_i = r_i + \gamma Q_{\theta'}\left(s_i', \mu_{\phi'}(s_i')\right)$, and the action a_i is the action produced by the actor network, that is, $a = \mu_\phi(s_i)$.

After computing the loss of the critic network, we compute the gradients $\nabla_\theta J(\theta)$ and update the critic network parameter θ using gradient descent:

$$\theta = \theta - \alpha \nabla_\theta J(\theta)$$

Now, let us update the actor network. We learned that the objective function of the actor network is:

$$J(\phi) = \frac{1}{K} \sum_i Q_\theta(s_i, a)$$

Note that in the above equation, we are only using the state (s_i) from the sampled K transitions (s, a, r, s'). The action a is selected by actor network, $a = \mu_\phi(s_i)$. Now, we need to maximize the preceding objective function. Maximizing the above objective function helps the actor to generate actions in such a way that it maximizes the Q value produced by the critic. We can maximize the objective function by computing the gradients of our objective function $\nabla_\phi J(\phi)$ and update the actor network parameter ϕ using gradient ascent:

$$\phi = \phi + \alpha \nabla_\phi J(\phi)$$

And then, in the final step, we update the parameter of the target critic network θ' and the parameter of the target actor network ϕ' by soft replacement:

$$\theta' = \tau\theta + (1 - \tau)\theta'$$

$$\phi' = \tau\phi + (1 - \tau)\phi'$$

We repeat these steps for several episodes. Thus, for each step in the episode, we update the parameter of our networks. Since the parameter gets updated at every step, our policy will also be improved at every step in the episode.

To have a better understanding of how DDPG works, let's look into the DDPG algorithm in the next section.

Algorithm – DDPG

The DDPG algorithm is given as follows:

1. Initialize the main critic network parameter θ and the main actor network parameter ϕ

2. Initialize the target critic network parameter θ' by just copying the main critic network parameter θ

3. Initialize the target actor network parameter ϕ' by just copying the main actor network parameter ϕ'

4. Initialize the replay buffer $\mathcal{D}$

5. For N number of episodes, repeat steps 6 and 7

6. Initialize an Ornstein-Uhlenbeck random process $\mathcal{N}$ for an action space exploration

7. For each step in the episode, that is, for $t = 0,...,T - 1$:

    1. Select action a based on the policy $\mu_\phi(s)$ and exploration noise, that is, $a = \mu_\phi(s) + \mathcal{N}$.

    2. Perform the selected action a, move to the next state s', get the reward r, and store this transition information in the replay buffer $\mathcal{D}$.

    3. Randomly sample a minibatch of K transitions from the replay buffer $\mathcal{D}$.

    4. Compute the target value of the critic, that is,
        $$y_i = r_i + \gamma Q_{\theta'}\left(s_i', \mu_{\phi'}(s_i')\right).$$

    5. Compute the loss of the critic network, $J(\theta) = \dfrac{1}{K}\sum_i (y_i - Q_\theta(s_i, a_i))^2$.

    6. Compute the gradient of the loss $\nabla_\theta J(\theta)$ and update the critic network parameter using gradient descent, $\theta = \theta - \alpha\nabla_\theta J(\theta)$.

    7. Compute the gradient of the actor network $\nabla_\phi J(\phi)$ and update the actor network parameter by gradient ascent, $\phi = \phi + \alpha\nabla_\phi J(\phi)$.

    8. Update the target critic and target actor network parameter as
        $\theta' = \tau\theta + (1 - \tau)\theta'$ and $\phi' = \tau\phi + (1 - \tau)\phi'$.

Swinging up a pendulum using DDPG

In this section, let's implement the DDPG algorithm to train the agent to swing up a pendulum. That is, we will have a pendulum that starts swinging from a random position and the goal of our agent is to swing the pendulum up so it stays upright.

First, let's import the required libraries:

```
import warnings
warnings.filterwarnings('ignore')

import tensorflow as tf
tf.compat.v1.disable_v2_behavior()
import numpy as np
import gym
```

Creating the Gym environment

Let's create a pendulum environment using Gym:

```
env = gym.make("Pendulum-v0").unwrapped
```

Get the state shape of the environment:

```
state_shape = env.observation_space.shape[0]
```

Get the action shape of the environment:

```
action_shape = env.action_space.shape[0]
```

Note that the pendulum is a continuous environment, and thus our action space consists of continuous values. Hence, we get the bounds of our action space:

```
action_bound = [env.action_space.low, env.action_space.high]
```

Defining the variables

Now, let's define some of the important variables.

Set the discount factor, γ:

```
gamma = 0.9
```

Set the value of τ, which is used for soft replacement:

```
tau = 0.001
```

Set the size of our replay buffer:

```
replay_buffer = 10000
```

Set the batch size:

```
batch_size = 32
```

Defining the DDPG class

Let's define the class called DDPG, where we will implement the DDPG algorithm. To aid understanding, let's look into the code line by line. You can also access the complete code from the GitHub repository of the book:

```
class DDPG(object):
```

Defining the init method

First, let's define the init method:

```
def __init__(self, state_shape, action_shape, high_action_value,):
```

Define the replay buffer for storing the transitions:

```
self.replay_buffer = np.zeros((replay_buffer, state_shape * 2 +
action_shape + 1), dtype=np.float32)
```

Initialize num_transitions to 0, which means that the number of transitions in our replay buffer is zero:

```
self.num_transitions = 0
```

Start the TensorFlow session:

```
self.sess = tf.Session()
```

We learned that in DDPG, instead of selecting the action *a* directly, to ensure exploration, we add some noise $\mathcal{N}$ using the Ornstein-Uhlenbeck process. So, we first initialize the noise:

```
self.noise = 3.0
```

Then, initialize the state shape, action shape, and high action value:

```
self.state_shape, self.action_shape, self.high_action_value =
state_shape, action_shape, high_action_value
```

Define the placeholder for the state:

```
self.state = tf.placeholder(tf.float32, [None, state_shape],
'state')
```

Define the placeholder for the next state:

```
self.next_state = tf.placeholder(tf.float32, [None, state_
shape], 'next_state')
```

Define the placeholder for the reward:

```
self.reward = tf.placeholder(tf.float32, [None, 1], 'reward')
```

With the actor variable scope:

```
with tf.variable_scope('Actor'):
```

Define the main actor network, which is parameterized by ϕ. The actor network takes the state as an input and returns the action to be performed in that state:

```
self.actor = self.build_actor_network(self.state,
scope='main', trainable=True)
```

Define the target actor network that is parameterized by ϕ'. The target actor network takes the next state as an input and returns the action to be performed in that state:

```
target_actor = self.build_actor_network(self.next_state,
scope='target', trainable=False)
```

With the critic variable scope:

```
with tf.variable_scope('Critic'):
```

Define the main critic network, which is parameterized by θ. The critic network takes the state and also the action produced by the actor in that state as an input and returns the Q value:

```
critic = self.build_critic_network(self.state, self.actor,
scope='main', trainable=True)
```

Define the target critic network, which is parameterized by θ'. The target critic network takes the next state and also the action produced by the target actor network in that next state as an input and returns the Q value:

```
target_critic = self.build_critic_network(self.next_state,
target_actor, scope='target', trainable=False)
```

Get the parameter of the main actor network ϕ:

```
self.main_actor_params = tf.get_collection(tf.GraphKeys.GLOBAL_
VARIABLES, scope='Actor/main')
```

Get the parameter of the target actor network ϕ':

```
self.target_actor_params = tf.get_collection(tf.GraphKeys.
GLOBAL_VARIABLES, scope='Actor/target')
```

Get the parameter of the main critic network θ:

```
self.main_critic_params = tf.get_collection(tf.GraphKeys.
GLOBAL_VARIABLES, scope='Critic/main')
```

Get the parameter of the target critic network θ':

```
self.target_critic_params = tf.get_collection(tf.GraphKeys.
GLOBAL_VARIABLES, scope='Critic/target')
```

Perform the soft replacement, update the parameter of the target actor network as $\phi' = \tau\phi + (1 - \tau)\phi'$, and update the parameter of the target critic network as $\theta' = \tau\theta + (1 - \tau)\theta'$:

```
self.soft_replacement = [

    [tf.assign(phi_, tau*phi + (1-tau)*phi_), tf.assign(theta_,
tau*theta + (1-tau)*theta_)]

    for phi, phi_, theta, theta_ in zip(self.main_actor_params,
self.target_actor_params, self.main_critic_params, self.target_critic_
params)

    ]
```

Compute the target Q value. We learned that the target Q value can be computed as the sum of reward and the discounted Q value of the next state-action pair, $y_i = r_i + \gamma Q_{\theta'}\left(s_i', \mu_{\phi'}(s_i')\right)$:

```
y = self.reward + gamma * target_critic
```

Now, let's compute the loss of the critic network. The loss of the critic network is the mean squared error between the target Q value and the predicted Q value:

$$J(\theta) = \frac{1}{K}\sum_i \left(y_i - Q_\theta(s_i, a_i)\right)^2$$

So, we can define the mean squared error as:

```
MSE = tf.losses.mean_squared_error(labels=y,
 predictions=critic)
```

Train the critic network by minimizing the mean squared error using the Adam optimizer:

```
self.train_critic = tf.train.AdamOptimizer(0.01).minimize(MSE,
 name="adam-ink", var_list = self.main_critic_params)
```

We learned that the objective function of the actor is to generate an action that maximizes the Q value produced by the critic network, as shown here:

$$J(\phi) = \frac{1}{K}\sum_i Q_\theta(s_i, a)$$

Where the action $a = \mu_\phi(s_i)$, and we can maximize this objective by computing gradients and by performing gradient ascent. However, it is a standard convention to perform minimization rather than maximization. So, we can convert the preceding maximization objective into a minimization objective by just adding a negative sign. Hence, we can define the actor network objective as:

$$J(\phi) = -\frac{1}{K}\sum_i Q_\theta(s_i, a)$$

Now, we can minimize the actor network objective by computing gradients and by performing gradient descent. Thus, we can write:

```
actor_loss = -tf.reduce_mean(critic)
```

Train the actor network by minimizing the loss using the Adam optimizer:

```
        self.train_actor = tf.train.AdamOptimizer(0.001).
    minimize(actor_loss, var_list=self.main_actor_params)
```

Initialize all the TensorFlow variables:

```
        self.sess.run(tf.global_variables_initializer())
```

Selecting the action

Let's define a function called `select_action` to select the action with the noise to ensure exploration:

```
        def select_action(self, state):
```

Run the actor network and get the action:

```
        action = self.sess.run(self.actor, {self.state: state[np.
    newaxis, :]})[0]
```

Now, we generate a normal distribution with the mean as the action and the standard deviation as the noise and we randomly select an action from this normal distribution:

```
        action = np.random.normal(action, self.noise)
```

We need to make sure that our action should not fall away from the action bound. So, we clip the action so that it lies within the action bound and then we return the action:

```
        action = np.clip(action, action_bound[0],action_bound[1])

        return action
```

Defining the train function

Now, let's define the train function:

```
        def train(self):
```

Perform the soft replacement:

```
        self.sess.run(self.soft_replacement)
```

Randomly select indices from the replay buffer with the given batch size:

```
indices = np.random.choice(replay_buffer, size=batch_size)
```

Select the batch of transitions from the replay buffer with the selected indices:

```
batch_transition = self.replay_buffer[indices, :]
```

Get the batch of states, actions, rewards, and next states:

```
batch_states = batch_transition[:, :self.state_shape]
batch_actions = batch_transition[:, self.state_shape: self.
state_shape + self.action_shape]
batch_rewards = batch_transition[:, -self.state_shape - 1:
-self.state_shape]
batch_next_state = batch_transition[:, -self.state_shape:]
```

Train the actor network:

```
self.sess.run(self.train_actor, {self.state: batch_states})
```

Train the critic network:

```
self.sess.run(self.train_critic, {self.state: batch_states,
self.actor: batch_actions, self.reward: batch_rewards, self.next_state:
batch_next_state})
```

Storing the transitions

Now, let's store the transitions in the replay buffer:

```
def store_transition(self, state, actor, reward, next_state):
```

First, stack the state, action, reward, and next state:

```
trans = np.hstack((state,actor,[reward],next_state))
```

Get the index:

```
index = self.num_transitions % replay_buffer
```

Store the transition:

```
self.replay_buffer[index, :] = trans
```

Update the number of transitions:

```
    self.num_transitions += 1
```

If the number of transitions is greater than the replay buffer, train the network:

```
    if self.num_transitions > replay_buffer:
        self.noise *= 0.99995
        self.train()
```

Building the actor network

We define a function called `build_actor_network` to build the actor network. The actor network takes the state and returns the action to be performed in that state:

```
def build_actor_network(self, state, scope, trainable):
    with tf.variable_scope(scope):
        layer_1 = tf.layers.dense(state, 30, activation = tf.nn.
tanh, name = 'layer_1', trainable = trainable)
        actor = tf.layers.dense(layer_1, self.action_shape,
activation = tf.nn.tanh, name = 'actor', trainable = trainable)
        return tf.multiply(actor, self.high_action_value, name =
"scaled_a")
```

Building the critic network

We define a function called `build_critic_network` to build the critic network. The critic network takes the state and the action produced by the actor in that state and returns the Q value:

```
def build_critic_network(self, state, actor, scope, trainable):
    with tf.variable_scope(scope):
        w1_s = tf.get_variable('w1_s', [self.state_shape, 30],
trainable = trainable)
        w1_a = tf.get_variable('w1_a', [self.action_shape, 30],
trainable = trainable)
        b1 = tf.get_variable('b1', [1, 30], trainable = trainable)
        net = tf.nn.tanh( tf.matmul(state, w1_s) + tf.matmul(actor,
w1_a) + b1 )

        critic = tf.layers.dense(net, 1, trainable = trainable)
        return critic
```

Training the network

Now, let's start training the network. First, let's create an object for our DDPG class:

```
ddpg = DDPG(state_shape, action_shape, action_bound[1])
```

Set the number of episodes:

```
num_episodes = 300
```

Set the number of time steps in each episode:

```
num_timesteps = 500
```

For each episode:

```
for i in range(num_episodes):
```

Initialize the state by resetting the environment:

```
state = env.reset()
```

Initialize the return:

```
Return = 0
```

For every step:

```
for t in range(num_timesteps):
```

Render the environment:

```
env.render()
```

Select the action:

```
action = ddpg.select_action(state)
```

Perform the selected action:

```
next_state, reward, done, info = env.step(action)
```

Store the transition in the replay buffer:

```
ddpg.store_transition(state, action, reward, next_state)
```

Update the return:

```
Return += reward
```

If the state is the terminal state, then break:

```
if done:
    break
```

Update the state to the next state:

```
state = next_state
```

Print the return for every 10 episodes:

```
if i %10 ==0:
    print("Episode:{}, Return: {}".format(i,Return))
```

By rendering the environment, we can observe how the agent learns to swing up the pendulum:

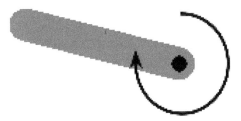

Figure 12.5: The Gym pendulum environment

Now that we have learned how DDPG works and how to implement it, in the next section, we will learn about another interesting algorithm called twin delayed DDPG.

Twin delayed DDPG

Now, we will look into another interesting actor-critic algorithm, known as TD3. TD3 is an improvement (and basically a successor) to the DDPG algorithm we just covered.

In the previous section, we learned how DDPG uses a deterministic policy to work on the continuous action space. DDPG has several advantages and has been successfully used in a variety of continuous action space environments.

We understood that DDPG is an actor-critic method where an actor is a policy network and it finds the optimal policy, while the critic evaluates the policy produced by the actor by estimating the Q function using a DQN.

One of the problems with DDPG is that the critic overestimates the target Q value. This overestimation causes several issues. We learned that the policy is improved based on the Q value given by the critic, but when the Q value has an approximation error, it causes stability issues to our policy and the policy may converge to local optima.

Thus, to combat this, TD3 proposes three important features, which are as follows:

1. Clipped double Q learning
2. Delayed policy updates
3. Target policy smoothing

First, we will understand how TD3 works intuitively, and then we will look at the algorithm in detail.

Key features of TD3

TD3 is essentially the same as DDPG, except that it proposes three important features to mitigate the problems in DDPG. In this section, let's first get a basic understanding of the key features of TD3. The three key features of TD3 are:

- **Clipped double Q learning**: Instead of using one critic network, we use two main critic networks to compute the Q value and also use two target critic networks to compute the target value.

  We compute two target Q values using two target critic networks and use the minimum value of these two while computing the loss. This helps to prevent overestimation of the target Q value. We will learn more about this in detail in the next section.

- **Delayed policy updates**: In DDPG, we learned that we update the parameter of both the actor (policy network) and critic (DQN) network at every step of the episode. Unlike DDPG, here we delay updating the parameter of the actor network.

  That is, the critic network parameter is updated at every step of the episode, but the actor network (policy network) parameter is delayed and updated only after every two steps of the episode.

- **Target policy smoothing**: The DDPG method produces different target values even for the same action. Hence, the variance of the target value will be high even for the same action, so we reduce this variance by adding some noise to the target action.

Now that we have a basic idea of the key features of TD3, we will get into more detail and learn how exactly these three key features work and how they solve the problems associated with DDPG.

Clipped double Q learning

Remember in *Chapter 9, Deep Q Network and Its Variants*, while learning about the DQN, we discovered that it tends to overestimate the Q value of the next state-action pair in the target? It is shown here:

$$y = r + \gamma \max_{a'} Q_{\theta'}(s', a')$$

Overestimates Q Value

In order to mitigate the overestimation, we used double Q learning. With double Q learning, we use two different networks, in other words, two different Q functions, one for selecting an action and the other to compute the Q value, as shown here:

$$y = r + \gamma Q_{\theta'}(s', \arg \max_{a'} Q_\theta(s', a'))$$

Thus, computing the target value by using the preceding equation prevents the overestimation of the Q value in the DQN.

We learned that in DDPG, the critic network is the DQN, and so it also suffers from the overestimation of the Q value in the target. Can we employ double Q learning in DDPG and try to solve the overestimation bias? Yes! But the problem is that in the actor-critic method, the policy and target network parameter updates happen slowly, and this will not help us in removing the overestimation bias.

So, we will use a slightly different version of double Q learning called *clipped double Q learning*. In clipped double Q learning, we use two target critic networks to compute the Q value.

We use the two target critic networks and compute the two Q values and select the minimum value out of these two to compute the target value. This helps to prevent overestimation bias. Let's understand this in more detail.

If we need two target critic networks, then we also need two main critic networks. We know that the target network parameter is just a time-delayed copy of the main network parameter. So, we define two main critic networks with the parameters θ_1 and θ_2 to compute the two Q values, that is, $Q_{\theta_1}(s, a)$ and $Q_{\theta_2}(s, a)$, respectively.

We also define the two target critic networks with parameters θ_1' and θ_2' to compute the two Q values of next state-action pair in the target, that is, $Q_{\theta_1'}(s', a')$ and $Q_{\theta_2'}(s', a')$, respectively. Let's understand this clearly step by step.

In DDPG, we learned that we compute the target value as:

$$y = r + \gamma Q_{\theta'}(s', \mu_{\phi'}(s'))$$

Computing the Q value of the next state-action pair in the target in this way creates overestimation bias:

$$y = r + \gamma \underline{Q_{\theta'}(s', \mu_{\phi'}(s'))}$$

↓
Creates overestimation bias

So, to avoid this, in TD3, first, we compute the Q value of the next state-action pair in the target using the first target critic network with a parameter θ_1', that is, $Q_{\theta_1'}(s', a')$, and then we compute the Q value of the next state-action pair in the target using the second target critic network with a parameter θ_2', that is, $Q_{\theta_2'}(s', a')$. Then, we use the minimum of these two Q values to compute the target value as expressed here:

$$y = r + \gamma \min \begin{pmatrix} Q_{\theta_1'}(s', a') \\ Q_{\theta_2'}(s', a') \end{pmatrix}$$

Where the action $a' = \mu_{\phi'}(s')$.

We can express the preceding equation simply as:

$$y = r + \gamma \min_{j=1,2} Q_{\theta_j'}(s', a')$$

Where the action $a' = \mu_{\phi'}(s')$.

Computing the target value in this way prevents overestimation of the Q value of the next state-action pair.

Okay, we computed the target value. How do we compute the loss and update the critic network parameter? We learned that we use two main critic networks, so, first, we compute the loss of the first main critic network, parameterized by θ_1:

$$J(\theta_1) = \frac{1}{K}\sum_i \left(y_i - Q_{\theta_1}(s_i, a_i)\right)^2$$

After computing the loss, we compute the gradients and update the parameter θ_1 using gradient descent as $\theta_1 = \theta_1 - \alpha\nabla_{\theta_1}J(\theta_1)$.

Next, we compute the loss of the second main critic network, parameterized by θ_2:

$$J(\theta_2) = \frac{1}{K}\sum_i \left(y_i - Q_{\theta_2}(s_i, a_i)\right)^2$$

After computing the loss, we compute the gradients and update the parameter θ_2 using gradient descent as $\theta_2 = \theta_2 - \alpha\nabla_{\theta_2}J(\theta_2)$.

We can simply express the preceding updates as:

$$J(\theta_j) = \frac{1}{K}\sum_i \left(y_i - Q_{\theta_j}(s_i, a_i)\right)^2 \quad \text{for } j = 1, 2$$

$$\theta_j = \theta_j - \alpha\nabla_{\theta_j}J(\theta_j) \qquad \text{for } j = 1, 2$$

After updating the two main critic network parameters, θ_1 and θ_2, we can update the two target critic network parameters, θ_1' and θ_2', by soft replacement, as shown here:

$$\theta_1' = \tau\theta_1 + (1 - \tau)\theta_1'$$

$$\theta_2' = \tau\theta_2 + (1 - \tau)\theta_2'$$

We can simply express the preceding updates as:

$$\theta_j' = \tau\theta_j + (1 - \tau)\theta_j' \quad \text{for } j = 1, 2$$

Delayed policy updates

Delayed policy updates imply that we update the parameters of our actor network (policy network) less frequently than the critic networks. But why do we want to do that? We learned that in DDPG, actor and critic network parameters are updated at every step of the episode.

When the critic network parameter is not good, then it estimates the incorrect Q values. If the Q value estimated by the critic network is not correct, then the actor network cannot update its parameter correctly. That is, we learned that the actor network learns based on feedback from the critic network. This feedback is just the Q value. When the critic network gives incorrect feedback (incorrect Q value), then the actor network cannot learn the correct action and cannot update its parameter correctly.

Thus, to avoid this, we hold updating the parameter of the actor network for a while and only update the critic network to make the critic estimate the correct Q value. That is, we update the parameter of the critic network at every step of the episode, and we delay updating the parameter of the actor network, and only update it for some specific steps of the episode because we don't want our actor to learn from the incorrect critic's feedback.

In a nutshell, the critic network parameter is updated at every step of the episode, but the actor network parameter update is delayed. We generally delay the update by two steps.

Okay, in DDPG, we learned that the objective of the actor network (policy network) is to maximize the Q value:

$$J(\phi) = \frac{1}{K} \sum_i Q_\theta(s_i, a)$$

The preceding objective of the actor network is the same in TD3 as well. That is, similar to DDPG, here, the objective of the actor is to generate actions in such a way that it maximizes the Q value produced by the critic. But wait! Unlike DDPG, here we have two Q values, $Q_{\theta_1}(s, a)$ and $Q_{\theta_2}(s, a)$, since we use two critic networks with parameters θ_1 and θ_2, respectively. So which Q value should our actor network maximize? Should it be $Q_{\theta_1}(s, a)$ or $Q_{\theta_2}(s, a)$? We can take either of these and maximize one. So, we can take $Q_{\theta_1}(s, a)$.

Thus, in TD3, the objective of the actor network is to maximize the Q value, $Q_{\theta_1}(s, a)$, as shown here:

$$J(\phi) = \frac{1}{K} \sum_i Q_{\theta_1}(s_i, a)$$

Remember that in the above equation, the action a is selected by actor network, $a = \mu_\phi(s_i)$. In order to maximize the objective function, we compute the gradients of our objective function, $\nabla_\phi J(\phi)$, and update the parameter of the network using gradient ascent:

$$\phi = \phi + \alpha \nabla_\phi J(\phi)$$

Now, instead of doing this parameter update of the actor network at every time step of the episode, we delay the updates and update the parameter only on every other step (every two steps). Let t be the time step of the episode and d denotes the number of time steps we want to delay the update by (usually d is set to 2); then we can write the following:

1. If t mod d =0, then:

    1. Compute the gradient of the objective function $\nabla_\phi J(\phi)$

    2. Update the actor network parameter using gradient ascent
        $\phi = \phi + \alpha \nabla_\phi J(\phi)$

This will be made clearer when we look at the final algorithm.

Target policy smoothing

To understand this, let's first recollect how we compute the target value in TD3. We learned that in TD3, we update the target value using clipped double Q learning with two target critic networks:

$$y = r + \gamma \min_{j=1,2} Q_{\theta'_j}(s', a')$$

Where the action $a' = \mu_{\phi'}(s')$.

As we can notice, we compute the target values with action a' generated by the target actor network, $\mu_{\phi'}(s)$. Instead of using the action given by the target actor network directly, we add some noise ϵ to the action and modify the action to $\tilde{a}$, as shown here:

$$\tilde{a} = \mu_{\phi'}(s') + \epsilon \quad \text{where} \quad \epsilon \sim (\mathcal{N}(0, \sigma), -c, +c)$$

Here, $-c$ to $+c$ indicates that noise is clipped, so that we can keep the target close to the actual action. Thus, our target value computation now becomes:

$$y = r + \gamma \min_{j=1,2} Q_{\theta'_j}(s', \tilde{a})$$

In the preceding equation, the action $\tilde{a} = \mu_{\phi'}(s') + \epsilon$.

But why are we doing this? Why do we need to add noise to the action and use it to compute the target value? Similar actions should have similar target values, right? However, the DDPG method produces target values with high variance even for similar actions. This is because deterministic policies overfit to the sharp peaks in the value estimate. So, we can smooth out these peaks for similar actions by adding some noise. Thus, target policy smoothing basically acts as a regularizer and reduces the variance in the target values.

Now that we have understood the key features of the TD3 algorithm, let's get clarity on what we have learned so far and how the TD3 algorithm works by putting all the concepts together.

Putting it all together

First, let's recollect the notations to understand TD3 better. We use six networks— four critic networks and two actor networks:

- The two main critic network parameters are represented by θ_1 and θ_2
- The two target critic network parameters are represented by θ_1' and θ_2'
- The main actor network parameter is represented by ϕ
- The target actor network parameter is represented by ϕ'

TD3 is an actor-critic method, and so the parameters of TD3 will get updated at every step of the episode, unlike the policy gradient method where we generate complete episodes and then update the parameter. Now, let's get started and understand how TD3 works.

First, we initialize the two main critic network parameters, θ_1 and θ_2, and the main actor network parameter ϕ with random values. We know that the target network parameter is just a copy of the main network parameter. So, we initialize the two target critic network parameters θ_1' and θ_2' by just copying θ_1 and θ_2, respectively. Similarly, we initialize the target actor network parameter ϕ' by just copying the main actor network parameter ϕ. We also initialize the replay buffer $\mathcal{D}$.

Now, for each step in the episode, first, we select an action a using the actor network:

$$a = \mu_\phi(s)$$

But instead of using the action a directly, to ensure exploration, we add some noise ϵ, where $\epsilon \sim \mathcal{N}(0, \sigma)$. Thus, our action now becomes:

$$a = \mu_\phi(s) + \epsilon$$

Then, we perform the action a, move to the next state s', and get the reward r. We store this transition information in a replay buffer $\mathcal{D}$.

Next, we randomly sample a minibatch of K transitions (s, a, r, s') from the replay buffer. These K transitions will be used for updating both our critic and actor network.

First, let us compute the loss of the critic networks. We learned that the loss function of the critic networks is:

$$J(\theta_j) = \frac{1}{K} \sum_i \left(y_i - Q_{\theta_j}(s_i, a_i) \right)^2 \quad \text{for } j = 1, 2$$

In the preceding equation, the following applies:

- The action a_i is the action produced by the actor network, that is, $a_i = \mu_\phi(s_i)$
- y_i is the target value of the critic, that is, $y_i = r_i + \gamma \min_{j=1,2} Q_{\theta'_j}(s'_i, \tilde{a})$, and the action $\tilde{a}$ is the action produced by the target actor network, that is, $\tilde{a} = \mu_{\phi'}(s'_i) + \epsilon$ where $\epsilon \sim (\mathcal{N}(0, \sigma), -c, +c)$

After computing the loss of the critic network, we compute the gradients $\nabla_{\theta_j} J(\theta_j)$ and update the critic network parameter using gradient descent:

$$\theta_j = \theta_j - \alpha \nabla_{\theta_j} J(\theta_j) \quad \text{for } j = 1, 2$$

Now, let us update the actor network. We learned that the objective function of the actor network is:

$$J(\phi) = \frac{1}{K} \sum_i Q_{\theta_1}(s_i, a)$$

Note that in the above equation, we are only using the state (s_i) from the sampled K transitions (s, a, r, s'). The action a is selected by actor network, $a = \mu_\phi(s_i)$. In order to maximize the objective function, we compute gradients of our objective function $\nabla_\phi J(\phi)$ and update the parameters of the network using gradient ascent:

$$\phi = \phi + \alpha \nabla_\phi J(\phi)$$

Instead of doing this parameter update of the actor network at every time step of the episode, we delay the updates. Let t be the time step of the episode and d denotes the number of time steps we want to delay the update by (usually d is set to 2); then we can write the following:

1. If $t \bmod d = 0$, then:

    1. Compute the gradient of the objective function $\nabla_\phi J(\phi)$

    2. Update the actor network parameter using gradient ascent
        $\phi = \phi + \alpha \nabla_\phi J(\phi)$

Finally, we update the parameter of the target critic networks θ_1' and θ_2' and the parameter of the target actor network ϕ' by soft replacement:

$$\theta_j' = \tau \theta_j + (1 - \tau)\theta_j' \quad \text{for } j = 1, 2$$

$$\phi' = \tau \phi_j + (1 - \tau)\phi'$$

There is a small change in updating the parameter of the target networks. Just like we delay updating the actor network parameter for d steps, we update the target network parameter for every d step; hence, we can write:

1. If $t \bmod d = 0$, then:

    1. Compute the gradient of the objective function $\nabla_\phi J(\phi)$ and update the actor network parameter using gradient ascent $\phi = \phi + \alpha \nabla_\phi J(\phi)$

    2. Update the target critic network parameter and target actor network parameter as $\theta_j' = \tau \theta_j + (1 - \tau)\theta_j' \quad$ for $j = 1,2$, and $\phi' = \tau \phi + (1 - \tau)\phi'$, respectively

We repeat the preceding steps for several episodes and improve the policy. To get a better understanding of how TD3 works, let's look into the TD3 algorithm in the next section.

Algorithm – TD3

The TD3 algorithm is exactly similar to the DDPG algorithm except that it includes the three key features we learned in the previous sections. So, before looking into the TD3 algorithm directly, you can revise all the key features of TD3.

The algorithm of TD3 is given as follows:

1. Initialize the two main critic network parameters θ_1 and θ_2 and the main actor network parameter ϕ

2. Initialize the two target critic network parameters θ_1' and θ_2' by copying the main critic network parameters θ_1 and θ_2, respectively

3. Initialize the target actor network parameter ϕ' by copying the main actor network parameter ϕ'

4. Initialize the replay buffer $\mathcal{D}$

5. For N number of episodes, repeat step 6

6. For each step in the episode, that is, for $t = 0,...,T-1$:

   1. Select the action a based on the policy $\mu_\phi(s)$ and with exploration noise ϵ, that is, $a = \mu_\phi(s) + \epsilon$ where, $\epsilon \sim (\mathcal{N}(0,\sigma)$

   2. Perform the selected action a, move to the next state s', get the reward r, and store the transition information in the replay buffer $\mathcal{D}$

   3. Randomly sample a minibatch of K transitions from the replay buffer $\mathcal{D}$

   4. Select the action $\tilde{a}$ to compute the target value, $\tilde{a} = \mu_{\phi'}(s_i') + \epsilon$, where $\epsilon \sim (\mathcal{N}(0,\sigma), -c, +c)$

   5. Compute the target value of the critic, that is,
   $y_i = r_i + \gamma \min_{j=1,2} Q_{\theta_j'}(s_i', \tilde{a})$

   6. Compute the loss of the critic network,
   $$J(\theta_j) = \frac{1}{K}\sum_i \left(y_i - Q_{\theta_j}(s_i, a_i)\right)^2 \quad \text{for } j = 1,2$$

   7. Compute the gradients of the loss $\nabla_{\theta_j} J(\theta_j)$ and minimize the loss using gradient descent, $\theta_j = \theta_j - \alpha \nabla_{\theta_j} J(\theta_j)$ for $j = 1,2$

   8. If $t \bmod d = 0$, then:

      1. Compute the gradient of the objective function $\nabla_\phi J(\phi)$ and update the actor network parameter using gradient ascent, $\phi = \phi + \alpha \nabla_\phi J(\phi)$

      2. Update the target critic network parameter and target actor network parameter as $\theta_j' = \tau \theta_j + (1-\tau)\theta_j'$ for $j = 1,2$, and $\phi' = \tau \phi + (1-\tau)\phi'$, respectively

Now that we have learned how TD3 works, in the next section, we will learn about another interesting algorithm, called SAC.

Soft actor-critic

Now, we will look into another interesting actor-critic algorithm, called SAC. This is an off-policy algorithm and it borrows several features from the TD3 algorithm. But unlike TD3, it uses a stochastic policy π. SAC is based on the concept of entropy. So first, let's understand what is meant by entropy. Entropy is a measure of the randomness of a variable. It basically tells us the uncertainty or unpredictability of the random variable and is denoted by $\mathcal{H}$.

If the random variable always gives the same value every time, then we can say that its entropy is low because there is no randomness. But if the random variable gives different values, then we can say that its entropy is high.

For an example, consider a dice throw experiment. Every time a dice is thrown, if we get a different number, then we can say that the entropy is high because we are getting a different number every time and there is high uncertainty since we don't know which number will come up on the next throw. But if we are getting the same number, say 3, every time the dice is thrown, then we can say that the entropy is low, since there is no randomness here as we are getting the same number on every throw.

We know that the policy π tells what action to perform in a given state. What happens when the entropy of the policy $\mathcal{H}(\pi(\cdot \,|s))$ is high or low? If the entropy of the policy is high, then this means that our policy performs different actions instead of performing the same action every time. But if the entropy of the policy is low, then this means that our policy performs the same action every time. As you may have guessed, increasing the entropy of a policy promotes exploration, while decreasing the entropy of the policy means less exploration.

We know that, in reinforcement learning, our goal is to maximize the return. So, we can define our objective function as shown here:

$$J(\phi) = E_{\tau \sim \pi_\phi}[R(\tau)]$$

Where ϕ is the parameter of our stochastic policy π.

We know that the return of the trajectory is just the sum of rewards, that is:

$$R(\tau) = \sum_{t=0}^{T-1} r_t$$

So, we can rewrite our objective function by expanding the return as:

$$J(\phi) = E_{\tau \sim \pi_\phi} \left[\sum_{t=0}^{T-1} r_t \right]$$

Maximizing the preceding objective function maximizes the return. In the SAC method, we use a slightly modified version of the objective function with the entropy term as shown here:

$$J(\phi) = E_{\tau \sim \pi_\phi} \left[\sum_{t=0}^{T-1} r_t + \alpha \mathcal{H}(\pi(\cdot \, | s_t)) \right]$$

As we can see, our objective function now has two terms; one is the reward and the other is the entropy of the policy. Thus, instead of maximizing only the reward, we also maximize the entropy of a policy. But what is the point of this? Maximizing the entropy of the policy allows us to explore new actions. But we don't want to explore actions that give us a bad reward. Hence, maximizing entropy along with maximizing reward means that we can explore new actions along with maintaining maximum reward. The preceding objective function is often referred to as **maximum entropy reinforcement learning**, or **entropy regularized reinforcement learning**. Adding an entropy term is also often referred to as an entropy bonus.

Also, the term α in the objective function is called temperature and is used to set the importance of our entropy term, or we can say that it is used to control exploration. When α is high, we allow exploration in the policy, but when it is low, then we don't allow exploration.

Okay, now that we have a basic idea of SAC, let's get into some more details.

Understanding soft actor-critic

SAC, as the name suggests, is an actor-critic method similar to DDPG and TD3 we learned in the previous sections. Unlike DDPG and TD3, which use deterministic policies, SAC uses a stochastic policy. SAC works in a very similar manner to TD3. We learned that in actor-critic architecture, the actor uses the policy gradient to find the optimal policy and the critic evaluates the policy produced by the actor using the Q function.

Similarly, in SAC, the actor uses the policy gradient to find the optimal policy and the critic evaluates the policy produced by the actor. However, instead of using only the Q function to evaluate the actor's policy, the critic uses both the Q function and the value function. But why exactly do we need both the Q function and the value function to evaluate the actor's policy? This will be explained in detail in the upcoming sections.

So, in SAC, we have three networks, one actor network (policy network) to find the optimal policy, and two critic networks—a value network and a Q network, to compute the value function and the Q function, respectively, to evaluate the policy produced by the actor.

Before moving on, let's look at the modified version of the value function and the Q function with the entropy term.

V and Q functions with the entropy term

We know that the value function (state value) is the expected return of the trajectory starting from state s following a policy π:

$$V^\pi(s) = \mathop{\mathbb{E}}_{\tau \sim \pi}[R(\tau)|s_0 = s]$$

We learned that the return is the sum of rewards of the trajectory, so we can rewrite the preceding equation by expanding the return as:

$$V(s) = \mathop{\mathbb{E}}_{\tau \sim \pi}\left[\sum_{t=0}^{T-1} r_t|s_0 = s\right]$$

Now, we can rewrite the value function by adding the entropy term as shown here:

$$V(s) = E_{\tau \sim \pi}\left[\sum_{t=0}^{T-1} r_t + \alpha \mathcal{H}(\pi(\cdot|s_t))|s_0 = s\right]$$

We know that the Q function (state-action value) is the expected return of the trajectory starting from state s and action a following a policy π:

$$Q^\pi(s,a) = [R(\tau)|s_0 = s, a_0 = a]$$

Expanding the return of the trajectory, we can write the following:

$$Q(s,a) = \underset{\tau \sim \pi}{\mathbb{E}}\left[\sum_{t=0}^{T-1} r_t|s_0 = s, a_0 = a\right]$$

Now, we can rewrite the Q function by adding the entropy term as shown here:

$$Q(s,a) = E_{\tau \sim \pi}\left[\sum_{t=0}^{T-1} r_t + \alpha \sum_{t=0}^{T-1} \mathcal{H}(\pi(\cdot|s_t))|s_0 = s, a_0 = a\right]$$

The modified Bellman equation for the preceding Q function with the entropy term is given as:

$$Q(s,a) = \underset{s' \sim P}{\mathbb{E}}[r + \gamma V(s')] \qquad (2)$$

Here, the value function can be computed using the relation between the Q function and the value function as:

$$V(s) = \mathbb{E}_{a \sim \pi}[Q(s,a) - \alpha \log \pi(a|s)] \qquad (3)$$

To learn how exactly we obtained the equations (2) and (3), you can check the derivation of soft policy iteration in the paper *Soft Actor-Critic: Off-Policy Maximum Entropy Deep Reinforcement Learning with a Stochastic Actor*, by Tuomas Haarnoja et.al.: https://arxiv.org/pdf/1801.01290.pdf

Components of SAC

Now that we have a basic idea of SAC, let's go into more detail and understand how exactly each component of SAC works by looking at them separately.

Critic network

We learned that unlike other actor-critic methods we have seen earlier, the critic in SAC uses both the value function and the Q function to evaluate the policy produced by the actor network. But why is that?

In the previous algorithms, we used the critic network to compute the Q function for evaluating the action produced by the actor. Also, the target Q value in the critic is computed using the Bellman equation. We can do the same here. However, here we have modified the Bellman equation of the Q function due to the entropy term, as we learned in equation (2):

$$Q(s, a) = \underset{s' \sim P}{E}[r + \gamma V(s')]$$

From the preceding equation, we can observe that in order to compute the Q function, first we need to compute the value function. So, we need to compute both the Q function and the value function in order to evaluate the policy produced by the actor. We can use a single network to approximate both the Q function and the value function. However, instead of using a single network, we use two different networks, the Q network to estimate the Q function, and the value network to estimate the value function. Using two different networks to compute the Q function and value function stabilizes the training.

As mentioned in the SAC paper, "*There is no need in principle to include a separate function approximator (neural network) for the state value since it is related to the Q function and policy according to Equation 2. But in practice, including a separate function approximator (neural network) for the state value can stabilize training and is convenient to train simultaneously with the other networks.*"

First, we will learn how the value network works and then we will learn about the Q network.

Value network

The value network is denoted by V, the parameter of the value network is denoted by ψ, and the parameter of the target value network is denoted by ψ'.

Thus, $V_\psi(s)$ implies that we approximate the value function (state value) using the neural network parameterized by ψ. Okay, how can we train the value network? We can train the network by minimizing the loss between the target state value and the state value predicted by our network. How can we obtain the target state value? We can use the value function given in equation (3) to compute the target state value.

We learned that according to equation (3), the value of the state is computed as:

$$V(s) = \mathbb{E}_{a \sim \pi}[Q(s, a) - \alpha \log \pi(a|s)]$$

In the preceding equation, we can remove the expectation. We will approximate the expectation by sampling K number of transitions from the replay buffer. So, we can compute the target state value y_v using the preceding equation as:

$$y_v = Q(s, a) - \alpha \log \pi(a|s)$$

If we look at the preceding equation, we have a Q function. In order to compute the Q function, we use a Q network parameterized by θ, and similarly, our policy is parameterized by ϕ, so we can rewrite the preceding equation with the parameterized Q function and policy as shown here:

$$y_v = Q_\theta(s, a) - \alpha \log \pi_\phi(a|s)$$

But if we use the preceding equation to compute the target value, the Q value will overestimate. So, to avoid this overestimation, we use clipped double Q learning, just like we learned in TD3. That is, we compute the two Q values using two Q networks parameterized by θ_1 and θ_2 and take the minimum value of these two, as shown here:

$$y_v = \min \begin{pmatrix} Q_{\theta_1}(s, a) \\ Q_{\theta_2}(s, a) \end{pmatrix} - \alpha \log \pi_\phi(a|s)$$

As we can observe in the preceding equation, for clipped double Q learning, we are using the two main Q networks parameterized by θ_1 and θ_2, but in TD3, we used two target Q networks parameterized by θ_1' and θ_2'. Why is that?

Because here, we are computing the Q value of a state-action pair $Q(s, a)$ so we can use the two main Q networks parameterized by θ_1 and θ_2, but in TD3, we compute the Q value of the next state-action pair $Q(s', a')$, so we used the two target Q networks parameterized by θ_1' and θ_2'. Thus, here, we don't need target Q networks.

We can simply express the preceding equation as:

$$y_v = \min_{j=1,2} Q_{\theta_j}(s, a) - \alpha \log \pi_\phi(a|s)$$

Now, we can define our objective function $J_V(\psi)$ of the value network as the mean squared difference between the target state value and the state value predicted by our network, as shown here:

$$J_V(\psi) = \frac{1}{K}\sum_i \left(y_{v_i} - V_\psi(s_i)\right)^2$$

Where K denotes the number of transitions we sample from the replay buffer.

We can calculate the gradients of our objective function and then update our main value network parameter ψ as:

$$\psi = \psi - \lambda\nabla_\psi J(\psi)$$

Note that we are using λ to represent the learning rate since we are already using α to denote the temperature.

We can update the parameter of the target value network ψ' using soft replacement:

$$\psi' = \tau\psi + (1 - \tau)\psi'$$

We will learn where exactly the target value network is used in the next section.

Q network

The Q network is denoted by Q and it is parameterized by θ. Thus, $Q_\theta(s, a)$ implies that we approximate the Q function using the neural network parameterized by θ. How can we train the Q network? We can train the network by minimizing the loss between the target Q value and the Q value predicted by the network. How can we obtain the target Q value? Here is where we use the Bellman equation.

We learned that according to the Bellman equation (2), the Q value can be computed as:

$$Q(s, a) = \underset{s' \sim P}{E}[r + \gamma V(s')]$$

We can remove the expectation in the preceding equation. We will approximate the expectation by sampling K number of transitions from the replay buffer. So, we can compute the target Q value y_q using the preceding equation as:

$$y_q = r + \gamma V(s')$$

If we look at the preceding equation, we have a value of next state $V(s')$. In order to compute the value of next state $V(s')$, we use a target value network parameterized by ψ', so we can rewrite the preceding equation with the parameterized value function as shown here:

$$y_q = r + \gamma V_\psi(s')$$

Now, we can define our objective function $J_Q(\theta)$ of the Q network as the mean squared difference between the target Q value and the Q value predicted by the network, as shown here:

$$J_Q(\theta) = \frac{1}{K} \sum_i \left(y_{q_i} - Q_\theta(s_i, a_i) \right)^2$$

Where K denotes the number of transitions we sample from the replay buffer.

In the previous section, we learned that we use two Q networks parameterized by θ_1 and θ_2 to prevent overestimation bias. So, first, we compute the loss of the first Q network, parameterized by θ_1:

$$J_Q(\theta_1) = \frac{1}{K} \sum_i \left(y_{q_i} - Q_{\theta_1}(s_i, a_i) \right)^2$$

Then, we compute the gradients and update the parameter θ_1 using gradient descent as $\theta_1 = \theta_1 - \lambda \nabla_{\theta_1} J(\theta_1)$.

Next, we compute the loss of the second Q network, parameterized by θ_2:

$$J_Q(\theta_2) = \frac{1}{K} \sum_i \left(y_{q_i} - Q_{\theta_2}(s_i, a_i) \right)^2$$

Then, we compute the gradients and update the parameter θ_2 using gradient descent as $\theta_2 = \theta_2 - \lambda \nabla_{\theta_2} J(\theta_2)$.

We can simply express the preceding updates as:

$$J_Q(\theta_j) = \frac{1}{K}\sum_i \left(y_{q_i} - Q_{\theta_j}(s_i, a_i)\right)^2 \quad \text{for } j = 1,2$$

$$\theta_j = \theta_j - \lambda \nabla_{\theta_j} J(\theta_j) \qquad \text{for } j = 1,2$$

Actor network

The actor network (policy network) is parameterized by ϕ. Let's recall the objective function of the actor network we learned in TD3:

$$J(\phi) = \frac{1}{K}\sum_i Q_\theta(s_i, a)$$

Where a is the action produced by the actor.

The preceding objective function means that the goal of the actor is to generate action in such a way that it maximizes the Q value computed by the critic.

The objective function of the actor network in SAC is the same as what we learned in TD3, except that here we use a stochastic policy $\pi_{\phi(a|s)}$, and also, we maximize the entropy. So, we can write the objective function of the actor network in SAC as:

$$J_\pi(\phi) = \frac{1}{K}\sum_i [Q_\theta(s_i, a) - \alpha \log \pi_\phi(a|s_i)]$$

Now, how can we compute the derivative of the preceding objective function? Because, unlike TD3, here, our action is computed using a stochastic policy. It will be difficult to apply backpropagation and compute gradients of the preceding objective function with the action computed using a stochastic policy. So, we use the reparameterization trick. The reparameterization trick guarantees that sampling from our policy is differentiable. Thus, we can rewrite our action as shown here:

$$a = f_\phi(\epsilon_i; s_i)$$

In the preceding equation, we can observe that we parameterize the policy with a neural network f and ϵ is the noise sampled from a spherical Gaussian distribution.

Thus, we can rewrite our objective function as shown here:

$$J_\pi(\phi) = \frac{1}{K}\sum_i [Q_\theta(s_i, a) - \alpha \log\pi_\phi(a|s_i)]$$

Note that in the preceding equation, our action is $a = f_\phi(\epsilon_i; s_i)$. Remember how we used two Q functions parameterized by θ_1 and θ_2 to avoid overestimation bias? Now, which Q function should we use in the preceding objective function? We can use either of the functions and so we use the Q function parameterized by θ_1 and write our final objective function as:

$$J_\pi(\phi) = \frac{1}{K}\sum_i [Q_{\theta_1}(s_i, a) - \alpha \log\pi_\phi(a|s_i)]$$

Now that we have understood how the SAC algorithm works, let's recap what we have learned so far and how the SAC algorithm works exactly by putting all the concepts together.

Putting it all together

First, let's recall the notations to understand SAC better. We use five networks—four critic networks (two value networks and two Q networks) and one actor network:

- The main value network parameter is represented by ψ
- The target value network parameter is represented by ψ'
- The two main Q network parameters are represented by θ_1 and θ_2
- The actor network (policy network) parameter is represented by ϕ
- The target state value is represented by y_v, and the target Q value is represented by y_q

SAC is an actor-critic method, and so the parameters of SAC will get updated at every step of the episode. Now, let's get started and understand how SAC works.

First, we initialize the main network parameter of the value network ψ, two Q network parameters θ_1 and θ_2, and the actor network parameter ϕ. Next, we initialize the target value network parameter ψ' by just copying the main network parameter ψ and then we initialize the replay buffer $\mathcal{D}$.

Now, for each step in the episode, first, we select an action a using the actor network:

$$a = \pi_\phi(s)$$

Then, we perform the action a, move to the next state s', and get the reward r. We store this transition information in a replay buffer $\mathcal{D}$.

Next, we randomly sample a minibatch of K transitions from the replay buffer. These K transitions (s, a, r, s') are used for updating our value, Q, and actor network.

First, let us compute the loss of the value network. We learned that the loss function of the value network is:

$$J_V(\psi) = \frac{1}{K} \sum_i \left(y_{v_i} - V_\psi(s_i) \right)^2$$

Where y_{v_i} is the target state value and it is given as
$$y_{v_i} = \min_{j=1,2} Q_{\theta_j}(s_i, a_i) - \alpha \log \pi_\phi(a_i | s_i).$$

After computing the loss, we calculate the gradients and update the parameter ψ of the value network using gradient descent: $\psi = \psi - \lambda \nabla_\psi J(\psi)$.

Now, we compute the loss of the Q networks. We learned that the loss function of the Q network is:

$$J_Q(\theta_j) = \frac{1}{K} \sum_i \left(y_{q_i} - Q_{\theta_j}(s_i, a_i) \right)^2 \quad \text{for } j = 1, 2$$

Where y_{q_i} is the target Q value and it is given as $y_{q_i} = r_i + \gamma V_{\psi'}(s_i')$.

After computing the loss, we calculate the gradients and update the parameter of the Q networks using gradient descent:

$$\theta_j = \theta_j - \lambda \nabla_{\theta_j} J(\theta_j) \quad \text{for } j = 1, 2$$

Next, we update the actor network. We learned that the objective of the actor network is:

$$J_\pi(\phi) = \frac{1}{K} \sum_i [Q_{\theta_1}(s_i, a) - \alpha \log \pi_\phi(a | s_i)]$$

Now, we calculate gradients and update the parameter ϕ of the actor network using gradient ascent:

$$\phi = \phi + \lambda \nabla_\phi J(\phi)$$

Finally, in the end, we update the target value network parameter by soft replacement, as shown here:

$$\psi' = \tau\psi + (1 - \tau)\psi'$$

We repeat the preceding steps for several episodes and improve the policy. To get a better understanding of how SAC works, let's look into the SAC algorithm in the next section.

Algorithm – SAC

The SAC algorithm is given as follows:

1. Initialize the main value network parameter ψ, the Q network parameters θ_1 and θ_2, and the actor network parameter ϕ

2. Initialize the target value network ψ' by just copying the main value network parameter ψ

3. Initialize the replay buffer $\mathcal{D}$

4. For N number of episodes, repeat step 5

5. For each step in the episode, that is, for $t = 0,..., T - 1$:

    1. Select an action a based on the policy $\pi_\phi(s)$, that is, $a = \pi_\phi(s)$

    2. Perform the selected action a, move to the next state s', get the reward r, and store the transition information in the replay buffer $\mathcal{D}$

    3. Randomly sample a minibatch of K transitions from the replay buffer

    4. Compute the target state value
    $$y_{v_i} = \min_{j=1,2} Q_{\theta_j}(s_i, a_i) - \alpha \log \pi_\phi(a_i|s_i)$$

    5. Compute the loss of value network $J_V(\psi) = \frac{1}{K}\sum_i \left(y_{v_i} - V_\psi(s_i)\right)^2$

       and update the parameter using gradient descent, $\psi = \psi - \lambda \nabla_\psi J(\psi)$

    6. Compute the target Q value $y_{q_i} = r_i + \gamma V_{\psi'}(s_i')$

7. Compute the loss of the Q networks

$$J_Q(\theta_j) = \frac{1}{K} \sum_i \left(y_{q_i} - Q_{\theta_j}(s_i, a_i) \right)^2 \quad \text{for } j = 1, 2 \text{ and update the}$$

parameter using gradient descent, $\theta_j = \theta_j - \lambda \nabla_{\theta_j} J(\theta_j)$ for $j = 1, 2$

8. Compute gradients of the actor objective function, $\nabla_\phi J(\phi)$ and

update the parameter using gradient ascent, $\phi = \phi + \lambda \nabla_\phi J(\phi)$

9. Update the target value network parameter as $\psi' = \tau\psi + (1 - \tau)\psi'$

Many congratulations on learning the several important state-of-the-art actor-critic algorithms, including DDPG, twin delayed DDPG, and SAC. In the next chapter, we will examine several state-of-the-art policy gradient algorithms.

Summary

We started off the chapter by understanding the DDPG algorithm. We learned that DDPG is an actor-critic algorithm where the actor estimates the policy using policy gradient and the critic evaluates the policy produced by the actor using the Q function. We learned how DDPG uses a deterministic policy and how it is used in environments with a continuous action space.

Later, we looked into the actor and critic components of DDPG in detail and understood how they work, before finally learning about the DDPG algorithm.

Moving on, we learned about the twin delayed DDPG, which is the successor to DDPG and constitutes an improvement to the DDPG algorithm. We learned the key features of TD3, including clipped double Q learning, delayed policy updates, and target policy smoothing, in detail and finally, we looked into the TD3 algorithm.

At the end of the chapter, we learned about the SAC algorithm. We learned that, unlike DDPG and TD3, the SAC method uses a stochastic policy. We also understood how SAC works with the entropy bonus in the objective function, and we learned what is meant by maximum entropy reinforcement learning.

In the next chapter, we will learn the state-of-the-art policy gradient algorithms such as trust region policy optimization, proximal policy optimization, and actor-critic using Kronecker-factored trust region.

Questions

Let's put our knowledge of actor-critic methods to the test. Try answering the following questions:

1. What is the role of actor and critic networks in DDPG?
2. How does the critic in DDPG work?
3. What are the key features of TD3?
4. Why do we need clipped double Q learning?
5. What is target policy smoothing?
6. What is maximum entropy reinforcement learning?
7. What is the role of the critic network in SAC?

Further reading

For more information, refer to the following papers:

- **Continuous Control with Deep Reinforcement Learning** by *Timothy P. Lillicrap, et al.,* https://arxiv.org/pdf/1509.02971.pdf
- **Addressing Function Approximation Error in Actor-Critic Methods** by *Scott Fujimoto, Herke van Hoof, David Meger,* https://arxiv.org/pdf/1802.09477.pdf
- **Soft Actor-Critic: Off-Policy Maximum Entropy Deep Reinforcement Learning with a Stochastic Actor** by *Tuomas Haarnoja, Aurick Zhou, Pieter Abbeel, Sergey Levine,* https://arxiv.org/pdf/1801.01290.pdf

13

TRPO, PPO, and ACKTR Methods

In this chapter, we will learn two interesting state-of-art policy gradient algorithms: trust region policy optimization and proximal policy optimization. Both of these algorithms act as an improvement to the policy gradient algorithm (REINFORCE with baseline) we learned in *Chapter 10, Policy Gradient Method.*

We begin the chapter by understanding the **Trust Region Policy Optimization (TRPO)** method and how it acts as an improvement to the policy gradient method. Later we will understand several essential math concepts that are required to understand TRPO. Following this, we will learn how to design and solve the TRPO objective function. At the end of the section, we will understand how the TRPO algorithm works step by step.

Moving on, we will learn about **Proximal Policy Optimization (PPO)**. We will understand how PPO works and how it acts as an improvement to the TRPO algorithm in detail. We will also learn two types of PPO algorithm called PPO-clipped and PPO-penalty.

At the end of the chapter, we will learn about an interesting actor-critic method called the **Actor-Critic using Kronecker-Factored Trust Region (ACKTR)** method, which uses Kronecker factorization to approximate the second-order derivative. We will explore how ACKTR works and how it uses the trust region in its update rule.

In this chapter, we will learn the following topics:

- Trust region policy optimization
- Designing the TRPO objective function
- Solving the TRPO objective function
- Proximal policy optimization
- The PPO algorithm
- Actor-critic using Kronecker-factored trust region

Trust region policy optimization

TRPO is one of the most popularly used algorithms in deep reinforcement learning. TRPO is a policy gradient algorithm and it acts as an improvement to the policy gradient with baseline method we learned in *Chapter 10, Policy Gradient Method*. We learned that policy gradient is an on-policy method, meaning that on every iteration, we improve the same policy with which we are generating trajectories. On every iteration, we update the parameter of our network and try to find the improved policy. The update rule for updating the parameter θ of our network is given as follows:

$$\theta = \theta + \alpha \nabla_\theta J(\theta)$$

Where $\nabla_\theta J(\theta)$ is the gradient and α is known as the step size or learning rate. If the step size is large then there will be a large policy update, and if it is small then there will be a small update in the policy. How can we find an optimal step size? In the policy gradient method, we keep the step size small and so on every iteration there will be a small improvement in the policy.

But what happens if we take a large step on every iteration? Let's suppose we have a policy π parameterized by θ. So, on every iteration, updating θ implies that we are improving our policy. If the step size is large, then the policy on every iteration varies greatly, meaning the old policy (the policy used in the previous iteration) and the new policy (the policy used in the current iteration) vary greatly. Since we are using a parametrized policy, it implies that if we make a large update (large step size) then the parameter of the old policy and the new policy vary heavily, and this leads to a problem called model collapse.

This is the reason that in the policy gradient method, instead of taking larger steps and updating the parameter of our network, we take small steps and update the parameter to keep the old policy and new policy close. But how can we improve this?

Can we take a larger step along with keeping the old and new policies close so that it won't affect our model performance and also helps us to learn quickly? Yes, this problem is solved by TRPO.

TRPO tries to make a large policy update while imposing a constraint that the old policy and the new policy should not vary too much. Okay, what is this constraint? But first, how can we measure and understand if the old policy and new policy are changing greatly? Here is where we use a measure called the **Kullback-Leibler (KL)** divergence. The KL divergence is ubiquitous in reinforcement learning. It tells us how two probability distributions are different from each other. So, we can use the KL divergence to understand if our old policy and new policy vary greatly or not. TRPO adds a constraint that the KL divergence between the old policy and the new policy should be less than or equal to some constant δ. That is, when we make a policy update, the old policy and the new policy should not vary more than some constant. This constraint is called the trust region constraint.

Thus, TRPO tries to make a large policy update while imposing the constraint that the parameter of the old policy and the new policy should be within the trust region. Note that in the policy gradient method, we use a parameterized policy. Thus, keeping the parameter of the old policy and the new policy within the trust region implies that the old and new policies are within the trust region.

TRPO guarantees monotonic policy improvement; that is, it guarantees that there will always be a policy improvement on every iteration. This is the fundamental idea behind the TRPO algorithm.

To understand how exactly TRPO works, we should understand the math behind TRPO. TRPO has pretty heavy math. But worry not! It will be simple if we understand the fundamental math concepts required to understand TRPO. So, before diving into the TRPO algorithm, first, we will understand several essential math concepts that are required to understand TRPO. Then we will learn how to design a TRPO objective function with the trust region constraint, and finally, we will see how to solve the TRPO objective function.

Math essentials

Before understanding how TRPO works, first, we will understand the following important math concepts:

- The Taylor series
- The trust region method
- The conjugate gradient method

- Lagrange multipliers
- Importance sampling

The Taylor series

The Taylor series is a series of infinite terms and it is used for approximating a function. Let's say we have a function $f(x)$ centered at $x = a$; we can approximate it using an infinite sum of polynomial terms as shown here:

$$f(x) = f(a) + \frac{f'(a)}{1!}(x - a) + \frac{f''(a)}{2!}(x - a)^2 + \frac{f'''(a)}{3!}(x - a)^3 + \cdots$$

The preceding equation can be represented in sigma notation as:

$$f(x) = \sum_{n=0}^{\infty} \frac{f^{(n)}(a)}{n!}(x - a)^n$$

So for each term in the Taylor series, we calculate the nth order derivative, divide them by $n!$, and multiply by $(x - a)^n$.

Let's understand how exactly the Taylor series approximates a function with an example. Let's say we have an exponential function e^x as shown in *Figure 13.1*:

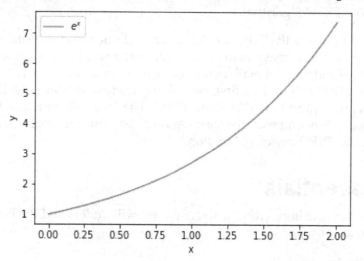

Figure 13.1: Exponential function

Can we approximate the exponential function e^x using the Taylor series? We know that the Taylor series is given as:

$$f(x) = f(a) + \frac{f'(a)}{1!}(x-a) + \frac{f''(a)}{2!}(x-a)^2 + \frac{f'''(a)}{3!}(x-a)^3 + \cdots \qquad (1)$$

Here, the function $f(x)$ we want to approximate is e^x, that is:

$$f(x) = e^x$$

Say our function $f(x) = e^x$ is centered at $x = a$, first, let's calculate the derivatives of the function up to 3 orders. The derivative of the exponential function is the function itself, so we can write:

$$f'(a) = e^a$$
$$f''(a) = e^a$$
$$f'''(a) = e^a$$

Substituting the preceding terms in the equation (1), we can write:

$$e^x = e^a + \frac{e^a}{1!}(x-a) + \frac{e^a}{2!}(x-a)^2 + \frac{e^a}{3!}(x-a)^3 + \cdots$$

Let's suppose $a = 0$; then our equation becomes:

$$e^x = e^0 + \frac{e^0}{1!}(x-0) + \frac{e^0}{2!}(x-0)^2 + \frac{e^0}{3!}(x-0)^3 + \cdots$$

We know that $e^0 = 1$; thus, the Taylor series of the exponential function is given as:

$$e^x = 1 + x + \frac{x^2}{2!} + \frac{x^3}{3!} + \cdots \qquad (2)$$

It implies that the sum of the terms on the right-hand side approximates the exponential function e^x. Let's understand this with the help of a plot. Let's take only the terms till the 0th order derivative from the Taylor series (equation 2), that is, $e^x = 1$, and plot them:

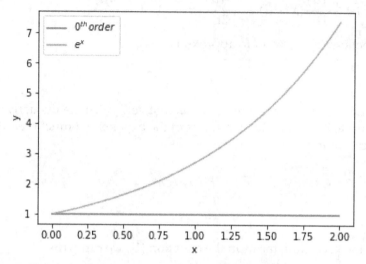

Figure 13.2: Taylor series approximation till the 0th order derivative

As we can observe from the preceding plot, just taking the 0th order derivative, we are far away from the actual function e^x. That is, our approximation is not good. So, let's take the sum of terms till the 1st order derivative from the Taylor series (equation 2), that is, $e^x = 1 + x$, and plot them:

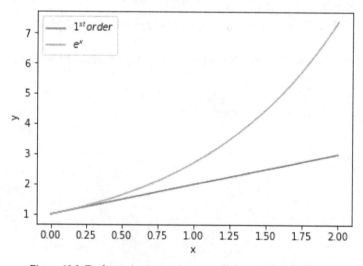

Figure 13.3: Taylor series approximation till the 1st order derivative

As we can observe from the preceding plot, including the terms till the 1st order derivative from the Taylor series gets us closer to the actual function e^x. So, let's take the sum of terms till the 2nd order derivative from the Taylor series (equation 2), that is, $e^x = 1 + x + \dfrac{x^2}{2!}$, and plot them. As we can observe from the following plot our approximation gets better and we reach closer to the actual function e^x:

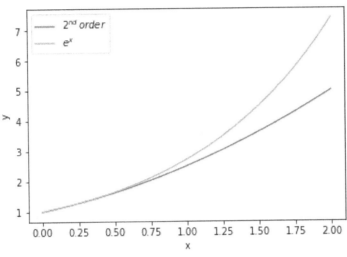

Figure 13.4: Taylor series approximation till the 2nd order derivative

Now, let's take the sum of terms till the 3rd order derivative from the Taylor series, that is, $e^x = 1 + x + \dfrac{x^2}{2!} + \dfrac{x^3}{3!}$, and plot them:

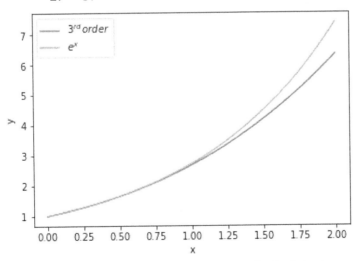

Figure 13.5: Taylor series approximation till the 3rd order derivative

By looking at the preceding graph, we can understand that our approximation is far better after including the sum of terms till the 3rd order derivative. As you might have guessed, adding more and more terms in the Taylor series makes our approximation of e^x better. Thus, using the Taylor series, we can approximate any function.

The Taylor polynomial till the first degree is called **linear approximation.** In linear approximation, we calculate the Taylor series only till the first-order derivative. Thus, the linear approximation (first-order) of the function $f(x)$ around the point a can be given as:

$$f(x) = f(a) + \frac{f'(a)}{1!}(x - a)$$

We can denote our first-order derivative by $\nabla f(a)$, so we can just replace $f'(a)$ by $\nabla f(a)$ and rewrite the preceding equation as:

$$f(x) = f(a) + \nabla f(a)(x - a)$$

The Taylor polynomial till the second degree is called **quadratic approximation**. In quadratic approximation, we calculate the Taylor series only till the second-order derivative. Thus, the quadratic approximation (second-order) of the function $f(x)$ around the point a can be given as:

$$f(x) = f(a) + \frac{f'(a)}{1!}(x - a) + \frac{f''(a)}{2!}(x - a)^2$$

We can denote our first-order derivative by $\nabla f(a)$ and second-order derivative by $\nabla^2 f(a)$; so, we can just replace $f'(a)$ with $\nabla f(a)$ and $f''(a)$ with $\nabla^2 f(a)$ and rewrite the preceding equation as:

$$f(x) = f(a) + \nabla f(a)(x - a) + \frac{1}{2!}(x - a)^T \nabla^2 f(a)(x - a)$$

A Hessian is a second-order derivative, so we can denote $\nabla^2 f(a)$ by $H(a)$ and rewrite the preceding equation as:

$$f(x) = f(a) + \nabla f(a)(x - a) + \frac{1}{2!}(x - a)^T H(a)(x - a)$$

Thus, to summarize, a **linear approximation** of the function $f(x)$ is given as:

$$f(x) = f(a) + \nabla f(a)(x - a)$$

The **quadratic approximation** of the function $f(x)$ is given as:

$$f(x) = f(a) + \nabla f(a)(x - a) + \frac{1}{2!}(x - a)^T H(a)(x - a)$$

The trust region method

Let's say we have a function $f(x)$ and we need to find the minimum of the function. Let's suppose it is difficult to find the minimum of the function $f(x)$. So, what we can do is that we can use the Taylor series and approximate the given function $f(x)$ and try to find the minimum value using the approximated function. Let's represent the approximated function with $\tilde{f}(x)$.

Say we use the quadratic approximation, we learned that with the quadratic approximation, we calculate the Taylor series only till the second-order derivative. Thus, the quadratic approximation (second-order) of the given function $f(x)$ around the region a can be given as:

$$\tilde{f}(x) = f(a) + \nabla f(a)(x - a) + \frac{1}{2!}(x - a)^T H(a)(x - a)$$

So, we can just use the approximated function $\tilde{f}(x)$ and compute the minimum value. But wait! What if our approximated function $\tilde{f}(x)$ is inaccurate at a particular point, say a^*, and if a^* is optimal, then we miss out on finding the optimal value.

So, we will introduce a new constraint called the trust region constraint. The trust region implies the region where our actual function $f(x)$ and approximated function $\tilde{f}(x)$ are close together. So, we can say that our approximation will be accurate if our approximated function $\tilde{f}(x)$ is in the trust region.

For instance, as shown in *Figure 13.6*, our approximated function $\tilde{f}(x)$ is in the trust region and thus our approximation will be accurate since the approximated function $\tilde{f}(x)$ is closer to the actual function $f(x)$:

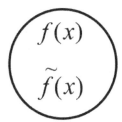

Figure 13.6: Approximated function is in the trust region

But when $\tilde{f}(x)$ is not in the trust region, then our approximation will not be accurate since the approximated function $\tilde{f}(x)$ is far from the actual function $f(x)$:

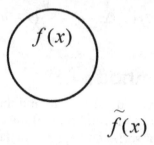

$$\tilde{f}(x)$$

Figure 13.7: Approximated function is not in the trust region

Thus, we need to make sure that our approximated function stays in the trust region so that it will be close to the actual function.

The conjugate gradient method

The conjugate gradient method is an iterative method used to solve a system of linear equations. It is also used to solve the optimization problem. The conjugate gradient method is used when a system is of the form:

$$Ax = b$$

Where A is the positive definite, square, and symmetric matrix, x is the vector we want to find, and b is the known vector. Let's consider the following quadratic function:

$$f(x) = \frac{1}{2}x^T Ax - b^T x + c$$

When A is the positive semi-definite matrix; finding the minimum of this function is equal to solving the system $Ax = b$. Just like gradient descent, conjugate gradient descent also tries to find the minimum of the function; however, the search direction of conjugate gradient descent will be different from gradient descent, and conjugate gradient descent attains convergence in N iterations. Let's understand how conjugate gradient descent differs from gradient descent with the help of a contour plot.

First, let's look at the contour plot of gradient descent. As we can see in the following plot, in order to find the minimum value of a function, gradient descent takes several search directions and we get a zigzag pattern of directions:

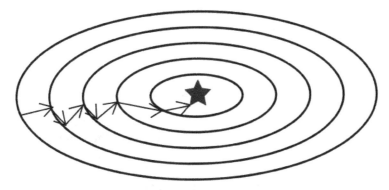

Figure 13.8: Contour plot of gradient descent

Unlike the gradient descent method, in the conjugate gradient descent, the search direction is orthogonal to the previous search direction as shown in *Figure 13.9*:

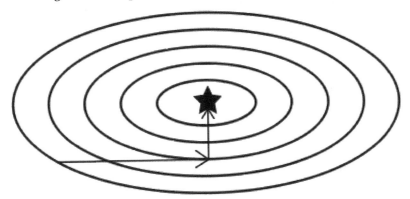

Figure 13.9: Contour plot of conjugate gradient descent

So, using conjugate gradient descent, we can solve a system of the form $Ax = b$.

Lagrange multipliers

Let's say we have a function $f(x) = x^2$: how do we find the minimum of the function? We can find the minimum of the function by finding a point where the gradient of the function is zero. The gradient of the function $f(x) = x^2$ is given as:

$$\nabla f(x) = 2x$$

When $x = 0$, the gradient of the function is zero; that is, $\nabla f(x) = 0$ when $x = 0$. So, we can say that the minimum of the function $f(x) = x^2$ is at $x = 0$. The problem we just saw is called the unconstrained optimization problem.

Consider a case where we have a constraint—say we need to minimize the function $f(x)$ subject to the constraint that $g(x) = 1$, as shown here:

$$\underset{x}{\text{minimize}} \qquad f(x) = 2x^2 + 1$$
$$\text{subject to} \qquad g(x) = 1$$

Now, how can we solve this problem? That is, how can we find the minimum of the function $f(x)$ while satisfying the constraint $g(x)$? We can find the minimum value when the gradient of the objective function $f(x)$ and the gradient of the constraint $g(x)$ point in the same direction. That is, we can find the minimum value when the gradient of $f(x)$ and the gradient of $g(x)$ are parallel or antiparallel to each other:

$$\nabla f(x) = \nabla g(x)$$

Although the gradients of $f(x)$ and $g(x)$ point in the same direction, their magnitude will not be the same. So, we will just multiply the gradient of $g(x)$ by a variable called λ as shown here:

$$\nabla f(x) = \lambda \nabla g(x)$$

Where λ is known as the Lagrange multiplier. So, we can rewrite the preceding equation as:

$$\nabla f(x) - \lambda \nabla g(x) = 0$$

Solving the preceding equation implies that we find the minimum of the function $f(x)$ along with satisfying the constraint $g(x)$. So, we can rewrite our objective function as:

$$L(x, \lambda) = f(x) - \lambda g(x)$$

The gradient of the preceding function is given as:

$$\nabla L(x, \lambda) = \nabla f(x) - \lambda \nabla g(x)$$

We can find the minimum value when $\nabla L(x, \lambda) = 0$. Lagrange multipliers are widely used for solving constrained optimization problems.

Let's understand this with one more example. Say we want to find the minimum of the function $3x^2 + 2y^2$ subject to the constraint $x^2 + y^2 \leq 3$, as the following shows:

$$\underset{x,y}{\text{minimize}} \qquad 3x^2 + 2y^2$$
$$\text{subject to} \qquad x^2 + y^2 \leq 3$$

We can rewrite our objective function with the constraint multiplied by the Lagrange multiplier as:

$$L(x, y, \lambda) = 3x^2 + 2y^2 - \lambda(x^2 + y^2 - 3)$$

Solving for $\nabla L(x, y, \lambda) = 0$, we can find the minimum of the function $3x^2 + 2y^2$ along with satisfying the constraint that $x^2 + y^2 \leq 3$.

Importance sampling

Let's recap the importance sampling method we learned in *Chapter 4, Monte Carlo Methods*. Say we want to compute the expectation of a function $f(x)$ where the value of x is sampled from the distribution $p(x)$, that is, $x \sim p(x)$; we can write:

$$\mathbb{E}_{x \sim p(x)}[f(x)] = \int_x p(x)f(x)dx$$

Can we approximate the expectation of a function $f(x)$? We learned that using the Monte Carlo method, we can approximate the expectation as:

$$\mathbb{E}_{x \sim p(x)}[f(x)] \approx \frac{1}{N} \sum_i f(x_i)$$

That is, using the Monte Carlo method, we sample x from the distribution $p(x)$ for N times and compute the average of $f(x)$ to approximate the expectation.

Instead of using the Monte Carlo method, we can also use importance sampling to approximate the expectation. In the importance sampling method, we estimate the expectation using a different distribution $q(x)$; that is, instead of sampling x from $p(x)$ we use a different distribution $q(x)$:

$$\mathbb{E}[f(x)] \approx \int_x f(x) \frac{p(x)}{q(x)} q(x)dx$$

$$\mathbb{E}[f(x)] \approx \frac{1}{N} \sum_i f(x_i) \frac{p(x_i)}{q(x_i)}$$

The ratio $\frac{p(x)}{q(x)}$ is called the importance sampling ratio or the importance correction.

Now that we have understood the several important math prerequisites, we will learn how the TRPO algorithm works in the next section.

Designing the TRPO objective function

At the beginning of the chapter, we learned that TRPO tries to make a large policy update while imposing the constraint that the parameter of the old policy and the new policy should stay within the trust region. In this section, we will learn how to design the TRPO objective function along with the trust region constraint so that the old policy and the new policy will not vary very much.

This section will be pretty dense and optional. If you are not interested in math you can directly navigate to the section *Solving the TRPO objective function*, where we learn how to solve the TRPO objective function step by step.

Let us say we have a policy π; we can express the expected discounted return η following the policy π as follows:

$$\eta(\pi) = \mathbb{E}_{\tau \sim \pi}\left[\sum_{t=0}^{\infty} \gamma^t r_t\right] \tag{1}$$

We know that in the policy gradient method, on every iteration, we keep on improving the policy π. Say we updated our old policy π and have a new policy $\tilde{\pi}$; then, we can express the expected discounted return η, following the new policy $\tilde{\pi}$ in terms of advantage over the old policy π, as follows:

$$\eta(\tilde{\pi}) = \eta(\pi) + \mathbb{E}_{\tau \sim \tilde{\pi}}\left[\sum_{t=0}^{\infty} \gamma^t A_\pi(s_t, a_t)\right] \tag{2}$$

As we can notice from the preceding equation, the expected return following the new policy $\tilde{\pi}$, that is, $\eta(\tilde{\pi})$, is just the sum of the expected return following the old policy π, that is, $\eta(\pi)$, and the expected discounted advantage of the old policy A_π. That is:

$$\eta(\tilde{\pi}) = \underbrace{\eta(\pi)}_{\substack{\text{Expected return of} \\ \text{old policy}}} + \underbrace{E_{T \sim \tilde{\pi}}\left[\sum_{t=0}^{\infty} \gamma^t A_\pi(s_t, a_t)\right]}_{\substack{\text{Expected discounted} \\ \text{advantage of old policy}}}$$

But, why are we using the advantage of the old policy? Because we are measuring how good the new policy $\tilde{\pi}$ is with respect to the average performance of the old policy π.

We can simplify the equation (2) and replace the sum over time steps with the sum over states and actions as shown here:

$$\eta(\tilde{\pi}) = \eta(\pi) + \sum_s \rho_{\tilde{\pi}}(s) \sum_a \tilde{\pi}(a|s) A_\pi(s,a) \qquad (3)$$

Where $\rho_{\tilde{\pi}}(s)$ is the discounted visitation frequency of the new policy. We already learned that the expected return of the new policy $\eta(\tilde{\pi})$ is obtained by adding the expected return of the old policy $\eta(\pi)$ and the advantage of the old policy A_π.

In the preceding equation (3), if the advantage $A_\pi(s,a)$ is always positive, then it means that our policy is improving and we have better $\eta(\tilde{\pi})$. That is, if the advantage $A_\pi(s,a)$ is always ≥ 0, then we will always have an improvement in our policy.

However, equation (3) is difficult to optimize, so we approximate $\eta(\tilde{\pi})$ by a local approximate $L_\pi(\tilde{\pi})$:

$$L_\pi(\tilde{\pi}) = \eta(\pi) + \sum_s \rho_\pi(s) \sum_a \tilde{\pi}(a|s) A_\pi(s,a) \qquad (4)$$

As you may notice, unlike equation (3), in equation (4) we use $\rho_\pi(s)$ instead of $\rho_{\tilde{\pi}}(s)$. That is, we use a discounted visitation frequency of the old policy $\rho_\pi(s)$ instead of the new policy $\rho_{\tilde{\pi}}(s)$. But why do we have to do that? Because we already have trajectories sampled from the old policy, so it is easier to obtain $\rho_\pi(s)$ than $\rho_{\tilde{\pi}}(s)$.

A surrogate function is a function that is an approximate of the objective function; so, we can call $L_\pi(\tilde{\pi})$ a surrogate function since it is the local approximate of our objective function $\eta(\tilde{\pi})$.

Thus, $L_\pi(\tilde{\pi})$ is the local approximate of our objective $\eta(\tilde{\pi})$. We need to make sure that our local approximate is accurate. Remember how, in the *The trust region method* section, we learned that the local approximation of the function will be accurate if it is in the trust region? So, our local approximate $L_\pi(\tilde{\pi})$ will be accurate if it is in the trust region. Thus, while updating the values of $L_\pi(\tilde{\pi})$, we need to make sure that it remains in the trust region; that is, the policy updates should remain in the trust region.

So, when we update the old policy π to a new policy $\tilde{\pi}$, we just need to ensure that the new policy update stays within the trust region. In order to do that, we have to measure how far our new policy is from the old policy, so, we use the KL divergence to measure this:

$$D_{KL}\big(\pi(\cdot|s)\|\tilde{\pi}(\cdot|s)\big)$$

Therefore, while updating the policy, we check the KL divergence between the policy updates and make sure that our policy updates are within the trust region. To satisfy this KL constraint, Kakade and Langford introduced a new policy updating scheme called conservative policy iteration and derived the following lower bound:

$$\eta(\tilde{\pi}) \geq L_\pi(\tilde{\pi}) - CD_{KL}^{\max}(\pi, \tilde{\pi})$$

$$\text{Where, } C = \frac{4\epsilon\gamma}{(1-\gamma)^2}$$

As we can observe, in the preceding equation, we have the KL divergence as the penalty term and C is the penalty coefficient.

Now, our surrogate objective function (4) along with the penalized KL term is written as:

$$\text{maximize}_{\tilde{\pi}}[L_\pi(\tilde{\pi}) - CD_{KL}^{\max}(\pi, \tilde{\pi})] \tag{5}$$

Maximizing the surrogate function $L(\tilde{\pi}) - CD_{KL}^{\max}(\pi, \tilde{\pi})$ improves our true objective function $\eta(\tilde{\pi})$ and guarantees a monotonic improvement in the policy. The preceding objective function is known as **KL penalized objective.**

Parameterizing the policies

We learned that maximizing the surrogate objective function maximizes our true objective function. We know that in the policy gradient method, we use a parameterized policy; that is, we use a function approximator like a neural network parameterized by some parameter θ and learn the optimal policy.

We parameterize the old policy with θ as $\pi_{\theta_{old}}$ and the new policy with θ as π_θ. So, we can rewrite our equation (5) in terms of parameterized policies as shown here:

$$\text{maximize}_{\theta}\left[L(\pi_\theta) - CD_{KL}^{\max}\left(\pi_{\theta_{old}}, \pi_\theta\right)\right] \tag{6}$$

As shown in the preceding equation, we are using the max KL divergence between the old and new policies, that is, $D_{KL}^{\max}\left(\pi_{\theta_{old}}, \pi_\theta\right)$. It is difficult to optimize our objective with the max KL term, so instead of using max KL, we can take the average KL divergence $\bar{D}_{KL}\left(\pi_{\theta_{old}}, \pi_\theta\right)$ and rewrite our surrogate objective as:

$$\text{maximize}_{\theta}\left[L(\pi_\theta) - C\bar{D}_{KL}\left(\pi_{\theta_{old}}, \pi_\theta\right)\right] \tag{7}$$

The issue with the preceding objective function is that when we substitute the value of the penalty coefficient C as $C = \dfrac{4\epsilon\gamma}{(1-\gamma)^2}$, it reduces the step size, and it takes us a lot of time to attain convergence.

So, we can redefine our surrogate objective function as a constrained objective function as:

$$\underset{\theta}{\text{maximize}} \; L(\pi_\theta)$$
$$\text{subject to } \bar{D}_{KL}\left(\pi_{\theta_{old}}, \pi_\theta\right) \leq \delta \tag{8}$$

The preceding equation implies that we maximize our surrogate objective function $L(\pi_\theta)$ while maintaining the constraint that the KL divergence between the old policy $\pi_{\theta_{old}}$ and new policy π_θ is less than or equal to a constant δ, and it ensures that our old policy and the new policy will not vary very much. The preceding objective function is called the **KL-constrained objective.**

Sample-based estimation

In the previous section, we learned how to frame our objective function as a KL-constrained objective with parameterized policies. In this section, we will learn how to simplify our objective function.

We learned that our KL constrained objective function is given as:

$$\underset{\theta}{\text{maximize}} \; L(\pi_\theta)$$
$$\text{subject to } \bar{D}_{KL}\left(\pi_{\theta_{old}}, \pi_\theta\right) \leq \delta$$

From equation (4), substituting the value of $L(\pi_\theta)$ with

$$\sum_s \rho_{\pi_{\theta_{old}}}(s) \sum_a \pi_\theta(a|s) A_{\pi_{\theta_{old}}}(s, a)$$ in the preceding equation, we can write:

$$\underset{\theta}{\text{maximize}} \; \sum_s \rho_{\pi_{\theta_{old}}}(s) \sum_a \pi_\theta(a|s) A_{\pi_{\theta_{old}}}(s, a)$$
$$\text{subject to } \bar{D}_{KL}\left(\pi_{\theta_{old}}, \pi_\theta\right) \leq \delta \tag{9}$$

Now we will see how we can simplify equation (9) by getting rid of the two summations using sampling.

The first sum $\sum_s \rho_{\pi_{\theta_{old}}}(s)$ expresses the summation over state visitation frequency; we can replace it by sampling states from state visitation as $\mathbb{E}_{s \sim \rho}(\pi_{\theta_{old}})$. Then, our equation becomes:

$$\mathbb{E}_{s \sim \rho(\pi_{\theta_{old}})} \left[\sum_a \pi_\theta(a|s) A_{\pi_{\theta_{old}}}(s, a) \right]$$

Next, we replace the sum over actions $\sum_a \pi_\theta(a|s)$ with an importance sampling estimator. Let q be the sampling distribution, and a is sampled from q, that is, $a \sim q$. Then, we can rewrite our preceding equation as:

$$\mathbb{E}_{s \sim \rho\left(\pi_{\theta_{old}}\right), a \sim q} \left[\frac{\pi_\theta(a|s)}{q(a|s)} A_{\pi_{\theta_{old}}}(s, a) \right]$$

Replacing the sampling distribution q with $\pi_{\theta_{old}}$, we can write:

$$\mathbb{E}_{s \sim \rho\left(\pi_{\theta_{old}}\right), a \sim \pi_{\theta_{old}}} \left[\frac{\pi_\theta(a|s)}{\pi_{\theta_{old}}(a|s)} A_{\pi_{\theta_{old}}}(s, a) \right]$$

Thus, our equation (9) becomes:

$$\underset{\theta}{\text{maximize }} \mathbb{E}_{s,a \sim \pi_{\theta_{old}}} \left[\frac{\pi_\theta(a|s)}{\pi_{\theta_{old}}(a|s)} A_{\pi_{\theta_{old}}}(s, a) \right]$$
$$\text{subject to } \mathbb{E}_{s \sim \pi_{\theta_{old}}} \left[D_{KL}\left(\pi_{\theta_{old}}(\cdot|s) \| \pi_\theta(\cdot|s) \right) \right] \leq \delta$$

In the next section, we will learn how to solve the preceding objective function to find the optimal policy.

Solving the TRPO objective function

In the previous section, we learned that the TRPO objective function is expressed as:

$$\underset{\theta}{\text{maximize }} \mathbb{E}_{s,a \sim \pi_{\theta_{old}}} \left[\frac{\pi_\theta(a|s)}{\pi_{\theta_{old}}(a|s)} A_{\pi_{\theta_{old}}}(s, a) \right]$$
$$\text{subject to } \mathbb{E}_{s \sim \pi_{\theta_{old}}} \left[D_{KL}\left(\pi_{\theta_{old}}(\cdot|s) \| \pi_\theta(\cdot|s) \right) \right] \leq \delta$$

The preceding equation implies that we try to find the policy that gives the maximum return along with the constraint that the KL divergence between the old and new policies should be less than or equal to δ. This KL constraint makes sure that our new policy is not too far away from the old policy.

For notation brevity, let us represent our objective with $L(\theta)$ and the KL constraint with $D(\theta)$ and rewrite the preceding equation as:

$$\underset{\theta}{\text{maximize }} L(\theta) \qquad\qquad (10)$$
$$\text{subject to } D(\theta) \leq \delta$$

By maximizing our objective function $L(\theta)$, we can find the optimal policy. We can maximize the objective $L(\theta)$ by calculating gradients with respect to θ and update the parameter using gradient ascent as:

$$\theta = \theta + \alpha\Delta\theta$$

Where $\Delta\theta$ is the search direction (gradient) and α is the backtracking coefficient.

That is, to update the parameter θ, we perform the two following steps:

- First, we compute the search direction $\Delta\theta$ using the Taylor series approximation
- Next, we perform the line search in the computed search direction $\Delta\theta$ by finding the value of α using the backtracking line search method

We will learn what the backtracking coefficient is and how exactly the backtracking line search method works in the *Performing a line search in the search direction* section. Okay, but why do we have to perform these two steps? If you look at our objective function (10), we have a constrained optimization problem. Our constraint here is that while updating the parameter θ, we need to make sure that our parameter updates are within the trust region; that is, the KL divergence between the old and new parameters should be less than or equal to δ.

Thus, performing these two steps and updating our parameter helps us satisfy the KL constraint and also guarantees monotonic improvement. Let's get into details and learn how exactly the two steps work.

Computing the search direction

It is difficult to optimize our objective function (10) directly, so first, we approximate our function using the Taylor series. We approximate the surrogate objective function $L(\theta)$ using linear approximation and we approximate our constraint $D(\theta)$ using quadratic approximation.

To better understand the upcoming steps, recap *The Taylor series* from the *Math essentials* section.

The **linear approximation** of our objective function at a point θ_k is given as:

$$L(\theta) = L(\theta_k) + \nabla_\theta L(\theta)(\theta - \theta_k)$$

We represent the gradient $\nabla_\theta L(\theta)$ with g, so the preceding equation becomes:

$$L(\theta) = L(\theta_k) + g^T(\theta - \theta_k)$$

While solving the preceding equation, the value of $L(\theta_k)$ becomes zero, so we can write:

$$L(\theta) = g^T(\theta - \theta_k) \tag{11}$$

The **quadratic approximation** of our constraint at point θ_k is given as:

$$D_{KL}(\theta_k\|\theta) = D_{KL}(\theta_k\|\theta_k) + \nabla_\theta D_{KL}(\theta_k\|\theta)(\theta - \theta_k) + \frac{1}{2}(\theta - \theta_k)^T H(\theta - \theta_k)$$

Where H is the second-order derivative, that is, $H = \nabla_\theta^2 D_{KL}(\theta_k, \theta)$. In the preceding equation, the first term $D_{KL}(\theta_k\|\theta_k)$ becomes zero as the KL divergence between two identical distributions is zero, and the first-order derivative $\nabla_\theta D_{KL}(\theta_k\|\theta)(\theta - \theta_k)$ becomes zero at $\theta = \theta_k$.

So, our final equation becomes:

$$D_{KL}(\theta_k\|\theta) = \frac{1}{2}(\theta - \theta_k)^T H(\theta - \theta_k) \tag{12}$$

Substituting (11) and (12) in the equation (10), we can write:

$$\max_\theta \; g^T(\theta - \theta_k)$$
$$\text{subject to } \frac{1}{2}(\theta - \theta_k)^T H(\theta - \theta_k) \leq \delta \tag{13}$$

Note that in the preceding equation, θ_k represents the parameter of the old policy and θ represents the parameter of the new policy.

As we can observe, in equation (13) we have a constrained optimization problem. How can we solve this? We can solve this using the Lagrange multiplier.

Thus, using the Lagrange multiplier λ, we can rewrite our objective function (13) as:

$$L(\theta,\lambda) = g^T(\theta - \theta_k) - \lambda\frac{1}{2}(\theta - \theta_k)^T H(\theta - \theta_k) - \delta \tag{14}$$

For notation brevity, let s represent $\theta - \theta_k$, so we can rewrite equation (14) as:

$$L = g^T s - \lambda\frac{1}{2}s^T H s - \delta \tag{15}$$

Our goal is to find the optimal parameter θ. So, we need to calculate the gradient of the preceding function and update our parameter using gradient ascent as follows:

$$\theta = \theta_k + \beta s \tag{16}$$

Where β is the learning rate and s is the gradient. Now we will look at how to determine the learning rate β and the gradient s.

First, we compute s. Calculating the derivative of the objective function L given in equation (15) with respect to gradient s, we can write:

$$\frac{dL}{ds} = g - \lambda H s = 0$$

Thus, we can write:

$$g = \lambda H s$$

λ is just our Lagrange multiplier and it will not affect our gradient, so we can write:

$$g = Hs \tag{17}$$

Thus, we can write:

$$s = H^{-1}g$$

However, computing the value of s directly in this way is not optimal. This is because in the preceding equation, we have H^{-1}, which implies the inverse of the second-order derivative. Computing the second-order derivative and its inverse is a expensive task. So, we need to find a better way to compute s; how we do that?

From (17), we learned that:

$$g = Hs$$

From the preceding equation, we can observe the equation is in the form of $Ax = B$. Thus, using conjugate gradient descent, we can approximate the value of s as:

$$s \approx H^{-1}g$$

Thus, our update equation becomes:

$$\theta = \theta_k + \beta s \qquad (18)$$

Where the value of $s \approx H^{-1}g$ is computed using conjugated gradient descent.

Now that we have calculated the gradient, we need to determine the learning rate β. We need to keep in mind that our update should be within the trust region, so while calculating the value of β, we need to maintain the KL constraint.

In equation (18), we learned that our update rule is:

$$\theta = \theta_k + \beta s$$

By rearranging the terms, we can write:

$$\theta - \theta_k = \beta s \qquad (19)$$

From equation (13), we can write our KL constraint as:

$$\frac{1}{2}(\theta - \theta_k)^T H(\theta - \theta_k) = \delta$$

Substituting (19) in the preceding equation, we can write:

$$\frac{1}{2}(\beta s)^T H(\beta s) = \delta$$

The preceding equation can be solved as:

$$\frac{1}{2}\beta^2 s^T Hs = \delta$$
$$\beta^2 s^T Hs = 2\delta$$

$$\beta^2 = \frac{2\delta}{s^T H s}$$

$$\beta = \sqrt{\frac{2\delta}{s^T H s}}$$

Thus, we can substitute the preceding value of the learning rate β in the equation (18) and rewrite our parameter update as:

$$\theta = \theta_k + \sqrt{\frac{2\delta}{s^T H s}} \, s$$

Where the value of $s \approx H^{-1}g$ is computed using conjugated gradient descent.

Thus, we have computed the search direction using the Taylor series approximation and the Lagrange multiplier:

$$\theta = \theta_k + \underbrace{\sqrt{\frac{2\delta}{s^T H s}} \, s}_{\text{search direction } (\Delta\theta)}$$

In the next section, let's learn how to perform a line search.

Performing a line search in the search direction

In order to make sure that our policy updates satisfy the KL constraint, we use a backtracking line search method. So, our update equation becomes:

$$\theta = \theta_k + \alpha^j \sqrt{\frac{2\delta}{s^T H s}} \, s$$

Okay, what does this mean? What's that new parameter α doing there? It is called the backtracking coefficient and the value of α ranges from 0 to 1. It helps us to take a large step to update our parameter. That is, we can set α to a high value and make a large update. However, we need to make sure that we are maximizing our objective $L(\theta) \geq 0$ along with satisfying our constraint $D(\theta) \leq \delta$.

So, we just try for different values of j from 0 to N and compute θ as

$$\theta = \theta_k + \alpha^j \sqrt{\frac{2\delta}{s^T H s}} \, s. \text{ If } L(\theta) \geq 0 \text{ and } D(\theta) \leq \delta \text{ for some values of } j, \text{ then we just}$$

stop and update our parameter as $\theta = \theta_k + \alpha^j \sqrt{\frac{2\delta}{s^T H s}} \, s$.

The following steps provide clarity on how the backtracking line search method works:

1. For iterations $j = 0, 1, 2, 3, \ldots, N$:

    1. Compute $\theta = \theta_k + \alpha^j \sqrt{\dfrac{2\delta}{s^T H s}} \, s$

    2. If $L(\theta) \geq 0$ and $D(\theta) \leq \delta$ then:

        1. Update $\theta = \theta_k + \alpha^j \sqrt{\dfrac{2\delta}{s^T H s}} \, s$

        2. Break

Thus, our final parameter update rule of TRPO is given as:

$$\theta = \theta_k + \alpha^j \sqrt{\frac{2\delta}{s^T H s}} \, s$$

In the next section, we will learn how exactly the TRPO algorithm works by using the preceding update rule.

Algorithm – TRPO

TRPO acts as an improvement to the policy gradient algorithm we learned in *Chapter 10, Policy Gradient Method*. It ensures that we can take large steps and update our parameter along with maintaining the constraint that our old policy and the new policy should not vary very much. The TRPO update rule is given as:

$$\theta = \theta_k + \alpha^j \sqrt{\frac{2\delta}{s^T H s}} \, s$$

Now, let's look at the algorithm of TRPO and see exactly how TRPO uses the preceding update rule and finds the optimal policy. Before going ahead, let's recap how we computed gradient in the policy gradient method. In the policy gradient method, we computed the gradient g as:

$$g = \frac{1}{N} \sum_{i=1}^{N} \left[\sum_{t=0}^{T-1} \nabla_\theta \log \pi_\theta \left(a_t | s_t \right) \left(R_t - V_\phi(s_t) \right) \right]$$

Where R_t is the reward-to-go. The reward-to-go is the sum of the rewards of the trajectory starting from a state s and action a; it is expressed as:

$$R_t = \sum_{t'=0}^{T-1} r(s_{t'}, a_{t'})$$

Isn't the reward-to-go similar to something we learned about earlier? Yes! If you recall, we learned that the Q function is the sum of rewards of the trajectory starting from the state s and action a. So, we can just replace the reward-to-go with the Q function and write our gradient as:

$$g = \frac{1}{N} \sum_{i=1}^{N} \left[\sum_{t=0}^{T-1} \nabla_\theta \log \pi_\theta \left(a_t | s_t \right) \left(Q(s_t, a_t) - V_\phi(s_t) \right) \right]$$

In the preceding equation, we have a difference between the Q function and the value function. We learned that the advantage function is the difference between the Q function and the value function and hence we can rewrite our gradient with the advantage function as:

$$g = \frac{1}{N} \sum_{i=1}^{N} \left[\sum_{t=0}^{T-1} \nabla_\theta \log \pi_\theta \left(a_t | s_t \right) A_t \right]$$

Now, let's look at the algorithm of TRPO. Remember that TRPO is the policy gradient method, so unlike actor-critic methods, here, first we generate N number of trajectories and then we update the parameter of the policy and value network.

The steps involved in the TRPO are given as follows:

1. Initialize the policy network parameter θ and value network parameter ϕ

2. Generate N number of trajectories $\{\tau^i\}_{i=1}^{N}$ following the policy π_θ

3. Compute the return (reward-to-go) R_t

4. Compute the advantage value A_t

5. Compute the policy gradients:

$$g = \frac{1}{N} \sum_{i=1}^{N} \left[\sum_{t=0}^{T-1} \nabla_\theta \log \pi_\theta (a_t | s_t) A_t \right]$$

6. Compute $s = H^{-1}g$ using the conjugate gradient method

7. Update the policy network parameter θ using the update rule:

$$\theta = \theta + \alpha^j \sqrt{\frac{2\delta}{s^T H s}} \, s$$

8. Compute the mean squared error of the value network:

$$J(\phi) = \frac{1}{N} \sum_{i=1}^{N} \sum_{t=0}^{T-1} \left(R_t - V_\phi(s_t) \right)^2$$

9. Update the value network parameter ϕ using gradient descent as
$\phi = \phi - \alpha \nabla_\phi J(\phi)$

10. Repeat steps 2 to 9 for several iterations

Now that we have understood how TRPO works, in the next section, we will learn another interesting algorithm called proximal policy optimization.

Proximal policy optimization

In the previous section, we learned how TRPO works. We learned that TRPO keeps the policy updates in the trust region by imposing a constraint that the KL divergence between the old and new policy should be less than or equal to δ. The problem with the TRPO method is that it is difficult to implement and is computationally expensive. So, now we will learn one of the most popular and state-of-the-art policy gradient algorithms called **Proximal Policy Optimization (PPO)**.

PPO improves upon the TRPO algorithm and is simple to implement. Similar to TRPO, PPO ensures that the policy updates are in the trust region. But unlike TRPO, PPO does not use any constraints in the objective function. Going forward, we will learn how exactly PPO works and how PPO ensures that the policy updates are in the trust region.

There are two different types of PPO algorithm:

- **PPO-clipped** – In the PPO-clipped method, in order to ensure that the policy updates are in the trust region (that the new policy is not far away from the old policy), PPO adds a new function called the clipping function, which ensures that the new and old policies are not far away from each other.
- **PPO-penalty** – In the PPO-penalty method, we modify our objective function by converting the KL constraint term to a penalty term and update the penalty coefficient adaptively during training by ensuring that the policy updates are in the trust region.

We will now look into the preceding two types of PPO algorithm in detail.

PPO with a clipped objective

First, let us recall the objective function of TRPO. We learned that the TRPO objective function is given as:

$$\underset{\theta}{\text{maximize}} \; \mathbb{E}_t \left[\frac{\pi_\theta(a_t|s_t)}{\pi_{\theta_{old}}(a_t|s_t)} A_t \right]$$
$$\text{subject to} \; \mathbb{E}_t \left[D_{KL} \big(\pi_{\theta_{old}}(\cdot|s_t) \| \pi_\theta(\cdot|s_t) \big) \right] \leq \delta$$

It implies that we try to maximize our policy along with the constraint that the old policy and the new policy stays within the trust region, that is, the KL divergence between the old policy and new policy should be less than or equal to δ.

Let us take only the objective without the constraint and write the PPO objective function as:

$$L(\theta) = \mathbb{E}_t \left[\frac{\pi_\theta(a_t|s_t)}{\pi_{\theta_{old}}(a_t|s_t)} A_t \right]$$

In the preceding equation, the term $\dfrac{\pi_\theta(a_t|s_t)}{\pi_{\theta_{old}}(a_t|s_t)}$ implies the probability ratio, that is,

the ratio of the new policy to the old policy. Let us denote this using $r_t(\theta)$ and write the PPO objective function as:

$$L(\theta) = \mathbb{E}_t \left[r_t(\theta) A_t \right] \tag{20}$$

If we update the policy using the preceding objective function then the policy updates will not be in the trust region. So, to ensure that our policy updates are in the trust region (that the new policy is not far from the old policy), we modify our objective function by adding a new function called the clipping function and rewrite our objective function as:

$$L(\theta) = \mathbb{E}_t[\min(r_t(\theta)A_t, \text{clip}(r_t(\theta), 1 - \epsilon, 1 + \epsilon)A_t)]$$

The preceding function implies that we take the minimum of two terms: one is $r_t(\theta) A_t$ and the other is $\text{clip}(r_t(\theta), 1 - \epsilon, 1 + \epsilon)A_t$.

We know that the first term $r_t(\theta) A_t$ is basically our objective, see equation (20), and the second term is called the clipped objective. Thus, our final objective function is just the minimum of the unclipped and clipped objectives. But what's the use of this? How does adding this clipped objective help us in keeping our new policy not far away from the old policy?

Let's understand this by taking a closer look:

$$L(\theta) = \mathbb{E}_t[\min(r_t(\theta)A_t, \text{clip}(r_t(\theta), 1 - \epsilon, 1 + \epsilon)A_t)]$$

We know that the first term (unclipped objective) is just given by equation (20). So, let's take a look into the second term, the clipped objective. It is given as:

$$\text{clip}(r_t(\theta), 1 - \epsilon, 1 + \epsilon)A_t$$

By looking at the preceding term, we can say that we are clipping the probability ratio $r_t(\theta)$ in the range of $[1 - \epsilon \text{ to } 1 + \epsilon]$. But why do we have to clip $r_t(\theta)$? This can be explained by considering two cases of the advantage function—when the advantage is positive and when it is negative.

Case 1: When the advantage is positive

When the advantage is positive, $A_t > 0$, then it means that the corresponding action should be preferred over the average of all other actions. So, we can increase the value of $r_t(\theta)$ for that action so that it will have a greater chance of being selected. However, while increasing the value of $r_t(\theta)$, we should not increase it too much that it goes far away from the old policy. So, to prevent this, we clip $r_t(\theta)$ at $1 + \epsilon$.

Figure 13.10 shows how we increase the value of $r_t(\theta)$ when the advantage is positive and how we clip it at $1 + \epsilon$:

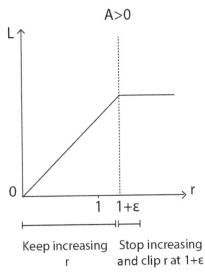

Figure 13.10: Value of $r_t(\theta)$ when the advantage is positive

Case 2: When the advantage is negative

When the advantage is negative, $A_t < 0$, then it means that the corresponding action should not be preferred over the average of all other actions. So, we can decrease the value of $r_t(\theta)$ for that action so that it will have a lower chance of being selected. However, while decreasing the value of $r_t(\theta)$, we should not decrease it too much that it goes far away from the old policy. So, in order to prevent that, we clip $r_t(\theta)$ at $1 - \epsilon$.

Figure 13.11 shows how we decrease the value of $r_t(\theta)$ when the advantage is negative and how we clip it at $1 - \epsilon$:

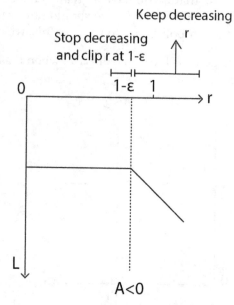

Figure 13.11: Value of $r_t(\theta)$ when the advantage is negative

The value of ϵ is usually set to 0.1 or 0.2. Thus, we learned that the clipped objective keeps our policy updates close to the old policy by clipping at $1 + \epsilon$ and $1 - \epsilon$ based on the advantage function. So, our final objective function takes the minimum value of the unclipped and clipped objectives as:

$$L(\theta) = \mathbb{E}_t[\min(r_t(\theta)A_t, \text{clip}(r_t(\theta), 1 - \epsilon, 1 + \epsilon)A_t)]$$

Now that we have learned how the PPO algorithm with a clipped objective works, let's look into the algorithm in the next section.

Algorithm – PPO-clipped

The steps involved in the PPO-clipped algorithm are given as follows:

1. Initialize the policy network parameter θ and value network parameter ϕ
2. Collect N number of trajectories $\{\tau^i\}_{i=1}^{N}$ following the policy π_θ
3. Compute the return (reward-to-go) R_t
4. Compute the gradient of the objective function $\nabla_\theta L(\theta)$

5. Update the policy network parameter θ using gradient ascent as
$$\theta = \theta + \alpha \nabla_\theta L(\theta)$$

6. Compute the mean squared error of the value network:

$$J(\phi) = \frac{1}{N} \sum_{i=1}^{N} \sum_{t=0}^{T-1} \left(R_t - V_\phi(s_t) \right)^2$$

7. Compute the gradient of the value network $\nabla_\phi J(\phi)$

8. Update the value network parameter ϕ using gradient descent as
$$\phi = \phi - \alpha \nabla_\phi J(\phi)$$

9. Repeat steps 2 to 8 for several iterations

Implementing the PPO-clipped method

Let's implement the PPO-clipped method for the swing-up pendulum task. The code used in this section is adapted from one of the very good PPO implementations (https://github.com/MorvanZhou/Reinforcement-learning-with-tensorflow/tree/master/contents/12_Proximal_Policy_Optimization) by Morvan.

First, let's import the necessary libraries:

```
import warnings
warnings.filterwarnings('ignore')
import tensorflow.compat.v1 as tf
tf.disable_v2_behavior()

import numpy as np
import matplotlib.pyplot as plt
import gym
```

Creating the Gym environment

Let's create a pendulum environment using Gym:

```
env = gym.make('Pendulum-v0').unwrapped
```

Get the state shape of the environment:

```
state_shape = env.observation_space.shape[0]
```

Get the action shape of the environment:

```
action_shape = env.action_space.shape[0]
```

Note that the pendulum is a continuous environment and thus our action space consists of continuous values. So, we get the bound of our action space:

```
action_bound = [env.action_space.low, env.action_space.high]
```

Set the epsilon value that is used in the clipped objective:

```
epsilon = 0.2
```

Defining the PPO class

Let's define a class called PPO where we will implement the PPO algorithm. For a clear understanding, let's take a look into the code line by line:

```
class PPO(object):
```

Defining the init method

First, let's define the init method:

```
    def __init__(self):
```

Start the TensorFlow session:

```
        self.sess = tf.Session()
```

Define the placeholder for the state:

```
        self.state_ph = tf.placeholder(tf.float32, [None, state_shape],
    'state')
```

Now, let's build the value network that returns the value of a state:

```
        with tf.variable_scope('value'):

            layer1 = tf.layers.dense(self.state_ph, 100, tf.nn.relu)
            self.v = tf.layers.dense(layer1, 1)
```

Define the placeholder for the Q value:

```
        self.Q = tf.placeholder(tf.float32, [None, 1],
  'discounted_r')
```

Define the advantage value as the difference between the Q value and the state value:

```
        self.advantage = self.Q - self.v
```

Compute the loss of the value network:

```
        self.value_loss = tf.reduce_mean(tf.square(self.advantage))
```

Train the value network by minimizing the loss using the Adam optimizer:

```
        self.train_value_nw = tf.train.AdamOptimizer(0.002).
  minimize(self.value_loss)
```

Now, we obtain the new policy and its parameter from the policy network:

```
        pi, pi_params = self.build_policy_network('pi', trainable=True)
```

Obtain the old policy and its parameter from the policy network:

```
        oldpi, oldpi_params = self.build_policy_network('oldpi',
  trainable=False)
```

Sample an action from the new policy:

```
        with tf.variable_scope('sample_action'):
            self.sample_op = tf.squeeze(pi.sample(1), axis=0)
```

Update the parameters of the old policy:

```
        with tf.variable_scope('update_oldpi'):
            self.update_oldpi_op = [oldp.assign(p) for p, oldp in
  zip(pi_params, oldpi_params)]
```

Define the placeholder for the action:

```
        self.action_ph = tf.placeholder(tf.float32, [None, action_
  shape], 'action')
```

Define the placeholder for the advantage:

```
        self.advantage_ph = tf.placeholder(tf.float32, [None, 1],
    'advantage')
```

Now, let's define our surrogate objective function of the policy network:

```
        with tf.variable_scope('loss'):
            with tf.variable_scope('surrogate'):
```

We learned that the objective of the policy network is:

$$L(\theta) = \mathbb{E}_t[\min(r_t(\theta)A_t, \text{clip}(r_t(\theta), 1 - \epsilon, 1 + \epsilon)A_t)]$$

First, let's define the ratio $r_t(\theta)$ as $\dfrac{\pi_\theta(a_t|s_t)}{\pi_{\theta_{old}}(a_t|s_t)}$:

```
            ratio = pi.prob(self.action_ph) / oldpi.prob(self.
    action_ph)
```

Define the objective by multiplying the ratio $r_t(\theta)$ and the advantage value A_t:

```
            objective = ratio * self.advantage_ph
```

Define the objective function with the clipped and unclipped objectives:

```
            L = tf.reduce_mean(tf.minimum(objective, tf.clip_by_
    value(ratio, 1.-epsilon, 1.+ epsilon)*self.advantage_ph))
```

Now, we can compute the gradient and maximize the objective function using gradient ascent. However, instead of doing that, we can convert the preceding maximization objective into the minimization objective by just adding a negative sign. So, we can denote the loss of the policy network as:

```
        self.policy_loss = -L
```

Train the policy network by minimizing the loss using the Adam optimizer:

```
        with tf.variable_scope('train_policy'):
            self.train_policy_nw = tf.train.AdamOptimizer(0.001).
    minimize(self.policy_loss)
```

Initialize all the TensorFlow variables:

```
        self.sess.run(tf.global_variables_initializer())
```

Defining the train function

Now, let's define the train function:

```
def train(self, state, action, reward):
```

Update the old policy:

```
self.sess.run(self.update_oldpi_op)
```

Compute the advantage value:

```
adv = self.sess.run(self.advantage, {self.state_ph: state,
self.Q: reward})
```

Train the policy network:

```
[self.sess.run(self.train_policy_nw, {self.state_ph: state,
self.action_ph: action, self.advantage_ph: adv}) for _ in range(10)]
```

Train the value network:

```
[self.sess.run(self.train_value_nw, {self.state_ph: state,
self.Q: reward}) for _ in range(10)]
```

Building the policy network

We define a function called build_policy_network for building the policy network. Note that our action space is continuous here, so our policy network returns the mean and variance of the action as an output and then we generate a normal distribution using this mean and variance and select an action by sampling from this normal distribution:

```
def build_policy_network(self, name, trainable):
    with tf.variable_scope(name):
```

Define the layer of the network:

```
layer = tf.layers.dense(self.state_ph, 100, tf.nn.relu,
trainable=trainable)
```

Compute the mean:

```
mu = 2 * tf.layers.dense(layer, action_shape, tf.nn.tanh,
trainable=trainable)
```

Compute the standard deviation:

```
sigma = tf.layers.dense(layer, action_shape, tf.nn.
softplus, trainable=trainable)
```

Compute the normal distribution:

```
norm_dist = tf.distributions.Normal(loc=mu, scale=sigma)
```

Get the parameters of the policy network:

```
params = tf.get_collection(tf.GraphKeys.GLOBAL_VARIABLES,
scope=name)
return norm_dist, params
```

Selecting the action

Let's define a function called `select_action` for selecting the action:

```
def select_action(self, state):
    state = state[np.newaxis, :]
```

Sample an action from the normal distribution generated by the policy network:

```
action = self.sess.run(self.sample_op, {self.state_ph: state})
[0]
```

We clip the action so that it lies within the action bounds and then we return the action:

```
action = np.clip(action, action_bound[0], action_bound[1])
return action
```

Computing the state value

We define a function called `get_state_value` to obtain the value of the state computed by the value network:

```
def get_state_value(self, state):

    if state.ndim < 2: state = state[np.newaxis, :]

    return self.sess.run(self.v, {self.state_ph: state})[0, 0]
```

Training the network

Now, let's start training the network. First, let's create an object for our PPO class:

```
ppo = PPO()
```

Set the number of episodes:

```
num_episodes = 1000
```

Set the number of time steps in each episode:

```
num_timesteps = 200
```

Set the discount factor, γ:

```
gamma = 0.9
```

Set the batch size:

```
batch_size = 32
```

For each episode:

```
for i in range(num_episodes):
```

Initialize the state by resetting the environment:

```
state = env.reset()
```

Initialize the lists for holding the states, actions, and rewards obtained in the episode:

```
episode_states, episode_actions, episode_rewards = [], [], []
```

Initialize the return:

```
Return = 0
```

For every step:

```
for t in range(num_timesteps):
```

Render the environment:

```
env.render()
```

Select the action:

```
action = ppo.select_action(state)
```

Perform the selected action:

```
next_state, reward, done, _ = env.step(action)
```

Store the state, action, and reward in the list:

```
episode_states.append(state)
episode_actions.append(action)
episode_rewards.append((reward+8)/8)
```

Update the state to the next state:

```
state = next_state
```

Update the return:

```
Return += reward
```

If we reached the batch size or if we reached the final step of the episode:

```
if (t+1) % batch_size == 0 or t == num_timesteps-1:
```

Compute the value of the next state:

```
v_s_ = ppo.get_state_value(next_state)
```

Compute the Q value as $r + \gamma V(s')$:

```
discounted_r = []
for reward in episode_rewards[::-1]:
    v_s_ = reward + gamma * v_s_
    discounted_r.append(v_s_)
discounted_r.reverse()
```

Stack the episodic states, actions, and rewards:

```
es, ea, er = np.vstack(episode_states), np.vstack(episode_
actions), np.array(discounted_r)[:, np.newaxis]
```

Train the network:

```
ppo.train(es, ea, er)
```

Empty the lists:

```
        episode_states, episode_actions, episode_rewards = [], [],
[]
```

Print the return for every 10 episodes:

```
    if i %10 ==0:
        print("Episode:{}, Return: {}".format(i,Return))
```

Now that we have learned how PPO with a clipped objective works and how to implement it, in the next section we will learn about another interesting type of PPO algorithm called PPO with a penalized objective.

PPO with a penalized objective

In the PPO-penalty method, we convert the constraint term into a penalty term. First, let us recall the objective function of TRPO. We learned that the TRPO objective function is given as:

$$\underset{\theta}{\text{maximize}}\ \mathbb{E}_t \left[\frac{\pi_\theta(a_t|s_t)}{\pi_{\theta_{old}}(a_t|s_t)} A_t \right]$$

$$\text{subject to}\ \mathbb{E}_t \left[D_{KL}\big(\pi_{\theta_{old}}(\cdot\,|s_t) \| \pi_\theta(\cdot\,|s_t)\big) \right] \leq \delta$$

In the PPO-penalty method, we can rewrite the preceding objective by converting the KL constraint term into a penalty term as shown here:

$$L(\theta) = \mathbb{E}_t \left[\frac{\pi_\theta(a_t|s_t)}{\pi_{\theta_{old}}(a_t|s_t)} A_t - \beta \text{KL}\big[\pi_{\theta_{old}}(\cdot\,|s_t), \pi_\theta(\cdot\,|s_t)\big] \right]$$

Where β is called the penalty coefficient.

Let $d = \text{KL}\big[\pi_{\theta_{old}}(\cdot\,|s_t), \pi_\theta(\cdot\,|s_t)\big]$ and let δ be the target KL divergence; then, we set the value of β adaptively as:

- If d is greater than or equal to 1.5 δ, then we set $\beta_{i+1} = 2\beta_i$
- If d is less than or equal to $\delta/1.5$, then we set $\beta_{i+1} = \beta_i/2$

We can understand how exactly this works by looking into the PPO-penalty algorithm in the next section.

Algorithm – PPO-penalty

The steps involved in the PPO-penalty algorithm are:

1. Initialize the policy network parameter θ and the value network parameter ϕ, and initialize the penalty coefficient β_1 and the target KL divergence δ

2. For iterations $i = 1, 2, \cdots, K$:

    1. Collect N number of trajectories following the policy π_θ
    2. Compute the return (reward-to-go) R_t
    3. Compute $L(\theta) = \mathbb{E}_t \left[\dfrac{\pi_\theta(a_t|s_t)}{\pi_{\theta_{old}}(a_t|s_t)} A_t - \beta_i \mathrm{KL}\left[\pi_{\theta_{old}}(\cdot \,|s_t), \pi_\theta(\cdot \,|s_t)\right] \right]$
    4. Compute the gradient of the objective function $\nabla_\theta L(\theta)$
    5. Update the policy network parameter θ using gradient ascent as
       $\theta = \theta + \alpha \nabla_\theta L(\theta)$
    6. If d is greater than or equal to 1.5 δ, then we set $\beta_{i+1} = 2\beta_i$; if d is less than or equal to $\delta/1.5$, then we set $\beta_{i+1} = \beta_i/2$
    7. Compute the mean squared error of the value network:

    $$J(\phi) = \frac{1}{N} \sum_{i=1}^{N} \sum_{t=0}^{T-1} \left(R_t - V_\phi(s_t) \right)^2$$

    8. Compute the gradients of the value network $\nabla_\phi J(\phi)$
    9. Update the value network parameter ϕ using gradient descent as
       $\phi = \phi - \alpha \nabla_\phi J(\phi)$

Thus, we learned how PPO-clipped and PPO-penalized objectives work. In general, PPO with a clipped objective is used more often than the PPO method with a penalized objective.

In the next section, we will learn another interesting algorithm called ACKTR.

Actor-critic using Kronecker-factored trust region

ACKTR, as the name suggests, is the actor-critic algorithm based on the Kronecker factorization and trust region.

We know that the actor-critic architecture consists of the actor and critic networks, where the role of the actor is to produce a policy and the role of the critic is to evaluate the policy produced by the actor network. We learned that in the actor network (policy network), we compute gradients and update the parameter of the actor network using gradient ascent:

$$\theta = \theta + \alpha \nabla_\theta J(\theta)$$

Instead of updating our actor network parameter using the preceding update rule, we can also update it by computing the natural gradients as:

$$\theta = \theta + \alpha F^{-1} \nabla_\theta J(\theta) \tag{21}$$

Where F is called the Fisher information matrix. Thus, the natural gradient is just the product of the inverse of the Fisher matrix and standard gradient:

$$\theta = \theta + \alpha \underbrace{F^{-1} \nabla_\theta J(\theta)}_{\text{Natural Gradient}}$$

The use of the natural gradient is that it guarantees a monotonic improvement in the policy. However, updating the actor network (policy network) parameter using the preceding update rule is a computationally expensive task, because computing the Fisher information matrix and then taking its inverse is a computationally expensive task. So, to avoid this tedious computation, we can just approximate the value of F^{-1} using a Kronecker-factored approximation. Once we approximate F^{-1} using a Kronecker-factored approximation, then we can just update our policy network parameter using the natural gradient update rule given in equation (21), and while updating the policy network parameter, we also ensure that the policy updates are in the trust region so that the new policy is not far from the old policy. This is the main idea behind the ACKTR algorithm.

Now that we have a basic understanding of what ACKTR is, let us understand how this works exactly in detail. First, we will understand what Kronecker factorization is, then we will learn how it is used in the actor-critic setting, and later we will learn how to incorporate the trust region in the policy updates.

Before going ahead, let's learn several math concepts that are required to understand ACKTR.

Math essentials

To understand how Kronecker factorization works, we will learn the following important concepts:

- Block matrix
- Block diagonal matrix
- The Kronecker product
- The vec operator
- Properties of the Kronecker product

Block matrix

A block matrix is defined as a matrix that can be broken down into submatrices called blocks, or we can say a block matrix is formed by a set of submatrices or blocks. For instance, let's consider a block matrix A as shown here:

$$A = \begin{bmatrix} 1 & 2 & 4 & 5 \\ 3 & 4 & 6 & 7 \\ 1 & 1 & 1 & 1 \\ 1 & 2 & 2 & 1 \end{bmatrix}$$

The matrix A can be broken into four 2×2 submatrices as shown here:

$$A_1 = \begin{bmatrix} 1 & 2 \\ 3 & 4 \end{bmatrix}, A_2 = \begin{bmatrix} 4 & 5 \\ 6 & 7 \end{bmatrix}, A_3 = \begin{bmatrix} 1 & 1 \\ 1 & 2 \end{bmatrix}, A_4 = \begin{bmatrix} 1 & 1 \\ 2 & 1 \end{bmatrix}$$

Now, we can simply write our block matrix A as:

$$A = \begin{bmatrix} A_1 & A_2 \\ A_3 & A_4 \end{bmatrix}$$

Block diagonal matrix

A block diagonal matrix is a block matrix that consists of a square matrix on the diagonals, and off-diagonal elements are set to 0. A block diagonal matrix A is represented as:

$$A = \begin{bmatrix} A_1 & 0 & \cdots & 0 \\ 0 & A_2 & \cdots & 0 \\ \vdots & \vdots & \ddots & \vdots \\ 0 & 0 & \cdots & A_n \end{bmatrix}$$

Where the diagonals $A_1, A_2, \cdots, A_n$ are the square matrices.

An example of a block diagonal matrix is shown here:

$$A = \begin{bmatrix} 1 & 2 & 0 & 0 & 0 & 0 \\ 3 & 4 & 0 & 0 & 0 & 0 \\ 0 & 0 & 4 & 5 & 0 & 0 \\ 0 & 0 & 6 & 7 & 0 & 0 \\ 0 & 0 & 0 & 0 & 7 & 8 \\ 0 & 0 & 0 & 0 & 9 & 0 \end{bmatrix}$$

As we can see, the diagonals are basically the square matrix and off-diagonal elements are set to zero:

$$A = \begin{bmatrix} \boxed{\begin{matrix} 1 & 2 \\ 3 & 4 \end{matrix}} & 0 & 0 & 0 & 0 \\ 0 & 0 & \boxed{\begin{matrix} 4 & 5 \\ 6 & 7 \end{matrix}} & 0 & 0 \\ 0 & 0 & 0 & 0 & \boxed{\begin{matrix} 7 & 8 \\ 9 & 0 \end{matrix}} \end{bmatrix}$$

Thus, we can write:

$$A_1 = \begin{bmatrix} 1 & 2 \\ 3 & 4 \end{bmatrix}, A_2 = \begin{bmatrix} 4 & 5 \\ 6 & 7 \end{bmatrix}, A_3 = \begin{bmatrix} 7 & 8 \\ 9 & 0 \end{bmatrix}$$

Now, we can simply denote our block diagonal matrix A as:

$$A = \begin{bmatrix} A_1 & 0 & 0 \\ 0 & A_2 & 0 \\ 0 & 0 & A_3 \end{bmatrix}$$

The Kronecker product

The Kronecker product is an operation performed between two matrices. The Kronecker product is not the same as matrix multiplication. When we perform the Kronecker product between two matrices, it will output the block matrix. The Kronecker product is denoted by $\otimes$. Let us say we have a matrix A of order $m \times n$ and a matrix B of order $p \times q$; the Kronecker product of matrices A and B is expressed as:

$$A \otimes B = \begin{pmatrix} a_{11}B & a_{12}B & \cdots & a_{1n}B \\ a_{21}B & a_{22}B & \cdots & a_{2n}B \\ \vdots & \vdots & \vdots & \vdots \\ a_{m1}B & a_{m2}B & \cdots & a_{mn}B \end{pmatrix}$$

This implies that we multiply every element in matrix A by matrix B. Let us understand this with an example. Say we have two matrices A and B as shown here:

$$A = \begin{bmatrix} 1 & 1 \\ 2 & 0 \end{bmatrix} \text{ and } B = \begin{bmatrix} 2 & 4 \\ 1 & 3 \end{bmatrix}$$

Then the Kronecker product of matrices A and B is given as:

$$A \otimes B = \begin{bmatrix} 1 & 1 \\ 2 & 0 \end{bmatrix} \otimes \begin{bmatrix} 2 & 4 \\ 1 & 3 \end{bmatrix}$$

$$= \begin{bmatrix} 1 \begin{bmatrix} 2 & 4 \\ 1 & 3 \end{bmatrix} & 1 \begin{bmatrix} 2 & 4 \\ 1 & 3 \end{bmatrix} \\ 2 \begin{bmatrix} 2 & 4 \\ 1 & 3 \end{bmatrix} & 0 \begin{bmatrix} 2 & 4 \\ 1 & 3 \end{bmatrix} \end{bmatrix}$$

$$= \begin{bmatrix} 1 \times 2 & 1 \times 4 & 1 \times 2 & 1 \times 4 \\ 1 \times 1 & 1 \times 3 & 1 \times 1 & 1 \times 3 \\ 2 \times 2 & 2 \times 4 & 0 \times 2 & 0 \times 4 \\ 2 \times 1 & 2 \times 3 & 0 \times 1 & 0 \times 3 \end{bmatrix}$$

$$= \begin{bmatrix} 2 & 4 & 2 & 4 \\ 1 & 3 & 1 & 3 \\ 4 & 8 & 0 & 0 \\ 2 & 6 & 0 & 0 \end{bmatrix}$$

The vec operator

The vec operator creates a column vector by stacking all the columns in a matrix below one another. For instance, let's consider a matrix A as shown here:

$$A = \begin{bmatrix} 1 & 2 \\ 3 & 4 \end{bmatrix}$$

Applying the vec operator on A stacks all the columns in the matrix one below the other as follows:

$$\text{vec(A)} = \begin{bmatrix} 1 \\ 3 \\ 2 \\ 4 \end{bmatrix}$$

Properties of the Kronecker product

The Kronecker product has several useful properties; these include:

- $A \otimes (B \otimes C) = (A \otimes B) \otimes C$
- $(A \otimes B)^{-1} = A^{-1} \otimes B^{-1}$
- $(A \otimes B)\,\text{vec}(C) = ACB^{T}$

Now that we have learned several important concepts, let's understand what Kronecker factorization is.

Kronecker-Factored Approximate Curvature (K-FAC)

Let's suppose we have a neural network parametrized by θ and we train the neural network using gradient descent. We can write our update rule, including the natural gradient, as:

$$\theta = \theta - \alpha F^{-1} \nabla_\theta J(\theta)$$

Where F is the Fisher information matrix. The problem is that computing F and finding its inverse is an expensive task. So to avoid that, we use a Kronecker-factored approximation to approximate the value of F^{-1}.

Let's learn how we approximate F^{-1} using Kronecker factors. Say our network has $1, 2, \ldots, l, \ldots, L$ layers and the weight of the network is represented by θ. Thus, $\theta_1, \theta_2, \ldots, \theta_l, \ldots, \theta_L$ denotes the weights of the layers $1, 2, \ldots, l, \ldots, L$ respectively. Let $p(y|x)$ denote the output distribution of the network, and we will use the negative log-likelihood as the loss function J:

$$J(\theta) = \mathbb{E}_{(x,y)} - [\log p(y|x; \theta)]$$

Then, the Fisher information matrix can be written as:

$$F_\theta = \mathbb{E}_{(x,y)}[\nabla_\theta \log p(y|x) \, \nabla_\theta \log p(y|x)^\mathsf{T}]$$

K-FAC approximates the Fisher information matrix, F, as a block diagonal matrix where each block refers to the gradients of the loss with respect to the weights of a particular layer. For example, the block F_1 denotes the gradients of the loss with respect to the weights of layer 1. The block F_2 denotes the gradients of the loss with respect to the weights of layer 2. The block F_l denotes the gradients of the loss with respect to the weights of layer l:

$$F \approx \begin{bmatrix} F_1 & & & & \\ & F_2 & & & \\ & & \ddots & & \\ & & & F_l & \\ & & & & \ddots \\ & & & & & F_L \end{bmatrix}$$

That is, $F \approx \text{diag}(F_1, F_2, \ldots, F_l, \ldots, F_L)$, where:

- $F_1 = \mathbb{E}\left[\text{vec}\{\nabla_{\theta_1} J\} \, \text{vec}\{\nabla_{\theta_1} J\}^\mathsf{T}\right]$
- $F_2 = \mathbb{E}\left[\text{vec}\{\nabla_{\theta_2} J\} \, \text{vec}\{\nabla_{\theta_2} J\}^\mathsf{T}\right]$
- $F_l = \mathbb{E}\left[\text{vec}\{\nabla_{\theta_l} J\} \, \text{vec}\{\nabla_{\theta_l} J\}^\mathsf{T}\right]$
- $F_L = \mathbb{E}\left[\text{vec}\{\nabla_{\theta_L} J\} \, \text{vec}\{\nabla_{\theta_L} J\}^\mathsf{T}\right]$

As we can observe, each block F_1 to F_L contains the derivatives of loss J with respect to the weights of the corresponding layer. Okay, how can we compute each block? That is, how can the values in the preceding block diagonal matrix be computed?

To understand this, let's just take one block, say, F_l, and learn how it is computed. Let's take a layer l. Let a be the input activation vector, let θ_l be the weights of the layer, and let s be the output pre-activation vector, and it can be sent to the next layer $l + 1$.

We know that in the neural network, we multiply the activation vector by weights and send that to the next layer; so, we can write:

$$s = \theta_l a \tag{22}$$

We can approximate the block F_l corresponding to layer l as:

$$F_l = \mathbb{E}\left[\text{vec}\{\nabla_{\theta_l}J\}\,\text{vec}\{\nabla_{\theta_l}J\}^{\mathsf{T}}\right] \tag{23}$$

The preceding equation F_l denotes the gradient of the loss with respect to the weights of layer l.

From (22), the partial derivative of the loss function J with respect to weights θ_l in layer l can be written as:

$$\nabla_{\theta_l}J = (\nabla_s J)a^T \tag{24}$$

Substituting (24) in (23), we can write:

$$\begin{aligned}
F_l &= \mathbb{E}[(\nabla_s J \otimes a)(\nabla_s J \otimes a)^T] \\
&= \mathbb{E}[(\nabla_s J \otimes a)(\nabla_s J^T \otimes a^T)] \\
F_l &= \mathbb{E}[aa^T \otimes \nabla_s J \, \nabla_s J^T]
\end{aligned}$$

The preceding equation implies that F_l is just the expected value of the Kronecker product. So, we can rewrite it as the Kronecker product of the expected value; that is, F_l can be approximated as the Kronecker product of the expected value:

$$F_l = \mathbb{E}[aa^T] \otimes \mathbb{E}[\nabla_s J \, \nabla_s J^T]$$

Let $A = \mathbb{E}[aa^T]$ and $S = \mathbb{E}[\nabla_s J \, \nabla_s J^T]$. We can write:

$$F_l = A \otimes S \tag{25}$$

This is known as Kronecker factorization and A and S are called the Kronecker factors. Now that we have learned how to compute the block F_l, let's learn how to update the weights θ_l of the layer l.

The update rule for updating the weights θ_l of the layer l is given as:

$$\theta_l = \theta_l - \alpha F_l^{-1}\nabla_{\theta_l}J(\theta_l)$$

Let $\Delta\theta_l = F_l^{-1}\nabla_{\theta_l}J(\theta_l)$. We can write:

$$\theta_l = \theta_l - \alpha\Delta\theta_l$$

Let's see how to compute the value of $\Delta\theta_l$:

$$\Delta\theta_l = F_l^{-1}\nabla_{\theta_l}J(\theta_l)$$

Applying the vec operator on both sides, we can write:

$$\text{vec}\{\Delta\theta_l\} = F_l^{-1}\text{vec}\{\nabla_{\theta_l}J(\theta_l)\}$$

From (25), we can substitute the value of F_l and write:

$$\text{vec}\{\Delta\theta_l\} = (A \otimes S)^{-1}\text{vec}\{\nabla_{\theta_l}J(\theta_l)\}$$

Using the properties $(A \otimes B)^{-1} = A^{-1} \otimes B^{-1}$ and $(A \otimes B)\,\text{vec}(C) = ACB^T$, we can write:

$$\text{vec}\{\Delta\theta_l\} = \text{vec}\{A^{-1}\nabla_{\theta_l}J S^{-1}\}$$

As you may observe, we have computed the value of $\Delta\theta_l$ without expensive computation of the inverse of the Fisher information matrix using Kronecker factors. Now, using the value of $\Delta\theta_l$ we just derived, we can update the weights θ_l of the layer l as:

$$\theta_l = \theta_l - \alpha\Delta\theta_l$$

In a nutshell, K-FAC approximates the Fisher information matrix as a block diagonal matrix where each block contains the derivatives. Then, each block is approximated as the Kronecker product of two matrices, which is known as Kronecker factorization.

Thus, we have learned how to approximate the natural gradient using Kronecker factors. In the next section, we will learn how to apply this in an actor-critic setting.

K-FAC in actor-critic

We know that in the actor-critic method, we have actor and critic networks. The role of the actor is to produce the policy and the role of the critic is to evaluate the policy produced by the actor network.

First, let's take a look at the actor network. In the actor network, our goal is to find the optimal policy. So, we try to find the optimal parameter θ with which we can obtain the optimal policy. We compute gradients and update the parameter of the actor network using gradient ascent:

$$\theta = \theta + \alpha \nabla_\theta J(\theta)$$

Instead of updating the actor network parameter using the preceding update rule, we can also update the parameter of the actor network by computing the natural gradients as:

$$\theta = \theta + \alpha F^{-1} \nabla_\theta J(\theta)$$

But computing F^{-1} is an expensive task. So, we can use Kronecker factorization for approximating the value of F^{-1}. We can define the Fisher information matrix for the actor network F as:

$$F = \mathbb{E}_{p(\tau)} \left[\nabla_\theta \log \pi \left(a_t | s_t \right) \left(\nabla_\theta \log \pi \left(a_t | s_t \right) \right)^{\mathrm{T}} \right]$$

Now, just as we learned in the previous section, we can approximate the Fisher information matrix as a block diagonal matrix where each block contains the derivatives, and then we can approximate each block as the Kronecker product of two matrices.

Let $\Delta\theta = F^{-1} \nabla_\theta J(\theta)$. We can write:

$$\theta = \theta + \alpha \Delta\theta$$

The value of $\Delta\theta$ can be computed using Kronecker factorization as:

$$\text{vec}\{\Delta\theta\} = \text{vec}\{A^{-1} \nabla_\theta J S^{-1}\}$$

This is exactly the same as what we learned in the previous section.

Now, let's look at the critic network. We know that the critic evaluates the policy produced by the actor network by estimating the Q function. So, we train the critic by minimizing the mean squared error between the target value and predicted value.

We minimize the loss using gradient descent and update the critic network parameter ϕ as:

$$\phi = \phi - \alpha \nabla_\phi J(\phi)$$

Where $\nabla_\phi J(\phi)$ is the standard first-order gradient.

Instead of using the first-order gradient, can we use the second-order gradient and update the critic network parameter ϕ, similar to what we did with the actor? Yes, in settings like least squares (MSE), we can use an algorithm called the Gauss-Newton method for finding the second-order derivative. You can learn more about the Gauss-Newton method here: http://www.seas.ucla.edu/~vandenbe/236C/lectures/ gn.pdf. Let's represent our error as $e(\phi) =$ target $-$ predicted. According to the Gauss-Newton method, the update rule for updating the critic network parameter ϕ is given as:

$$\phi = \phi - \alpha G^{-1} J^T (-e(\phi))$$

Where G is called the Gauss-Newton matrix, and it is given as $G = \mathbb{E}[JJ^T]$, and J is the Jacobian matrix. (A Jacobian matrix is a matrix that contains a first-order partial derivative for a vector-valued function.)

If you look at the preceding equation, computing G^{-1} is equivalent to computing the F^{-1} we saw in the actor network. That is, computing the inverse of the Gauss-Newton matrix is equivalent to computing the inverse of the Fisher information matrix. So, we can use the Kronecker factor (K-FAC) to approximate the value of G^{-1} just like we approximated the value of F^{-1}.

Instead of applying K-FAC to the actor and critic separately, we can also apply them in a shared mode. As specified in the paper **Scalable trust-region method for deep reinforcement learning using Kronecker-factored approximation** by Yuhuai Wu, Elman Mansimov, Shun Liao, Roger Grosse, Jimmy Ba (https://arxiv.org/ pdf/1708.05144.pdf), *"We can have a single architecture where both actor and critic share the lower layer representations but they have different output layers."*

In a nutshell, in the ACKTR method, we update the parameters of the actor and critic networks by computing the second-order derivatives. Since computing the second-order derivative is an expensive task, we use a method called Kronecker-factored approximation to approximate the second-order derivative.

In the next section, we will learn how to incorporate the trust region into our update rule so that our new and old policy updates will not be too far apart.

Incorporating the trust region

We learned that we can update the parameter of our network with a natural gradient as:

$$\theta = \theta + \alpha F^{-1} \nabla_\theta J(\theta)$$

In the previous section, we learned how we can use K-FAC to approximate the F^{-1} matrix. While updating the policy, we need to make sure that our policy updates are in the trust region; that is, our new policy should not be too far away from the old policy. So to ensure this, we can choose the step size α as

$$\alpha = \min\left(\alpha_{\max}, \sqrt{\frac{2\delta}{\Delta\theta^T \hat{F} \Delta\theta}} \right),$$ where α and the trust region radius δ are the

hyperparameters, as mentioned in the ACKTR paper (refer to the *Further reading* section). Updating our network parameters with this step size ensures that our policy updates are in the trust region.

Summary

We started off the chapter by understanding what TRPO is and how it acts as an improvement to the policy gradient algorithm. We learned that when the new policy and old policy vary greatly then it causes model collapse.

So in TRPO, we make a policy update while imposing the constraint that the parameters of the old and new policies should stay within the trust region. We also learned that TRPO guarantees monotonic policy improvement; that is, it guarantees that there will always be a policy improvement on every iteration.

Later, we learned about the PPO algorithm, which acts as an improvement to the TRPO algorithm. We learned about two types of PPO algorithm: PPO-clipped and PPO-penalty. In the PPO-clipped method, in order to ensure that the policy updates are in the trust region, PPO adds a new function called the clipping function that ensures the new and old policies are not far away from each other. In the PPO-penalty method, we modify our objective function by converting the KL constraint term to a penalty term and update the penalty coefficient adaptively during training by ensuring that the policy updates are in the trust region.

At the end of the chapter, we learned about ACKTR. In the ACKTR method, we update the parameters of the actor and critic networks by computing the second-order derivative. Since computing the second-order derivative is an expensive task, we use a method called Kronecker-factored approximation to approximate the second-order derivatives, and while updating the policy network parameter, we also ensure that the policy updates are in the trust region so that the new policy is not far from the old policy.

In the next chapter, we will learn about several interesting distributional reinforcement learning algorithms.

Questions

Let's evaluate our understanding of the algorithms we learned in this chapter. Try answering the following questions:

1. What is a trust region?
2. Why is TRPO useful?
3. How does the conjugate gradient method differ from gradient descent?
4. What is the update rule of TRPO?
5. How does PPO differ from TRPO?
6. Explain the PPO-clipped method.
7. What is Kronecker factorization?

Further reading

For more information, refer to the following papers:

- **Trust Region Policy Optimization** by *John Schulman, Sergey Levine, Philipp Moritz, Michael I. Jordan, Pieter Abbeel,* https://arxiv.org/pdf/1502.05477.pdf

- **Proximal Policy Optimization Algorithms** by *John Schulman, Filip Wolski, Prafulla Dhariwal, Alec Radford, Oleg Klimov,* https://arxiv.org/pdf/1707.06347.pdf

- **Scalable trust-region method for deep reinforcement learning using Kronecker-factored approximation** by *Yuhuai Wu, Elman Mansimov, Shun Liao, Roger Grosse, Jimmy Ba,* https://arxiv.org/pdf/1708.05144.pdf

14

Distributional Reinforcement Learning

In this chapter, we will learn about distributional reinforcement learning. We will begin the chapter by understanding what exactly distributional reinforcement learning is and why it is useful. Next, we will learn about one of the most popular distributional reinforcement learning algorithms called **categorical DQN**. We will understand what a categorical DQN is and how it differs from the DQN we learned in *Chapter 9, Deep Q Networks and Its Variants*, and then we will explore the categorical DQN algorithm in detail.

Following this, we will learn another interesting algorithm called **Quantile Regression DQN (QR-DQN)**. We will understand what a QR-DQN is and how it differs from a categorical DQN, and then we will explore the QR-DQN algorithm in detail.

At the end of the chapter, we will learn about the policy gradient algorithm called the **Distributed Distributional Deep Deterministic Policy Gradient (D4PG)**. We will learn what the D4PG is and how it differs from the DDPG we covered in *Chapter 12, Learning DDPG, TD3, and SAC*, in detail

In this chapter, we will cover the following topics:

- Why distributional reinforcement learning?
- Categorical DQN
- Quantile regression DQN
- Distributed distributional deep deterministic policy gradient

Let's begin the chapter by understanding what distributional reinforcement learning is and why we need it.

Why distributional reinforcement learning?

Say we are in state *s* and we have two possible actions to perform in this state. Let the actions be *up* and *down*. How do we decide which action to perform in the state? We compute Q values for all actions in the state and select the action that has the maximum Q value. So, we compute $Q(s, up)$ and $Q(s, down)$ and select the action that has the maximum Q value.

We learned that the Q value is the expected return an agent would obtain when starting from state *s* and performing an action *a* following the policy π:

$$Q^{\pi}(s, a) = \underset{\tau \sim \pi}{\mathbb{E}} [R(\tau)|s_0 = s, a_0 = a]$$

But there is a small problem in computing the Q value in this manner because the Q value is just an expectation of the return, and the expectation does not include the intrinsic randomness. Let's understand exactly what this means with an example.

Let's suppose we want to drive from work to home and we have two routes **A** and **B**. Now, we have to decide which route is better, that is, which route helps us to reach home in the minimum amount of time. To find out which route is better, we can calculate the Q values and select the route that has the maximum Q value, that is, the route that gives us the maximum expected return.

Say the Q value of choosing route *A* is $Q(s, A) = 31$, and the Q value of choosing route *B* is $Q(s, B) = 28$. Since the Q value (the expected return of route **A**) is higher, we can choose route **A** to travel home. But are we missing something here? Instead of viewing the Q value as an expectation over a return, can we directly look into the distribution of return and make a better decision?

Yes!

But first, let's take a look at the distribution of route **A** and route **B** and understand which route is best. The following plot shows the distribution of route **A**. It tells us with 70% probability we reach home in 10 minutes, and with 30% probability we reach home in 80 minutes. That is, if we choose route **A** we usually reach home in 10 minutes but when there is heavy traffic we reach home in 80 minutes:

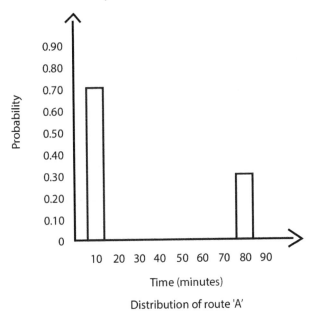

Distribution of route 'A'

Figure 14.1: Distribution of route A

Figure 14.2 shows the distribution of route **B**. It tells us that with 80% probability we reach home in 20 minutes and with 20% probability we reach home in 60 minutes.

That is, if we choose route **B** we usually reach home in 20 minutes but when there is heavy traffic we reach home in 60 minutes:

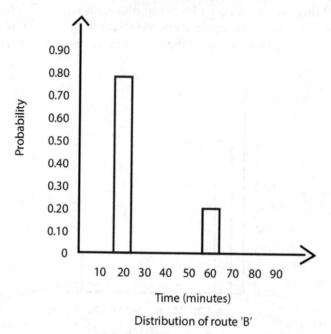

Distribution of route 'B'

Figure 14.2: Distribution of route B

After looking at these two distributions, it makes more sense to choose route **B** instead of choosing route **A**. With route **B**, even in the worst case, that is, even when there is heavy traffic, we can reach home in 60 minutes. But with route **A**, when there is heavy traffic, we reach home in 80 minutes. So, it is a wise decision to choose route **B** rather than **A**.

Similarly, if we can observe the distribution of return of route **A** and route **B**, we can understand more information and we will miss out on these details when we take actions just based on the maximum expected return, that is, the maximum Q value. So, instead of using the expected return to select an action, we use the distribution of return and then select optimal action based on the distribution.

This is the basic idea and motivation behind distributional reinforcement learning. In the next section, we will learn one of the most popular distributional reinforcement learning algorithms, called categorical DQN, which is also known as the C51 algorithm.

Categorical DQN

In the last section, we learned why it is more beneficial to choose an action based on the distribution of return than to choose an action based on the Q value, which is just the expected return. In this section, we will understand how to compute the distribution of return using an algorithm called categorical DQN.

The distribution of return is often called the value distribution or return distribution. Let Z be the random variable and $Z(s, a)$ denote the value distribution of a state s and an action a. We know that the Q function is represented by $Q(s, a)$ and it gives the value of a state-action pair. Similarly, now we have $Z(s, a)$ and it gives the value distribution (return distribution) of the state-action pair.

Okay, how can we compute $Z(s, a)$? First, let's recollect how we compute $Q(s, a)$.

In DQN, we learned that we use a neural network to approximate the Q function, $Q(s, a)$, Since we use a neural network to approximate the Q function, we can represent the Q function by $Q_\theta(s, a)$, where θ is the parameter of the network. Given a state as an input to the network, it outputs the Q values of all the actions that can be performed in that state, and then we select the action that has the maximum Q value.

Similarly, in categorical DQN, we use a neural network to approximate the value of $Z(s, a)$. We can represent this by $z_\theta(s, a)$, where θ is the parameter of the network. Given a state as an input to the network, it outputs the value distribution (return distribution) of all the actions that can be performed in that state as an output and then we select an action based on this value distribution.

Let's understand the difference between the DQN and categorical DQN with an example. Suppose we are in the state s and say our action space has two actions a and b. Now, as shown in *Figure 14.3*, given the state s as an input to the DQN, it returns the Q value of all the actions, then we select the action that has the maximum Q value, whereas in the categorical DQN, given the state s as an input, it returns the value distribution of all the actions, then we select the action based on this value distribution:

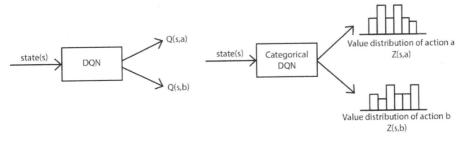

Figure 14.3: DQN vs categorical DQN

Okay, how can we train the network? In DQN, we learned that we train the network by minimizing the loss between the target Q value and the Q value predicted by the network. We learned that the target Q value is obtained by the Bellman optimality equation. Thus, we minimize the loss between the target value (the optimal Bellman Q value) and the predicted value (the Q value predicted by the network) and train the network.

Similarly, in categorical DQN, we train the network by minimizing the loss between the target value distribution and the value distribution predicted by the network. Okay, how can we obtain the target value distribution? In DQN, we obtained the target Q value using the Bellman equation; similarly in categorical DQN, we can obtain the target value distribution using the distributional Bellman equation. What's the distributional Bellman equation? First, let's recall the Bellman equation before learning about the distributional Bellman equation.

We learned that the Bellman equation for the Q function $Q(s, a)$ is given as:

$$Q^*(s, a) = \mathbb{E}_{s' \sim P}[R(s, a, s') + \gamma \max_{a'} Q^*(s', a')]$$

Similarly, the Bellman equation for the value distribution $Z(s, a)$ is given as:

$$Z(s, a) \equiv R(s, a, s') + \gamma Z(s', a')$$

This equation is called the distributional Bellman equation. Thus, in categorical DQN, we train the network by minimizing the loss between the target value distribution, which is given by the distributional Bellman equation, and the value distribution predicted by the network.

Okay, what loss function should we use? In DQN, we use the **mean squared error (MSE)** as our loss function. Unlike a DQN, we cannot use the MSE as the loss function in the categorical DQN because in categorical DQN, we predict the probability distribution and not the Q value. Since we are dealing with the distribution we use the cross entropy loss as our loss function. Thus, in categorical DQN, we train the network by minimizing the cross entropy loss between the target value distribution and the value distribution predicted by the network.

In a nutshell, a categorical DQN is similar to DQN, except that in a categorical DQN, we predict the value distribution whereas in a DQN we predict the Q value. Thus, given a state as an input, a categorical DQN returns the value distribution of each action in that state. We train the network by minimizing the cross entropy loss between the target value distribution, which is given by the distributional Bellman equation, and the value distribution predicted by the network.

Now that we have understood what a categorical DQN is and how it differs from a DQN, in the next section we will learn how exactly the categorical DQN predicts the value distribution.

Predicting the value distribution

Figure 14.4 shows a simple value distribution:

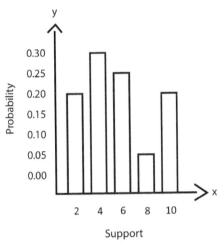

Figure 14.4: Value distribution

The horizontal axis values are called support or atoms and the vertical axis values are the probability. We denote the support by Z and the probability by P. In order to predict the value distribution, along with the state, our network takes the support of the distribution as input and it returns the probability of each value in the support.

So, now, we will see how to compute the support of the distribution. To compute support, first, we need to decide the number of values of the support N, the minimum value of the support V_{min}, and the maximum value of the support V_{max}. Given a number of support N, we divide them into N equal parts from V_{min} to V_{max}.

Let's understand this with an example. Say the number of support $N = 5$, the minimum value of support $V_{min} = 2$, and the maximum value of the support $V_{max} = 10$. Now, how can we find the values of the support? In order to find the values of the support, first, we will compute the step size called $\triangle z$. The value of $\triangle z$ can be computed as:

$$\triangle z = \frac{V_{max} - V_{min}}{N - 1}$$

$$\triangle z = \frac{10 - 2}{5 - 1}$$

$$\triangle z = {}^{8}/_{4} = 2$$

Now, to compute the values of support, we start with the minimum value of support V_{min} and add $\triangle z$ to every value until we reach the number of support N. In our example, we start with V_{min}, which is 2, and we add $\triangle z = 2$ to every value until we reach the number of support N. Thus, the support values become:

$$\text{Support} = [2, 4, 6, 8, 10]$$

Thus, we can write the value of support as $z_i = V_{min} + i \triangle z : 0 \leq i < N$. The following Python snippet gives us more clarity on how to obtain the support values:

```python
def get_support(N, V_min, V_max):
    dz = (V_max - V_min) / (N-1)
    return [V_min + i * dz for i in range(N)]
```

Okay, we have learned how to compute the support of the distribution, now how does the neural network take this support as input and return the probabilities?

In order to predict the value distribution, along with the state, we also need to give the support of the distribution as input and then the network returns the probabilities of our value distribution as output. Let's understand this with an example. Say we are in a state s and we have two actions to perform in this state, and let the actions be *up* and *down*. Say our calculated support values are $z_1, z_2,$ and z_3.

As *Figure 14.5* shows, along with giving the state s as input to the network, we also give the support of our distribution $z_1, z_2,$ and z_3. Then our network returns the probabilities $p_i(s, a)$ of the given support for the distribution of action *up* and distribution of action *down*:

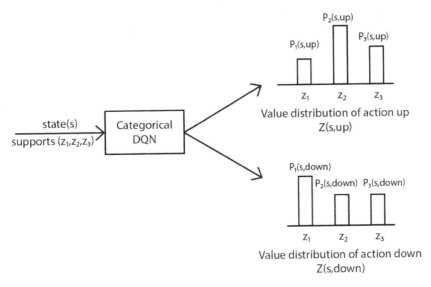

Figure 14.5: A categorical DQN

The authors of the categorical DQN paper (see the *Further reading* section for more details) suggest that it will be efficient to set the number of support N as 51, and so the categorical DQN is also known as the C51 algorithm. Thus, we have learned how categorical DQN predicts the value distribution. In the next section, we will learn how to select the action based on this predicted value distribution.

Selecting an action based on the value distribution

We have learned that a categorical DQN returns the value distribution of each action in the given state. But how can we select the best action based on the value distribution predicted by the network?

We generally select an action based on the Q value, that is, we usually select the action that has the maximum Q value. But now we don't have a Q value; instead, we have a value distribution. How can we select an action based on the value distribution?

First, we will extract the Q value from the value distribution and then we select the action as the one that has the maximum Q value. Okay, how can we extract the Q value? We can compute the Q value by just taking the expectation of the value distribution. The expectation of the distribution is given as the sum of support z_i multiplied by their corresponding probability p_i. So the expectation of the value distribution Z is given as:

$$\mathbb{E}[Z] = \sum_i z_i p_i$$

Where z_i is the support and p_i is the probability.

Thus, the Q value of the value distribution can be computed as:

$$Q(s, a) = \sum_i z_i p_i(s, a)$$

After computing the Q value, we select the best action as the one that has the maximum Q value:

$$a^* = \arg\max_a Q(s, a)$$

Let's understand how this works exactly. Suppose we are in the state s and say we have two actions in the state. Let the actions be *up* and *down*. First, we need to compute support. Let the number of support $N = 3$, the minimum value of the support $V_{min} = 2$, and the maximum value of the support $V_{max} = 4$. Then, our computed support values will be [2,3,4].

Now, along with the state s, we feed the support, then the categorical DQN returns the probabilities $p_i(s, a)$ of the given support for the value distribution of action *up* and distribution of action *down* as shown here:

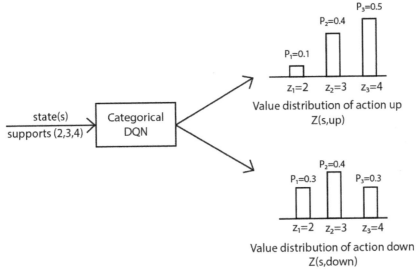

Figure 14.6: Categorical DQN

Now, how can we select the best action, based on these two value distributions? First, we will extract the Q value from the value distributions and then we select the action that has the maximum Q value.

We learned that the Q value can be extracted from the value distribution as the sum of support multiplied by their probabilities:

$$Q(s, a) = \sum_i z_i p_i(s, a)$$

So, we can compute the Q value of action *up* in state *s* as:

$$Q(s, \text{up}) = \sum_i z_i p_i(s, \text{up})$$
$$= z_1 p_1(s, \text{up}) + z_2 p_2(s, \text{up}) + z_3 p_3(s, \text{up})$$
$$= (2 \times 0.1) + (3 \times 0.4) + (4 \times 0.5)$$
$$= 3.4$$

Now, we can compute the Q value of action *down* in state s as:

$$Q(s, \text{down}) = \sum_i z_i p_i(s, \text{down})$$

$$= z_1 p_1(s, \text{down}) + z_2 p_2(s, \text{down}) + z_3 p_3(s, \text{down})$$
$$= (2 \times 0.3) + (3 \times 0.4) + (4 \times 0.3)$$
$$= 3.0$$

Now, we select the action that has the maximum Q value. Since the action *up* has the high Q value, we select the action *up* as the best action.

Wait! What makes categorical DQN special then? Because just like DQN, we are selecting the action based on the Q value at the end. One important point we have to note is that, in DQN, we compute the Q value based on the expectation of the return directly, but in categorical DQN, first, we learn the return distribution and then we compute the Q value based on the expectation of the return distribution, which captures the intrinsic randomness.

We have learned that the categorical DQN outputs the value distribution of all the actions in the given state and then we extract the Q value from the value distribution and select the action that has the maximum Q value as the best action. But the question is how exactly does our categorical DQN learn? How do we train the categorical DQN to predict the accurate value distribution? Let's discuss this in the next section.

Training the categorical DQN

We train the categorical DQN by minimizing the cross entropy loss between the target value distribution and the predicted value distribution. How can we compute the target distribution? We can compute the target distribution using the distributional Bellman equation given as follows:

$$\tau Z(s, a) \equiv R(s, a, s') + \gamma Z(s', a')$$

Where $R(s, a, s')$ represents the immediate reward r, which we obtain while performing an action a in the state s and moving to the next state s', so we can just denote $R(s, a, s')$ by r:

$$\tau Z(s, a) \equiv r + \gamma Z(s', a')$$

Remember in DQN we computed the target value using the target network parameterized by θ'? Similarly, here, we use the target categorical DQN parameterized by θ' to compute the target distribution.

After computing the target distribution, we train the network by minimizing the cross entropy loss between the target value distribution and the predicted value distribution. One important point we need to note here is that we can apply the cross entropy loss between any two distributions only when their supports are equal; when their supports are not equal we cannot apply the cross entropy loss.

For instance, *Figure 14.7* shows the support of both the target and predicted distribution is the same, (1,2,3,4). Thus, in this case, we can apply the cross entropy loss:

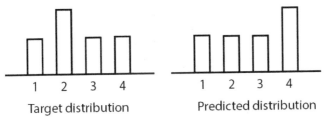

Figure 14.7: Target and predicted distribution

In *Figure 14.8*, we can see that the target distribution support (1,3,4,5) and the predicted distribution support (1,2,3,4) are different, so in this case, we cannot apply the cross entropy loss.

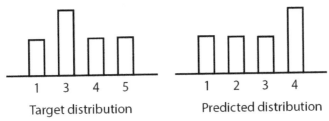

Figure 14.8: Target and predicted distribution

So, when the support of the target and prediction distribution is different, we perform a special step called the projection step using which we can make the support of the target and prediction distribution equal. Once we make the support of the target and prediction distribution equal then we can apply the cross entropy loss.

In the next section, we will learn how exactly the projection works and how it makes the support of the target and prediction distribution equal.

Projection step

Let's understand how exactly the projection step works with an example. Suppose the input support is $z = [1, 2]$.

Let the probability of predicted distribution be $p = [0.5, 0.5]$. *Figure 14.9* shows the predicted distribution:

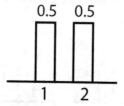

Figure 14.9: Predicted distribution

Let the probability of target distribution be $p = [0.3, 0.7]$. Let the reward $r = 0.1$ and the discount factor $\gamma = 0.9$. The target distribution support value is computed as $\tau z_j = r_t + \gamma_t z_j$, so, we can write:

$$\tau z_1 = r + \gamma z_1$$
$$= 0.1 + (0.9 * 1) = 1.0$$

$$\tau z_2 = r + \gamma z_2$$
$$= 0.1 + (0.9 * 2) = 1.9$$

Thus, the target distribution becomes:

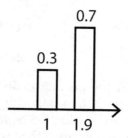

Figure 14.10: Target distribution

As we can observe from the preceding plots, the supports of the predicted distribution and target distribution are different. The predicted distribution has the support [1, 2] while the target distribution has the support [1, 1.9], so in this case, we cannot apply the cross entropy loss.

Now, using the projection step we can convert the support of our target distribution to be the same support as the predicted distribution. Once the supports of the predicted and target distribution are the same then we can apply the cross entropy loss.

Okay, what's that projection step exactly? How can we apply it and convert the support of the target distribution to match the support of the predicted distribution?

Let's understand this with the same example. As the following shows, we have the target distribution support [1, 1.9] and we need to make it equal to the predicted distribution support [1, 2], how can we do that?

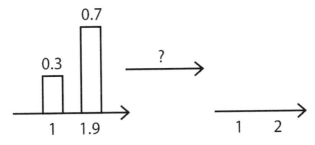

Figure 14.11: Target distribution

So, what we can do is that we can distribute the probability 0.7 from the support 1.9 to the support 1 and 2:

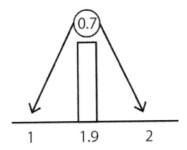

Figure 14.12: Target distribution

Okay, but how can we distribute the probabilities from the support 1.9 to the support 1 and 2? Should it be an equal distribution? Of course not. Since 2 is closer to 1.9, we distribute more probability to 2 and less to 1.

As shown in *Figure 14.13*, from 0.7, we will distribute 0.63 to support 2 and 0.07 to support 1.

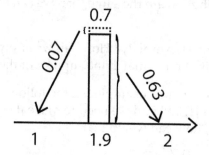

Figure 14.13: Target distribution

Thus, now our target distribution will look like:

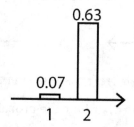

Figure 14.14: Target distribution

From *Figure 14.14*, we can see that support of the target distribution is changed from [1, 1.9] to [1, 2] and now it matches the support of the predicted distribution. This step is called the projection step.

What we learned is just a simple example, consider a case where our target and predicted distribution support varies very much. In this case, we cannot manually determine the amount of probability we have to distribute across the supports to make them equal. So, we introduce a set of steps to perform the projection, as the following shows. After performing these steps, our target distribution support will match our predicted distribution by distributing the probabilities across the support.

First, we initialize an array m with its shape as the number of support with zero values. The m denotes the distributed probability of the target distribution after the projection step.

For *j* in range of the number of support:

1. Compute the target support value: $\hat{\tau}z_j = [r_t + \gamma_t z_j]_{V_{min}}^{V_{max}}$
2. Compute the value of *b*: $b_j = (\hat{\tau}z_j - V_{min})/\triangle z$
3. Compute the lower bound and the upper bound: $l = \lfloor b_j \rfloor, u = \lceil b_j \rceil$
4. Distribute the probability on the lower bound: $m_l = m_l + p_j(u - b_j)$
5. Distribute the probability on the upper bound: $m_u = m_u + p_j(b_j - l)$

Understanding how exactly these projection steps work is a little tricky! So, let's understand this by considering the same example we used earlier. Let z = [1, 2], N = 2, V_{min} = 1, and V_{max} = 2.

Let the probability of predicted distribution be p = [0.5, 0.5]. *Figure 14.15* shows the predicted distribution:

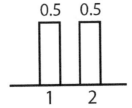

Figure 14.15: Predicted distribution

Let the probability of target distribution be p = [0.3, 0.7]. Let the reward r = 0.1 and the discount factor γ = 0.9, and we know $\tau z_j = r_t + \gamma_t z_j$, thus, the target distribution becomes:

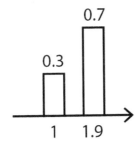

Figure 14.16: Target distribution

From *Figure 14.16*, we can infer that support in target distribution is different from the predicted distribution. Now, we will learn how to perform the projection using the preceding steps.

First, we initialize an array m with its shape as the number of support with zero values. Thus, $m = [0, 0]$.

Iteration, j=0:

1. Compute the target support value:

$$\hat{t}z[0] = r + \gamma z[0]$$
$$= 0.1 + 0.9 \times 1$$
$$= 1.0$$

2. Compute the value of b:

$$b[0] = (\hat{t}z[0] - V_{\min})/\triangle z$$
$$= (1 - 1)/1$$
$$= 0$$

3. Compute the lower and upper bound:

$$l = 0, u = 0$$

4. Distribute the probability on the lower bound:

$$m_l = m_l + p_j(u - b_j)$$

$$m[0] = m[0] + p[0](b[0] - l)$$
$$= 0 + 0.3(0 - 0)$$
$$= 0$$

5. Distribute the probability on the upper bound:

$$m_u = m_u + p_j(b_j - l)$$

$$m[0] = m[0] + p[0](b[0] - l)$$
$$= 0 + 0.3(0 - 0)$$
$$= 0$$

After the 1st iteration, the value of m becomes $[0, 0]$.

Iteration, j=1:

1. Compute the target support value:

    $$\hat{t}z[1] = r + \gamma z[1]$$
    $$= 0.1 + 0.9 \times 2$$
    $$= 1.9$$

2. Compute the value of b:

    $$b[1] = (\hat{t}z[1] - V_{min})/\triangle z$$
    $$= (1.9 - 1)/1$$
    $$= 0.9$$

3. Compute the lower and upper bound of b:

    $$l = 0, u = 1$$

4. Distribute the probability on the lower bound:

    $$m_l = m_l + p_j(u - b_j)$$

    $$m[0] = m[0] + p[1](u - b[1])$$
    $$= 0 + 0.7(1 - 0.9)$$
    $$= 0.06999$$
    $$= 0.07$$

5. Distribute the probability on the upper bound:

    $$m_u = m_u + p_j(b_j - l)$$

    $$m[1] = m[1] + p[1](b[1] - l)$$
    $$= 0 + 0.7(0.9 - 0)$$
    $$= 0.63$$

After the second iteration, the value of m becomes [0.07, 0,63]. The number of iterations = the length of our support. Since the length of our support is 2, we will stop here and thus the value of m becomes our new distributed probability for the modified support, as *Figure 14.17* shows:

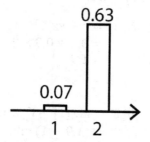

Figure 14.17: Target distribution

The following snippet will give us more clarity on how exactly the projection step works:

```
m = np.zeros(num_support)

for j in range(num_support):
    Tz = min(v_max,max(v_min,r+gamma * z[j]))
    bj = (Tz - v_min) / delta_z
    l,u = math.floor(bj),math.ceil(bj)
    pj = p[j]
    m[int(l)] += pj * (u - bj)
    m[int(u)] += pj * (bj - 1)
```

Now that we have understood how to compute the target value distribution and how we can make the support of target value distribution equal to the support of predicted value distribution using the projection step, we will learn how to compute the cross entropy loss. Cross entropy loss is given as:

$$\text{Cross Entropy} = -\sum_i y_i \log{(\hat{y}_i)}$$

Where y is the actual value and $\hat{y}$ is the predicted value. Thus, we can write:

$$\text{Cross Entropy} = -\sum_i m_i \log{p_i(s, a)}$$

Where m is the target probabilities from the target value distribution and $p(s, a)$ is the predicted probabilities from the predicted value distribution. We train our network by minimizing the cross entropy loss.

Thus, using a categorical DQN, we select the action based on the distribution of the return (value distribution). In the next section, we will put all these concepts together and see how a categorical DQN works.

Putting it all together

First, we initialize the main network parameter θ with random values, and we initialize the target network parameter θ' by just copying the main network parameter θ. We also initialize the replay buffer $\mathcal{D}$.

Now, for each step in the episode, we feed the state of the environment and support values to the main categorical DQN parameterized by θ. The main network takes the support and state of the environment as input and returns the probability value for each support. Then the Q value of the value distribution can be computed as the sum of support multiplied by their probabilities:

$$Q(s, a) = \sum_i z_i p_i(s, a)$$

After computing the Q value of all the actions in the state, we select the best action in the state s as the one that has the maximum Q value:

$$a^* = \arg\max_a Q(s, a)$$

However, instead of selecting the action that has the maximum Q value all the time, we select the action using the epsilon-greedy policy. With the epsilon-greedy policy, we select a random action with probability epsilon and with the probability 1-epsilon, we select the best action that has the maximum Q value. We perform the selected action, move to the next state, obtain the reward, and store this transition information (s, a, r, s') in the replay buffer $\mathcal{D}$.

Now, we sample a transition (s, a, r, s') from the replay buffer $\mathcal{D}$ and feed the next state s' and support values to the target categorical DQN parameterized by θ'. The target network takes the support and next state s' as input and returns the probability value for each support.

Then the Q value can be computed as the sum of support multiplied by their probabilities:

$$Q(s', a) = \sum_i z_i p_i(s', a)$$

After computing the Q value of all next state-action pairs, we select the best action in the state s' as the one that has the maximum Q value:

$$a^* = \arg\max_a Q(s', a)$$

Now, we perform the projection step. The m denotes the distributed probability of the target distribution after the projection step.

For j in range of the number of support:

1. Compute the target support value: $\hat{t}z_j = [r_t + \gamma_t z_j]_{V_{min}}^{V_{max}}$
2. Compute the value of b: $b_j = (\hat{t}z_j - V_{min})/\triangle z$
3. Compute the lower bound and the upper bound: $l = \lfloor b_j \rfloor, u = \lceil b_j \rceil$
4. Distribute the probability on the lower bound: $m_l = m_l + p_j(s', a^*)(u - b_j)$
5. Distribute the probability on the upper bound: $m_u = m_u + p_j(s', a^*)(b_j - l)$

After performing the projection step, compute the cross entropy loss:

$$\text{Cross Entropy} = -\sum_i m_i \log p_i(s, a)$$

Where m is the target probabilities from the target value distribution and $p(s, a)$ is the predicted probabilities from the predicted value distribution. We train our network by minimizing the cross entropy loss.

We don't update the target network parameter θ' in every time step. We freeze the target network parameter θ' for several time steps, and then we copy the main network parameter θ to the target network parameter θ'. We keep repeating the preceding steps for several episodes to approximate the optimal value distribution. To give us a more detailed understanding, the categorical DQN algorithm is given in the next section.

Algorithm – categorical DQN

The categorical DQN algorithm is given in the following steps:

1. Initialize the main network parameter θ with random values

2. Initialize the target network parameter θ' by copying the main network parameter θ

3. Initialize the replay buffer $\mathcal{D}$, the number of support (atoms), and also V_{min} and V_{max}

4. For N number of episodes perform *step 5*

5. For each step in the episode, that is, for $t = 0, \dots, T - 1$:

    1. Feed the state s and support values to the main categorical DQN parameterized by θ and get the probability value for each support.
    Then compute the Q value as $Q(s, a) = \sum_i z_i p_i(s, a)$

    2. After computing the Q value, select an action using the epsilon-greedy policy, that is, with the probability epsilon, select random action a and with probability 1-epsilon, select the action as $a^* = \arg\max_a Q(s, a)$

    3. Perform the selected action and move to the next state s' and obtain the reward r

    4. Store the transition information in the replay buffer $\mathcal{D}$

    5. Randomly sample a transition from the replay buffer $\mathcal{D}$

    6. Feed the next state s' and support values to the target categorical DQN parameterized by θ' and get the probability value for each support. Then compute the value as $Q(s', a) = \sum_i z_i p_i(s', a)$

    7. After computing the Q value, we select the best action in the state s' as the one that has the maximum Q value $a^* = \arg\max_a Q(s', a)$

    8. Initialize the array m with zero values with its shape as the number of support

    9. For j in range of the number of support:

        1. Compute the target support value: $\hat{t}z_j = [r_t + \gamma_t z_j]_{V_{min}}^{V_{max}}$

        2. Compute the value of b: $b_j = (\hat{t}z_j - V_{min})/\Delta z$

3. Compute the lower bound and upper bound: $l = \lfloor b_j \rfloor, u = \lceil b_j \rceil$

4. Distribute the probability on the lower bound:
$$m_l = m_l + p_j(s', a^*)(u - b_j)$$

5. Distribute the probability on the upper bound:
$$m_u = m_u + p_j(s', a^*)(b_j - l)$$

10. Compute the cross entropy loss: Cross Entropy $= -\sum_i m_i \log p_i(s, a)$

11. Minimize the loss using gradient descent and update the parameter of the main network

12. Freeze the target network parameter θ' for several time steps and then update it by just copying the main network parameter θ

Now that we have learned the categorical DQN algorithm, to understand how a categorical DQN works, we will implement it in the next section.

Playing Atari games using a categorical DQN

Let's implement the categorical DQN algorithm to play Atari games. The code used in this section is adapted from an open-source categorical DQN implementation, `https://github.com/princewen/tensorflow_practice/tree/master/RL/Basic-DisRL-Demo`, provided by Prince Wen.

First, let's import the necessary libraries:

```
import numpy as np
import random
from collections import deque
import math
import tensorflow.compat.v1 as tf
tf.disable_v2_behavior()

import gym
from tensorflow.python.framework import ops
```

Defining the variables

Now, let's define some of the important variables.

Initialize the V_{min} and V_{max}:

```
v_min = 0
v_max = 1000
```

Initialize the number of atoms (supports):

```
atoms = 51
```

Set the discount factor, γ:

```
gamma = 0.99
```

Set the batch size:

```
batch_size = 64
```

Set the time step at which we want to update the target network:

```
update_target_net = 50
```

Set the epsilon value that is used in the epsilon-greedy policy:

```
epsilon = 0.5
```

Defining the replay buffer

First, let's define the buffer length:

```
buffer_length = 20000
```

Define the replay buffer as a deque structure:

```
replay_buffer = deque(maxlen=buffer_length)
```

We define a function called `sample_transitions` that returns the randomly sampled minibatch of transitions from the replay buffer:

```
def sample_transitions(batch_size):
    batch = np.random.permutation(len(replay_buffer))[:batch_size]
    trans = np.array(replay_buffer)[batch]
    return trans
```

Defining the categorical DQN class

Let's define a class called `Categorical_DQN` where we will implement the categorical DQN algorithm. Instead of looking into the whole code at once, we will look into only the important parts. The complete code used in this section is available in the GitHub repo of the book.

For a clear understanding, let's take a look into the code line by line:

```
class Categorical_DQN():
```

Defining the init method

First, let's define the init method:

```
    def __init__(self,env):
```

Start the TensorFlow session:

```
        self.sess = tf.InteractiveSession()
```

Initialize the V_{min} and V_{max}:

```
        self.v_max = v_max
        self.v_min = v_min
```

Initialize the number of atoms:

```
        self.atoms = atoms
```

Initialize the epsilon value:

```
        self.epsilon = epsilon
```

Get the state shape of the environment:

```
        self.state_shape = env.observation_space.shape
```

Get the action shape of the environment:

```
self.action_shape = env.action_space.n
```

Initialize the time step:

```
self.time_step = 0
```

Initialize the target state shape:

```
target_state_shape = [1]
target_state_shape.extend(self.state_shape)
```

Define the placeholder for the state:

```
self.state_ph = tf.placeholder(tf.float32,target_state_shape)
```

Define the placeholder for the action:

```
self.action_ph = tf.placeholder(tf.int32,[1,1])
```

Define the placeholder for the *m* value (the distributed probability of the target distribution):

```
self.m_ph = tf.placeholder(tf.float32,[self.atoms])
```

Compute the value of $\triangle z$ as $\triangle z = V_{max} - V_{min}/N - 1$:

```
self.delta_z = (self.v_max - self.v_min) / (self.atoms - 1)
```

Compute the support values as $z_i = V_{min} + i \triangle z : 0 \leq i < N$:

```
self.z = [self.v_min + i * self.delta_z for i in range(self.
atoms)]
```

Build the categorical DQN:

```
self.build_categorical_DQN()
```

Initialize all the TensorFlow variables:

```
self.sess.run(tf.global_variables_initializer())
```

Building the categorical DQN

Let's define a function called `build_network` for building a deep network. Since we are dealing with Atari games, we use the convolutional neural network:

```
def build_network(self, state, action, name, units_1, units_2,
weights, bias):
```

Define the first convolutional layer:

```
with tf.variable_scope('conv1'):
    conv1 = conv(state, [5, 5, 3, 6], [6], [1, 2, 2, 1],
weights, bias)
```

Define the second convolutional layer:

```
with tf.variable_scope('conv2'):
    conv2 = conv(conv1, [3, 3, 6, 12], [12], [1, 2, 2, 1],
weights, bias)
```

Flatten the feature maps obtained as a result of the second convolutional layer:

```
with tf.variable_scope('flatten'):
    flatten = tf.layers.flatten(conv2)
```

Define the first dense layer:

```
with tf.variable_scope('dense1'):
    dense1 = dense(flatten, units_1, [units_1], weights, bias)
```

Define the second dense layer:

```
with tf.variable_scope('dense2'):
    dense2 = dense(dense1, units_2, [units_2], weights, bias)
```

Concatenate the second dense layer with the action:

```
with tf.variable_scope('concat'):
    concatenated = tf.concat([dense2, tf.cast(action,
tf.float32)], 1)
```

Define the third layer and apply the softmax function to the result of the third layer and obtain the probabilities for each of the atoms:

```
with tf.variable_scope('dense3'):
    dense3 = dense(concatenated, self.atoms, [self.atoms],
```

```
weights, bias)

        return tf.nn.softmax(dense3)
```

Now, let's define a function called `build_categorical_DQN` for building the main and target categorical DQNs:

```
def build_categorical_DQN(self):
```

Define the main categorical DQN and obtain the probabilities:

```
with tf.variable_scope('main_net'):
    name = ['main_net_params',tf.GraphKeys.GLOBAL_VARIABLES]
    weights = tf.random_uniform_initializer(-0.1,0.1)
    bias = tf.constant_initializer(0.1)

    self.main_p = self.build_network(self.state_ph,self.action_
ph,name,24,24,weights,bias)
```

Define the target categorical DQN and obtain the probabilities:

```
with tf.variable_scope('target_net'):
    name = ['target_net_params',tf.GraphKeys.GLOBAL_VARIABLES]

    weights = tf.random_uniform_initializer(-0.1,0.1)
    bias = tf.constant_initializer(0.1)

    self.target_p = self.build_network(self.state_ph,self.
action_ph,name,24,24,weights,bias)
```

Compute the main Q value with the probabilities obtained from the main categorical DQN as $Q(s, a) = \sum_i z_i P_i(s, a)$:

```
self.main_Q = tf.reduce_sum(self.main_p * self.z)
```

Similarly, compute the target Q value with probabilities obtained from the target categorical DQN as $Q(s', a) = \sum_i z_i p_i(s', a)$:

```
self.target_Q = tf.reduce_sum(self.target_p * self.z)
```

Define the cross entropy loss as $\text{Cross Entropy} = -\sum_i m_i \log p_i(s, a)$:

```
self.cross_entropy_loss = -tf.reduce_sum(self.m_ph *
tf.log(self.main_p))
```

Define the optimizer and minimize the cross entropy loss using the Adam optimizer:

```
self.optimizer = tf.train.AdamOptimizer(0.01).minimize(self.
cross_entropy_loss)
```

Get the main network parameters:

```
main_net_params = tf.get_collection("main_net_params")
```

Get the target network parameters:

```
target_net_params = tf.get_collection('target_net_params')
```

Define the `update_target_net` operation for updating the target network parameters by copying the parameters of the main network:

```
self.update_target_net = [tf.assign(t, e) for t, e in
zip(target_net_params, main_net_params)]
```

Defining the train function

Let's define a function called `train` to train the network:

```
def train(self,s,r,action,s_,gamma):
```

Increment the time step:

```
self.time_step += 1
```

Get the target Q values:

```
list_q_ = [self.sess.run(self.target_Q,feed_dict={self.state_
ph:[s_],self.action_ph:[[a]]}) for a in range(self.action_shape)]
```

Select the next state action a' as the one that has the maximum Q value:

```
a_ = tf.argmax(list_q_).eval()
```

Initialize an array m with its shape as the number of support with zero values. The m denotes the distributed probability of the target distribution after the projection step:

```
m = np.zeros(self.atoms)
```

Get the probability for each atom using the target categorical DQN:

```
        p = self.sess.run(self.target_p,feed_dict = {self.state_
ph:[s_],self.action_ph:[[a_]]})[0]
```

Perform the projection step:

```
    for j in range(self.atoms):
        Tz = min(self.v_max,max(self.v_min,r+gamma * self.z[j]))
        bj = (Tz - self.v_min) / self.delta_z
        l,u = math.floor(bj),math.ceil(bj)

        pj = p[j]

        m[int(l)] += pj * (u - bj)
        m[int(u)] += pj * (bj - l)
```

Train the network by minimizing the loss:

```
        self.sess.run(self.optimizer,feed_dict={self.state_ph:[s] ,
    self.action_ph:[action], self.m_ph: m })
```

Update the target network parameters by copying the main network parameters:

```
        if self.time_step % update_target_net == 0:
            self.sess.run(self.update_target_net)
```

Selecting the action

Let's define a function called `select_action` for selecting the action:

```
    def select_action(self,s):
```

We generate a random number, and if the number is less than epsilon we select the random action, else we select the action that has the maximum Q value:

```
        if random.random() <= self.epsilon:
            return random.randint(0, self.action_shape - 1)
        else:
            return np.argmax([self.sess.run(self.main_Q,feed_
    dict={self.state_ph:[s],self.action_ph:[[a]]}) for a in range(self.
    action_shape)])
```

Training the network

Now, let's start training the network. First, create the Atari game environment using gym. Let's create a Tennis game environment:

```
env = gym.make("Tennis-v0")
```

Create an object to our Categorical_DQN class:

```
agent = Categorical_DQN(env)
```

Set the number of episodes:

```
num_episodes = 800
```

For each episode:

```
for i in range(num_episodes):
```

Set done to False:

```
done = False
```

Initialize the return:

```
Return = 0
```

Initialize the state by resetting the environment:

```
state = env.reset()
```

While the episode is not over:

```
while not done:
```

Render the environment:

```
env.render()
```

Select an action:

```
action = agent.select_action(state)
```

Perform the selected action:

```
next_state, reward, done, info = env.step(action)
```

Update the return:

```
Return = Return + reward
```

Store the transition information in the replay buffer:

```
replay_buffer.append([state, reward, [action], next_state])
```

If the length of the replay buffer is greater than or equal to the buffer size then start training the network by sampling transitions from the replay buffer:

```
if len(replay_buffer) >= batch_size:
    trans = sample_transitions(batch_size)
    for item in trans:
        agent.train(item[0],item[1], item[2], item[3],gamma)
```

Update the state to the next state:

```
state = next_state
```

Print the return obtained in the episode:

```
print("Episode:{}, Return: {}".format(i,Return))
```

Now that we have learned how a categorical DQN works and how to implement it, in the next section, we will learn about another interesting algorithm.

Quantile Regression DQN

In this section, we will look into another interesting distributional RL algorithm called QR-DQN. It is a distributional DQN algorithm similar to the categorical DQN; however, it has several features that make it more advantageous than a categorical DQN.

Math essentials

Before going ahead, let's recap two important concepts that we use in QR-DQN:

- **Quantile**
- **Inverse cumulative distribution function (Inverse CDF)**

Quantile

When we divide our distribution into equal areas of probability, they are called quantiles. For instance, as *Figure 14.18* shows, we have divided our distribution into two equal areas of probabilities and we have two quantiles with 50% probability each:

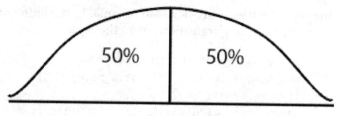

Figure 14.18: 2-quantile plot

Inverse CDF (quantile function)

To understand an **inverse cumulative distribution function (inverse CDF)**, first, let's learn what a **cumulative distribution function (CDF)** is.

Consider a random variable X, and $P(X)$ denotes the probability distribution of X. Then the cumulative distribution function is expressed as:

$$F(x) = P(X \leq x)$$

It basically implies that $F(x)$ can be obtained by adding up all the probabilities that are less than or equal to x.

Let's look at the following CDF:

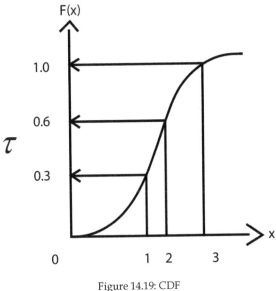

Figure 14.19: CDF

In the preceding plot, τ_i represents the cumulative probability, that is, $\tau_i = F(x_i)$. Say $i = 1$, then $\tau_1 = F(1) = 0.3$.

The CDF takes x as an input and returns the cumulative probability τ. Hence, we can write:

$$\tau = F(x)$$

Say $x = 2$, then we get $\tau = 0.6$.

Now, we will look at the inverse CDF. Inverse CDF, as the name suggests, is the inverse of the CDF. That is, in CDF, given the support x, we obtain the cumulative probability τ, whereas in inverse CDF, given the cumulative probability τ, we obtain the support x. Inverse CDF can be expressed as:

$$x = F^{-1}(\tau)$$

The following plot shows the inverse CDF:

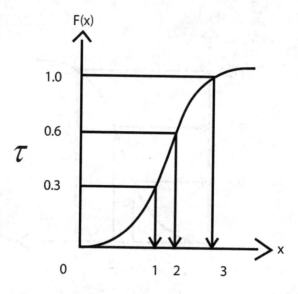

Figure 14.20: Inverse CDF

As shown in *Figure 14.20*, given the cumulative probability τ, we obtain the support x.

Say $\tau = 0.6$, then we get $x = 2$.

We have learned that the quantiles are equally divided probabilities. As *Figure 14.20* shows, we have three quantiles q_1 to q_3 with equally divided probabilities and the quantile values are [0.3,0.6,1.0], which are just our cumulative probabilities. Hence, we can say that the inverse CDF (quantile function) helps us to obtain the value of support given the equally divided probabilities. Note that in inverse CDF, the support should always be increasing as it is based on the cumulative probability.

Now that we have learned what the quantile function is, we will gain an understanding of how we can make use of the quantile function in the distributional RL setting using an algorithm called QR-DQN.

Understanding QR-DQN

In categorical DQN (C51), we learned that in order to predict the value distribution, the network takes the support of the distribution as input and returns the probabilities.

To compute the support, we also need to decide the number of support N, the minimum value of support V_{min}, and the maximum value of support V_{max}.

If you recollect in C51, our support values are equally spaced at fixed locations $(z_1, z_2, \ldots, z_n)$ and we feed this equally spaced support as input and obtained the non-uniform probabilities $(p_1, p_2, \ldots, p_n)$. As *Figure 14.21* shows, in C51, we feed the equally spaced support (z_1, z_2, z_3, z_4) as input to the network along with the state(s) and obtain the non-uniform probabilities (p_1, p_2, p_3, p_4) as output:

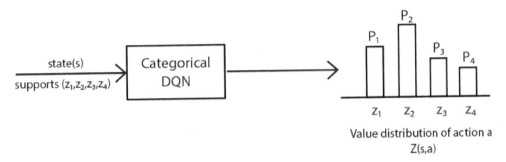

Figure 14.21: Categorical DQN

QR-DQN can be viewed just as the opposite of C51. In QR-DQN, to estimate the value distribution, we feed the uniform probabilities $(p_1, p_2, \ldots, p_n)$ and the network outputs the supports at variable locations $(z_1, z_2, \ldots, z_n)$. As shown in the following figure, we feed the uniform probabilities (p_1, p_2, p_3, p_4) as input to the network along with the state(s) and obtain the support (z_1, z_2, z_3, z_4) placed at variable locations as output:

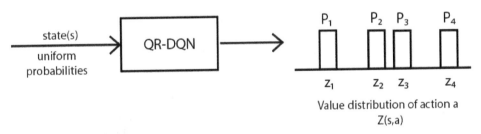

Figure 14.22: QR-DQN

Thus, from the two preceding figures we can observe that, in a categorical DQN, along with the state, we feed the fixed support at equally spaced intervals as input to the network and it returns the non-uniform probabilities, whereas in a QR-DQN, along with the state, we feed the fixed uniform probabilities as input to the network and it returns the support at variable locations (unequally spaced support).

Okay, but what's the use of this? How does a QR-DQN work exactly? Let's explore this in detail.

We understood that a QR-DQN takes the uniform probabilities as input and returns the support values for estimating the value distribution. Can we make use of the quantile function to estimate the value distribution? Yes! We learned that the quantile function helps us to obtain the values of support given the equally divided probabilities. Thus, in QR-DQN, we estimate the value distribution by estimating the quantile function.

The quantile function is given as:

$$z = F^{-1}(\tau)$$

Where z is the support and τ is the equally divided cumulative probability. Thus, we can obtain the support z given τ.

Let N be the number of quantiles, then the probability can be obtained as:

$$p_i = \frac{1}{N} \text{ for } i = 1, 2, ..., N$$

For example, if $N = 4$, then $p = [0.25, 0.25. 0.25, 0.25]$. If $N = 5$, then p = [0.20, 0.20, 0.20, 0.20, 0.20].

Once we decide the number of quantiles N, the cumulative probabilities τ (quantile values) can be obtained as:

$$\tau_i = \frac{i}{N} \text{ for } i = 1, ..., N$$

For example, if $N = 4$, then $\tau = [0.25, 0.50, 0.75, 1.0]$. If $N = 5$, then $\tau = [0.2, 0.4, 0.6, 0.8, 1.0]$.

We just feed this equally divided cumulative probability τ (quantile values) as input to the QR-DQN and it returns the support value. That is, we have learned that the QR-DQN estimates the value distribution as the quantile function, so we just feed the τ and obtain the support values z of the value distribution.

Let's understand this with a simple example. Say we are in a state s and we have two possible actions *up* and *down* to perform in the state. As shown in the following figure, along with giving the state s as input to the network, we also feed the quantile value τ, which is just the equally divided cumulative probability. Then our network returns the support for the distribution of action *up* and the distribution of action *down*:

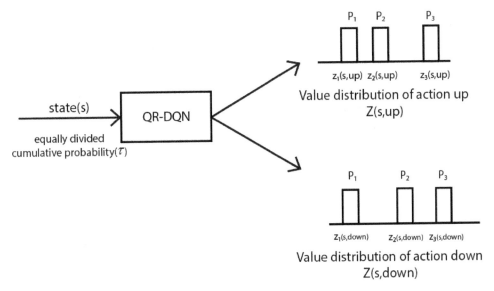

Figure 14.23: QR-DQN

If you recollect, in C51, we computed the probability $p(s, a)$ for the given state and action, whereas here in QR-DQN, we compute the support $z(s, a)$ for the given state and action.

 Note that we use capital $Z(s, a)$ to represent the value distribution and small $z(s, a)$ to represent the support of the distribution.

Similarly, we can also compute the target value distribution using the quantile function. Then we train our network by minimizing the distance between the predicted quantile and the target quantile distribution.

Still, the fundamental question is why are we doing this? How it is more beneficial than C51? There are several advantages of quantile regression DQN over categorical DQN. In quantile regression DQN:

- We don't have to choose the number of supports and the bounds of support, which is V_{min} and V_{max}.
- There are no limitations on the bounds of support, thus the range of returns can vary across states.
- We can also get rid of the projection step that we performed in the C51 to match the supports of the target and predicted distribution.

One more important advantage of a QR-DQN is that it minimizes the p-Wasserstein distance between the predicted and target distribution. But why is this important? Minimizing the Wasserstein distance between the target and predicted distribution helps us in attaining convergence better than minimizing the cross entropy.

Okay, what exactly is the p-Wasserstein distance? The p-Wasserstein distance, W_p, is characterized as the L^p metric on inverse CDF. Say we have two distributions U and V, then the p-Wasserstein metric between these two distributions is given as:

$$W_p(U,V) = \left(\int_0^1 |F_V^{-1}(\omega) - F_U^{-1}(\omega)|^p d\omega \right)^{\frac{1}{p}}$$

Where $F_U^{-1}(\omega)$ and $F_V^{-1}(\omega)$ denote the inverse CDF of the distributions U and V respectively. Thus, minimizing the distance between two inverse CDFs implies that we minimize the Wasserstein distance.

We learned that in QR-DQN, we train the network by minimizing the distance between the predicted and target distribution, and both of them are quantile functions (inverse CDF). Thus, minimizing the distance between the predicted and target distribution (inverse CDFs) implies that we minimize the Wasserstein distance.

The authors of the QR-DQN paper (see the *Further reading* section for more details) also highlighted that instead of computing the support for the quantile values τ, they suggest using the quantile midpoint values $\hat{\tau}$. The quantile midpoint can be computed as:

$$\hat{\tau}_i = \frac{\tau_{i-1} + \tau_i}{2}$$

That is, the value of the support z can be obtained using quantile midpoint values as $z = F^{-1}(\hat{\tau})$ instead of obtaining support using the quantile values as $z = F^{-1}(\tau)$.

But why the quantile midpoint? The quantile midpoint acts as a unique minimizer, that is, the Wasserstein distance between two inverse CDFs will be less when we use quantile midpoint values $\hat{\tau}$ instead of quantile values τ. Since we are trying to minimize the Wasserstein distance between the target and predicted distribution, we can use quantile midpoints $\hat{\tau}$ so that the distance between them will be less. For instance, as *Figure 14.24* shows, the Wasserstein distance is less when we use the quantile midpoint values $\hat{\tau}$ instead of quantile values τ:

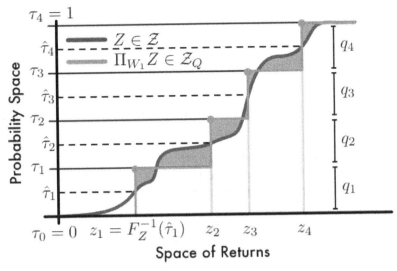

Figure 14.24: Using quantile midpoint values instead of quantile values

Source (`https://arxiv.org/pdf/1710.10044.pdf`)

In a nutshell, in QR-DQNs, we compute the value distribution as a quantile function. So, we just feed the cumulative probabilities that are equally divided probabilities into the network and obtain the support values of the distribution and we train the network by minimizing the Wasserstein distance between the target and predicted distribution.

Action selection

Action selection in QR-DQN is just the same as in C51. First, we extract Q value from the predicted value distribution and then we select the action as the one that has the maximum Q value. We can extract the Q value by just taking the expectation of the value distribution. The expectation of distribution is given as a sum of support multiplied by their corresponding probability.

In C51, we computed the Q value as:

$$Q(s, a) = \sum_i z_i p_i(s, a)$$

Where $p_i(s, a)$ is the probability given by the network for state s and action a and z_i is the support.

Whereas in a QR-DQN, our network outputs the support instead of the probability. So, the Q value in the QR-DQN can be computed as:

$$Q(s,a) = \sum_i p_i z_i(s,a)$$

Where $z_i(s, a)$ is the support given by the network for state s and action a and p_i is the probability.

After computing the Q value, we select the action that has the maximum Q value. For instance, let's say, we have a state s and two actions in the state, let them be *up* and *down*. The Q value for action *up* in the state s is computed as:

$$Q(s,\text{up}) = \sum_i p_i z_i(s,\text{up})$$

The Q value for action *down* in the state s is computed as:

$$Q(s,\text{down}) = \sum_i p_i z_i(s,\text{down})$$

After computing the Q value, we select the optimal action as the one that has the maximum Q value:

$$a^* = \arg\max_a Q(s,a)$$

Now that we have learned how to select actions in QR-DQN, in the next section, we will look into the loss function of QR-DQN.

Loss function

In C51, we used cross entropy loss as our loss function because our network predicts the probability of the value distribution. So we used the cross entropy loss to minimize the probabilities between the target and predicted distribution. But in QR-DQN, we predict the support of the distribution instead of the probabilities. That is, in QR-DQN, we feed the probabilities as input and predict the support as output. So, how can we define the loss function for a QR-DQN?

We can use the quantile regression loss to minimize the distance between the target support and the predicted support. But first, let's understand how to calculate the target support value.

Before going ahead, let's recall how we compute the target value in a DQN. In DQN, we use the Bellman equation and compute the target value as:

$$y = r + \gamma \max_{a'} Q(s', a')$$

In the preceding equation, we select action a' by taking the maximum Q value over all possible next state-action pairs.

Similarly, in QR-DQN, to compute the target value, we can use the distributional Bellman equation. The distributional Bellman equation can be given as:

$$\tau Z(s, a) \equiv r + \gamma Z(s' + a')$$

So, the target support z_j can be computed as:

$$\tau z_j = r + \gamma z_j(s', a')$$

To compute support z_j for the state s', we also need to select some action a'. How can we select an action? We just compute the return distribution of all next state-action pairs using the target network and select the action a^* that has the maximum Q value:

$$\tau z_j = r + \gamma z_j(s', a^*)$$

Now that we have learned how to compute the target support value, let's see how to compute the quantile regression loss. The advantage of using the quantile regression loss is that it adds a penalty to the overestimation and underestimation error. Let's understand this with an example.

Let's say the target support value is [1, 5, 10, 15, 20] and the predicted support value is [100, 5, 10, 15, 20]. As we can see, our predicted support has a very high value in the initial quantile and then it is decreasing. In the inverse CDF section, we learned that support should always be increasing as it is based on the cumulative probability. But if you look at the predicted values the support starts from 100 and then decreases.

Let's consider another case. Suppose the target support value is [1, 5, 10, 15, 20] and the predicted support value is [1, 5, 10, 15, 4]. As we can see, our predicted support value is increasing from the initial quantile and then it is decreasing to 4 in the final quantile. But this should not happen. Since we are using inverse CDF, our support values should always be increasing.

Thus, we need to make sure that our support should be increasing and not decreasing. So, if the initial quantile values are overestimated with high values and if the later quantile values are underestimated with low values, we can penalize them. That is, we multiply the overestimated value by τ and the underestimated value by $(\tau - 1)$. Okay, how can we determine if the value is overestimated or underestimated?

First, we compute the difference between the target and the predicted value. Let u be the difference between the target support value and the predicted support value. Then, if the value of u is less than 0, we multiply u by $(\tau - 1)$, else we multiply u by τ. This is known as **quantile regression loss**.

But the problem with quantile regression loss is that it will not be smooth at 0 and it makes the gradient stay constant. So, instead of using quantile regression loss, we use a new modified version of loss called quantile Huber loss.

To understand how exactly quantile Huber loss works, first, let's look into the Huber loss. Let's denote the difference between our actual and predicted values as u. Then the Huber loss $\mathcal{L}_\kappa(u)$ can be given as:

$$\mathcal{L}_\kappa(u) = \begin{cases} 0.5\,u^2 & , & if\,|u| \leq \kappa \\ \kappa(|u| - 0.5\kappa), & & \text{otherwise} \end{cases}$$

Let $\kappa = 1$, then, when the absolute value, $|u|$, is less than or equal to κ, the Huber loss is given as the quadratic loss, $0.5\,u^2$, else it is a linear loss, $K(|u| - 0.5\kappa)$.

The following Python snippet helps us to understand Huber loss better:

```python
def huber_loss(target,predicted, kappa=1):

    #compute u as difference between target and predicted value
    u = target - predicted

    #absolute value of u
    abs_u = abs(u)

    #compute quadratic loss
    quad_loss = 0.5 * (abs_u ** 2)

    #compute linear loss
    linear_loss = kappa * (abs_u - 0.5 * kappa)

    #true where the absolute value is less than or equal to kappa
    flag = abs_u <= kappa
```

```
    #Loss is the quadratic loss where the absolute value is less than
kappa
    #else it is linear loss

    loss = (flag) * quad_loss + (~flag) * linear_loss

    return loss
```

Now that we have understood what the Huber loss $\mathcal{L}_\kappa(u)$ is, let's look into the quantile Huber loss. In the quantile Huber loss, when the value of u (the difference between target and predicted support) is less than 0, then we multiply the Huber loss $\mathcal{L}_\kappa(u)$ by $1 - \tau$, and when the value of u is greater than or equal to 0, we multiply the Huber loss $\mathcal{L}_\kappa(u)$ by τ.

Now that we have understood how a QR-DQN works, in the next section, we will look into another interesting algorithm called D4PG.

Distributed Distributional DDPG

D4PG, which stands for **D**istributed **D**istributional **D**eep **D**eterministic **P**olicy **G**radient, is one of the most interesting policy gradient algorithms. We can make a guess about how D4PG works just by its name. As the name suggests, D4PG is basically a combination of **deep deterministic policy gradient (DDPG)** and distributional reinforcement learning, and it works in a distributed fashion. Confused? Let's go deeper and understand how D4PG works in detail.

To understand how D4PG works, it is highly recommended to revise the DDPG algorithm we covered in *Chapter 12, Learning DDPG, TD3, and SAC*. We learned that DDPG is an actor critic method where the actor tries to learn the policy while the critic tries to evaluate the policy produced by the actor using the Q function. The critic uses the deep Q network for estimating the Q function and the actor uses the policy network for computing the policy. Thus, the actor performs an action while the critic gives feedback to the action performed by the actor and, based on the critic feedback, the actor network will be updated.

D4PG works just like DDPG but in the critic network, instead of using a DQN for estimating the Q function, we can use our distributional DQN to estimate the value distribution. That is, in the previous sections, we have learned several distributional DQN algorithms, such as C51 and QR-DQN. So, in the critic network, instead of using a regular DQN, we can use any distributional DQN algorithm, say C51.

Apart from this, D4PG also proposes several changes to the DDPG architecture. So, we will get into the details and learn how exactly D4PG differs from DDPG. Before going ahead, let's be clear with the notation:

- The policy network parameter is represented by ϕ and the target policy network parameter is represented by ϕ'.

- The critic network parameter is represented by θ and the target critic network parameter is represented by θ'.

- Since we are talking about a deterministic policy, let's represent it by μ, and our policy is parameterized by the policy network, so we can denote the policy by μ_ϕ.

Now, we will understand how exactly the critic and actor network in D4PG works.

Critic network

In DDPG, we learned that we use the critic network to estimate the Q function. Thus, given a state and action, the critic network estimates the Q function as $Q_\theta(s, a)$. To train the critic network we minimize the MSE between the target Q value given by the Bellman optimality equation and the Q value predicted by the network.

The target value in DDPG is computed as:

$$y_i = r_i + \gamma Q_{\theta'}\left(s_i', \mu_{\phi'}(s_i')\right) \tag{1}$$

Once we compute the target value, we compute the loss as the MSE between the target value and the predicted value as:

$$J(\theta) = \frac{1}{K}\sum_i \left(y_i - Q_\theta(s_i, a_i)\right)^2$$

Where K denotes the number of transitions randomly sampled from the replay buffer. After computing the loss, we compute the gradients $\nabla_\theta J(\theta)$ and update the critic network parameter using gradient descent:

$$\theta = \theta - \alpha\nabla_\theta J(\theta)$$

Now, let's talk about the critic in D4PG. As we learned in D4PG, we use the distributional DQN to estimate the Q value. Thus, given a state and action, the critic network estimates the value distribution as $Z_\theta(s, a)$.

To train the critic network, we minimize the distance between the target value distribution given by the distributional Bellman equation and the value distribution predicted by the network.

The target value distribution in D4PG is computed as:

$$y_i = r_i + \gamma Z_{\theta'}\left(s_i', \mu_{\phi'}(s_i')\right) \tag{2}$$

As you can observe, equation (2) is similar to (1) except that we just replaced Q with Z, indicating that we are computing the target value distribution. D4PG proposes one more change to the target value computation (2). Instead of using the one-step return r, we use the **N-step return**, and it can be expressed as:

$$y_i = \left(\sum_{n=0}^{N-1} \gamma^n r_{i+N}\right) + \gamma^N Z_{\theta'}(s_{i+N}', \mu_{\theta'}(s_{i+N}'))$$

Where N is the length of the transition, which we sample from the replay buffer.

After computing the target value distribution, we can compute the distance between the target value distribution and the predicted value distribution as:

$$J(\theta) = \frac{1}{K}\sum_i d(y_i, Z_\theta(s, a))$$

Where d denotes any distance measure for measuring the distance between two distributions. Say we are using C51, then d denotes the cross entropy and K denotes the number of transitions sampled from the replay buffer. After computing the loss, we calculate the gradients and update the critic network parameter. The gradients can be computed as:

$$\nabla_\theta J(\theta) = \frac{1}{K}\sum_i \nabla_\theta d\left(y_i, Z_\theta(s, a)\right)$$

D4PG proposes a small change to our gradient updates. In D4PG, we use a **prioritized experience replay.** Let's say we have an experience replay buffer of size R. Each transition in the replay buffer will have a non-uniform probability p_i. The non-uniform probability helps us to give more importance to one transition than the other. Say we have a sample i, then its probability can be given as $\frac{1}{Rp_i}$ or Rp_i^{-1}.

While updating the critic network, we weight the updates using $(Rp_i)^{-1}$, which gives importance to the updates.

Thus our gradient computation becomes:

$$\nabla_\theta J(\theta) = \frac{1}{K} \sum_i \nabla_\theta (Rp_i)^{-1} d\left(y_i, Z_\theta(s, a)\right)$$

After computing the gradient, we can update the critic network parameter using gradient descent as $\theta = \theta - \alpha \nabla_\theta J(\theta)$. Now that we have understood how the critic network works in D4PG, let's look into the actor network in the next section.

Actor network

First, let's quickly recap how the actor network in DDPG works. In DDPG, we learned that the actor network takes the state as input and returns the action:

$$a = \mu_\phi(s)$$

Note that we are using the deterministic policy in the continuous action space, and to explore new actions we just add some noise $\mathcal{N}$ to the action produced by the actor network since the action is a continuous value.

So, our modified action can be represented as:

$$a = \mu_\phi(s) + \mathcal{N}$$

Thus, the objective function of the actor is to generate an action that maximizes the Q value produced by the citric network:

$$J(\phi) = \frac{1}{K} \sum_i Q_\theta(s_i, a)$$

Where $a = \mu_\phi(s_i)$.

We learned that to maximize the objective, we compute the gradients of our objective function $\nabla_\phi J(\phi)$ and update the actor network parameter by performing gradient ascent.

Now let's come to D4PG. In D4PG we perform the same steps with a little difference. Note that here we are not using the Q function in the critic. Instead, we are computing the value distribution and thus our objective function becomes:

$$J(\phi) = \frac{1}{K} \sum_i Z_\theta(s_i, a)$$

Where the action, $a = \mu_\phi(s_i)$ and just like we saw in DDPG, to maximize the objective, first, we compute the gradients of our objective function $\nabla_\phi J(\phi)$. After computing the gradients we update the actor network parameter by performing gradient ascent:

$$\phi = \phi + \alpha \nabla_\phi J(\phi)$$

We learned that D4PG is a **distributed** algorithm, meaning that instead of using one actor, we use L **number of actors**, each of which acts parallel and is independent of the environment, collects experience, and stores the experience in the replay buffer. Then we update the network parameter to the actors periodically.

Thus, to summarize, D4PG is similar to DDPG except for the following:

1. We use the distributional DQN in the critic network instead of using the regular DQN to estimate the Q values.

2. We calculate N-step returns in the target instead of calculating the one-step return.

3. We use a prioritized experience replay and add importance to the gradient update in the critic network.

4. Instead of using one actor, we use **L** independent actors, each of which acts in parallel, collects experience, and stores the experience in the replay buffer.

Now that we have understood how D4PG works, putting together all the concepts we have learned, let's look into the algorithm of D4PG in the next section.

Algorithm – D4PG

Let t_{target} denote the time steps at which we want to update the target critic and actor network parameters. We set $t_{target} = 2$, which states that we update the target critic network and target actor network parameter for every 2 steps of the episode. Similarly, let t_{actors} denote the time steps at which we want to replicate the network weights to the L actors. We set $t_{actors} = 2$, which states that we replicate the network weights to the actors on every 2 steps of the episode.

The algorithm of D4PG is given as follows:

1. Initialize the critic network parameter θ and actor network parameter ϕ
2. Initialize target critic network parameter θ' and target actor network parameter ϕ' by copying from θ and ϕ respectively
3. Initialize the replay buffer $\mathcal{D}$
4. Launch the L number of actors
5. For N number of episodes, repeat *step 6*
6. For each step in the episode, that is, for $t = 0, \dots, T-1$:

    1. Randomly sample a minibatch of K transitions from the replay buffer $\mathcal{D}$
    2. Compute the target value distribution of the critic, that is,

    $$y_i = \left(\sum_{n=0}^{N-1} \gamma^n r_{i+N} \right) + \gamma^N Z_{\theta'}(s'_{i+N}, \mu_{\theta'}(s'_{i+N}))$$

    3. Compute the loss of the critic network and calculate the gradient as

    $$\nabla_\theta J(\theta) = \frac{1}{K} \sum_i \nabla_\theta (Rp_i)^{-1} d\left(y_i, Z_\theta(s,a) \right)$$

    4. After computing the gradients, update the critic network parameter using gradient descent: $\theta = \theta - \alpha \nabla_\theta J(\theta)$
    5. Compute the gradient of the actor network $\nabla_\phi J(\phi)$
    6. Update the actor network parameter by gradient ascent:
       $\phi = \phi + \alpha \nabla_\phi J(\phi)$
    7. If $t \bmod t_{target} = 0$, then:

Update the target critic and target actor network parameter using soft replacement as $\theta' = \tau\theta + (1 - \tau)\theta'$ and $\phi' = \tau\phi + (1 - \tau)\phi'$ respectively

8. If $t \bmod t_{actors} = 0$, then:

Replicate the network weights to the actors

And we perform the following steps in the actor network:

1. Select action a based on the policy $\mu_\phi(s)$ and exploration noise, that is, $a = \mu_\phi(s) + \mathcal{N}$

2. Perform the selected action a, move to the next state s', get the reward r, and store the transition information in the replay buffer $\mathcal{D}$

3. Repeat *steps 1* to *2* until the learner finishes

Thus, we have learned how D4PG works.

Summary

We started the chapter by understanding how distributional reinforcement learning works. We learned that in distributional reinforcement learning, instead of selecting an action based on the expected return, we select the action based on the distribution of return, which is often called the value distribution or return distribution.

Next, we learned about the categorical DQN algorithm, also known as C51, where we feed the state and support of the distribution as the input and the network returns the probabilities of the value distribution. We also learned how the projection step matches the support of the target and predicted the value distribution so that we can apply the cross entropy loss.

Going ahead, we learned about quantile regression DQNs, where we feed the state and also the equally divided cumulative probabilities τ as input to the network and it returns the support value of the distribution.

At the end of the chapter, we learned about how D4PG works, and we also learned how it varies from DDPG.

Questions

Let's test our knowledge of distributional reinforcement learning by answering the following questions:

1. What is distributional reinforcement learning?
2. What is a categorical DQN?
3. Why is the categorical DQN called the C51 algorithm?
4. What is the quantile function?
5. How does a QR-DQN differ from a categorical DQN?
6. How does D4PG differ from DDPG?

Further reading

For more information, refer to the following papers:

*   **A Distributional Perspective on Reinforcement Learning** by *Marc G. Bellemare, Will Dabney, Remi Munos*, https://arxiv.org/pdf/1707.06887.pdf

*   **Distributional Reinforcement Learning with Quantile Regression** by *Will Dabney, Mark Rowland, Marc G. Bellemare, Rémi Munos*, https://arxiv.org/pdf/1710.10044.pdf

*   **Distributed Distributional Deep Deterministic Policy Gradient** by *Gabriel Barth-Maron, et al.*, https://arxiv.org/pdf/1804.08617.pdf

15

Imitation Learning and Inverse RL

Learning from demonstration is often called imitation learning. In the imitation learning setting, we have expert demonstrations and train our agent to mimic those expert demonstrations. Learning from demonstrations has many benefits, including helping an agent to learn more quickly. There are several approaches to perform imitation learning, and two of them are **supervised imitation learning** and **Inverse Reinforcement Learning (IRL)**.

First, we will understand how we can perform imitation learning using supervised learning, and then we will learn about an algorithm called **Dataset Aggregation (DAgger)**. Next, we will learn how to use demonstration data in a DQN using an algorithm called **Deep Q Learning from Demonstrations (DQfD)**.

Moving on, we will learn about IRL and how it differs from reinforcement learning. We will learn about one of the most popular IRL algorithms called **maximum entropy IRL**. Toward the end of the chapter, we will understand how **Generative Adversarial Imitation Learning (GAIL)** works.

In this chapter, we will learn about the following topics:

- Supervised imitation learning
- DAgger
- Deep Q learning from demonstrations
- Inverse reinforcement learning

- Maximum entropy inverse reinforcement learning
- Generative adversarial imitation learning

Let's begin our chapter by understanding how supervised imitation learning works.

Supervised imitation learning

In the imitation learning setting, our goal is to mimic the expert. Say, we want to train our agent to drive a car. Instead of training the agent from scratch by having them interact with the environment, we can train them with expert demonstrations. Okay, what are expert demonstrations? An expert demonstrations are a set of trajectories consisting of state-action pairs where each action is performed by the expert.

We can train an agent to mimic the actions performed by the expert in various respective states. Thus, we can view expert demonstrations as training data used to train our agent. The fundamental idea of imitation learning is to imitate (learn) the behavior of an expert.

One of the simplest and most naive ways to perform imitation learning is to treat the imitation learning task as a supervised learning task. First, we collect a set of expert demonstrations, and then we train a classifier to perform the same action performed by the expert in the respective states. We can view this as a big multiclass classification problem and train our agent to perform the action performed by the expert in the respective states.

Our goal is to minimize the loss $L(a^*, \pi_\theta(s))$ where a^* is the expert action and $\pi_\theta(s)$ denotes the action performed by our agent.

Thus, in supervised imitation learning, we perform the following steps:

1. Collect the set of expert demonstrations
2. Initialize a policy π_θ
3. Learn the policy by minimizing the loss function $L(a^*, \pi_\theta(s))$

However, there exist several challenges and drawbacks with this method. The knowledge of the agent is limited only to the expert demonstrations (training data), so if the agent comes across a new state that is not present in the expert demonstrations, then the agent will not know what action to perform in that state.

Say, we train an agent to drive a car using supervised imitation learning and let the agent perform in the real world. If the training data has no state where the agent encounters a traffic signal, then our agent will have no clue about the traffic signal.

Also, the accuracy of the agent is highly dependent on the knowledge of the expert. If the expert demonstrations are poor or not optimal, then the agent cannot learn correct actions or the optimal policy.

To overcome the challenges in supervised imitation learning, we introduce a new algorithm called DAgger. In the next section, we will learn how DAgger works and how it overcomes the limitations of supervised imitation learning.

DAgger

DAgger is one of the most-used imitation learning algorithms. Let's understand how DAgger works with an example. Let's revisit our example of training an agent to drive a car. First, we initialize an empty dataset $\mathcal{D}$.

In the first iteration, we start off with some policy π_1 to drive the car. Thus, we generate a trajectory τ using the policy π_1. We know that the trajectory consists of a sequence of states and actions—that is, states visited by our policy π_1 and actions made in those states using our policy π_1. Now, we create a new dataset $\mathcal{D}_1$ by taking only the states visited by our policy π_1 and we use an expert to provide the actions for those states. That is, we take all the states from the trajectory and ask the expert to provide actions for those states.

Now, we combine the new dataset $\mathcal{D}_1$ with our initialized empty dataset $\mathcal{D}$ and update $\mathcal{D}$ as:

$$\mathcal{D} = \mathcal{D} \cup \mathcal{D}_1$$

Next, we train a classifier on this updated dataset $\mathcal{D}$ and learn a new policy π_2.

In the second iteration, we use the new policy π_2 to generate trajectories, create a new dataset $\mathcal{D}_2$ by taking only the states visited by the new policy π_2, and ask the expert to provide the actions for those states.

Now, we combine the dataset $\mathcal{D}_2$ with $\mathcal{D}$ and update $\mathcal{D}$ as:

$$\mathcal{D} = \mathcal{D} \cup \mathcal{D}_2$$

Next, we train a classifier on this updated dataset $\mathcal{D}$ and learn a new policy π_3.

In the third iteration, we use the new policy π_3 to generate trajectories and create a new dataset $\mathcal{D}_3$ by taking only the states visited by the new policy π_3, and then we ask the expert to provide the actions for those states.

Now, we combine the dataset $\mathcal{D}_3$ with $\mathcal{D}$ and update $\mathcal{D}$ as:

$$\mathcal{D} = \mathcal{D} \cup \mathcal{D}_3$$

Next, we train a classifier on this updated dataset $\mathcal{D}$ and learn a new policy π_4. In this way, DAgger works in a series of iterations until it finds the optimal policy.

Now that we have a basic understanding of Dagger; let's go into more detail and learn how DAgger finds the optimal policy.

Understanding DAgger

Let's suppose we have a human expert, and let's denote the expert policy with π_E. We initialize an empty dataset $\mathcal{D}$ and also a novice policy $\hat{\pi}_1$.

Iteration 1:

In the first iteration, we create a new policy π_1 as:

$$\pi_1 = \beta_1 \pi_E + (1 - \beta_1)\hat{\pi}_1 \qquad (1)$$

The preceding equation implies that we create a new policy π_1 by taking some amount of expert policy π_E and some amount of novice policy $\hat{\pi}_1$. How much of the expert policy and novice policy we take is decided by the parameter β. The value of β is given as:

$$\beta_i = p^{i-1}$$

The value of p is chosen between 0.1 and 0.9. Since we are in iteration 1, substituting $i = 1$, we can write:

$$\beta_1 = p^0 = 1$$

Thus, substituting $\beta_1 = 1$ in equation (1), we can write:

$$\pi_1 = \pi_E$$

As we can observe, in the first iteration, the policy π_1 is just an expert policy π_E. Now, we use this policy π_1 and generate trajectories. Next, we create a new dataset $\mathcal{D}_1$ by collecting all the states visited by our policy π_1 and ask the expert to provide actions of those states. So, our dataset will consist of $\mathcal{D}_1 = \{(s, \pi_E(s))\}$.

Now, we combine the dataset $\mathcal{D}_1$ with our initialized empty dataset $\mathcal{D}$ and update $\mathcal{D}$ as:

$$\mathcal{D} = \mathcal{D} \cup \mathcal{D}_1$$

Now that we have an updated dataset $\mathcal{D}$, we train a classifier on this new dataset and extract a new policy. Let the new policy be $\hat{\pi}_2$.

Iteration 2:

In the second iteration, we create a new policy π_2 as:

$$\pi_2 = \beta\pi_E + (1 - \beta)\hat{\pi}_2$$

The preceding equation implies that we create a new policy π_2 by taking some amount of expert policy π_E and some amount of policy $\hat{\pi}_2$ that we obtained in the previous iteration. We know that the value of beta is chosen as: $\beta_i = p^{i-1}$. Thus, we have $\beta_2 = p^1$.

Now, we use this policy π_2 and generate trajectories. Next, we create a new dataset $\mathcal{D}_2$ by collecting all the states visited by our policy π_2 and ask the expert to provide actions of those states. So, our dataset will consist of $\mathcal{D}_2 = \{(s, \pi_E(s))\}$.

Now, we combine the dataset $\mathcal{D}_2$ with $\mathcal{D}$ and update $\mathcal{D}$ as:

$$\mathcal{D} = \mathcal{D} \cup \mathcal{D}_2$$

Now that we have an updated dataset $\mathcal{D}$, we train a classifier on this new dataset and extract a new policy. Let that new policy be $\hat{\pi}_3$.

We repeat these steps for several iterations to obtain the optimal policy. As we can observe in each iteration, we aggregate our dataset $\mathcal{D}$ and train a classifier to obtain the new policy. Notice that the value of β is decaying exponentially. This makes sense as over a series of iterations, our policy will become better and so we can reduce the importance of the expert policy.

Now that we have understood how DAgger works, in the next section, we will look into the algorithm of DAgger for a better understanding.

Algorithm – DAgger

The algorithm of DAgger is given as follows:

1. Initialize an empty dataset $\mathcal{D}$
2. Initialize a policy $\hat{\pi}_1$
3. For iterations $i = 1$ to N:

    1. Create a policy $\pi_i = \beta_i\pi_E + (1 - \beta_i)\hat{\pi}_i$.
    2. Generate a trajectory using the policy π_i.

3. Create a dataset $\mathcal{D}_i$ by collecting states visited by the policy π_i and actions of those states provided by the expert π_E. Thus, $\mathcal{D}_i = \{(s, \pi_E(s))\}$.

4. Aggregate the dataset as $\mathcal{D} = \mathcal{D} \cup \mathcal{D}_i$.

5. Train a classifier on the updated dataset $\mathcal{D}$ and extract a new policy $\hat{\pi}_{i+1}$.

Now that we have learned the DAgger algorithm, in the next section, we will learn about DQfD.

Deep Q learning from demonstrations

We learned that in imitation learning, we try to learn from expert demonstrations. Can we make use of expert demonstrations in DQN and perform better? Yes! In this section, we will learn how to make use of expert demonstrations in DQN using an algorithm called DQfD.

In the previous chapters, we have learned about several types of DQN. We started off with vanilla DQN, and then we explored various improvements to the DQN, such as double DQN, dueling DQN, prioritized experience replay, and more. In all these methods, the agent tries to learn from scratch by interacting with the environment. The agent interacts with the environment and stores their interaction experience in a buffer called a replay buffer and learns based on their experience.

In order for the agent to perform better, it has to gather a lot of experience from the environment, add it to the replay buffer, and train itself. However, this method costs us a lot of training time. In all the previous methods we have learned so far, we have trained our agent in a simulator, so the agent gathers experience in the simulator environment to perform better. To learn the optimal policy, the agent has to perform a lot of interactions with the environment, and some of these interactions give the agent a very bad reward. This is tolerable in a simulator environment. But how can we train the agent in a real-world environment? We can't train the agent by directly interacting with the real-world environment and by making a lot of bad actions in the real-world environment.

So, in those cases, we can train the agent in a simulator that corresponds to the particular real-world environment. But the problem is that it is hard to find an accurate simulator corresponding to the real-world environment for most use cases. However, we can easily obtain expert demonstrations.

For instance, let's suppose we want to train an agent to play chess. Let's assume we don't find an accurate simulator to train the agent to play chess. But we can easily obtain good expert demonstrations of an expert playing chess.

Now, can we make use of these expert demonstrations and train our agent? Yes! Instead of learning from scratch by interacting with the environment, if we add the expert demonstrations directly to the replay buffer and pre-train our agent based on these expert demonstrations, then the agent can learn better and faster.

This is the fundamental idea behind DQfD. We fill the replay buffer with expert demonstrations and pre-train the agent. Note that these expert demonstrations are used only for pre-training the agent. Once the agent is pre-trained, the agent will interact with the environment and gather more experience and make use of it for learning. Thus DQfD consists of two phases, which are pre-training and training.

First, we pre-train the agent based on the expert demonstrations, and then we train the agent by interacting with the environment. When the agent interacts with the environment, it collects some experience, and the agent's experience (self-generated data) also gets added to the replay buffer. The agent makes use of both the expert demonstrations and also the self-generated data for learning. We use a prioritized experience replay buffer and give more priority to the expert demonstrations than the self-generated data. Now that we have a basic understanding of DQfD, let's go into detail and learn how exactly it works.

Phases of DQfD

DQfD consists of two phases:

- Pre-training phase
- Training phase

Pre-training phase

In the pre-training phase, the agent does not interact with the environment. We directly add the expert demonstrations to the replay buffer and the agent learns by sampling the expert demonstrations from the replay buffer.

The agent learns from expert demonstrations by minimizing the loss $J(Q)$ using gradient descent. However, pre-training with expert demonstrations alone is not sufficient for the agent to perform better because the expert demonstrations will not contain all possible transitions. But the pretraining with expert demonstrations acts as a good starting point to train our agent. Once the agent is pre-trained with demonstrations, then during the training phase, the agent will perform better actions in the environment from the initial iteration itself instead of performing random actions, and so the agent can learn quickly.

Training phase

Once the agent is pre-trained, we start the training phase, where the agent interacts with the environment and learns based on its experience. Since the agent has already learned some useful information from the expert demonstrations in the pre-training phase, it will not perform random actions in the environment.

During the training phase, the agent interacts with the environment and stores its transition information (experience) in the replay buffer. We learned that our replay buffer will be pre-filled with the expert demonstrations data. So, now, our replay buffer will consist of a mixture of both expert demonstrations and the agent's experience (self-generated data). We sample a minibatch of experience from the replay buffer and train the agent. Note that here we use a prioritized replay buffer, so while sampling, we give more priority to the expert demonstrations than the agent-generated data. In this way, we train the agent by sampling experience from the replay buffer and minimize the loss using gradient descent.

We learned that the agent interacts with the environment and stores the experience in the replay buffer. If the replay buffer is full, then we overwrite the buffer with new transition information generated by the agent. However, we won't overwrite the expert demonstrations. So, the expert demonstrations will always remain in the replay buffer so that the agent can make use of expert demonstrations for learning.

Thus, we have learned how to pre-train and train an agent with expert demonstrations. In the next section, we will learn about the loss function of DQfD.

Loss function of DQfD

The loss function of DQfD comprises the sum of four losses:

1. Double DQN loss
2. N-step double DQN loss
3. Supervised classification loss
4. L2 loss

Now, we will look at each of these losses.

Double DQN loss – $J_{DQ}(Q)$ represents the 1-step double DQN loss.

N-step double DQN loss – $J_n(Q)$ represents the n-step double DQN loss.

Supervised classification loss – $J_E(Q)$ represents the supervised classification loss. It is expressed as:

$$J_E(Q) = \max_{a \in A}[Q(s, a) + l(a_E, a)] - Q(s, a_E)$$

Where:

- a_E is the action taken by the expert.
- $l(a_E, a)$ is known as the margin function or margin loss. It will be 0 when the action taken is equal to the expert action $a = a_E$; else, it is positive.

L2 regularization loss – $J_{L2}(Q)$ represents the L2 regularization loss. It prevents the agent from overfitting to the demonstration data.

Thus, the final loss function will be the sum of all the preceding four losses:

$$J(Q) = J_{DQ}(Q) + \lambda_1 J_n(Q) + \lambda_2 J_E(Q) + \lambda_3 J_{L2}(Q)$$

Where the value of λ acts as a weighting factor and helps us to control the importance of the respective loss.

Now that we have learned how DQfD works, we will look into the algorithm of DQfD in the next section.

Algorithm – DQfD

The algorithm of DQfD is given as follows:

1. Initialize the main network parameter θ
2. Initialize the target network parameter θ' by copying the main network parameter θ
3. Initialize the replay buffer $\mathcal{D}$ with the expert demonstrations
4. Set d: the number of time steps we want to delay updating the target network parameter
5. **Pre-training phase**: For steps $t = 1, 2, \dots, T$:
    1. Sample a minibatch of experience from the replay buffer $\mathcal{D}$
    2. Compute the loss $J(Q)$
    3. Update the parameter of the network using gradient descent
    4. If $t \bmod d = 0$:

        Update the target network parameter θ' by copying the main network parameter θ

6. **Training phase**: For steps $t = 1, 2, ..., T$:

   1. Select an action

   2. Perform the selected action and move to the next state, observe the reward, and store this transition information in the replay buffer $\mathcal{D}$

   3. Sample a minibatch of experience from the replay buffer $\mathcal{D}$ with prioritization

   4. Compute the loss $J(Q)$

   5. Update the parameter of the network using gradient descent

   6. If $t \bmod d = 0$:

      Update the target network parameter θ' by copying the main network parameter θ

That's it! In the next section, we will learn about a very interesting concept called IRL.

Inverse reinforcement learning

Inverse Reinforcement Learning (IRL) is one of the most exciting fields of reinforcement learning. In reinforcement learning, our goal is to learn the optimal policy. That is, our goal is to find the optimal policy that gives the maximum return (sum of rewards of the trajectory). In order to find the optimal policy, first, we should know the reward function. A reward function tells us what reward we obtain by performing an action a in the state s. Once we have the reward function, we can train our agent to learn the optimal policy that gives the maximum reward. But the problem is that designing the reward function is not that easy for complex tasks.

Consider designing the reward function for tasks such as an agent learning to walk, self-driving cars, and so on. In these cases, designing the reward function is not that handy and involves assigning rewards to a variety of agent behaviors. For instance, consider designing the reward function for an agent learning to drive a car. In this case, we need to assign a reward for every behavior of the agent. For example, we can assign a high reward if the agent follows the traffic signal, avoids pedestrians, doesn't hit any objects, and so on. But designing the reward function in this way is not optimal, and there is also a good chance that we might miss out on several behaviors of an agent.

Okay, now the question is can we learn the reward function? Yes! If we have expert demonstrations, then we can learn the reward function from the expert demonstrations. But how can we do that exactly? Here is where IRL helps us. As the name suggests, IRL is the inverse of reinforcement learning.

In RL, we try to find the optimal policy given the reward function, but in IRL, we try to learn the reward function given the expert demonstrations. Once we have derived the reward function from the expert demonstrations using IRL, we can use the reward function to train our agent to learn the optimal policy using any reinforcement learning algorithm.

IRL consists of several interesting algorithms. In the next section, we will learn one of the most popular IRL algorithms, called maximum entropy IRL.

Maximum entropy IRL

In this section, we will learn how to extract a reward function from the given set of expert demonstrations using an IRL algorithm called maximum entropy IRL. Before diving into maximum entropy IRL, let's learn some of the important terms that are required to understand how maximum entropy IRL works.

Key terms

Feature vector – We can represent the state by a feature vector f. Let's say we have a state s; its feature vector can then be defined as f_s.

Feature count – Say we have a trajectory τ; the feature count of the trajectory is then defined as the sum of the feature vectors of all the states in the trajectory:

$$f_\tau = \sum_{s \in \tau} f_s \qquad (2)$$

Where f_τ denotes the feature count of the trajectory τ.

Reward function – The reward function can be defined as the linear combination of the features, that is, the sum of feature vectors multiplied by a weight θ:

$$R_\theta(\tau) = \theta_1 f_{s_1} + \theta_2 f_{s_2} + \cdots + \theta_T f_{s_T}$$

Where θ denotes the weight and f_s denotes the feature vector. Note that this θ is what we are trying to learn. When we obtain the optimal θ, then we will have a correct reward function. We will learn how we can find the optimal θ in the next section.

We can represent the preceding equation in sigma notation as:

$$R_\theta(\tau) = \sum_{s \in \tau} \theta^T f_s$$

We know that the feature count is the sum of feature vectors of all the states in the trajectory, so from (2), we can rewrite the preceding equation as:

$$R_\theta(\tau) = \theta^T f_\tau$$

Thus, the reward of the trajectory is just the weight multiplied by the feature count of the trajectory.

Back to maximum entropy IRL

Now, let's learn how maximum entropy IRL works. Consider that we have expert demonstrations $\mathcal{D}$. Our goal is to learn the reward function from the given expert demonstrations. How can we do that?

We have already learned that the reward function is given as $R_\theta(\tau) = \theta^T f_\tau$. Finding the optimal parameter θ helps us to learn the correct reward function. So, we will sample a trajectory τ from the expert demonstrations $\mathcal{D}$ and try to find the reward function by finding the optimal parameter θ.

The probability of a trajectory being sampled from the expert demonstrations is directly proportional to the exponential of the reward function. That is, trajectories that obtain more rewards are more likely to be sampled from our demonstrations than those trajectories that obtain less rewards:

$$p(\tau) = \exp(R_\theta(\tau))$$

The probability should be in the range of 0 to 1, right? But the value of $\exp(R_\theta(\tau))$ will not be in the range of 0 to 1. So, in order to normalize that, we introduce z, which acts as the normalization constant and is given as $z = \sum_\tau \exp(R_\theta(\tau))$. We can rewrite our preceding equation with z as:

$$p(\tau) = \frac{\exp(R_\theta(\tau))}{z} \qquad (3)$$

Now, our objective is to maximize $p(\tau)$, that is, to maximize the log probability of selecting trajectories that give more rewards. So, we can define our objective function as:

$$L(\theta) = \frac{1}{M} \log p(\tau) \qquad (4)$$

Where M denotes the number of demonstrations.

Substituting (3) in (4), we can write:

$$L(\theta) = \frac{1}{M} \log \left(\frac{\exp(R_\theta(\tau))}{z} \right)$$

Based on the log rule, $\log a/b = \log a - \log b$, we can write:

$$L(\theta) = \frac{1}{M} (\log \exp(R_\theta(\tau)) - \log z)$$

The logarithmic and exponential terms cancel each other out, so the preceding equation becomes:

$$L(\theta) = \frac{1}{M} (R_\theta(\tau) - \log z)$$

We know that $z = \sum_\tau \exp(R_\theta(\tau))$; substituting the value of z, we can rewrite the preceding equation as:

$$L(\theta) = \frac{1}{M} \left(R_\theta(\tau) - \log \sum_\tau \exp(R_\theta(\tau)) \right)$$

We know that $R_\theta(\tau) = \theta^T f_\tau$; substituting the value of $R_\theta(\tau)$, our final simplified objective function is given as:

$$L(\theta) = \frac{1}{M} \left(\theta^T f_\tau - \log \sum_\tau \exp(\theta^T f_\tau) \right)$$

To find the optimal parameter θ, we compute the gradient of the preceding objective function $\nabla_\theta L(\theta)$ and update the value of θ as $\theta = \theta + \alpha \nabla_\theta L(\theta)$. In the next section, we will learn how to compute the gradient $\nabla_\theta L(\theta)$.

Computing the gradient

We learned that our objective function is given as:

$$L(\theta) = \frac{1}{M} \left(\theta^T f_\tau - \log \sum_\tau \exp(\theta^T f_\tau) \right)$$

Now, we compute the gradient of the objective function with respect to θ. After computation, our gradient is given as:

$$\nabla_\theta L(\theta) = \frac{1}{M} \left(\sum_\tau f_\tau - \sum_\tau p(\tau|\theta) f_\tau \right)$$

$$\nabla_\theta L(\theta) = \frac{1}{M} \sum_\tau f_\tau - \frac{1}{M} \sum_\tau p(\tau|\theta) f_\tau$$

The average of the feature count is just the feature expectation $\tilde{f}$, so we can substitute $\frac{1}{M} \sum_\tau f_\tau = \tilde{f}$ and rewrite the preceding equation as:

$$\nabla_\theta L(\theta) = \tilde{f} - \frac{1}{M} \sum_\tau p(\tau|\theta) f_\tau$$

We can rewrite the preceding equation by combining all the states of the trajectories as:

$$\nabla_\theta L(\theta) = \tilde{f} - \sum_s p(s|\theta) f_s \tag{5}$$

Thus, using the preceding equation, we compute gradients and update the parameter θ. If you look at the preceding equation, we can easily compute the first term, which is just the feature expectation $\tilde{f}$, but what about the $p(s|\theta)$ in the second term? $p(s|\theta)$ is called the state visitation frequency and it represents the probability of being in a given state. Okay, how can we compute $p(s|\theta)$?

If we have a policy π, then we can use the policy to compute the state visitation frequency. But we don't have any policy yet. So, we can use a dynamic programming method, say, value iteration, to compute the policy. However, in order to compute the policy using the value iteration method, we require a reward function. So, we just feed our reward function $R_\theta(\tau)$ and extract the policy using the value iteration. Then, using the extracted policy, we compute the state visitation frequency.

The steps involved in computing the state visitation frequency using the policy π are as follows:

1. Let the probability of visiting a state s at a time t be $\mu_t(s)$. We can write the probability of visiting the initial state s_1 at a first time step $t = 1$ as:
    $\mu_1(s) = p(s = s_1)$

2. Then for time steps $t = 1$ to T:

Compute $\mu_{t+1}(s) = \sum_a \sum_{s'} \mu_t(s')\pi(a|s')p(s|s',a)$

3. Compute the state visitation frequency as $p(s|\theta) = \sum_t \mu_t(s)$.

To get a clear understanding of how maximum entropy IRL works, let's look into the algorithm in the next section.

Algorithm – maximum entropy IRL

The algorithm of maximum entropy IRL is given as follows:

1. Initialize the parameter θ and gather the demonstrations $\mathcal{D}$
2. For N number of iterations:
   1. Compute the reward function $R_\theta(\tau) = \theta^T f_\tau$
   2. Compute the policy using value iteration with the reward function obtained in the previous step
   3. Compute state visitation frequency $p(s|\theta)$ using the policy obtained in the previous step
   4. Compute the gradient with respect to θ, that is,
      $$\nabla_\theta L(\theta) = \tilde{f} - \sum_s p(s|\theta) f_s$$
   5. Update the value of θ as $\theta = \theta + \alpha\nabla_\theta L(\theta)$

Thus, over a series of iterations, we will find an optimal parameter θ. Once we have θ, we can use it to define the correct reward function $R_\theta(\tau)$. In the next section, we will learn about GAIL.

Generative adversarial imitation learning

Generative Adversarial Imitation Learning (GAIL) is another very popular IRL algorithm. As the name suggests, it is based on **Generative Adversarial Networks (GANs)**, which we learned about in *Chapter 7, Deep Learning Foundations*. To understand how GAIL works, we should first recap how GANs work.

In a GAN, we have two networks: one is the generator and the other is the discriminator. The role of the generator is to generate new data points by learning the distribution of the input dataset. The role of the discriminator is to classify whether a given data point is generated by the generator (learned distribution) or whether it is from the real data distribution.

Minimizing the loss function of a GAN implies minimizing the **Jensen Shannon (JS) divergence** between the real data distribution and the fake data distribution (learned distribution). The JS divergence is used to measure how two probability distributions differ from each other. Thus, when the JS divergence between the real and fake distributions is zero, it means that the real and fake data distributions are equal, that is, our generator network has successfully learned the real distribution.

Now, let's learn how to make use of GANs in an IRL setting. First, let's introduce a new term called **occupancy measure**. It is defined as the distribution of the states and actions that our agent comes across while exploring the environment with some policy π. In simple terms, it is basically the distribution of state-action pairs following a policy π. The occupancy measure of a policy π is denoted by ρ_π.

In the imitation learning setting, we have an expert policy, and let's denote the expert policy by π_E. Similarly, let's denote the agent's policy by π_θ. Now, our goal is to make our agent learn the expert policy. How can we do that? If we make the occupancy measure of the expert policy and the agent policy equal, then it implies that our agent has successfully learned the expert policy. That is, the occupancy measure is the distribution of the state-action pairs following a policy. If we can make the distribution of state-action pairs of the agent's policy equal to the distribution of state-action pairs of the expert's policy, then it means that our agent has learned the expert policy. Let's explore how we can do this using GANs.

We can perceive the occupancy measure of the expert policy as the real data distribution and the occupancy measure of the agent policy as the fake data distribution. Thus, minimizing the JS divergence between the occupancy measure of the expert policy $\rho_{\pi E}$ and the occupancy measure of the agent policy $\rho_{\pi\theta}$ implies that the agent will learn the expert policy.

With GANs, we know that the role of the generator is to generate new data points by learning the distribution of a given dataset. Similarly, in GAIL, the role of the generator is to generate a new policy by learning the distribution (occupancy measure) of the expert policy. The role of the discriminator is to classify whether the given policy is the expert policy or the agent policy.

With GANs, we know that, for a generator, the optimal discriminator is the one that is not able to distinguish between the real and fake data distributions; similarly, in GAIL, the optimal discriminator is the one that is unable to distinguish whether the generated state-action pair is from the agent policy or the expert policy.

To make ourselves clear, let's understand the terms we use in GAIL by relating to GAN terminology:

- **Real data distribution** – Occupancy measure of the expert policy
- **Fake data distribution** – Occupancy measure of the agent policy
- **Real data** – State-action pair generated by the expert policy
- **Fake data** – State-action pair generated by the agent policy

In a nutshell, we use the generator to generate the state-action pair in a way that the discriminator is not able to distinguish whether the state-action pair is generated using the expert policy or the agent policy. Both the generator and discriminator are neural networks. We train the generator to generate a policy similar to the expert policy using TRPO. The discriminator is a classifier, and it is optimized using Adam. Thus, we can define the objective function of GAIL as:

$$\max_\theta \min_\omega \mathbb{E}_{\pi_\theta}\left[\log\big(D_\omega(s,a)\big)\right] + \mathbb{E}_{\pi_E}[\log(1 - D_\omega(s,a))]$$

Where θ is the parameter of the generator and ω is the parameter of the discriminator.

Now that we have an understanding of how GAIL works, let's get into more detail and learn how the preceding equation is derived.

Formulation of GAIL

In this section, we explore the math of GAIL and see how it works. You can skip this section if you are not interested in math. We know that in reinforcement learning, our objective is to find the optimal policy that gives the maximum reward. It can be expressed as:

$$\mathrm{RL}(r) = \arg\max_\pi \mathbb{E}_\pi\left[r(s,a)\right]$$

We can rewrite our objective function by adding the entropy of a policy as shown here:

$$\mathrm{RL}(r) = \arg\max_\pi H(\pi) + \mathbb{E}_\pi[r(s,a)]$$

The preceding equation tells us that we can maximize the entropy of the policy while also maximizing the reward. Instead of defining the objective function in terms of the reward, we can also define the objective function in terms of cost.

That is, we can define our RL objective function in terms of cost, as our objective is to find an optimal policy that minimizes the cost; this can be expressed as:

$$RL(c) = \arg\min_{\pi \in \Pi} - H(\pi) + \mathbb{E}_{\pi}[c(s, a)] \tag{6}$$

Where c is the cost. Thus, given the cost function, our goal is to find the optimal policy that minimizes the cost.

Now, let's talk about IRL. We learned that in IRL, our objective is to find the reward function from the given set of expert demonstrations. We can also define the objective of IRL in terms of cost instead of reward. That is, we can define our IRL objective function in terms of cost, as our objective is to find the cost function under which the expert demonstration is optimal. The objective can be expressed using maximum causal entropy IRL as:

$$IRL(\pi_E) = \arg\max_{c} \left(\min_{\pi} - H(\pi) + \mathbb{E}_{\pi}[c(s, a)] \right) - \mathbb{E}_{\pi_E}[c(s, a)]$$

What does the preceding equation imply? In the IRL setting, our goal is to learn the cost function given the expert demonstrations (expert policy). We know that the expert policy performs better than the other policy, so we try to learn the cost function c, which assigns low cost to the expert policy and high cost to other policies. Thus, the preceding objective function implies that we try to find a cost function that assigns low cost to the expert policy and high cost to other policies.

To reduce overfitting, we introduce the regularizer ψ and rewrite the preceding equation as:

$$IRL_{\psi}(\pi_E) = \arg\max_{c} - \psi(c) + \left(\min_{\pi} - H(\pi) + \mathbb{E}_{\pi}[c(s, a)] \right) - \mathbb{E}_{\pi_E}[c(s, a)] \tag{7}$$

From equation (6), we learned that in a reinforcement learning setting, given a cost, we obtain the optimal policy, and from (7), we learned that in an IRL setting, given an expert policy (expert demonstration), we obtain the cost. Thus, from (6) and (7), we can observe that the output of IRL can be sent as an input to the RL. That is, IRL results in the cost function and we can use this cost function as an input in RL to learn the optimal policy. Thus, we can write $RL(IRL(\pi_E))$, which implies that the result of IRL is fed as an input to the RL.

We can express this in a functional composition form as $RL \circ IRL_{\psi}(\pi_E)$:

$$RL \circ IRL_{\psi}(\pi_E) = \arg\min_{\pi} - H(\pi) + \psi^{\star}(\rho_{\pi} - \rho_{\pi_E}) \tag{8}$$

In equation (8), the following applies:

- ψ^* is the convex conjugate of the regularizer ψ
- ρ_π is the occupancy measure of the agent policy
- ρ_{π_E} is the occupancy measure of the expert policy

To learn how exactly the equation (8) is derived, you can refer to the GAIL paper given in the *Further reading* section at the end of the chapter. The objective function (equation (8)) implies that we try to find the optimal policy whose occupancy measure is close to the occupancy measure of the expert policy. The occupancy measure between the agent policy and the expert policy is measured by ψ^*. There are several choices for the regularizer ψ^*. We use a generative adversarial regularizer ψ^*_{GA} and write our equation as:

$$\text{RL} \circ \text{IRL}_\psi(\pi_E) = \arg\min_\pi -H(\pi) + \psi^*_{GA}(\rho_\pi - \rho_{\pi_E}) \tag{9}$$

Thus, minimizing $\psi^*_{GA}(\rho_\pi - \rho_{\pi_E})$ basically implies that we minimize the JS divergence between the occupancy measure of the agent policy ρ_π and the expert policy $\rho_{\pi E}$. Thus, we can rewrite the RHS of the equation (9) as:

$$\min_\pi -\lambda H(\pi) + \psi^*_{GA}(\rho_\pi - \rho_{\pi_E}) = -\lambda H(\pi) + D_{JS}(\rho_\pi, \rho_{\pi_E})$$

$$\min_\pi \psi^*_{GA}(\rho_\pi - \rho_{\pi_E}) - \lambda H(\pi) = D_{JS}(\rho_\pi, \rho_{\pi_E}) - \lambda H(\pi)$$

Where λ is just the policy regularizer. We know that the JS divergence between the occupancy measure of the agent policy ρ_π and the expert policy $\rho_{\pi E}$ is minimized using the GAN, so we can just replace $D_{JS}\left(\rho_\pi, \rho_{\pi_E}\right)$ in the preceding equation with the GAN objective function as:

$$\min_\pi \psi^*_{GA}(\rho_\pi - \rho_{\pi_E}) - \lambda H(\pi) = \max_\theta \min_\omega \mathbb{E}_{\pi_\theta}\left[\log(D_\omega(s,a))\right] + \mathbb{E}_{\pi_E}\left[\log(1 - D_\omega(s,a))\right] - \lambda H(\pi) \tag{10}$$

Where θ is the parameter of the generator and ω is the parameter of the discriminator.

Thus, our final objective function of GAIL becomes:

$$\text{RL} \circ \text{IRL}_\psi(\pi_E) = \max_\theta \min_\omega \mathbb{E}_{\pi_\theta}\left[\log(D_\omega(s,a))\right] + \mathbb{E}_{\pi_E}\left[\log(1 - D_\omega(s,a))\right] - \lambda H(\pi) \tag{11}$$

The objective equation implies that we can find the optimal policy by minimizing the occupancy measure of the expert policy and the agent policy, and we minimize that using GANs.

The role of the generator is to generate a policy by learning the occupancy measure of the expert policy, and the role of the discriminator is to classify whether the generated policy is from the expert policy or the agent policy. So, we train the generator using TRPO and the discriminator is basically a neural network that tells us whether the policy generated by the generator is the expert policy or the agent policy.

Summary

We started the chapter by understanding what imitation learning is and how supervised imitation learning works. Next, we learned about the DAgger algorithm, where we aggregate the dataset obtained over a series of iterations and learn the optimal policy.

After looking at DAgger, we learned about DQfD, where we prefill the replay buffer with expert demonstrations and pre-train the agent with expert demonstrations before the training phase.

Moving on, we learned about IRL. We understood that in reinforcement learning, we try to find the optimal policy given the reward function, but in IRL, we try to learn the reward function given the expert demonstrations. When we have derived the reward function from the expert demonstrations using IRL, we can use the reward function to train our agent to learn the optimal policy using any reinforcement learning algorithm. We then explored how to learn the reward function using the maximum entropy IRL algorithm.

At the end of the chapter, we learned about GAIL, where we used GANs to learn the optimal policy. In the next chapter, we will explore a reinforcement learning library called Stable Baselines.

Questions

Let's assess our understanding of imitation learning and IRL. Try answering the following questions:

1. How does supervised imitation learning work?
2. How does DAgger differ from supervised imitation learning?
3. Explain the different phases of DQfD.
4. Why do we need IRL?
5. What is a feature vector?
6. How does GAIL work?

Further reading

For more information, refer to the following papers:

- **A Reduction of Imitation Learning and Structured Prediction to No-Regret Online Learning** by *Stephane Ross, Geoffrey J. Gordon, J. Andrew Bagnell,* `https://arxiv.org/pdf/1011.0686.pdf`

- **Deep Q-learning from Demonstrations** by *Todd Hester, et al.,* `https://arxiv.org/pdf/1704.03732.pdf`

- **Maximum Entropy Inverse Reinforcement Learning** by *Brian D. Ziebart, Andrew Maas, J.Andrew Bagnell, Anind K. Dey,* `https://www.aaai.org/Papers/AAAI/2008/AAAI08-227.pdf`

- **Generative Adversarial Imitation Learning** by *Jonathan Ho, Stefano Ermon,* `https://arxiv.org/pdf/1606.03476.pdf`

16

Deep Reinforcement Learning with Stable Baselines

So far, we have learned various deep **reinforcement learning** (**RL**) algorithms. Wouldn't it be nice if we had a library to easily implement a deep RL algorithm? Yes! There are various libraries available to easily build a deep RL algorithm.

One such popular deep RL library is OpenAI Baselines. OpenAI Baselines provides an efficient implementation of many deep RL algorithms, which makes them easier to use. However, OpenAI Baselines does not provide good documentation. So, we will look at the fork of OpenAI Baselines called **Stable Baselines**.

Stable Baselines is an improved implementation of OpenAI Baselines. Stable Baselines is easier to use and it also includes state-of-the-art deep RL algorithms along with several useful features. We can use Stable Baselines for quickly prototyping the RL model.

Let's start off the chapter by installing Stable Baselines, and then we will learn how to create our first agent using the library. Next, we will learn about vectorized environments. Going further, we will learn to implement several deep RL algorithms using Stable Baselines along with exploring various functionalities of baselines.

In this chapter, we will learn the following topics:

- Installing Stable Baselines
- Creating our first agent with Stable Baselines
- Multiprocessing with vectorized environments
- Playing Atari games with DQN and its variants
- Lunar lander using A2C
- Swinging up a pendulum using DDPG
- Training an agent to walk using TRPO
- Implementing GAIL

Let's begin the chapter by installing Stable Baselines.

Installing Stable Baselines

First, let's install the dependencies:

```
sudo apt-get update && sudo apt-get install cmake libopenmpi-dev
zlib1g-dev
```

Several deep RL algorithms require MPI to run, so, let's install MPI:

```
sudo pip install mpi4py
```

Now, we can install Stable Baselines through `pip`:

```
pip install stable-baselines[mpi]
```

Note that currently, Stable Baselines works only with TensorFlow version 1.x. So, make sure you are running the Stable Baselines experiment with TensorFlow 1.x.

Now that we have installed Stable Baselines, let's see how to create our first agent using it.

Creating our first agent with Stable Baselines

Now, let's build our first deep RL algorithm using Stable Baselines. Let's create a simple agent using a **Deep Q Network (DQN)** for the mountain car climbing task. We know that in the mountain car climbing task, a car is placed between two mountains and the goal of the agent is to drive up the mountain on the right.

First, let's import gym and DQN from `stable_baselines`:

```
import gym
from stable_baselines import DQN
```

Create a mountain car environment:

```
env = gym.make('MountainCar-v0')
```

Now, let's instantiate our agent. As we can observe in the following code, we are passing `MlpPolicy`, which implies that our network is a multilayer perceptron:

```
agent = DQN('MlpPolicy', env, learning_rate=1e-3)
```

Now, let's train the agent by specifying the number of time steps we want to train:

```
agent.learn(total_timesteps=25000)
```

That's it. Building a DQN agent and training it is that simple.

Evaluating the trained agent

We can also evaluate the trained agent by looking at the mean rewards using `evaluate_policy`:

```
from stable_baselines.common.evaluation import evaluate_policy
```

In the following code, agent is the trained agent, `agent.get_env()` gets the environment we trained our agent in, and `n_eval_episodes` represents the number of episodes we need to evaluate our agent:

```
mean_reward, n_steps = evaluate_policy(agent, agent.get_env(), n_eval_
episodes=10)
```

Storing and loading the trained agent

With Stable Baselines, we can also save and load our trained agent to and from disk.

We can save the agent as follows:

```
agent.save("DQN_mountain_car_agent")
```

After saving, we can load the agent as follows:

```
agent = DQN.load("DQN_mountain_car_agent")
```

Viewing the trained agent

After training, we can also have a look at how our trained agent performs in the environment.

Initialize the state:

```
state = env.reset()
```

For 5,000 steps:

```
for t in range(5000):
```

Predict the action to perform in the given state using our trained agent:

```
action, _ = agent.predict(state)
```

Perform the predicted action:

```
next_state, reward, done, info = env.step(action)
```

Update state to the current state:

```
state = next_state
```

Render the environment:

```
env.render()
```

Now, we can see how our trained agent performs in the environment:

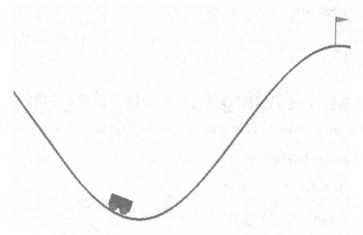

Figure 16.1: Agent learning to climb mountain

Putting it all together

Now, let's look at the final code combining everything we learned so far:

```python
#import the libraries
import gym
from stable_baselines import DQN
from stable_baselines.common.evaluation import evaluate_policy

#create the gym environment
env = gym.make('MountainCar-v0')

#instantiate the agent
agent = DQN('MlpPolicy', env, learning_rate=1e-3)

#train the agent
agent.learn(total_timesteps=25000)

#evaluate the agent
mean_reward, n_steps = evaluate_policy(agent, agent.get_env(), n_eval_
episodes=10)

#save the trained agent
agent.save("DQN_mountain_car_agent")

#view the trained agent
state = env.reset()

for t in range(5000):
    action, _ = agent.predict(state)
    next_state, reward, done, info = env.step(action)
    state = next_state
    env.render()
```

Now that we have a basic idea of how to use Stable Baselines, let's explore it in detail.

Vectorized environments

One of the very interesting and useful features of Stable Baselines is that we can train our agent in multiple independent environments either in separate processes (using **SubprocVecEnv**) or in the same process (using **DummyVecEnv**).

For example, say we are training our agent in a cart pole balancing environment – instead of training our agent only in a single cart pole balancing environment, we can train our agent in the multiple cart pole balancing environments.

We generally train our agent in a single environment per step but now we can train our agent in multiple environments per step. This helps our agent to learn more quickly. Now, our state, action, reward, and done will be in the form of a vector since we are training our agent in multiple environments. So, we call this a vectorized environment.

There are two types of vectorized environment offered by Stable Baselines:

- SubprocVecEnv
- DummyVecEnv

SubprocVecEnv

In the subproc vectorized environment, we run each environment in a **separate** process (taking advantage of multiprocessing). Now, let's see how to create the subproc vectorized environment.

First, let's import `SubprocVecEnv`:

```
from stable_baselines.common.vec_env import SubprocVecEnv
from stable_baselines.common import set_global_seeds
```

Next, we create a function called `make_env` for initializing our environment:

```
def make_env(env_name, rank, seed=0):
    def _init():
        env = gym.make(env_name)
        env.seed(seed + rank)
        return env
    set_global_seeds(seed)
    return _init
```

Then, we can create the subproc vectorized environment as follows:

```
env_name = 'Pendulum-v0'
num_process = 2
env = SubprocVecEnv([make_env(env_name, i) for i in range(num_process)])
```

DummyVecEnv

In the dummy vectorized environment, we run each environment in sequence on the current Python process. It does not support multiprocessing. Now, let's see how to create the dummy vectorized environment.

First, let's import DummyVecEnv:

```
from stable_baselines.common.vec_env import DummyVecEnv
```

Next, we can create the dummy vectorized environment as follows:

```
env_name = 'Pendulum-v0'
env = DummyVecEnv([lambda: gym.make(env_name)])
```

Now that we have learned to train the agent in multiple independent environments using vectorized environments, in the next section, we will see how to integrate custom environments into Stable Baselines.

Integrating custom environments

We can also use Stable Baselines to train an agent in our own environment. While creating our own environment, we need to make sure that our custom environment follows the Gym interface. That is, our environment should include methods such as step, reset, render, and so on.

Suppose the name of our custom environment is CustomEnv. First, we instantiate our custom environment as follows:

```
env = CustomEnv()
```

Next, we can train our agent in the custom environment as usual:

```
agent = DQN('MlpPolicy', env, learning_rate=1e-3)
agent.learn(total_timesteps=25000)
```

That's it. In the next section, let's learn how to play Atari games using a DQN and its variants.

Playing Atari games with a DQN and its variants

Now, let's learn how to create a DQN to play Atari games with Stable Baselines. First, let's import the necessary modules:

```
from stable_baselines import DQN
```

Since we are dealing with Atari games, we can use a convolutional neural network instead of a vanilla neural network. So, we use CnnPolicy:

```
from stable_baselines.deepq.policies import CnnPolicy
```

We learned that we preprocess the game screen before feeding it to the agent. With Stable Baselines, we don't have to preprocess manually; instead, we can make use of the make_atari module, which takes care of preprocessing the game screen:

```
from stable_baselines.common.atari_wrappers import make_atari
```

Now, let's create an Atari game environment. Let's create the Ice Hockey game environment:

```
env = make_atari('IceHockeyNoFrameskip-v4')
```

Instantiate the agent:

```
agent = DQN(CnnPolicy, env, verbose=1)
```

Train the agent:

```
agent.learn(total_timesteps=25000)
```

After training the agent, we can have a look at how our trained agent performs in the environment:

```
state = env.reset()
while True:
    action, _ = agent.predict(state)
    next_state, reward, done, info = env.step(action)
    state = next_state
    env.render()
```

The preceding code displays how our trained agent plays the ice hockey game:

Figure 16.2: Agent playing the Ice Hockey game

Implementing DQN variants

We just learned how to implement DQN using Stable Baselines. Now, let's see how to implement the variants of DQN, such as double DQN, DQN with prioritized experience replay, and dueling DQN. Implementing DQN variants is very simple with Baselines.

First, we define our keyword arguments as follows:

```
kwargs = {"double_q": True, "prioritized_replay": True, "policy_
kwargs": dict(dueling=True)}
```

Now, while instantiating our agent, we just need to pass the keyword arguments:

```
agent = DQN(CnnPolicy, env, verbose=1, **kwargs)
```

Then, we can train the agent as usual:

```
agent.learn(total_timesteps=25000)
```

That's it! Now we have the dueling double DQN with prioritized experience replay. In the next section, we will learn how to play the lunar lander game using the **Advantage Actor-Critic Algorithm (A2C)**.

Lunar lander using A2C

Let's learn how to implement A2C with Stable Baselines for the lunar landing task. In the lunar lander environment, our agent drives the space vehicle, and the goal of the agent is to land correctly on the landing pad. If our agent (lander) lands away from the landing pad, then it loses the reward, and the episode will get terminated if the agent crashes or comes to rest. The action space of the environment includes four discrete actions, which are: do nothing, fire left orientation engine, fire main engine, and fire right orientation engine. Now, let's see how to train the agent using A2C to correctly land on the landing pad.

First, let's import the necessary libraries:

```
import gym
from stable_baselines.common.policies import MlpPolicy
from stable_baselines.common.vec_env import DummyVecEnv
from stable_baselines.common.evaluation import evaluate_policy
from stable_baselines import A2C
```

Create the lunar lander environment using Gym:

```
env = gym.make('LunarLander-v2')
```

Let's use the dummy vectorized environment. We learned that in the dummy vectorized environment, we run each environment in the same process:

```
env = DummyVecEnv([lambda: env])
```

Create the agent:

```
agent = A2C(MlpPolicy, env, ent_coef=0.1, verbose=0)
```

Train the agent:

```
agent.learn(total_timesteps=25000)
```

After training, we can evaluate our agent by looking at the mean rewards:

```
mean_reward, n_steps = evaluate_policy(agent, agent.get_env(), n_eval_
episodes=10)
```

We can also have a look at how our trained agent performs in the environment:

```
state = env.reset()
while True:
    action, _states = agent.predict(state)
    next_state, reward, done, info = env.step(action)
    state = next_state
    env.render()
```

The preceding code will show how well our trained agent lands on the landing pad:

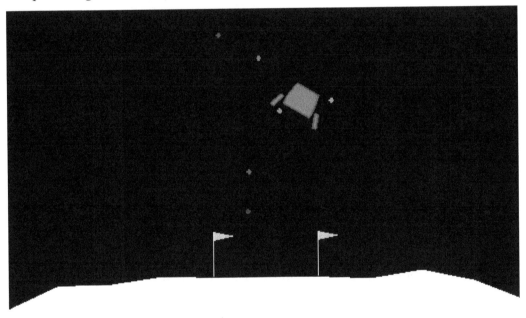

Figure 16.3: Agent playing the lunar lander game

Creating a custom network

In the previous section, we learned how to create an A2C using Stable Baselines. Instead of using the default network, can we customize the network architecture? Yes! With Stable Baselines, we can also use our own custom architecture. Let's see how to do that.

First, let's import the feedforward policy (feedforward network):

```
from stable_baselines.common.policies import FeedForwardPolicy
```

Now, we can define our custom policy (custom network) as shown in the following snippet. As we can observe in the following code, we are passing net_arch=[dict(pi=[128, 128, 128], vf=[128, 128, 128])], which specifies our network architecture. pi represents the architecture of the policy network and vf represents the architecture of value network:

```
class CustomPolicy(FeedForwardPolicy):
    def __init__(self, *args, **kargs):
        super(CustomPolicy, self).__init__(*args, **kargs,
                                net_arch=[dict(pi=[128, 128,
128], vf=[128, 128, 128])], feature_extraction="mlp")
```

We can instantiate the agent with the custom policy as follows:

```
agent = A2C(CustomPolicy, 'LunarLander-v2', verbose=1)
```

Now, we can train the agent as usual:

```
agent.learn(total_timesteps=25000)
```

That's it. Similarly, we can create our own custom network. In the next section, let's learn how to perform the *inverted pendulum swing-up* task using the **Deep Deterministic Policy Gradient (DDPG)** algorithm.

Swinging up a pendulum using DDPG

Let's learn how to implement the DDPG for the inverted pendulum swing-up task using Stable Baselines. First, let's import the necessary libraries:

```
import gym
import numpy as np

from stable_baselines.ddpg.policies import MlpPolicy
from stable_baselines.common.noise import NormalActionNoise,
OrnsteinUhlenbeckActionNoise, AdaptiveParamNoiseSpec
from stable_baselines import DDPG
```

Create the pendulum environment using Gym:

```
env = gym.make('Pendulum-v0')
```

Get the number of actions:

```
n_actions = env.action_space.shape[-1]
```

We know that in DDPG, instead of selecting the action directly, we add some noise using the Ornstein-Uhlenbeck process to ensure exploration. So, we create the action noise as follows:

```
action_noise = OrnsteinUhlenbeckActionNoise(mean=np.zeros(n_actions),
sigma=float(0.5) * np.ones(n_actions))
```

Instantiate the agent:

```
agent = DDPG(MlpPolicy, env, verbose=1, param_noise=None, action_
noise=action_noise)
```

Train the agent:

```
agent.learn(total_timesteps=25000)
```

After training the agent, we can also look at how our trained agent swings up the pendulum by rendering the environment. Can we also look at the computational graph of DDPG? Yes! In the next section, we will learn how to do that.

Viewing the computational graph in TensorBoard

With Stable Baselines, it is easier to view the computational graph of our model in TensorBoard. In order to that, we just need to pass the directory where we will store our log files while instantiating the agent, as shown here:

```
agent = DDPG(MlpPolicy, env, verbose=1, param_noise=None, action_
noise=action_noise, tensorboard_log="logs")
```

Then, we can train the agent:

```
agent.learn(total_timesteps=25000)
```

After training, open the terminal and type the following command to run TensorBoard:

```
tensorboard --logdir logs
```

As we can observe, we can now see the computational graph of the DDPG model (agent):

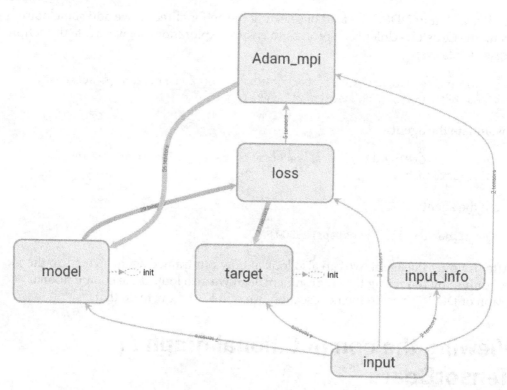

Figure 16.4: Computational graph of DDPG

From *Figure 16.4*, we can understand how the DDPG computational graph is generated just as we learned in *Chapter 12, Learning DDPG, TD3, and SAC*.

Now, let's expand and look into the model node for more clarity:

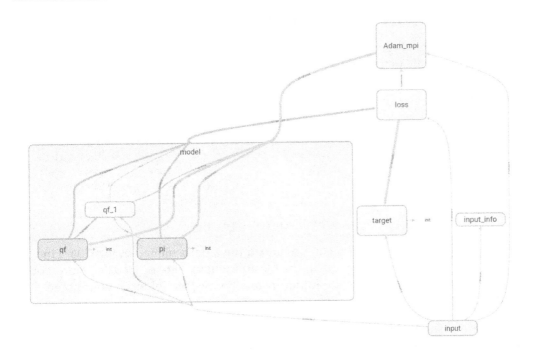

Figure 16.5: Computational graph of DDPG

As we can observe from *Figure 16.5*, our model includes the policy (actor) and Q (critic) network.

Now that we have learned how to use Stable Baselines to implement DDPG for the inverted pendulum swing-up task, in the next section we will learn how to implement TRPO using Stable Baselines.

Training an agent to walk using TRPO

In this section, let's learn how to train the agent to walk using **Trust Region Policy Optimization (TRPO)**. Let's use the MuJoCo environment for training the agent. **MuJoCo** stands for **Multi-Joint dynamics with Contact** and is one of the most popular simulators used for training agents to perform continuous control tasks.

Note that MuJoCo is a proprietary physics engine, so we need to acquire a license to use it. Also, MuJoCo offers a free 30-day trial period. Installing MuJoCo requires a specific set of steps. So, in the next section, we will see how to install the MuJoCo environment.

Installing the MuJoCo environment

First, in your home directory, create a new hidden folder called .mujoco. Next, go to the MuJoCo website (https://www.roboti.us/) and download MuJoCo according to your operating system. As shown in *Figure 16.6*, MuJoCo provides support for Windows, Linux, and macOS:

Download				
	mujoco200 win64	mjpro150 win32	mjpro140 win32	mjpro131 win32
	mujoco200 linux	mjpro150 win64	mjpro140 win64	mjpro131 win64
	mujoco200 macos	mjpro150 linux	mjpro140 linux	mjpro131 linux
		mjpro150 osx	mjpro140 osx	mjpro131 osx

Figure 16.6: Different MuJoCo versions

If you are using Linux, then you can download the zip file named mujoco200 linux. After downloading the zip file, unzip the file and rename it to mujoco200. Now, copy the mujoco200 folder and place the folder inside the .mujoco folder in your home directory.

As *Figure 16.7* shows, now in our home directory, we have a .mujoco folder, and inside the .mujoco folder, we have a mujoco200 folder:

```
sudharsan@Sudharsan:~$ cd .mujoco/
sudharsan@Sudharsan:~/.mujoco$ ls
mujoco200
sudharsan@Sudharsan:~/.mujoco$ 
```

Figure 16.7: Installing MuJoCo

Now, we need to obtain a trial license. First, go to https://www.roboti.us/license.html and register for the trial license, as *Figure 16.8* shows:

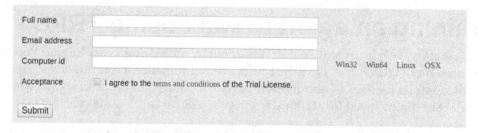

Figure 16.8: Registering for the trial license

To register, we also need the computer id. As *Figure 16.8* shows, to the right of the **Computer id** field, we have the name of different platforms. Now, just click on your operating system and you will obtain the relevant executable getid file. For instance, if you are using Linux, then you will obtain a file named getid_linux.

After downloading the getid_linux file, run the following command on your terminal:

```
chmod +x getid_linux
```

Then, run the following command:

```
./getid_linux
```

The preceding command will display your computer id. After getting the computer id, fill in the form and register to obtain a license. Once you click on the **Submit** button, you will get an email from Roboti LLC Licensing.

From the email, download the file named mjkey.txt. Next, place the mjkey.txt file in the .mujoco folder. As *Figure 16.9* shows, now our .mujoco hidden folder contains the mjkey.txt file and a folder named mujoco200:

```
sudharsan@Sudharsan:~$ cd .mujoco/
sudharsan@Sudharsan:~/.mujoco$ ls
mjkey.txt  mujoco200
sudharsan@Sudharsan:~/.mujoco$ []
```

Figure 16.9: Installing MuJoCo

Next, open your terminal and run the following command to edit the bashrc file:

```
nano ~/.bashrc
```

Copy the following line to the bashrc file and make sure to replace the username text with your own username:

```
export LD_LIBRARY_PATH=$LD_LIBRARY_PATH:/home/username/.mujoco/
mujoco200/bin
```

Next, save the file and exit the nano editor. Now, run the following command on your terminal:

```
source ~/.bashrc
```

Well done! We are almost there. Now, clone the MuJoCo GitHub repository:

```
git clone https://github.com/openai/mujoco-py.git
```

Navigate to the `mujoco-py` folder:

```
cd mujoco-py
```

Update the packages:

```
sudo apt-get update
```

Install the dependencies:

```
sudo apt-get install libgl1-mesa-dev libgl1-mesa-glx libosmesa6-dev
python3-pip python3-numpy python3-scipy
```

Finally, install MuJoCo:

```
pip3 install -r requirements.txt
sudo python3 setup.py install
```

To test the successful installation of MuJoCo, let's run a Humanoid agent by taking a random action in the environment. So, create the following Python file named `mujoco_test.py` with the following code:

```python
import gym
env = gym.make('Humanoid-v2')
env.reset()
for t in range(1000):
  env.render()
  env.step(env.action_space.sample())

env.close()
```

Next, open the terminal and run the Python file:

```
python mujoco_test.py
```

The preceding code will render the Humanoid environment as *Figure 16.10 shows*:

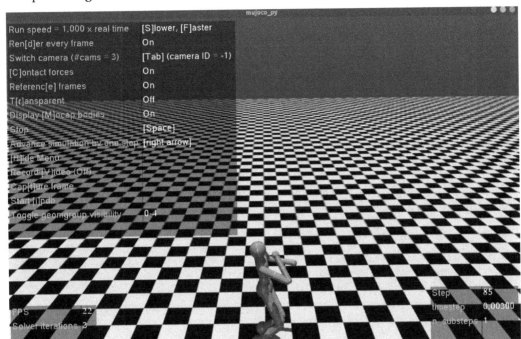

Figure 16.10: Humanoid environment

Now that we have successfully installed MuJoCo, let's start implementing TRPO to train our agent to walk in the next section.

Implementing TRPO

Import the necessary libraries:

```
import gym

from stable_baselines.common.policies import MlpPolicy
from stable_baselines.common.vec_env import DummyVecEnv, VecNormalize
from stable_baselines import TRPO
from stable_baselines.common.vec_env import VecVideoRecorder
```

Create a vectorized Humanoid environment using DummyVecEnv:

```
env = DummyVecEnv([lambda: gym.make("Humanoid-v2")])
```

Normalize the states (observations):

```
env = VecNormalize(env, norm_obs=True, norm_reward=False,
                   clip_obs=10.)
```

Instantiate the agent:

```
agent = TRPO(MlpPolicy, env)
```

Train the agent:

```
agent.learn(total_timesteps=250000)
```

After training the agent, we can see how our trained agent learned to walk by rendering the environment:

```
state = env.reset()
while True:
    action, _ = agent.predict(state)
    next_state, reward, done, info = env.step(action)
    state = next_state
    env.render()
```

Save the whole code used in this section in a Python file called `trpo.py` and then open the terminal and run the file:

```
python trpo.py
```

We can see how our trained agent learned to walk in *Figure 16.11*:

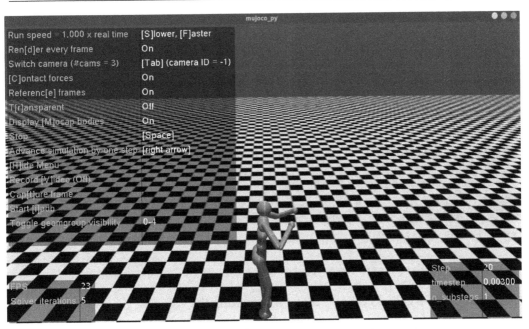

Run speed = 1.000 x real time	[S]lower, [F]aster
Ren[d]er every frame	On
Switch camera (#cams = 3)	[Tab] (camera ID = -1)
[C]ontact forces	On
Referenc[e] frames	On
T[r]ansparent	Off
Display [M]ocap bodies	On
Stop	[Space]
Advance simulation by one step	[right arrow]
[H]ide Menu	
Record [V]ideo (Off)	
Cap[t]ure frame	
Start [i]pdb	
Toggle geomgroup visibility	0-4

Figure 16.11: Agent learning to walk using TRPO

 Always use the terminal to run the program that uses the MuJoCo environment.

That's it. In the next section, we will learn how to record our trained agent's actions as a video.

Recording the video

In the previous section, we trained our agent to learn to walk using TRPO. Can we also record a video of our trained agent? Yes! With Stable Baselines, we can easily record a video of our agent using the `VecVideoRecorder` module.

Note that to record the video, we need the `ffmpeg` package installed in our machine. If it is not installed, then install it using the following set of commands:

```
sudo add-apt-repository ppa:mc3man/trusty-media
sudo apt-get update
sudo apt-get dist-upgrade
sudo apt-get install ffmpeg
```

Now, let's import the `VecVideoRecorder` module:

```
from stable_baselines.common.vec_env import VecVideoRecorder
```

Define a function called `record_video` for recording the video:

```
def record_video(env_name, agent, video_length=500, prefix='', video_
folder='videos/'):
```

Create the environment:

```
env = DummyVecEnv([lambda: gym.make(env_name)])
```

Instantiate the video recorder:

```
env = VecVideoRecorder(env, video_folder=video_folder,
        record_video_trigger=lambda step: step == 0, video_
length=video_length, name_prefix=prefix)
```

Select actions in the environment using our trained agent where the number of time steps is set to the video length:

```
state = env.reset()
for t in range(video_length):
    action, _ = agent.predict(state)
    next_state, reward, done, info = env.step(action)
    state = next_state
env.close()
```

That's it! Now, let's call our `record_video` function. Note that we are passing the environment name, our trained agent, the length of the video, and the name of our video file:

```
record_video('Humanoid-v2', agent, video_length=500, prefix='Humanoid_
walk_TRPO')
```

Now, we will have a new file called `Humanoid_walk_TRPO-step-0-to-step-500.mp4` in the videos folder:

Figure 16.12: Recorded video

In this way, we can record our trained agent's action. In the next section, we will learn how to implement PPO using Stable Baselines.

Training a cheetah bot to run using PPO

In this section, let's learn how to train the 2D cheetah bot to run using **Proximal Policy Optimization (PPO)**. First, import the necessary libraries:

```
import gym
from stable_baselines.common.policies import MlpPolicy
from stable_baselines.common.vec_env import DummyVecEnv, VecNormalize
from stable_baselines import PPO2
```

Create a vectorized environment using `DummyVecEnv`:

```
env = DummyVecEnv([lambda: gym.make("HalfCheetah-v2")])
```

Normalize the state:

```
env = VecNormalize(env,norm_obs=True)
```

Instantiate the agent:

```
agent = PPO2(MlpPolicy, env)
```

Train the agent:

```
agent.learn(total_timesteps=250000)
```

After training, we can see how our trained cheetah bot learned to run by rendering the environment:

```
state = env.reset()
while True:
    action, _ = agent.predict(state)
    next_state, reward, done, info = env.step(action)
    state = next_state
    env.render()
```

Save the whole code used in this section in a Python file called `ppo.py` and then open the terminal and run the file:

```
python ppo.py
```

We can see how our trained cheetah bot learned to run, as *Figure 16.13* shows:

Figure 16.13: 2D cheetah bot learning to run

Making a GIF of a trained agent

In the previous section, we learned how to train the cheetah bot to run using PPO. Can we also create a GIF file of our trained agent? Yes! Let's see how to do that.

First, import the necessary libraries:

```
import imageio
import numpy as np
```

Initialize the list for storing images:

```
images = []
```

Initialize the state by resetting the environment, where agent is the agent we trained in the previous section:

```
state = agent.env.reset()
```

Render the environment and get the image:

```
img = agent.env.render(mode='rgb_array')
```

For every step in the environment, save the image:

```
for i in range(500):
    images.append(img)
    action, _ = agent.predict(state)
    next_state, reward, done ,info = agent.env.step(action)
    state = next_state
    img = agent.env.render(mode='rgb_array')
```

Create the GIF file as follows:

```
imageio.mimsave('HalfCheetah.gif', [np.array(img) for i, img in
enumerate(images) if i%2 == 0], fps=29)
```

Now, we will have a new file called HalfCheetah.gif, as *Figure 16.14* shows:

Figure 16.14: GIF of the trained agent

In this way, we can obtain a GIF of our trained agent. In the next section, we will learn how to implement GAIL using Stable Baselines.

Implementing GAIL

In this section, let's explore how to implement **Generative Adversarial Imitation Learning (GAIL)** with Stable Baselines. In *Chapter 15, Imitation Learning and Inverse RL*, we learned that we use the generator to generate the state-action pair in a way that the discriminator is not able to distinguish whether the state-action pair is generated using the expert policy or the agent policy. We train the generator to generate a policy similar to an expert policy using TRPO, while the discriminator is a classifier and it is optimized using Adam.

To implement GAIL, we need expert trajectories so that our generator learns to mimic the expert trajectory. Okay, so how can we obtain the expert trajectory? First, we use the TD3 algorithm to generate expert trajectories and then create an expert dataset. Then, using this expert dataset, we train our GAIL agent. Note that instead of using TD3, we can also use any other algorithm for generating expert trajectories.

First, let's import the necessary libraries:

```
import gym
from stable_baselines import GAIL, TD3
from stable_baselines.gail import ExpertDataset, generate_expert_traj
```

Instantiate the TD3 agent:

```
agent = TD3('MlpPolicy', 'MountainCarContinuous-v0', verbose=1)
```

Generate the expert trajectories:

```
generate_expert_traj(agent, 'expert_traj', n_timesteps=100, n_
episodes=20)
```

Create the expert dataset using the expert trajectories:

```
dataset = ExpertDataset(expert_path='expert_traj.npz', traj_
limitation=10, verbose=1)
```

Instantiate the GAIL agent with the expert dataset (expert trajectories):

```
agent = GAIL('MlpPolicy', 'MountainCarContinuous-v0', dataset,
verbose=1)
```

Train the GAIL agent:

```
agent.learn(total_timesteps=25000)
```

After training, we can also render the environment and see how our trained agent performs in the environment. That's it, implementing GAIL using Stable Baselines is that simple.

Summary

We started the chapter by understanding what Stable Baselines is and how to install it. Then, we learned to create our first agent with Stable Baselines using a DQN. We also learned how to save and load an agent. Next, we learned how to create multiple independent environments using vectorization. We also learned about two types of vectorized environment called SubprocVecEnv and DummyVecEnv.

We learned that in SubprocVecEnv, we run each environment in a different process, whereas in DummyVecEnv, we run each environment in the same process.

Later, we learned how to implement a DQN and its variants to play Atari games using Stable Baselines. Next, we learned how to implement A2C and also how to create a custom policy network. Moving on, we learned how to implement DDPG and also how to view the computational graph in TensorBoard.

Going further, we learned how to set up the MuJoCo environment and how to train an agent to walk using TRPO. We also learned how to record a video of a trained agent. Next, we learned how to implement PPO and how to make a GIF of a trained agent. At the end of the chapter, we learned how to implement generative adversarial imitation learning using Stable Baselines.

Questions

Let's put our knowledge of Stable Baselines to the test. Try answering the following questions:

1. What is Stable Baselines?
2. How do you store and load a trained agent?
3. What is a vectorized environment?
4. What is the difference between the SubprocVecEnv and DummyVecEnv environments?
5. How do you visualize a computational graph in TensorBoard?
6. How do you record a video of a trained agent?

Further reading

To learn more, check the following resource:

- Check out the Stable Baselines documentation, available at `https://stable-baselines.readthedocs.io/en/master/index.html`

17
Reinforcement Learning Frontiers

Congratulations! You have made it to the final chapter. We have come a long way. We started off with the fundamentals of reinforcement learning and gradually we learned about the state-of-the-art deep reinforcement learning algorithms. In this chapter, we will look at some exciting and promising research trends in reinforcement learning. We will start the chapter by learning what meta learning is and how it differs from other learning paradigms. Then, we will learn about one of the most used meta-learning algorithms, called **Model-Agnostic Meta Learning (MAML)**.

We will understand MAML in detail, and then we will see how to apply it in a reinforcement learning setting. Following this, we will learn about hierarchical reinforcement learning, and we look into a popular hierarchical reinforcement learning algorithm called MAXQ value function decomposition.

At the end of the chapter, we will look at an interesting algorithm called **Imagination Augmented Agents (I2As)**, which makes use of both model-based and model-free learning.

In this chapter, we will learn about the following topics:

- Meta reinforcement learning
- Model-agnostic meta learning
- Hierarchical reinforcement learning

- MAXQ value function decomposition
- Imagination Augmented Agents

Let's begin the chapter by understanding meta reinforcement learning.

Meta reinforcement learning

In order to understand how meta reinforcement learning works, first let's understand meta learning.

Meta learning is one of the most promising and trending research areas in the field of artificial intelligence. It is believed to be a stepping stone for attaining **Artificial General Intelligence (AGI)**. What is meta learning? And why do we need meta learning? To answer these questions, let's revisit how deep learning works.

We know that in deep learning, we train a deep neural network to perform a task. But the problem with deep neural networks is that we need to have a large training dataset to train our network, as it will fail to learn when we have only a few data points.

Let's say we trained a deep learning model to perform task **A**. Suppose we have a new task **B**, which is closely related to task **A**. Although task **B** is closely related to task **A**, we can't use the model we trained for task **A** to perform task **B**. We need to train a new model from scratch for task **B**. So, for each task, we need to train a new model from scratch although they might be related. But is this really true AI? Not really. How do we humans learn? We generalize our learning to multiple concepts and learn from there. But current learning algorithms master only one task. So, here is where meta learning comes in.

Meta learning produces a versatile AI model that can learn to perform various tasks without having to be trained from scratch. We train our meta-learning model on various related tasks with few data points, so for a new related task, it can make use of the learning achieved in previous tasks. Many researchers and scientists believe that meta learning can get us closer to achieving AGI. Learning to learn is the key focus of meta learning. We will understand how exactly meta learning works by looking at a popular meta learning algorithm called MAML in the next section.

Model-agnostic meta learning

Model-Agnostic Meta Learning (MAML) is one of the most popular meta-learning algorithms and it has been a major breakthrough in meta-learning research. The basic idea of MAML is to find a better initial model parameter so that with a good initial parameter, a model can learn quickly on new tasks with fewer gradient steps.

So, what do we mean by that? Let's say we are performing a classification task using a neural network. How do we train the network? We start off by initializing random weights and train the network by minimizing the loss. How do we minimize the loss? We minimize the loss using gradient descent. Okay, but how do we use gradient descent to minimize the loss? We use gradient descent to find the optimal weights that will give us the minimal loss. We take multiple gradient steps to find the optimal weights so that we can reach convergence.

In MAML, we try to find these optimal weights by learning from the distribution of similar tasks. So, for a new task, we don't have to start with randomly initialized weights; instead, we can start with optimal weights, which will take fewer gradient steps to reach convergence and doesn't require more data points for training.

Let's understand how MAML works in simple terms. Let's suppose we have three related tasks: T_1, T_2, and T_3.

First, we randomly initialize our model parameter (weight), θ. We train our network on task T_1. Then, we try to minimize the loss L by gradient descent. We minimize the loss by finding the optimal parameter. Let θ_1' be the optimal parameter for the task T_1. Similarly, for tasks T_2 and T_3, we will start off with a randomly initialized model parameter θ and minimize the loss by finding the optimal parameters by gradient descent. Let θ_2' and θ_3' be the optimal parameters for tasks T_2 and T_3, respectively.

As we can see in the following figure, we start off each task with the randomly initialized parameter θ and minimize the loss by finding the optimal parameters θ_1', θ_2', and θ_3' for the tasks T_1, T_2, and T_3 respectively:

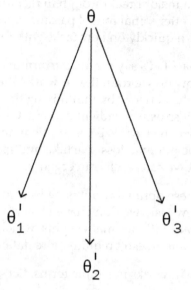

Figure 17.1: θ is initialized at a random position

However, instead of initializing θ in a random position, that is, with random values, if we initialize θ in a position that is common to all three tasks, then we don't need to take many gradient steps and it will take us less time to train. MAML tries to do exactly this. MAML tries to find this optimal parameter θ that is common to many of the related tasks, so we can train a new task relatively quick with few data points without having to take many gradient steps.

As *Figure 17.2* shows, we shift θ to a position that is common to all different optimal θ' values:

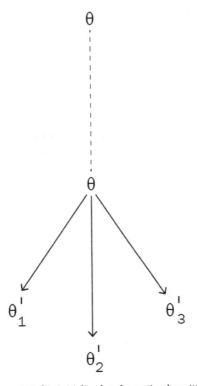

Figure 17.2: θ is initialized at the optimal position

So, for a new related task, say, T_4, we don't have to start with a randomly initialized parameter, θ. Instead, we can start with the optimal θ value (shifted θ) so that it will take fewer gradient steps to attain convergence.

Thus, in MAML, we try to find this optimal θ value that is common to related tasks to help us learn from fewer data points and minimize our training time. MAML is model-agnostic, meaning that we can apply MAML to any models that are trainable with gradient descent. But how exactly does MAML work? How do we shift the model parameters to an optimal position? Now that we have a basic understanding of MAML, we will address all these questions in the next section.

Understanding MAML

Suppose we have a model f parameterized by θ, that is, f_θ, and we have a distribution over tasks, $p(T)$. First, we initialize our parameter θ with some random values. Next, we sample a batch of tasks T_i from a distribution over tasks—that is, $T_i \sim p(T)$. Let's say we have sampled five tasks: T_1, T_2, T_3, T_4, T_5.

Now, for each task T_i, we sample k number of data points and train the model f parameterized by θ, that is, f_θ. We train the model by computing the loss $L_{T_i}(f_\theta)$ and we minimize the loss using gradient descent and find the optimal parameter θ'_i. The parameter update rule using gradient descent is given as:

$$\theta'_i = \theta - \alpha \nabla_\theta L_{T_i}(f_\theta) \tag{1}$$

In the preceding equation, the following applies:

- θ'_i is the optimal parameter for a task T_i
- θ is the initial parameter
- α is the learning rate
- $\nabla_\theta L_{T_i}(f_\theta)$ is the gradient of loss for a task T_i with the model parameterized as f_θ

So, after the preceding parameter update using gradient descent, we will have optimal parameters for all five tasks that we have sampled. That is, for the tasks T_1, T_2, T_3, T_4, T_5, we will have the optimal parameters $\theta'_1, \theta'_2, \theta'_3, \theta'_4, \theta'_5$, respectively.

Now, before the next iteration, we perform a meta update or meta optimization. That is, in the previous step, we found the optimal parameter θ'_i by training on each of the tasks, T_i. Now we take some new set of tasks and for each of these new tasks T_i, we don't have to start from the random position θ; instead, we can start from the optimal position θ'_i to train the model.

That is, for each of the new tasks $T_{i'}$ instead of using the randomly initialized parameter θ, we use the optimal parameter θ'_i. This implies that we train the model f parameterized by θ'_i, that is, $f_{\theta'_i}$ instead of using f_θ. Then, we calculate the loss $L_{T_i}(f_{\theta'_i})$, compute the gradients, and update the parameter θ. This makes our randomly initialized parameter θ move to an optimal position where we don't have to take many gradient steps. This step is called a meta update, meta optimization, or meta training. It can be expressed as follows:

$$\theta = \theta - \beta \nabla_\theta \sum_{T_i \sim p(T)} L_{T_i}\left(f_{\theta'_i}\right) \tag{2}$$

In equation (2), the following applies:

- θ is the initial parameter
- β is the learning rate
- $\nabla_\theta \sum_{T_i \sim p(T)} L_{T_i}\left(f_{\theta'_i}\right)$ is the gradient of loss for each of the new tasks $T_{i'}$ with the model parameterized as $f_{\theta'_i}$

If you look at our previous meta update equation (2) closely, we can see that we are updating our model parameter θ by merely taking an average of gradients of each new task T_i with the model f parameterized by θ'_i.

Figure 17.3 helps us to understand the MAML algorithm better. As we can observe, our MAML algorithm has two loops—an **inner loop** where we find the optimal parameter θ'_i for each of the tasks T_i using the model f parameterized by initial parameter θ, that is, f_θ, and an **outer loop** where we use the model f parameterized by the optimal parameter θ'_i obtained in the previous step, that is $f_{\theta'_i}$, and train the model on the new set of tasks, calculate the loss, compute the gradient of the loss, and update the randomly initialized model parameter θ:

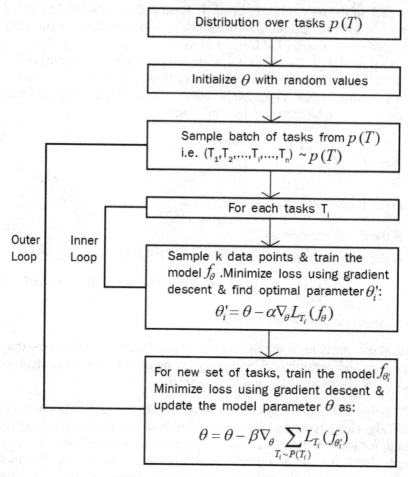

Figure 17.3: The MAML algorithm

 Note that we should not use the same set of tasks we used to find the optimal parameter θ_i' when updating the model parameter θ in the outer loop.

In a nutshell, in MAML, we sample a batch of tasks and for each task T_i in the batch, we minimize the loss using gradient descent and get the optimal parameter θ_i'. Then, we update our randomly initialized model parameter θ by calculating gradients for each new task T_i with the model parameterized as $f_{\theta_i'}$.

Still not clear how exactly MAML works? Worry not! Let's look in even more detail at the steps and understand how MAML works in a supervised learning setting in the next section.

MAML in a supervised learning setting

As we learned, MAML is model-agnostic and so we can apply MAML to any model that can be trained with gradient descent. In this section, let's learn how to apply the MAML algorithm in a supervised learning setting. Before going ahead, let's define our loss function.

If we are performing regression, then we can use mean squared error as our loss function:

$$L_{T_i}(f_\theta) = \sum_{x_j, y_j \sim T_i} \|f_\theta(x_i) - y_i\|_2^2$$

If we are performing classification, then we can use cross-entropy loss as our loss function:

$$L_{T_i}(f_\theta) = \sum_{x_j, y_j \sim T_i} y_j \log f_\theta(x_j) + (1 - y_j) \log\left(1 - f_\theta(x_j)\right)$$

Now let's see step by step how exactly MAML is used in supervised learning.

Let's say we have a model f parameterized by a parameter θ, and we have a distribution over tasks $p(T)$. First, we randomly initialize the model parameter θ.

Next, we sample a batch of tasks T_i from a distribution of tasks, that is, $T_i \sim p(T)$. Let's say we have sampled three tasks; then, we have T_1, T_2, T_3.

Inner loop: For each task T_i, we sample k data points and prepare our training and test datasets:

$$D_i^{train} = \{(x_1, y_1), (x_2, y_2) \ldots (x_k, y_k)\}$$
$$D_i^{test} = \{(x_1, y_1), (x_2, y_2) \ldots (x_k, y_k)\}$$

Wait! What are the training and test datasets? We use the training dataset in the inner loop for finding the optimal parameter θ_i' and the test set in the outer loop for finding the optimal parameter θ. The test dataset does not mean that we are checking the model's performance. It basically acts as a training set in the outer loop. We can also call our test set a meta-training set.

Now, we train the model f_θ on the training dataset D_i^{train}, calculate the loss, minimize the loss using gradient descent, and get the optimal parameter θ_i' as $\theta_i' = \theta - \alpha\nabla_\theta L_{T_i}(f_\theta)$.

That is, for each of the tasks T_i, we sample k data points and prepare D_i^{train} and D_i^{test}. Next, we minimize the loss on the training dataset D_i^{train} and get the optimal parameter θ_i'. As we sampled three tasks, we will have three optimal parameters, $\theta_1', \theta_2', \theta_3'$.

Outer loop: Now, we perform meta optimization on the test set (meta-training set); that is, we try to minimize the loss in the test set D_i^{test}. Here, we parameterize our model f by the optimal parameter θ_i' calculated in the previous step. So, we compute the loss of the model $L_{T_i}(f_{\theta_i'})$ and the gradients of the loss and update our randomly initialized parameter θ using our test dataset (meta-training dataset) as:

$$\theta = \theta - \beta\nabla_\theta \sum_{T_i \sim p(T)} L_{T_i}(f_{\theta_i'})$$

We repeat the preceding steps for several iterations to find the optimal parameter. For a clear understanding of how MAML works in supervised learning, let's look into the algorithm in the next section.

Algorithm – MAML in supervised learning

The algorithm of MAML in a supervised learning setting is given as follows:

1. Say that we have a model f parameterized by a parameter θ and we have a distribution over tasks $p(T)$. First, we randomly initialize the model parameter θ.

2. Sample a batch of tasks T_i from a distribution of tasks, that is, $T_i \sim p(T)$.

3. For each task T_i:

    1. Sample k data points and prepare our training and test datasets:

       $$D_i^{train} = \{(x_1, y_1), (x_2, y_2) \dots (x_k, y_k)\}$$
       $$D_i^{test} = \{(x_1, y_1), (x_2, y_2) \dots (x_k, y_k)\}$$

    2. Train the model f_θ on the training dataset D_i^{train} and compute the loss.

    3. Minimize the loss using gradient descent and get the optimal parameter θ_i' as $\theta_i' = \theta - \alpha\nabla_\theta L_{T_i}(f_\theta)$.

4. Now, minimize the loss on the test set D_i^{test}. Parameterize the model f with the optimal parameter θ_i' calculated in the previous step, compute loss $L_{T_i}(f_{\theta_i'})$. Calculate gradients of the loss and update our randomly initialized parameter θ using our test (meta-training) dataset as:

$$\theta = \theta - \beta \nabla_\theta \sum_{T_i \sim p(T)} L_{T_i}(f_{\theta_i'}).$$

5. Repeat *steps* 2 to 4 for several iterations.

The following figure gives us an overview of how the MAML algorithm works in supervised learning:

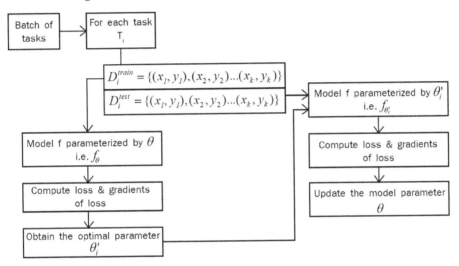

Figure 17.4: Overview of MAML

Now that we have learned how to use MAML in a supervised learning setting, in the next section, we will see how to use MAML in a reinforcement learning setting.

MAML in a reinforcement learning setting

Now, let's learn how to apply the MAML algorithm in a reinforcement learning setting. We know that the objective of reinforcement learning is to find the optimal policy, that is, the policy that gives the maximum return. We've learned about several reinforcement learning algorithms for finding the optimal policy, and we've also learned about several deep reinforcement learning algorithms for finding the optimal policy, where we used the neural network parameterized by θ.

We can apply MAML to any algorithm that can be trained with gradient descent. For instance, let's take the policy gradient method. In the policy gradient method, we use a neural network parameterized by θ to find the optimal policy and we train our network using gradient descent. So, we can apply the MAML algorithm to the policy gradient method.

Let's understand how MAML works in reinforcement learning step by step.

Let's say we have a model (policy network) f parameterized by a parameter θ. The model (policy network) f tries to find the optimal policy by learning the optimal parameter θ. Suppose, we have a distribution over tasks $p(T)$. First, we randomly initialize the model parameter θ.

Next, we sample a batch of tasks T_i from a distribution of tasks, that is, $T_i \sim p(T)$. Let's say we have sampled three tasks; then, we have T_1, T_2, T_3.

Inner loop: For each task T_i, we prepare our train dataset D_i^{train}. Okay, how can we create the training dataset in a reinforcement learning setting?

We have the model (policy network) f_θ. So, we generate k number of trajectories using our model f_θ. We know that the trajectories consist of a sequence of state-action pairs. So, we have:

$$D_i^{train} = \{(\mathbf{s}_1^1, \mathbf{a}_1^1, \dots \mathbf{s}_T^1), \dots, (\mathbf{s}_1^k, \mathbf{a}_1^k, \dots \mathbf{s}_T^k)$$

Now, we compute the loss and minimize it using gradient descent and get the optimal parameter θ_i' as $\theta_i' = \theta - \alpha \nabla_\theta L_{T_i}(f_\theta)$.

That is, for each of the tasks T_i, we sample k trajectories and prepare the training dataset D_i^{train}. Next, we minimize the loss on the training dataset D_i^{train} and get the optimal parameter θ_i'. As we sampled three tasks, we will have three optimal parameters, $\theta_1', \theta_2', \theta_3'$.

We also need the test dataset D_i^{test}, which we use in the outer loop. How do we prepare our test dataset? Now, we use our model f parameterized by the optimal parameter θ_i'; that is, we use $f_{\theta_i'}$ and generate k number of trajectories. So, we have:

$$D_i^{test} = \{(\mathbf{s}_1^1, \mathbf{a}_1^1, \dots \mathbf{s}_T^1), \dots, (\mathbf{s}_1^k, \mathbf{a}_1^k, \dots \mathbf{s}_T^k)\}$$

Remember that D_i^{train} is created by f_θ and the test (meta-training) dataset D_i^{test} is created by $f_{\theta_i'}$.

Outer loop: Now, we perform meta optimization on the test (meta-training) dataset; that is, we try to minimize the loss in the test dataset D_i^{test}. Here, we parameterize our model f by the optimal parameter θ_i' calculated in the previous step. So, we compute the loss of the model $L_{T_i}(f_{\theta_i'})$ and the gradients of the loss and update our randomly initialized parameter θ using our test (meta-training) dataset as:

$$\theta = \theta - \beta \nabla_\theta \sum_{T_i \sim p(T)} L_{T_i}(f_{\theta_i'})$$

We repeat the preceding step for several iterations to find the optimal parameter. For a clear understanding of how MAML works in reinforcement learning, let's look into the algorithm in the next section.

Algorithm – MAML in reinforcement learning

The algorithm of MAML in a reinforcement learning setting is given as follows:

1. Say, we have a model f parameterized by a parameter θ and we have a distribution over tasks $p(T)$. First, we randomly initialize the model parameter θ.

2. Sample a batch of tasks T_i from a distribution of tasks, that is, $T_i \sim p(T)$.

3. For each task T_i:

    1. Sample k trajectories using f_θ and prepare the training dataset:
    $D_i^{train} = \{(\mathbf{s}_1^1, \mathbf{a}_1^1, ... \mathbf{s}_T^1), ..., (\mathbf{s}_1^k, \mathbf{a}_1^k, ... \mathbf{s}_T^k)\}$.
    2. Train the model f_θ on the training dataset D_i^{train} and compute the loss.
    3. Minimize the loss using gradient descent and get the optimal parameter θ_i' as $\theta_i' = \theta - \alpha \nabla_\theta L_{T_i}(f_\theta)$.
    4. Sample k trajectories using $f_{\theta_i'}$ and prepare the test dataset:
    $D_i^{test} = \{(\mathbf{s}_1^1, \mathbf{a}_1^1, ... \mathbf{s}_T^1), ..., (\mathbf{s}_1^k, \mathbf{a}_1^k, ... \mathbf{s}_T^k)\}$.

4. Now, we minimize the loss on the test dataset D_i^{test}. Parameterize the model f with the optimal parameter θ_i' calculated in the previous step and compute the loss $L_{T_i}(f_{\theta_i'})$. Calculate the gradients of the loss and update our randomly initialized parameter θ using our test (meta-training) dataset as:

$$\theta = \theta - \beta \nabla_\theta \sum_{T_i \sim p(T)} L_{T_i}(f_{\theta_i'})$$

5. Repeat *steps 2* to *4* for several iterations.

That's it! Meta learning is a growing field of research. Now that we have a basic idea of meta learning, you can explore more about meta learning and see how meta learning is used in reinforcement learning. In the next section, we will learn about hierarchical reinforcement learning.

Hierarchical reinforcement learning

The problem with reinforcement learning is that it cannot scale well with a large number of state spaces and actions, which ultimately leads to the problem called curse of dimensionality. **Hierarchical reinforcement learning (HRL)** is proposed to solve the curse of dimensionality, where we decompose large problems into small subproblems in a hierarchy. Let's suppose the goal of our agent is to reach home from school. Now, our goal is split into a set of subgoals, such as going out of the school gate, booking a cab, and so on.

There are different methods used in HRL, such as state-space decomposition, state abstraction, and temporal abstraction. In state-space decomposition, we decompose the state space into different subspaces and try to solve the problem in a smaller subspace. Breaking down the state space also allows faster exploration, as the agent does not want to explore the entire state space. In state abstraction, the agent ignores the variables that are irrelevant to achieving the current subtasks in the current state space. In temporal abstraction, the action sequence and action sets are grouped, which divides the single step into multiple steps.

We will now look into one of the most commonly used algorithms in HRL, called MAXQ value function decomposition.

MAXQ value function Decomposition

MAXQ value function decomposition is one of the most frequently used algorithms in HRL. In this section, let's get a basic idea and overview of how MAXQ value function decomposition works. Let's understand how MAXQ value function decomposition works with an example. Let's take a taxi environment as shown in *Figure 17.5*:

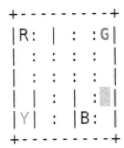

Figure 17.5: Taxi environment

Let's suppose our agent is driving a taxi. As *Figure 17.5* shows, the tiny, yellow-colored rectangle is the taxi driven by our agent. The letters (**R, G, Y, B**) represent the different locations. Thus we have four locations in total, and the agent has to pick up a passenger at one location and drop them off at another location. The agent will receive +20 points as a reward for a successful drop-off and -1 point for every time step it takes. The agent will also lose -10 points for illegal pickups and drop-offs.

So the goal of our agent is to learn to pick up and drop off passengers at the correct location in a short time without adding illegal passengers.

Now we break the goal of our agent into four subtasks as follows:

- **Navigate**: In the Navigate subtask, the goal of our agent is to drive the taxi from the current location to one of the target locations. The Navigate(t) subtask will use the four primitive actions: *north, south, east,* and *west*.

- **Get**: In the Get subtask, the goal of our agent is to drive the taxi from its current location to the passenger's location and pick up the passenger.

- **Put**: In the Put subtask, the goal of our agent is to drive the taxi from its current location to the passenger's destination and drop off the passenger.

- **Root**: Root is the whole task.

We can represent all these subtasks in a directed acyclic graph called a task graph, as *Figure 17.6* shows:

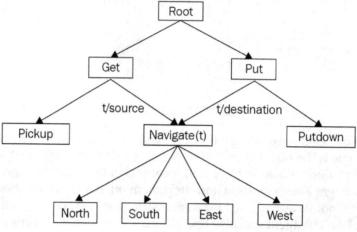

Figure 17.6: Task graph

As we can observe from the preceding figure, all the subtasks are arranged hierarchically. Each node represents a subtask or primitive action and each edge connects in such a way that a subtask can call its child subtask. As shown, the **Navigate(t)** subtask has four primitive actions: **East**, **West**, **North**, and **South**. The **Get** subtask has a **Pickup** primitive action and a **Navigate(t)** subtask. Similarly, the **Put** subtask has a **Putdown** (drop) primitive action and **Navigate(t)** subtask.

In MAXQ value function decomposition, we decompose the value function into a set of value functions for each of the subtasks. For the efficient designing and debugging of MAXQ decompositions, we can redesign our task graphs as *Figure 17.7* shows:

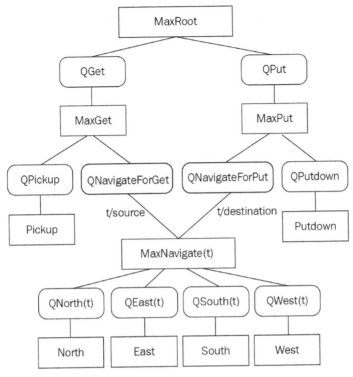

Figure 17.7: Task graph

As we can observe from *Figure 17.7*, our redesigned graph contains two special types of nodes: max nodes and Q nodes. The max nodes define the subtasks in the task decomposition and the Q nodes define the actions that are available for each subtask.

Thus, in this section, we got a basic idea of MaxQ value function decomposition. In the next section, we will learn about I2A.

Imagination augmented agents

Are you a fan of chess? If I asked you to play chess, how would you play it? Before moving any chess piece on the chessboard, you might imagine the consequences of moving a chess piece and move the chess piece that you think would help you to win the game. So, basically, before taking any action, we imagine the consequence and, if it is favorable, we proceed with that action, else we refrain from performing that action.

Similarly, **Imagination Augmented Agents (I2As)** are augmented with imagination. Before taking any action in an environment, the agent imagines the consequences of taking the action and if they think the action will provide a good reward, they will perform the action. The I2A takes advantage of both model-based and model-free learning. *Figure 17.8* shows the architecture of I2As:

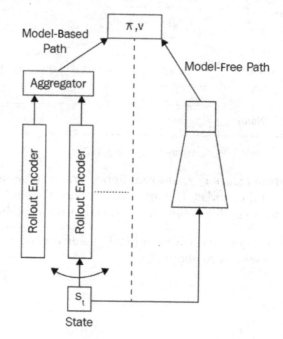

I2A architecture

Figure 17.8: I2A architecture

As we can observe from *Figure 17.8*, I2A architecture has both model-based and model-free paths. Thus, the action the agent takes is the result of both the model-based and model-free paths. In the model-based path, we have rollout encoders.

These rollout encoders are where the agent performs imagination tasks, so let's take a closer look at the rollout encoders. *Figure 17.9* shows a single rollout encoder:

Single Imagination Rollout

Figure 17.9: Single imagination rollout

From *Figure 17.9*, we can observe that the rollout encoders have two layers: the imagine future layer and the encoder layer. The imagine future layer is where the imagination happens. The imagine future layer consists of the imagination core.

When we feed the state s_t to the imagination core, we get the next state $\hat{s}_{t+1}$ and the reward $\hat{r}_{t+1}$, and when we feed this next state $\hat{s}_{t+1}$ to the next imagination core, we get the next state $\hat{s}_{t+2}$ and reward $\hat{r}_{t+2}$. If we repeat these for n steps, we get a rollout, which is basically a pair of states and rewards, and then we use encoders such as **Long Short-Term Memory (LSTM)** to encode this rollout. As a result, we get rollout encodings. These rollout encodings are actually the embeddings describing the future imagined path. We will have multiple rollout encoders for different future imagined paths, and we use an aggregator to aggregate this rollout encoder.

Okay, but how exactly does the imagination happen in the imagination core? What is actually in the imagination core? *Figure 17.10* shows a single imagination core:

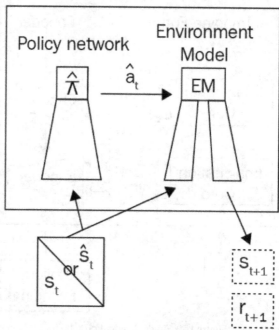

Figure 17.10: The imagination core

As we can observe from *Figure 17.10*, the imagination core consists of a policy network and an environment model. The environment model learns from all the actions that the agent has performed so far. It takes information about the state $\hat{s}_t$, imagines all the possible futures considering the experience, and chooses the action $\hat{a}_t$ that gives a high reward.

Figure 17.11 shows the complete architecture of I2As with all components expanded:

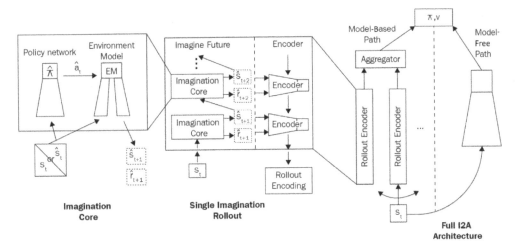

Figure 17.11: Full I2A architecture

Have you played Sokoban before? Sokoban is a classic puzzle game where the player has to push boxes to a target location. The rules of the game are very simple: boxes can only be pushed and cannot be pulled. If we push a box in the wrong direction then the puzzle becomes unsolvable:

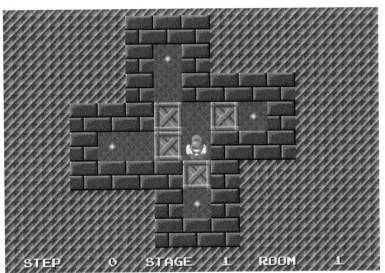

Figure 17.12: Sokoban environment

The I2A architecture provides good results in these kinds of environments, where the agent has to plan in advance before taking an action. The authors of the paper tested I2A performance on Sokoban and achieved great results.

There are various exciting research advancements happening around deep reinforcement learning. Now that you have finished reading the book, you can start exploring such advancements and experiment with various projects. Learn and reinforce!

Summary

We started this chapter by understanding what meta learning is. We learned that with meta learning, we train our model on various related tasks with a few data points, such that for a new related task, our model can make use of the learning obtained from the previous tasks.

Next, we learned about a popular meta-learning algorithm called MAML. In MAML, we sample a batch of tasks and for each task T_i in the batch, we minimize the loss using gradient descent and get the optimal parameter θ_i'. Then, we update our randomly initialized model parameter θ by calculating the gradients for each of the new tasks T_i with the model parameterized as $f_{\theta_i'}$.

Moving on, we learned about HRL, where we decompose large problems into small subproblems in a hierarchy. We also looked into the different methods used in HRL, such as state-space decomposition, state abstraction, and temporal abstraction. Next, we got an overview of MAXQ value function decomposition, where we decompose the value function into a set of value functions for each of the subtasks.

At the end of the chapter, we learned about I2As, which are augmented with imagination. Before taking any action in an environment, the agent imagines the consequences of taking the action, and if they think the action will provide a good reward, they will perform the action.

Deep reinforcement learning is evolving every day with interesting advancements. Now that you have learned about the various state-of-the-art deep reinforcement learning algorithms, you can start building interesting projects and also contribute to deep reinforcement learning research.

Questions

Let's test the knowledge you gained in this chapter; try answering the following questions:

1. Why do we need meta learning?
2. What is MAML?
3. What is the meta objective?
4. What is the meta training set?
5. Define HRL.
6. How does an I2A work?

Further reading

For more information, we can refer to the following papers:

- **Model-Agnostic Meta-Learning for Fast Adaptation of Deep Networks** by *Chelsea Finn, Pieter Abbeel, Sergey Levine,* https://arxiv.org/pdf/1703.03400.pdf
- **Hierarchical Reinforcement Learning with the MAXQ Value Function Decomposition** by *Thomas G. Dietterich,* https://arxiv.org/pdf/cs/9905014.pdf
- **Imagination-Augmented Agents for Deep Reinforcement Learning** by *Théophane Weber, et al.,* https://arxiv.org/pdf/1707.06203.pdf

Appendix 1 – Reinforcement Learning Algorithms

Let's have a look at all the reinforcement learning algorithms we have learned about in this book.

Reinforcement learning algorithm

The steps involved in a typical reinforcement learning algorithm are given as follows:

1. First, the agent interacts with the environment by performing an action.
2. The agent performs an action and moves from one state to another.
3. Then the agent will receive a reward based on the action it performed.
4. Based on the reward, the agent will understand whether the action is good or bad.
5. If the action was good, that is, if the agent received a positive reward, then the agent will prefer performing that action, else the agent will try performing other actions that can result in a positive reward. So reinforcement learning is basically a trial-and-error learning process.

Value Iteration

The algorithm of value iteration is given as follows:

1. Compute the optimal value function by taking maximum over the Q function, that is, $V^*(s) = \max_a Q^*(s, a)$
2. Extract the optimal policy from the computed optimal value function

Policy Iteration

The algorithm of policy iteration is given as follows:

1. Initialize a random policy
2. Compute the value function using the given policy
3. Extract a new policy using the value function obtained from *step 2*
4. If the extracted policy is the same as the policy used in *step 2* then stop, else send the extracted new policy to *step 2* and repeat *steps 2* to *4*

First-Visit MC Prediction

The algorithm of first-visit MC prediction is given as follows:

1. Let total_return(s) be the sum of the return of a state across several episodes and $N(s)$ be the counter, that is, the number of times a state is visited across several episodes. Initialize total_return(s) and $N(s)$ as zero for all the states. The policy π is given as input.

2. For M number of iterations:
    1. Generate an episode using the policy π
    2. Store all rewards obtained in the episode in a list called rewards
    3. For each step t in the episode:

        If the state s_t is occurring for the first time in the episode:
        1. Compute the return of the state s_t as $R(s_t) = \text{sum(rewards[t:])}$
        2. Update the total return of the state s_t as total_return(s_t) = total_return(s_t) + $R(s_t)$
        3. Update the counter as $N(s_t) = N(s_t) + 1$

3. Compute the value of a state by just taking the average, that is:

$$V(s) = \frac{\text{total\_return}(s)}{N(s)}$$

Every-Visit MC Prediction

The algorithm of every-visit MC prediction is given as follows:

1. Let total_return(s) be the sum of the return of a state across several episodes and $N(s)$ be the counter, that is, the number of times a state is visited across several episodes. Initialize total_return(s) and $N(s)$ as zero for all the states. The policy π is given as input.

2. For M number of iterations:

    1. Generate an episode using the policy π
    2. Store all the rewards obtained in the episode in the list called rewards
    3. For each step t in the episode:

        1. Compute the return of the state s_t as $R(s_t) = \text{sum}(\text{rewards}[t:])$
        2. Update the total return of the state s_t as
           total_return(s_t) = total_return(s_t) + $R(s_t)$
        3. Update the counter as $N(s_t) = N(s_t) + 1$

3. Compute the value of a state by just taking the average, that is:

$$V(s) = \frac{\text{total\_return}(s)}{N(s)}$$

MC Prediction – the Q Function

The algorithm for MC prediction of the Q function is given as follows:

1. Let total_return(s, a) be the sum of the return of a state-action pair across several episodes and $N(s, a)$ be the number of times a state-action pair is visited across several episodes. Initialize total_return(s, a) and $N(s, a)$ for all state-action pairs to zero. The policy π is given as input.

2. For M number of iterations:

    1. Generate an episode using policy π
    2. Store all the rewards obtained in the episode in the list called rewards
    3. For each step t in the episode:

1. Compute the return for the state-action pair,
   $R(s_t, a_t) = \text{sum(rewards[t:])}$

2. Update the total return of the state-action pair,
   $\text{total\_return}(s_t, a_t) = \text{total\_return}(s_t, a_t) + R(s_t, a_t)$

3. Update the counter as $N(s_t, a_t) = N(s_t, a_t) + 1$

3. Compute the Q function (Q value) by just taking the average, that is:

$$Q(s, a) = \frac{\text{total\_return}(s, a)}{N(s, a)}$$

MC Control Method

The algorithm for the MC control method is given as follows:

1. Let total_return(s, a) be the sum of the return of a state-action pair across several episodes and N(s, a) be the number of times a state-action pair is visited across several episodes. Initialize total_return(s, a) and N(s, a) for all state-action pairs to zero and initialize a random policy π.

2. For M number of iterations:

   1. Generate an episode using policy π

   2. Store all the rewards obtained in the episode in the list called rewards

   3. For each step t in the episode:

      If (s_t, a_t) is occurring for the first time in the episode:

      1. Compute the return of a state-action pair,
         $R(s_t, a_t) = \text{sum(rewards[t:])}$

      2. Update the total return of the state-action pair as
         $\text{total\_return}(s_t, a_t) = \text{total\_return}(s_t, a_t) + R(s_t, a_t)$

      3. Update the counter as $N(s_t, a_t) = N(s_t, a_t) + 1$

      4. Compute the Q value by just taking the average, that is,
         $$Q(s_t, a_t) = \frac{\text{total\_return}(s_t, a_t)}{N(s_t, a_t)}$$

   4. Compute the new updated policy from π using the Q function:

$$\pi = \arg\max_a Q(s, a)$$

On-Policy MC Control – Exploring starts

The algorithm for on-policy MC control by exploring the starts method is given as follows:

1. Let total_return(s, a) be the sum of the return of a state-action pair across several episodes and $N(s, a)$ be the number of times a state-action pair is visited across several episodes. Initialize total_return(s, a) and $N(s, a)$ for all state-action pairs to zero and initialize a random policy π.

2. For M number of iterations:

    1. Select the initial state s_0 and initial action a_0 randomly such that all state-action pairs have a probability greater than 0

    2. Generate an episode from the selected initial state s_0 and action a_0 using policy π

    3. Store all the rewards obtained in the episode in the list called rewards

    4. For each step t in the episode:

        If (s_t, a_t) is occurring for the first time in the episode:

        1. Compute the return of a state-action pair,
            $R(s_t, a_t) = \text{sum}(\text{rewards}[t:])$

        2. Update the total return of the state-action pair as
            total_return(s_t, a_t) = total_return(s_t, a_t) + $R(s_t, a_t)$

        3. Update the counter as $N(s_t, a_t) = N(s_t, a_t) + 1$

        4. Compute the Q value by just taking the average, that is,

            $$Q(s_t, a_t) = \frac{\text{total\_return}(s_t, a_t)}{N(s_t, a_t)}$$

    5. Compute the updated policy from π using the Q function:

        $$\pi(s) = \arg\max_a Q(s, a)$$

On-Policy MC Control – Epsilon-Greedy

The algorithm for on-policy MC control with the epsilon-greedy policy is given as follows:

1. Let total_return(s, a) be the sum of the return of a state-action pair across several episodes and $N(s, a)$ be the number of times a state-action pair is visited across several episodes. Initialize total_return(s, a) and $N(s, a)$ for all state-action pairs to zero and initialize a random policy π.

2. For M number of iterations:

    1. Generate an episode using policy π

    2. Store all the rewards obtained in the episode in the list called rewards

    3. For each step t in the episode:

        If (s_t, a_t) is occurring for the first time in the episode:

        1. Compute the return of a state-action pair,
            $R(s_t, a_t) = \text{sum(rewards[t:])}$.

        2. Update the total return of the state-action pair as
            $\text{total\_return}(s_t, a_t) = \text{total\_return}(s_t, a_t) + R(s_t, a_t)$.

        3. Update the counter as $N(s_t, a_t) = N(s_t, a_t) + 1$.

        4. Compute the Q value by just taking the average, that is,

            $$Q(s_t, a_t) = \frac{\text{total\_return}(s_t, a_t)}{N(s_t, a_t)}$$

    4. Compute the updated policy π using the Q function. Let
        $a^* = \arg\max_a Q(s, a)$. The policy π selects the best action a^*
        with probability $1 - \epsilon$, and a random action with probability ϵ.

Off-Policy MC Control

The algorithm for the off-policy MC control method is given as follows:

1. Initialize the Q function $Q(s, a)$ with random values and set the behavior
    policy b to be epsilon-greedy, set the target policy π to be greedy policy
    and initialize the cumulative weights as $C(s, a) = 0$

2. For M number of episodes:

    1. Generate an episode using the behavior policy b

    2. Initialize return R to 0 and weight W to 1

    3. For each step t in the episode, $t = T - 1, T - 2, \ldots, 0$:

        1. Compute the return as $R = R + r_{t+1}$

        2. Update the cumulative weights to $C(s_t, a_t) = C(s_t, a_t) + W$

        3. Update the Q value to

            $$Q(s_t, a_t) = Q(s_t, a_t) + \frac{W}{C(s_t, a_t)}(R_t - Q(s_t, a_t))$$

4. Compute the target policy $\pi(s_t) = \arg\max_a Q(s_t, a)$

5. If $a_t \neq \pi(s_t)$ then break

6. Update the weight to $W = W \dfrac{1}{b(a_t|s_t)}$

3. Return the target policy π

TD Prediction

The algorithm for the TD prediction method is given as follows:

1. Initialize the value function $V(s)$ with random values. A policy π is given.

2. For each episode:

    1. Initialize the state s

    2. For each step in the episode:

        1. Perform an action a in the state s according to given policy π, get the reward r, and move to the next state s'

        2. Update the value of the state to
        $V(s) = V(s) + \alpha(r + \gamma V(s') - V(s))$

        3. Update $s = s'$ (this step implies we are changing the next state s' to the current state s)

        4. If s is not a terminal state, repeat *steps 1 to 4*

On-Policy TD Control – SARSA

The algorithm for on-policy TD control – SARSA is given as follows:

1. Initialize the Q function $Q(s, a)$ with random values

2. For each episode:

    1. Initialize the state s

    2. Extract a policy from $Q(s, a)$ and select an action a to perform in the state s

    3. For each step in the episode:

        1. Perform the action a, move to the new state s', and observe the reward r

        2. In the state s', select the action a' using the epsilon-greedy policy

3. Update the Q value to

$$Q(s, a) = Q(s, a) + \alpha(r + \gamma Q(s', a') - Q(s, a))$$

4. Update $s = s'$ and $a = a'$ (update the next state s'-action a' pair to the current state s-action a pair)

5. If s is not the terminal state, repeat *steps 1 to 5*

Off-Policy TD Control – Q Learning

The algorithm for off-policy TD control – Q learning is given as follows:

1. Initialize a Q function $Q(s, a)$ with random values

2. For each episode:

    1. Initialize the state s

    2. For each step in the episode:

        1. Extract a policy from $Q(s, a)$ and select an action a to perform in the state s

        2. Perform the action a, move to the new state s', and observe the reward r

        3. Update the Q value to

        $$Q(s, a) = Q(s, a) + \alpha(r + \gamma \max_{a'} Q(s', a') - Q(s, a))$$

        4. Update $s = s'$ (update the next state s' to the current state s)

        5. If s is not a terminal state, repeat *steps 1 to 5*

Deep Q Learning

The algorithm for deep Q learning is given as follows:

1. Initialize the main network parameter θ with random values

2. Initialize the target network parameter θ' by copying the main network parameter θ

3. Initialize the replay buffer $\mathcal{D}$

4. For N number of episodes, perform *step 5*

5. For each step in the episode, that is, for $t = 0, \ldots, T - 1$:

    1. Observe the state s and select an action using the epsilon-greedy policy, that is, with probability epsilon, select random action a, and with probability 1-epsilon, select the action as $a = \arg\max\limits_{a} Q_\theta(s, a)$

    2. Perform the selected action and move to the next state s' and obtain the reward r

    3. Store the transition information in the replay buffer $\mathcal{D}$

    4. Randomly sample a minibatch of K transitions from the replay buffer $\mathcal{D}$

    5. Compute the target value, that is, $y_i = r_i + \gamma \max\limits_{a'} Q_{\theta'}(s'_i, a')$

    6. Compute the loss, $L(\theta) = \dfrac{1}{K} \sum\limits_{i=1}^{K} (y_i - Q_\theta(s_i, a_i))^2$

    7. Compute the gradients of the loss and update the main network parameter θ using gradient descent, $\theta = \theta - \alpha \nabla_\theta L(\theta)$

    8. Freeze the target network parameter θ' for several time steps and then update it by just copying the main network parameter θ

Double DQN

The algorithm for double DQN is given as follows:

1. Initialize the main network parameter θ with random values

2. Initialize the target network parameter θ' by copying the main network parameter θ

3. Initialize the replay buffer $\mathcal{D}$

4. For N number of episodes, repeat *step 5*

5. For each step in the episode, that is, for $t = 0, \ldots, T - 1$:

    1. Observe the state s and select an action using the epsilon-greedy policy, that is, with probability epsilon, select random action a with probability 1-epsilon, and select the action as $a = \arg\max\limits_{a} Q_\theta(s, a)$

    2. Perform the selected action and move to the next state s' and obtain the reward r

    3. Store the transition information in the replay buffer $\mathcal{D}$

4. Randomly sample a minibatch of K transitions from the replay buffer $\mathcal{D}$

5. Compute the target value, that is, $y_i = r_i + \gamma Q_{\theta'}(s_i', \arg\max_{a'} Q_\theta(s_i', a'))$

6. Compute the loss, $L(\theta) = \dfrac{1}{K} \sum_{i=1}^{K} (y_i - Q_\theta(s_i, a_i))^2$

7. Compute the gradients of the loss and update the main network parameter θ using gradient descent: $\theta = \theta - \alpha \nabla_\theta L(\theta)$

8. Freeze the target network parameter θ' for several time steps and then update it by just copying the main network parameter θ

REINFORCE Policy Gradient

The algorithm for REINFORCE policy gradient is given as follows:

1. Initialize the network parameter θ with random values

2. Generate some N number of trajectories $\{\tau^i\}_{i=1}^{N}$ following the policy π_θ

3. Compute the return of the trajectory $R(\tau)$

4. Compute the gradients

$$\nabla_\theta J(\theta) = \frac{1}{N} \sum_{i=1}^{N} \left[\sum_{t=0}^{T-1} \nabla_\theta \log \pi_\theta(a_t|s_t) R(\tau) \right]$$

5. Update the network parameter, $\theta = \theta + \alpha \nabla_\theta J(\theta)$

6. Repeat *steps* 2 to 5 for several iterations

Policy Gradient with Reward-To-Go

The algorithm for policy gradient with reward-to-go is given as follows:

1. Initialize the network parameter θ with random values

2. Generate some N number of trajectories $\{\tau^i\}_{i=1}^{N}$ following the policy π_θ

3. Compute the return (reward-to-go) R_t

4. Compute the gradients $\nabla_\theta J(\theta) = \dfrac{1}{N} \sum_{i=1}^{N} \left[\sum_{t=0}^{T-1} \nabla_\theta \log \pi_\theta(a_t|s_t) R_t \right]$

5. Update the network parameter: $\theta = \theta + \alpha \nabla_\theta J(\theta)$

6. Repeat *steps* 2 to 5 for several iterations

REINFORCE with Baseline

The algorithm for REINFORCE with baseline is given as follows:

1. Initialize the policy network parameter θ and value network parameter ϕ

2. Generate some N number of trajectories $\{\tau^i\}_{i=1}^N$ following the policy π_θ

3. Compute the return (reward-to-go) R_t

4. Compute the policy gradient,

$$\nabla_\theta J(\theta) = \frac{1}{N} \sum_{i=1}^{N} \left[\sum_{t=0}^{T-1} \nabla_\theta \log \pi_\theta (a_t | s_t) \ (R_t - V_\phi(s_t)) \right]$$

5. Update the policy network parameter θ using gradient ascent,
   $\theta = \theta + \alpha \nabla_\theta J(\theta)$

6. Compute the mean squared error of the value network,

$$J(\phi) = \frac{1}{N} \sum_{i=1}^{N} \sum_{t=0}^{T-1} (R_t - V_\phi(s_t))^2$$

7. Update the value network parameter ϕ using gradient descent,
   $\phi = \phi - \alpha \nabla_\phi J(\phi)$

8. Repeat *steps* 2 to 7 for several iterations

Advantage Actor Critic

The algorithm for the advantage actor critic method is given as follows:

1. Initialize the actor network parameter θ and critic network parameter ϕ

2. For N number of episodes, repeat *step* 3

3. For each step in the episode, that is, for, $t = 0, \ldots, T - 1$:

   1. Select an action using the policy $a_t \sim \pi_\theta(s_t)$

   2. Take the action a_t in the state s_t, and observe the reward r and move to the next state s_t'

3. Compute the policy gradients:

$$\nabla_\theta J(\theta) = \nabla_\theta \log \pi_\theta \left(a_t | s_t\right)\left(r + \gamma V_\phi(s_t') - V_\phi(s_t)\right)$$

4. Update the actor network parameter θ using gradient ascent:

$$\theta = \theta + \alpha \nabla_\theta J(\theta)$$

5. Compute the loss of the critic network:

$$J(\phi) = r + \gamma V_\phi(s_t') - V_\phi(s_t)$$

6. Compute gradients $\nabla_\phi J(\phi)$ and update the critic network parameter ϕ using gradient descent: $\phi = \phi - \alpha \nabla_\phi J(\phi)$

Asynchronous Advantage Actor-Critic

The steps involved in **Advantage Actor-Critic (A3C)** are given below:

1. The worker agent interacts with its own copies of the environment
2. Each worker follows a different policy and collects the experience
3. Next, the worker agents compute the loss of the actor and critic networks
4. After computing the loss, they calculates the gradients of the loss and sends those gradients to the global agent asynchronously
5. The global agent updates its parameter with the gradients received from the worker agents
6. Now, the updated parameter from the global agent will be sent to the worker agents periodically

Deep Deterministic Policy Gradient

The algorithm for **Deep Deterministic Policy Gradient (DDPG)** is given as follows:

1. Initialize the main critic network parameter θ and main actor network parameter ϕ
2. Initialize the target critic network parameter θ' by just copying the main critic network parameter θ
3. Initialize the target actor network parameter ϕ' by just copying the main actor network parameter ϕ.
4. Initialize the replay buffer $\mathcal{D}$

5. For N number of episodes, repeat *steps 6 to 7*

6. Initialize an Ornstein-Uhlenbeck random process $\mathcal{N}$ for action space exploration

7. For each step in the episode, that is, for $t = 0, \ldots, T-1$:

   1. Select action a based on the policy $\mu_\phi(s)$ and exploration noise, that is, $a = \mu_\phi(s) + \mathcal{N}$

   2. Perform the selected action a, move to the next state s' and get the reward r, and store this transition information in the replay buffer $\mathcal{D}$

   3. Randomly sample a minibatch of K transitions from the replay buffer $\mathcal{D}$

   4. Compute the target value of the critic, that is,
   $$y_i = r_i + \gamma Q_{\theta'}\left(s_i', \mu_{\phi'}(s_i')\right)$$

   5. Compute the loss of the critic network $J(\theta) = \frac{1}{K}\sum_i (y_i - Q_\theta(s_i, a_i))^2$

   6. Compute the gradient of the loss $\nabla_\theta J(\theta)$ and update the critic network parameter using gradient descent, $\theta = \theta - \alpha\nabla_\theta J(\theta)$

   7. Compute the gradient of the actor network $\nabla_\phi J(\phi)$ and update the actor network parameter using gradient ascent, $\phi = \phi + \alpha\nabla_\phi J(\phi)$

   8. Update the target critic and target actor network parameters, $\theta' = \tau\theta + (1-\tau)\theta'$ for $j = 1,2$ and $\phi' = \tau\phi + (1-\tau)\phi'$

Twin Delayed DDPG

The algorithm for **Twin Delayed DDPG (TD3)** is given as follows:

1. Initialize two main critic networks parameters, θ_1 and θ_2, and the main actor network parameter ϕ

2. Initialize two target critic networks parameters, θ_1' and θ_2', by copying the main critic network parameters θ_1 and θ_2, respectively

3. Initialize the target actor network parameter ϕ' by copying the main actor network parameter ϕ

4. Initialize the replay buffer $\mathcal{D}$

5. For N number of episodes, repeat *step 6*

6.   For each step in the episode, that is, for $t = 0, \ldots, T-1$:

    1.   Select action a based on the policy $\mu_\phi(s)$ and with exploration noise ϵ, that is, $a = \mu_\phi(s) + \epsilon$ where, $\epsilon \sim (\mathcal{N}(0, \sigma))$

    2.   Perform the selected action a, move to the next state s', get the reward r, and store the transition information in the replay buffer $\mathcal{D}$

    3.   Randomly sample a minibatch of K transitions from the replay buffer $\mathcal{D}$

    4.   Select the action $\tilde{a}$ for computing the target value $\tilde{a} = \mu_{\phi'}(s') + \epsilon$ where $\epsilon \sim (\mathcal{N}(0, \sigma)), -c, +c)$

    5.   Compute the target value of the critic, that is,

$$y_i = r_i + \gamma \min_{j=1,2} Q_{\theta'_j}(s'_i, \tilde{a})$$

    6.   Compute the loss of the critic network

$$J(\theta_j) = \frac{1}{K} \sum_i \left(y_i - Q_{\theta_j}(s_i, a_i) \right)^2 \quad \text{for } j = 1, 2.$$

    7.   Compute the gradients of the loss $\nabla_{\theta_j} J(\theta_j)$ and minimize the loss using gradient descent, $\theta_j = \theta_j - \alpha \nabla_{\theta_j} J(\theta_j)$ for $j = 1, 2$

    8.   If $t \bmod d = 0$, then:

        1.   Compute the gradient of the objective function $\nabla_\phi J(\phi)$ and update the actor network parameter using gradient ascent, $\phi = \phi + \alpha \nabla_\phi J(\phi)$

        2.   Update the target critic networks parameter and target actor network parameter as $\theta' = \tau\theta + (1 - \tau)\theta'$ for $j = 1, 2$ and $\phi' = \tau\phi + (1 - \tau)\phi'$, respectively

Soft Actor-Critic

The algorithm for **Soft Actor-Critic (SAC)** is given as follows:

1.   Initialize the main value network parameter ψ, the Q network parameters θ_1 and θ_2, and the actor network parameter ϕ

2.   Initialize the target value network ψ' by just copying the main value network parameter ψ

3.   Initialize the replay buffer $\mathcal{D}$

4. For N number of episodes, repeat *step 5*

5. For each step in the episode, that is, for $t = 0, \ldots, T - 1$

   1. Select action a based on the policy $\pi_\phi(s)$, that is, $a = \pi_\phi(s)$

   2. Perform the selected action a, move to the next state s', get the reward r, and store the transition information in the replay buffer $\mathcal{D}$

   3. Randomly sample a minibatch of K transitions from the replay buffer

   4. Compute target state value $y_{v_i} = \min_{j=1,2} Q_{\theta_j}(s_i, a_i) - \alpha \log \pi_\phi(a_i|s_i)$

   5. Compute the loss of value network $J_V(\psi) = \frac{1}{K} \sum_i \left(y_{v_i} - V_\psi(s_i) \right)^2$

      and update the parameter using gradient descent, $\psi = \psi - \lambda \nabla_\psi J(\psi)$

   6. Compute the target Q value $y_{q_i} = r_i + \gamma V_{\psi'}(s_i')$

   7. Compute the loss of the Q networks

      $J_Q(\theta_j) = \frac{1}{K} \sum_i \left(y_{q_i} - Q_{\theta_j}(s_i, a_i) \right)^2$ for $j = 1, 2$ and update the

      parameter using gradient descent, $\theta_j = \theta_j - \lambda \nabla_{\theta_j} J(\theta_j)$ for $j = 1, 2$

   8. Compute gradients of the actor objective function, $\nabla_\phi J(\phi)$ and update the parameter using gradient ascent, $\phi = \phi + \lambda \nabla_\phi J(\phi)$

   9. Update the target value network parameter, $\psi' = \tau\psi + (1 - \tau)\psi'$

Trust Region Policy Optimization

The algorithm for **Trust Region Policy Optimization (TRPO)** is given as follows:

1. Initialize the policy network parameter θ and value network parameter ϕ

2. Generate N number of trajectories $\{\tau^i\}_{i=1}^N$ following the policy π_θ

3. Compute the return (reward-to-go) R_t

4. Compute the advantage value A_t

5. Compute the policy gradients $g = \frac{1}{N} \sum_{i=1}^{N} \left[\sum_{t=0}^{T-1} \nabla_\theta \log \pi_\theta (a_t|s_t) A_t \right]$

6. Compute $s = H^{-1}g$ using the conjugate gradient method

7. Update the policy network parameter θ using the update rule

$$\theta = \theta + \alpha^j \sqrt{\frac{2\delta}{s^T H s}} \, s$$

8. Compute the mean squared error of the value network,

$$J(\phi) = \frac{1}{N} \sum_{i=1}^{N} \sum_{t=0}^{T-1} (R_t - V_\phi(s_t))^2$$

9. Update the value network parameter ϕ using gradient descent,

$\phi = \phi - \alpha \nabla_\phi J(\phi)$

10. Repeat *steps* 2 to 9 for several iterations

PPO-Clipped

The algorithm for the PPO-clipped method is given as follows:

1. Initialize the policy network parameter θ and value network parameter ϕ

2. Collect some N number of trajectories $\{\tau^i\}_{i=1}^{N}$ following the policy π_θ

3. Compute the return (reward-to-go) R_t

4. Compute the gradient of the objective function $\nabla_\theta L(\theta)$

5. Update the policy network parameter θ using gradient ascent,
$\theta = \theta + \alpha \nabla_\theta L(\theta)$

6. Compute the mean squared error of the value network,

$$J(\phi) = \frac{1}{N} \sum_{i=1}^{N} \sum_{t=0}^{T-1} \left(R_t - V_\phi(s_t)\right)^2$$

7. Compute the gradient of the value network $\nabla_\phi J(\phi)$

8. Update the value network parameter ϕ using gradient descent,
$\phi = \phi - \alpha \nabla_\phi J(\phi)$

9. Repeat *steps* 2 to 8 for several iterations

PPO-Penalty

The algorithm for the PPO-penalty method is given as follows:

1. Initialize the policy network parameter θ and value network parameter ϕ and initialize the penalty coefficient β_1 and the target KL divergence δ

2. For iterations $i = 1, 2, \cdots, K$:

    1. Collect some N number of trajectories following the policy π_θ

    2. Compute the return (reward-to-go) R_t

    3. Compute $L(\theta) = \mathbb{E}_t \left[\frac{\pi_\theta(a_t|s_t)}{\pi_{\theta_{old}}(a_t|s_t)} A_t - \beta_i \text{KL}[\pi_{\theta_{old}}(\cdot\,|s_t), \pi_\theta(\cdot\,|s_t)] \right]$

    4. Compute the gradient of the objective function $\nabla_\theta L(\theta)$

    5. Update the policy network parameter θ using gradient ascent, $\theta = \theta + \alpha \nabla_\theta L(\theta)$

    6. If d is greater than or equal to 1.5δ, then we set $\beta_{i+1} = 2\beta_i$; if d is lesser than or equal to $\delta/1.5$, then we set, $\beta_{i+1} = \beta_i/2$

    7. Compute the mean squared error of the value network:

    $$J(\phi) = \frac{1}{N} \sum_{i=1}^{N} \sum_{t=0}^{T-1} \left(R_t - V_\phi(s_t) \right)^2$$

    8. Compute the gradients of the value network $\nabla_\phi J(\phi)$

    9. Update the value network parameter ϕ using gradient descent, $\phi = \phi - \alpha \nabla_\phi J(\phi)$

Categorical DQN

The algorithm for a categorical DQN is given as follows:

1. Initialize the main network parameter θ with random values

2. Initialize the target network parameter θ' by copying the main network parameter θ

3. Initialize the replay buffer $\mathcal{D}$, the number of atoms, and also V_{min} and V_{max}

4. For N number of episodes, perform *step 5*

5. For each step in the episode, that is, for $t = 0, \ldots, T - 1$:

   1. Feed the state s and support values to the main categorical DQN parameterized by θ, and get the probability value for each support value. Then compute the Q value as $Q(s, a) = \sum_i z_i p_i(s, a)$.

   2. After computing the Q value, select an action using the epsilon-greedy policy, that is, with probability epsilon, select a random action a and with probability 1-epsilon, select an action as $a^* = \arg\max_a Q(s, a)$.

   3. Perform the selected action and move to the next state s' and obtain the reward r.

   4. Store the transition information in the replay buffer $\mathcal{D}$.

   5. Randomly sample a transition from the replay buffer $\mathcal{D}$.

   6. Feed the next state s' and support values to the target categorical DQN parameterized by θ' and get the probability value for each support. Then compute the value as $Q(s', a) = \sum_i z_i p_i(s', a)$.

   7. After computing the Q value, we select the best action in the state s' as the one that has the maximum Q value $a^* = \arg\max_a Q(s', a)$.

   8. Initialize the array m with zero values with its shape as the number of support.

   9. For j in the range of the number of support values:

      1. Compute the target support value: $\hat{t}z_j = [r_t + \gamma_t z_j]_{V_{min}}^{V_{max}}$

      2. Compute the value of b: $b_j = (\hat{t}z_j - V_{min})/\Delta z$

      3. Compute the lower bound and upper bound: $l = \lfloor b_j \rfloor, u = \lceil b_j \rceil$

      4. Distribute the probability on the lower bound:
         $m_l = m_l + p_j(s', a^*)(u - b_j)$

      5. Distribute the probability on the upper bound:
         $m_u = m_u + p_j(s', a^*)(b_j - l)$

   10. Compute the cross entropy loss Cross Entropy $= -\sum_i m_i \log p_i(s, a)$.

   11. Minimize the loss using gradient descent and update the parameter of the main network

   12. Freeze the target network parameter θ' for several time steps and then update it by just copying the main network parameter θ

Distributed Distributional DDPG

The **Distributed Distributional Deep Deterministic Policy Gradient (D4PG)** algorithm is given as follows:

1. Initialize the critic network parameter θ and the actor network parameter ϕ

2. Initialize the target critic network parameter θ' and the target actor network parameter ϕ' by copying from θ and ϕ, respectively

3. Initialize the replay buffer $\mathcal{D}$

4. Launch L number of actors

5. For N number of episodes, repeat *step 6*

6. For each step in the episode, that is, for $t = 0, \ldots, T - 1$:

    1. Randomly sample a minibatch of K transitions from the replay buffer $\mathcal{D}$

    2. Compute the target value distribution of the critic, that is,

    $$y_i = \left(\sum_{n=0}^{N-1} \gamma^n r_{i+N} \right) + \gamma^N Z_{\theta'}(s'_{i+N}, \mu_{\phi'}(s'_{i+N}))$$

    3. Compute the loss of the critic network and calculate the gradient as

    $$\nabla_\theta J(\theta) = \frac{1}{K} \sum_i \nabla_\theta (Rp_i)^{-1} d\left(y_i, Z_\theta(s, a) \right)$$

    4. After computing gradients, update the critic network parameter using gradient descent: $\theta = \theta - \alpha \nabla_\theta J(\theta)$

    5. Compute the gradient of the actor network $\nabla_\phi J(\phi)$

    6. Update the actor network parameter by gradient ascent:
    $\phi = \phi + \alpha \nabla_\phi J(\phi)$

    7. If $t \bmod t_{target} = 0$ then:

        Update the target critic and target actor network parameters using soft replacement as $\theta' = \tau\theta + (1 - \tau)\theta'$ and $\phi' = \tau\phi + (1 - \tau)\phi'$, respectively

    8. If $t \bmod t_{actors} = 0$ then:

        Replicate the network weights to the actors

We perform the following steps in the actor network:

1. Select action a based on the policy $\mu_\phi(s)$ and exploration noise, that is,
    $a = \mu_\phi(s) + \mathcal{N}$

2. Perform the selected action a, move to the next state s' and get the reward r, and store the transition information in the replay buffer $\mathcal{D}$

3. Repeat *steps 1* and *2* until the learner finishes

DAgger

The algorithm for DAgger is given as follows:

1. Initialize an empty dataset $\mathcal{D}$
2. Initialize a policy $\hat{\pi}_1$
3. For iterations $i = 1$ to N:

    1. Create a policy $\pi_i = \beta_i \pi_E + (1 - \beta_i)\hat{\pi}_i$.
    2. Generate a trajectory using the policy π_i.
    3. Create a dataset $\mathcal{D}_i$ by collecting states visited by the policy π_i and the actions of those states provided by the expert π_E. Thus, $\mathcal{D}_i = \{(s, \pi_E(s))\}$.
    4. Aggregate the dataset as $\mathcal{D} = \mathcal{D} \cup \mathcal{D}_i$.
    5. Train a classifier on the updated dataset $\mathcal{D}$ and extract a new policy $\hat{\pi}_{i+1}$.

Deep Q learning from demonstrations

The algorithm for **Deep Q Learning from Demonstrations (DQfD)** is given as follows:

1. Initialize the main network parameter θ
2. Initialize the target network parameter θ' by copying the main network parameter θ
3. Initialize the replay buffer $\mathcal{D}$ with the expert demonstrations
4. Set d, the number of time steps we want to delay updating the target network parameter

5. **Pre-training phase**: For steps $t = 1, 2, \ldots, T$:

    1. Sample a minibatch of experience from the replay buffer $\mathcal{D}$
    2. Compute the loss $J(Q)$
    3. Update the parameter of the network using gradient descent
    4. If $t \bmod d = 0$:

        Update the target network parameter θ' by copying the main network parameter θ

6. **Training phase**: For steps $t = 1, 2, \ldots, T$:

    1. Select an action
    2. Perform the selected action and move to the next state, observe the reward, and store this transition information in the replay buffer $\mathcal{D}$
    3. Sample a minibatch of experience from the replay buffer $\mathcal{D}$ with prioritization
    4. Compute the loss $J(Q)$
    5. Update the parameter of the network using gradient descent
    6. If $t \bmod d = 0$:

        Update the target network parameter θ' by copying the main network parameter θ

MaxEnt Inverse Reinforcement Learning

The algorithm for maximum entropy inverse reinforcement learning is given as follows:

1. Initialize the parameter θ and gather the expert demonstrations $\mathcal{D}$
2. For N number of iterations:

    1. Compute the reward function $R_\theta(\tau) = \theta^T f_\tau$
    2. Compute the policy using the value iteration with the reward function obtained in the previous step
    3. Compute the state visitation frequency $p(s|\theta)$ using the policy obtained in the previous step

4. Compute the gradient with respect to θ, that is,

$$\nabla_\theta L(\theta) = \tilde{f} - \sum_s p(s|\theta) f_s$$

5. Update the value of θ as $\theta = \theta + \alpha \nabla_\theta L(\theta)$

MAML in Reinforcement Learning

The algorithm for MAML in the reinforcement learning setting is given as follows:

1. Say we have a model f parameterized by a parameter θ and we have a distribution over tasks $p(T)$. First, we randomly initialize the model parameter θ.

2. Sample a batch of tasks T_i from a distribution of tasks, that is, $T_i \sim p(T)$.

3. For each task T_i:

    1. Sample k trajectories using f_θ and prepare the training dataset:
    $$D_i^{train} = \{(\mathbf{s}_1^1, \mathbf{a}_1^1, \dots \mathbf{s}_T^1), \dots, (\mathbf{s}_1^k, \mathbf{a}_1^k, \dots \mathbf{s}_T^k)\}$$

    2. Train the model f_θ on the training dataset D_i^{train} and compute the loss

    3. Minimize the loss using gradient descent and get the optimal parameter θ_i' as $\theta_i' = \theta - \alpha \nabla_\theta L_{T_i}(f_\theta)$

    4. Sample k trajectories using $f_{\theta_i'}$ and prepare the test dataset:
    $$D_i^{test} = \{(\mathbf{s}_1^1, \mathbf{a}_1^1, \dots \mathbf{s}_T^1), \dots, (\mathbf{s}_1^k, \mathbf{a}_1^k, \dots \mathbf{s}_T^k)\}$$

4. Now, we minimize the loss on the test dataset D_i^{test}. Parameterize the model f with the optimal parameter θ_i' calculated in the previous step and compute the loss $L_{T_i}(f_{\theta_i'})$. Calculate the gradients of the loss and update our randomly initialized parameter θ using our test (meta-training) dataset:

$$\theta = \theta - \beta \nabla_\theta \sum_{T_i \sim p(T)} L_{T_i}\left(f_{\theta_i'}\right)$$

5. Repeat *steps 2 to 4* for several iterations.

Appendix 2 – Assessments

The following are the answers to the questions mentioned at the end of each chapter.

Chapter 1 – Fundamentals of Reinforcement Learning

1. In supervised and unsupervised learning, the model (agent) learns based on the given training dataset, whereas, in **reinforcement learning (RL)**, the agent learns by directly interacting with the environment. Thus RL is essentially an interaction between the agent and its environment.

2. The environment is the world of the agent. The agent stays within the environment. For instance, in the chess game, the chessboard is the environment since the chess player (agent) learns to play chess within the chessboard (environment). Similarly, in the Super Mario Bros game, the world of Mario is called the environment.

3. The deterministic policy maps the state to one particular action, whereas the stochastic policy maps the state to the probability distribution over an action space.

4. The agent interacts with the environment by performing actions, starting from the initial state until they reach the final state. This agent-environment interaction starting from the initial state until the final state is called an episode.

5. The discount factor helps us in preventing the return reaching up to infinity by deciding how much importance we give to future rewards and immediate rewards.

6. The value function (value of a state) is the expected return of the trajectory starting from that state whereas the Q function (the Q value of a state-action pair) is the expected return of the trajectory starting from that state and action.

7. In a deterministic environment, we can be sure that when an agent performs an action a in state s, then it always reaches state s'. In a stochastic environment, we cannot say that by performing some action a in state s, the agent always reaches state s' because there will be some randomness associated with the stochastic environment.

Chapter 2 – A Guide to the Gym Toolkit

1. The Gym toolkit provides a variety of environments for training the RL agent ranging from classic control tasks to Atari game environments. We can train our RL agent to learn in these simulated environments using various RL algorithms.

2. We can create a Gym environment using the make function. The make function requires the environment ID as a parameter.

3. We learned that the action space consists of all the possible actions in the environment. We can obtain the action space by using env.action_space.

4. We can visualize the Gym environment using the render() function.

5. Some classic control environments offered by Gym include the cart pole balancing environment, the pendulum, and the mountain car environment.

6. We can generate an episode by selecting an action in each state using the step() function.

7. The state space of the Atari environment will be either the game screen's pixel values or the RAM of the Atari machine.

8. We can record the agent's gameplay using the Monitor wrapper. It takes three parameters—the environment, the directory where we want to save our recordings, and the force option.

Chapter 3 – The Bellman Equation and Dynamic Programming

1. The Bellman equation states that the value of a state can be obtained as a sum of the immediate reward and the discounted value of the next state. Similar to the Bellman equation of the value function, the Bellman equation of the Q function states that the Q value of a state-action pair can be obtained as a sum of the immediate reward and the discounted Q value of the next state-action pair.

2. The Bellman expectation equation gives the Bellman value and Q functions whereas the Bellman optimality equation gives the optimal Bellman value and Q functions.

3. The value function can be derived from the Q function as $V^*(s) = \max_a Q^*(s, a)$.

4. The Q function can be derived from the value function as
$$Q^*(s, a) = \sum_{s'} P(s'|s, a)[R(s, a, s') + \gamma V^*(s')]$$

5. In the value iteration method, we perform the following steps:

   1. Compute the optimal value function by taking maximum over Q function, that is, $V^*(s) = \max_a Q^*(s, a)$

   2. Extract the optimal policy from the computed optimal value function

6. In the policy iteration method, we perform the following steps:

   1. Initialize the random policy

   2. Compute the value function using the given policy

   3. Extract a new policy using the value function obtained from *step 2*

   4. If the extracted policy is the same as the policy used in *step 2* then stop, else send the extracted new policy to *step 2* and repeat *steps* 2 to 4

7. In the value iteration method, first, we compute the optimal value function by taking the maximum over the Q function iteratively. Once we find the optimal value function then we will use it to extract the optimal policy. In the policy iteration method, we will try to compute the optimal value function using the policy iteratively. Once we have found the optimal value function then the policy that was used to create the optimal value function will be extracted as the optimal policy.

Chapter 4 – Monte Carlo Methods

1. In the Monte Carlo method, we approximate the value of a state by taking the average return of a state across N episodes instead of taking the expected return.

2. To compute the value function using the dynamic programming method, we need to know the model dynamics, and when we don't know the model dynamics, we use model-free methods. The Monte Carlo method is a model-free method meaning that it doesn't require the model dynamics (transition probability) to compute the value function.

3. In a prediction task, we evaluate the given policy by predicting the value function or Q function, which helps us to understand the expected return an agent would get if it used the given policy. However, in a control task, our goal is to find the optimal policy and are not given any policy as input, so we start by initializing a random policy and try to find the optimal policy iteratively.

4. In the MC prediction method, the value of a state and value of a state-action pair can be computed by just taking the average return of the state and an average return of state-action pair across several episodes respectively.

5. In first-visit MC, we compute the return only for the first time the state is visited in the episode. In every-visit MC, we compute the return every time the state is visited in the episode.

6. When the environment is non-stationary, we don't have to take the return of the state from all the episodes and compute the average. As the environment is non-stationary, we can ignore returns from earlier episodes and use only the returns from the latest episodes for computing the average. Thus, we can compute the value of the state using the incremental mean.

7. In the on-policy method, we generate episodes using one policy and also improve the same policy iteratively to find the optimal policy, while with the off-policy Monte Carlo control method, we use two different policies for generating the episode (the behavior policy) and for finding the optimal policy (the target policy).

8. An epsilon-greedy policy is one where we select a random action (exploration) with probability epsilon, and we select the best action (exploitation) with probability 1-epsilon.

Chapter 5 – Understanding Temporal Difference Learning

1. Unlike the Monte Carlo method, the **Temporal Difference (TD)** learning method makes use of bootstrapping so that we don't have to wait until the end of the episode to compute the value of a state.

2. The TD learning algorithm takes the benefits of both the dynamic programming and the Monte Carlo methods into account. That is, just like the dynamic programming method, we perform bootstrapping so that we don't have to wait till the end of an episode to compute the state value or Q value and just like the Monte Carlo method, it is a model-free method, and so it does not require the model dynamics of the environment to compute the state value or Q value.

3. The TD error can be defined as the difference between the target value and predicted value.

4. The TD learning update rule is given as $V(s) = V(s) + \alpha(r + \gamma V(s') - V(s))$.

5. In a TD prediction task, given a policy, we estimate the value function using the given policy. So, we can say what the expected return an agent can obtain in each state if it acts according to the given policy.

6. **SARSA** is an on-policy TD control algorithm and it stands for **State-Action-Reward-State-Action**. The update rule for computing the Q function using SARSA is given as $Q(s, a) = Q(s, a) + \alpha(r + \gamma Q(s', a') - Q(s, a))$.

7. SARSA is an on-policy algorithm, meaning that we use a single epsilon-greedy policy for selecting an action in the environment and also to compute the Q value of the next state-action pair, whereas Q learning is an off-policy algorithm meaning that we use an epsilon-greedy policy for selecting an action in the environment, but to compute the Q value of the next state-action pair we use a greedy policy.

Chapter 6 – Case Study – The MAB Problem

1. The **Multi-Armed Bandit (MAB)** problem is one of the classic problems in RL. A MAB is a slot machine where we pull the arm (lever) and get a payout (reward) based on some probability distribution. A single slot machine is called a one-armed bandit, and when there are multiple slot machines, it is called a MAB or k-armed bandit, where k denotes the number of slot machines.

2. With the epsilon-greedy policy, we select the best arm with probability 1-epsilon, and we select the random arm with probability epsilon.

3. In softmax exploration, the arm will be selected based on the probability. However, in the initial rounds we will not know the correct average reward of each arm, so selecting the arm based on the probability of average reward will be inaccurate in the initial rounds. So to avoid this we introduce a new parameter called T. T is called the temperature parameter.

4. The upper confidence bound is computed as $\text{UCB}(a) = Q(a) + \sqrt{\dfrac{2\log(t)}{N(a)}}$.

5. When the value of α is higher than β, then we will have a high probability closer to 1 than 0.

6. The steps involved in the Thomson sampling method are as follows:

    1. Initialize the beta distribution with alpha and beta set to equal values for all the k arms

    2. Sample a value from the beta distribution of all the k arms

    3. Pull the arm whose sampled value is high

    4. If we win the game then update the alpha value of the distribution as $\alpha = \alpha + 1$

    5. If we lose the game then update the beta value of the distribution as $\beta = \beta + 1$

    6. Repeat *steps* 2 to 5 for several numbers of rounds

7. With contextual bandits, we take actions based on the state of the environment and the state holds the context. Contextual bandits are widely used for personalizing content according to the user's behavior. They are also used to solve the cold-start problems faced in recommendation systems.

Chapter 7 – Deep Learning Foundations

1. The activation function is used to introduce non-linearity to neural networks.

2. The softmax function is basically a generalization of the sigmoid function. It is usually applied to the final layer of the network and while performing multi-class classification tasks. It gives the probabilities of each class being output and thus, the sum of softmax values will always equal 1.

3. The epoch specifies the number of times the neural network sees our whole training data. So, we can say one epoch is equal to one forward pass and one backward pass for all training samples.

4. RNNs are widely applied for use cases that involve sequential data, such as time series, text, audio, speech, video, weather, and much more. They have been greatly used in various **Natural Language Processing** (NLP) tasks, such as language translation, sentiment analysis, text generation, and so on.

5. While backpropagating the RNN, we multiply the weights and derivative of the tanh function at every time step. When we multiply smaller numbers at every step while moving backward, our gradient becomes infinitesimally small and leads to a number that the computer can't handle; this is called the vanishing gradient problem.

6. The pooling layer reduces spatial dimensions by keeping only the important features. The different types of pooling operation include max pooling, average pooling, and sum pooling.

7. Suppose, we want our GAN to generate handwritten digits. First, we will take a dataset containing a collection of handwritten digits; say, the MNIST dataset. The generator learns the distribution of images in our dataset. It learns the distribution of handwritten digits in our training set. We feed random noise to the generator and it will convert the random noise into a new handwritten digit similar to the one in our training set. The goal of the discriminator is to perform a classification task. Given an image, it classifies it as real or fake; that is, whether the image is from the training set or has been generated by the generator.

Chapter 8 – A Primer on TensorFlow

1. A TensorFlow session is used to execute computational graphs with operations on the node and tensors to its edges.

2. Variables are the containers used to store values. Variables will be used as input to several other operations in the computational graph. We can think of placeholders as variables, where we only define the type and dimension, but will not assign the value. Values for the placeholders will be fed at runtime. We feed the data to the computational graphs using placeholders. Placeholders are defined with no values.

3. TensorBoard is TensorFlow's visualization tool that can be used to visualize the computational graph. It can also be used to plot various quantitative metrics and the results of several intermediate calculations. When we are training a really deep neural network, it would become confusing when we have to debug the model. As we can visualize the computational graph in TensorBoard, we can easily understand, debug, and optimize such complex models. It also supports sharing.

4. Eager execution in TensorFlow is more Pythonic and allows for rapid prototyping. Unlike the graph mode, where we need to construct a graph every time to perform any operation, eager execution follows the imperative programming paradigm, where any operation can be performed immediately without having to create a graph, just like we do in Python.

5. Building a model in Keras involves four important steps:
    1. Defining the model
    2. Compiling the model
    3. Fitting the model
    4. Evaluating the model

6. A functional model provides more flexibility than a sequential model. For instance, in a functional model, we can easily connect any layer to another layer, whereas, in a sequential model, each layer is in a stack of one above another.

Chapter 9 – Deep Q Network and Its Variants

1. When the environment consists of a large number of states and actions, it will be very expensive to compute the Q value of all possible state-action pairs in an exhaustive fashion. So, we use a deep Q network for approximating the Q function.

2. We use a buffer called the replay buffer to collect the agent's experience and based on this experience, we train our network. The replay buffer is usually implemented as a queue structure (first in, first out) rather than a list. So, if the buffer is full and the new experience comes in, we remove the old experience and add the new experience into the buffer.

3. When the target and predicted values depend on the same parameter θ, it will cause instability in the mean squared error and the network will learn poorly. It also causes a lot of divergence during training. So, we use a target network.

4. Unlike with DQNs, in double DQNs, we compute the target value using two Q functions. One Q function parameterized by the main network parameter θ selects the action that has the maximum Q value, and the other Q function parameterized by the target network parameter θ' computes the Q value using the action selected by the main network.

5. A transition with a high TD error implies that the transition is not correct and so we need to learn more about that transition to minimize the error. A transition with a low TD error implies that the transition is already good. We can always learn more from our mistakes rather than only focusing on what we are already good at, right? Similarly, we can learn more from the transitions with a high TD error than those with a low TD error. Thus, we can assign a higher priority to the transitions with a high TD error and a lower priority to transitions that got a low TD error.

6. The advantage function can be defined as the difference between the Q function and the value function.

7. The LSTM layer is in the DQN so that we can retain information about the past states as long as it is required. Retaining information about the past states helps us when we have the problem of **Partially Observable Markov Decision Processes (POMDPs)**.

Chapter 10 – Policy Gradient Method

1. In the value-based method, we extract the optimal policy from the optimal Q function (Q values).

2. It is difficult to compute optimal policy using the value-based method when our action space is continuous. So, we use the policy-based method. In the policy-based method, we compute the optimal policy without the Q function.

3. In the policy gradient method, we select actions based on the action probability distribution given by the network and if we win the episode, that is, if we get a high return, then we assign high probabilities to all the actions of the episode, else we assign low probabilities to all the actions of the episode.

4. The policy gradient is computed as

$$\nabla_\theta J(\theta) = \frac{1}{N} \sum_{i=1}^{N} \left[\sum_{t=0}^{T-1} \nabla_\theta \log \pi_\theta(a_t|s_t) R(\tau) \right].$$

5. Reward-to-go is basically the return of the trajectory starting from the state s_t. It is computed as
$$R_t = \sum_{t'=0}^{T-1} r(s_{t'}, a_{t'})$$

6. The policy gradient with the baseline function is a policy gradient method that uses the baseline function to reduce the variance in the return.

7. The baseline function b gives us the expected return from the state the agent is in, then subtracting b on every step will reduce the variance in the return.

Chapter 11 – Actor-Critic Methods – A2C and A3C

1. The actor-critic method is one of the most popular algorithms in deep RL. Several modern deep RL algorithms are designed based on the actor-critic method. The actor-critic method lies at the intersection of value-based and policy-based methods. That is, it takes advantage of both value-based and policy-based methods.

2. In the actor-critic method, the actor computes the optimal policy and the critic evaluates the policy computed by the actor network by estimating the value function.

3. In the policy gradient method with baseline, first, we generate complete episodes (trajectories), and then we update the parameter of the network, whereas, in the actor-critic method, we update the network parameter at every step of the episode.

4. In the actor network, we compute the gradient as

$$\nabla_\theta J(\theta) = \nabla_\theta \log \pi_\theta (a_t|s_t)(r + \gamma V_\phi(s_t') - V_\phi(s_t))$$.

5. In **advantage actor-critic (A2C)**, we compute the policy gradient with the advantage function and the advantage function is the difference between the Q function and the value function, that is, $Q(s, a) - V(s)$.

6. The word asynchronous implies the way A3C works. That is, instead of having a single agent that tries to learn the optimal policy, here, we have multiple agents that interact with the environment. Since we have multiple agents interacting with the environment at the same time, we provide copies of the environment to every agent so that each agent can interact with its own copy of the environment. So, all these multiple agents are called worker agents and we have a separate agent called the global agent. All the worker agents report to the global agent asynchronously and the global agent aggregates the learning.

7. In A2C, we can have multiple worker agents, each interacting with its own copies of the environment, and all the worker agents perform the synchronous updates, unlike A3C where the worker agents perform asynchronous updates.

Chapter 12 – Learning DDPG, TD3, and SAC

1. DDPG consists of an actor and critic. The actor is a policy network and uses the policy gradient method for learning the optimal policy. The critic is a DQN and it evaluates the action produced by the actor.

2. The critic is basically a DQN. The goal of the critic is to evaluate the action produced by the actor network. The critic evaluates the action produced by the actor using the Q value computed by the DQN.

3. The key features of TD3 includes clipped double Q learning, delayed policy updates, and target policy smoothing.

4. Instead of using one critic network, we use two main critic networks for computing the Q value and we use two target critic networks for computing the target value. We compute two target Q values using two target critic networks and use the minimum value out of these two while computing the loss. This helps in preventing the overestimation of the target Q value.

5. The DDPG method produces different target values even for the same action, thus the variance of the target value will be high even for the same action, so we reduce this variance by adding some noise to the target action.

6. In the SAC method, we use a slightly modified version of the objective function with the entropy term as $J(\phi) = E_{\tau \sim \pi_\phi} \left[\sum_{t=0}^{T-1} \left(r_t + \alpha \mathcal{H} \left(\pi(\cdot \mid s_t) \right) \right) \right]$ and it is often called **maximum entropy RL** or **entropy regularized RL**.

    Adding an entropy term is also often referred to as an entropy bonus.

7. The role of the critic network is to evaluate the policy produced by the actor. Instead of using only the Q function to evaluate the actor's policy, the critic in SAC uses both the Q function and the value function.

Chapter 13 – TRPO, PPO, and ACKTR Methods

1. The trust region implies the region where our actual function $f(x)$ and approximated function $\tilde{f}(x)$ are close together. So, we can say that our approximation will be accurate if our approximated function $\tilde{f}(x)$ is in the trust region.

2. TRPO is a policy gradient algorithm, and it acts as an improvement to policy gradient with baseline. TRPO tries to make a large policy update while imposing a KL constraint that the old policy and the new policy should not vary from each other too much. TRPO guarantees monotonic policy improvement, guaranteeing that there will always be a policy improvement on every iteration.

3. Just like gradient descent, conjugate gradient descent also tries to find the minimum of the function; however, the search direction of conjugate gradient descent will be different from gradient descent and conjugate gradient descent attains convergence in N iterations.

4. The update rule of TRPO is given as $\theta = \theta + \alpha^j \sqrt{\dfrac{2\delta}{s^T H s}} s$.

5. PPO acts as an improvement to the TRPO algorithm and is simple to implement. Similar to TRPO, PPO ensures that the policy updates are in the trust region. But unlike TRPO, PPO does not use any constraint in the objective function.

6. In the PPO clipped method, in order to ensure that the policy updates are in the trust region, that is, the new policy is not far away from the old policy, PPO adds a new function called the clipping function, which ensures that the new and old policies are not far away from each other.

7. K-FAC approximates the Fisher information matrix as a block diagonal matrix where each block contains the derivatives. Then each block is approximated as a Kronecker product of two matrices, which is known as Kronecker factorization.

Chapter 14 – Distributional Reinforcement Learning

1. In a distributional RL, instead of selecting an action based on the expected return, we select the action based on the distribution of the return, which is often called the value distribution or return distribution.

2. In categorical DQN, we feed the state and support of the distribution as the input and the network returns the probabilities of the value distribution.

3. The authors of the categorical DQN suggest that it will be efficient to choose the number of support N as 51 and so the categorical DQN is also known as the C51 algorithm.

4. Inverse CDF is also known as the quantile function. Inverse CDF as the name suggests is the inverse of the cumulative distribution function. That is, in CDF, given the support x, we obtain the cumulative probability τ, whereas in inverse CDF, given cumulative probability τ, we obtain the support x.

5. In a categorical DQN, along with the state, we feed the fixed support at equally spaced intervals as an input to the network, and it returns the non-uniform probabilities. However, in a QR-DQN, along with the state, we feed the fixed uniform probabilities as an input to the network and it returns the support at variable locations (unequally spaced support).

6. The D4PG is similar to DDPG except for the following:

   1. We use a distributional DQN in the critic network instead of using the regular DQN to estimate the Q values.

   2. We calculate N-step returns in the target instead of calculating one-step returns.

3. We use prioritized experience replay and add importance to the gradient updates in the critic network.

4. Instead of using one actor, we use L independent actors, each of which acts in parallel, collecting experience and storing the experience in the replay buffer.

Chapter 15 – Imitation Learning and Inverse RL

1. One of the simplest and most naive ways to perform imitation learning is by treating an imitation learning task as a supervised learning task. First, we collect a set of expert demonstrations, then we train a classifier to perform the same action performed by the expert in a particular state. We can view this as a big multiclass classification problem and train our agent to perform the action performed by the expert in the respective state.

2. In DAgger, we aggregate the dataset over a series of iterations and train the classifier on the aggregated dataset.

3. In DQfD, we fill the replay buffer with expert demonstrations and pre-train the agent. Note that these expert demonstrations are used only for pretraining the agent. Once the agent is pre-trained, the agent will interact with the environment and gather more experience and make use of it for learning. Thus DQfD consists of two phases, which are pre-training and training.

4. IRL is used when it is hard to design the reward function. In RL, we try to find the optimal policy given the reward function but in IRL, we try to learn the reward function given the expert demonstrations. Once we have derived the reward function from the expert demonstrations using IRL, then we can use the reward function to train our agent to learn the optimal policy using any RL algorithm.

5. We can represent the state with a feature vector f. Let's say we have a state s; then its feature vector can be defined as f_s.

6. In GAIL, the role of the generator is to generate a policy by learning the occupancy measure of the expert policy, and the role of the discriminator is to classify whether the generated policy is from the expert policy or the agent policy. So, we train the generator using TRPO. The discriminator is basically a neural network that tells us whether the policy generated by the generator is the expert policy or the agent policy.

Chapter 16 – Deep Reinforcement Learning with Stable Baselines

1. Stable Baselines is an improved implementation of OpenAI Baselines. Stable Baselines is a high-level library that is easier to use than OpenAI Baselines, and it also includes state-of-the-art deep RL algorithms along with offering several useful features.

2. We can save the agent as `agent.save()` and load the trained agent as `agent.load()`.

3. We generally train our agent in a single environment per step but with Stable Baselines, we can train our agent in multiple environments per step. This helps our agent to learn quickly. Now, our states, actions, reward, and done will be in the form of a vector since we are training our agent in multiple environments. So, we call this a vectorized environment.

4. In SubprocVecEnv, we run each environment in a different process, whereas in DummyVecEnv, we run each environment in the same process.

5. With Stable Baselines, it is easier to view the computational graph of our model in TensorBoard. In order to do that, we just need to pass the directory where we need to store our log files while instantiating the agent.

6. With Stable Baselines, we can easily record a video of our agent using the `VecVideoRecorder` module.

Chapter 17 – Reinforcement Learning Frontiers

1. Meta learning produces a versatile AI model that can learn to perform various tasks without having to train them from scratch. We train our meta-learning model on various related tasks with a few data points, so for a new but related task, it can make use of the learning obtained from the previous tasks and we don't have to train it from scratch.

2. **Model-Agnostic Meta Learning (MAML)** is one of the most popularly used meta-learning algorithms and it has created a major breakthrough in meta-learning research. The basic idea of MAML is to find a better initial model parameter so that with good initial parameters, the model can learn quickly on new tasks with fewer gradient steps.

3. In the outer loop of MAML, we update the model parameter as

    $\theta = \theta - \beta \nabla_\theta \sum_{T_i \sim p(T)} L_{T_i}(f_{\theta_i'})$ and it is known as a meta objective.

4. The meta training set basically acts as a training set in the outer loop and is used to update the model parameter in the outer loop.

5. In hierarchical RL, we decompose a large problem into small subproblems in a hierarchy. The different methods used in hierarchical RL include state-space decomposition, state abstraction, and temporal abstraction.

6. With an imagination augmented agent, before taking any action in an environment, the agent imagines the consequences of taking the action and if they think the action will provide a good reward, they will perform the action.

Other Books You May Enjoy

If you enjoyed this book, you may be interested in these other books by Packt:

Deep Reinforcement Learning Hands-On

Maksim Lapan

ISBN: 978-1-83882-699-4

- Understand the deep learning context of RL and implement complex deep learning models
- Evaluate RL methods including cross-entropy, DQN, actor-critic, TRPO, PPO, DDPG, D4PG, and others
- Build a practical hardware robot trained with RL methods for less than $100

- Discover Microsoft's TextWorld environment, which is an interactive fiction games platform
- Use discrete optimization in RL to solve a Rubik's Cube
- Teach your agent to play Connect 4 using AlphaGo Zero
- Explore the very latest deep RL research on topics including AI chatbots
- Discover advanced exploration techniques, including noisy networks and network distillation techniques

Python Machine Learning - Third Edition

Sebastian Raschka, Vahid Mirjalili

ISBN: 978-1-78995-575-0

- Master the frameworks, models, and techniques that enable machines to 'learn' from data
- Use scikit-learn for machine learning and TensorFlow for deep learning
- Apply machine learning to image classification, sentiment analysis, intelligent web applications, and more
- Build and train neural networks, GANs, and other models
- Discover best practices for evaluating and tuning models
- Predict continuous target outcomes using regression analysis
- Dig deeper into textual and social media data using sentiment analysis

Leave a review - let other readers know what you think

Please share your thoughts on this book with others by leaving a review on the site that you bought it from. If you purchased the book from Amazon, please leave us an honest review on this book's Amazon page. This is vital so that other potential readers can see and use your unbiased opinion to make purchasing decisions, we can understand what our customers think about our products, and our authors can see your feedback on the title that they have worked with Packt to create. It will only take a few minutes of your time, but is valuable to other potential customers, our authors, and Packt. Thank you!

Index

optimal policy, extracting from optimal value
    function 112-114
optimal value function, computing 110-112
fully connected layer 305, 306
functional model 349, 350

G

gates 294
Gaussian policy 22
Gauss-Newton method
    reference link 548
Generative Adversarial Imitation Learning
        (GAIL) 617-619, 651
    formulation 619-621
    implementing 651
Generative Adversarial Networks
        (GANs) 307-309, 617
    architecture 313
    discriminative model 310
    generative model 309, 310
    generator and discriminative model,
        learning 311, 312
    loss function, examining 314
generative model, types
    explicit density model 309
    implicit density model 309
generator loss function 316
gradient descent 274
gym environment
    action selection 56-58
    Atari game environment 69, 70
    classic control environment 62, 63
    creating 47-49
    episode, generating 56-61
    exploring 50, 62
Gym toolkit
    error fixes 46
    installing 45
    used, for creating bandit environment 228

H

handwritten digit classification, using
        TensorFlow 330
    accuracy, computing 334, 335
    dataset, loading 330, 331
    forward propagation 333

graphs, visualizing in TensorBoard 338-342
loss and backpropagation, computing 334
model, training 336, 337
number of neurons, defining in each
        layer 331
placeholders, defining 332, 333
required libraries, importing 330
summary, creating 335, 336
hidden layer 267
hierarchical reinforcement learning
        (HRL) 668
horizon 25, 40
hyperbolic tangent (tanh) 269

I

Imagination Augmented Agents
        (I2As) 672-676
importance sampling method 511
incremental mean updates 167
indirect dependency 322
infinite horizon 26
init method
    defining 441-444
inner loop 661
input gate 295
input layer 267
inverse cumulative distribution function
        (inverse CDF) 584-586
Inverse Reinforcement Learning (IRL) 612
    maximum entropy IRL 613

J

Jensen Shannon (JS) divergence 618

K

k-armed bandit 226
Keras 348
kernel 298
key features, TD3
    clipped double Q learning 475-477
    delayed policy updates 477-479
    target policy smoothing 479, 480
KL-constrained objective 515
KL penalized objective 514
Kronecker-Factored Approximate Curvature

CPSIA information can be obtained
at www.ICGtesting.com
Printed in the USA
LVHW100745231021
701273LV00009B/46

9 781839 210686